Forensic Child and Adolescent Mental Health

Meeting the Needs of Young Offenders

Edited by

Susan Bailey
Chair, Academy Of Medical Royal Colleges

Prathiba Chitsabesan
University of Manchester

Paul Tarbuck
Former Chairperson of the Royal College of Nursing Controlled Environments Forum

CAMBRIDGE
UNIVERSITY PRESS

University Printing House, Cambridge CB2 8BS, United Kingdom

One Liberty Plaza, 20th Floor, New York, NY 10006, USA

477 Williamstown Road, Port Melbourne, VIC 3207, Australia

4843/24, 2nd Floor, Ansari Road, Daryaganj, Delhi – 110002, India

79 Anson Road, #06–04/06, Singapore 079906

Cambridge University Press is part of the University of Cambridge.

It furthers the University's mission by disseminating knowledge in the pursuit of education, learning, and research at the highest international levels of excellence.

www.cambridge.org
Information on this title: www.cambridge.org/9781107003644
10.1017/9780511777127

First published 2017

Printed in the United States of America by Sheridan Books, Inc.

A catalogue record for this publication is available from the British Library.

Library of Congress Cataloging-in-Publication Data
Names: Bailey, Susan, 1950– editor. | Tarbuck, Paul, editor. | Chitsabesan, Prathiba, editor.
Title: Forensic child and adolescent mental health : meeting the needs of young offenders / edited by Susan Bailey, Paul Tarbuck, Prathiba Chitsabesan.
Description: Cambridge, United Kingdom ; New York, NY, USA : Cambridge University Press, 2017. | Includes bibliographical references.
Identifiers: LCCN 2016046816 | ISBN 9781107003644 (hardback)
Subjects: | MESH: Criminals – psychology | Adolescent | Criminal Behavior | Mental Disorders – psychology | Mental Disorders – diagnosis | Needs Assessment
Classification: LCC RA1151 | NLM WM 605 | DDC 614/.15–dc23
LC record available at https://lccn.loc.gov/2016046816

ISBN 978-1-107-00364-4 Hardback

In memory of Richard Marley and 'inspired' by Dorothy Tonak

Contents

List of Contributors ix
Foreword xiii
Preface xv

Prologue: Understanding Adolescence 1
Mike and Mary Shooter

Section 1 Developmental Pathways

1 **Origins of Offending in Young People** 11
Barbara Maughan

2 **Psychosocial Resilience, Psychosocial Care and Forensic Mental Healthcare** 24
Richard Williams and Verity Kemp

Section 2 Assessment and Needs of Young Offenders

3 **Assessment of Young Offenders: Mental Health, Physical, Educational and Social Needs** 41
Prathiba Chitsabesan and Lorraine Khan

4 **Risk Assessment and Management Approaches with Adolescent Offenders** 55
James Millington and Charlotte Lennox

5 **The Influence of Neurodevelopmental Impairment on Youth Crime** 68
Nathan Hughes, Huw Williams and Prathiba Chitsabesan

Section 3 Serious Offences: Origins, Nature and Treatment

6 **Serious Offences: Origins and Nature of Individual Violence** 83
Charlotte Lennox and Rajan Nathan

7 **Childhood Predictors of Young Homicide Offenders and Victims and Their Implications for Interventions** 94
Lia Ahonen, David P. Farrington, Rolf Loeber, Rebecca Stallings and Dustin Pardini

8 **Group Violence and Youth Gangs** 107
Heather Law, Lorraine Khan and Sally Zlotowitz

9 **Sexually Harmful Behaviour in Young People** 121
Maeve Murphy, Kenny Ross and Simon Hackett

Section 4 Assessment and Management

10 **Depression, Self-Harm and Suicidal Behaviour in Young Offenders** 135
Gemma Trainor, Justine Rothwell and Heidi Hales

11 **Post-Traumatic Stress Disorder, Adjustment Disorder and Complex Trauma in Young People at Risk of Entering the Criminal Justice System** 152
Shreeta Raja and Andrew Rogers

12 **Young People with Schizophrenia in Forensic Settings** 166
Enys Delmage

13 **Substance Misuse in Young People with Antisocial Behaviour** 177
Louise Theodosiou

14 **Attention Deficit Hyperactivity Disorder and Antisocial Behaviour** 190
Susan Young, Ben Greer and Oliver White

15 **Autism Spectrum Disorders in Young People in the Criminal Justice System** 201
Ernest Gralton and Gillian Baird

16 **Youth Psychopathy: a Developmental Perspective** 217
Lorraine Johnstone

Section 5 Therapeutic Approaches

17 **Early Interventions in Conduct Disorder and Oppositional Defiant Disorder** 239
Stephen Scott, Leena K. Augimeri and Justine Fifield

18 **Cognitive, Behavioural and Related Approaches in Young Offenders** 254
Paul Mitchell and Charlotte Staniforth

19 **Systemic Treatment Approaches in Young People with Risky Behaviours** 266
Simone Fox and Helen Jones

20 **Sounding the Picture – Drawing Out the Sound: Music Therapy and Art Therapy with Young People Who Have Committed Serious Criminal Offences** 278
Lynn Aulich and Joanna Holroyd

Section 6 Legal Frameworks, Organisations and Systems

21 **Children and the Law** 289
Enys Delmage, Hannele Variend and Mike Shaw

22 **Youth Justice Services in England and Wales** 300
Paul Tarbuck

23 **Working with Young People in a Secure Environment** 312
Jim Rose, Pam Hibbert and Paul Mitchell

Epilogue 321
Maggie Atkinson

Index 323

Contributors

Lia Ahonen Visiting Researcher, University of Pittsburgh, Department of Psychiatry, Pittsburgh, PA, USA and Assistant Professor of Criminology, Örebro University, Sweden.

Maggie Atkinson Honorary Professor at Keele University, Chair of New Direction, former Children's Commissioner for England and former Director of Children's Services, Gateshead Council, UK.

Leena Augimeri Director, SNAP Scientific and Program Development and Centre for Children Committing Offences, Child Development Institute; Adjunct Professor, University of Toronto, Toronto, ON, Canada.

Lynn Aulich Art Therapist, Adolescent Forensic Services, Greater Manchester West Mental Health NHS Trust, Manchester, UK.

Sue Bailey Professor Dame, DBE, Chair of the Children and Young People's Mental Health Coalition, Vice Chair of the Centre for Mental Health and Chair of the Academy of Medical Royal Colleges, UK.

Gillian Baird Professor in Paediatric Neurodisability, Guy's & St Thomas NHS Trust and King's Health Partners, London, UK.

Prathiba Chitsabesan Consultant Child and Adolescent Psychiatrist and Clinical Director, Pennine Care NHS Trust; Honorary Research Fellow and Lecturer, Centre for Mental Health and Risk, Manchester Academic Health Science Centre, University of Manchester, UK.

Enys Delmage Consultant in Adolescent Forensic Psychiatry, St Andrew's Healthcare, Northampton, and Honorary Assistant Professor, University of Nottingham, UK.

David Farrington OBE, Emeritus Professor of Psychological Criminology, Institute of Criminology, University of Cambridge, Cambridge, UK.

Justine Fifield Research Assistant, Centre for Children Committing Offences, Child Development Institute, Toronto, ON, Canada.

Simone Fox Senior Lecturer and Deputy Clinical Director, Department of Clinical Psychology, Royal Holloway, University of London, Egham, UK and Consultant Clinical and Forensic Psychologist, Multisystemic Therapy Expert, National Implementation Service, South London and Maudsley NHS Foundation Trust, London, UK.

Ernest Gralton Consultant Forensic Psychiatrist in Adolescent Developmental Disabilities, St Andrew's Healthcare, Scotland, UK.

Ben Greer Research Assistant, Broadmoor Hospital, West London Mental Health NHS Trust, Crowthorne, UK.

John Gunn CBE, Emeritus Professor of Forensic Psychiatry at the Institute of Psychiatry, Kings College, London, UK.

Simon Hackett Professor of Applied Social Sciences, Durham University, Durham, UK.

Heidi Hales Consultant Adolescent Forensic Psychiatrist, CNWL NHS Foundation Trust and HMYOI Cookham Wood, London, UK.

Pam Hibbert OBE Independent Specialist and Chair of the National Association for Youth Justice, UK.

Joanna Holroyd Case Manager/Therapist, East Cheshire 0–16 CAMHS and Music Therapist, UK.

Nathan Hughes Senior Lecturer, School of Social Policy, University of Birmingham, UK, and Marie Curie Research Fellow, Murdoch Childrens Research Institute, Melbourne, Australia.

Lorraine Johnstone Consultant Clinical and Forensic Psychologist; Head of Child and Family Clinical Psychology, NHS Forth Valley; Clinical Lead, the Interventions for Vulnerable Youth Project (IVY Project), Centre for Youth and Criminal Justice, Strathclyde University, UK.

Helen Jones Associate, National Implementation Service Evidence Based Interventions for Children Looked After or on the Edge of Care or Custody, South London and Maudsley NHS Foundation Trust, National and Specialist CAMHS, Michael Rutter Centre, Maudsley Hospital, London, UK.

Verity Kemp Associate, Welsh Institute for Health and Social Care, University of South Wales and Director, Health Planning Ltd, UK.

Lorraine Khan Associate Director, Children and Young People, Centre for Mental Health, London, UK.

Heather Law Research Coordinator at the Psychosis Research Unit, Greater Manchester West Mental Health NHS Foundation Trust and Honorary Research Fellow, School of Psychological Sciences, University of Manchester, Manchester, UK.

Charlotte Lennox, Research Fellow and Lecturer, Faculty of Biology, Medicine and Health, Division of Psychology and Mental Health, University of Manchester, Manchester, UK.

Rolf Loeber Distinguished Emeritus Professor of Psychiatry and Psychology, Departments of Psychiatry and Psychology, University of Pittsburgh, Pittsburgh, PA, USA.

Barbara Maughan Professor of Developmental Epidemiology, MRC Social, Genetic and Developmental Psychiatry Centre, Institute of Psychiatry, Psychology and Neuroscience, King's College London, UK.

James Millington Consultant Clinical and Forensic Psychologist, Greater Manchester West, Mental Health NHS Foundation Trust, Prestwich, UK.

Paul Mitchell Independent Consultant in Mental Health and Social Care and former Clinical Lead for the National Secure Forensic Mental Health Service for Young People, UK.

Maeve Murphy Clinical Nurse Specialist, FACTS Team, Greater Manchester Mental Health NHS Foundation Trust, Manchester, UK.

Dustin Pardini Associate Child Clinical Psychologist, Professor, School of Criminology and Criminal Justice, Arizona State University, USA.

Rajan Nathan Consultant Forensic Psychiatrist and Clinical Director, Mersey Care NHS Trust, UK and Honorary Senior Research Fellow, University of Liverpool, Liverpool, UK.

Shreeta Raja Chartered Clinical Psychologist, Changing Minds Limited, Warrington, UK.

Andrew Rogers Consultant Clinical and Forensic Psychologist and Clinical Director, Changing Minds Limited, Warrington, UK.

Jim Rose Director, Responsive Solutions UK Ltd., UK.

Kenny Ross Consultant Adolescent Forensic Psychiatrist, FACTS Team, Greater Manchester Mental Health NHS Foundation Trust, Manchester, UK.

Justine Rothwell Cognitive Behavioural Therapist, Meadows Care, Rochdale, UK.

Stephen Scott Professor of Child Health and Behaviour and Director, National Academy for Parenting Research, Institute of Psychiatry, King's College London, London, UK.

Mike Shaw Consultant in Child and Adolescent Psychiatry and Co-Director FDAC National Unit, Tavistock and Portman NHS Foundation Trust, FDAC National Unit, Coram Community Campus, London, UK.

Mary Shooter Magistrate and Chair of the Magistrates Association Training Committee for South Wales and Member of the Training and Development Committee for the Gwent Magistrates Bench, Wales, UK.

Mike Shooter CBE, FRCPsych President of the British Association for Counselling and Psychotherapy, UK.

Rebecca Stallings Data Management Specialist, UPMC Pittsburgh Youth Study, Department of Psychiatry, University of Pittsburgh, Pittsburgh, PA, USA.

Charlotte Staniforth Consultant Clinical Psychologist, Adolescent Service, St Andrew's Healthcare, and Visiting Research Associate, Department of Forensic Mental Health, Institute of Psychiatry, King's College London, UK.

Paul Tarbuck Mental Health Nurse Practitioner, Inspector of health services within places of custody including young offender institutions. Formerly Director of NHS Forensic CAMHS, Forensic Adult and Specialist Mental Health Services in the UK and Chairperson of the Royal College of Nursing Forum for Nurses Working in Controlled Environments

Louise Theodosiou Consultant Child and Adolescent Psychiatrist, Central Manchester University Hospitals NHS Foundation Trust, Manchester, UK.

Gemma Trainor Lecturer, Florence Nightingale Faculty of Nursing and Midwifery, King's College London, UK.

Hannele Variend Consultant in General Adult Psychiatry, Derbyshire Healthcare NHS Foundation Trust, Matlock, UK.

Oliver White Consultant Child and Adolescent Forensic Psychiatrist, Southern Health NHS Foundation Trust, Bluebird House Medium Secure Forensic Adolescent Psychiatric Unit, Southampton, UK, and Oxford Health NHS Foundation Trust, Thames Valley Community Forensic CAMHS Team, Oxford, UK.

Huw Williams Associate Professor of Clinical Neuropsychology and Co-Director of the Centre for Clinical Neuropsychology Research, Exeter University, UK.

Richard Williams OBE, Emeritus Professor of Mental Health Strategy, Welsh Institute for Health and Social Care, University of South Wales, and former Consultant in Child and Adolescent Psychiatry, UK.

Susan Young Senior Lecturer in Forensic Clinical Psychology, Imperial College London, London, and Forensic Research and Development Director, Broadmoor Hospital, West London Mental Health NHS Trust, Crowthorne, UK.

Sally Zlotowitz Clinical and Community Psychologist, INTEGRATE Clinical Director (Interim), MAC-UK, UK. Honorary Research Associate, University College London.

Foreword

Professor Dame Sue Bailey has done a great deal for psychiatry, and in so many ways. She was a pioneer as a practising child and adolescent forensic psychiatrist and an academic in the field. She has gone on to leadership roles in the UK and overseas, perhaps most notably as president of the Royal College of Psychiatrists and then of the Academy of all the British Medical Royal Colleges.

Sue Bailey and her co-editors are now to be congratulated for this textbook. It is an important book which indicates that forensic psychiatry has come of age. Every mental health worker knows that 'the child is father of the man' and that adult behaviour has its roots in the developmental mix of genetics, intrauterine climate and parenting and other environmental factors through childhood. There is a long and painful history regarding children as the architects of their own failings and thus neglecting to care for them appropriately. Sue Bailey, in her introduction, gives a good, brief synopsis of how that neglect affected thinking about forensic child and adolescent mental health in Europe until the 1980s. Then changes began to gather pace in the UK, with the overhaul of the English and Welsh youth justice system in 1998. We can be justly proud of some of the recent advances in this work, a brief history of which is set out later in this volume. Even so, we need to remain aware of the huge tasks still in front of society and our profession. This volume points to the interesting, but stony road ahead.

I have to confess that I have long believed, and taught, that considering adult forensic psychiatry to be a separate specialty, distinct from child and adolescent forensic psychiatry, is a serious mistake. I understand how this arose. Children's services of all kinds, including paediatrics and child psychiatry, have traditionally been separated from adult services. There is, indeed, specialist knowledge that applies to each, but there is also a terrible barrier to good practice in this separation. There is little will or capacity for ensuring continuity of treatment between youth

and adulthood, but biology does not recognise a sharp distinction. It is essential for anyone who claims to practise forensic psychiatry to be familiar with the problems presenting in individuals at all stages of their life. Forensic psychiatry can be regarded as the study and management of behaviours which stop the individual from reaching his or her full potential while posing risks of harm to others. Such behaviours usually begin early, and we probably have a better chance of changing them in their early stages than we do when they are well established in adult life.

Future generations of mental health workers may give more emphasis to behaviour problems and less to the strange so-called diagnostic system to which we seem currently wedded. I have long thought that clinics specialising in the assessment and treatment of particular behaviours are at least as useful as clinics purporting to focus on particular diagnoses. This book rightly deals with violence, harmful sexual behaviour, substance misuse and self-destructive behaviour as problems in their own right. Investment in services for such complex problems is likely to pay handsome dividends in adult life. Investment in research studying both causes and the management of many of the problems outlined in this book could lead to greatly improved outcomes, as has happened elsewhere in medicine. A difficulty is that the timescale for research, and consequently evidence-based change, will be longer than muddling on with containment strategies, and thus less politically attractive. We have some of the building blocks in place, in the form of longitudinal, prospective studies, from birth, such as the one in this book by Barbara Maughan, and these have not only taught us about environmental influences on development, but many have incorporated genetic and other physical measures too. The area in which we are lacking is translation from the findings of these studies to widely effective interventions. Nevertheless, I think this book indicates that there is a vigorous task force available to carry such research forward given an appropriate academic environment and sufficient resources. I hope it will help to persuade society to provide those essential resources.

The book should, thus, be read by influential people in all walks of life. Care for children, and their treatment if things go wrong, should be everyone's concern. Nevertheless I think it should be on the essential reading list for all mental health professionals. In particular, in my view, beyond the core readership, forensic mental health professionals working with adults should pay particular attention to its content and should consider ways in which they can collaborate with their colleagues dealing with younger patients and vice versa.

John Gunn, CBE, FRCPsych, FMedSci
Emeritus Professor of Forensic Psychiatry
Institute of Psychiatry, King's College London

Preface

Few dilemmas have challenged the ideas of society about the nature of human development and the nature of justice more than children and young people in the juvenile justice system, especially those who have mental health problems, neurodevelopmental disorders and learning disabilities. In the eighteenth and nineteenth centuries children were seldom distinguished from adults and were placed with adults in prison. In the England of 1823, boys as young as nine years of age were held in solitary confinement for their own protection in ships retired from the Battle of Trafalgar. In the nineteenth century, legislation regarding children's rights was tied to the need for labour.

There have been periodic reactions against convicting, imprisoning and punishing young people. The pioneers who sought to rescue both young offenders and those children offended against provided the beginnings of youth justice, care and child protection. Both community and secure residential innovations in youth justice have been characterised by patterns of reforming zeal followed by the gradual embedding of scientific evidence base from the dual fields of juvenile justice and the assessment and treatment of mental health problems in children and young people.

The overhaul of the youth justice system in England and Wales in 1998 with the introduction of the then multiagency youth justice teams proved a turning point for progress in youth justice, paralleled across the UK, many parts of Europe, Australia and New Zealand. Ten years earlier the development of Forensic Child and Adolescent Mental Health Services (FCAMHS) started to emerge with a now vibrant European Association for Forensic Child & Adolescent Psychiatry, Psychology and other involved Professions (EFCAP).

Hence the time seemed right to bring together researchers, educationalists, those shaping policy and service development and, above all, practitioners who are actively contributing to the knowledge base and practice in the field of child and adolescent forensic mental health in the development of a textbook which summarises the evidence base in the assessment and treatment of mental health needs in young people in the criminal justice system, service models of care and likely future directions of travel in the field.

In its scope this textbook therefore provides a developmental approach to understanding the needs of adolescents and how young people within and at risk of entering the criminal justice system may differ. It recognises the importance of prevention, early intervention and the building of psychosocial resilience through the delivery of values-based practice. It highlights the need for comprehensive assessment for young people across the multiple domains of their lives, given their complex and multiple co-morbid needs, and how in day-to-day practice this can be achieved by multiagency services. A range of evidence-based interventions for specific mental disorders are described but in the context of meeting holistic psychosocial needs. Case examples have been provided to illustrate how theoretical principles may be put into practice for clinicians and staff working with young people.

We fully recognise the challenges faced by those who chose to work in this field and the absolute importance of practitioners being supported and equipped to enable children and young people to develop well in the face of often accumulative negative experiences across their early years.

Our hope is this book will be of interest and of help to a wide range of professionals working across the field both in community and secure settings and across health, education, social care and juvenile justice services. The policy and legal framework has been illustrated by reference to the system in England but will have relevance to readers from across the UK, Europe and further afield.

The editors are very grateful to the contributors for all their patience and hard work, and I am personally hugely grateful to my fellow editors.

Sue Bailey, DBE, FRCPsych
Chair of the Children and Young People's Mental Health Coalition,
Vice Chair of the Centre for Mental Health and
Chair of the Academy of Medical Royal Colleges

Prologue
Understanding Adolescence

Mike and Mary Shooter

Introduction

This chapter will discuss three main questions: What is adolescence all about? How may it go wrong? And what can we do to put it right if it does? But first we need to address a deeper issue: is adolescence a universal concept or is it so dependent on the surrounding context that it ceases to have any validity?

Does Adolescence Exist?

Historically, can there have been such a thing as adolescence when young boys were sent up chimneys, girls were having babies and life was brutish and brief? Culturally, is there room for adolescence when children of a certain age are subjected to initiation rights and are expected to emerge as fully fledged adults on the other side? Is adolescence possible only where young people remain in school or higher education long enough for idle self-absorption? What happens to adolescence in austerity, when young people are obliged to remain as children in the parental home long after they might have found their feet in better times? Can adolescence be said to have been invented by the media and by commercial industries seeking to make money out of young people's wish to follow peer-group fashion? And is adolescence the politicians' last opportunity to exploit an age group without giving them the vote to express what they feel about it?

In other words, is adolescence a relatively modern, Western and artificial construct about which there is very little academic study until the late nineteenth century (Demos and Demos, 1969)? Or is there something universal about a stage of development that may be unique to human animals and which we all experience whatever the context in which we live? The answer, we would contend, is a mixture of both those views. Yes, there is something so specific about adolescence that it has engaged the attention of writers and philosophers from Plato 2500 years ago to the current explosion of coming-of-age novels and films.

And this has been so, whether or not the word itself has been in common usage, whether academics have deemed it worthy of study and whether practitioners have felt it necessary to provide specific facilities for adolescents or crammed them onto the paediatric or the adult ward with equal embarrassment. But the surface reflections of adolescence will change from time to time and culture to culture as young people themselves come to terms with it in their particular surroundings.

It is a mistake to assume that adults are in charge of the maturation process. Young people everywhere are 'constructing their own adolescence' (Coleman, 2011). They will find their own way of expressing what is happening to them, whether their development is on the right or the wrong track and however difficult the adults around them seem to make it. And the adults, in their turn, will react with pride or consternation. As Shakespeare's Old Shepherd put it, there are times when we might wish that children went straight to adulthood after all 'or that youth would sleep out the rest; for there is nothing in the between but getting wenches with child, wronging the ancientry, stealing, fighting' (*A Winter's Tale* III. iii. 58). A little harsh, perhaps, but many adults would share the feeling!

Question 1: What's It All About?

Addressing this question could occupy the entire book and still not result in an answer that would satisfy everyone. So let's settle for a few key issues.

Schools of Thought: Rival Perspectives

There are many different schools of thought about adolescence, as there are indeed about all human development – physical, cognitive, psychological, social, spiritual and many more. All of us will have memories of the trials and tribulations of puberty, however hard we may have tried to suppress them, and of the bodily changes that go with it. Our parents may have been more aware of the cognitive changes we were going through as we passed from Piaget's 'concrete thinking' to 'formal operations', in which we began to play around with abstract concepts in the same way that a child might do with physical objects, and were often accused of being 'lost in thought'. Freud explored the 'genital' stage of psychosexual development, the influence it has on the adolescent's self-image and all the specific tensions and general moodiness that goes with it.

For Freud, these emotional changes were rooted in genetics and had little to do with the environment; but classic thinkers like Erik Erikson set the adolescent's struggle to discover a sense of identity within the social relationships being forged outside the home in peer group and community. Later, attachment theorists suggested that the consistency of care in infancy can influence social relationships in adolescence. Those who emerge from secure attachments to their parental figures with a positive sense of themselves will be eager to explore new relationships. Those whose early care was fraught with insecurities will doubt both themselves and the trustworthiness of others. They will be anxious about making relationships or avoid them altogether (Mikulincer et al., 2013).

Meanwhile, increasing attention is being paid to the spiritual aspects of development, to the sense of adolescence being part of a journey towards some distant goal, in which moral values in their widest sense are as important as the basic tasks of reproduction and survival that monopolise the lives of other animals (Shooter, 2009). For a long time such a concept was frustrated by its association with religion or by misunderstanding of religious-sounding metaphors likening young people to 'pilgrims' (Coles, 1990). This has given way to all sorts of research, including claims that spiritual development leads to decreased rates of delinquency and even that delinquent behaviour itself is a search for spiritual meaning (Blakeney and Blakeney, 2006).

Stages of Development: Clarity and Complications

The word 'adolescence' comes from the Latin *adolescere*, meaning to grow to maturity. All of the schools of thought are stage theories, in which human beings pass from stage to stage, completing the developmental tasks appropriate to each stage and then moving on. Each stage demands a greater maturity than the one before and, if completed successfully, paves the way for an even greater level of maturity in the next – until we reach old age and begin the long slide down into what Shakespeare called, with typical pessimism, 'second childishness and mere oblivion, sans teeth, sans eyes, sans taste, sans everything' (*As You Like It* II. vii. 139). Modern medicine has done much to improve the final prognosis, but we all get the general gist.

However, in real life, things are not quite so clearcut in the early stages. Reading Piaget, for example, one could be forgiven for imagining that children and young people develop in a staccato fashion, suddenly becoming capable of a whole new set of cognitive functions overnight, as they pass from sensorimotor to pre-operational to concrete operational to formal operational thinking, at successive ages. But development is much more gradual than that and subject to all sorts of surrounding influences. Anyone who has worked with bereaved families will know that children who are given straightforward information about what has happened and the opportunity to share in the rituals and emotions involved will have a far more mature understanding of death than someone older who has been 'protected' from their grief. And all of us have islands of magical thinking that survive into adulthood in the form of harmless superstitions or a more destructive sense of guilt that we have caused something to happen because we wanted it to.

We have all heard some children being described as 'old for their age' or adults being accused of 'behaving childishly'. What that usually means is that the child is showing surprising emotional maturity though they may not grasp the full facts of a situation, while the adult may know what is happening intellectually but be unable to deal with it emotionally. In other words, different aspects of development may get out of phase with each other, and adolescents, classically, are capable of swinging from one complete set of thinking, beliefs, emotions and behaviours to another, and from one moment to the next. On the hospital ward, this can confuse doctors and nurses who have insightfully included a 16-year-old in discussions about treatment, only to have him retreat into a helpless childhood on the end of a needle. At home, such confusion infuriates parents who are apt to prop the teenager up against the wall, metaphorically at least, and demand to know why. But the teenager may not know why, and be as scared by this apparent lack of control as the parents are angry.

Challenging Our Stereotypes

So far we have looked at commonalities, as if all adolescents were the same. At a recent workshop the participants were asked to shout out words to describe adolescents. In truth, we could have written the list beforehand because they were all stereotypes. Teenagers are 'stroppy', 'lazy' and 'self-centred' and that's putting it mildly. They take issue with everything, they would stay in bed all day if you let them and they do what they want to do, irrespective of the risks involved and everyone else's wishes. And, of course, they do it all deliberately, just to annoy us! There are several things wrong with this picture.

To begin with, adolescents differ in all sorts of ways. There are huge variations, for example, in the speed of sexual maturation. As a general rule, 'mid-teenage girls are tall, slightly curvy, and have breasts … the average mid-teenage boy is short, weedy and has a light dusting of unimpressive body hair' (Bainbridge, 2009: 71). Bainbridge argues that there may be evolutionary advantages to this disparity. Perhaps girls are built to look more mature and to begin their adult roles earlier in life; boys remain less impressive and less challenging to adult males until they are older. But, in the meantime, this helps to explain why girls look so terrifying to boys in the first few years at secondary school, and girls may get into trouble with parents for dating older men.

Yet this itself is a stereotype. Even within the sexes, individuals mature at different ages and may hover on the edge of the shower, reluctant to show how more or less developed they are from their peers. At best this may make both girls and boys squirm with embarrassment in games lessons; at worst it may lead girls in particular into sexual activity long before they are emotionally able to deal with it. And this leads to the next point: it is not acne but attitude that is the problem.

The Teenage Brain: A New Enlightenment

Adults can come to terms with the physical manifestations of adolescence, but it is the behaviour that drives them up the wall and which they see as consciously designed to do so. In fact, some of the most exciting research on adolescence shows what astonishing things are going on in the teenage brain and how little choice adolescents may have in the sort of behaviours for which they attract such criticism (Jensen and Nutt, 2014) (see also Chapter 20 by Aulich and Holroyd).

In short, the human brain is never larger compared to body size than it is in the teenage years, and all sorts of changes are going on within its increasing convolutions. An over-abundance of grey matter connections is being pruned and the growth of key white matter fibres speeded up. Vital dopamine pathways are being laid down as the focus of brain activity shifts from the archaic, brain-stem pathways we once needed for primitive survival to more sophisticated links with the huge but as yet ill-directed adolescent pre-frontal cortex. It is possible to see the teenage brain as caught somewhere in between, as the old pathways are dying out and the new ones are not yet mature, leaving adolescents with a 'dangerous combination of inquisitiveness and carelessness' (Bainbridge, 2009: 121) that could explain their risk-taking behaviours.

A more positive way of looking at it would be to say that the teenage brain is in a state of 'receptive plasticity', somewhere between the tumultuous growth of childhood and the more settled but inflexible state of adulthood. Its structure is capable of influencing the teenager's behaviour and being influenced by that behaviour in turn, in a sort of virtuous circle. Thus research is beginning to show that play in adolescence, not structured sport or isolated computer games but free play that involves risk-taking and risk-mastery, is essential for the laying down of nerve pathways for social competence.

In other words, the teenage brain is not a mere halfway house between childhood and adulthood, but a vital and necessary stage in its own right. Meanwhile, whatever is happening inside, things may get quite difficult on the surface. The combination of a jealous streak, the effects of sex hormones and shaky brain processes for dealing with fear may render the adolescent impetuous, oppositional and liable to fly off the handle at the slightest provocation. And the circadian rhythms that govern sleep patterns are subtly different in adolescents, in response to shrinkage of the pineal gland and shifts in the night-time peaks and daytime troughs of the melatonin hormone that it secretes. Teenagers do indeed find it difficult to get up in the morning and are less alert and grumpier if forced to do so, through no fault of their own (Morgan, 2013). Some schools are already adjusting their timetables to accommodate these findings but it is asking a lot of parents to remember what is happening in their teenagers' brain when arguments rage over the breakfast table. We do not give up our stereotypes so easily!

Towards a Healthy Outcome: The Meaning of Well-Being

Amongst all the angst and annoyance, we need to remember the positive qualities towards which adolescent development is heading and from which, with a bit of luck, most teenagers will emerge with a sense of well-being and parents, teachers and all the adults around them with a sigh of relief! And that takes us back to those rival schools of thought with which we began. At first glance, they may seem to clash with each other and the debate between their protagonists has often been fierce. But child development can best be understood 'as a process of dynamic transaction between multiple factors' (Gibbs et al., 2015). The schools of thought are not only complementary in many aspects but may all be needed, together, to fully explain what is happening in the experience of adolescence and the outcome if all goes well.

Armed with an increasing sense of physical mastery over the world, a growing, if sometimes anxiety-provoking, awareness of sexual prowess and the experience of success and the congratulations that go with it, the healthy adolescent develops a reasonably secure self-image. Gradually, he learns to recognise, label and come to terms with his own most primitive feelings and to recognise and appreciate the feelings of others. He has the cognitive ability to think in the abstract about himself and the world, to make plans for the future and to work towards them with the sort of values that he thinks are worth standing up for. He can put himself in the shoes of others who may have different views and find ways of maintaining relationships nonetheless. In other words, the adolescent develops the four essential components of well-being – control, communication, cooperation and compromise. What could possibly go wrong?

Question 2: How May It Go Wrong?

Adolescent Turmoil: Normal and Pathological

Not surprisingly, in the light of what we have said already, some writers have seen a certain amount of conflict as a normal part of adolescence. G. Stanley Hall, one of the first academics to study adolescence, thought that it reflected the turbulent history of the human race over the last two millennia: Sturm und Drang (storm and stress). Many parents might agree with him but two classic research studies have undermined the notion of adolescent turmoil. The first (Bandura and Walters, 1959) found no greater stress in adolescence than at any other stage of life. The second (Rutter et al., 1976) uncovered only a small increase in disturbance that had usually been present from much earlier in childhood and in response to parental conflict rather than psychological problems in the adolescent per se.

Nevertheless, the complicated processes of adolescent development give ample opportunity for it to go off the rails in one way or another. Take, for example, the concept of identity formation, Erik Erikson's stage 5 of human development (Erikson, 1963). The majority of adolescents emerge with what he called an 'adaptive' response, a coherent sense of self in relation to peer group, adults and the community. But 'maladaptive' responses could result in role confusion and aimless drifting in which pathological clinging to delinquent gangs or teenage pregnancy might seem preferable to loneliness and despair. At least they would give the adolescent some sense of identity, and we have all seen how attractive that might be to teenagers out of school, out of work and out on the streets in modern sink estates.

The idea of an 'identity crisis' in adolescence has led to further research on how it might be resolved (Marcia, 1980). Speaking to 18- to 22-year-old college students, Marcia found that most of them had developed a firm commitment to their path in life or had suspended a decision while they tried out a variety of roles for a while. But some seemed totally unable to work things out (role diffusion), and others had opted for safety too early in life, had avoided all experiment and had settled for conventional goals (role foreclosure). These concepts may be complicated by the effects of economically hard times, when there are less career opportunities available and many adolescents are forced to grab at whatever comes along. Meanwhile, the educational system has been accused of compounding all this by stressing the need for academic achievement rather than creativity, keeping adolescents' noses to the grindstone and increasing the sense of failure in those who fall off the ladder.

In-born and Acquired Obstacles

The tasks of adolescence are difficult enough in themselves; for some adolescents they are made almost impossible by internal and external factors, either innate or thrust upon them through circumstances beyond their control. A child on the autistic spectrum, for example, will find it very difficult to deal with abstract concepts or to see the world through the eyes of anyone but himself. He might survive in primary school, where teachers in more intimate classes might accommodate difficult behaviour, but adolescence is often a nightmare for the child and all the adults around him.

We would be hard put to design a stage more difficult for him than that of teenage relationships and the appreciation of other people's feelings, tolerance of difference, flexibility of attitude to unfairness, control of temper and the abstract thinking that they entail. Secondary schools, with their own rigidities, are often unable to cope.

Illnesses, first occurring in adolescence or increasing in severity, can cut across all the normal processes of adolescent development. How is it possible to feel part of her peer group if the teenager spends most of her life in a wheelchair and out of school? How can a teenager - disfigured by illness and its treatment - feel part of the crowd when she is so obviously and embarrassingly different in the eyes of both herself and those around her? How can she establish her independence when she is becoming increasingly reliant on parents and medical experts for her very survival? And how can she commit herself to any sort of life plan when the future is so uncertain? Thankfully, such questions have encouraged the development of specialist facilities for adolescents in hospital and the inclusion of psychiatrists, psychologists and youth workers in the medical teams working within them and out in the community; but there is still a long way to go before institutions like hospitals and schools can cope with the issues involved.

Family Reactions: Conflict and Consequences

Most adolescents, of course, do not live in a vacuum. They live at home, in families of one sort or another, subject to all the family tensions that might surround the adolescent's behaviour. How families resolve these tensions is critical to everyone concerned. To put it bluntly, parents of a teenager get another shot at the 'terrible twos'. You will remember that the two-year-old, with his newfound ability to get around physically and a biological urge to explore the world, provided he has a secure-enough sense of attachment to believe that his mother has not ceased to exist just because she is out of sight, will push the boundaries of safety. And the good-enough mother, aware of the dangers, will encourage her toddler's exploration, dust him off when he falls over and send him off again until the risks are too great. When the toddler becomes frustrated, he has a tantrum, is cuddled, and the process continues until the growing child develops his own awareness of the dangers to be avoided (Bailey and Shooter, 2009).

Without being patronising (or matronising for that matter), much the same battles can recur in adolescence. The normal teenager, alone or led on as part of her peer group, has the same urge to explore the world, apparently heedless of the dangers involved. The parents, knowing better of course, are faced with the dilemma of how to reward healthy risk-taking while maintaining an envelope of security. This is a tightrope that is easy to fall off on both sides, if you will forgive a mixed metaphor or two! Under-reactive parents will suffer fewer arguments, but their teenagers may have to resort to ever more dangerous behaviour, serious drug abuse or sexual activity for example, to get any idea of where the boundaries might be. The adolescents of over-restrictive parents may kick against the boundaries with all sorts of pathological attempts, such as the eating disorders, to wrest any sort of control over their lives.

Again, the good-enough parent will get by with a skirmish or two but be rewarded with offspring thankful that they were there when it all got too much. Parents may worry that their sons and daughters are about to overthrow everything they have worked for, but most of them will grow up with much the same view of life and pass it on to their own offspring in turn. That sounds comforting, but it also means that when things go wrong, the problems will be passed on from one generation to another in cycles of pathology that may be very difficult to break and which entail huge *costs* in terms of both human misery and service involvement.

Serious Situations

The following are typical scenarios where things have gone seriously awry across the lifespan and a young adult has ended up before the courts.

A 20-year-old before the Magistrates Court, charged with assault.

Dean was admitted to the paediatric ward of his local hospital at the age of four with 'failure to thrive'. He was pale, thin and small for his age, wet the bed every night, was clumsy, had a stutter and was generally unkempt. He was alternately tearful and aggressive to the other children but responded well to being 'mothered' by the nurses. His own mother was a single parent with three children, all with special needs, by three different fathers, none of whom took a responsible role in their parenting. Dean's mother was reported to have had a puerperal depression after his birth. Her relationship with Dean was difficult from the start. 'He'll turn out just like his father . . . you wait and see!' she said to one of the nurses on the ward. A case conference considered the possibility of neglect but no further action was taken.

Dean was referred to the Child and Adolescent Mental Health Team at the age of seven. The educational psychologist described him as 'destructive to everyone and everything around him . . . he can't concentrate for more than a few seconds, plays the fool to get attention and is impossible to teach . . . he must have that ADHD'. He was seen by a consultant child and adolescent psychiatrist who suggested a trial of medication but Dean's mother 'failed' to bring him to further appointments and he was lost to follow-up.

Records of Dean's history from there on proved fragmentary, just like his life. He spent several brief episodes in Local Authority care, was thrown out of secondary school and into Special Education, but was on the streets at 16 with a drug habit and stealing to support the habit, and in a criminal peer group. He was admitted to an Accident and Emergency department on at least two occasions with 'accidental' overdoses but not followed up. He had increasing contact with the police and received several cautions for minor offences.

Dean has now been arrested when trying to steal drugs from an ambulance that had stopped to treat an old lady who had fallen in the street. He knocked the old lady over again as he ran off but gave himself up when challenged just a few streets away. The old lady fractured her hip but may have done so in the original fall. Reports reveal that Dean's father was imprisoned at the age of 18, for aggravated burglary.

A 19-year-old university student before the Magistrates Court, charged with shoplifting and possession.

Leanne was brought up in a middle-class, professional household with an emphasis on hard work, academic achievement and little time for play. Her mother was a teacher but had spent long periods off work with depression. Her father had his own business, which was failing. By the time Leanne reached secondary school, there were large debts building up and the father was drinking heavily. Tensions in the house may have led to domestic violence, and neighbours telephoned the police on several occasions. The parents were interviewed but Leanne's mother denied any problems.

Leanne was sent home from school on an increasing number of mornings with headaches and stomach aches, investigated by the GP (general practitioner) with nothing serious being discovered. She became unable to walk after a brief bout of influenza and was admitted to hospital with a diagnosis of Chronic Fatigue Syndrome (CFS).

She was weaned slowly out of hospital and back to school by interventions from the Child and Adolescent Mental Health Services (CAMHS), whilst adult mental health services treated her mother's depression – all against the father's initial opposition. 'I hope you're not accusing me of being the cause of all this', he said threateningly to the consultant paediatrician who assessed Leanne. 'Because I'll take you to court if you do and that'll be your career finished!'

Leanne obtained sufficient A-level grades to get to university – the first time she had ever been away from home. But she became increasingly anxious in her first term, she had few friends and her work was suffering. She saw the local GP for a repetition of her aches and pains but there had been no link between her home and university records for 'confidentiality reasons'. The supermarket pressed charges when she was caught with a bizarre selection of items in her possession and a substantial quantity of cannabis which she said a colleague had given her 'to look after'.

A 21-year-old before the Magistrates Court, charged with soliciting and possession with intent to deal.

Subash comes from an Anglo-Indian family with strict cultural rules. His two elder sisters both entered arranged marriages without apparent complaint, and there was immense pressure on Subash to become a doctor 'just like his grandfather back home'. Subash's father failed to gain entrance to medical school and is now a drug company representative. His mother told Subash that it was up to him to retrieve the family's honour.

Subash did well at primary school, although the teachers worried about his lack of social outlets. His achievement began to fall off rapidly at secondary school, where he was teased unmercifully by his peer group because of his effeminate behaviour. He became increasingly isolated and withdrawn, retreating into his bedroom whenever he could to make contact with largely older men on the internet. At 16 he was 'caught' by his mother trying on his sister's clothes. She challenged him after reading in his diary that he was having secret meetings with men when he should have been in school, and he 'confessed' to being gay. His mother told his father, there was a huge family row and Subash was thrown out of the house and 'disowned' after refusing to be sent back to the grandfather to 'knock some sense' into him.

Subash has survived since as a rent boy and by dealing in drugs.

A 19-year-old before the Magistrates Court, charged with arson.

Tracy appears as an overweight, unkempt and physically unattractive young woman with some degree of learning difficulties and what an expert witness (the local CAMHS psychologist) calls a 'typical fire-setter's background'.

Tracy had a history of early neglect at the hands of a single-parent mother who had herself been in Local Authority care and gave birth to Tracy at the age of 16. There were strong suspicions that Tracy was sexually abused when her mother was living with a man who was subsequently imprisoned for abusing other girls. She was a socially isolated young girl with little education and low self-esteem. Her behaviour was impulsive, with poor anger management and explosive outbursts whenever frustrated. She began drinking increasingly heavily in her early teenage

years, encouraged to steal alcohol from supermarkets by those in her peer group who regularly took advantage of her.

Tracy was taken into Local Authority care with multiple failed foster placements punctuated by stormy returns to her mother. Her 'favourite game' when in care was to abscond on a Friday night, get as far away as she could, then give herself up at the local police station. It happened so often that the local social services had a special Tracy-duty-roster to go out and pick her up. She had fleeting contact with psychiatric services because of self-harming (cutting) behaviour and was briefly treated by her GP for depression. After years of sexual behaviour with older men, she became pregnant at 16. The baby was taken into care at birth.

Tracy was said by her mother to have had a history of fire setting as a child. At 14 she had a short spell in a secure children's home after setting fire to her bedclothes while in a Local Authority hostel. She had told the staff she was going to do it because she felt 'out of control of my feelings'. She has now been arrested and charged with setting fire to an old, boarded-up terrace house shortly after being told that she would not be allowed to have any contact with her now-adopted baby. A homeless old man who had been dossing in the terraced house suffered extensive burns in the fire.

Question 3: How Can We Help to Put It Right If It Does go wrong?

It is not the remit of this chapter to look in detail at the pathways to young offending and how to prevent or deal with it. But the four scenarios above are typical of the life stories of young people who end up before the courts. We can use them to pick out some key aspects of those stories, where they went wrong, the repercussions for the adolescents involved and how they might have been retold with a happier ending.

A Jigsaw of Understanding: Where It Went Wrong

To understand those stories, we need to put together a jigsaw of individual, circumstantial, family and wider systemic pieces that together make up the full picture of the young person's plight. And to start with, the development of all four of the young people had been undermined by early deprivation. It is always tempting to blame this on material poverty; on sink estates with their accompanying stereotypes of single parenthood; downtrodden mothers with little or no parental support of their own, struggling with children with special needs and from multiple, feckless fathers – as in the background of Dean and Tracy.

But poverty does not necessarily mean deprivation. One of the joys of working with families in poor areas is the finding of families who have not been ground down by their circumstances but have prospered, emotionally if not materially. Much work is now being done on the factors that give those families and their offspring greater resilience (Southwick et al., 2011). Correspondingly, material prosperity does not necessarily lead to well-being. Deprivation can exist in middle-class, professional families with large houses, large mortgages and large debts; with a tense and sterile atmosphere; huge academic expectancies; and little time for play. Both Leanne and Subash suffered such deprivation that it crushed their individuality just as surely as poverty might have done.

In addition, the lives of these young people have been compromised by innate, constitutional factors or by events and circumstances thrust upon them from outside. None of Dean's minor physical problems seemed worth treating, but together they must have been crippling to his self-esteem. How do you achieve any sort of popularity with your peer group if you can't express yourself clearly because of a stutter, if you are too clumsy to be good at games and if you are always smelly and unkempt? In those circumstances, playing the fool in a destructive way may not be part of an organic disorder such as Attention Deficit Hyperactivity Disorder but a last, desperate attempt to get attention of any sort.

Similarly, an illness like Leanne's CFS needed addressing in its own right, of course, but we also need to work out what 'meaning' it might have had within her life. We know that the situation in her home was dire and that an adolescent like Leanne might well feel responsible for sorting it out. We could make out a case for her emotional stress being converted into aches and pains which then carried her out of school and back home to help out and protect a depressed mother – until it all got too much and her full-blown CFS alerted the services to the need for their intervention.

Repercussions for Relationships

All this has left our four young people with major problems in coming to terms with the normal tasks of adolescent development. Far from forming healthy relationships with their peer group and the outside world, Dean and Tracy drifted ever more dangerously around in their search for the sort of boundaries that their parents failed to provide – the sort of drifting in which playing the fool or fall guy at best, and joining criminal gangs and sexual exploitation at worst, must have at least offered some sort of perverted 'security'. Unable to understand, control, express and communicate their feelings coherently, their behaviour spoke for them. And sometimes this was bound to be explosive and destructive in ways that would damage themselves or others, as in Tracy's cutting and fire setting.

Meanwhile, Subash and Leanne struggled to find their independence in a web of cultural and family rules that first entrapped them in the home, isolated from peer-group relationships, then 'spat' them out precipitately, Subash onto the streets and Leanne to a university life for which she was totally unprepared. And in both cases, the end result of this over-restriction was just as dangerous as the neglect suffered by Dean and Tracy. None of them received the sort of good-enough care in which they could learn the balance between healthy experimentation and dangerous risk-taking, with disastrous consequences.

In such circumstances, the wider 'family' of services, local authority social services, schools and their attendant psychology services, Child and Adolescent and Adult Mental Health Teams, hospital paediatric and Accident and Emergency services, GPs, the police and many more, may all have become involved, as they did at various times with our four young people. But just like the families of origin, they also have their relationships, within and between them, that may replicate and reinforce the dynamics within the family, and the internal, psychological dynamics within the young person in turn.

Thus the multiple failed school and foster placements in the lives of Dean and Tracy, and the insecurities, false hopes and rejections they entailed, must have reinforced everything they experienced at home and the sense of worthlessness and guilt with which they emerged. Several people expressed worries about Subash and Leanne, at various points in their lives, but the services tended to be involved for brief periods only, at times of crisis, then hand them on like relay batons, without offering the sort of long-term, coordinated vision that they required. Services, in their eyes, were not to be trusted.

Ways of Helping: Safety – the First Consideration

The corollary of all this is that by acting more responsibly the services may set a positive example to families and help to repair some of the damage done to the young people within them. So what sort of help might our four young people have needed? First of all, we need to recognise that the behaviour of all of them could be seen not just as a 'cry for help' but, at times, a scream – and a scream that too often went unheeded because it was seen as some sort of social problem that was not part of service responsibility or turned into a diagnosis for treatment. And much as we would like to work with a situation, sometimes the only answer to the scream is to remove the child or young person to a safer place.

It is easy to point the finger at struggling single parents, though too often services fail to act upon neglect that is obvious in the lives of children like Dean and Tracy until it is almost too late. But services are much warier of tackling abusive situations in middle-class families with different cultural values, such as Subash's family, or hostile, litigious parents like Leanne's father. Once removed, we must make sure that the alternative care offered does not replicate the abuse from which the child has been rescued, that they do not pass from the frying pan into the fire. Someone like Dean or Tracy, who had been so scarred by family breakdown, would be bound to test out foster placements to the limit. They might have benefitted, first, from the less intimate and intensive relationships in an old-style family group home.

Early Intervention – Flexibility of Approach

Next, we need to move away from 'a one size fits all approach, in which any one practice is seen as being most suitable for all clients' (Cooper and McLeod, 2011). Young people in trouble, living in pathological family situations or fragmented care, need the coordinated involvement of many services and many forms of help in many formats (Geldart and Geldart, 2010). Early intervention schemes like Sure Start (Glass, 1999) are built around a combination of parenting programmes, practical help like child-minding and educational and play opportunities for children. They have been successful in turning around the lives of families in severely deprived areas like those in which Dean and Tracy grew up. In other words, if we want to help young people like them, the earlier the better.

Where adolescents are still trapped in families like those of Subash and Leanne, work may have to be done with a parent struggling with their own problem, like the depression of Leanne's mother, and in marital or family therapy before the tensions can be lifted from the young person's shoulders and they can get on with their own lives. School counselling, now available in every secondary school in Wales, offers many adolescents an opportunity to share problems they may have at home or in their peer group, free from the trespass of others.

And, above all, we need to ask what help young people themselves are looking for. They are experts in their own predicament and can be self-taught a range of strategies to deal with 'normal' stresses (Morgan, 2014). Those in therapy need to be addressed as partners to be empowered in the search for their own solutions rather than 'cases' in passive receipt of treatment doled out by adults. Much has been written about the skills of counselling with adolescents (Hanley et al., 2013), but purist approaches in cognitive, psychodynamic and Rogerian therapies may need to give way to innovative formats such as music and film, that fit young people's needs and lifestyles rather than fitting the young person to what the therapist has been trained to give (Hadley and Yancy, 2011).

Conclusions

In the end, what seems to matter most is the quality of the relationship offered to them, irrespective of the discipline of origin of the counsellor involved. What adolescents value is the chance to talk about their problems and to explore their feelings, to be listened to, understood and accepted for what they are, not what someone wants them to be. Within the security of that therapeutic alliance, they can try out new ways of working towards short-term goals and then face the world outside with the confidence that those successes would bring. This requires the counsellor to steer a difficult path between, for example, the need for closeness and the dangers of becoming the good-enough parent the young person lacked, the need for unconditional regard while simultaneously disapproving of some of the young person's behaviour and the courage to take the sort of risks in therapy without which the young person might not develop whist being aware of the need for an envelope of safety. But the rewards are huge.

One thing is certain: without such a reparative experience the adolescent is likely to repeat the pathology of the previous generation and to pass it on to the next in a vicious cycle of thwarted development. It is no surprise that Leanne showed the signs of entrapment that her mother did before her, that Subash found his own way of disappointing family expectations, as his father had done, that Tracy became pregnant at the same young age as her mother did and her own baby began a similar lifetime of Local Authority care, and that Dean fulfilled his mother's angry prophecy that he would end up before the courts, just like his father. Without help rather than simple punishment, all four will be condemned to hand on the pathology in their turn.

It is the financial cost of such a cycle of family breakdown, abuse, school dropout, unemployment, divorce, mental health problems and criminal justice involvement that is beginning to persuade governments to put money into early intervention schemes and adolescent services. But it is the human misery of young people, the children they once were and the adults they will become, that matters most.

References

Bailey, S. and Shooter, M. S. Editors. (2009). *The Young Mind: An Essential Guide to Mental Health for Young Adults, Parents and Teachers*. London: Amazon.

Bainbridge, D. (2009). *Teenagers: A Natural History*. London: Portobello Books.

Bandura, A. and Walters, R. H. (1959). *Adolescent Aggression*. New York: Ronald Press.

Blakeney, R. F. and Blakeney, C. D. (2006). Delinquency: a quest for moral and spiritual integrity? In Roehlkepartain, E. C., Ebstyne King, P., Wagener, L. and Benson, Peter L. Editors. *The Handbook of Spiritual Development in Childhood and Adolescence*. Thousand Oaks: Sage Publications.

Coleman, J. C. (2011). *The Nature of Adolescence*. 4th Edition. Hove, East Sussex: Routledge.

Coles, R. (1990). *The Spiritual Life of Children*. Boston: Houghton Mifflin Company.

Cooper, M. and McLeod, J. (2011). *Pluralistic Counselling and Psychotherapy*. London: Sage Publications.

Demos, J. and Demos, V. (1969). Adolescence in a historical perspective. *Journal of Marriage and Family*, **31**(4), 632–638.

Erikson, E. (1963). *Childhood and Society*. 2nd Edition. New York: Norton.

Geldart, K. and Geldart, D. (2010). *Counselling Adolescents: The Proactive Approach for Young People*. 3rd Edition. London: Sage.

Gibbs, S., Barrow, W. and Parker, R. (2015). Child development and attachment. In chapter 1, Pattison, S., Robson, M. and Beynon, A. Editors. *The Handbook of Counselling Children and Young People*. London: Sage Publications.

Glass, N. (1999). Sure Start: the development of an early intervention programme for young children in the United Kingdom. *Children & Society*, **13**, 257–264.

Hadley, S. and Yancy, G. (2011). *Therapeutic Uses of Rap and Hip-Hop*. New York: Routledge.

Hanley, T., Humphrey, N. and Lennie, C. Editors. (2013). *Adolescent Counselling Psychology: Theory, Research and Practice*. Hove, East Sussex: Routledge.

Jensen, F. E. and Nutt, A. E. (2014). *The Teenage Brain: A Neuroscientist's Survival Guide to Raising Adolescents and Young Adults*. London: Harper.

Marcia, J. E. (1980). Identity in adolescence. In Andelson, J. Editor. *Handbook of Adolescent Psychology*. New York: Wiley.

Mikulincer, M., Shaver, P. R. and Berant, E. (2013). An attachment perspective on therapeutic processes and outcomes. *Journal of Personality*, **81**(6), 606–616.

Morgan, N. (2013). *Blame My Brain: The Amazing Teenage Brain Revealed*. 3rd Edition. London: Walker Books Ltd.

Morgan, N. (2014). *The Teenage Guide to Stress*. London: Walker Books Ltd.

Rutter, M., Graham, P., Chadwick D. F. D. and Yule, W. (1976). Adolescent turmoil: fact or fiction? *Journal of Child Psychology and Psychiatry*, **17**, 35–56.

Shooter, M. S. (2009). Child and adolescent psychiatry. In chapter 5, Cook, C., Powell, A. and Sims, A. Editors. *Spirituality and Psychiatry*. London: R.C. Psych. Publications.

Southwick, S. M., Litz, B. T., Charney, D. and Friedman, M. J. Editors. (2011). *Resilience and Mental Health: Challenges Across the Lifespan*. Cambridge: Cambridge University Press.

Chapter

1

Origins of Offending in Young People

Barbara Maughan

Introduction

Some antisocial behaviour begins in adolescence, but for many young offenders – including many of those seen in the juvenile justice system and adolescent forensic services – the origins of their difficulties may lie much earlier in development. There is now clear evidence, for example, that adolescent offending and conduct problems can show links with adverse exposures as early as the prenatal period; that they are associated with neurological impairments, temperamental features, and aspects of parenting, family relationships and social circumstances in infancy and early childhood; that they are influenced by progress in schooling and peer relationships, and by the multiple biological, psychological and social changes of adolescence; and that heritable influences may impact on, and interact with, many of these (see Hill, 2002; Murray and Farrington, 2010 for reviews). The pathways linking influences at these different developmental stages are complex, and far from completely understood; different types of influence may interact, or lay down vulnerabilities that are only expressed in face of later risks, or cumulate in their effects over time. Not surprisingly, such complex chains of influence are also difficult to investigate, and – given the problems of establishing causality in any aspects of human behaviour – it is rare that we are able to say definitively that any particular influence is *causal*. Despite this, information about early origins that is potentially informative for clinical practice is accumulating at a rapid rate. This chapter provides an overview of the range of factors now thought to be involved; many of the issues raised here will be taken up in more detail in other chapters in this volume.

Heterogeneity of Adolescent Antisocial Behaviour

The search for the causes of offending has a long history, with contributions from a number of different disciplines; as a result, there are now huge literatures charting associations between adolescent offending and a wide spectrum of potential risks. For many years studies focused on broadly defined young offender samples, on the premise that most antisocial behaviour stemmed from the same roots. Yet as clinicians will be all too well aware, this may not be the case; in practice, there is often marked heterogeneity in adolescent offender populations, and this in turn may point to equally important variability in early origins. If that is so, advances in understanding the origins of offending, and in developing effective treatments, will depend on identifying more homogeneous subsets of antisocial youth (Klahr and Burt, 2014). In current literature, three main approaches to subtyping predominate: distinctions based on age at onset; distinctions based on behavioural manifestations, in particular between physically aggressive and non-aggressive ('rule-breaking') behaviours; and distinctions based on variations in levels of associated callous-unemotional (CU) traits. Though many risk factors for offending may be shared by young people in these different subgroups, others clearly differ; we thus begin by providing a brief sketch of these three different models as a background to the remainder of the discussion.

First, in relation to age at onset, Moffitt (1993: 677) proposed a developmental taxonomy whereby early onset conduct problems, evident in the form of disruptive behaviours that begin in childhood, are seen as distinct from adolescent onset delinquency in both aetiology and course. Aetiologically, Moffitt argued that the roots of early onset conduct problems could be traced to individually based characteristics – including neurocognitive deficits, under-controlled temperament and hyperactivity – that increase vulnerability to the development of behaviour problems in the context of adverse family and parenting conditions. In adolescent onset conduct problems, by contrast, individual vulnerabilities of this kind are thought to be less marked. Instead, social factors – and in particular, the influence of deviant peers – are argued to be more salient, along with frustrations arising from the 'adolescent maturity gap', whereby, in many societies, young people achieve biological maturity well before they are accorded mature status in social terms. This model (mirrored in the age at onset subtypes in the DSM-IV criteria for conduct disorder [American Psychiatric Association, 1994]) has generated major bodies of both criminological and developmental research. Key elements of the model have received extensive support, though some qualifications have also emerged (Fairchild et al., 2013: 940).

Next, in terms of behavioural manifestations, many investigators have argued the importance of differentiating physical aggression from non-aggressive/rule-breaking or 'covert' antisocial behaviours (see e.g. Tremblay, 2010). Although many young offenders show both types of behavioural difficulty, developmental variations between the two are clear. Physical aggression emerges early in childhood, and shows highly stable individual differences over time; rule-breaking and delinquency, by contrast, are more common in adolescence, and typically follow a more benign later course. In addition, aetiological factors have been found to vary, with behaviour genetic studies suggesting that both the genetic and the non-shared environmental influences on these two dimensions of antisocial behaviour are largely distinct (Burt, 2013). To an extent, however, behavioural and age at onset distinctions may overlap, with aggression more marked among young people with early onset difficulties, and rule-breaking more common in adolescent onset groups.

Third, and from a somewhat different perspective, recent research has included a major focus on the subgroup of antisocial youth who show features that might be labelled psychopathy in adulthood, and in childhood are regarded as showing high levels of CU traits: a lack of guilt and remorse, a lack of concern for the feelings of others, shallow or superficial expressions of affect and a lack of concern over performance in important activities (see e.g. Frick et al., 2014). In antisocial samples CU traits are predictive of more severe aggression, and more persistent antisocial behaviour problems, and high levels of CU traits – now reflected in the 'limited prosocial emotions' specifier for conduct disorder in DSM-5 (American Psychiatric Association, 2013) – are thought to index a further subtype of early onset conduct problems, with particular early origins and treatment needs.

With these distinctions in mind we turn to an overview of the key individual, family-level and broader social risk factors for youth offending identified in current research. Because many young offenders show behaviours typical of conduct disorder, we draw on literatures that take offending, disruptive behaviour disorders and broader designations of 'externalising' behaviour as their focus of interest. By risk factors, we mean factors that have been found in the research literature to be associated with an increased risk of offending – that is, they have *correlational* links with adverse behavioural outcomes. As noted above, establishing *causality* in this area is inevitably difficult, though investigators are increasingly using more complex designs in an attempt to rule out, or at least evaluate the effects of, established sources of confounding. A second general issue to bear in mind here is that, although the risk factors discussed here are all indeed associated with an increased likelihood of offending, there are nonetheless marked individual differences in response to almost all known risks. This suggests that some young people benefit from protective factors, or factors that promote resilience in the face of risk (see e.g. Rutter, 2013; also Williams and Kemp, Chapter 2). In this chapter different risk factors are considered in turn. Much theory and empirical evidence in this area supports biosocial models whereby antisocial behaviour is seen as the outcome of an interplay between individual, developmental and social risks. And, finally, where evidence points to differing associations with different subtypes of adolescent offending, these are noted. At the end of the chapter findings on a range of risk factors are drawn together in a more speculative way to sketch in possible developmental pathways to youth offending for young people with aggressive behaviours, and with high levels of CU traits.

Risk Factors for Youth Offending

Individual Level Factors

Temperament

Individual differences in temperament are evident from very early in development, and have been implicated in many models of antisocial behaviour. Once thought to be largely heritable, temperament is now known to be responsive to social influences, such that particular temperamental features may be most salient in conjunction with other risks; differing aspects of temperament may also interact to influence antisocial propensities. Lahey et al. (1999), for example, proposed a model combining elements of oppositional/'difficult' temperament in infancy (including irritability, resistance to control and anger); behavioural inhibition (thought to protect against the development of conduct problems); and callousness/low reward dependence, associated with low levels of empathy and concern for others. More recent discussions (see e.g. Hill and Maughan, 2015: 48; Pardini and Frick, 2013: 21) have posited differing biosocial pathways to early onset conduct problems associated with different temperamental origins. For children who show reactive aggression and oppositionality, such models propose that vulnerability to antisocial behaviour is set in train by a combination of infant anger-proneness and negative, intrusive parenting that serves to increase negative mood in the child. For children who show proactive aggression and lack empathy, by contrast, their lack of emotional responsiveness may be associated with a quite different temperamental profile, centring on fearlessness. Infant fearfulness is important in the development of conscience and guilt, and may also be linked with reduced behavioural inhibition; a fearless temperament may thus mean that children miss out on the developmental advantages that a more fearful disposition can convey. Finally, though individual temperamental traits have typically been regarded as either advantageous or disadvantageous, this may not always be the case; instead, consistent with models of differential susceptibility, some traits may be maladaptive under adverse conditions, but more adaptive in others. Scott and O'Connor (2012), for example, found that emotionally dysregulated children were more responsive to improvements in parenting following a parenting intervention than their more 'headstrong' counterparts, suggesting that temperamental features may not only be important in the early development of conduct problems, but may also moderate treatment effects.

Autonomic Reactivity

Low resting heart rate – now listed as a putative biomarker for conduct disorder in DSM-5 (American Psychiatric Association, 2013) – is among the best-replicated biological correlate of antisocial behaviour in young people. The mechanisms underlying this association are not fully understood, but two main models have been proposed: first, that low autonomic nervous system (ANS) arousal indexes a relative lack of fear; or second, that it constitutes an unpleasant physiological state that prompts individuals to engage in stimulating behaviours (some of which may be antisocial) in order to increase levels of arousal. A recent meta-analysis of over 100 independent reports (Portnoy and Farrington, 2015) reported a small summary effect size (d = −0.20) for associations between low resting heart rate and antisocial behaviour; and that this overall effect was similar for males and females, and did not vary systematically by age; it was also observed for a range of types of antisocial behaviour, including both aggression and psychopathy. They noted that it could also have clinical implications, as some cognitive/behavioural interventions for conduct problems have shown increases in levels of autonomic arousal among their outcomes, while others suggest that autonomic activity may moderate intervention effects.

Neurobiological Correlates

In addition to ANS activity, serotonergic functioning and stress-regulating mechanisms, including the hypothalamic-pituitary-adrenal (HPA) axis, have also been explored as neurobiological correlates of antisocial behaviour in childhood and adolescence (van Goozen et al., 2007). In adults, there is strong evidence for an inverse relationship between serotonin (5-HT) measures and antisocial behaviour. Van Goozen et al., concluded that the direction of the association is less straightforward; as noted below, however, the MAO-A (monoamine oxidase-A) genotype has been implicated in a range of gene–environment interaction studies, with individuals with the low activity form of the gene showing much elevated levels of antisocial behaviour in conjunction with maltreatment or other adverse experiences. Associations with HPA axis activity are complex, presenting a range of measurement challenges, and findings have been somewhat mixed. In general, however, studies of school-aged children have reported negative relationships between conduct problems and both basal and stress-induced cortisol levels, stronger in clinic-referred, than in community, samples (see Fairchild et al., 2013: 932).

Neuropsychological and Psychophysiological Correlates

There is extensive evidence that many delinquents and young people with severe antisocial behaviour have lower IQ scores than their non-delinquent peers, with verbal deficits being especially marked (see e.g. Rutter et al., 1998). Verbal deficits also appear to be associated with the persistence of antisocial behaviour, and have been theorised to be important because of their involvement in the development of self-control; they may be less evident in young people with high levels of CU traits than in other antisocial groups. Deficits in executive functioning (concerned with problem-solving, planning and inhibitory control) are also widely supported, and young people with conduct disorder seem especially likely to show altered decision-making under 'hot' or motivational conditions. Moffitt (1993: 680) argued that neuropsychological difficulties of this kind are especially characteristic of early onset and persistent conduct problems; some studies suggest that they may also be apparent, though to a less marked degree, in adolescent onset groups (Fairchild et al., 2013: 934).

A good deal of evidence now suggests that children and young people with antisocial behaviour and high levels of CU traits also show specific profiles in relation to emotion processing: they are poor at modulating their behaviour in response to punishment, and have difficulties in processing sad and fearful emotional expressions in others. By contrast, those without CU traits may show exaggerated responses to anger or social threat (Viding et al., 2012). Consistent with these findings, functional neuroimaging studies have reported lower amygdala activity in response to others' distress in samples of antisocial children high in CU traits, along with abnormal responses to punishment cues in a number of brain regions. Structural imaging studies suggest that boys high in CU traits have increased grey matter and decreased white matter concentrations in fronto-temporal circuitry involved in emotion processing and decision-making. In more general conduct problem samples, however, antisocial children and adolescents have been found to have decreased grey matter in several fronto-temporal areas. More generally, the burgeoning neuroimaging literature suggests that children with conduct disorder show alterations in paralimbic system regions (ventromedial, lateral orbitofrontal and superior temporal cortices together with specific underlying limbic regions) regulating motivation and emotion control (Arnsten and Rubia, 2012), along with changes in cortical thickness and folding indicated by Fairchild et al. (2013: 934).

Information Processing and Social Cognition

Deficits in social-cognitive abilities – the skills involved in attending to, interpreting and responding to social cues – have been implicated in a range of childhood disorders. Dodge (1993), in an influential early model, proposed that aggressive children – many of whom grow up in threatening or abusive environments – are more likely to attend to threatening aspects of others' actions, to interpret hostile intent in neutral or ambiguous situations (that is, develop hostile attributional biases), and to favour aggressive solutions when faced with social challenges. Many (though not all) aspects of this model have received empirical support, and provide a persuasive basis for understanding the difficulties many antisocial young people face in relationships with adults and peers, and the processes that may contribute to the persistence of their difficulties over time. Recent evidence suggests that social-cognitive deficits are most pronounced in early onset and persistent conduct problems, but also apparent in groups with later-emerging difficulties, perhaps via influences on the quality of relationships with peers (Oliver et al., 2011).

Family-Level Factors

Heritable Influences

Antisocial behaviour and offending run in families, and there is by now extensive evidence from twin and adoption studies that genetic factors are contributors to these effects, accounting for some 40–50% of population variation in antisocial outcomes (see e.g. Rhee and Waldman, 2002). Other genetically informative designs lead to similar conclusions: Kendler et al. (2015), for example, using criminal record data on full- and half-siblings in a large Swedish population, found that between 35 and 55% of individual differences in risk for officially recorded crime were attributable to heritable factors. Longitudinal twin studies suggest that genetic influences are also implicated in the continuity of antisocial behaviour from late childhood to early adulthood, with new genetic and environmental factors coming on stream in adolescence (Wichers et al., 2013: 198). And heritability estimates vary for different subtypes of antisocial behaviour, with physical aggression, high levels of CU traits and early onset conduct problems all associated with stronger genetic influence than rule-breaking or adolescent onset delinquency.

Beyond these general estimates, genetically informative research has also cast light on the ways in which genetic and environmental risks intertwine across development. First, the extent of genetic influence on externalising behaviours appears to vary with social and contextual factors, such that deviant peer affiliations, for example, can amplify genetic risk, while prosocial affiliations may suppress it (Burt and Klump, 2014). At the individual level, theoretically informed tests of measured gene–environment interactions (GxE) have also been informative, suggesting that genetic factors *moderate* young people's susceptibility to other risks (Taylor and Kim-Cohen, 2007). In one long-term longitudinal study, for example, variations in MAO-A genotype showed pervasive effects on risk for adolescent and early adult offending, interacting with factors as varied as maternal smoking in pregnancy, material deprivation in childhood, maltreatment, childhood IQ and leaving school without qualifications (Fergusson et al., 2012).

Second, it is also clear that genetically influenced traits can affect *exposure* to adverse environments. It has long been known that aspects of children's temperament and behaviour can evoke negative reinforcing responses from parents (an evocative gene–environment correlation – rGE). More recent evidence suggests that similar processes occur in other relationships, including those with peers: as early as the kindergarten years, genetically influenced hyperactive and disruptive behaviours have been found to evoke peer victimisation and rejection (Boivin et al., 2013), while later in development genetic factors contribute to affiliations with deviant peers (Kendler et al., 2007).

Third, behaviour geneticists have highlighted a further type of gene–environment correlation that may complicate interpretation of associations with many other family factors once assumed to be purely environmental in origin. Because the same gene variants that are transmitted from parents to children may also influence the family environments those parents provide, apparently 'environmental' factors may actually show genetic mediation. Active gene–environment correlations of this kind are likely to be ubiquitous, and may be especially salient in relation to antisocial child outcomes: antisocial parents often provide less than optimal rearing environments for their children, but confounding from genetic influences makes it difficult to determine how far these are indeed implicated in the development of children's difficulties or largely a reflection of genetic transmission. This issue is explored below. Finally, consistent with findings from animal models, evidence is now beginning to emerge that epigenetic mechanisms such as DNA methylation, that are responsive to environmental influence, may play a role in the biological pathways linking adverse environmental exposures and behavioural outcomes (McGowan and Roth, 2015; Provençal et al., 2015).

Prenatal and Perinatal Influences

Early brain development is especially sensitive to the effects of environmental stressors; as a result, adverse pre- and perinatal exposures (including effects of toxins, maternal diet in pregnancy, prenatal maternal substance use and obstetric complications) have attracted attention as potential risks for behavioural outcomes. Isolating the specific effects of such early risks presents challenges; birth complications, for example – of interest as possible contributors to neuropsychological deficits, and identified as risk factors in a number of studies – are often associated with other adverse circumstances, making it difficult to detect their specific effects. Similar cautions apply to findings on maternal smoking in pregnancy, which has repeatedly been shown to be associated with offspring behavioural outcomes including delinquency and crime (Wakschlag et al., 2002). Yet mothers who smoke in pregnancy differ from other mothers in a multitude of ways, and confounding from the effects of these associated factors is difficult to rule out. One recent study using a genetically informative design (Kuja-Halkola et al., 2014) found effects consistent with a causal role for prenatal tobacco exposure on birth outcomes (birth weight, pre-term birth and small-for-dates), but not in relation to cognitive outcomes or crime; instead, the pattern of associations was more suggestive of genetic effects influencing behaviours in both maternal and offspring generations. As noted earlier, however, pregnancy smoking has been implicated in some studies of gene–environment interactions, leaving open the possibility that – in addition to its adverse impact on physical health outcomes – it may be implicated in behavioural outcomes via more complex pathways.

One further prenatal influence that has received particular attention in the child development field concerns the impact of exposure to maternal anxiety, depression or stress in pregnancy. Much of the impetus for this work derives from evidence from animal studies showing sizeable and lasting effects of exposure to prenatal stress on offspring neurogenesis, immunity and stress physiology. Building on foetal programming models for physical health (whereby in utero exposures are thought to initiate adaptive responses in the organism that are then carried forward in development), investigators have queried whether similar programming effects might apply in the psychological and behavioural domains.

Findings from a wide range of studies do now provide evidence that mothers' emotional well-being in pregnancy is associated with neurodevelopmental, endocrine, immune, and behavioural and emotional outcomes in children (Talge et al., 2007). In the main, however, these findings relate to outcomes measured at a single point in time, whereas a programming hypothesis posits persisting effects. The longest-term evidence available to date comes from a prospective study beginning in pregnancy and tracking offspring emotional/behavioural outcomes repeatedly to age 13 (O'Donnell et al., 2014). Children of mothers with high levels of anxiety and depression in pregnancy showed significantly elevated levels of emotional and behavioural difficulties in early childhood that persisted, with no appreciable attenuation of effects, to early adolescence, and were robust to controls for a wide range of potential confounders. While much still needs to be learned about the mechanisms involved here, evidence of this kind provides strong support for a role for prenatal exposures in the development of behavioural outcomes, and for the need for interventions – such as the Nurse-Family Partnership (Miller, 2015) – that begin at the earliest stages of development.

Parenting

Decades of longitudinal research in many countries has confirmed that variations in parenting are strongly associated with risk for delinquency and crime. Numerous authoritative reviews have synthesised findings from this large body of research (see e.g. Patterson et al., 1992). Parenting influences begin early in development, and continue into adolescence, with evidence suggesting that adolescent outcomes are influenced by earlier as well as more proximal aspects of parenting. Parenting practices have been argued to account for considerable proportions of the variation in childhood conduct problems; in relation to delinquency, one recent review put the figure at around 11% (Hoeve et al., 2009).

Despite the consistency of these findings, interpretation of their meaning is not straightforward; in addition to the possibility of reverse causation (child behaviours evoking differing patterns of response from parents), variations in parenting may also be confounded with other risks for delinquency, including heritable effects. As many commentators have noted, support for causal inferences is strengthened when evidence from studies with different designs converge on the same conclusions. For some aspects of parenting converging evidence of this kind is now becoming available: in addition to longitudinal studies (valuable in determining the temporal ordering of effects), evidence from natural/quasi-experiments (including to explore issues of genetic confounding, adoption studies, studies of discordant monozygotic twins and children of twins designs) along with evidence from parenting interventions can be drawn upon to clarify effects.

Most theoretical models highlight two core dimensions of parenting: first, a positive dimension tapping warmth, availability, positive engagement and support; and second, a dimension reflecting behavioural control that includes discipline, monitoring and behaviour management. In terms of positive parenting, longitudinal studies have identified links between early parental involvement and fewer conduct problems in adolescence; parental warmth and responsiveness show similar patterns of association, and have emerged as key mediators of effects in successful parenting interventions with younger children. In relation to discipline and control, extensive evidence supports links between harsh and coercive disciplinary strategies and children's risk for conduct problems. One of the best-established bodies of research stems from Patterson et al.'s (1992) 'coercive family process' model, whereby child problem behaviour comes to be learned during episodes of parent–child conflict via negative reinforcement processes whereby the parent becomes angry, but then gives in to the child's demands to buy short-term relief. A key feature of effective parenting interventions is to help parents become aware of such coercive cycles and learn alternative strategies including, in adolescence, building good communication, monitoring young people's behaviour and using consistent limit setting. Harsh discipline and rejecting parenting have consistently been associated with increased risk for conduct problems and delinquency. Here, however, problems of reverse causation and confounding may be especially acute. In a review of evidence from a variety of research designs Jaffee et al. (2012) concluded that there are reciprocal relationships between youth antisocial behaviour and harsh discipline: child effects on parents are present, but there is also evidence for environmentally mediated effects of harsh discipline in increasing levels of child and adolescent conduct problems.

Finally we turn to an aspect of parenting of particular salience in adolescence: parents' monitoring of their children's activities and whereabouts. Here too there is considerable evidence for links with youth antisocial behaviour, but also debates over their meaning, in this case centring on the possibility that effects are largely child-driven, reflecting a greater willingness among better behaved young people to share information about their activities and lives. A recent study using the extended children of twins design (which can account for both active and evocative gene–environment correlations) did, however, document an environmentally mediated association between parental knowledge and adolescents' externalising behaviours in a relatively low-risk sample (Marceau et al., 2015). In high-risk samples longitudinal studies have found that some parents *reduce* their levels of monitoring and guidance as their children reach adolescence. Interventions targeted at maintaining parental monitoring in high-risk groups have shown beneficial effects, with evidence that change in parental monitoring is a key mediator of intervention outcomes.

We conclude by noting that while these various aspects of parenting have been seen as important contributors to the development and maintenance of both aggressive and rule-breaking behaviours, it has often been assumed that antisocial young people with high levels of CU traits are less susceptible to parental discipline, and show attenuated responses to punishment cues. Recent evidence, however, is beginning to question that view. A systematic review of findings from longitudinal and intervention studies (Waller et al., 2013) found consistent associations between dimensions of parenting and increases in CU traits in both childhood and adolescence, with evidence that positive, affective dimensions of parenting may be of particular relevance to the development or prevention of CU traits.

Attachment Security

Since the time of Bowlby's early studies of 'juvenile thieves' (Bowlby, 1944), there has been strong interest in the possibility that attachment insecurity contributes to risk for antisocial behaviour. Reviews and meta-analyses drawing together findings from the large literatures in this area have generally supported that view. Fearon et al. (2010), for example, reported a medium effect size ($d = 0.31$) from a meta-analysis of associations between insecurity and externalising outcomes in childhood (up to age 12); within the overall insecure category, disorganised attachment patterns seemed most strongly implicated in links with disruptive behaviours. Savage (2014), focusing specifically on aggression and violence, extended the picture to older ages, and to a range of approaches to assessing attachment security. Most findings were in the expected direction, and many confirmed statistically significant associations between insecure attachment and increased risks of aggressive behaviour. A key question in this area is, of course, whether attachment predicts behavioural outcomes independent of other aspects of the parent–child relationship. Scott et al. (2011), examining adolescents' own representations of attachment in three independent samples, found that it did – suggesting in turn that attachment patterns could play a valuable role in clinical assessment and treatment models.

Maltreatment

There is also strong evidence for associations between more severely negative experiences within the family and risk for antisocial behaviour and delinquency (Jaffee et al., 2004); one meta-analysis estimated a moderate to large effect size associated with exposure to violence, primarily reflecting maltreatment. In interpreting these findings much the same concerns arise as in relation to other aspects of parenting: might the association arise from evocative effects of aversive behaviours on the part of the child, or from family confounding, including effects of parents' genetic propensities? Jaffee et al. (2012: 9) reviewed evidence from appropriately designed studies on these questions, and concluded that – though the evidence base is less extensive than for other aspects of parenting, and derives from studies using informant reports of maltreatment rather than official records – available findings do clearly point to environmentally mediated effects of maltreatment on risk for antisocial outcomes.

Other Family-level Influences

Numerous other family-level influences including teen parenting, marital discord and parental divorce (Bornovalova et al., 2013), parental psychopathology, including maternal depression (Barker et al., 2012), and family poverty all show consistent associations with increased levels of antisocial behaviour in children and adolescents. In each case, however, problems of confounding arise, making it uncertain whether the documented associations do indeed reflect environmentally mediated effects. Jaffee et al. (2012: 5) reviewed evidence from quasi-experimental and other studies in each of these areas. In the main they concluded that though familial (including genetic) confounding might play a part, there was also evidence of environmentally mediated effects of family-related adversity. The main exception to this pattern concerned parental alcohol problems, where links with antisocial behaviour in offspring seem primarily reflective of genetic transmission.

Influences beyond the Family

Peer Deviance

Aggressive and oppositional children are often rejected by their more prosocial peers, and associate mainly with other children with similar difficulties. As a result, they may both lack the advantages of positive peer interactions, and be at increased risk of having their own antisocial tendencies maintained or amplified through interactions with deviant peers. Peer deviance is a strong correlate and predictor of antisocial behaviour in both childhood and adolescence, whether it occurs in the context of dyadic or small group relationships or, at older ages, in delinquent gangs.

A long-standing debate in this area concerns the direction and meaning of these associations: do they reflect selection effects (birds of a feather flocking together) – or do they suggest that peer deviance plays an independent role in maintaining or exacerbating risks for delinquency and crime? As noted earlier, genetically informative studies provide clear evidence of evocative effects of individual characteristics on selection into deviant peer groups, suggesting that at least part of the association reflects processes of this kind. But this does not, of course, rule out the possibility that once established, deviant peer relations do work to exacerbate individuals' own antisocial activities via modelling and related processes. Recent studies have provided support, for example, for a role for peer influences in very specific processes such as deviancy training (the amount of talk between peers about aggression, rule-breaking, defiance of authority and property destruction), and the extent to which peers respond positively to such talk (Dishion and Tipsord, 2011). Findings from broader-range longitudinal studies have been more mixed, though there is evidence that joining gangs is associated with at least short-term increases in antisocial behaviour. Reviewing this and other evidence, Jaffee et al. (2012: 20) concluded that both social selection and social causation processes are implicated in the relationship between antisocial behaviour and peer deviance.

Schooling and Education

School-related influences may be implicated in risk for disruptive and antisocial behaviours in a variety of ways. Schools vary in their social and organisational 'climates', and these variations show modest associations with indicators of children's academic progress and behaviour (Rutter and Maughan, 2002). In part, school climate may reflect variations in the background characteristics of the children a school admits; in part, they seem attributable to differences in organisational characteristics and the tenor of day-to-day school life. For behavioural outcomes, the composition of pupil groupings may be especially important: young children are more likely to become aggressive in classes with other very aggressive children, and risks of delinquency may be increased in secondary schools with large proportions of low achievers or other delinquent youth. As we have seen, many young people with behavioural difficulties may also be low achievers; as a result, especially as they enter their teens, many may become disengaged from school. Henry et al. (2012) found that a school disengagement 'warning index' predicted delinquency in adolescence and into early adulthood, suggesting that school disengagement may form part of a 'cascade' of processes that contribute to vulnerability to crime. By the same token, however, school- and classroom-based interventions can prove highly effective in behaviour management, and for some severely disadvantaged children schooling can be an important source of positive experiences and support. In addition, experimental studies of preschool programmes have documented important long-term gains in terms of reduced risks of delinquency and unemployment many years after participants left school (see e.g. Schweinhart et al., 2005).

Neighbourhood Influences

Criminologists have long posited that characteristics of neighbourhoods, including 'collective efficacy' – the sense of social cohesion among neighbours, and their willingness to intervene for the common good – have independent influences on risks for delinquency and crime (see e.g. Sampson et al., 1997). Longitudinal studies (Odgers et al., 2009) suggest that collective efficacy may have a protective effect on children living in deprived contexts, but experimental evidence is less clear-cut in its effects. Jaffee et al. (2012: 24) report on findings from two US randomised studies where families were moved from less to more affluent areas; at best, outcomes some years after the moves showed slight reductions in risk of antisocial behaviours for girls, but equivocal, or possibly worsened, effects for boys. The meaning of these findings has been much debated, however, and further evidence would be valuable before drawing definitive conclusions.

Early Developmental Pathways

For many young people, risk factors from these differing domains may converge, interact or accumulate across development to contribute to risk for offending via distinct developmental pathways. Though evidence linking all the proposed elements in each pathway is still limited, commentators are beginning to draw them together into illustrative scenarios that may be valuable in generating further hypotheses (see e.g. Hill and Maughan, 2015: 49; Pardini and Frick, 2013: 22). Two of these elements are explored below.

The first, a 'high reactive' pathway, is thought to arise from a combination of temperamental anger-proneness/emotional dysregulation in the infant and negative, intrusive experiences within the family; this pathway is especially relevant to the development of early aggression. In part, extended displays of anger in a young child may evoke negative responses from parents; in part, negative emotionality in both parent and child may reflect shared genetic vulnerabilities; and in part, punitive responses from parents may exacerbate negative mood in the child and undermine the development of emotion regulation skills. Maternal depression, marital discord and physical abuse are also likely to be implicated in this pathway, though studies that bring all these elements together are still limited. Exposure to maternal anxiety and depression in utero may increase initial risks for infant negative emotionality (Davis et al., 2007), and gene–environment interactions such as those described in relation to MAO-A may also be especially relevant to the high reactive pathway. Outside the family, and somewhat later in development, anger-prone responses by the child can lead to difficulties in interactions with other adults, and to negative interactions with, or rejection by, peers; over time, the hostile environment within the family can thus extend to the child's wider social world. And from a social-cognitive perspective children with high levels of anger may be especially prone to develop hostile attributional biases, providing a further impetus to maintain their aggressive responses.

The second, 'low reactive' pathway, relating to young people who show high levels of CU traits, is thought to differ from this progression in a number of key ways. There are few developmental studies of the very early origins of CU traits, but several lines of evidence suggest possible elements in the pathway. First, vulnerable infants may make less eye contact with parents than other children, possibly leading to less engagement with caregivers and hence fewer opportunities to acquire an understanding of others' emotions. Second, lack of emotional responsiveness to others' emotions may be increased by temperamental fearlessness, which may inhibit the development of responsiveness to others' distress and may also be associated with reduced behavioural inhibition. The infant who experiences fear less frequently, or at low levels, may also be less likely to look to a parent for comfort in the face of threat, and so may experience fewer parent–child attachment sequences, further reducing emotional contact. Finally, early physiological under-arousal may contribute to risk for CU traits, further contributing to processes such as reduced fear conditioning.

Adolescent Onset and Adolescent Risks

Rates of delinquency rise sharply across the teens, and fall back equally clearly in the early adult years. These near-universal trends – recognised in criminological theory as the age–crime curve – suggest that though much disruptive behaviour has roots in childhood, new processes relevant to the expression of antisocial tendencies come on-stream in adolescence.

As outlined above, Moffitt (1993: 686) proposed that adolescent onset delinquency emerges with the onset of puberty, and has origins in the adolescent maturity gap, in cultural and historical contexts influencing adolescence, and in mimicry of the behaviour of deviant peers. Though initially viewed as less ominous for later development than its early onset counterpart, subsequent evidence has somewhat modified that view (Odgers et al., 2008); whatever its origins, delinquency in adolescence can result in 'snares' such as poor school achievement, problematic relationships or substance use that may constrain later opportunities and perpetuate antisocial lifestyles.

Ideally, strong tests of 'adolescent-specific' risks for delinquency would require long-term studies tracking samples prospectively from childhood; at this stage, evidence of this kind is still relatively limited. As we have seen, genetically informative longitudinal studies suggest that, alongside genetic factors that influence risk continuing from childhood, new genetic and environmental influences on externalising behaviours emerge in adolescence (Wichers et al., 2013: 200). The social, relational and psychological changes that accompany adolescence are legion. In addition, evidence is accumulating that the onset of puberty is associated with a range of neurobiological changes that are likely to be implicated in the overall rise in antisocial behaviour in the teens. Much of this work has focused on the broader category of risk-taking, and the reasons why, across a range of contexts, adolescents appear to take 'risky' decisions (Blakemore and Robbins, 2012). Neuroimaging studies highlight two features of particular importance here. First, the brain regions involved in cognitive control (including the prefrontal cortex) show a protracted period of structural development that continues throughout adolescence and into early adult life. At the same time, however, heightened brain responses to socially relevant, reward-related cues are more adolescence-specific, and prompted by the hormonal changes of puberty (Peper and Dahl, 2013).

From an evolutionary perspective such heightened sensitivity to social stimuli should carry adaptive advantages, preparing adolescents to meet the new demands of the adult world. In some contexts, however, it can prove more problematic. Experimental research provides graphic evidence that adolescents are more susceptible to peer influence in risky situations than are adults (Gardner and Steinberg, 2005), the presence of peers appearing to 'prime' motivations to immediately available, even if risky, rewards. Given that much adolescent delinquency takes place in peer contexts, the implications for antisocial behaviour are clear. Peer influences (along with other social-contextual factors) also appear to moderate hormone–behaviour associations in the teens, with evidence, for example, that high testosterone levels are associated with non-aggressive conduct problems in boys with deviant peers, but with prosocial leadership in those with more conventional friends (Rowe et al., 2004). Finally, the timing of puberty may also be salient, with early timing in particular being associated with increased risk for antisocial behaviour (and other difficulties) in both girls (Mendle et al., 2007) and boys (Mendle and Ferrero, 2010). The mechanisms involved here are not fully understood; biologically based influences may be involved, but commentators have also proposed a 'maturation disparity' hypothesis (whereby the gap between early maturers' physical and psychosocial development puts them at risk of adverse outcomes), or the possibility that pre-existing behavioural difficulties may be exacerbated by the new social challenges of adolescence (Ge and Natsuaki, 2009).

Conclusions

As this brief overview suggests, many differing domains of risk are implicated in the origins of adolescent offending. For many young people, vulnerabilities may be set in train very early in development; for others, risks may accumulate later in childhood or in the adolescent years. While researchers have made considerable progress in documenting risk associations in these differing domains, the developmental pathways involved are still in many ways speculative. In addition, risks for antisocial behaviour need to be viewed in the context of the moderating effects of the resilience-related factors that appear to buffer some young people against effects of adversity, and the range of influences that contribute to many young people's eventual desistance from crime. The research literature on early origins has already contributed extensively to the development of clinical practice and policy in relation to youth offending: much of the rationale for parenting programmes, for policies to support troubled families and reduce school exclusions, as well as for child-focused and multimodal interventions draws heavily on the literature reviewed here. As our understanding of developmental pathways increases, implications for prevention and treatment can also be expected to become clearer in their turn.

References

American Psychiatric Association. (1994). *Diagnostic and Statistical Manual of Mental Disorders*. 4th Edition. Washington, DC: American Psychiatric Association Publishing.

American Psychiatric Association. (2013). *Diagnostic and Statistical Manual of Mental Disorders*. 5th Edition. Arlington, VA: American Psychiatric Association Publishing.

Arnsten, A. F. T. and Rubia, K. (2012). Neurobiological circuits regulating attention, cognitive control, motivation, and emotion: disruptions in neurodevelopmental psychiatric disorders. *Journal of the American Academy of Child and Adolescent Psychiatry*, **51**, 356–367.

Barker, E. D., Copeland, W., Maughan, B., Jaffee, S. R. and Uher, R. (2012). Relative impact of maternal depression and associated risk factors on offspring psychopathology. *British Journal of Psychiatry*, **200**, 124–129.

Blakemore, S. J. and Robbins, T. W. (2012). Decision-making in the adolescent brain. *Nature Neuroscience*, **15**, 1184–1191.

Boivin, M., Brendgen, M., Vitaro, F., Forget-Dubois, N., Feng, B., Tremblay, R. E. and Dionne, G. (2013). Evidence of gene-environment correlation for peer difficulties: disruptive behaviors predict early peer relation difficulties in school through genetic effects. *Development and Psychopathology*, **25**, 79–92.

Bowlby, J. (1944). Forty-four juvenile thieves: their characters and home life. *International Journal of Psychoanalysis*, **25**, 19–52.

Burt, S. A. (2013). Do etiological influences on aggression overlap with those on rule breaking? a meta-analysis. *Psychological Medicine*, **43**, 1801–1812.

Burt, S. A. and Klump, K. (2014). Prosocial peer affiliation suppresses genetic influences on non-aggressive antisocial behaviors during childhood. *Psychological Medicine*, **44**, 821–830.

Davis, E. P., Glynn, L. M., Schetter, C. D., Hobel, C., Chicz-Demet, A. and Sandman, C. A. (2007). Prenatal exposure to maternal depression and cortisol influences infant temperament. *Journal of the American Academy of Child and Adolescent Psychiatry*, **46**, 737–746.

Dishion, T. J. and Tipsord, J. M. (2011). Peer contagion in child and adolescent social and emotional development. *Annual Review of Psychology*, **62**, 189–214.

Dodge, K. A. (1993). Social-cognitive mechanisms in the development of conduct disorder and depression. *Annual Review of Psychology*, **44**, 559–584.

Fairchild, G., van Goozen, S. H. M., Calder, A. J. and Goodyer, I. M. (2013). Research review: evaluating and reformulating the developmental taxonomic theory of antisocial behaviour. *Journal of Child Psychology and Psychiatry*, **54**, 924–940.

Fearon, R. P., Bakermans-Kranenburg, M. J., van IJzendoorn, M. H., Lapsley, A-M. and Roisman, G. I. (2010). The significance of insecure attachment and disorganization in the development of children's externalizing behavior: a meta-analytic study. *Child Development*, **81**, 435–456.

Fergusson, D. M., Boden, J. M., Horwood, L. J., Miller, A. and Kennedy, M. A. (2012). Moderating role of the MAOA genotype in antisocial behaviour. *British Journal of Psychiatry*, **200**, 116–123.

Frick, P. J., Ray, J. V., Thornton, L. C. and Kahn, R. E. (2014). Can callous-unemotional traits enhance the understanding, diagnosis, and treatment of serious conduct problems in children and adolescents? a comprehensive review. *Psychological Bulletin*, **140**, 1–57.

Gardner, M. and Steinberg, L. (2005). Peer influence on risk taking, risk preference, and risky decision making in adolescence and adulthood: an experimental study. *Developmental Psychology*, **41**, 625–635.

Ge, X. and Natsuaki, M. N. (2009). In search of explanations for early pubertal timing effects on developmental psychopathology. *Current Directions in Psychological Science*, **18**, 327–331.

Henry, K. L., Knight, K. E. and Thornberry, T. P. (2012). School disengagement as a predictor of dropout, delinquency, and problem substance use during adolescence and early adulthood. *Journal of Youth and Adolescence*, **41**, 156–166.

Hill, J. (2002). Biological, psychological and social processes in the conduct disorders. *Journal of Child Psychology and Psychiatry*, **43**, 133–164.

Hill, J. and Maughan, B. (2015). Conceptual issues and empirical challenges in the disruptive behavior disorders. In Thapar, A., Pine, D. S., Leckman, J., Snowling, M. J., Scott, S. and Taylor, E. Editors. *Rutter's Child and Adolescent Psychiatry*. 6th Edition (pp. 37–48). Chichester: Wiley.

Hoeve, M., Dubas, J. S., Eichelsheim, V. I., van der Laan, P. H., Smeenk, W. and Gerris, J. R. M. (2009). The relationship between parenting and delinquency: a meta-analysis. *Journal of Abnormal Child Psychology*, **37**, 749–775.

Jaffee, S. R., Caspi, A., Moffitt, T. E., Polo-Tomas, M., Price, T. S. and Taylor, A. (2004). Physical maltreatment victim to antisocial child: evidence of an environmentally mediated process. *Journal of Abnormal Psychology*, **113**, 44–55.

Jaffee, S. R., Strait, L. B. and Odgers, C. L. (2012). From correlates to causes: can quasi-experimental studies and statistical innovations bring us closer to identifying the causes of antisocial behavior? *National Institute of Health Public Access Author Manuscript – NIHMS328571 finally edited and published in Psychological Bulletin*, **138**, 272–295.

Kendler, K. S., Jacobson, K. C., Gardner, C. O., Gillespie, N., Aggen, S. A. and Prescott, C. A. (2007). Creating a social world – a developmental twin study of peer-group deviance. *Archives of General Psychiatry*, **64**, 958–965.

Kendler, K. S., Lonn, S. L., Maes, H. H., Sundquist, J. and Sundquist, K. (2015). The etiologic role of genetic and environmental factors in criminal behavior as determined from full- and half-sibling pairs: an evaluation of the validity of the twin method. *Psychological Medicine*, **45**, 1873–1880.

Klahr, A. M. and Burt, S. A. (2014). Practitioner Review: evaluation of the known behavioral heterogeneity in conduct disorder to improve its assessment and treatment. *Journal of Child Psychology and Psychiatry*, **55**, 1300–1310.

Kuja-Halkola, R., D'Onofrio, B. M., Larsson, H. and Lichtenstein, P. (2014). Maternal smoking during pregnancy and adverse outcomes in offspring: genetic and environmental sources of covariance. *Behavior Genetics*, **44**, 456–467.

Lahey, B. B., Waldman, I. D. and McBurnett, K. (1999). Annotation: the development of antisocial behavior: an integrative causal model. *Journal of Child Psychology and Psychiatry*, **40**, 669–682.

Marceau, K., Narusyte, J., Lichtenstein, P., Ganiban, J. M., Spotts, E. L., Reiss, D. and Neiderhiser, J. M. (2015). Parental knowledge is an environmental influence on adolescent externalizing. *Journal of Child Psychology and Psychiatry*, **56**, 130–137.

McGowan, P. O. and Roth, T. L. (2015). Epigenetic pathways through which experiences become linked with biology. *Development and Psychopathology*, **27**, 637–648.

Mendle, J. and Ferrero, J. (2010). Detrimental psychological outcomes associated with pubertal timing in adolescent boys. *Developmental Review*, **32**, 49–66.

Mendle, J., Turkheimer, E. and Emery, R. E. (2007). Detrimental psychological outcomes associated with pubertal timing in adolescent girls. *Developmental Review*, **21**, 151–171.

Miller, T. R. (2015). Projected outcomes of nurse-family partnership home visitation during 1996–2013, USA. *Prevention Science*, **16**, 765–777.

Moffitt, T. E. (1993). Adolescence-limited and life-course-persistent antisocial behavior – a developmental taxonomy. *Psychological Review*, **100**, 674–701.

Murray, J. and Farrington, D. P. (2010). Risk factors for conduct disorder and delinquency: key findings from longitudinal studies. *Canadian Journal of Psychiatry*, **55**, 633–42.

O'Donnell, K. J., Glover, V., Barker, E. D. and O'Connor, T. G. (2014). The persisting effect of maternal mood in pregnancy on childhood psychopathology. *Development and Psychopathology*, **26**, 393–403.

Odgers, C. L., Moffitt, T. E., Broadbent, J. M., Dickson, N., Hancox, R. J., Harrington, H., Poulton, R., Sears, M. R., Thomson, W. M. and Caspi, A. (2008). Female and male antisocial trajectories: from childhood origins to adult outcomes. *Development and Psychopathology*, **20**, 673–716.

Odgers, C. L., Moffitt, T. E., Tach, L. M., Sampson, R. J., Taylor, A., Matthews, C. L. and Caspi, A. (2009). The protective effects of neighborhood collective efficacy on British children growing up in deprivation: a developmental analysis. *Developmental Psychology*, **45**, 942–957.

Oliver, B. R., Barker, E. D., Mandy, W. P. L., Skuse, D. H. and Maughan, B. (2011). Social cognition and conduct problems: a developmental approach. *Journal of the American Academy of Child and Adolescent Psychiatry*, **50**, 385–394.

Pardini, D. and Frick, P. J. (2013). Multiple developmental pathways to conduct disorder: current conceptualizations and clinical implications. *Journal of the Canadian Academy of Child and Adolescent Psychiatry*, **22**, 20–25.

Patterson, G., Reid, J. and Dishion, T. (1992) *Antisocial Boys*. Eugene, OR: Castalia.

Peper, J. S. and Dahl, R. E. (2013). The teenage brain: surging hormones–brain-behavior interactions during puberty. *Current Directions in Psychological Science*, **22**, 134–139.

Portnoy, J. and Farrington, D. P. (2015). Resting heart rate and antisocial behavior: an updated systematic review and meta-analysis. *Aggression and Violent Behavior*, **22**, 33–45.

Provençal, N., Booij, L. and Tremblay, R. E. (2015). The developmental origins of chronic physical aggression: biological pathways triggered by early life adversity. *Journal of Experimental Biology*, **218**, 123–133.

Rhee, S. H. and Waldman, I. D. (2002). Genetic and environmental influences on antisocial behavior: a meta-analysis of twin and adoption studies. *Psychological Bulletin*, **128**, 490–529.

Rowe, R., Maughan, B., Worthman, C., Costello, E. J. and Angold, A. (2004). Testosterone, conduct disorder and social dominance in boys: pubertal development and biosocial interaction. *Biological Psychiatry*, **55**, 546–552.

Rutter, M. (2013). Annual research review: resilience – clinical implications. *Journal of Child Psychology and Psychiatry* **54**, 474–487.

Rutter, M., Giller, H. and Hagell, A. (1998). *Antisocial Behaviour by Young People*. Cambridge, UK: Cambridge University Press.

Rutter, M. and Maughan, B. (2002). School effectiveness findings 1979–2002. *Journal of School Psychology*, **40**, 451–475.

Sampson, R. J., Raudenbush, S. W. and Earls, F. (1997). Neighborhoods and violent crime: a multilevel study of collective efficacy. *Science*, **277**, 918–924.

Savage, J. (2014). The association between attachment, parental bonds and physically aggressive and violent behavior: a comprehensive review. *Aggression and Violent Behavior*, **19**, 164–178.

Schweinhart, L. J., Montie, J., Xiang, Z., Barnett, W. S., Belfield, C. R. and Nores, M. (2005). *Life-Time Effects: The High/Scope Perry Preschool Study Through Age 40*. Ypsilanti: High/Scope Press.

Scott, S., Briskman, J., Woolgar, M., Humayun, S. and O'Connor, T. G. (2011). Attachment in adolescence: overlap with parenting and unique prediction of behavioural adjustment. *Journal of Child Psychology and Psychiatry*, **52**, 1052–1062.

Scott, S. and O'Connor, T. G. (2012). An experimental test of differential susceptibility to parenting among emotionally-dysregulated children in a randomized controlled trial for oppositional behavior. *Journal of Child Psychology and Psychiatry*, **53**, 1184–1193.

Talge, N. M., Neal, C. and Glover, V. (2007). Antenatal maternal stress and long-term effects on child neurodevelopment: how and why? *Journal of Child Psychology and Psychiatry*, **48**, 245–261.

Taylor, A. and Kim-Cohen, J. (2007). Meta-analysis of gene–environment interactions in developmental psychopathology. *Development and Psychopathology*, **19**, 1029–1037.

Tremblay, R. E. (2010). Developmental origins of disruptive behaviour problems: the 'original sin' hypothesis, epigenetics and their consequences for prevention. *Journal of Child Psychology and Psychiatry*, **51**, 341–367.

van Goozen, S. H. M., Fairchild, G., Snoek, H. and Harold, G. T. (2007). The evidence for a neurobiological model of childhood antisocial behavior. *Psychological Bulletin*, **133**, 149–182.

Viding, E., Fontaine, N. M. G. and McCrory, E. J. (2012). Antisocial behaviour in children with and without callous-unemotional traits. *Journal of the Royal Society of Medicine*, **105**, 195–200.

Wakschlag, L. S., Pickett, K. E., Cook, E. Benowitz, N. L. and Leventhal, B. L. (2002). Maternal smoking during pregnancy and severe antisocial behavior in offspring: a review. *American Journal of Public Health*, **92**, 966–974.

Waller, R., Gardner, F. and Hyde, L. W. (2013). What are the associations between parenting, callous-unemotional traits, and antisocial behavior in youth? a systematic review of evidence. *Clinical Psychology Review*, **33**, 593–608.

Wichers, M., Gardner, C., Maes, H. H., Lichtenstein, P., Larsson, H. and Kendler, K. S. (2013). Genetic innovation and stability in externalizing problem behavior across development: a multi-informant twin study. *Behavior Genetics*, **43**, 191–201.

Psychosocial Resilience, Psychosocial Care and Forensic Mental Healthcare

Richard Williams and Verity Kemp

This chapter provides an overview of the construct of psychosocial resilience, and makes the case for its relevance to forensic mental healthcare for younger people. We argue that three core usages of the concept, in child development, ecology and economics, and also with regard to emergencies, disasters and more sustained adversity, are linked by research on the needs of children and young people (Panter-Brick and Leckman, 2013: 333–336; Tol et al., 2013). We bring together these areas of research and practice, consider the interfaces between them and commend taking the notions of psychosocial resilience into forensic practice and research as a benefit for the young people involved. We are in the company of Robinson in adopting this aspiration (Robinson, 2016: 18). She says, 'There is wide variation in what is taken to represent resilience' and that

> Resilience . . . as a consistent theme for youth justice system[s] has considerable value, emphasising health, wellbeing and empowerment. Practice approaches focused narrowly on offending miss vital opportunities to engage young people and to build supportive relationships that enable young people to resolve the . . . difficulties that they feel stand in their way. The resilience perspective . . . is inherently more appreciative of young people's views and the meaning they give to their actions and their relationships (Robinson, 2016: 30).

Yet, Robinson says, 'resilience remains marginal in youth justice literature' (Robinson, 2016: 18).

The NATO Guidance on Psychosocial Care for People Affected by Disasters and Major Incidents says, 'Substantial resilience of persons and communities is the expected response to a disaster, but is not inevitable' (Department of Health, 2009; North Atlantic Treaty Organization [NATO/EAPC], 2009). Southwick, Litz, Charney and Friedman write, 'Children, in general, are remarkably resilient' (Southwick et al., 2011: xiv). Despite controversy over the years, in which it has been argued that

children and young people are less resilient than are adults, there is also evidence to suggest that 'What information that does exist suggests that children cope as well as, if not better than adults' (Southwick et al., 2011: xii). But, a subsequently published collection of papers in a special issue of the *Journal of Child Psychology and Psychiatry* (JCPP) on the effects of early trauma and deprivation on human development allows the editors to conclude that 'This set of papers provide compelling cross-sectional and longitudinal evidence that early experiences of inadequate input (neglect/deprivation) and unwanted input (threat/trauma) – remembered or not – led to long-term developmental and clinical abnormalities. They also add to a growing body of evidence about the neurodevelopmental pathways involved in psychopathology' (Zeanah and Sonuga-Barke, 2016: 1101). However, these editors also say that '. . . a number of papers demonstrate that the presence and behavior of caretakers moderate the effects of early adversity and response to interventions' (Zeanah and Sonuga-Barke, 2016: 1101). This chapter focuses on a number of these moderating and mitigating factors from a social science perspective.

By contrast, pathways that protect children and young people and enable them to develop well and express resilience include a wide variety of experiences and relationships involving their having supportive parents and/or carers, healthy and safe environments to live in, good experiences of education, satisfying relationships, and 'factors such as attachment[s], social support, religion, intelligence and problem-solving ability, and cognitive flexibility' (Southwick et al., 2011: xii). It is now accepted widely that people, families and communities should build and sustain their capacities for psychosocial resilience if they are to cope well with the demands on them that arise throughout their lives.

We think that these social understandings begin to resolve certain of the tensions between recognising why children and young people are widely held to be more vulnerable to adversity and major incidents than are adults, while some researchers assert that they can cope as well as do adults. Psychosocial resilience rests on social identity, relational skills, attachment capacities, dependable social networks and availability of social support as well as certain other personal attributes. These requirements, which are ordinarily intense in children and young people who are developing rapidly, may be threatened by the impacts on adults' abilities to offer parenting and social support during austerity and after major incidents. Furthermore, it is all too evident that not all children have the advantages of well-founded social identities, good-enough parenting or sufficient freedom from recurrent, repeated or long-term adversity. The editorial in the JCPP's special issue draws attention to the cumulative risk model – '. . . long-term adverse outcomes are better predicted by the total number, rather than the specific nature of environmental risk exposures' becoming the dominant thesis as to how '. . . environmental exposures to different adverse experiences and events early in life produce negative outcomes many years later' (Zeanah and Sonuga-Barke, 2016: 1099).

Young people who require forensic mental healthcare stand out from their peers in a number of ways, and not least is the matter of offending. So, we consider what impacts past experiences may have on troubled young people's needs. We suggest how endeavours of young people to draw on collective sources of psychosocial resilience might put them at risk of mixing with people who may not help them to escape from circles of misfortune, deprivation, unmet need and/or offending.

We draw on four constructs in which we bring together learning gathered about:

(1) Resilience as a general ecological construct;
(2) Psychosocial resilience as a construct that is in prominent use in the fields relating to disasters, emergencies and adversity;
(3) Psychosocial resilience as a construct in child development;
(4) The backgrounds and vertical and horizontal epidemiologies that impact on the needs of children and young people who are in contact with youth justice and forensic mental health services;

Necessarily and appropriately, our discourse reaches into the areas of concern about social care, education, public mental healthcare, and primary and specialist mental healthcare. It sits within the boundaries of the conceptual bases, roles and work of many different disciplines. Great steps have been made in recent decades in both the conceptual strategic frameworks for understanding the roles and design of child and adolescent mental health services as well as specialist forensic mental health services, on one hand, and in mental health responses to the needs of people who are affected by all manner of adversities, on the other (NHS Health Advisory Service, 1995; National Assembly for Wales, 2001; Williams, 2004: 315–335; Bailey and Williams, 2005; North Atlantic Treaty Organization, 2009; Williams et al., 2014).

We recommend that young people who are in contact with forensic mental health services require a mix of the components of psychosocial care as well as effective mental healthcare if services are to meet their needs. We take the adjective 'psychosocial' to refer to:

the cognitive, emotional, social and physical experiences of particular people and of collectives of people . . . in the context of particular social and physical environments. It . . . is used to describe the psychological and social processes that occur within and between people and across groups of people . . . [and] these processes as they occur before, during and after events that may be variously described as emergencies, disasters and major incidents.

(Department of Health, 2009)

We use 'psychosocial' in this chapter to refer to the same four domains: the emotional, cognitive, social and physical experiences of young people who face the kinds of problems that bring them into contact with forensic mental health services.

Psychosocial care describes interventions that offer comfort, improve how people cope with adverse events and reduce the risks of them developing psychiatric disorders. Most people derive the support they require from their families, friends and colleagues. Mental healthcare refers to bio-social-medical interventions from which people who have disorders may benefit. Usually, they also require psychosocial care as a platform on which their mental healthcare is based.

Next, we clarify what we mean by resilience, psychosocial resilience, distress and disorders. Then, we revisit past research on the kinds of problems that fall within the remit of forensic mental health services. Subsequently, we identify the complementary roles of psychosocial care and mental healthcare. We show how both relate to meeting the needs of young people with the intention that they cope more effectively and with greater resilience when they meet challenges in life.

Resilience

Resilience concerns how people, groups of people, communities and systems cope with and spring back from major problems, adversity and untoward events to regain effective functioning. It is defined by the UN as: 'The ability of a system, community or society exposed to hazards to resist, absorb, accommodate to and recover from the effects of a hazard in a timely and efficient manner, including through the preservation and restoration of its essential basic structures and functions' (UNISDR, 2009). Thus, many definitions that are based on ecological concepts emphasise resilience as describing how systems and communities resist, absorb, accommodate to, and recover from the effects of hazards. This way of using the construct of resilience in emergency preparedness and the rule of law describes approaches to securing societal and state assets that may come under threat from natural and human-made threats.

Psychosocial Resilience

While the construct of human resilience draws on these ecological roots, studies of how humans behave during and after situations that are complex, complicated or demand change show that tipping the definition of resilience towards adaptability and transformation in addition to absorbing stress provides a more substantial model for understanding how people cope and a more adequate picture of their needs. Our use of the term 'psychosocial resilience' embraces this approach.

Interestingly, Omand presents an approach to resilience that is founded on three generations of objectives (Omand, 2010). As a result, we identify three generations of psychosocial resilience:

- First-generation resilience: the ability to cope well with events and their immediate aftermath.
- Second-generation resilience: the ability to adapt to and recover from events.
- Third-generation resilience: the ability of people to transform their social connections, relationships, roles, communities and organisations in the light of lessons learned from the events that affect them.

Psychosocial resilience includes all three generations and, in this chapter, relates to how young people cope with, adapt and recover from adversities that impact on them and whether or not they can transform their relationships and become more resilient in the future as a consequence.

Broadly, there are two main streams of research regarding the construct of psychosocial resilience. The first relates to how people develop through childhood into adulthood and the second concerns how people process the more traumatic and tragic crises in their lives and present their experiences through their emotional, cognitive and social behavioural responses. In our opinion, these are not discrete conceptual approaches that should be used separately, but they relate to the same aspects of people's lives and experiences when they are faced with events that are of sudden onset or longer-term aversive circumstances. The cumulative risk model supports this position. Masten et al. offer examples of resilience pathways, which have similarities with what Norris et al. describe as trajectories, in the context of acute trauma and chronic adversity (Norris et al., 2009: 2191; Masten et al., 2011). Masten et al. also describe resilience models, which show the potential effects of risk factors, assets, protective factors and interventions.

Both groups of authors paint a picture of resilience as a construct that describes how people adapt to challenges, acute and/or chronic, over time rather than it indicating solely a set of personal traits or attributes. Theirs is a dynamic approach to considering how people cope, adapt and recover, which is supported by Rutter and many other researchers (Rutter, 2012). We commend this approach.

Defining Psychosocial Resilience

There are challenges in defining psychosocial resilience (Department of Health, 2009). Southwick et al. report that Layne and colleagues have found at least eight distinct meanings (Layne et al., 2007; Southwick et al., 2011). The American Psychological Association has defined it as 'the process of adapting well in the face of adversity, trauma, tragedy, threats or even significant sources of threat' (American Psychological Association, 2010). The editors of the *Journal of Psychology and Psychiatry*'s annual research review for 2013 define resilience as 'the process of harnessing psychosocial, structural and cultural resources to sustain wellbeing' (Panter-Brick and Leckman, 2013: 334).

Sapienza and Masten have reported four waves of research into resilience that have ensued since its importance to psychiatry and psychology was recognised (Masten, et al., 2011: 103; Sapienza and Masten, 2011: 267–268). These four waves are as follows:

- Descriptive: asking what seems to make a difference;
- Process: how does it make a difference?
- Promotion: which interventions promote or protect mental health and development?
- Interaction: the processes of interaction across system levels.

The observation of Sapienza and Masten is that models of psychosocial resilience have become more dynamic and systemic with time. They report that approaches to research on psychosocial resilience and young people have shifted progressively from: work to identify the nature and properties of what constitutes resilience; how it operates through interactive, multilevel and multidisciplinary processes; through to the current concern with the 'dominant models of resilience [which are] . . . dynamic, focused on processes linking neurobiology to behavior [and] to environmental conditions' (Sapienza and Masten, 2011: 267). This analysis is reflected in the spread of papers in the annual research review in the *Journal of Psychology and Psychiatry* in 2013. Research on psychosocial resilience shows that the potentially adverse effects on persons, families and communities of disasters and emergencies can be mitigated by dynamic human social systems (Williams and Hazell, 2011).

When facing stressful challenges, people may show capabilities in some domains, but not in others, and they may show uneven functioning. Some researchers define resilience as 'excellence in one salient domain with at least average adjustment in other domains' (Southwick et al., 2011: xi). The dynamic theories explain why these characteristics may vary with time and may be specific to particular circumstances, social networks and events (Masten et al., 2011: 103–119).

Thus, we conclude from our surveys of a selection of the research that psychosocial resilience is not best understood as a trait within persons but represents interactions between each person's capabilities, other people, and the circumstances in which they find themselves. As a construct that summarises a series of social processes, psychosocial resilience is difficult to measure. Robinson says, 'Rutter . . . draws on research to propose a series of mechanisms that might mediate the interaction of the risk and

protective variables in a positive direction'. She summarises these mechanisms as being:

- 'Reducing the risk impact, possibly by altering the risk or by reducing exposure to the risk;
- Reduction of negative chain reactions;
- Promoting self-esteem and self-efficacy;
- Providing opportunities' (Robinson, 2016: 23–24; Rutter, 1987)

Panter-Brick and Leckman opine that

Resilience offers the promise of a paradigm shift in many fields of research, clinical practice, and policy. A lens on resilience shifts the focus of attention–from efforts to appraise risk or vulnerability, towards concerted efforts to enhance strength or capability. It also shifts the focus of analysis . . . to asking more complex questions regarding wellbeing, such as when, how, why and for whom do resources truly matter.

(Panter-Brick and Leckman, 2013: 333)

Accordingly, we see psychosocial resilience as a systemic, dynamic process in which people's social identities and relationships play strong parts. Thus, resilience describes social processes by which people act singly or together to mitigate, moderate or adapt to the effects of events. We assert that each of the approaches that we have introduced here is relevant to forensic mental healthcare.

Williams and Drury have identified two interactive components of resilience: personal and collective psychosocial resilience.

Personal Psychosocial Resilience

Personal psychosocial resilience describes a person's capacity for adapting emotionally, cognitively, socially and physically reasonably well and without lasting detriment to self, relationships or personal development in the face of adversity, threat or challenge (adapted from Williams, 2007).

There has been substantial research into certain personal attributes and capabilities of people who appear to cope well with the stressors consequent on disasters and adversity and which may put people at advantage. We conclude that resilience is not a trait within persons but represents interactions between each person, other people and the circumstances in which they find themselves. Box 2.1 lists an adaptation of the factors Southwick and Charney have identified (Southwick and Charney, 2012).

A number of concepts overlap with, or are included within, the attributes of personal

Box 2.1 Resilience Factors

Realistic optimism

Facing fear

Having strong guiding values

Spirituality

Social support

Physical fitness

Mental fitness

Cognitive and emotional flexibility and the ability to improvise

Creating meaning and purpose from events through personal growth

Source: Modified after Southwick and Charney (2012) and included here with the permission of Cambridge University Press.

psychosocial resilience. They include hardiness, sense of coherence (SoC), adaptation, recovery, cognitive emotion regulation and engagement theory.

'Hardiness', a term that is close, but not limited, to the ecological approach to resilience, has three elements: commitment, control and challenge. People who are hardy demonstrate commitment by considering stressful events as being interesting and meaningful and are able to envisage themselves as being in control of what happens to them (i.e. they express agency or have an internal locus of control to use the metaphors from other theoretical stances). So, challenge is part of the normal processes of life for a hardy person, and it provides opportunities for their development (Kobasa, 1979; Kobasa et al., 1982).

People with SoC also see what happens to them as having meaning. They view their circumstances as capable of being managed, and themselves as able to comprehend events. They tend to feel that their physical and mental health is protected, regardless of known risks and adverse events, and they are less likely to experience distress (Antonovsky, 1987).

Adaptation implies that the object of recovery after an adverse event is not to return to the previous circumstances through processes of restoration. Rather, people who adapt well are able to adjust well to changed circumstances and express agency in moulding them to improve their capabilities and environment.

We see these outcomes as also describing the goals of recovery, which is a word that is often used in relationship to both traumatic events and mental ill health. Each use describes active, positive approaches

taken by particular people to managing their environments in the context of supportive groups of other people and the resources that they have available. Thus, depending on the models of care used, there may be similarities in the conceptual meanings and the practical expressions of the ways in which the term 'recovery' is used in trauma care and mental healthcare. Meyer and Mueser quote Anthony and Deegan who define recovery in the mental health context (Meyer and Mueser, 2011). Anthony defines recovery as involving 'the development of a new meaning and purpose in one's life as one grows beyond the catastrophic effects of mental illness' (Anthony, 1993). Deegan describes recovery 'as a process, a way of life, an attitude and a way of approaching the day's challenges. It is not a perfectly linear process. At times our course is erratic and we falter, slide back, regroup, and start again … The need is to re-establish a new and valued sense of integrity and purpose within and beyond the limits of the disability' (Deegan, 1988). People who are resilient have similar attributes and experiences.

The cognitive emotional regulation framework is based on people using regulation of their emotions to change adaptively their appraisal of the stressors they experience and, thereby, moderate those stressors' impacts on their coping (Troy and Mauss, 2011). The aspiration of that framework, and there is evidence to support it, is that assisting people to use cognitive approaches to regulate their emotions may alter their appraisal of a stressor and, thereby, improve their resilience and reduce the potential for longer-term negative outcomes.

Engagement theory considers that resilience describes processes that people use in the face of stress that regulate the distress they experience and their trajectories of engagement and adaptation. Engagement is defined by Schaufeli et al. as a persistent, pervasive and positive affective-motivational state of fulfilment in people who are reacting to challenging circumstances (Schaufeli et al., 2002). It has three dimensions: vigour, dedication and absorption. Thus, it overlaps with hardiness and SoC. Hobfoll et al. commend distinguishing engagement trajectories from distress trajectories (Hobfoll et al., 2011). They also offer principles, which show how engagement and distress interact, that have much in common with the pathways described by Masten et al. (2011: 108–111) and the trajectories described by Norris et al. (2009: 2191).

The concept of resilience has moved from focusing solely on personal attributes through dynamic processes and relationships to become a systemic and multidimensional notion. Our review of the personal domain shows that the personal attributes that are a part of resilience are also ones through which people see themselves in relation to their worlds, external events and other people. This shows clearly that there are intrapersonal and interpersonal features in resilience. Research reported recently has focused on transpersonal processes and so, now, we turn to collective psychosocial resilience and social identity theory.

Collective Psychosocial Resilience

Williams and Drury define collective psychosocial resilience as 'the way in which groups of people and crowds of people express and expect solidarity and cohesion, and thereby coordinate and draw upon collective sources of support and other practical resources adaptively to deal with adversity' (Department of Health, 2009; Williams and Drury, 2011: 63–66).

Collective psychosocial resilience is used to express the way people behave when they are in groups, and how they deal together with and recover from adverse events. The term is variously used as a description (Hernández, 2002; Almedon, 2005; Kahn, 2005), to refer to social connections and forms of social capital that are already in existence (Fielding and Anderson, 2008), or to denote theories about why people behave as they do when groups of them are faced with adversity or traumatic events.

An important development in the research on collective resilience has described a dynamic model based on a social identity theory (Turner et al., 1987; Haslam, 2004). This approach has developed from studying how crowds respond to crises. It describes and explains why people help one another during and after events, and how this contributes to people's short- and longer-term capacities for coping with, and recovering from stress and distress. The social identity model suggests that there is a move from focusing on 'me' to focusing on 'we' and, thereby, a shared social identity when people suffer extreme events together (Drury et al., 2009a). Shared social identity results in people, for example, sharing possessions, and offering social support to people to whom they might otherwise not have talked, even to the point of putting themselves at risk (Williams and Drury, 2010, 2011: 65).

Research indicates that other benefits for people of creating a shared social identity include making available to them the perceptions and appraisals of risk of peers against which they can calibrate their own judgements and perceptions of how the world is, and how it should be. This can be the basis of group consensus (Haslam et al., 1998). Also, stress is reduced when collective support is forthcoming.

Previously, social identity and the related social supportive actions that people in mass emergencies exhibit was thought to be dependent on pre-existing social relationships (Mawson, 2005), but recent emergencies (e.g. the London Bombings in 2005) have shown that strangers formed a shared social identity as a result of their shared experience (Cocking et al., 2009; Drury et al., 2009b). In July 2005, they gave and received emotional support, water, first aid and reassurance. This has been attributed to the sense of the common fate shared by all of the people involved, itself a form of collective resilience. This research illustrated that resilient, adaptive behaviours do develop without social relationships that have been established before events occur.

This review of collective psychosocial resilience illustrates the relationship between social context, culture and how people respond to, and cope with crises and adversity. We note that there are links between this domain within psychosocial resilience and concepts of social capital and the mental health recovery model.

Horizontal Epidemiology

The concepts of resilience and recovery also have a shared focus on horizontal as well as vertical epidemiology.

> Although it is well known that the burden and costs of ... [psychiatric] disorders are high, there is evidence that [their] overall, personal, social and economic costs ... have been underestimated because of the lack of valid and reliable information regarding the full range of psychosocial difficulties that actually shape the lived experience[s] of persons with these disorders ... that affect their quality of life. [The] ... innovative theoretical premise of horizontal epidemiology ... [is] the view that psychosocial difficulties associated with mental ... disorders are not exclusively determined by the diagnosis of ... particular disorder[s] in ... vertical, silo-like pattern[s], but horizontally in a manner that reflects commonalities in the lived experience[s] of people who have ... diverse mental health problems.

Since … horizontal epidemiology accounts for the psychosocial difficulties that are actually experienced by people with … disorders, independently of the … disorder associated with them, it concentrates on what is more relevant to the lives of people with … [these] disorders. This [could well] lead to more effective intervention planning and management, and, therefore, to improved quality of life along the continuum of care, in the community, and across … people's life span[s].

(Cieza, Personal communication)

An Integrated Approach: Adaptive Capacities

We concur with Robinson who points out that Rutter argued around 30 years ago that vulnerability and protection are two ends of the same concept and that 'The vulnerability or protective effect is event only in combination with the risk variable … the terms "process" and "mechanism" are preferable to "variable" or "factor" because any one variable may act as a risk factor in one situation but as a vulnerability factor in another' (Rutter, 1987: 317; Robinson, 2016: 23).

Thus, it is inappropriate to describe people as inherently resilient or vulnerable without referring to their particular circumstances and the risks that they face. But, as regards the mechanisms of resilience, the recent literature suggests that the core features of people who have good psychosocial resilience are that they:

- Perceive that they have, and actually receive support. The abilities of people to accept and use social support and the availability of it are two of the core features of resilience.
- Tend to show acceptance of reality.
- Have belief in themselves that is supported by strongly held values.
- Have abilities to improvise.

Thus, people respond to stressors by mobilising their inner, personal resources and, in parallel, the support provided by their families, colleagues, friends and the people with whom they are in contact when untoward events occur is critically important. Together, these resources allow people, families and communities to generate adaptive capacities that enable them to cope reasonably well, recover from events and learn lessons for the future. Figure 2.1 illustrates this approach.

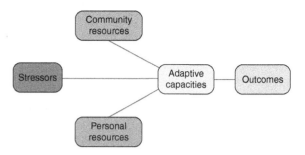

Figure 2.1 Adaptive Capacities

Source: Reproduced with the permission of the copyright holders, Williams R and Kemp V.

The annual research review published by the *Journal of Child Psychology and Psychiatry* in 2013 focuses on resilience in child development. It presents reviews of research on neurobiology, social ecology, nutrition and adjustment that impact on resilience and considers resilience in a variety of circumstances that impact on children. As one of the papers says, aptly we think, 'this body of knowledge supports a perspective of resilience as a complex dynamic process driven by time- and context-dependent variables, rather than the balance between risk and protective factors with known impacts on mental health' (Tol et al., 2013: 445). The approach of looking at people's histories to understand the risk and protective factors that have impacted on them raises the importance of people's past narratives and vertical epidemiology.

Furthermore, a number of strands of research indicate that resilience may be context specific (Panter-Brick and Leckman, 2013: 333–336). In other words, the contemporary circumstances in which people find themselves, the people with whom they relate at the time and their present needs have enormous impacts on how well they cope. These horizontal epidemiological factors resonate with what we know of the power of young people's peer groups, and especially so when they are socially alienated. They also reflect the matters that adolescent users of mental health services report as important in other people appropriately understanding their needs. Certainly, this approach is not intended to diminish the 'profound influence of early life experiences (biological embedding) as another predisposing factor for life stressors and the cumulative burden' (Karatsoreos and McEwen, 2013: 343) or awareness 'of the capacity of the brain to store memories of a lifetime, as well as the capacity of the brain for plasticity' (Karatsoreos and McEwen, 2013: 344), but it does argue for a broad approach in which resilience is considered among a range of factors that influence people's needs and responses to events (Sapienza and Masten, 2011).

First-generation psychosocial resilience describes securing robustness, and that has overlaps with the concepts of hardiness and SoC. The second generation focuses on recovery or bouncing back with fortitude without giving up cherished values, which we see as core to psychosocial resilience, and third-generation psychosocial resilience concerns how people cope better in the future through their transformed social relations and continuing adaptability. Thus, we see adaptability, transformability and sustainability as components of third-generation psychosocial resilience. We assert that these concepts, and our understanding of psychosocial resilience, apply fully to adolescents and the process of growing up in adolescence.

Distress, Disorders and Psychosocial Resilience

Being resilient at a specified time and in an identified environmental and social context does not imply that any person is unaffected by traumatic and tragic events or adversity. Rather, it proposes processes by which people who are affected experience distress followed by their coping, adaptation and recovery if the environment and circumstances are supportive.

When there are adverse circumstances, people are likely to experience psychosocial distress because these situations may undermine people's perceptions of the environment and themselves, their senses of control and feelings of worth. At least temporarily, people may have insufficient emotional, cognitive, social or physical resources to cope with events. Typically these experiences are described as distress, which describes 'the experiences and feelings of people after external events that challenge their tolerance and adaptation ... Distress is an anticipated human emotion, not a disorder, when it and any associated psychosocial dysfunction emerges and persists in proportion to external stressful situations' (Horwitz, 2007; North Atlantic Treaty Organization, 2009: 1–38).

Resilient people may suffer transient distress after encountering crises or adversity. The term derives from Latin in which 'resilere' means the ability to recoil or leap back. So, the construct is entirely compatible with short-term distress that is not associated with prolonged or sustained dysfunction.

It is important, but it can be difficult, to distinguish people's distress, consequent on their involvement in a crisis or longer-standing adversity, from mental disorder. Their experiences or symptoms may be similar. The distinction turns on the pathways or trajectories of people's responses over time and the severity and duration of any associated dysfunction. Furthermore, distress may lead to the development of dysfunction, which may be temporary, or more sustained and can, in some circumstances, lead to, or may be, a component of mental disorders.

As we have already seen, the extent to which people are able to display psychosocial resilience is influenced by many factors: relationships and attachments, events that affect people throughout their lives; how people are able to adapt and use their experiences; the particularities of the events and circumstances; and how all these elements interplay. Genetics and neurobiology are important in determining how resilient people may be (Levin, 2009). Thus, the adaptive capacities that comprise psychosocial resilience are of genetic, psychological, social and environmental origins.

Summary

In this section, we have surveyed a number of concepts, theories and processes taken from a variety of scientific disciplines that all contribute to the overarching concept of resilience. This part of the chapter can be summed up well by quoting from Southwick et al., who say children's 'resilience develops as a set of abilities and processes including positive attachment, the capacity to attract social support, self-motivating rewards [that are] critical for mastery and self-efficacy, effective modulation of the stress response, and successful monitoring and regulation of emotions' (Southwick et al., 2011: xiv). The trajectories or pathways of people's distressed responses to crises and adversity are important in determining how best to intervene to assist people because psychosocial resilience is now considered to be an interactive, dynamic, systemic concept.

Children and Young People and Forensic Mental Health Services

Next, we summarise the needs of young people who use forensic mental health services in England and Wales.

At its core, forensic mental healthcare is a specialisation that is based on assessing and treating people who are mentally disordered and whose behaviour has led, or could lead, to offending (Mullen, 2000). However, we have found that defining forensic mental health services in terms of assessing and treating mentally abnormal offenders narrows the roles that those services are asked to play. Williams, for example, has surveyed the tasks that may face comprehensive forensic child and adolescent mental health services. They include delivering (Williams, 2004: 322–323):

- Diagnostic and advisory services;
  - Ambulatory, community and outpatient assessments;
  - Consultation within and between agencies in planning care delivered by the state;
  - Preparation and presentation of opinions, including report preparation;
  - Attendance at courts to give professional evidence or expert opinion;
  - Advising other professionals in the course of their work.
- Therapeutic services;
  - Ambulatory, community and outpatient therapeutic interventions;
  - Residential and/or inpatient assessments, care and treatments;
- Teaching, training and supporting other professionals;
- Research.

In its review of the Gardener Unit in Salford of 1994 (Williams et al., 1994), the NHS Health Advisory Service (NHS HAS) described the priority client groups for medium secure inpatients services as including:

- Mentally disordered offenders;
- Sex offenders and abusers;
- Severely suicidal and self-harming adolescents;
- Very severely mentally ill adolescents;
- Adolescents who need to begin psychiatric rehabilitation in secure circumstances;
- Brain injured adolescents and young people who have severe organic disorders.

Subsequent research by the Health Services Management Centre in the University of Birmingham analysed information relating to referrals to highly specialised forensic mental health inpatients services for adolescents in England and Wales, and presents a similar picture to the findings of the NHS HAS (Williams and Barnes, 1997).

All three sets of findings are significant because they indicate the broad nature of the behaviours of, stressors faced by, and the problems and needs of children and young people who are in contact with forensic mental health services.

Better Mental Health Outcomes for Children and Young People identified groups of children and young people who are at risk (National CAMHS Support Service, 2011). The guide describes one group as composed of people engaged in the criminal justice system who are 'far more likely to experience mental health problems than their peers. In secure settings, mental health needs are known to be considerable, severe and complex ... [and with] complicating factors of substance misuse and learning difficulties, and ... distress and anxiety at being locked up and away from home'.

Williams (2004: 326) has summarised the features that research has shown as common to young people in contact with forensic mental health services. They include:

- Very poor educational attainments, poor basic educational skills including low levels of literacy;
- Chaotic relationships;
- High levels of exclusion from school and from other services;
- High levels of psychiatric symptoms and disorders;
- Poor prospects of their needs having been met previously despite high levels of investment of professional time.

Forensic mental health services are provided principally for two groups of young people: a relatively small number with a range of serious problems treated as inpatients, and a not insubstantial number who are treated as outpatients. Research by Chitsabesan et al. suggests that the experiences and needs of the two groups are similar.

Chitsabesan et al., (2006) conducted a cross-sectional survey of 301 young offenders in six geographically representative areas across England and Wales who were resident in custody ($n = 151$) or attending Youth Offending Teams in their communities ($n = 150$). High levels of, often unmet, needs were identified arising from: social relationships (48%); education/work (36%); violence to people and property (35%); mental health (31%) and risky behaviour (29%). More than three quarters of the sample were males (77%), and one third (37%) had been in the care of the state at some time previously.

About 20% of the young people met the criteria for having a learning disability, 52% had severe problems with reading and 61% with reading comprehension (Chitsabesan et al., 2007). We think that these results show that a large majority of these juvenile offenders, whether in the secure estate or living in communities, had serious problems with literacy to the point that they would be unlikely to benefit from the full range of the national curricula in England and Wales.

Cumulatively, these studies show that young people who are in contact with the forensic mental health services have substantial unmet needs and that they come from backgrounds in which they experience continuing adversity. Interestingly, there were no significant differences between the young offenders in custody and those in the community in respect of their mental health other than that the members of the latter group had significantly more needs than those in custody and more problems arising from substance and alcohol misuse.

How Psychosocial Resilience and Psychosocial Care Fit with Forensic Mental Healthcare

At first sight, it might appear that young people who are in contact with forensic mental health services are unlikely to have many of the characteristics, circumstances or experiences of young people who are most likely to behave resiliently. This book provides powerful pictures of the users of forensic mental health services as perpetrators, victims and survivors of violence and as having experienced multiple hardships, chronic life strains, long-term disadvantage and many sources of adversity. Some, though not all of them, have serious mental disorders and most have been through repeated distress and frustration of their aspirations. Often, they lack the material and personal resources with which to mitigate some of the effects of the challenges that they have faced and continue to face.

Elements of psychosocial resilience that have been shown to be fundamental in protecting people from the effects of trauma include the capacity to accept social and emotional support from other people and the abilities to form and sustain effective relationships and attachments to other people. Yet, poor attachment capabilities and unsatisfactory relationships are well within the range of problems that many young people in contact with the youth justice and adolescent forensic mental health services are likely to have experienced.

Within this systemic context, it is likely that many young people who require forensic mental healthcare have had many fewer opportunities to develop or express psychosocial resilience when compared with adolescents who cope well. But, this analysis tends to play down the importance of collective sources of support and resilience. In the course of our clinical work, we have noticed that many disadvantaged young people endeavour to recruit social support from groups of peers. However, young people who are offenders or mentally disordered offenders are more likely than are their less troubled and troublesome peers to use defensive coping by attempting to recruit collective support from gangs and peers who are themselves in serious trouble and who also have serious problems. The price of this form of collective support may be to commit crime and/or consume drugs and alcohol as raisons d'être or tickets of entry. Some young people's well-being may be boosted, albeit temporarily and in costly ways, by wider recognition of their crimes to the point that they might be described as surviving on the basis of their notoriety.

While this analysis portrays a grim picture, a number of authorities, including Masten and her colleagues, point out that some young people whose lives are going in a bad direction in adolescence become successful adults. They may show dramatic declines in some forms of bad behaviour during their transitions from adolescence to adulthood after a sharp increase in those behaviours earlier in adolescence (Masten et al., 2011: 107). These observations remind us of the importance of adopting a realistic but optimistic approach by developing the psychosocial resilience, and the adaptive capacities and capabilities associated with it, of the young people, but also of the policy makers, service designers, services and practitioners whose work is with, for or about troubled young people.

The concepts and science that lie within or are closely related to the systemic notions of psychosocial resilience offer us two other advantages in understanding the needs of young people who are in contact with adolescent forensic mental health services. First, we suggest that studying resilience provides an insight into the needs of young people, which, if met, might assist them to deal better with their current problems and also set out on a path towards avoiding serious problems and offending in the future. Second is our opinion that studying resilience suggests a range of psychosocial interventions, termed psychosocial care, which could underpin and provide a platform for specialised mental healthcare with a view to both acting synergistically to improve the effectiveness of each. We style this the psychosocial approach.

Study of psychosocial resilience in the arena of disasters indicates that there are factors that protect people from developing disorders and that outcomes are better if they are offered psychosocial care. The Sendai Framework for Disaster Risk Reduction 2015–2030 recognises that providing coordinated psychosocial and mental healthcare in disasters has become a critical part of preparing for, responding to and recovering from disasters. Science suggests that similar considerations are also relevant to people who have experienced sustained or repeated adversity and who have a lack of personal and material resources (Buckner and Waters, 2011: 264–275). We commend ensuring that the focus of intervention for young people who use forensic mental health services is broad and goes beyond their treatment for psychopathology to include meeting a much wider array of their psychosocial needs.

The work of Chitsabesan and her colleagues shows that young people's mental health needs, though prominent in her survey, lie within their subjects' broad range of, if anything, more prevalent social, education and risk-taking problems. Assisting young people to achieve functional literacy, for example, by enabling them to comprehend what they read, and, thereby, benefit from education must be high-priority matters. The concepts within resilience predict these skills as offering young people ways out of their problems and ways in which they might develop the capacity to resist being drawn back into crime and mental disorder.

In the last 25 years, good self-regulation has been recognised as a predictor of positive outcomes in children (Masten and Coatsworth, 1998). Emotional and functional self-regulation requires cognitive skills and we have already linked them with resilience (Buckner and Waters, 2011: 267–268). We think that many young people who are in contact with the youth justice and forensic mental health services require interventions to assist them with better regulating their emotions and actions. They also require adaptive coping skills if they are to deal effectively with their distress not only at the time, but also when they, inevitably, meet challenges in the future.

On the basis of the profile of past experiences and current needs of young offenders, which is provided

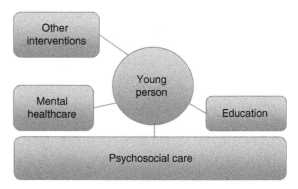

Figure 2.2 Psychosocial Care as a Platform for Mental Healthcare and Other Interventions

Source: Reproduced with the permission of the copyright holders, Williams R and Kemp V

by the research that we have summarised briefly, we suggest that mental healthcare interventions for young mentally disordered offenders should build on, and be integrated with a platform of psychosocial care and education interventions. Figure 2.2 illustrates this concept.

A Model of Care

In our opinion, Masten et al. suggest the components of a framework for policy, service design and practice. It is based on research on resilience (Masten et al., 2011: 114). It includes the following five elements:

Mission:	Frame positive goals
Models:	Include strengths, promotive and protective processes in models of change
Measures:	Include assessments of positive predictors, outcomes and change
Methods:	Consider strategies that reduce risk, boost resources, mobilise/protect fundamental adaptive systems and generate positive cascades
Multilevel approaches:	Consider multiple systems that may influence human resilience

Recommendations for young offenders and mentally disordered offenders that include elements of these kinds are not new. However, this approach is evidence-based and it allows us to draw into consideration lessons from studying psychosocial resilience. It also allows interventions to be planned into comprehensive care plans that are intended to assist people to be more resilient in the future as well as dealing with young people's unmet needs.

Interventions for Young Offenders Suggested by Studying Resilience

Our introduction to psychosocial resilience emphasises the importance of people's attachment capabilities and the social support that they receive. Building resilience requires interventions to develop these abilities. Our overview of young offenders' unmet needs shows the importance of these capabilities for young offenders.

Self-regulation, Adaptive Coping and Psychological First Aid

Similarly, we have identified self-regulation as a component of resilience, and this is another area of capability with which many young offenders also require assistance. We have identified the tendency for young offenders who are seriously at risk of repeated offending and mental disorders to adopt defensive coping. Psychosocial care recognises the importance to people's recovery of adaptation to their changed circumstances, and adaptive coping is an important aspect of the principles that underpin psychological first aid (PFA). PFA covers both social and psychological support and involves provision of humane, supportive and practical help for people who are affected by serious crises (World Health Organization et al., 2011). The British Red Cross has developed the CALMER model of PFA: Consider; Acknowledge; Listen; Manage; Enable; and Resources. This model asks people who use it to: Consider the situation, and the needs of the other person(s) and yourself; Acknowledge the situation and who you are, your intent and what has happened; deploy Listening skills and Learn from what people say; Manage the situation, safety, needs and any changes; Enable explanation, decision-making and contact with others; and know where to get Resources for support (Davidson, 2010). We think that it could be adapted to assist young people to cope adaptively with challenges and stress and as an intervention that is preliminary to cognitive work on self-regulation.

Social Support and Social Identity

The importance to young people of collective sources of support for their development and coping is clear. In this regard, social support means social interactions that provide people with actual assistance, but also embed them in a web of relationships that they perceive to be caring and readily available in times of need. Haslam et al. summarise, 'a growing body of work [which] indicates [that] social support is more likely to be given, received, and interpreted in the spirit in which it is intended to the extent that those who are in a position to provide and receive that support perceive themselves to share a sense of social identity' (Haslam et al., 2009: 11). They also say, 'Alongside evidence of the relationship between social identity and social support, research has also shown that a sense of shared identity underpins the capacity for members of disadvantaged groups to work together to buffer themselves from the negative consequences of their circumstances' (Haslam et al., 2009: 12). A book on The Social Cure shows that the effect sizes of social support should not be underestimated (Jetten et al., 2012).

While adolescents who use forensic mental health services are likely to have brought disadvantage to other people through offending, they are also, evidently, members of groups that are disadvantaged. Thus, social identity theories help to explain why and how some adolescent offenders draw support from groups of their peers who have similar experiences and problems. In some circumstances, though, the price may be high. Social identity theory also explains how some people may get into trouble partially as a consequence of their attempts to meet their own needs and particularly so when their personal psychosocial resources and opportunities to call on adults and successful peers for support run thin.

Martinez and Abrams identify that 'A burgeoning, yet underdeveloped, literature base has suggested that . . . young offenders [who return to communities after incarceration] receive important benefits . . . from informal support – the tangible and/or intangible resources, real or perceived, exchanged by individuals without pre-prescribed regulations – that family members, friends, and neighbourhood social networks can offer' (Martinez and Abrams, 2011: 170). The authors of this meta-synthesis of literature say that 'The overriding theme in this synthesis was that young offenders who confront their friends must "walk a fine line" between isolation and belonging, the latter side of which tempted the youth to re-engage in crime' (Martinez and Abrams, 2011: 183). Overall they found that, 'In some, . . . family support was overwhelmingly identified as critical to returning young offenders for material support, motivation, and emotional support. Extended family connections were a source of employment, gifts, and occasional goodwill support. Conversely, these "ties" also could exert pressure and the overbearing sense of expectations. This ... led some of the youth into a cycle of a "self-fulfilling" prophecy of return' to crime. Thus, there is, indeed, a tricky line for adolescents to manage between accepting support and resisting returning to crime both when they are treated in the community and when they return from residential care and treatment.

We conclude that research and theory suggest interventions that are important. They should be orientated to helping young people to develop their judgement about other people and to choose effectively the peer groups with which they associate. There are also roles for services to work with families to ensure that the support they offer to young people is truly supportive and not productive of expectations that are so high that the young people choose to move back towards patterns of criminal behaviour and activity.

Interventions for the Staff of Services That Work with and Treat Young Offenders

The concepts of horizontal epidemiology and resilience also have implications for staff who work in forensic mental health services. Søndenaa et al. say, 'Staff in forensic services for people with intellectual disabilities are expected to deal with a wide range of emotional challenges when providing care. The potential impact of this demanding work has not been systematically explored previously' (Søndenaa et al., 2013). We have highlighted research that suggests that a substantial proportion of young people who are treated by forensic mental health services have intellectual disabilities. So the work of Søndenaa et al. is highly relevant to this chapter.

Søndenaa et al. report research on professional quality of life and the resilience of the staff who work in these settings. They emphasise the importance of providing adequate support services for staff. They face substantial pressures arising from their work as well as whatever else occurs in their professional and personal lives. They are likely to benefit from social support and effective professional leadership in dealing well with the challenges they face. Many of the supporting facilities, attitudes and support from which they can benefit are likely to be influenced by similar factors and principles that we have applied in this chapter to designing psychosocial services for the young people in their care.

A parallel approach to sustaining the resilience of staff is that from Edmondson relating to teams and teamwork. She has researched the psychosocial safety of the environments in which practitioners work and the leadership and peer support that practitioners require if they are to build on their strengths and sustain their resilience (Edmondson, 2003). She says that 'in psychologically safe environments, people believe that if they make a mistake others will not penalize or think less of them for it. They also believe that others will not resent or penalize them for asking for help, information or feedback. This belief fosters the confidence to take the risks described ... and thereby ... gain from the associated benefits of learning'. There is evidence that psychologically safe working environments are not only better for the wellbeing and welfare of the staff, but also less likely to result in errors of judgement or mistakes.

Edmondson argues 'creating conditions of psychological safety is essential to laying a foundation for effective learning in organizations' (Edmondson, 2003: 257). She finds that 'Team leaders have a powerful effect on psychological safety' and places responsibilities on leaders for creating working environments that are as psychologically safe as is possible. She says, 'The actions and attitudes of the team leader are ... important determinants of the team learning process' (Edmondson, 2003: 265). This requires leaders to: be accessible; acknowledge fallibility; balance empowering other people with managing the tendencies for certain people to dominate discussions; balance psychological safety with accountability and other components of strategic and clinical governance; guide team members through talking about and learning from their uncertainties; and balance opportunities for their teams' reflection with action.

Conclusions

This chapter draws on a series of concepts: resilience as a construct that is prominent in the field of crises; psychosocial resilience as a concept in child development and knowledge of the backgrounds of, adversities, and contemporary sources of support and demand that are faced by young people who are in contact with forensic mental health services.

We identify two important aspects of planning care for young offenders and young people who use forensic mental health services that we think are vitally important to ensuring more successful outcomes, and reducing risks of their reoffending and offenders developing recurring mental health needs. They are:

- Recognising and responding to the psychosocial needs of the young people; and
- Founding a comprehensive approach to mental healthcare that is likely to be most effective on a solid platform of psychosocial care and education in which consideration of the systemic concepts within the notions of psychosocial care, resilience and recovery are included alongside effective specialist treatments for mental disorders.

There are other learning points that emerge from the science of resilience and psychosocial care. While none is new, they are nonetheless important.

- First, we should not fall into the trap of considering resilience to be solely a trait that results from the actions of individual persons: rather, it is best considered as a series of interacting and systemic dimensions. They include people's personal capabilities, their capacities for forming and sustaining relationships and the sources of personal and collective social support that are available to them from peers and adults.
- Second, studies of resilience suggest an approach to psychosocial care, which reminds us of the importance to young people of narrative and ecological approaches that stress trajectories of response to crises and adversity, and the interdependencies between young people and the contexts in which they live.
- Third, interventions that are designed to respond to young people's unmet needs, bolster their resilience and help them to avoid the suction power of recidivism and the possibilities of continuing ill health should address capacities and skills that are appropriate to the social, emotional, cognitive and physical maturities and needs of the particular young people involved.
- Fourth, staff are key to delivering the kinds of care that we describe in this chapter. Their needs are important. Effective psychosocial care that is well integrated with focused mental healthcare for young people requires that we also consider the needs of staff and that we plan to offer them social support and good leadership in order to sustain their psychosocial resilience.

A key challenge is how we embed this approach across training and in day-to-day practice. Evidently, staff should be well led and be members of teams that offer psychological safety to their members in which the positive power of their social identities and role modelling can be offered to the young people with whom they work.

References

Almedon, A. M. (2005). Social capital and mental health: an interdisciplinary review of primary evidence. *Social Science & Medicine*, **61**, 943–964.

American Psychological Association. (2010). *The Road to Resilience*. Washington, DC: American Psychological Association. Available from: www.apa.org/helpcenter/road-resilience.aspx. Accessed on 23 December, 2016.

Anthony, W. A. (1993). Recovery from mental illness: the guiding vision of the mental health service system in the 1990s. *Psychosocial Rehabilitation Journal*, **16**, 11–23.

Antonovsky, A. (1987). *Unravelling the Mystery of Health: How People Manage Stress and Stay Well*. San Francisco: Jossey-Bass.

Bailey, S. and Williams, R. (2005). Forensic mental health services for children and adolescents. In Williams, R. and Kerfoot, M. Editors. *Child and Adolescent Mental Health Services: Strategy, Planning, Delivery and Evaluation* (pp. 271–298). Oxford: Oxford University Press.

Buckner, J. C. and Waters, J. S. (2011). Resilience in the context of poverty. In Southwick, S. M., Litz, B. T., Charney, D. and Friedman, M. J. Editors. *Resilience and Mental Health: Challenges across the Lifespan* (pp. 264–275). Cambridge: Cambridge University Press.

Chitsabesan, P., Kroll, L., Bailey, S., Kenning, C., Sneider, S., MacDonald, W. and Theodosiou, L. (2006). Mental health needs of young offenders in custody and in the community. *British Journal of Psychiatry*, **188**, 534–540.

Chitsabesan, P., Bailey, S., Williams, R., Kroll, L., Kenning, C. and Talbot, L. (2007). Learning disabilities and educational needs of juvenile offenders. *Journal of Children's Services*, **24**, 4–17.

Cocking, C., Drury, J. and Reicher, S. (2009). The psychology of crowd behaviour in emergency evacuations: results from two interview studies and implications for the Fire & Rescue Services. *Irish Journal of Psychology*, **30**, 59–73.

Davidson, S. (2010). The development of the British Red Cross' psychosocial framework: CALMER. *Journal of Social Work Practice*, **24**(1), 29–42.

Deegan, P. E. (1988). Recovery: the lived experience of rehabilitation. *Psychosocial Rehabilitation Journal*, **11**, 11–19.

Department of Health. (2009). *NHS Emergency Planning Guidance: Planning for the Psychosocial and Mental Health Care of People Affected by Major Incidents and Disasters*. London: Department of Health.

Drury, J., Cocking, C. and Reicher, S. (2009a). Everyone for themselves? A comparative study of crowd solidarity among emergency survivors. *British Journal of Social Psychology*, **48**, 487–506.

Drury, J., Cocking, C. and Reicher, S. (2009b). The nature of collective resilience: survivor reactions to the 2005 London bombings. *International Journal of Mass Emergencies and Disasters*, 27, 66–95.

Edmondson, A. (2003). Managing the risk of learning: psychological safety in work teams. Chapter 13 in West, M. A., Tjosveld, D. and Smith, K. G. Editors. *International Handbook of Organizational Teamwork and Cooperative Working*. Oxford: Wiley.

Fielding, A. and Anderson, J. (2008). *Occasional Paper 2: Working with Refugee Communities to Build Collective Resilience*. Perth, Australia: Association for Services to Torture and Trauma Survivors.

Haslam, S. A. (2004). *Psychology in Organizations: The Social Identity Approach*. London: Sage.

Haslam, S. A., Turner, J. C., Oakes, P., McGarty, C. and Reynolds, K. (1998). The group as a basis for emergent stereotype consensus. *European Review of Social Psychology*, **28**, 203–239.

Haslam, S. A., Jetten, J., Postmes, T. and Haslam, C. (2009). Social identity, health and well-being: an emerging agenda for applied psychology. *Applied Psychology: An International Review*, **58**(1), 1–23.

Hernández, P. (2002). Resilience in families and communities: Latin American contributions from the psychology of liberation. *The Family Journal*, **10**(3), 334–343.

Hobfoll, S.E., Hall, B., Horsey, K. J. and Lamaoureux, B. E. (2011). Resilience in the face of terrorism: linking resource investment with engagement. In Southwick, S. M., Litz, B. T., Charney, D. and Friedman, M. J. Editors. *Resilience and Mental Health: Challenges across the Lifespan*. Cambridge: Cambridge University Press.

Horwitz, A. V. (2007). Distinguishing distress from disorder as psychological outcomes of stressful social arrangements. *Health*, **11**, 273–289.

Jetten, J., Haslam, C. and Haslam, S. A. (2012). *The Social Cure: Identity, Health and Well-being*. Hove and New York: Psychology Press.

Kahn, W. A. (2005). *Holding Fast: The Struggle to Create Resilient Caregiving Organizations*. Hove, East Sussex: Brunner-Routledge.

Karatsoreos, I.N. and McEwen, B.S. (2013). Annual Research Review: The neurobiology and physiology of resilience and adaptation across the life course. *Journal of Child Psychology and Psychiatry* 54(4), 337–347.

Kobasa, S. C. (1979). Stressful life events, personality, and health: an inquiry into hardiness. *Journal of Personal and Social Psychology*, **37**(1), 1–11.

Kobasa, S. C., Maddi, S. R. and Kahn, S. (1982). Hardiness and health: a prospective study. *Journal of Personal and Social Psychology*, **42**(1):168–177.

Layne, C. M., Warren, J. S., Watson, P. J. an Shalev, A. Y. (2007). Risk, vulnerability, resistance, and resilience: towards an integrative conceptualization of posttraumatic adaptation. In Friedman, T. K. M. and Resick, P. Editors. *Handbook of PTSD: Science and Practice* (pp. 497–520). New York: Guilford Press.

Levin, A. (2009). Genes influence vulnerability to posttrauma disorders. *Psychiatric News*, **44**(3), 17.

Martinez, D. J. and Abrams, L. S. (2011). Informal social support among returning young offenders: a metasynthesis of the literature. *International Journal of Offender Therapy and Comparative Criminology*, **57**(2), 169–190.

Masten, A. S. and Coatsworth, D. (1998). The development of competence in favorable and unfavorable environments: lessons from research on successful children. *American Psychologist*, **53**, 205–220.

Masten, A. S., Monn, A. R. and Supkoff, L. M. (2011). Resilience in children and adolescents. In Southwick, S. M., Litz, B. T., Charney, D. and Friedman, M. J. Editors. *Resilience and Mental Health: Challenges across the Lifespan*. Cambridge: Cambridge University Press.

Mawson, A. R. (2005). Understanding mass panic and other collective responses to threat and disaster. *Psychiatry*, **68**, 95–113.

Meyer, P. S. and Mueser, K. T. (2011). Resiliency in individuals with serious mental illness. In Southwick, S. M., Litz, B. T., Charney, D. and Friedman, M. J. Editors. *Resilience and Mental Health: Challenges across the Lifespan*. Cambridge: Cambridge University Press.

Mullen, P. E. (2000). Forensic mental health. *British Journal of Psychiatry*, **176**, 307–311.

National Assembly for Wales. (2001). *Everybody's Business: Child and Adolescent Mental Health Services in Wales: Strategy Document*. Cardiff: National Assembly for Wales.

National CAMHS Support Service. (2011). *Better Mental Health Outcomes for Children and Young People: A Resource Directory for Commissioners*. London: National CAMHS Support Services.

NHS Health Advisory Service. (1995). *Together We Stand: The Commissioning, Role and Management of Child and Adolescent Mental Health Services*. London: HMSO.

Norris, F. H., Tracy, M. and Galea, S. (2009). Looking for resilience: Understanding the longitudinal trajectories of responses to stress. *Social Science & Medicine*, **68**, 2190–2198.

North Atlantic Treaty Organization. (NATO/EAPC) (2009). *Psychosocial Care for People Affected by Disasters and Major Incidents*. Brussels: NATO. Available from: www .healthplanning.co.uk/media/1962/NATO_Guidance_Psyc hosocial_Care_for_People_Affected_by_Disasters_and_ Major_Incidents.pdf. Accessed 20 October 2016.

Omand, D. (2010). *Securing the State*. London: C. Hurst & Co (Publishers) Ltd.

Panter-Brick, C. and Leckman, J. F. (2013). Editorial commentary: resilience in child development – interconnected pathways to wellbeing. *Journal of Child Psychology and Psychiatry*, 54(4), 333–336.

Robinson, A. (2016). The resilience motif: implications for youth justice. *Youth Justice* 16(1), 18–33.

Rutter, M. (1987). Psychosocial resilience and protective mechanisms. *American Journal of Orthopsychiatry*, 57(3), 316–331.

Rutter, M. (2012). Resilience as a dynamic concept. *Development and Psychopathology* 24, 335–344.

Sapienza, J. K. and Masten, A. S. (2011). Understanding and promoting resilience in children and youth. *Current Opinion in Psychiatry*, 24(4), 267–273.

Schaufeli, W. B., Salanova, M., Gonzáles-Romá, V. and Bakker, A. B. (2002). The measurement of burnout and engagement; a confirmatory factor analytic approach. *Journal of Happiness Studies*, 3, 71–92.

Søndenaa, E., Lauvrud, C., Sandvik, M., Nonstad, K. and Whittington, R. (2013). Resilience and professional quality of life in staff working with people with intellectual disabilities and offending behavior in community based and institutional settings. *Health Psychology Research*, 1(e3), 11–15.

Southwick, S. M. and Charney, D. S. (2012). *Resilience: The Science of Mastering Life's Greatest Challenges.* Cambridge: Cambridge University Press.

Southwick, S. M., Litz, B. T., Charney, D. and Friedman, M. J. Editors. (2011). Preface. In *Resilience and Mental Health: Challenges across the Lifespan* (pp. xi–xv). Cambridge: Cambridge University Press.

Tol, W. A., Song, S. and Jordans, M. J. D. (2013). Annual research review: resilience and mental health in children and adolescents living in areas of armed conflict – a systematic review of findings in low- and middle-income countries. *The Journal of Child Psychology and Psychiatry*, 54, 445–460.

Troy, A. S. and Mauss, I. B. (2011). Resilience in the face of stress: emotion regulation as a protective factor. In Southwick, S. M., Litz, B. T., Charney, D. and Friedman, M. J. Editors. *Resilience and Mental Health: Challenges across the Lifespan*. Cambridge: Cambridge University Press.

Turner, J C., Hogg, M. A., Oakes, P. J., Reicher, S. D. and Wetherell, M. S. (1987). *Rediscovering the Social Group: A Self-categorization Theory*. Oxford: Blackwell.

UNISDR. (2009). *UNISDR Terminology on Disaster Risk Reduction*. Geneva: United Nations Office for Disaster Risk Reduction.

Williams, R. (2004). A strategic approach to commissioning and delivering forensic child and adolescent mental health services. In Bailey, S. and Dolan, M. Editors. *Adolescent Forensic Psychiatry* (pp. 315 to 335). London: Butterworth-Heinemann.

Williams, R. (2007). The psychosocial consequences for children of mass violence, terrorism and disasters. *International Review of Psychiatry*, 19(3), 263–277.

Williams, R. and Barnes, M. (1997). Commissioning adolescent forensic mental health services. Health Services Management Centre in the University of Birmingham, unpublished.

Williams, R. and Drury, J. (2010). The nature of psychosocial resilience and its significance for managing mass emergencies, disasters and terrorism. In Awotona, A. Editor. *Rebuilding Sustainable Communities for Children and Their Families After Disasters: A Global Survey.* Newcastle upon Tyne: Cambridge Scholars Publishing.

Williams, R. and Drury, J. (2011). Personal and collective psychosocial resilience: implications for children, young people and their families involved in war and disasters. In Cook, D., Wall, J. and Cox, P. Editors. *Children and Armed Conflict*. Basingstoke and New York: Palgrave McMillan.

Williams, R. and Hazell, P. (2011). Austerity, poverty, resilience, and the future of mental health services for children and adolescents. *Current Opinion in Psychiatry*, 24(4), 263–266.

Williams, R., Bates, P., Farrar, M., Gay, M., George, D., Owen, E. and White, R. (1994). *A review of the adolescent forensic psychiatry service based on the Gardener Unit, Prestwich Hospital, Salford, Manchester.* London: NHS Health Advisory Service, Mental Health Act Commission, Social Services Inspectorate of the Department of Health.

Williams, R., Bisson, J. and Kemp, V. (2014). *OP 94 Principles for Responding to the Psychosocial and Mental Health Needs of People Affected by Disasters or Major Incidents.* London: The Royal College of Psychiatrists.

World Health Organization, War Trauma Foundation, World Vision International. (2011). Psychological first aid: Guide for field workers. Geneva: WHO. Available from: http://apps.who.int/iris/bitstream/10665/44615/1/9789241548205_eng.pdf. Accessed 20 October 2016.

Zeanah, C. H. and Sonuga-Barke, J. S. (2016). The effects of early trauma and deprivation on human development – from measuring cumulative risk to characterizing specific mechanisms. *Journal of Child Psychology and Psychiatry*, 57 (10), 1099–1102.

Chapter

Assessment of Young Offenders

Mental Health, Physical, Educational and Social Needs

3

Prathiba Chitsabesan and Lorraine Khan

Introduction

Young people who end up in the youth justice system have well-documented multiple vulnerabilities affecting their life chances (Centre for Mental Health, 2010), including a higher level of mental health need. Politicians and professionals have begun to recognise the importance of meeting the needs of offenders, as long-term costs to society become increasingly apparent. Studies to date suggest that one of the most common reasons for unmet need is lack of appropriate and timely assessment (Kroll et al., 2002; Harrington and Bailey, 2005; Centre for Mental Health, 2010). A recent review by the Office of the Children's Commissioner (Hughes et al., 2012) raised concerns about the significant number of young people within the secure estate who demonstrated symptoms indicating potential neurodisability that were undetected.

However, assessment can be complicated by a number of factors including the non-clear-cut nature of emerging poor mental health in comparison to presentations in adults (Vikram et al., 2007), the minimisation of symptoms by young offenders and the disinclination of young people to engage with mental health services due to fear of stigma.

Initial assessment is a key factor in the successful treatment of mental or physical health needs for young offenders. Early identification of mental health needs may also reduce the later risk of mental disorders and their related health costs (Knapp et al., 2011). Timely assessment may inform risk assessment processes as well as increasing engagement in offence-related interventions. Learning disabilities and language disorders are also more common in this group of young people and are likely to affect many aspects of their life and functioning.

However, identification of mental disorders in young children and adolescents can be complex. A normal childhood may be hard to define and can be influenced by a number of different variables, including gender and culture. It is therefore unclear whether childhood psychopathology should be defined by categorical disorders or symptoms. Additionally, the developmental trajectory of psychopathology from childhood into adulthood is complex, as different pathways can lead to the same adult outcomes and vice versa.

While a detailed assessment of every offender's mental health would be helpful, it would be costly to implement given the number of young people in contact with the justice system and the pressures on the police and the courts to deliver justice expediently. Instead a two-tiered approach providing a universal screen to all juvenile offenders but a more detailed assessment of those highlighted in the initial screen is likely to be more cost-effective.

There has been much confusion in the juvenile justice system between the terms 'screening' and 'assessment', and often the terms are used interchangeably. Grisso et al. (2005) attempt a clearer definition. They argue that screening is a briefer process that helps to identify current needs or symptoms and should be applied to all offenders in the juvenile justice system at the point of entry. It helps to differentiate young people into two main categories: those at higher risk and requiring more detailed assessment, and those whose needs are more minor. Screening tools should ideally demonstrate good reliability and validity. Reliability ensures that the screening tool produces consistent results irrespective of the person administering it, while validity ensures that the screening tool measures what it's supposed to.

Assessment involves a more comprehensive evaluation of symptoms identified in the initial screening process and facilitates a response which is more pertinent to the needs of that particular individual. For example, a young person may require a full physical examination, a more thorough mental health assessment or referral for psychometric assessment to identify any learning disabilities. Assessment may therefore involve a standardised tool or a clinical interview with a trained juvenile justice worker or professional from another discipline, for example psychologist or speech and language therapist. It usually requires training and expertise to be administered appropriately and often takes longer to perform. However, the advantage of an assessment is its ability to provide a more reliable perspective of the needs of an individual which can be helpful in recommendations regarding treatment.

In this chapter we have attempted to provide a brief overview of the existing literature and its implications for policy and practice.

Mental Health Needs

Over the last ten years a number of international studies have examined the prevalence rates of psychiatric disorders among juvenile offenders (Table 3.1). The prevalence of any mental disorder in the general youth population is about 16% (Roberts et al., 1998).

The high rate of psychopathology in juvenile offenders may be the consequence of shared risk factors in the development of both antisocial behaviour and psychiatric disorders. The lives of these young people are often characterised by attachment difficulties, trauma, familial psychopathology and disadvantage (Loeber and Farrington, 2000; McCabe et al., 2002). Unsurprisingly rates of disruptive disorders such as conduct disorder are particularly high, ranging from 24% to 73% (Teplin et al., 2002; Vreugdenhil et al., 2004). Conduct disorder is also associated with high comorbidity for other psychiatric disorders, including Attention Deficit Hyperactivity Disorder (ADHD) and substance misuse. While studies consistently show high rates of psychiatric disorders among young offenders, prevalence rates are diverse due to differences in methodology between studies. This includes differences in sampling techniques and assessment tools, as well as variations in sample sizes (see Table 3.1).

The North West Juvenile Project (NWJP) attempted to address some of the limitations of previous studies by including a large random sample of offenders detained at Cook County Juvenile Temporary Detention Center (Teplin et al., 2002;

Abram et al., 2003). Juvenile offenders (1172 males) were assessed using the Diagnosis Interview Schedule for Children–Version 2.3 (DISC-2.3). Excluding conduct disorder, 60% of offenders met the diagnostic criteria for one or more disorders. Affective (16%) and anxiety disorders (21%) were common, while 51% had a substance misuse disorder (Table 3.1). ADHD was found in 11% of young offenders. Comorbidity was frequent, with 17% of male offenders presenting with three or more types of disorders. Overlap between substance misuse disorders and ADHD or conduct disorder was particularly common (31%). Research findings have consistently shown that juvenile offenders are characterised by high comorbidity, contributing to complexity in both their assessment and treatment. Rates of comorbidity are especially high among offenders misusing substances (Domalanta et al., 2003).

Within the remit of this chapter we have not explored substance misuse by juvenile offenders, as this is covered comprehensively elsewhere (please refer to Chapter 13 by Theodosiou).

The NWJP study also explored rates of trauma and Post-Traumatic Stress Disorder (PTSD) and found that the majority of young male offenders had experienced at least one trauma in their lifetime (93%), while 11% met the criteria for PTSD. However, rates of PTSD were found to be much higher in a study of 370 male juvenile offenders in custody in Russia (Ruchkin et al., 2002). Most offenders reported some post-traumatic stress symptoms, with 25% meeting full DSM-IV criteria. Higher PTSD scores were found to be related to higher scores of violence exposure.

Autistic Spectrum Disorder (ASD) is used to describe a group of disorders, including autism and Asperger's Syndrome. It is a lifelong condition affecting communication, relationships with others and how young people make sense of the world around them. Males are more likely to be affected by autism than females.

Knowledge of the prevalence rate of ASD in the youth justice system is generally poor (please refer to Chapter 15 by Gralton and Baird). There is some concern that young people who experience autism may be over-represented among offending populations (Cashin and Newman, 2009). Howlin (1997) suggested that certain features of ASD could predispose some young people to offend in particular

Table 3.1 Comparison of Prevalence Rates of Psychiatric Disorders in Male Juvenile Offenders

Study	Country	Site	Males (n)	Mean Age (yrs)	Measure	Prevalence Rates of Disorders
Wasserman et al., 2002	USA	Custody	292	17	DISC-IV	MDD 8% Any anxiety disorder 20% ADHD 2% Any SUD 50%
McCabe et al., 2002	USA	Adjudicated	513	16	DISC-IV	MDD 3% Any anxiety disorder 10% ADHD 15% Any SUD 37%
Kroll et al., 2002	UK	Custody	97	15	K-SADS	MDD 22% GAD 17% ADHD 11% Schizophrenia 1% Drug abuse 69% Alcohol abuse 48%
Ruchkin et al., 2002	Russia	Custody	330	16	K-SADS-PL	MDD 10% GAD 12% ADHD 14% Drug abuse 27% Alcohol abuse 56%
Domalanta et al., 2003	USA	Custody	750	15	PHQ	MDD 10% Any anxiety disorder 13% Drug Abuse 43% Alcohol Abuse 27%
Teplin et al., 2002	USA	Custody	1172	15	DISC 2.3	Affective disorder 11% Any anxiety disorder 21% ADHD 11% Any SUD 51%
Gosden et al., 2003	Denmark	Custody	100	Not specified 15–17	KSADS-PL	Mild depression 2% Any anxiety disorder 5% ADHD 1% Schizophrenia 2% Any SUD 41%
Vreugdenhil et al., 2004	Holland	Custody	204	16	DISC-IV	MDD 6% Any anxiety disorder 9% ADHD 8% SUD 55%
Chitsabesan et al., 2006	UK	Custody and community	232	16	SNASA	Depression 13% GAD 16% ADHD 8% Psychotic symptoms 4% Drug Misuse 21% Alcohol Misuse 9%
Fazel et al., 2008 Meta-regression analysis	Varied	Custody	13,778	Varied	Varied	MDD 11% ADHD 12% Psychotic Illness 3%

Table 3.1 (cont.)

Study	Country	Site	Males (n)	Mean Age (yrs)	Measure	Prevalence Rates of Disorders
Colins et al., 2010	Varied	Custody	3401	Varied	Varied	MDD 12%
Systematic literature review						GAD 16% ADHD 14% SUD 45%

Note: ADHD = Attention Deficit Hyperactivity Disorder; DISC = Diagnostic Interview Schedule for Children; GAD = Generalised Anxiety Disorder; K-SADS-PL = Kiddie-Schedule for Affective Disorders, Present and Lifetime Version; MDD = Major Depressive Disorder; PHQ = Patient Health Questionnaire; SNASA = Salford Needs Assessment Schedule for Adolescents; SUD = Substance Use Disorder.

ways. These include their social naivety which could lead to suggestibility and a tendency to be influenced by others, antisocial behaviour stemming from poor understanding or misinterpretation of social cues, and crimes reflecting obsessions. In response to these concerns, the National Autistic Society has developed information and guidance on autism for professionals working within the criminal justice system (The National Autistic Society, 2008).

Self-harm is also under-investigated by many studies as research tools evaluating mental disorders primarily focus on psychiatric diagnoses. Studies have shown that self-harm is more prevalent among offenders as certain risk factors for self-harm are more common among this group (please refer to Chapter 10 by Trainor, Rothwell and Hales). Predictors of an increased risk include previous attempts, prolonged low mood, ADHD, having a bad temper (impulsive aggression) and substance use frequency (Putnins, 2005).

The literature similarly demonstrates that suicide rates are much higher in the offender population compared with non-antisocial peers. This may be partially explained by their tendency to use violent methods, for example hanging and stabbing, rather than taking an overdose. Lifetime risk of suicide attempts was found to be high at 12% (Wasserman et al., 2002) Studies suggest that risk factors for suicidal behaviour may be different for juvenile offenders compared with the wider population. Ruchkin et al. (2003) found that ADHD, but not depression, independently predicted suicidal behaviour. However, findings from studies are inconsistent and more research in this area is essential as suicide risk is a significant problem in this population.

There have also been few longitudinal studies that have explored how mental health needs change over time, particularly for offenders as they move between custody and community settings. Kroll et al. (2002) followed a sample of 97 male juvenile offenders admitted to secure care using the Salford Needs Assessment Schedule for Adolescents (SNASA) (Kroll et al., 1999). Three months after admission, rates of depression, PTSD and anxiety disorders had increased. One explanation for the increase in mental health needs may be the use of alcohol and drugs by young offenders in the community to manage their mental health symptoms. These symptoms become increasingly apparent following admission to custody due to reduced access to these substances. The offenders were reassessed two years later when many offenders had been released back into the community (Harrington et al., 2005). Rates of substance abuse increased to 31% on discharge compared with 21% following initial admission. Anxiety disorder including PTSD was also more common at follow-up in young people who remained in custody, although this may be partially attributed to the association with violent crime as high rates of PTSD have been found in violent offenders (Ruchkin et al., 2002).

Mental Health Screening

Mental health screening can focus on diagnostic labels or symptoms; it can focus on broader problem areas affecting a child's well-being; or alternatively it can map risk and protective factors associated with mental health and emotional well-being. Ideally screening tools should have both high sensitivity (measure of true positives) and specificity (measure of true negatives), although this is difficult to achieve in practice.

Instead, many screening tools often have low sensitivity (high false positives), but high specificity (low false negatives). Consequently, many young people may screen positive who have some mental health symptoms but who are below threshold to meet the criteria for a mental health diagnosis. However, this is essential to ensure that offenders with possible mental disorders are not missed.

Internationally, there have been a number of mental health screening tools developed for use within the youth justice system. Any tool selected should be feasible for use and therefore administered relatively easily and quickly by juvenile justice staff. Mental health screening tools should also have defined processes to differentiate those at risk that require further assessment. Grisso et al. (2005) define a minimum set of requirements for a mental health screening tool for juvenile offenders. They include the assessment of affective and anxiety symptoms, indicators of risk of aggression, self-harm or suicide as well as alcohol and drug misuse.

Diagnosis and Symptom-Focused Approaches

One of the most widely used screening tools in the USA is the Massachusetts Youth Screening Instrument – Version 2 (MAYSI-2) (Grisso and Barnum, 2006), which is recommended for use for all offenders on initial contact with the juvenile justice system. The MAYSI-2 is a 52-item self-report tool that takes 15 minutes to complete with 'yes/no' response. Each of the seven scales has two suggested cut-off scores: the 'warning' cut-off indicates high risk (above 90% of normative sample), while the 'caution' cut-off indicates young people with clinically significant symptoms.

Most validated tools screening for ASD have been designed to identify the syndrome in childhood rather than in adolescence. The Social Communication Questionnaire (SCQ) (formerly the Autism Screening Questionnaire) has demonstrated good sensitivity and specificity in a number of studies and can be used for both children and adults (Berument et al., 1999). However, it requires completion by a parent or primary caregiver who can provide information on the young person's early developmental history which may be difficult to achieve in practice. The Autism Spectrum Quotient (AQ) – adolescent version (Baron-Cohen et al., 2001) was developed to meet the needs of under-16-year-olds, while the Gilliam Autism Rating Scale – Third Edition (GARS-3) (Gilliam, 2014) is valid for those between the ages of three and 22. The screening tools are completed by either a caregiver or a professional who knows the young person well, although their psychometric profile may be less favourable than the SCQ.

Needs Assessment Approaches

Instead of screening solely for mental disorders, some screening tools focus on broader needs which have the capacity to undermine a young person's mental health and emotional well-being. These tools typically cover a wider range of functioning such as education and social areas which are often impaired in young offenders. Needs assessment can therefore be a more useful measure of problems in young people with complex needs, as comorbidity such as learning needs can affect every day functioning as well as the ability to engage in treatment.

Needs assessment has also become more important as the cost of healthcare is rising in contrast to resources which are limited. In planning services the prevalence of a disorder does not necessarily equate to the services that are required. This is influenced by a number of factors, including the availability of an effective intervention as well as a willingness to accept that intervention (Harrington et al., 1999).

The Salford Needs Assessment Schedule for Adolescents (Kroll et al., 1999) defines 'need' as a significant problem that can benefit from an intervention or persists despite intervention. The SNASA is administered as a semi-structured interview with the young person and carer. The 17 items cover five domains (mental health, risky behaviours including self-harm and substance misuse, education/work, violence and relationships). Clinicians consider what interventions have been offered to the young person and its effectiveness against other appropriate interventions. Depending on their judgement as to whether an appropriate intervention has been offered, a final needs status is generated. Possible needs status includes no need, unmet need, suspended need or persistent need despite intervention.

The SNASA is also the basis of a mental health screening tool used by youth offending teams within England and Wales. A universal screening tool, the SQIFA (Screening Questionnaire Interview for Adolescents) is administered to all young offenders on initial contact. The eight items cover a range of mental health problems including substance misuse and self-harm. If a young person is identified with needs they are referred for the second stage assessment. The SIFA (Screening Interview for Adolescents) (SIFA) is based on the SNASA and covers the same eight areas of mental health as the SQIFA. It also explores the motivation of the young person to change and a review of previous interventions. The SIFA is administered by the health worker within the Youth Offending Team, and young people are referred to the appropriate specialist services locally, dependent on the severity of the symptoms and their motivation to engage.

In a comparison study, the psychometric properties of the MAYSI-2, SDQ (Strengths Difficulties Questionnaire) and SIFA were evaluated against each other (Bailey et al., 2006). The SIFA demonstrated moderately good sensitivity and specificity in comparison with the MAYSI-2 which had high sensitivity but low specificity.

Risk and Resilience Approach

There has been some criticism of systems and approaches which are too heavily weighted towards mental health diagnosis and needs. Such approaches are seen to be reactive rather than preventative and underestimate the strengths which promote recovery and the social determinants of good mental and physical health (Morgan and Ziglio, 2007). An important underpinning principle of the risk and resilience approach is that it focuses on building important 'assets' in the child's health and emotional wellbeing (see Figure 3.1). Activity can include strengthening the child's internal resources, as well as resilience in their families, their communities and their broader environment. However, this approach requires more extensive evaluation to test its impact on subsequent mental health and social outcomes.

Social Needs

A number of different factors have been identified in the development of antisocial behaviour, including familial dysfunction, poverty and poor child-rearing behaviour (Loeber and Farrington, 2000). The latter includes difficulties with supervision, warmth and responsiveness to conflict resolution and can lead to an insecure attachment style. The effects of delinquent peers, particularly in adolescence can also be influential.

Consequently, many juvenile offenders have difficulties in social aspects of their lives, both with family and peer relationships. Two UK studies using the SNASA, found that relationship needs were among

the most common domains of need with 72% and 48% of juvenile offenders respectively (Kroll et al., 2002; Chitsabesan et al., 2006). About 29% of young people experienced difficulties with family relationships and 35% with relationships with peers (Chitsabesan et al., 2006). Almost one in ten offenders had problems with weekday occupation or accommodation. A number of offenders had received interventions around peer and family relationships, although this was often not structured.

The Asset assessment tool used by youth offending teams in the UK predominantly focuses on criminogenic risks and needs. It has been criticised for omitting speech and communication needs and for inadequate attention to learning disabilities, although this has been addressed in the AssetPlus. Practitioners using the Asset were found to under identify mental health needs, highlighting training needs among youth justice professionals (Harrington and Bailey, 2005).

In the Netherlands, the BARO was developed to standardise assessments for all young people on initial contact with the criminal justice system. The BARO covers nine domains of functioning, including physical and psychosocial development and functioning within the family and school. It incorporates informant history (parent and teacher) where possible and demonstrates good psychometric properties in identifying underlying psychopathology (Doreleijers and Spaander, 2002).

Physical Health Needs

Health inequalities tend to be high among offending groups. Longitudinal studies indicate that children with conduct disorders have poorer physical health outcomes as adults than their peers (Scott, 2008). Children and young people who offend are also more likely to engage in risky behaviours such as violence, alcohol and drug misuse, and sexually promiscuous behaviour. Cigarette smoking, poor diet and lack of exercise are also common. Almost one in five offenders were found to have sexually transmitted infections, including chlamydia and gonorrhoea (Golzari et al., 2006). These disorders are more common in juvenile offenders as they are more likely to become sexually active young, have multiple partners and are less likely to use condoms.

A study of 197 young offenders and those attending a special needs school found that 46% reported a Traumatic Brain Injury (TBI) involving loss of consciousness (Williams et al., 2010). The majority of

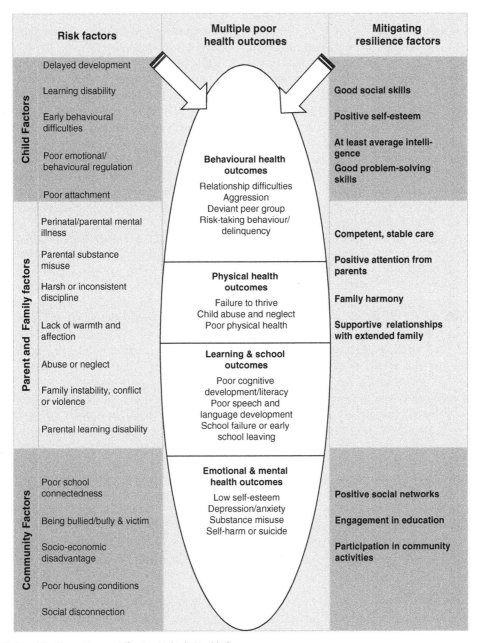

Figure 3.1 Risk and Resilience Factors Affecting Multiple Health Outcomes

these events were the results of fights. Young people with more self-reported TBIs were found to be at greater risk of mental health problems and of cannabis misuse (please refer to Chapter 5 by Hughes, Williams and Chitsabesan). Moderate to severe loss of consciousness has been associated with neuropsychological, behavioural and social problems (Stambrook et al., 1990).

Few health practitioners in contact with young offenders use validated tools for comprehensively assessing physical health needs. The 12-item Short Form Physical Health Survey Subscale (Ware et al., 1996) was used in a cross-sectional survey of juvenile offenders (223 males) in custody in New South Wales, Australia (Butler et al., 2008). A physical assessment including blood and urine analysis was also conducted. Three-quarters of offenders (79%) reported some health symptoms, while 36% reported at least five symptoms. The most chronic condition was asthma in almost a third of offenders. About one in ten offenders tested positive for both hepatitis B and C, and almost half of those found to be positive for hepatitis C were unaware of the diagnosis. Prevalence rates for hepatitis C were three times higher for those injecting drugs. The authors concluded that contact with the youth justice system provides an opportunity to screen young offenders for physical health problems and to also initiate contact with health services.

Awareness of the importance of screening for mental and physical health needs has improved within the last decade. A survey of healthcare policies for juvenile offenders across 83 juvenile detention centres across the USA found that 90% had a physical and mental health screening policy and that 95% of detention centres provided non-emergency medical care on site (Pajer et al., 2007). However, utilisation of health services in the community is often poor with many offenders not seeking medical care when symptomatic. Reasons varied from problems with transport and organising an appointment, to lack of a family member to accompany them and fear of what the doctor might say (Butler et al., 2008). Additionally, not all custody or community sites routinely obtain previous medical or psychiatric records as part of their assessment process (Pajer et al., 2007). Poor continuity of care is a common reason for unmet needs, as information from previous assessments is not always transferred with the young person, especially as they move between custody and community sites (Harrington and Bailey, 2005).

Educational Needs

The association between academic problems and antisocial behaviour has been well established. Young offenders are frequently excluded from school, propelling them towards the company of other antisocial peers (Chitsabesan et al., 2007). Detachment from school increases the risk of offending through reduced supervision, loss of any positive socialisation effects of school and by creating delinquent groups of young people (Stevenson, 2006).

While studies have been helpful in highlighting the numbers of juvenile offenders with learning disabilities and academic underachievements, definitions and terminology have varied, and a number of different tools have been used to measure learning needs making comparisons difficult.

A study of 802 male and female offenders (aged 12–21 years) serving community orders in Australia found that 15% had an intellectual disability (IQ<70) using the Wechsler Abbreviated Scale for Intelligence (Wechsler, 1999), while 21% had significant reading difficulties (Kenny et al., 2006).

The neurocognitive profiles of juvenile offenders include deficits in verbal skills, attention and impulse control as well as low IQ scores (Moffitt, 1993; Loeber and Farrington, 2000). Language and communication problems have also been identified in studies of juvenile offenders, although often poorly recognised in practice (Bryan et al., 2007). Meanwhile, deficits in executive function including poor impulse control and attention can affect the young person's ability to regulate their behaviours, plan and generate alternative strategies. Specific deficits in verbal-based tasks can be identified in intelligence (IQ) assessments through a discrepancy in verbal and performance scores with a typically lower verbal score (P>V) (Moffitt, 1993). However, the association between learning disabilities and academic underachievement is complex. A meta-analysis of 131 studies exploring verbal and performance discrepancy in IQ found that the discrepancy was largest for adolescent offenders but negligible for younger offenders (Isen, 2010). Verbal subtests are more strongly influenced by schooling and consequently verbal deficits may accumulate with time secondary to school failure.

Reading and reading comprehension difficulties are also common. One study found that almost half of juvenile offenders had a reading or reading comprehension age below ten years (Chitsabesan et al., 2007). The age of criminal responsibility within England and Wales is ten years; this finding therefore raises questions about a young person's ability to follow the legal processes and make informed decisions (please refer to Chapter 21 by Delmage, Variend and Shaw). Identifying offenders with learning disabilities is therefore essential not only to tailor interventions appropriately, but also because children and adults with intellectual disabilities have a different legal status dependent on the severity of their impairment.

Well established validated tools to measure IQ include the Wechsler Intelligence Scale for Children (Wechsler, 1991), the Stanford-Binet fifth edition

(Roid, 2003) and Woodcock Johnson-III (WJ-III) (Woodcock et al., 2001). These tests measure different facets of intelligence (crystalline and fluid) and include normative data across the lifespan. The Wechsler scales and WJ-III additionally measure aspects of executive function, including working memory, although more specific tools to test executive function also exist. Assessment of specific learning difficulties, for example reading and spelling can also be made through scales attached to the general IQ assessment measure, making interpretation easier. The Wechsler Abbreviated Scale for Intelligence (WASI) (Wechsler, 1999) provides a reliable but briefer measure of intelligence.

However, many of these tools require specialist training to be administered and there is often limited access to such professionals within the youth justice system. Youth justice staff also frequently lack training to identify these needs (Harrington and Bailey, 2005).

The Hayes Ability Screening Index (HASI) (Hayes, 2000) is a short screen for hidden developmental disabilities, developed in Australia. This tool has demonstrated reasonable reliability in identifying those requiring further assessment and takes 5–10 minutes to administer. In Australia it has been used in police custody suites before police interview to ensure the offender has full capacity for participation in the criminal justice process. The tool has been validated with adult and teenage populations. One study, however, has raised questions about the reliability of the tool for children in the youth justice system in England (Ford et al., 2008). Within the UK, the Child and Adolescent Intellectual Disability Screening Questionnaire (CAIDS-Q) has recently been developed for young people 8–18 years of age and shown good sensitivity and specificity as well as inter-rater reliability (McKenzie et al., 2012).

Screening for speech and language difficulties amongst juvenile offenders is at an early stage of development within the UK. Bryan et al's prevalence study (Bryan et al., 2007) in custodial settings indicate that the Test of Adolescent and Adult Language, third Edition (TOAL-3) (Wiig and Secord, 1989) has some potential with young people in the youth justice system, but further work is needed to test its validity and reliability more extensively. Meanwhile, the Children's Communication Checklist Questionnaire (CCC-2) is a popular screening questionnaire for communication problems in children aged 4–16 years (Bishop, 2006). Work is currently progressing to develop a shortened version of the tool (CCC-S) for easier use within a universal setting as an initial screening tool.

Gender and Ethnicity Differences

Rates of mental disorder in adolescents in the general population suggest that some disorders are more common in girls than boys. A study of adjudicated adolescent offenders in San Diego explored gender differences in psychopathology and functioning (McCabe et al., 2002) using the DISC. The study found that female offenders had higher rates of most DSM-IV disorders (except substance misuse disorder), although this was significant only for mood disorders and separation anxiety disorder. Girls also experienced more abuse and neglect than male offenders and were more likely to experience multiple disorders (69% compared with 53%). This is consistent with the findings of other studies and supports the view that female offenders are a high-risk group in terms of their mental health needs.

With respect to educational needs, a Swedish study of 163 male and female young offenders found that girls performed significantly better than boys in reading and spelling (Svensson et al., 2001). Similar results were found in a UK study of 301 juvenile offenders. Male offenders had significantly lower verbal and Full-Scale IQs than female offenders, although both groups were below the average score for the general population (Chitsabesan et al., 2007). Male offenders were also more likely to have a significant verbal and performance IQ discrepancy (54% compared with 31%) as well as significantly lower reading and reading comprehension ages.

Girls have historically been found to have a later onset to their antisocial behaviour compared with boys. This has led to the suggestion by Moffitt et al. (2001) that one form of antisocial behaviour occurs in the context of deviant peer relationships and affects girls as well as boys, while the other (early onset, life course persistent) is neurodevelopmental in origin and predominantly affects boys. Boys whose behavioural difficulties start early have some of the worst prospects in terms of their mental health, physical health and employment prospects (Fergusson et al., 2005).

Studies exploring differences in mental disorders among juvenile offenders of different race and ethnicity have been sparse and not always easy to interpret. The Cook Study in the USA found that non-Hispanic white male offenders had the highest rates for many disorders and African American the lowest (Abram et al., 2003). The MAYSI-2 national study found a similar picture nationally, but found that ethnicity differences varied across sites and were generally small (Vincent et al., 2008).

There is generally an over-representation of some ethnic minority groups within the criminal justice system and concerns that these groups of young people have poorer access to services (Shelton, 2005). Young offenders from ethnic minorities may be less likely to report mental health symptoms (Domalanta et al., 2003; Gosden et al., 2003), possibly as a consequence of the stigma associated with mental illness. Subsequently, ethnicity differences in rates of mental disorders are likely to be influenced by a number of factors, including differences in presentation of underlying mental health problems, differences in self-reporting and difficulties in accessing services.

Conclusions

Over the last decade, international studies have highlighted that young people with disproportionately high and multiple needs have clustered in juvenile justice systems. These young people generally experience higher levels of diagnosable mental health problems than the general population as well as facing a wide range of other co-existing challenges such as elevated rates of learning disability, speech and communication problems, academic under-attainment, physical health difficulties and social exclusion.

Many of these needs go unrecognised in the system. Lack of identification hampers opportunities for early intervention and promotion of healthy development and resilience in young people and it can undermine due process in the criminal justice system. Policy makers in many countries have become increasingly aware of the need to work with local commissioners and services to address this over-representation of children with multiple needs in the criminal justice system. Historically, screening and assessment tools have been developed focusing on single problem areas. However, young people who offend often possess multiple problems which in aggregate undermine

their mental and physical health and their life chances as well as affecting numerous agencies' budgets.

Research has focused on developing and refining validated screening and assessment tools as well as providing pointers as to how identification, support and intervention might most effectively be improved.

There is a need to develop a single comprehensive and reliable screening tool in juvenile justice which addresses the overlapping risk factors for a range of poor outcomes. The aim of this tool would be twofold. First, to accurately identify flags for immediate risk to self or others, current mental and physical health needs, and risks relating to capacity which may undermine understanding of the offence itself or the criminal justice process. Second, it would provide a vehicle for picking up young people with risk factors which are known to jeopardise their future life chances and outcomes. This would include those with early starting behavioural difficulties and those under-attaining or disengaging from school.

Where flags for concern emerge, this should prompt a more specialist and detailed fast-track assessment. When concerns about capacity arise or where risk is high, screening staff will need swift backup from specialist professionals who can recognise and advise on the impact of these disorders. In some instances, young people may need to be adjourned before being charged for a more detailed assessment which may clash with drives to administer justice swiftly, but could possibly save money in the longer term through a reduction in breach of bail conditions.

In recognition of these difficulties, the Comprehensive Health Assessment Tool (CHAT) was developed for use with young offenders in custody across England and Wales (Offender Health Research Network, 2013; Chitsabesan et al., 2014). The CHAT is a semi-structured assessment developed to provide a standardised approach to health screening for all young offenders admitted to the secure estate. It consists of five parts: an initial reception screen, followed by a physical health, mental health and substance misuse screen for all offenders. Part 5 is a neurodevelopmental and TBI section which includes screening for speech and language difficulties, learning disability, ASD and TBI. The reception health screen (part 1) is conducted on admission to custody and aims to identify those at risk of serious physical, mental health or substance misuse needs. The subsequent sections (parts 2–5) are completed within a suggested timeframe and it is recommended that the complete tool should be embedded within local pathways with access to staff training and supervision, although, this can sometimes be a challenge to implement in practice. Assessing and managing unmet health needs can inform individual care plans, help to address offending behaviour and provide a valuable opportunity to re-engage young people with health and educational services to address unmet needs.

When and How Should Screening Occur?

US developmental work identifies several windows of opportunity for screening throughout the criminal justice pathway. There is growing academic evidence of the benefits of early intervention for mental health and emotional well-being, and therefore screening should occur at the earliest point of contact with the system. Such opportunities can vary in their timing dependent on the legislative framework governing different international justice systems. In the USA, the first opportunity for screening occurs when a young person offends and has contact with the probation service; probation officers in some states complete screening systematically at this stage (Grisso et al., 2005).

In England and Wales, there is a more complex informal system of cautioning before the young person first has contact with youth justice workers. At this earlier stage in the system, the young person often has limited access to professionals other than the police and there is pressure to complete screening speedily. Consequently, professionals need to find ways of working flexibly to cover police custody settings beyond office hours and to screen young people in less than ideal environments. Screening and assessment should inform police and prosecution decision making, diverting young people where appropriate to evidence-based interventions or to packages of care designed to decrease risk factors and promote resilience.

Other key opportunities for screening across the youth justice pathway include when the young person enters court, faces remand into custody, is sentenced to a community order or to custody or is being released from secure settings back to the community. Building on assessments rather than repeating screening and assessment is crucial as young people move in and out of custody. The recent development of healthcare quality standards for all young offenders within the secure estate in England and Wales is a joint intercollegiate initiative led by Royal College of Paediatrics and Child Health (2013). It demonstrates the increasing importance of providing a standardised and evidence-based approach to screening and intervention for a variety of health needs whilst young people remain within the secure estate.

Creating Child-Centred Screening and Assessment

Based on a prevention and early intervention paradigm, screening and assessment processes for children and young people who offend should be different from those designed for adults. It should be suited to their developmental stage and reflect the different evidence-base for effective interventions. Difficulties can present in less clear-cut and more confusing ways, often masked by other behavioural difficulties such as aggression or by the neurological changes which are associated with adolescent brain development. Furthermore, young people will also have different physical health risk factors in comparison to adults. Much of the literature on effective screening and assessment emphasises the importance of seeking additional information from key informants in the young person's life to build a clearer picture of strengths and needs. This may be a carer or teacher who has knowledge of their developmental history, who can observe their progress and pick up any changes during day-to-day contact.

When developing a system of screening, priority should also be placed on how the process is experienced by young people. Many young people in the criminal justice system can be nervous of formal statutory services, particularly mental health services or may be chaotic attendees of clinic-based appointments. Some validated tools can be too complex in their wording or too lengthy, risking alienating young people. Finally, for those with hidden disabilities, it is considered advisable to arrange more than one interview. Effective screening relies not just on having validated tools, but also on the skill of an engaging and therapeutically skilled workforce (Vikram et al., 2007), who can see the young person in the round and build a picture of strengths and risk factors. All of these issues have implications for workforce development as well as for service design if these processes are to be effectively implemented in the juvenile justice system.

Screening and Assessment: Shared Accountability for Children's Healthy Development

Finally, screening and assessment of young people's needs in the youth justice system should be based upon a firm foundation of multiagency and integrated whole-system accountability for building emotional resilience and promoting healthy development in children and young people. For children and young people with conduct problems and multiple needs, it should be backed up by effective pathways to a range of evidence-based interventions including engaging parenting programmes. In the youth justice system, particular attention is required to the very high needs of young women and those with early onset antisocial behaviour. Finally, greater integration should exist between services within the youth justice system and those outside, particularly joint work with schools, mental health services, paediatrics and the voluntary sector to support a culture where risk factors such as school exclusion are jointly prevented and where resilience building and early intervention is a shared priority.

This chapter has outlined the importance of developing validated screening tools which reflect the full range of well-documented needs experienced by children who offend. Screening should occur at the earliest point of contact with the youth justice system and should link to timely fuller assessment and engaging evidence-based intervention where this is needed. Both screening and assessment should be delivered by appropriately skilled practitioners who are able to involve young people and their families and empower young people to build on their strengths, improve their mental health and well-being, and enhance their life chances.

References

Abram, K. M., Teplin, L. A., McClelland, G. M. and Dulcan, M. K. (2003). Co-morbid psychiatric disorders in youth in juvenile detention. *Archives of General Psychiatry*, **60**, 1097–1108.

Bailey, S., Doreleijers, T. and Tarbuck, P. (2006). Recent developments in mental health screening and assessment in juvenile justice systems. *Child and Adolescent Psychiatric Clinics of North America*, **15**, 391–406.

Baron-Cohen, S., Wheelwright, S., Skinner, R. and Martin, C. E. (2001). The autistic spectrum quotient. *Journal of Autism and Developmental Disorders*, **36**(3), 343–350.

Berument, S., Rutter, M., Lord, C., Pickles, A. and Bailey, A. (1999). Autism screening questionnaire: diagnostic validity. *British Journal of Psychiatry*, **175**, 444–451.

Bishop, D. (2006). *Children's Communication Checklist-2nd Edition*. San Antonio: Pearson.

Bryan, K., Freer, J. and Furlong, C. (2007). Prevalence of speech and language difficulties in young offenders. *International Journal of Language and Communication Disorders*, **39**, 391–400.

Butler, T., Belcher, J. M., Chapman, U., Kenny, D., Allerton, M. and Fasher, M. (2008). The physical health status of young Australian offenders. *Australian and New Zealand Journal of Public Health*, **32**(1), 73–80.

Cashin, A. and Newman, C. (2009). Autism in the criminal justice detention system: a review of the literature. *Journal of Forensic Nursing*, **5**(2), 70–75.

Centre for Mental Health. (2010). *You Just Get On and Do It: Healthcare Provision in Youth Offending Teams*. London: Centre for Mental Health.

Chitsabesan, P., Kroll, L., Bailey, S., Kenning, C., Sneider, S., MacDonald, W. and Theodosiou, L. (2006). National study of mental health provision for young offenders. Part 1: Mental health needs of young offenders in custody and in the community. *British Journal of Psychiatry*, **188**, 534–540.

Chitsabesan, P., Bailey, S., Williams, R., Kroll, L., Kenning, C. and Talbot, L. (2007). Learning disabilities and educational needs of juvenile offenders. *Journal of Children's Services*, **2**(4), 4–14.

Chitsabesan, P., Lennox, C., Theodosiou, L., Law, H., Bailey, S. and Shaw, J. (2014). The development of the comprehensive health assessment tool for young offenders within the secure estate. *Journal of Forensic Psychiatry and Psychology*, **25**(1), 1–25.

Colins, O., Vermeiren, R., Vreugdenhil, C., Van den Brink, W., Doreleijers, T. and Broekaert, E. (2010). Psychiatric disorders in detained male adolescents in custody: a systematic literature review. *Canadian Journal of Psychiatry*, **55**(4), 255–263.

Domalanta, D. D., Rissler, W. L., Roberts, R. E. and Risser, J. M. (2003). Prevalence of depression and other psychiatric disorders among incarcerated youths. *Journal of the American Academy of Child and Adolescent Psychiatry*, **42**, 477–484.

Doreleijers, T. A. H. and Spannder, M. (2002). The development and implementation of the BARO; a new device to detect psychopathology in minors with first police contacts. In Corrado, R. and Roesch, R. Editors. *Multi-problem Violent Youths. A Foundation for Comparative Research Needs, Interventions and Outcomes*. Washington, DC: IOC Press.

Fazel, S., Doll, H. and Langstrom, N. (2008). Mental disorders among adolescents in juvenile detention and correctional facilities: a systematic review and metaregression analysis of 25 surveys. *Journal of the American Academy of Child and Adolescent Psychiatry*, **47**, 1010–1019.

Fergusson, D., Horwood, L. J. and Ridder, E. M. (2005). Show me the child at seven: the consequences of conduct problems in childhood for psychosocial functioning in adulthood. *Journal of Child Psychology and Psychiatry* **46**, 837–849.

Ford, G., Andrews, R., Booth, A., Dibdin, J., Hardingham, S. and Kelly, T. P. (2008). Screening for learning disability in an adolescent forensic population. *Journal of Forensic Psychiatry and Psychology*, **19**(3), 371–381.

Gilliam, J. (2014). *Gilliam Autism Rating Scale – Third Edition.* Austin, TX: PRO-ED.

Golzari, M., Hunt, S. J. and Anushiravani, A. (2006). The health status of youth in juvenile detention facilities. *Journal of Adolescent Health*, **38**, 776–782.

Gosden, N., Kramp, P., Gabrielsen, G. and Sestoft, D. (2003). Prevalence of mental disorders among 15–17 year old male adolescent remand prisoners in Denmark. *Acta Psychiatric Scandinavia*, **107**, 102–110.

Grisso, T., Vincent, G. and Seagrave, D. Editors. (2005). *Mental Health Screening and Assessment in Juvenile Justice.* New York: Guilford Press.

Grisso, T. and Barnum, R. (2006) *Massachusetts Youth Screening Instrument- Version 2: User Manual and Technical Report.* Sarasota, FL: Professional Resource Press.

Harrington, R. and Bailey, S. (2005). *Mental Health Needs and Effectiveness of Provision for Young People in the Youth Justice System.* London: Youth Justice Board.

Harrington, R. C., Kerfoot, M. and Verduyn, C. (1999). Developing needs-led child and adolescent mental health services: issues and prospects. *European Journal of Child and Adolescent Psychiatry*, **8**, 1–10.

Harrington, R. C., Kroll, L., Rothwell, J., McCarthy, K., Bradley, D. and Bailey, S. (2005). Psychosocial needs of boys in secure care for serious or persistent offending. *Journal of Child Psychology and Psychiatry*, **45**, 1–8.

Hayes, S. C. (2000). *Hayes Ability Screening Index (HASI) Manual.* Sydney: University of Sydney, Behavioural Sciences in Medicine.

Howlin, P. (1997). *Autism: Preparing for Adulthood.* Oxon: Routledge.

Hughes, N., Williams, P., Chitsabesan, P., Davies, R. and Mounce, L. (2012). *Nobody Made the Connection; The Prevalence of Neurodisability in Young People Who Offend.* London: Office for the Children's Commissioner.

Isen, J. (2010). A meta-analytic assessment of Wechsler's P&>V sign in antisocial populations. *Clinical Psychology Review*, **30**, 428–435.

Kenny, D., Nelson, P., Butler, T., Lennings, C., Allerton, M. and Champion, U. (2006). *NSW Young People on Community Orders Health Survey 2003–2006: Key Findings Report.* Sydney: The University of Sydney.

Knapp, M., McDaid, D. and Parsonage, M. (2011). *Mental Health Promotion and Prevention: The Economic Case.* London: Department of Health. Available from: www.pssru .ac.uk/index.php. Accessed 22 February 2011.

Kroll, L., Woodham, A., Rothwell, J., Bailey, S., Tobias, C., Harrington, R. and Marshall, M. (1999). Reliability of the Salford needs assessment schedule for adolescents. *Psychological Medicine*, **29**, 891–902.

Kroll, L., Rothwell, J., Bradley, D., Shah, P., Bailey, S. and Harrington, R. C. (2002). Mental health needs of boys in secure care for serious or persistent offending: a prospective longitudinal study, *Lancet*, **359**, 1975–1979.

Loeber, R. and Farrington, D. P. (2000). Young people who commit crime: epidemiology, developmental origins, risk factors, early interventions, and policy implications. *Development and Psychopathology*, **12**, 737–762.

McCabe, K. M., Lansing, A. E., Garland, A. N. N. and Hough, R. (2002). Gender differences in psychopathology, functional impairment, familial risk factors among adjudicated delinquents. *Journal of the American Academy of Child and Adolescent Psychiatry*, **41**, 860–867.

McKenzie, K., Paxton, D., Murray, G. C., Milanesi, P. and Murray, A. L. (2012). The evaluation of a screening tool for children with an intellectual disability: the Child and Adolescent Intellectual Disability Screening Questionnaire. *Research in Developmental Disabilities*, **33**, 1068–1075.

Moffitt, T. (1993). Adolescent limited and life course persistent antisocial behaviour: a developmental taxonomy. *Psychological Review*, **1000**, 674–701.

Moffitt, T., Caspi, A., Rutter, M. and Silva, P. A. (2001). *Sex Differences in Antisocial Behaviour: Conduct Disorder and Delinquency and Violence in the Dunedin Longitudinal Study.* Cambridge: Cambridge University Press.

Morgan, A. and Ziglio, E. (2007). Revitalising the evidence base for public health: an assets model. *Promotion and Education* **14**(2 Suppl.), 17–22.

Offender Health Research Network. (2013). *The Comprehensive Health Assessment Tool (CHAT): Young People in the Secure Estate – Version 3.* Manchester: University of Manchester.

Pajer, K. A., Kelleher, K., Gupta, R. A., Rolls, J. and Gardner, W. (2007). Psychiatric and medical healthcare policies in juvenile detention facilities. *Journal of the American Academy of Child and Adolescent Psychiatry*, **46**(12), 1660–1667.

Putnins, A. L. (2005). Correlates and predictors of self-reported suicide attempts among incarcerated youths. *International Journal of Offenders Therapy and Comparative Criminology*, **49**(2), 143–157.

Roberts, R. E., Atkinson, C. C. and Rosenblatt, A. (1998). Prevalence of psychopathology among children and adolescents. *American Journal of Psychiatry*, **155**, 715–725.

Roid, G. H. (2003). *Stanford-Binet Intelligence Scales*, Fifth Edition. Itasca, IL: Riverside.

Royal College of Paediatrics and Child Health. (2013). *Healthcare Standards for Children and Young People in Secure Settings*. London: Royal College of Paediatrics and Child Health.

Ruchkin, V., Schwab-Stone, M., Koposov, R. A., Vermeiren, R. and King, R. A. (2003). Suicidal ideations and attempts in juvenile delinquents. *Journal of Child Psychology Psychiatry*, 44, 1058–1066.

Ruchkin, V., Schwab-Stone, M., Koposov, R. A., Vermeiren, R. and Steiner, H. (2002). Violence exposure, post-traumatic stress and personality in juvenile delinquents. *Journal of the American Academy of Child and Adolescent Psychiatry*, 41, 322–329.

Scott, S. (2008). An update on interventions for conduct disorder. *Advances in Psychiatric Treatment*, 14, 61–70.

Shelton, D. (2005). Patterns of treatment and service costs for young offenders with mental disorders. *Journal of Child and Adolescent Psychiatric Nursing*, 18, 103–112.

Stambrook, M., Moore, A. D., Peters, L. C., Deviaene, C. and Hawryluk, G. A. (1990). Effects of mild, moderate and severe closed head injury on long-term vocational status. *Brain Injury*, 4(2), 183–190.

Stevenson, M. (2006). *Young People and Offending: Education, Youth Justice and Social Care Inclusion*. London: Williams.

Svensson, I., Lundberg, I. and Jacobson, C. (2001). The prevalence of reading and spelling difficulties among inmates of institutions for compulsory care of juvenile delinquents. *Dyslexia*, 7, 62–76.

Teplin, L. A., Abram, K. M., McCelland, G. M., Dulcan, M. K. and Mericle, A. A. (2002). Psychiatric disorders in youth in detention. *Archives of General Psychiatry*, 59, 1133–1143.

The National Autistic Society. (2008). *Autism: A Guide for Criminal Justice Professionals*. London: NAS752.

Vikram, P., Flisher, A. J., Hetrick, S. and McGorry, P. (2007). Mental health of young people: a global public-health challenge. *Lancet*, 369, 1302–1313.

Vincent, G. M., Grisso, T., Terry, A. and Banks, S. (2008). Sex and race differences in mental health symptoms in juvenile justice: the MAYSI-2 National Meta-analysis. *Journal of the American Academy of Child and Adolescent Psychiatry*, 47, 282–290.

Vreugdenhil, C., Doreleijers, T., Vermeiren, R., Wouters, L. F. and Van Den Brink, W. (2004). Psychiatric disorders in a representative sample of incarcerated boys in the Netherlands. *Journal of the American Academy of Child and Adolescent Psychiatry*, 43, 97–104.

Ware, J. E., Kosinski, M. and Keller, S. D. (1996). A 12-item short-form health survey. *Med Care*, 34(3), 220–223.

Wasserman, G. A., McReynolds, L. S., Lucas, C. P., Fisher, P. and Santos, L. (2000). The Voice DISC-IV with incarcerated male youths: prevalence of disorder. *Journal of the American Academy of Child and Adolescent Psychiatry*, 41(3), 314–321.

Wechsler, D. (1991). *Wechsler Intelligence Scale for Children*. London: Psychological Corporation.

Wechsler, D. (1999). *Wechsler Abbreviated Scale for Intelligence*. London: Psychological Corporation.

Wiig, E. H. and Secord, W. (1989). *Test of Language Competence – Expanded Edition*. San Antonio, TX: Psychological Corporation.

Williams, H. W., Giray, C., Mewse, A. J., Tonks, J. and Burgess, C. N. W. (2010). Self-reported traumatic brain injury in male young offenders: a risk factor for re-offending, poor mental health and violence? *Neuropsychological Rehabilitation*, 20(6), 801–812.

Woodcock, R. W., McGrew, K. S. and Mather, N. (2001). *Woodcock-Johnson-III*. Itasca, IL: Riverside.

Risk Assessment and Management Approaches with Adolescent Offenders

James Millington and Charlotte Lennox

The formulation of the problem is often more essential than its solution, which may be merely a matter of mathematical or experimental skill.
(Albert Einstein)

Introduction

High-risk behaviours, including violence, offending, suicide and self-harm, can significantly impact the lives of children and young people (CYP) and those around them. The assessment and management of risk has become an essential part of treatment planning for CYP displaying high-risk behaviours, and in the past decade, there have been considerable advances in the development of tools to help identify those CYP most at risk.

Risk assessment with CYP is a unique field and those embarking upon it need to reflect upon their own competencies, knowledge and experiences before commencing. Those familiar with adults may underestimate the significance of developmental factors. They may also not be familiar with the different language, tools, processes, systems and laws that apply to CYP within social, educational, mental health and criminal justice services.

Conversely, CYP professionals may lack experience of forensic practice and be reluctant to embark upon risk assessment for fear of condemning, labelling and stigmatising CYP. Nor may they be familiar with risk assessment tools and procedures as they are not routinely part of their role, historically reserved for CYP in secure settings or specialist forensic services.

This chapter sets out first to describe the approach to risk assessment and management, briefly summarise the range of risk assessment tools for high-risk behaviours in CYP and signpost the reader to the relevant research evidence. The main focus of the chapter will be to outline the core processes using a five-step model for assessing and managing risk with CYP.

Risk Assessment Tools with Children and Young People

There are a number of different approaches to risk assessments, and these different approaches are well documented in detail elsewhere (Otto and Douglas, 2010). In brief, there are two main approaches – non-discretionary versus discretionary – referring to how information is weighted and a final decision reached. Within these two main approaches there are a number of different variants (e.g. discretionary approaches include unaided clinical judgement, structured professional judgement and anamnestic risk assessment). The most commonly discussed are actuarial (non-discretionary) and structured professional judgement (SPJ) (discretionary). Actuarial risk assessments use statistical techniques to generate risk predictions. These assessments focus on a relatively small number of risk factors that are known, or are thought, to predict risk in groups as opposed to individuals. Actuarial tools do not predict individual risk but only make comparisons between individuals and groups of people with known re-offending. The actuarial approach is particularly limited when applied to CYP.

SPJ approaches represent a composite of empirical knowledge and clinical/professional expertise. The main difference between the two approaches is the changed focus on risk formulation and management. For actuarial assessments, the decision is made according to a fixed algorithm. For SPJ approaches, the professionals involved can make risk decisions having followed a transparent process based on the structured assessment of all risk and protective factors to inform the formulation. This enables flexibility to account for case-specific influences.

There are a number of different risk assessment tools in contemporary use with CYP.

Youth Level of Service/Case Management Inventory (YLS/CMI)

The Youth Level of Service/Case Management Inventory (YLS/CMI) (Hoge and Andrews, 2002) is a generic risk assessment tool assessing risk of future general offending. It contains 42 dichotomous items addressing eight domains: offence history, family circumstances/parenting, education/employment, peer relations, substance abuse, leisure/recreation, personality/behaviour and attitudes/orientation. The tool was initially developed as an actuarial tool and is more widely used in this way, but it can also function as an SPJ tool. To date the research evidence supporting the predictive accuracy of the YLS/CMI is mixed (Schwalbe, 2007; Olver et al., 2009; Rennie and Dolan, 2010; Hilterman et al., 2014).

Early Assessment Risk List for Boys (EARL-20B)

The Early Assessment Risk List for Boys (EARL-20B) (Augimeri et al., 2001) is designed specifically to assess the risk for violence among boys under the age of 13 years. It is composed of 20 items, each with general coding guidelines. There are six family items, which evaluate household characteristics, caregiver continuity, parenting style and the presence or absence of supports, stressors and antisocial values and conflict. There are 12 child items, which evaluate developmental problems, maltreatment and trauma, hyperactivity and attention deficits, likeability, peer socialisation, academic performance, neighbourhood characteristics, contact with authority, antisocial attitudes and behaviours, coping ability and early onset behavioural difficulties. The EARL-20B also includes two responsivity items, which evaluate child and family willingness to participate in treatment. Currently there is very little published research on the EARL-20B (Enebrink et al., 2006a, 2006b).

This is also a version of the EARL for girls (EARL-21 G) (Levene et al., 2001). The basic framework of the girls' version is similar, but contains 21 items, some of which are labelled and defined differently. This takes into account the evidence that girls express antisocial behaviour differently from boys. Research evidence using the EARL-G is even more scant than for the EARL-B.

The Structured Assessment of Violence Risk in Youth (SAVRY)

The Structured Assessment of Violence Risk in Youth (SAVRY) (Borum et al., 2003) assesses 24 risk factors (ten historical risk factors, six social/contextual risk factors, eight individual/clinical risk factors) and six protective factors. Each of the 24 risk factors is coded as low, moderate or high, and each of the six protective factors as present/absent. There is now an ever-increasing evidence base to support the predictive accuracy and clinical applicability of the SAVRY in a range of settings, not just forensic and criminal justice settings (Dolan and Rennie, 2008; Gammelgård et al., 2008, 2015; Welsh et al., 2008; Penney et al., 2010; McGowan et al., 2011; Singh et al., 2011).

The Structured Assessment of Protective Factors for Violence Risk – Youth Version (SAPROF-YV)

The Structured Assessment of Protective Factors for Violence Risk – Youth Version (SAPROF-YV) (de Vries Robbé et al., 2015c) is a tool specifically designed for the structured assessment of protective factors for violence risk. The tool is intended to be used alongside commonly used (primarily) risk-focused tools, such as the SAVRY. The SAPROF-YV aims to contribute to an increasingly accurate and balanced assessment of juvenile violence risk. The SAPROF-YV includes 16 protective factors divided into four groups, all are dynamic in nature. These are resilience factors, which include social competence, coping, self-control, perseverance and being future-orientated; motivational factors, which include motivation for treatment, compliance agreements, medication, school/work and leisure activities; relational factors which include relationships with parents/caretakers, peers and other supportive relationships; and finally external factors which include home or treatment environment, professional support and court orders. They are intended to provide positive guidelines for treatment planning, risk management and clinical evaluation. While to date there is no youth data, research using the adult tool is showing promising predictive validity (Abidin et al. 2013; de Vries Robbé et al., 2015a, 2015b).

Short-Term Assessment of Risk and Treatability: Adolescent Version (START: AV)

The Short-Term Assessment of Risk and Treatability: Adolescent Version (START: AV) (Viljoen et al., 2014) is an SPJ approach designed to assess short-term risks for multiple adverse outcomes, including risk of violence towards others, suicide, self-harm, victimisation, substance abuse, unauthorised leave, self-neglect and general offending. The START: AV includes 23 dynamic and treatment-relevant items that pertain to the youth and his/her social context (e.g., Social Skills, Emotional State, Substance Use, Support from Caregivers and Other Adults, Support from Peers, Parenting and Home Environment). Each item is rated based on the past three months. Very limited research has so far been undertaken using the START: AV and to date only from the authors. Viljoen et al. (2012) found that START: AV Risk estimates and Vulnerability total scores predicted multiple adverse outcomes, including violence towards others, offending, victimisation, suicidal ideation and substance abuse. In addition, Strength total scores inversely predicted violence, offending and street drug use.

Principles of Practice in Risk Assessment and Management

SPJ tools help the assessor to have a systematic and evidence-based transparent process; however, a great deal of clinical expertise is required to convert this process into a coherent and organised document of practical utility.

A five-step approach to this can assist the risk assessor to gather, process and communicate risk information:

- Step 1: Case Information;
- Step 2: Presence and Relevance of Risk Factors;
- Step 3: Presence and Relevance of Protective Factors;
- Step 4: Risk Formulation;
- Step 5: Management Plan.

The assessor will move through the steps in sequence, but they should consider that this is an iterative process and may require to move back and forth through the steps. For example, having gathered some evidence in Step 1 and considered this against the factors in the SPJ being used (Steps 2 and 3), gaps in information may be identified, and therefore the assessor may go back to Step 1 and start the process over.

An illustration of the five-step process is shown using the SAVRY in the case of Mike (see Box 4.1). The SAVRY is one of the most widely used SPJ tools with CYP given its applicability to both genders and across a range of settings.

Step 1: Case Information

Interviews

Interviews may be conducted with a range of people, for example young person, family members, victim(s). Interviewing the young person can help to engage her/him in her/his risk management; however, this may be experienced as traumatic, stigmatising, critical, shameful, and therefore needs to be planned thoroughly.

Questions asked by the assessor can be based around an assessment tool or be used to fill gaps and clarify discrepancies. There may be a range of independent accounts gathered at different times, so early evidence (e.g. victim(s) accounts, arresting officer account) may differ from later evidence (solicitor's statement of facts, expert witness summary, testimony in court). In the case of interviewing a young person after a lengthy stay in a secure setting, interviews may also allow for assessment of insight into her/his future risk, and/or level of motivation to change.

In recording the interview it is important that self-report and third-party information be clearly marked as such. Although interview questions should be carefully balanced with information from other sources, carelessness in questioning may damage relationships. The SAVRY manual contains further guidance about interviewing.

Collateral Information

Collateral information is crucial to obtaining a clear account and begins with gathering information from all services as soon as possible. These may include: police, prison, mental health services, Youth Offending Teams, school and education services, Social Services and the voluntary sector.

Original documents are often better (e.g. school records and reports, details of incidents and exclusions, Police National Computer records, Pre-Sentence Reports) than summary reports. Be mindful that summary accounts may drift in their recording

BOX 4.1 Background History

Mike's Story

Mike is 16 years old and currently serving a 12-month Detention and Training Order (DTO) for making threats with a weapon and assault. He was recently released under licence but was breached due to violent behaviour and excessive drinking. Prior to this his first conviction at age 13 was for vehicle theft and assaulting a police officer, for which he received a 12-month Supervision Order which he completed. Reports indicate he had started to recognise his anger issues by identifying triggers and had adopted some effective strategies, such as relaxation and distraction techniques.

Mike's early home environment was settled. Mike's dad was described as authoritarian and Mike's mum as a submissive character who struggled to set boundaries. When Mike was aged six, his dad lost his job and began drinking heavily and was physically violent towards Mike's mum. Mike's mum was hospitalised on a number of occasions due to the domestic violence, and Mike and his older brother often stayed with their maternal aunt during these times. His dad left the family home when Mike was aged eight and he has not had contact with him since. The family home was sold, but debts remained, meaning the family were housed by the local authority. Their new house was in a high-crime area known for drug and gang problems.

Mike became very distressed in the period leading up to his father leaving the family home. A school report indicated that he was disruptive in class and ran out on several occasions following being prompted for not paying attention. GP records show a referral to the school Attention Deficit Hyperactivity Disorder (ADHD) link nurse; ADHD was ruled out, although reference was made to impulsive behaviour and anger problems. Between the ages of seven and eight Mike was taken to Accident and Emergency (A&E) on six occasions due to injuries he had received at home. Reports also suggest he ran away from his aunt's home on two occasions and stayed out overnight. Police were called to help locate him. Mike struggled with the strict rules and boundaries set by his aunt.

Mike is of average intelligence. He is a skilful and popular member of the school football team and has a good relationship with his coach, who believes Mike has considerable potential as a footballer. During secondary school his grades have progressively worsened and he skipped some classes. Mike reports being involved in fights and causing facial injuries to another boy. He said the fights often started because other boys were picking on him or his friends. He has begun associating with a delinquent peer group and has been temporarily excluded on three occasions, for smashing windows, disruptive behaviour and fighting.

Mike's mum in now in a long-term relationship with another partner. He recently served a two-year prison sentence for assault. Mike's older brother is doing well; he works and is in a stable relationship; he has recently moved out to live with his girlfriend. Mike has a very good relationship with his brother but is very upset that he has moved out.

Mike pleaded guilty to making threats with a weapon and assault on his mum's partner by punching and kicking. Mike and his mum's partner had been arguing after Mike returned home late and had been drinking excessively. In sentencing the Judge commented on his lack of remorse for his actions, and disrespectful behaviour in Court. While in custody Mike continued to be involved in violent incidents and extra days were added to his sentence. He was seen by the Mental Health In-reach Team following concerns about violence, anger, avoidance, low mood and incidents of Deliberate Self-Harm (DSH) in the form of cutting. He was subject to an open Assessment and Care in Custody Teamwork (ACCT) document for a week. When seen by the in-reach team he was described as hyper-vigilant with high levels of anger. He denied any ongoing mental health issues. He denied low mood and stated he preferred to stay in his cell to keep safe.

Mike attacked a peer in the showers with an improvised bladed weapon causing minor cuts. At interview with the in-reach nurse he stated he deserved it as he had been bullying on the wing. He assaulted a prison officer during a restraint by kicking him in the head causing bruising. He barricaded himself in a room with another peer and beat him up using punches and kicks causing severe bruising to the face and body, plus cuts to face requiring treatment. The young person refused to press charges. Mike again cited bullying as the reason for the assault.

Mike is about to be released again, and a review of his risk of violence to others is required in order to manage any identified risks.

and also be sanitised. Going back to original accounts, while time-consuming, may reveal inaccuracies that have since been added to the account of the offence. The legal process, for example plea bargaining, may also inadvertently contribute to this.

Recording Information

The collection of detailed information is crucial, in order to more effectively manage and re-assess any future risk. Modern electronic record systems may facilitate more transparent governance regarding incidents – but the content needs to be of sufficient quality for the risk assessor to use. Providing a comprehensive package of information can also help any future service tasked with assessing the young person's needs and risks.

Verbal expressions of concern, uncorroborated allegations and hearsay may be deemed unreliable or prejudicial. Incidents not thoroughly investigated are also of limited value. Therefore a systematic and comprehensive collection of independent accounts of offences, incidents, investigations and adjudications will assist those tasked with future assessments.

Steps 2 and 3: Presence and Relevance of Risk and Protective Factors

Risk assessments can vary in the type of risk they assess, for example the YLS/CMI assesses general offending, while the SAVRY assesses interpersonal violence. It is important that the assessor is clear about the type of risk being assessed and how each item within the assessment is related to the outcome in question. For example, targeted violence to an identifiable other will require further consideration as the factors within the SAVRY may or may not be as relevant. Targeted violence against a parent or a sexual partner may require other risk assessment processes, although the SAVRY and the five-step process are an important starting point.

Also, depending on the item, consideration needs to be given to the presence and relevance of the item as well as its severity and frequency. Determining relevance and relationship to a risk outcome rather than mere presence is a critical step that can make the evaluation meaningful to the individual. For example, although substance misuse may be present for a young person, the evidence recorded and the rating should determine the link that substance misuse has to violence.

Each item may require further assessment through seeking more information, or administration of psychometrics, neuropsychological assessment or interview such as the Psychopathy Checklist: Youth Version (Forth et al., 2003). It is important to record the evidence for each factor. Merely making a rating (low, moderate or high for risk factors and either absent or present for protective factors) does not fully inform the subsequent risk formulation, the risk management plans or communicate risk usefully to others. A summary risk judgement of 'high' may mean different things to different assessors and services. For example, a rating of 'high' on item 1 of the SAVRY requires just three acts of violence. These acts of violence can range from a threat made with a weapon to homicide, and therefore, the assessor must include ALL relevant detail. The SAVRY manual is available with a set of rating forms; however, there is not sufficient space on these to record the evidence. Assessors should develop their own reports so that the evidence can be transparently detailed for each factor (see Tables 4.1 and 4.2 as examples of the differences).

As the assessor will be following a systematic process, there may be additional risk and protective factors to consider. There are a number of risk factors not included in the SAVRY as there is insufficient empirical evidence at a population level to support their inclusion. However, at an individual level these factors may be relevant to a young person's risk of violence, for example mental illness, animal cruelty and fire setting. Other additional protective factors might include faith, insight, motivation and parental responsivity.

It is good practice to use both the SAVRY and the HCR-20 V3 (Douglas et al., 2013) for 18- to 21-year-olds and perhaps up to the age of 25 years with people with an intellectual disability given the developmental aspects of the factors within the SAVRY.

Step 4: Risk Formulation

The aim of a risk formulation is to provide a better understanding of the origins of violence and how it has developed, is maintained and changes. SPJ tools do not automatically generate formulations and risk management plans; therefore, the onus is on the skilled professional with expertise in the area to develop practical plans. A formulation has benefits over using a numerical or categorical summary in that it:

- Is explanatory;
- Is evidence-based;

Table 4.1 Summary of Ratings in Relation to the Coding and Critical Items to Mike of Each SAVRY Risk and Protective Factor

Historical Risk Factors	Coding	Critical Item
History of violence	High	Yes
History of non-violent offending	Moderate	
Early initiation of violence	Moderate	
Past supervision/intervention failures	High	Yes
History of self-harm and suicide attempts	Moderate	
Exposure to violence in the home	High	Yes
Childhood history of maltreatment	High	Yes
Parental/caregiver criminality	High	
Early caregiver disruption	Moderate	
Poor school achievement	Moderate	
Social/Contextual Risk Factors	**Coding**	**Critical Item**
Peer delinquency	High	Yes
Peer rejection	Moderate	
Stress and poor coping	High	Yes
Poor parental Management	Moderate	
Lack of personal and social support	Moderate	
Community disorganisation	Moderate	
Individual/Clinical Risk Factors	**Coding**	**Critical Item**
Negative attitude	High	Yes
Risk taking/impulsivity	High	Yes
Substance use difficulties	High	Yes
Anger management	High	Yes
Lack of empathy/remorse	Moderate	
Attention deficit	Low	
Poor compliance	High	
Low interest/commitment to school	Moderate	
Protective Factors	**Coding**	**Critical Item**
Prosocial involvement	Absent	
Strong social support	Absent	Yes
Strong attachments and bonds	Absent	Yes
Positive attitude towards intervention and authority	Absent	
Strong commitment to school	Absent	
Resilient personality factors	Absent	

After Borum et al. (2003).

- Is personalised and idiosyncratic;
- Enables the application of theory to practice;
- Identifies targets for intervention;
- Aids communication; and
- Is collaborative and can involve the person being assessed.

There are a number of frameworks which can be used to help explain and communicate risk. One

Table 4.2 An Example of a SAVRY Template for Mike Which Includes Evidence for Each Coding

Factors	Coding	Critical Item	Evidence
History of violence	High	Yes	Convictions: Assault on police officer (Age 13); threats with a weapon and assault (punching and kicking). School: Fights (multiple) – caused facial injury to boy – seek more information on age and frequency/severity Custody: x 3 – peer with improvised blade causing minor cuts; assault of prison officer (in restraint)- kicked in head causing bruised; peer (barricaded himself in a room and beat –punches and kicks causing severe bruising
Poor parental management	Moderate		Mum struggles to set boundaries – unclear how consistent boundaries are? Dad described as authoritarian – unclear how strict? Aunt tried to set strict rules. Need more information – interview mum, Mike and Aunt
Negative attitude	High	Yes	Struggles to generate non-aggressive solutions. Tends to react to situations with violence e.g. violence when challenged by authority – police officer (assault) – Not recent; reaction to bullying in custody. Need more information regarding the context of events to help identify trigger-plan to interview Mike Attitudes: Blames others for past violence, and also legitimises violence (he deserved it as had been bullying). Judge's comments about disrespectful behaviour at court.
Strong social support	Absent	Yes	Not currently but possible capacity to build supportive relationships – evidenced by sports coach. Prosocial brother with whom he has a 'good' relationship but need more info – no evidence that this has been a buffer/mitigated risk – should be considered in treatment planning.

After Borum et al. (2003).

approach is called the '5Ps' model: problem (risk of what?), predisposing (vulnerability) factors, precipitating factors (triggers to harm), perpetuating (maintenance) factors and protective factors. This was originally described as a '4Ps' model by Weerasekera (1996), and later a fifth P for problem was added.

Another model is the '3Ds' model, which represents drivers, destabilisers and disinhibitors (Hart and Logan, 2011; Johnstone, 2013). There are similarities between the 5Ps model and the 3Ds model, but the advantage of the 3Ds is the focus on drivers, for example what does a young person expect to achieve from being violent? (Logan, 2013). Either or both of

these models can be used by the assessor in structuring risk information. In the case formulation for Mike (see Box 4.2) the authors have used both.

A risk formulation can be said to have various aspects, but to develop a report of quality and utility more recently attempts have been made to establish a formulation quality checklist. Sturmey and McMurran (2011) initiated efforts to define, describe and evaluate features of formulation in forensic work. Hart et al. (2011) subsequently developed ten standards for case formulations: Narrative; External coherence, Factual foundation; Internal coherence; Explanatory breadth; Diachronicity; Simplicity; Generativity; Action-oriented; and Acceptability and quality.

BOX 4.2 Mike's Risk Formulation

Mike is at particular risk of being physically violent again in the future in situations in which he feels threatened or perceives others to be threatened. He presents a risk to peers and adult males, especially those in authority roles. Why?

There appear to be a number of interrelated factors that help explain why Mike might be physically violent. In terms of predisposing factors his early history suggests that he was exposed to violence and witnessed his dad be violent in the home towards his mum with his mum then being hospitalised on a number of occasions. Mike also attended A&E on multiple occasions between the ages of six and eight due to injuries he sustained at home. While the circumstances of Mike's injuries are not known, and more information is being sought, it is clear that his experiences are likely to have been traumatic, and at the very least disruptive given he needed to live with his aunt when his mother was hospitalised. As a consequence it is likely, and understandable, that Mike would view the world as an unsafe place and that he needs to be hyper-vigilant to threat, and particularly of males, in order to feel safe and/or to reduce anxiety. Given violence in the home appears to have been the norm, with his dad seemingly having difficulties with alcohol and managing anger, it is likely that Mike has been unable to learn how to regulate his own emotions and develop effective coping strategies, which appear also to contribute to his externalising violent expressions of anger. Whilst the focus of this formulation is Mike's violence risk, his underlying difficulties managing stress and regulating difficult emotions show themselves in poor coping, evidenced by his DSH (cutting) while in custody. These vulnerabilities are therefore considered to be critical factors for both violence and self-harm. His mum's difficulties setting boundaries and Mike's underlying behaviour difficulties may also help explain his apparent difficulties with authority and limited range of coping strategies.

For Mike there appears to be a number of clear precipitating factors or triggers for violence. In situations where he perceives peers as bullies he is at increased risk of violence as perceiving bullying triggers feelings of anger, with him then reacting impulsively, with violence appearing to be motivated by a need for justice; negative attitudes, that is violence was 'deserved', serving to help maintain the violence. Additionally, in situations where he perceives hostile intent, this is likely to lead to violence in order to show superiority or status, with violence here serving as a coping strategy, that is, making him feel less likely that he will be victimised. Within the custody setting these risks are exacerbated by an environment that he experiences as highly stressful, with deterioration in his mental state being an associated compounding factor. Mike's level of violence appears to be escalating in the custody setting; the recent barricading and hostage-taking behaviour represents a serious risk to himself and others and organisations tasked with caring for him. These issues underline the need for high levels of supervision, and that Mike might benefit from relocation to the vulnerable persons unit. Here he would be able to access supportive interventions that might enable him to reflect on his concerns in order to develop safe coping strategies.

Boundary setting is also a specific trigger for violence and threats of violence. In the community Mike's alcohol intoxication was a specific disinhibiting factor, which increased the severity of his violence towards his step-father when he set boundaries.

Mike would appear to find it difficult to generate alternative solutions and is perhaps currently not motivated to do so either, believing violence to be an effective strategy. However, it is notable that Mike successfully completed a 12-month Supervision Order previously where he was able to recognise anger issues and had adopted some effective strategies.

Relationships are important to Mike. He has positive support from his mum and older brother, but it is unclear how available and consistent this can be. In addition he has in the past had positive relationships with a football coach and some success as a team player; however, it is uncertain if these potential protective links can be (re) developed.

In risk assessment and management with CYP, as in both mental health and forensic practice, the downward projection of adult concepts should be done with caution. One particular aspect that is perhaps more challenging in working with CYP is the concept of diachronicity or how events are understood over time. As CYP are still developing (biologically, physically and psychologically), and are yet to complete a range of stages of development and experiences, their patterns of thinking and behaviour are more difficult to predict and determine. Emerging patterns of offending, if indeed a pattern can be identified, may yet be formative and even experimental. Further revisions of risk formulation standards are anticipated which will lead to further research on the utility of formulaic practice.

Adding scenarios to a formulation can assist the assessor to communicate how specific situations may arise in the future and what might be the likely triggers to this. As services will seek to anticipate situations and prevent a negative outcome, consideration of various scenarios helps to manage possible events and the consideration of risk formulation(s) in different contexts.

The assessor may consider a 'Repeat scenario' one in which a similar violent incident occurs as if the young person will do it again. In addition 'Escalation scenarios' where the young person may do something more serious, perhaps use the weapon they were carrying, may assist. A 'Twist Scenario' where something similar, but different, occurs may also lead to a stronger management plan. The use of a 'Best Case' scenario may often be helpful for intervention work, as a positive choice or option can be explored (See Box 4.2 for an example formulation for Mike).

Step 5: Management Plan

The key components of a risk management plan are treatment interventions, supervision, monitoring and victim safety plans. The details of how a young person should be *monitored* (both in terms of surveillance and when a repeated assessment) should be included. The plan should include what the *intervention* (or treatment) aspects are, for example, to improve deficits in the individual's psychosocial adjustment and address any underlying mental health condition. Details of how the young person should be *supervised* should be incorporated, including any details of restrictions that make it (more) difficult for the individual to engage in further violence. Consideration should also be given to *victim safety planning* to minimise the impact of any future violence on the victims' psychological and physical well-being.

Depending on the nature of the past violence and the legal framework in place around the young person, the nature of the obligations may vary. For example, a mental health clinician may have a formal duty to consider the impact of their decision making should the young person be formally detained in hospital. Similarly any bail or licence conditions may specify places where the young person may be or limit who they may contact. Should the young person be managed in a residential setting (this includes any secure or hospital environment), consideration should be given to any impact on risk of living with other young people that might either present as potential victims or be a threat. Violent behaviour which had up to that point not been observed due to the absence of a vulnerable peer or a threatening peer may emerge with their introduction.

All risk management plans should include the circumstances associated with previous risk and early warning signs of the indicated risks. All the agreed methods, interventions and strategies to reduce risk of harm should be clearly documented. In addition these details should also feature in any care plan which may exist as a separate document. It is important to crossmatch risk assessments to the care plans.

The risk management plan should detail the roles and responsibilities of those involved in the care of patient and specify how emergency situations or a crisis should be managed. The plan should include an indication of when risk should be reviewed and who will have the responsibility for ensuring this occurs.

There may be a need for immediate action to be taken at any step in the risk assessment process to safeguard the subject or other vulnerable people. There may also need to be an immediate change in how the young person is managed on discovering key information. The risk for serious physical harm should be made explicit, and if there are other risks indicated or revealed due to having been systematic in reviewing all documentation, then this too should be clearly actioned.

All cases should be subject to review. Although the date for a regular scheduled review of risk (including the management plans) should be set, the circumstances that would trigger an immediate review should also be clear. Examples include a change in legal status, receipt of new information, upon transfer to another unit including an adult setting where a review of risk may incorporate adult tools, a new incident, a change in mental health, prior to leave commencing or being considered, prior to discharge, release or transfer.

BOX 4.3 Mike's Risk Management Plan

In terms of treatment strategies for Mike he may benefit from programmes to address problem solving, anger and threat sensitivity. Mike warrants specific intervention to address his use of alcohol. Sessions to educate regarding weapon carrying and use may help deter him from carrying such weapons. As he is particularly impulsive consideration should be given to preventative measures that he agrees to, rather than expect him to, alter behaviour when in crisis. Over the longer term work on his attachment and relationship with others may be considered, including relationship to members of his family. This work should be considered only following a period of settling and stabilisation. Similarly Mike may be experiencing significant problems regarding past trauma that he may have witnessed or experienced directly – which may serve to reinforce his belief that the world is unsafe and unpredictable.

In terms of supervision for Mike, on release from custody a structured supervised accommodation setting may be more suitable than returning to the family home. To limit Mike's opportunity to be violent while promoting the effectiveness of protective factors, intensive support which serves to contain his instability, help normalise his interpretations of others and manage his emotions in an adaptive way will be key. More information is required regarding his family and local community, including possibilities of returning to some prosocial habits.

In terms of monitoring, Mike's drinking should be monitored, as well as contact with antisocial peers and likely victims (e.g. mum's partner). On release an updated risk assessment is required regarding violence and should be subject to at least weekly review. The lead professional responsible for this should be his YOT officer in conjunction with Mike and staff/manager in the accommodation setting. The YOT is responsible for coordinating and communicating risk assessments and risk management plans in conjunction with licence conditions. It is expected that the accommodation manager will adopt the risk management plan locally.

In terms of victim safety planning, Mike may represent a targeted threat to authoritative parental figures, and their attention should be drawn to the potential risk that may arise when working with Mike.

The communication of risk assessments and risk management plans to those tasked with supervising and supporting the young person is vital. It is partly the responsibility of the risk assessor to make sure that her/his work does not exist solely as a document in an electronic records system or in a paper file that nobody reads. A risk assessment should inform and influence the care of the young person and equip the team with the knowledge to keep all involved safe.

The pursuit of criminal convictions for antisocial behaviour, in part due to the reason that quality evidence will be gathered as part of any investigation process, will assist in establishing a richer understanding of risk and dangerousness. For many reasons further convictions and even police investigation may not occur if the young person is already in a detained setting. It may therefore be the responsibility of the institution to investigate and record thoroughly.

Additional Processes in risk assessment

In all SPJ tools, while the process is systematic and each factor is considered in turn, there remains a key role for the risk assessor to use her/his clinical judgement. There is still much work for the clinician to do in developing the formulation and risk management process. Although additional risk and protective factors can be added, the content is not exhaustive and assessors must consider additional case-specific factors.

The SAVRY is used to assess general interpersonal violence, not targeted violence (e.g. against a parent). Although a SAVRY assessment will be useful and help construct an assessment, the clinician should consider any risks to a replacement victim such as foster parent, professional carer or other authority figure.

Through being systematic the assessor may identify risk in areas other than interpersonal violence. In addition gaps in knowledge or other risk processes may also be identified. The use of more specific processes to explore stalking behaviour, fire setting, sexual violence or sexually harmful behaviour may also be considered. For more serious violent offences the use of offence analysis in addition is indicated.

An offence analysis includes the collation of all information relevant to the offence and a formulation. The process is often best supported by use of the SAVRY initially, but with a greater focus on the victim details and relationship to the offender. The assessor should consider:

- The victims' details (e.g. age, gender, relationship);
- Why they were selected (e.g. lifestyle, attractiveness);
- Previous patterns (e.g. threats, try outs, fantasy);
- The offender's behaviour on the day (e.g. thinking patterns, drug/alcohol or medication use);
- Location of offence (e.g. use of transport, attack vs deposition sites);
- Description of violence used (e.g. weapons used, pattern of injury, time spent with victim);
- Type and function of sexually aggressive behaviours;
- Level of planning and preparation;
- Level of impulsivity;
- Level of fantasy re-enactment (media, internet, games);
- Behaviour after offence (e.g. anything done to avoid detection);
- Knowledge of previous convictions and relationship of past offences to index;
- Knowledge of past victims (e.g. age, gender).

If a CYP presents with bizarre or unusual behaviour, the assessor should consider her/his developmental level or whether the presentation represents an emerging mental illness or disorder. A fixed pattern of offending is not expected with CYP. The assessor should evaluate the developmental level of intent and knowledge of harm (physical and psychological) to the victim. For example, an adult sex offender may not have always had the same pattern and type of offending – especially as a CYP. There may be a risk that cruel or unusual behaviour has a different explanation. Post-crime-phase behaviour may be used to repair damage, to seek help or relieve suffering rather than as a way to evade capture.

The assessor should consider level of emotional development on the subject's capacity to show and describe remorse, anger, impulsivity and control. This may be mistaken for callous indifference, but might have another explanation. The assessor should consider the subject's psychosexual development and their knowledge of physical and psychological harm. The involvement of peers in the commission of the offence should be carefully evaluated given the greater influence of peers in the everyday lives of CYP.

The assessor should note: the use of any objects or rituals; any aspects of humiliation, bullying or shaming and any lower level offending trends. The levels of denial, amnesia and arousal at the time of the offence

and at subsequent interviews should also be considered. A review of police interview transcripts against statements of outcome in court and against latest account may reveal important detail or omissions.

School threat assessment processes are used where planned school attacks are a concern as distinguished from other forms of violence. Those involved in such attacks are a small, behaviourally and psychologically heterogeneous group. However, there may be a pattern of thinking and behaviour which suggests events may be preventable. An assessment would attempt to determine a subject's:

- Motivation;
- Communication;
- Unusual interest in targeted violence;
- Evidence of attack-related behaviour and planning;
- Mental condition;
- Level of cognitive sophistication to plan and execute an attack;
- Recent losses (including loss of status);
- Consistency between communication and behaviour
- Concern expressed by others;
- Factors that might increase/decrease likelihood of attack.

A clearly communicated threat is not usual, but discussion of ideas amongst others may occur. Like other acts of extreme violence a pattern of the same behaviour is not anticipated given perpetrators often do not survive or, if they do, are detained. The focus of the assessment is therefore on the progression of the behaviour from idea to plan. The outcome may be whether to take action or not or monitor the CYP.

Common Mistakes

The definitions of risk factors are imperfect, and therefore, users must read the manual carefully and discuss ambiguities about evidence and ratings with colleagues. Risk management decisions are not prescribed; the SAVRY (or any other SPJ tool) will not tell you what decision to make, and therefore, users must consider appropriate interventions.

The link between risk factors and the outcome is non-linear, and therefore, a higher number of risk factors present does not necessarily imply that the subject is a higher risk. Similarly a young person that may only have a small number of risk factors present may actually be particularly risky. This issue highlights the problems in communicating risk by adding up the number of risk factors that are rated as high or ascribing a probability or percentage. The subsequent formulation and risk management plan should address the challenge in how risk is communicated by the clinician. A CYP who has been identified as needing significant security, supervision and monitoring may also paradoxically be lower in risk due to the comprehensive management plan in place.

Many SPJ tools also contain an overall categorical value (red, amber or green, or Low-Medium-High-Very High). These categories provide limited information about how a young person should be understood and managed. The definition of what is 'high, medium or low' will vary between individuals, services and systems, thus rendering such categorical conclusions as misleading. An alternative approach advocated in this chapter is to communicate risk by providing an explanatory risk formulation that includes the nature of violence, its severity, imminence, and any risk-reducing and risk-enhancing factors. The hazard of trying to sum up complexities within a single category or word is a practice that has been rectified in revised versions of other SPJ tools.

Failure to communicate the outcome of risk assessment, inadequately review it or re-assess at a key time, for example prior to release, might render management plans inadequate and subsequently attract professional criticism. The SAVRY is a tool and, like other assessments, should be used to assist clinical judgements rather than replace them. Whilst its use is part of defensible practice, its use should be one component of an array of wider, good forensic clinical practices.

A failure to work in collaboration (with the young person, family and colleagues) may also result in a deficient understanding and management plan. Although some young people may not cooperate, or not be in a position to do so due to their legal status, mental health or ability, this may not always be the case. If these contexts exist then they should be clearly evidenced as part of the process. A young person may not be able to work at the formulaic level, but may more readily engage at a factor level.

All violence risk assessment can be potentially harmful to the assessor. Consideration should be given to ensure that clinicians are not only competent

but also have access to supervision in ensuring good quality of practice and maintaining well-being.

Conclusions

SPJ approaches are a significant improvement on the previous attempts to assess and manage risk. The inclusion of risk formulation has been key to this. However, clinical expertise is still required to create and communicate a risk assessment and link this to risk management plans. It is anticipated that improvements in the risk assessment and management process will lead to an improvement in the quality of outcomes for young people. In order to improve practice in this area, clinicians should consider auditing their risk formulations against identified standards. Further research is still required to explore whether risk formulations and management plans make any difference in practice.

Acknowledgements

The authors would like to thank Dr Caroline Logan (Consultant Clinical Psychologist) and Paulette Farnworth (Clinical Nurse Specialist), both of Greater Manchester West, Mental Health NHS Foundation Trust and the University of Manchester, for their support, guidance and advice on earlier drafts.

References

Abidin, Z., Davoren, M., Naughton, L. et al. (2013). Susceptibility (risk and protective) factors for in-patient violence and self-harm: prospective study of structured professional judgement instruments START and SAPROF, DUNDRUM-3 and DUNDRUM-4 in forensic mental health services. *BMC Psychiatry*, **13**, 197.

Augimeri, L., Webster, C., Koegl, C. et al. (2001). *Early Assessment Risk List for Boys: EARL-20B, Version 2*. Toronto: Earlscourt Child and Family Centre.

Borum, R., Bartel, P. and Forth, A. (2003). *Manual for the Structured Assessment for Violence Risk in Youth (SAVRY) Version 1.1*. Tampa: Florida Mental Health Institute, University of South Florida.

de Vries Robbé, M., de Vogel, V., Douglas, K. S. et al. (2015a). Changes in dynamic risk and protective factors for violence during inpatient forensic psychiatric treatment: Predicting reductions in postdischarge community recidivism. *Law and Human Behavior*, **39**(1), 53–61.

de Vries Robbé, M., de Vogel, V., Koster, K. et al. (2015b). Assessing protective factors for sexually violent offending with the SAPROF. *Sex Abuse*, **27**(1), 51–70.

de Vries Robbé, M., Geers, M., Stapel, M. et al. (2015c). *SAPROF: Youth Version. Structured Assessment of Protective Factors for Violence risk – Guidelines for the Assessment of Protective Factors for Violence Risk*. Netherlands: Van der Hoeven Kliniek.

Dolan, M. C. and Rennie, C. E. (2008). The structured assessment of violence risk in youth as a predictor of recidivism in a United Kingdom cohort of adolescent offenders with conduct disorder. *Psychological Assessment*, **20**, 35–46.

Douglas, K. S., Hart, S. D., Webster, C. D. et al. (2013). *HCR-20V3: Assessing Risk for Violence – User Guide*. Burnaby, Canada: Mental Health, Law, and Policy Institute, Simon Fraser University.

Enebrink, P., Långström, N. and Gumpert, C. H. (2006a). Predicting aggressive and disruptive behaviour in referred 6–12 year-old boys: prospective validation of the EARLB-20B risk/needs checklist. *Assessment*, **13**, 356–367.

Enebrink, P., Långström, N., Hultén, A. et al. (2006b). Swedish validation of the Early Assessment Risk List for boys (EARL-20B), a decision-aid for use with children presenting with 239 conduct-disordered behaviour. *Nordic Journal of Psychiatry*, **60**, 438–446.

Forth, A., Kosson, D. and Hare, R. (2003). *The Hare Psychopathy Checklist: Youth Version, Technical Manual*. New York: Multi-Health Systems, Inc.

Gammelgård, M., Koivisto, A. M., Eronen, M. et al. (2008). The predictive validity of the structured assessment of violence risk in youth (SAVRY) among institutionalised adolescents. *Journal of Forensic Psychiatry & Psychology*, **19**(3), 352–370.

Gammelgård, M., Koivisto, A. M., Eronen, M. et al. (2015). Predictive validity of the structured assessment of violence risk in youth: a 4-year follow-up. *Criminal Behaviour and Mental Health*, **25**(3), 192–206.

Hart, S. D. and Logan, C. (2011). Formulation of violence risk using evidence-based assessments: the structured professional judgment approach. In Sturmey, P. and McMurran, M. Editors. *Forensic Case Formulation* (pp. 83–106). Chichester: Wiley-Blackwell.

Hart, S., Sturmey, P., Logan, C. et al. (2011) Forensic case formulation. *International Journal of Forensic Mental Health*, **10**, 118–128.

Hilterman, E. L., Nicholls, T. L. and van Nieuwenhuizen, C. (2014). Predictive validity of risk assessments in juvenile offenders: comparing the SAVRY, PCL: YV and YLS/CMI with unstructured clinical assessments. *Assessment* **21**(3), 324–339.

Hoge, R. and Andrews, D. (2002). *The Youth Level of Service/Case Management Inventory*. Toronto: Multi-Health Systems.

Johnstone, L. (2013). Working with complex cases: mental disorder and violence. In Logan, C. and Johnstone, L.

Editors. *Managing Clinical Risk: A Guide to Effective Practice* (pp. 56–88). Oxford, UK: Routledge.

Levene, K. S., Augimeri, L. K., Pepler, D. J. et al. (2001). *Early Assessment Risk List for Girls (EARL-21 G), Version 1, Consultation Edition*. Toronto: Earlscourt Child and Family Centre.

Logan, C. (2013). The HCR-20 version 3: a case study in risk formulation. *International Journal of Forensic Mental Health*, **13**, 1–9.

McGowan, M. R., Horn, R. A. and Mellott, R. N. (2011). The predictive validity of the Structured Assessment of Violence Risk in Youth in secondary educational settings. *Psychological Assessment*, **23**(2), 478–86.

Olver, M. E. Stockdale, K. C. and Wormith, J. S. (2009). Risk assessment with young offenders: a meta-analysis of three assessment measures. *Criminal Justice and Behavior*, **36**, 329–353.

Otto, R. and Douglas, K. (2010). *Handbook of Violence Risk Assessment*. New York: Routledge.

Penney, R. S., Lee, Z. and Moretti, M. M. (2010). Gender differences in risk factors for violence: an examination of the predictive validity of the Structured Assessment of Violence Risk in youth. *Aggressive Behaviour*, **36**, 390–404.

Rennie, C. and Dolan, M. (2010). Predictive validity of the youth level of service/case management inventory in custody sample in England. *Journal of Forensic Psychiatry & Psychology*, **21**(3), 407–425.

Schwalbe, C. S. (2007). Risk assessment for juvenile justice: a meta-analysis. *Law and Human Behavior*, **31**, 449–462.

Singh, J. P., Grann, M. and Fazel, S. (2011). A comparative study of violence risk assessment tools: a systematic review and metaregression analysis of 68 studies involving 25,980 participants. *Clinical Psychology Review*, **31**, 499–513.

Sturmey, P. and McMurran, M. (2011). *Forensic Case Formulation*. Chichester: Wiley-Blackwell.

Viljoen, J., Beneteau, J., Gulbransen, E. et al. (2012). Assessment of multiple risk outcomes, strengths, and change with the START: AV: a short-term prospective study with adolescent offenders. *International Journal of Forensic Mental Health*, **11**, 165–180.

Viljoen, J., Nicholls, K., Cruise, K. et al. (2014). *Short-Term Assessment of Risk and Treatability: Adolescent Version (START: AV)*. Vancouver, British Columbia: Mental Health, Law, and Policy Institute, Simon Fraser University.

Welsh, J. L., Schmidt, F., McKinnon, L. et al. (2008). A comparative study of adolescent risk assessment instruments: predictive and incremental validity. *Assessment*, **15**, 104–117.

Weerasekera, P. (1996). *Multiperspective Case Formulation: A Step toward Treatment Integration*. Malabar, FL: Krieger.

Chapter 5

The Influence of Neurodevelopmental Impairment on Youth Crime

Nathan Hughes, Huw Williams and Prathiba Chitsabesan

Introduction

Childhood neurodevelopmental impairments are physical, mental or sensory functional deficits caused by disruption in the development of the central nervous system – which consists of the brain, the spinal cord and a related set of neurons – or peripheral nervous system – which sends sensory information to the brain and controls the functioning of organs and muscles (Patel et al., 2011). Such disruptions are often the result of a complex mix of influences, including: genetics; pre-birth or birth trauma; illness or injury in childhood; or nutritional, educational or emotional deprivation; and might result in one or more of a wide range of physical, mental or sensory functional difficulties.

Common impairments include cognitive deficits; specific learning difficulties; communication difficulties; and emotional and behavioural problems (Patel et al., 2011; APA, 2013). Such symptoms can occur in combination, as evidenced in a wide range of clinically defined disorders or conditions, including (though not restricted to): Attention Deficit Hyperactivity Disorder (ADHD); Autistic Spectrum Disorder (ASD); learning (or intellectual) disability; communication disorders; Foetal Alcohol Syndrome Disorders (FASDs) and Traumatic Brain Injury (TBI) (Patel et al., 2011; APA, 2013).

The particular symptoms associated with each of these conditions are briefly outlined in Table 5.1. While these descriptions utilise clinical definitions, it is important to acknowledge that the clinical presentation of many of these conditions can change over time. For example, social communication disorders may become more evident during periods of transition, such as in starting secondary school (NICE, 2011), while overt hyperactivity symptoms in young people with ADHD frequently diminish in adolescence (Schmidt and Petermann, 2009). Impairments associated with many of these conditions are frequently on a spectrum, with many young people presenting with subclinical levels of need that do not meet diagnostic criteria or threshold for individual disorders, though still significantly affected by multiple symptoms and complex expressions of impairment. Similarly, given overlap in cause and expression, young people may experience various conditions in parallel. As such, a particular label or 'disorder' may not always adequately express the functional needs and difficulties experienced by a young person.

The Prevalence of Neurodevelopmental Impairment among Young People in Custody

A recent review of evidence across a range of international contexts reveals a consistently high incidence rate of neurodevelopmental impairment among incarcerated young people. Following an extensive, structured literature review of research, we have compared the rates of specific neurodevelopmental disorders and conditions amongst young people in custodial institutions to equivalent rates established in studies of young people in the general population (Hughes et al., 2012). In doing so, we demonstrate a disproportionate prevalence of a range of conditions amongst young people in custody. The findings of this review are summarised in Table 5.2.

These data clearly require careful interpretation given the methodological and analytical challenges in combining and comparing such a diverse range of research. Varying classifications or definitions of specific neurodevelopmental disorders are apparent, creating difficulties in the interpretation and direct comparison of findings. This variability is reflected in the numerous measures, tools and methods used to assess prevalence rates of specific disorders, which include: analyses of records of previous clinical diagnoses; self-report surveys of specific symptoms; qualitative interviews with young people and the use of

Table 5.1 Core Symptoms of Common Neurodevelopmental Conditions

Neurodevelopmental Condition	Definition
Attention Deficit Hyperactivity Disorder	Persistence in multiple symptoms of inattention, hyperactivity and/or impulsivity. Apparent in childhood, and present across more than one setting or context (APA, 2013)
Autistic Spectrum Disorder	Qualitative abnormalities in reciprocal social interactions and communication, and markedly restricted repetitive and stereotyped patterns of behaviour and interests Originally manifested in early childhood, and present across more than one setting or context (APA, 2013)
Intellectual (or Learning) Disability	Deficits in: – cognitive capacity (measured by an IQ score of less than 70) and – adaptive functioning (significant difficulties with everyday tasks) Can be mild, moderate, severe or profound in level of severity Onset occurs prior to adulthood (APA, 2013)
Communication Disorders	Persistent deficits in aspects of speech, language or hearing that significantly impact upon an individual's academic achievement or day-to-day social interactions. Levels of development are substantially below age-appropriate levels and are not explained by other disorders or conditions. Includes: – language disorder (expressive and receptive-expressive language) – speech sound disorder – childhood-onset fluency disorder (stuttering) – social (pragmatic) communication disorder (APA, 2013)
Foetal Alcohol Syndrome Disorder	Permanent birth defects resulting from prenatal alcohol exposure due to maternal consumption during pregnancy. Can include 'growth retardation' regarding height, weight and/or head circumference, developmental delays, behavioural dysfunction and/or learning difficulties (Chartrand and Forbes-Chilibeck, 2003)
Traumatic Brain Injury	Any injury to the brain caused by impact. Severity is typically measured by the length and depth of loss of consciousness. Common effects include: cognitive difficulties, including regarding memory, attention and executive functioning; irritability and anger; impulsivity; headaches and depression (Williams, 2013).

validated instruments or clinical tests. These varied approaches can potentially lead to very different assessments of levels of prevalence (Fazel et al., 2008). Comparisons are also made difficult by the variation in samples and populations on which individual studies are focused. This includes variation in the age range considered, which is typically dependent on the age of young people within a particular custodial setting.

Notwithstanding these challenges, and the caveats to interpretation that they require, the evidence available consistently suggests a disproportionately high rate of neurodevelopmental disorders amongst incarcerated young people. Indeed, it suggests that a significant proportion of young people in the custodial estate have one or more neurodevelopmental disorders, signifying high levels of need. What's more, the prevalence of clinically defined disorders is likely to be an underestimate of the proportion of young people affected by particular symptoms or subclinical levels of impairment.

This weight of evidence therefore suggests a widespread failure of current practices and interventions intended to prevent offending and re-offending to recognise and meet the needs of these vulnerable young people. Consequently, this evidence promotes a rethinking of the approaches of the youth justice system, and of policy and services more generally. This chapter seeks to inform this process through an examination of the multifarious

Table 5.2 Comparing the Prevalence of Neurodevelopmental Conditions

Neurodevelopmental Condition	Prevalence Rates amongst Young People in the General Population* (%)	Prevalence Rates amongst Young People in Custody* (%)
Attention Deficit Hyperactivity Disorder	1.7–9	12
Autistic Spectrum Disorder	0.6–1.2	15
Intellectual (or Learning) Disability	2–4	23–32
Communication Disorders	5–7	60–90
Foetal Alcohol Syndrome Disorder	0.1–5	10.9–11.7
Traumatic Brain Injury	24–31.6	65.1–72.1

* References are provided and studies summarised by Hughes et al. (2012).

explanations as to why young people with certain childhood neurodevelopmental impairments may be at greater risk of criminality, criminalisation and, ultimately, custodial intervention. In particular we consider:

- antisocial or aggressive behavioural traits that can result from cognitive or emotional deficits;
- the increased exposure to social and environmental risk for offending resulting from neurodevelopmental impairment; and
- disabling and criminalising processes, including within the criminal justice system.

Analysis of these interrelated explanations supports subsequent consideration to their implications for policy and practice responses. Throughout the article we draw on illustrative examples in relation to four of the conditions outlined in Table 5.1: learning disability; communication disorders; FASD and TBI. In parallel, we also draw your attention to the chapters in this edition examining other neurodevelopmental disorders; including ADHD (please refer to Chapter 14 by Young, Greer and White) and ASD (please refer to Chapter 15 by Gralton and Baird).

Antisocial Behavioural Traits Resulting from Cognitive or Emotional Deficits

Neurodevelopmental impairments are expressed through a wide range of symptoms, including deficits in cognitive functions (reasoning, thinking and perception) and social-affective functions (the expression of emotion and formation of relationships). Such deficits can affect a child's 'daily functioning in the social world' (Yeates et al., 2007), giving rise to certain

behavioural traits in particular contexts. Specifically, cognitive and emotional traits associated with particular neurodevelopmental disorders can directly influence propensity towards aggressive and antisocial behaviour in particular social situations, and therefore increase vulnerability towards criminality. In this regard, aggressive or antisocial behaviour, and therefore criminality, can be interpreted as an inappropriate response to a social situation that is indicative of a specific deficit in social functioning. This suggests that whilst young people with neurodevelopmental impairments may commit crime for exactly the same reasons as other young people, there may also be certain additional triggers or particular patterns of behaviour related to cognitive and emotional deficits. The following examples are chosen so as to illustrate the range of such deficits.

Executive Functioning

'Executive functioning' is an umbrella term describing the various, multifaceted cognitive processes used to enable complex goal-oriented thought and action, and the self-regulation of socially appropriate behaviour. Such processes include the initiation, planning and sequencing of complex tasks, the utilisation of long-term memory, concentration, inhibitory and attention control, and responsivity to novel or changing circumstances (Funahashi, 2001; Meltzer, 2007).

Deficits in executive functions are known to influence certain forms of antisocial behaviour. Two systematic reviews have suggested a robust and statistically significant association between executive functioning and various measures of antisocial, aggressive or criminal behaviour (Morgan and

Lilienfeld, 2000; Ogilvie et al., 2011). Ogilvie et al. (2011) summarise the hypothesised influences of executive functioning on antisocial behaviour as including: 'decreasing behavioral inhibition, impairing the ability to anticipate behavioral consequences and assess punishment and reward, [and] damaging the capability to generate socially appropriate behavior in challenging contexts' (Ogilvie et al., 2011:1064).

Deficits in executive functions are associated with a range of neurodevelopmental disorders. For example, the above descriptions of deficits in executive functioning closely relate to descriptions of the difficulties faced by those with learning disabilities, which include: setting goals and planning activity; organising and prioritising information; moving attention from one activity to another and maintaining information in the working memory (British Psychological Society, 2001).

A similar pattern of difficulties are apparent among young people with FASD (Burd et al., 2004; Greenbaum et al., 2009). FASD encompasses several different conditions related to permanent birth defects resulting from prenatal alcohol exposure due to maternal consumption during pregnancy (Burd et al., 2004), including FASD and alcohol-related neurodevelopmental disorder. Young people with FASD can demonstrate a range of cognitive functioning deficits, including with regard to reasoning, planning ahead, anticipating and learning from consequences of actions (Burd et al., 2010).

Deficits in executive functioning are similarly related to TBI. A TBI is any injury to the brain caused by impact. Typically this may occur from a direct blow to the head or a force that causes the brain to move around inside the skull, as in a road traffic accident (RTA), fall or assault (Faul et al., 2010). The frontal and temporal areas of the brain are common sites of injury due to their location at the front of the brain and their proximity to the skull (Catroppa and Anderson, 2009; Williams, 2013). These regions are 'intimately associated with' executive functioning (Morgan and Lilienfeld, 2000) and include the dorsolateral prefrontal cortex, associated with working memory, sustained attention, memory retrieval, abstraction and problem solving, and the orbitofrontal cortex, associated with emotional and social responses (Ganesalingam et al., 2007). Indeed, Sesma et al. (2008) report that between 20% and 40% of children aged between 5 and 15 years demonstrate 'significant executive dysfunction' within the

first year of injury. Furthermore, whilst motor deficits associated with TBI improve over time, there is evidence that executive functioning deficits are more enduring and can even worsen over time (Catroppa et al., 2008; Fay et al., 2009). In particular, Catroppa and Anderson (2009) highlight 'life-long difficulties' resulting from childhood TBI in relation to 'capacity for abstract thought, planning and problem-solving, mental flexibility, knowledge appraisal and metacognitive skills'.

Cognitive Empathy

In the context of antisocial behaviour, a deficit in cognitive empathy refers to 'poor ability to foresee the consequences of . . . offending and to appreciate the feelings of victims' (Farrington and Welsh, 2007: 41). Low cognitive empathy is theorised as related to offending 'on the assumption that people who can appreciate or experience a victim's feelings (or both) are less likely to victimize someone' (Farrington and Welsh, 2007: 47). Indeed, low cognitive empathy was identified as strongly related to offending in a systematic review of 35 studies (Jolliffe and Farrington, 2004). However, elsewhere the relationship was found to be 'greatly reduced after controlling for intelligence or socio-economic status' (Jolliffe and Farrington, 2010: 49), suggesting low empathy to be a mediating or moderating variable in the presence of these other factors.

Whilst its specific influence as a risk factor is unclear, poor cognitive empathy is a characteristic of several neurodevelopmental disorders, including learning disabilities, ADHD and autism. Cognitive empathy is also related to TBI that affects frontal lobes (Tonks et al., 2009). Various methods have been employed to demonstrate inhibited ability amongst those who have experienced severe TBI to recognise and appropriately respond to other people's emotions (Catroppa and Anderson, 2009), for example in selecting an appropriate emotional facial expression when listening to a particular tone of voice (Ryan et al., 2014) or in recognising the emotions being portrayed in facial expressions (Tonks et al., 2011). Such studies demonstrate that 'poorer emotional perception creates social misunderstandings that lead to generation of ineffective or inappropriate responses' (Ryan et al., 2013: 816). This in turn may heighten the likelihood of 'rejection' by peers and/or 'elicit psychological distress reflected in externalizing behaviors that include aggression, rule breaking and intrusive conduct' (Ryan et al., 2013: 817).

Emotional Regulation

Emotional regulation involves complex conscious and unconscious processes, including cognitive and physiological components which modulate affective states. Emotional regulation strategies develop throughout an individual's lifetime, but most critically during childhood, and reflect an interaction between intrinsic factors, such as temperament, and prior experience (Bradley and Corwyn, 2002). Regulatory systems develop during adolescence through functional and structural changes within the brain, including within the prefrontal cortex and amygdala. The prefrontal cortex is associated with the integration of emotional experiences and cognition, including emotion regulation (Davidson et al., 2000), while the amygdala is an important region for emotion recognition of fear as well as emotion regulation (Davidson et al., 2000).

Abnormalities in these regions have been shown in children with conduct disorder (Fairchild et al., 2011) as well as children with neurodevelopmental disorders. Consequently, children with a range of neurodevelopmental impairment are at risk of difficulties with emotional regulation, including those with; ADHD (Barkley, 2009), language impairment (Prizent and Wetherby, 1992), learning disability (Wishart et al., 2007) and TBI (Ganesalingam et al., 2007). Therefore problems with emotional recognition and regulation may be contributing mechanisms to the development of behavioural difficulties for this particular group of children and young people.

These illustrative examples offer a brief insight into the diverse and complex ways in which cognitive and emotional difficulties that are symptomatic of neurodevelopmental impairment might, in particular social contexts, give rise to the expression of aggressive or antisocial behaviour associated with criminality. The existence of such a trait is, of course, not deterministic of offending behaviour and future criminality. Such characteristics are therefore not sufficient explanation for the heightened risk of serious and persistent offending amongst those with neurodevelopmental impairments. The next two sections examine evidence of a parallel heightened susceptibility to social experiences that can lead to a greater risk of both criminality and criminalisation, and therefore begin to illustrate the potential developmental pathways into offending for young people made vulnerable by underlying emotional or cognitive deficits.

Increased Exposure to Social and Environmental Risk Factors for Offending

In addition to cognitive and emotional deficits that are directly implicated in offending behaviour, it is also possible to identify a range of social or environmental risk factors for criminality that either affect or interact with symptoms of impairment. The influence of neurodevelopmental impairment may be more greatly realised among young people experiencing adverse social and environmental conditions. In parallel, neurodevelopmental impairment may increase the likelihood of exposure to social and environmental risk or increase susceptibility to a range of negative social experiences that further heighten risk of criminality. The following examples consider the associations with three well-established social and environmental risk factors for offending: educational disengagement, negative peer group influences and problematic parenting practices.

Educational Disengagement

The relationship between neurodevelopmental impairment and social and environmental risk is most apparent in relation to education, with the links between various neurodevelopmental disorders and experiences of disengagement well established. This is, of course, starkly evident in relation to young people with learning disability, who can experience deficits in memory and problem-solving skills, which inhibit academic performance (British Psychological Society, 2001). For many young people with neurodevelopmental impairments, difficulties apparent prior to starting school can therefore be seen to potentially inhibit 'school readiness'. For example, a variety of symptoms associated with FASD develop in the pre-school phase, including impulse control, a short attention span, an inability to concentrate and poor memory (Green, 2007).

Difficulties in pre-school and early educational experiences can have a cumulative effect on educational careers, with difficulties prior to the age of eight leading to subsequent challenges in engaging with further stages of education. For example, Snow and Powell (2012) describe the cumulative challenges facing young people with oral language deficits, as experienced by those with particular communication disorders or learning difficulties. Recognising the shift from 'learning to read' to 'reading to learn' that typically occurs in the fourth year of formal education, Snow and Powell (2012) argue that those who have struggled to successfully engage with the formal literacy instruction of the first three years of school may 'struggle enormously' in entering this second phase. 'For boys in particular, this is often a time (around 8 years of age) when externalising behaviour difficulties becomes apparent in the classroom' (Snow and Powell, 2012: 2). A potential association between early difficulties in engaging with education due to impairment and subsequent classroom misbehaviour is therefore apparent.

Such difficulties engaging in education are apparent throughout school careers, though in particular again as young people transition from primary into secondary education. Here studies suggest particular problems with more subtle aspects of communication such as the understanding of pragmatics, and 'on access to increasingly demanding curriculum subjects where language is central' (Dockrell et al., 2007: 4). Furthermore the transition from the more nurturing environment of primary school to a secondary school that places significant academic, organisational and social demands on the student can be particularly challenging for young people with impairment (Pfiffner et al., 2006). Problematic transitions into secondary school can escalate disengagement from education and therefore represent a key developmental phase with regard to the risk of future criminal behaviour (National Crime Prevention, 1999).

Whilst young people with FASD, learning disabilities or communication disorders may more typically suffer such cumulative educational difficulties and disadvantage, young people who experience TBI in childhood may also be prone to sudden and unanticipated educational problems, particularly during secondary education. A head injury in childhood may affect parts of the brain associated with higher cognitive functions, and this may be fully realised only when the child reaches an age of maturity at which such functions are assumed to be developed and are called upon in the classroom. If a brain injury has inhibited the development of such skills, the young person may suddenly begin to struggle to effectively engage. What's more, the cause of this difficulty may not be attributed to an earlier head injury from which the young person appears to have recovered.

Peer Group Influence

A heightened risk of detachment from school, whether through disaffection, truancy or exclusion, can further act to increase the risk of offending (Patterson, 1996; Stevenson, 2006). There is evidence that susceptibility to risk factors associated with delinquent peer groups and a loss of positive socialisation through schools is itself heightened by the existence of specific neurodevelopmental impairments. This is supported by research studies that indicate challenges in peer group formation, and associated susceptibility to bullying and negative peer pressure.

In the previous section we noted the relationship between social communication and social interaction. Deficits in social communication can influence the formation and maintenance of peer relationships by reducing the capacity for peer negotiation and effective interaction (Botting and Conti-Ramsden, 2000). In particular, Baldry et al. (2011) argue that such deficits can promote a heightened desire in a young person to want to be accepted by their peer group, and therefore argue that such deficits can increase the risk of engagement in criminality, if associating with criminal peers. Indeed, Conti-Ramsden and Botting (2004) suggest that young people with speech and language difficulties are approximately three times more likely to be regular targets for victimization when compared to those without such difficulties. A similar finding has been established in relation to young people with a learning disability (Mishna, 2003; Baumeister et al., 2008). This suggests that young people with neurodevelopmental impairments may be readily targeted and manipulated by peers. Rejection by a child's peer group in middle childhood has been shown to be associated with later externalising problems (Kupersmidt et al., 1995). This may contribute to the initiation or escalation of antisocial behaviour through a greater association with other deviant peers as rejected children may avoid environments that they perceive as punishing or negative and seek environments and people that are supportive of their characteristics and interests (Patterson et al., 1989).

Parenting Practices

Parenting a child with a neurodevelopmental disorder can clearly bring a range of challenges, particularly when that disorder is not diagnosed or support services are not adequate. Such challenges can inadvertently lead to the use of parenting practices that serve to increase the risk of antisocial behaviour and offending. In particular, approaches to parenting that are excessively permissive or authoritarian may be adopted in response to the challenges of parenting a child with challenging behaviour with negative consequences.

Wade et al. (2003) suggest that children who have experienced TBI may be particularly vulnerable to negative effects associated with 'maladaptive parent-child interactions'. This is reflected in a range of studies that highlight particular correlations between various indicators of family functioning and long-term behavioural problems amongst young people who have experienced TBI. Wade et al. (2011) demonstrate 'parental warmness' to be associated with lower levels of externalising behaviour, when controlling for socio-economic status and other measures of family functioning. In parallel, parental 'negativity' is similarly associated with forms of externalising behaviour. A study tracking the ten-year developmental trajectories of young people who experienced TBI during their school years found that poor long-term behavioural outcomes were predicted by such parenting approaches (Anderson et al., 2012). Similarly, Yeates et al. (2010) found an association between authoritarian parenting practices and behavioural problems 18 months after injury, as well as echoing Kurowski et al. (2011) in finding a similar association with permissive practices.

'Neurodisability', Discrimination and Criminalisation

The discussion so far has focused on neurodevelopmental impairment as experienced through various functional limitations, highlighting both the direct impact of functional deficits on aggressive or antisocial behavioural traits, and the indirect relationship with social experiences known to increase risk of future criminality. In this section the focus now shifts from experiences of impairment to experiences of disability, defined as 'the loss or limitation of opportunities to take part in the normal life of the community on an equal level with others due to physical and social barriers' (Barnes, 1991: 2). Adopting the lens of disability therefore focuses attention on how an individual with impairment experiences their environment, including day-to-day functioning, social relations and services and support.

Perhaps the most obvious example of the experience of disability is in the ways in which neurodevelopmental disorders are defined and diagnosed, and the associated labels and categories are applied (Dowse et al., 2009). Diagnosis (or lack of) and classification determines the extent and nature of recognition and response to neurodevelopmental impairment. It determines service eligibility and subsequent support. It drives how a young person's needs are understood and responded to by a range of professionals. A lack of diagnosis can be central to the experiences that can serve to increase risk of offending discussed in the previous section. Parents may not receive the support needed to effectively care for their children. The school's failure to identify and respond to the learning needs resulting from neurodevelopmental impairment may be the origin of potential disengagement with education. It may also be directly implicated in the onset of problem behaviour. Without an awareness of an underlying cognitive or emotional deficit, classroom misbehaviour may simply be interpreted as an attitudinal or behavioural problem, with the root cause unaddressed (Law et al., 2013).

Where an impairment is frequently not diagnosed or is typically assessed as insufficient to meet eligibility criteria for service provision, there appears to be a particular subsequent impact on prevalence data among young people in custody. This is most apparent in relation to learning disability. Chitsabesan et al. (2007) found that the majority of young offenders with a learning disability identified in their study had an IQ in the 'mild range', and were therefore less likely to have had their learning needs identified in mainstream schools (Bailey et al., 2008). This is supported by Herrington's (2009: 398) suggestion that those with more severe learning disabilities are more likely to either have their 'challenging and/or offending behaviour … excused by care providers' or to be diverted towards specialist services if their needs were identified through contact with criminal justice services. As a result, the population within the youth justice system might be expected to demonstrate disproportionately high levels of mild or borderline intellectual functioning.

Disabling processes are equally apparent in experiences of the criminal justice system, with various practices serving to increase the risk of criminalisation of young people with neurodevelopmental impairments. Inadequate assessment and screening tools (Harrington and Bailey, 2005) and insufficient knowledge or training regarding the expression of neurodevelopmental impairment (McKenzie et al., 2000) lead to poor recognition of impairment and a failure of services to identify and appropriately support those with a neurodevelopmental impairment (Hayes, 2002).

Specialist service provision within the youth justice system is limited (Talbot, 2010). Instead young people with neurodevelopmental impairment are typically subject to generic youth justice interventions which assume typical levels of verbal and cognitive competence and are intended to 'tap important metacognitive skills, that is, "thinking about one's own thinking", so that unhelpful beliefs can be identified and modified' (Snow and Powell, 2012). Such approaches may therefore be inappropriate for some young people with neurodevelopmental impairment, leading to difficulties engaging with and completing court orders, and therefore an increased risk of breach and return to court for further sentencing.

Young people with particular neurodevelopmental impairments are also known to struggle to effectively understand and engage in various aspects of the criminal justice process. For example, cognitive impairment can inhibit narrative language skills, or the ability to tell one's story or version of events. Such skills are imperative given the forensic interviewing techniques applied in court or by police (Snow and Powell, 2005, 2011). What's more, the young person's reaction to this inability to participate may be misinterpreted. Snow and Powell (2012: 3) observe how low expressive vocabulary and poor narrative language skills can mean 'monosyllabic, poorly elaborated and non-specific responses that may be accompanied by poor eye-contact and occasional shrugs of the shoulders'. As in the case of misbehaviour in the classroom, if the underlying cause of these responses is not understood, they 'may be mistaken for deliberate rudeness and wilful non-compliance when being interviewed by police or cross-examined in court' (Snow and Powell, 2011: 482). If interpreted

as behavioural and attitudinal, difficulties in communication may therefore lead to greater risk of criminalisation.

Implications for Policy and Practice

The disproportionately high prevalence of neurodevelopmental disorders among young people in custody in numerous countries suggests a heightened vulnerability to serious and/or persistent offending coupled with a failure of various policy and practice systems to address complex needs in seeking to prevent offending and re-offending. In this chapter we have provided some insight into the multifarious ways in which cognitive and emotional impairments might give rise to antisocial or aggressive behaviour in particular contexts or situations, increasing risk of criminality. In parallel we have demonstrated how neurodevelopmental impairment may increase exposure to social and environmental risk factors for offending. This includes potential challenges to effective educational engagement and attainment, family functioning and negative peer group influences. We have also argued that experiences of neurodevelopmental impairment must be considered in parallel to experiences of neurodisability. Systemic failures to recognise and address the needs of young people with neurodevelopmental impairment have been shown to add further disadvantage and vulnerability, and ultimately to increase the likelihood of criminalisation.

Whilst painting a picture of vulnerability, disadvantage and discrimination, an appreciation of the array of cognitive and emotional, social and environmental, and systemic factors and experiences interacting to greatly increase risk of offending amongst young people with neurodevelopmental disorders offers insight into various potential means to intervene so as to reduce or counter this risk. In this concluding section we highlight a selection of policy and practice implications, emphasising the need for early intervention, responsive and tailored intervention, and reform to criminal justice processes all of which must be underpinned by effective screening and assessment to improve awareness of impairment.

Early Intervention through Educational and Family Support

An awareness of the developmental pathways of young people with neurodevelopmental impairments who offend necessitates earlier intervention through family and educational support, so as to prevent the development of secondary risk such as problematic family functioning, detachment from education or negative peer group influence.

Families are a valuable resource in supporting young people; however, families need to be supported if they are to maintain an effective level of care to a child with complex needs such as those associated with neurodevelopmental impairment (Hughes, 2010). This might include greater investment in parenting support programmes known to be effective for young people with specific disorders, as well as ongoing engagement with and support to parents, through the provision of information regarding potential future symptoms and expressions of particular impairments or disorders that can support the identification and appropriate response to functional and behavioural difficulties that may emerge during childhood and adolescence.

Young people at risk of later antisocial behaviour can often be identified early within the education system by their challenging behaviour or problems with academic engagement or attainment. Indeed, young people exhibiting early signs of difficulty should be routinely assessed for underlying cognitive and emotional needs so as to support appropriate attempts to maintain educational engagement, with the aim of not only reducing offending but also promoting better educational outcomes. For example, identification of neurodevelopmental difficulties with early signs of language difficulties can promote support during changes to classroom teaching at age eight, while awareness of need at primary school can allow young people to be appropriately supported on transition to secondary school.

Where neurodevelopmental impairment has been identified, early and sustained interventions to maintain attachment to school have been shown to have a greater chance of success compared with attempting to re-engage young people (Youth Justice Board, 2006). Access to specialist consultation with health and educational professionals, such as educational psychologists, child and adolescent mental health professionals, and speech therapists, is also key. Given their complex needs and potential for associated challenging behaviour, young people with neurodevelopmental impairment may benefit from support provided within a specialist educational placement

that is able to provide a small, flexible environment, and an adapted timetable with trained staff, as well as the acquisition of life skills that could contribute to better social adaptation in later life.

This suggests a significant set of training needs across a range of services in order to ensure appropriate assessment and response. Staff in education services, family intervention projects, social services and primary healthcare settings, as well as in community youth justice services, require support to recognise and understand issues relating to neurodevelopmental impairment. Awareness raising across a range of practitioners and professionals will also support more appropriate referral to relevant specialist services for further assessment and intervention.

Responsive Youth Justice Interventions

As we have highlighted, young people with neurodevelopmental impairments typically have specific needs and learning styles that can affect an ability to engage in interventions intended to support rehabilitation or to address identified behavioural, educational or mental health needs. Recognition of these varied needs directly contradicts current use of generic approaches which assume typical levels of verbal and cognitive competence, and which those with atypical neurodevelopment struggle to adhere to, resulting in experiences of neurodisability fuelling further criminalisation. For example, research has suggested that individuals with a history of TBI may find it more difficult to engage with offence-related rehabilitation due to information processing difficulties or disinhibited behaviour (Williams et al., 2010).

Recognition is therefore essential in order to develop individual care plans for the young person, allowing for services that are responsive to specific cognitive and emotional deficits. Awareness of a young person's needs can help practitioners in regular contact with them to offer appropriate support in the development of better life skills and more adaptive coping mechanisms with appropriate supervision and training. For example, the education of prison staff around the impact of TBI and management strategies to support offenders can have positive outcomes for both staff and prisoners, leading to a reduction in the number of negative interactions (Ferguson et al., 2012). Additionally, Tonks et al. (2011) suggest that individual rehabilitation programmes for young offenders with a history of TBI may help reduce their vulnerability to depression, anxiety and negative behavioural outcomes in later life.

Guidelines on how to support young people with specific neurodevelopmental disorders are already established and can be readily utilised, including, for example those published by the National Institute for Health and Care Excellence regarding ADHD (NICE, 2008) and ASD (NICE, 2011) (please refer to Chapter 14 by Young, Greer and White and Chapter 15 by Gralton and Baird). An example of a specialist pathway for young offenders with TBI has also been developed by the Disabilities Foundation (Chitsabesan et al., 2015). The service pathway is based on a successful model of interventions for adult offenders with TBI in an adult custodial secure facility (www.thedtgroup.org/foundation/offenders-with-brain-injury.aspx). There are also guidelines with specific reference to offending behaviour. For example, NICE recently published advice regarding 'recognition, intervention and management' of antisocial behaviour and conduct disorders (NICE, 2013). There is also growing evidence of the efficacy of individual therapeutic approaches to address and manage aspects of the disorder and associated risk of offending; for example adapted cognitive behaviour therapy (Hare and Paine, 1997) and skills development using social stories and comic strip cartoons address emotional recognition and help develop coping strategies to manage stress and conflict (Murphy, 2010). A case example in which some of these suggested approaches have been utilised is presented in Box 5.1.

Screening and Assessment

Our calls for early intervention and responsive youth justice provision repeatedly illustrate the importance of effective screening and assessment for neurodevelopmental impairment and associated needs. Routine screening and assessment can ensure the timely identification of needs which are secondary to neurodevelopmental impairment and the subsequent provision of appropriate support, enabling early intervention prior to the involvement of criminal justice agencies, as well as responsive criminal justice interventions, alert to and able to address the underlying causes of offending behaviour, and to tailor any subsequent interventions appropriately. Screening should inform legal decision making, diverting young people where appropriate to evidence-based interventions and away from the youth justice system, towards more specialist support. Recent advances in assessment in the criminal justice system within the UK have begun to recognise these needs, including through the implementation of screening for neurodevelopment disorders within the secure estate in England and Wales (Offender Health Research Network, 2013). These reforms are described elsewhere in this book (please refer to Chapter 3 by Chitsabesan and Khan).

Whilst recognition of the possible relationship between offending behaviour and these underlying needs is key, recognition of need does not necessarily imply diagnosis of a disorder. Assessments should emphasise function and need rather than diagnosis, and should maintain a holistic rather than medical approach. Brief screening tools that can be utilised by non-clinicians to identify functional needs would support early identification of difficulties as well as a differentiation of those who are at higher risk and require more detailed assessment.

Identifying offenders with neurodevelopmental impairment is also essential in order to ensure a young person's capacity to engage in the legal process, and consequently to effectively defend themselves. Only by recognising and responding to the specific needs of young people with neurodevelopmental impairment can we counter experiences of neurodisability and criminalisation. However, even without the introduction of robust screening, an awareness of the disabling processes and practices leading to potential criminalisation gives sufficient impetus for generic reform. An awareness of the potential impact of neurodevelopmental impairment, even when it is not diagnosed in a young person, suggests a need for revised practices within the criminal justice system so as not to assume cognitive competence or understanding of procedures, and therefore to support better engagement and access to justice for all young people.

Whilst these suggestions pose considerable challenges in reforming criminal justice practices and place further pressures on a range of universal and targeted services for young people and their families, not to act is to be in breach of our duties of care and to continue to criminalise a highly vulnerable population of young people as a result of neurodevelopmental impairment.

BOX 5.1 Case Example

Background

John is a 17-year-old boy who was given a custodial sentence for aggravated burglary and with a previous history of theft and fighting. John lives with his mother and three younger siblings, and has a long history of behavioural difficulties. He had previously attended a specialist educational school for children with emotional and behavioural difficulties but frequently truanted with friends.

Assessment

John was assessed by a nurse using the Comprehensive Health Assessment Tool (England) soon after admission to custodial care. The neurodisability (TBI subsection) section of the CHAT identified that John had experienced three TBIs during his childhood; two were secondary to fighting and one occurred after an road traffic accident (RTA) when he was knocked off his bike at eight years. Further information was sought from his mother, and his medical records were also requested. John had experienced loss of consciousness on two occasions and was admitted to hospital after the RTA. On the TBI section of the CHAT, John reported some ongoing problems with his attention and memory, and his mother reported that John had difficulties controlling his anger and would often get into fights with other children.

Staff liaison identified that John had difficulties in engaging in education and particularly concentrating and remembering things. There were no physical or neurological symptoms noted during his physical assessment.

Formulation

John has experienced a TBI with loss of consciousness and ongoing post-concussion symptoms (moderate impairment). He was referred to the multidisciplinary team for further assessment. John was assessed using the Wechsler Intelligence Scale for Children (WISC) which showed he had uneven cognitive profile, while further neurocognitive assessments identified particular deficits in attention and working memory.

Management

A multidisciplinary approach was used to manage John's needs. A nurse discussed the impact of John's TBI with him and identified areas of functioning that John was particularly struggling with. Direct interventions with John included strategies for relaxation, anger management and tips to improve his memory. Information was passed to professionals working with John on his particular profile of impairment and the need to use specific strategies (short, clear information, visual prompts, reminders and support for organisational skills). His educational needs were reviewed and additional support provided within lessons. Information was included in his care plan and discussed with his general practitioner (primary care physician) and community youth offending team prior to discharge.

References

Anderson, V., Godfrey, C., Rosenfeld, J. V. and Catroppa, C. (2012). Predictors of cognitive function and recovery 10 years after traumatic brain injury in young children. *Pediatrics*, **129**(2), 254–261.

American Psychiatric Association. (2013). *Diagnostic and Statistical Manual of Mental Disorders*. 5th Edtion (text rev.). Washington, DC: APA.

Bailey, S., Shaw, J., Tarbuck, P., Law, H., Turner, O., Alam, F., McCartan, F., Seethapathy, V., and Thomas, R. (2008). *Health Needs Identification and Assessment within the Custodial Youth Justice System*. London: Youth Justice Board.

Baldry, E., Dowse, L. and Clarence, M. (2011). People with mental and cognitive disabilities: pathways into prison. Background Paper for National Legal Aid Conference Darwin 2011. Australia. The University of New South Wales.

Barkley, R. A. (2009). Deficient emotional self regulation is a core component of ADHD. *Journal of ADHD and Related Disorders*, **1**(2), 5–37.

Barnes, C. (1991). *Disabled People in Britain and Discrimination: A Case for Anti-Discrimination Legislation*. London: Hurst and Co.

Baumeister, A., Storch, E. and Geffken, G. (2008). Peer victimization in children with learning disabilities. *Child and Adolescent Social Work Journal*, **25**, 11–23.

Botting, N. and Conti-Ramsden, G. (2000). Social and behavioural difficulties in children with language impairment. *Child Language Teaching and Therapy*, **16**(2), 105–120

Bradley, R. H. and Corwyn, R. F. (2002). Socioeconomic status and child development. *Annual Review of Psychology*, **53**, 371–399.

British Psychological Society. (2001). *Learning Disability: Definitions and Contexts*. Leicester: British Psychological Society.

Burd, L., Selfridge, R., Klug, M. and Bakko, S. (2004). Fetal alcohol syndrome in the United States corrections system. *Addiction Biology*, **9**(2), 169–176.

Burd, L., Fast, D. K., Conry, J. and Williams, A. (2010). Fetal alcohol spectrum disorder as marker for increased risk of involvement with correction systems. *Journal of Psychiatry and Law*, **38**(4), 559–583.

Catroppa, C. and Anderson, V. (2009). Neurodevelopmental outcomes of pediatric traumatic brain injury. *Future Neurology*, **4**(6), 811–821.

Catroppa, C., Anderson, V. A., Morse, S. A., Haritou, F. and Rosenfeld, J. V. (2008). Outcome and predictors of functional recovery 5 years following pediatric traumatic brain injury. *Journal of Pediatric Psychology*, **33**, 707–718.

Chartrand, L. N. and Forbes-Chilibeck, E. M. (2003). The sentencing of offenders with fetal alcohol syndrome. *Health Law Journal*, **11**, 35–70.

Chitsabesan, P., Bailey, S., Williams, R., Kroll, L., Kenning, C. and Talbot, L. (2007). Learning disabilities and educational needs of juvenile offenders. *Journal of Children's Services*, **2**(4), 4–14.

Chitsabesan, P., Lennox, C., Williams, H., Tariq, O., Shaw, J. (2015). Traumatic brain injury in juvenile offenders: findings from the comprehensive health assessment tool study and the development of a specialist linkworker service. *Journal of Head Trauma Rehabilitation*, **30**(2), 106–115.

Conti-Ramsden, G. and Botting, N. (2004). Social difficulties and victimization in children with SLI at 11 years of age. *Journal of Speech, Language, and Hearing Research*, **47**, 145–161.

Davidson, R. J., Putnam, K. M. and Larson, C. L. (2000). Dysfunction in the neural circuitry of emotion regulation – a possible prelude to violence. *Science*, **289**, 591–594.

Dockrell, J., Lindsay, G., Palikara, O. and Cullen, M. A. (2007). *Raising the Achievements of Children and Young People with Specific Speech and Language Difficulties and other Special Educational Needs through School to Work and College*. London: Department for Education and Skills.

Dowse, L., Baldry, E. and Snoyman, P. (2009). Disabling criminology: conceptualising the intersections of critical disability studies and critical criminology for people with mental health and cognitive disabilities in the criminal justice system. *Australian Journal of Human Rights*, **15**(1), 29–46.

Fairchild, G., Passamonti, L., Hurford, G., Hagan, C. C., von dem Hagen, E. A. H., van Goozen, S. H. M., Goodyer, A. J. and Calder, A. J. (2011). Brain structure abnormalities in early onset and adolescent onset conduct disorder. *American Journal of Psychiatry*, **168**, 624–633.

Farrington, D. P. and Welsh, B. C. (2007). *Saving Children From a Life of Crime: Early Risk Factors and Effective Interventions*. Oxford: Oxford University Press.

Faul, M., Xu, L., Wald, M. M. and Coronado, V. G. (2010). *Traumatic Brain Injury in the United States: Emergency Department Visits, Hospitalizations and Deaths 2002–2006*. Atlanta, GA: Centres for Disease Control and Prevention, National Centre for Injury Prevention and Control.

Fay, T. B., Yeates, K. O., Wade, S. L., Drotar, D., Stancin, T. and Taylor, H. G. (2009). Predicting longitudinal patterns of functional deficits in children with traumatic brain injury. *Neuropsychology*, **23**, 271–282.

Fazel, S., Doll, H. and Langstrom, N. (2008). Mental disorders among adolescents in juvenile detention and correctional facilities: a systematic review and metaregression analysis of 25 surveys. *Journal of the American Academy of Child and Adolescent Psychiatry*, **47**, 1010–1019.

Ferguson, P. L., Pickelsimer, E. E., Corrigan, J. D., Bogner, J. A., Wald, M. (2012). Prevalence of traumatic brain injury among prisoners in South Carolina. *Journal of Head Trauma Rehabilitation*, **27**, E11–20.

Funahashi, S. (2001). Neuronal mechanisms of executive control by the prefrontal cortex. *Neuroscience Research*, **39**, 147–165.

Ganesalingam, K., Sanson, A., Anderson, V. and Yeates, K. O. (2007). Self-regulation as a mediator of the effects of childhood traumatic brain injury on social and behavioural functioning. *Journal of the International Neuropsychological Society*, **13**(12), 298–311.

Green, J. H. (2007). Fetal alcohol spectrum disorders: understanding the effects of prenatal alcohol exposure and supporting students. *Journal of School Health*, **77**(3), 103–108.

Greenbaum, R. L., Stevens, S. A., Nash, K., Koren, G., and Rovet, J. (2009). Social cognitive and emotion processing abilities of children with fetal alcohol spectrum disorders: a comparison with attention deficit hyperactivity disorder. *Alcohol Clinical and Experimental Research*, **33**(10), 1656–1670.

Hare, D. J. and Paine, C. (1997). Developing cognitive behavioural treatments for people with Asperger's syndrome. *Clinical Psychology Forum*, **110**, 5–8.

Harrington, R. and Bailey, S. (2005). *Mental Health Needs and Effectiveness of Provision for Young People in the Youth Justice System*. London: Youth Justice Board.

Hayes, S. (2002). Early intervention or early incarceration? using a screening test for intellectual disability in the criminal justice system. *Journal of Applied Research in Intellectual Disabilities*, **15**, 120–128.

Herrington, V. (2009). Assessing the prevalence of intellectual disability among young male prisoners. *Journal of Intellectual Disability Research*, **53**(5), 397–410.

Hughes, N. (2010). Models and approaches to family-focused policy and practice. *Social Policy and Society*, **9**(4), 527–532.

Hughes, N., Williams, H., Chitsabesan, P., Davies, R. and Mounce, L. (2012). *Nobody Made the Connection: The Prevalence of Neurodisability in Young People Who Offend*. London: Office of the Children's Commissioner for England.

Jolliffe, D. and Farrington, D. P. (2004). Empathy and offending: a systematic review and meta-analysis. *Aggression and Violent Behaviour*, **9**, 441–476.

Jolliffe, D. and Farrington, D. P. (2010). Individual differences and offending. In McLaughlin, E. and Newburn, T. Editors. *The SAGE Handbook of Criminological Theory* (pp. 40–56). London: Sage.

Kupersmidt, J. B., Burchinal, M. and Patterson, C. J. (1995). Developmental patterns of childhood peer relations as predictors of externalizing behavior problems. *Development and Psychopathology*, **7**, 825–843.

Kurowski, B. G., Taylor, H. G., Yeates, K. O., Walz, N. C., Stancin, T. and Wade, S. L. (2011). Caregiver ratings of long-term executive dysfunction and attention problems after early childhood traumatic brain injury: family functioning is important. *Physical Medicine and Rehabilitation*, **3**, 836–845.

Law, J., Reilly, S. and Snow, P. C. (2013). Child speech, language and communication need re-examined in a public health context: a new direction for the speech and language therapy profession. *International Journal of Language and Communication Disorders*, **48**(5), 486–496.

McKenzie, K., Matheson, E., Patrick, S., Paxton, D. and Murray, G. C. (2000). An evaluation of the impact of a one day training course on the knowledge of health, day care and social care staff working in learning disability services. *Journal of Learning Disabilities*, **4**(2), 153–156.

Meltzer, L. Editor. (2007). *Executive Function in Education: From Theory to Practice*. New York: Guilford Press.

Mishna, F. (2003). Learning disabilities and bullying: double jeopardy. *Journal of Learning Disabilities*, **36**, 336–347.

Morgan, A. B. and Lilienfeld, S. O. (2000). A meta-analytic review of the relation between antisocial behavior and neuropsychological measures of executive function. *Clinical Psychology Review*, **20**, 113–156.

Murphy, D. (2010). Extreme violence in a man with an autistic spectrum disorder: Assessment and treatment within high-security psychiatric care. *Journal of Forensic Psychiatry and Psychology*, **21**, 462–477.

National Crime Prevention. (1999). *Pathways to Prevention: Developmental and Early Intervention Approaches to Crime in Australia*. Canberra: National Crime Prevention, Attorney-General's Department.

National Institute for Health and Care Excellence. (2008). *Attention deficit hyperactivity disorder: diagnosis and management of ADHD in children, young people and adults*. NICE Clinical Guideline 72. London: NICE.

National Institute for Health and Care Excellence. (2011). *Autism: recognition, referral and diagnosis in children and young people on the autism spectrum*. NICE Clinical Guideline 128. London: NICE.

National Institute for Health and Care Excellence. (2013). *Antisocial behaviour and conduct disorders in children and young people: recognition, intervention and management*. NICE Clinical Guideline 158. London: NICE.

Offender Health Research Network. (2013). *The Comprehensive Health Assessment Tool (CHAT): Young People in the Secure Estate – Version 3*. Manchester: University of Manchester.

Ogilvie, J. M., Stewart, A. L., Chan, R. C. K. and Shum, D. H. K. (2011). Neuropsychological measures of executive function and antisocial behavior: a meta-analysis. *Criminology*, **49**, 1063–1107.

Patel, D. P., Greydanus, D. E., Omar, H. A. and Merrick, J. Editors. (2011). *Neurodevelopmental Disabilities: Clinical Care for Children and Young Adults*. New York: Springer.

Patterson, G. (1996). Some characteristics of a developmental theory for early onset delinquency. In Lenzenweger, M. and Haugaard, J. Editors. *Frontiers of Developmental Psychopathology* (pp. 81–124). New York: Oxford University Press.

Patterson, G. R., DeBaryshe, B. D. and Ramsey, E. (1989). A developmental perspective on antisocial behavior. *American Psychologist*, **44**, 329–335.

Pfiffner, L., Barkley, R. A. and DuPaul, G. J. (2006). Treatment of ADHD in school settings. In Barkley, R. A. Editor. *Attention Deficit Hyperactivity Disorder: A Handbook for Diagnosis and Treatment*. 3rd edition. New York: Guilford.

Prizent, B. and Wetherby, A. (1992). Toward an integrated view of early language and communication development and socioemotional development. *Topics in Language Disorders*, **10**, 11–16.

Ryan, N.P., Anderson, V., Godfrey, C., Eren, S., Rosema, S., Taylor, K. and Catroppa, C. (2013). Social communication mediates the relationship between emotion perception and externalizing behaviors in young adult survivors of pediatric traumatic brain injury. *International Journal of Developmental Neuroscience*, **31**, 811–819

Ryan, N. P., Anderson, V., Godfrey, C., Beauchamp, M. H., Coleman, L., Eren, S., Rosema, S., Taylor, K. and Catroppa, C. (2014). Predictors of very-long-term sociocognitive function after pediatric traumatic brain injury: evidence for the vulnerability of the immature 'social brain'. *Journal of Neurotrauma*, **31**, 649–657.

Schmidt, S. and Petermann, F. (2009). Developmental psychopathology: Attention Deficit Hyperactivity Disorder (ADHD), *BMC Psychiatry*, **9**, 58.

Sesma, H. W., Slomine, B. S., Ding, R. and McCarthy, M. L. (2008). Children's Health After Trauma (CHAT) study group. Executive functioning in the first year after pediatric traumatic brain injury. *Pediatrics*, **121**, E1686–1695.

Snow, P. C. and Powell, M. B. (2005). What's the story? An exploration of narrative language abilities in male juvenile offenders. *Psychology, Crime and Law*, **11**(3), 239–253.

Snow, P. C. and Powell, M. B. (2011). Oral language competence in incarcerated young offenders: links with offending severity. *International Journal of Speech-Language Pathology*, **13**(6), 480–489.

Snow, P. and Powell, M. (2012). Youth (in)justice: oral language competence in early life and risk for engagement in antisocial behaviour in adolescence. *Australian Institute of Criminology, Trends and Issues in Crime and Criminal Justice, No. 435* (April), 421–444.

Stevenson, M. (2006). *Young People and Offending: Education, Youth Justice and Social Care Inclusion*. London: Williams.

Talbot, J. (2010). Prisoner' voices: experience of the criminal justice system by prisoners with learning disabilities. *Tizard Learning Disability Review*, **15**, 33–41.

Tonks, J., Slater, A., Frampton, I., Wall, S. E., Yates, P. and Williams, W. H. (2009). The development of emotion and empathy skills after childhood brain injury. *Developmental Medicine and Child Neurology*, **51**, 8–16.

Tonks, J., Yates, P., Frampton, I., Williams, W. H., Harris, D. and Slater, A. (2011). Resilience and the mediating effects of executive dysfunction after childhood brain injury: a comparison between children aged 9–15 years with brain injury and non-injured controls. *Brain Injury*, **25**, 870–881.

Wade, S. L., Taylor, H. G., Drotar, D., Stancin, T., Yeates, K. O. and Minich, N. M. (2003). Parent-adolescent interactions after traumatic brain injury: their relationship to family adaptation and adolescent adjustment. *Journal of Head Trauma Rehabilitation*, **18**, 164–176.

Wade, S. L., Cassedy, A., Walz, N. C., Taylor, H. G., Stancin, T. and Yeates, K. O. (2011). The relationship of parental warm responsiveness and negativity to emerging behavior problems following traumatic brain injury in young children. *Developmental Psychology*, **47**, 119–133.

Williams, H. W., Giray, C., Mewse, A. J., Tonks, J. and Burgess, C. N. W. (2010). Self-reported traumatic brain injury in male young offenders: a risk factor for re-offending, poor mental health and violence? *Neuropsychological Rehabilitation*, **20**(6), 801–812.

Williams, W. H. (2013). *Repairing Shattered Lives: Brain Injury and Its Implications for Criminal Justice*. London: Transition to Adulthood Alliance.

Wishart, J. G., Cebula, K. R., Willis, D. S. and Pitcairn, T. K. (2007). Understanding of facial expressions of emotion by children with intellectual disabilities of differing etiology. *Journal of Intellectual Disability Research*, **51**, 551–563.

Yeates, K. O., Bigler, E. D., Dennis, M., Gerhardt, C. A., Rubin, K. H., Stancin, T., Taylor, H. G. and Vannatta, K. (2007). Social outcomes in childhood brain disorder: a heuristic integration of social neuroscience and developmental psychology. *Psychological Bulletin*, **133**, 535–556.

Yeates, K. O., Taylor, H. G., Walz, N. C., Stancin, T. and Wade, S. L. (2010). The family environment as a moderator of psychosocial outcomes following traumatic brain injury in young children. *Neuropsychology*, **24**, 345–356.

Youth Justice Board. (2006). *Barriers to Engagement in Education, Training and Employment*. London: Youth Justice Board.

Serious Offences
Origins and Nature of Individual Violence

Charlotte Lennox and Rajan Nathan

The twentieth century will be remembered as a century marked by violence.
Nelson Mandela

The World Health Organisation states that violence ranks as the third leading cause of death in Europe among people aged 15–29 years after road traffic injuries and suicide, accounting for nearly 15,000 deaths in 2004. For each death as a result of violence there are an additional 20–40 hospital admissions as a result of non-fatal violence, and it ranks as the eighth leading cause of the burden of disease in the world, with 766,000 disability-adjusted life-years (DALYs) lost. About 11% of all UK hospital admissions result from violent assaults among young people, against a European average of 8% (World Health Organisation, 2010). Violence therefore results in large direct and indirect costs borne by health, criminal justice and social services.

Individual violence is represented in statistics of violent crime, including: murder, robbery, assault and sexual offences. Although violence associated with organised crime groups and gangs makes some contribution to these statistics, the overwhelming majority of violent crime offences are individual offences. Young people involved in committing serious individual violence tend to have a number of shared risk factors, including dispositional (e.g. demographic and personality), historical (e.g. history of violence and family maladjustment), contextual (e.g. negative peer relations and poor parental management) and individual/clinical factors (e.g. substance misuse, mental disorder, impulsivity and genetic factors). The origins, nature and treatment of individual violence are thought to be different to group violence.

In 2014–2015 in England and Wales there were 87,160 proven offences committed by 10- to 17-year-olds. Of these 24% were violent offences, a 4% increase over 2010 (Youth Justice Board, 2016). Preventing violence is one of the most important global concerns, but there is no single factor that explains why some

people behave violently towards others or why violence is more prevalent in some communities than in others. Violence is the result of a complex interaction of factors.

The purpose of this chapter is to highlight recent developments and the aims are twofold: (1) to describe the aetiological mechanisms of antisocial behaviour which can lead to individual violence with a primary focus on neurobiology and neuropsychology and (2) to discuss the implications for prevention and treatment.

Developmental Pathways to Violence

Since the 1990s, there have been numerous well-designed prospective longitudinal birth-cohort studies that have mapped the trajectories of adolescent violence and identified risk factors for future violence. Within the academic literature various theories have been developed in an attempt to explain the cause and continuation of violence. This chapter will briefly describe a few of the main theories.

The seminal work by Terrie Moffitt on a developmental taxonomy of antisocial behaviour proposed two distinct prototypes: the life-course-persistent versus the adolescence-limited offender. This theory suggests that for life-course-persistent offenders' antisocial behaviour is the result of neuro-development deficits in childhood (cognitive deficits, difficult temperament and hyperactivity) and a high-risk social environment (inadequate parenting, disrupted attachment and poverty). Life-course-persistent offenders are few in number and pathological in nature. In contrast, antisocial behaviour in the adolescence-limited offenders is the result of social processes in adolescence, which desist in young adulthood. Adolescence-limited offending occurs during puberty, as young people find the behaviour of other adolescence-limited offenders appealing and mimic it in order to express autonomy from parents and acquire affiliation with peers (Moffitt, 2003).

BOX 6.1 Mark's Story

Mark is a 17-year-old man who is in an institution for young offenders having been charged with armed robbery and wounding. It is alleged that he threatened a sales assistant in a garage with a knife and demanded money. When the assistant, who was in the customer area, tried to return to the secure 'staff only' area, Mark lunged with the knife and stabbed the assistant in the leg. It is thought that he may have continued the attack had a car not driven onto the forecourt. An assessment following his detention in custody revealed a history of problems from an early age. Aged seven years, he was briefly accommodated in care when it was reported by neighbours that he had been left on his own at home. His mother was known to the drug services for opiate abuse and her relationship with Mark's father only lasted a matter of weeks. There was continued social service involvement and in the records it is noted that teachers at primary school reported that Mark was difficult to manage within the classroom and these problems were evident soon after he started there. He was disruptive and distractible, and he did not get on well with the other children. Problems continued into secondary school and at the age of 13 he was excluded for aggression towards staff. Review of the medical records revealed that he sustained a head injury when he was eight years old having run into the path of a car. When he was 11 years old he was referred to child mental health services and a provisional diagnosis of Attention Deficit Hyperactivity Disorder (ADHD) was made. Further assessment was recommended but he and his mother did not attend appointments. He has been arrested before in relation to offences of theft, criminal damage and assault.

BOX 6.2 Sean's Story

Sean, who is 16, was assessed by the Youth Offending Team in relation to an assault offence. He was with a group of friends on a shopping parade when a confrontation occurred between one of his friends and a member of a group of teenagers from a nearby estate. Sean intervened and, egged on by his friends, he punched the other boy to the head. In the course of the assessment by the Youth Offending Team, Sean and his parents were interviewed. His parents reported that there were some problems at school from about the age of 12. He was prone to cheekiness and some truancy was reported. He was well liked within his group which included some boys who had also been reported for truancy and disruptiveness in school. Sean's father was often away from home with work during the week. His mother commented that she had noticed that since around the time he started secondary school (age 11 years) she found he became more challenging of her authority. He had not been convicted of any offences before, but he had been cautioned in relation to an act of vandalism when he was 14 years of age.

The case examples of Mark (Box 6.1) and Sean (Box 6.2) clearly highlight these distinct prototypes and the associated factors.

This history illustrates the role of peer influences at an age when the youngster is trying to establish autonomy from his/her parents. Moffitt's taxonomy has been very influential and was integrated into the DSM-IV diagnosis for conduct disorder, which has been retained in DSM-V. Childhood-onset conduct disorder is defined by the presence of symptoms before the age of ten years. Poor peer and family relationships are present, and these problems tend to persist through adolescence into adulthood. These children are more likely to develop adult Antisocial Personality Disorder (ASPD) than individuals with adolescent-onset conduct disorder. Adolescent-onset is defined by the absence of symptoms before the age of ten years. These individuals tend to be less

aggressive and have more normative peer relationships. They often display conduct behaviours in the company of a peer group engaged in these behaviours, such as a gang. Antisocial and offending behaviour tends to reduce with age and will have stopped by late adolescence/early adulthood. The prognosis for adolescent-onset is much better than for a person with the childhood-onset (Barker et al., 2010). While influential, Moffitt's taxonomy has come under recent criticism, and Skardhamar (2009) presents a critical review of the taxonomic theory and its empirical evidence.

A developmental pathway approach provides a useful framework both to explore the causal explanations of psychopathology (Drabick and Kendall, 2010) and to delineate the trajectories to particular types of psychopathology (Tremblay, 2010). The results of prospective longitudinal studies of representative community samples have revealed the developmental continuity of the antisocial groups where age of onset is critical. Loeber (1985) suggested that, in predicting future antisocial behaviour, we should look not only at the age of onset in general but at the age of onset of specific sets of behaviours. He proposed an 'overt' pathway of escalating aggression from minor to more serious aggression, distinguished from a 'covert' pathway involving non-confrontational antisocial behaviour, such as theft and fraud. Overt behaviour is confrontational in nature and involves direct contact with another for the purpose of controlling one's social environment. This category includes behaviours such as bullying, fighting, arguing, demand for attention, disobedience at home and school, impulsivity, stubbornness, temper tantrums and threats. Covert behaviour, on the other hand, is concealed in nature and consists of behaviours such as stealing, lying, truancy, fire setting, substance use, antisocial peer selection and running away from home. Serious overt antisocial behaviour gradually decreases as the child matures and, therefore, is temporary for most youths. However, covert antisocial behaviour gradually increases.

The identification of callous-unemotional traits has also been influential in the development of anti-social behaviour and violence. Callous-unemotional traits in adolescence have been found to be a strong predictor of antisocial behaviour (McMahon et al., 2010), involving a lack of guilt, absence of empathy and a callous use of others. Callous-unemotional traits are prominent in most conceptualisations of psychopathy in adults, and callous-unemotional traits in children may be important for the development of psychopathy. Current models of psychopathy suggest a four-factor model, including interpersonal, affective, lifestyle and antisocial dimensions. Callous-unemotional traits are best reflected within the affective domain on psychopathy.

A number of theories of the developmental pathways to violence exist that are supported by empirical evidence and that are relevant to understanding the pathways to serious outcomes. To date it cannot be said that any one is more valid, and they are not mutually exclusive, but they look at heterogeneity of pathways to antisocial behaviour/violence from different perspectives. To review the evidence of all the types is not possible within the constraints of this chapter, but the authors would refer readers to the following (Frick and Viding, 2009; Moffitt, 2009;

Loeber and Burke, 2011; Frick, 2012). Also most clinicians recognise that children do not often fall neatly into the prototypes suggested by research. Therefore, these descriptions serve as hypotheses around which to organise assessment.

The developmental pathway analysis demonstrates that there are complex interactions over time between biological and environmental correlates of violence. It should also be recognised that violence is not a unitary phenomenon. An influential dichotomy distinguishes violence involving an impulsive emotional reaction (reactive violence) from violence for which there is premeditation (instrumental or proactive violence) (Babcock et al., 2014). There is evidence to suggest that callous-unemotional traits are differentially related to proactive and reactive aggression. Youth with callous-unemotional traits tend to show both types of aggression, whereas antisocial youth without callous-unemotional traits show largely reactive aggression. The case examples of Sean and Mark illustrate the difference between instrumental and reactive violence. The violent act referred to in Sean's case example is an example of reactive violence, whereas the index offence in Mark's case has an instrumental motivation. Mark's history also reveals some of the typical features of the life-course persistent pathway, including early onset, manifestations of neuropsychological variation (in this case in the form of hyperactivity) and a high-risk social environment.

The biological and environmental factors responsible for the development and maintenance of antisocial behaviour and violence are not well understood. Studies in children and adolescents indicate that several family background variables (e.g. parental rejection, inconsistent discipline and abuse) are associated with the development of conduct disorder and callous-unemotional traits. The literature also suggests that children with conduct disorder, particularly those with a history of repeated violent behaviour, exhibit a range of deficits on neuropsychological tests, indicating a role for neurobiological factors, particularly executive (prefrontal) and temporolimbic (amygdala) dysfunction, in the aetiology of conduct disorder and callous-unemotional traits. Research has also shown children with conduct disorder to have reduced arousal levels, including reduced cortisol levels and high testosterone levels. The following sections will provide an overview of just some of the neurobiology and neuropsychology factors, beginning with evidence for deficit in specific brain regions.

Neurobiological Factors

Understanding behaviour, particularly violent behaviour, is complex, and is influenced by complex stimuli and circumstances. Understanding how the brain is involved in violent behaviour is also complex and involves many different structures. For example, the limbic system has been particularly associated with both emotion and aggressive behaviour. The limbic system was recognised as being composed of anatomically discrete structures, such as the amygdala, hippocampus and orbital frontal cortex. Recently, the use of the term 'limbic system' has fallen out of favour, not because the structures in this region are not involved in emotion but because, given the diversity of emotions, there is no reason to think that only one system, rather than several, is involved. Although there is evidence that certain brain regions are involved in violent behaviour, they are better understood as a complex integrated model, than as distinct regions.

Siever (2008: 431) describes an integrated model of aggression and violence, whereby an emotional stimulus, triggered by an aggressive event, will initially be processed by sensory processing centres, that is, auditory and visual. Sensory deficits such as hearing or visual impairment, as well as sensory distortions caused by drugs or alcohol, may result in distorted sensory impressions which can increase the likelihood of events being perceived as threatening. After sensory processing, the assessment of the stimulus will occur in early social information processing centres in visual and auditory integration areas and, finally, in higher association regions, including the prefrontal, temporal and parietal cortices. These stages can be influenced by cultural and social factors that might change the perception of the event, may become distorted by cognitive impairment deficits leading to a tendency to paranoid ideation and/or may be biased by negative schema that might be a function of a developmental stress/ trauma leading to diminished trust. Ultimately, processing of these stimuli in relation to past emotional conditioning encoded in the amygdala and related limbic regions will trigger the 'drive' to an aggressive action, while the orbital frontal cortex and anterior cingulate gyrus will provide 'top-down' modulation of these emotional responses and behaviours and serve to suppress behaviours with negative consequences.

Neurocircuitry

Left Cerebral Hemisphere

The brain is divided into two hemispheres, the left and right. Each hemisphere has an outer layer of grey matter, the cerebral cortex, supported by an inner layer of white matter. The hemispheres are linked by the corpus callosum. Broad generalisations have been made about the function or lateralisation of the right and left sides of the brain. The best evidence of lateralisation is language; both of the major areas involved in language skills, Broca's area and Wernicke's area, are in the left hemisphere.

There is substantial research showing that children displaying antisocial behaviour and conduct disorder have deficits in verbal skills in comparison to healthy controls (Teichner et al., 2000; see Lynam and Henry, 2001 for a review). Moreover, there is evidence to suggest a specific relationship between childhood aggression and impaired language skills (Séguin et al., 2009). Several theorists have described ways in which verbal neuropsychological deficits might be linked to antisocial behaviour and violence. The inhibition of aggression responding to social problems may be, in part, dependent on the development of adaptive skills required to negotiate interpersonal interactions, such as verbal skills. For example, deficits in verbal skills may preclude the ability to fully perceive/interpret the emotions expressed by others (victims). These deficits might also limit their response options in threatening or ambiguous social situations, predisposing them to quick physical reactions rather than more laborious verbal responses.

Cortex

The dorsolateral prefrontal cortex is located in the superior, lateral portion of the prefrontal area of the brain. The dorsolateral prefrontal cortex is responsible for motor planning, organisation and regulation. It plays an important role in the integration of sensory and mnemonic information. It is also involved in working memory. The dorsolateral prefrontal cortex is not exclusively responsible for the executive functions, and is interconnected with the cortical association areas and the orbitofrontal cortex. Executive function is broadly described as the abilities required to achieve and maintain a problem-solving set, and include functions such as planning, organisational skills, selective attention and inhibitory control.

Executive dysfunction may be particularly related to impulsivity and antisocial behaviour (Moffitt and Henry, 1991; Morgan and Lilienfeld, 2000), rather than premeditated violence and aggression.

Evidence that prefrontal brain regions were important in aggression was first recognised by brain lesions to this area resulting in notable disinhibited aggressive behaviour. An example often cited is the case of Phineas Gage, a railroad worker who was injured in an accident by a large iron rod that was driven through his skull damaging his orbitofrontal cortex. Following the injury Gage became angry and irritable. Studies have also shown that patients with ventromedial prefrontal cortex and orbitofrontal cortex injuries exhibit severe disruption in emotion and are more likely to use physical intimidation and threats in conflict situations (Siever, 2008: 432).

Despite a strong theoretical base for hypothesising prefrontal dysfunction a review of executive function deficits in antisocial children stated that the findings across studies were inconsistent although, whilst neuropsychological deficits do not necessarily lead to violent behaviour, it appears that many children who exhibit such behaviour suffer from certain deficits in the brain (Teichner and Golden, 2000). A meta-analysis of executive dysfunction and antisocial behaviour found that overall effect sizes for conduct disorder were small to medium (Cohen's d = 0.40; Morgan and Lilienfeld, 2000, see Lynam and Henry, 2001 for a review of the empirical evidence for executive dysfunction and Ishikawa and Raine, 2003 for a review of prefrontal deficits). Children exhibiting high levels of aggressive behaviour have been found to experience difficulties with sequential and recall memory, the ability to effectively use feedback to correct responses and cognitive perseveration. Recent studies looking at brain structure abnormalities in early-onset and adolescent-onset conduct disorder have failed to find significant differences, suggesting that brain structural abnormalities may contribute to the emergence of both onset types (Fairchild et al., 2009; Fairchild et al., 2011), thus supporting Skardhamar's (2009) critical review of Moffitt's taxonomic theory.

Although research has linked executive functioning and social information processing deficits to aggressive behaviour, relatively little attention has been focused on deficits between the typologies of reactive and proactive aggression. There is however a growing body of evidence to suggest that executive functioning deficits may be specifically related to reactive, rather than proactive, aggression (Ellis et al., 2009).

While executive dysfunction as measured by traditional neuropsychological tests suggests prefrontal dysfunction, executive function may also involve non-frontal brain regions; therefore, prefrontal dysfunction cannot necessarily be determined by poor performance on neuropsychological tests alone (Ishikawa and Raine, 2003). It may also be that executive function deficits associated with conduct disorder may be due to comorbid ADHD.

Brain imaging studies make it possible to examine brain structure and function directly. However, to date there have been very few imaging studies of children with conduct disorder (see Vloet et al., 2008 for a review). Recent developments (Rubia et al., 2010) suggest that inferior prefrontal under-activation appears to be disorder-specific, a neurofunctional biomarker for ADHD and not conduct disorder. There is preliminary evidence of an association in adolescents between conduct disorder and microstructural changes of the uncinate fasciculus which connects the amygdala and the frontal lobe (Sarkar et al., 2013).

The evidence for prefrontal dysfunction in antisocial children is mixed. However, there are a number of theorists that have described ways in which dysfunction might be linked to antisocial behaviour and violence. Of those focusing on the prefrontal cortex, the most prominent are the somatic marker hypothesis (Damasio, 1996) and the response modulation deficit hypothesis (see Newman, 1998 for a review).

The somatic marker hypothesis suggests that damage to the ventromedial cortex results in a failure to mark experiences as good or bad, and consequently there is no mechanism for learning to avoid aversive situations. This model receives some support from studies of acquired psychopathy, where subjects show an attenuated autonomic response to aversive social stimuli. Research has also shown that the amygdala, which is interconnected with the orbitofrontal and ventromedial prefrontal, is implicated. The response modulation deficit hypothesis also focuses on the ventromedial prefrontal cortex and accounts for risk-taking behaviour and failure to learn from experience seen in criminals with psychopathic personality performing laboratory-based tasks of passive-avoidance learning. Some support for the response modulation deficit hypothesis comes from studies which demonstrate children with marked callous-unemotional traits show insensitivity to punishment cues on gambling tasks.

The Amygdala

There is substantial evidence of a link between orbito-frontal cortex or amygdala dysfunction and deficits in emotional information processing by children and young people with antisocial behaviour. Studies have shown that they have social cognitive deficits, poor processing of punishment information, poor emotional memory (e.g. Dolan and Fullam, 2010), insensitivity to punishment cues, deficits in processing cues of fear (e.g. Fairchild et al., 2008) and distress and emotional words. Research has also investigated facial expression recognition in children with antisocial behaviour; in particular studies have shown that children with callous-unemotional traits have difficulties in recognising fearful and sad expressions (e.g. Blair et al., 2001). More recently, imaging studies have shown differential amygdala activity to preattentively presented fear in boys with conduct problems grouped by callous-unemotional traits, with high callous-unemotional traits associated with lower amygdala reactivity (Viding et al., 2012). However studies (e.g. Passamonti et al., 2010) have failed to find differences in facial expression recognition in early- versus late-onset conduct disorder.

Recently functional magnetic resonance imaging studies have confirmed amygdala dysfunction (e.g. Huebner et al., 2008). Sterzer et al. (2005) demonstrated a negative relationship between aggressive behaviour and the responsiveness of the left amygdala to strong negative affective pictures. Jones et al. (2009) found reduced right-sided amygdala activation to fearful expressions in children with aggressive conduct problems and callous-unemotional traits.

Blair (2005) proposed the Integrated Emotional System (IES), suggesting adolescents with callous-unemotional traits have diminished ability to form stimulus–punishment associations. The ability to form associations between moral transgressions and others' distress is vital for moral socialisation. Individuals with psychopathic traits find the distress cues in others less aversive and therefore are less likely to learn to avoid actions that bring about a negative response. Socialisation by punishment also relies on an ability to form stimulus–punishment associations.

Genetic Factors

As well as imaging studies, over the last decade, genetic studies have been vital in the advancement of our understanding of the origins of violence. Investigating biological risk factors may help to explain individual differences in predisposition to violence and may also highlight risk factors previously believed to have social or environmental origins to actually reflect a genetic vulnerability. Twin and adoption studies are important as they can reveal the relative importance of genetic and environmental factors, but also develop understanding of the aetiological differences between sub-groups of individuals (see Viding et al., 2008 for a review).

There have been numerous twin studies showing individual differences in antisocial behaviour and callous-unemotional traits are heritable. In a meta-analysis of 51 studies Rhee and Waldman (2002) reported that antisocial behaviour had a genetic influence, with 41% of variance being the result of genetic factors, 16% attributable to shared environmental factors and 43% to non-shared environmental factors. There is a growing evidence base from the UK focusing on genetic factors and the aetiology of antisocial behaviour and callous-unemotional traits. This UK research utilises The Twins Early Development Study, a birth record–based representative sample of twins born in the UK between 1994 and 1996. The study included teacher assessments of callous-unemotional as well as antisocial behaviour for twins. Viding et al. (2005) studied 3,687 twin pairs and found that extreme levels of callous-unemotional traits had a strong genetic influence (67% of variation). The authors then examined the heritability of extreme antisocial behaviour with the addition of callous-unemotional traits and again found a strong genetic influence (81% of variation) and no influence of shared environment. By comparison, children with low levels of callous-unemotional traits showed moderate genetic (30% of variation) and shared environmental influence. The authors replicated the finding of different heritability magnitudes in high and low levels of callous-unemotional traits using nine-year teacher data and the difference in heritability held even after hyperactivity was controlled for (Viding et al., 2008: 2520).

As mentioned previously, violence is the result of a complex interaction of factors, while antisocial behaviour and callous-unemotional traits clearly have a genetic influence and given that genetic effects can influence the likelihood of environmental risk, so can environmental risks influence genetic factors. The study of gene–environment interaction can further our understanding of the origins and nature of antisocial behaviour and violence. Gene–environment interaction research attempts to identify genetic sensitivity or susceptibility to environments, so that only children with certain genotypes will develop an antisocial outcome after exposure to environmental risk. For example Tuvblad et al. (2006) looked at the importance of socio-economic status on a sample of 1,133 pairs of twins aged 16–17 years from Sweden. They found that genetic influences on antisocial behaviour were more important in adolescents from high socio-economic environments, whereas shared environment was more important in low socio-economic groups. They suggest that different intervention policies should be considered in different socio-economic areas, that is, individually based interventions in high socio-economic areas and community level interventions for low socio-economic areas (see Viding et al., 2008: 2523) for a review of gene–environment interplay).

The next step for research is to identify specific/candidate genes that are located in specific brain regions and associated with violent behaviour. There is emerging evidence to suggest that a number of candidate genes in the serotoninergic system may be associated with antisocial and violent behaviour, in particular monoamine oxidase-A (MAO-A) and serotonin transporter polymorphism (5HTT) (Caspi et al., 2008). Caspi et al. (2002) examined whether antisocial behaviour could be predicted by an interaction between MAO-A and maltreatment. A birth cohort of 1,037 children was assessed from ages 3 to 26 years. They found a significant gene–environment interaction showing that the effect of childhood maltreatment on antisocial behaviour was significantly weaker among males with high MAO-A activity than males with low MAO-A activity. For adult violent conviction, maltreated males with the low MAO-A activity genotype were more likely than non-maltreated with this genotype to be convicted of a violent crime by a significant odds ratio of 9.8 (95% CI 3.1–31.1). In comparison, maltreatment was not significant for violence in males with high MAO-A activity (see Craig, 2007, for a review of MAO-A as a candidate gene for antisocial behaviour). The interaction between childhood abuse and MAO-A activity has been replicated recently in another longitudinal prospective study in which a representative community sample was followed up from birth to age 30 (Fergusson et al.,

2011). Individuals with low MAO-A activity who had experienced abuse were more likely to display adolescent conduct disorder and violence between the ages of 16 and 30. More recently Viding et al. (2010) used teacher ratings at age seven to screen 8,374 twins with DNA samples that were high versus low on both antisocial behaviour and callous-unemotional traits. They conducted a genome-wide association scan to identify the most associated single-nucleotide polymorphisms. While none of the associations reached genome-wide statistical significance, they did find that within the 'top-30' ranked associations included single-nucleotide polymorphisms near several neurodevelopmental genes, such as ROB02. This list of single-nucleotide polymorphisms is potentially associated with the aetiology of callous-unemotional traits and therefore further research is needed to verify and replicate the study on a larger scale. A note of caution in this area of research is introduced by a recent systematic review which did not find strong associations between any of a range of previously identified polymorphisms and aggression (Vassos et al., 2014). This may be a reflection of the difficulty of trying to uncover the potentially small effects of specific polymorphisms on complex heterogeneous phenotypes.

Treatment

The research reviewed above suggests that there may be particular sub-groups of young people who are at increased risk of serious violence and for whom early intervention is likely to be vital. Antisocial and violent behaviour, conduct disorder and callous-unemotional traits are associated with high personal and societal costs. Not only is there a substantial risk for persistence into adult life, they are associated with relationship problems with parents, teachers and peers, poor academic performance and poor self-esteem. In later life such behaviours contribute to parenting problems, unemployment, relationship breakdowns, increased risk for suicide and the development of substance misuse problems. There are also huge costs to society associated with such crimes; therefore, effective interventions would likely have both social and economic benefits.

Although there is a growing evidence base in this area, researchers are still attempting to identify the aetiology of serious violence and to understand individual differences in predisposition to violence. Such understandings are needed to establish interventions that effectively reduce aggressive behaviour.

Rehabilitation programmes that target underlying mechanisms of violence are yet to be developed. Prevention and intervention programmes that address the needs of impulsive antisocial behaviour are more widely available than for callous-unemotional traits. Behavioural parent training is the most extensively studied treatment for younger children's conduct problems, and there is considerable empirical support for its effectiveness (see Scott, 2008 for a review). For older children and adolescents multisystemic therapy is the best developed. Multisystemic therapy is an intensive, family-focused and community-based treatment programme based on nine treatment principles. Therapy is closely controlled, with weekly monitoring of progress. Clinicians take on only four to six cases at a time, since the work is intensive; there is close attention to quality control by weekly supervision along prescribed lines; and parents and adolescents fill in weekly questionnaires on whether they have been receiving therapy as planned. Therapy is given for three months and then stopped. There is now a body of evidence demonstrating the efficacy of multisystemic therapy (Henggeler, 2011).

There are only a few intervention programmes available for adults with ASPD and/or psychopathy and those that have been empirically tested have generally been limited (Dolan et al., 2010; Tarrier et al., 2010). However, Salekin's (2002) meta-analytic review suggests that there may be evidence of short-term effects using cognitive-behavioural techniques and interventions that specifically address perceptions of the self and the world, cognitive processes and core belief systems. The National Institute for Health and Care Excellence (NICE) reviewed all available high-quality evidence for the treatment of people with ASPD and as a result recommended group-based cognitive and behavioural interventions which, for those who have a history of offending behaviour, focus on reducing re-offending and antisocial behaviour (NICE, 2009).

Within the adult literature there is a perception of psychopathy and personality traits as 'untreatable'. Within child and adolescent research the belief is that there is scope for changing and modifying behaviour, that the brain may be more malleable and at its greatest potential for change in the early years of life; thus there may be an opportunity for interventions that limit the effects of genes that give rise to vulnerabilities for antisocial behaviour and violence.

Most clinicians view callous-unemotional and psychopathic traits in adolescents as potentially treatable, and there is some evidence to suggest that the identification of psychopathic traits in young people has many benefits, including the identification of high-risk offenders, reducing misclassifications and improving and optimising treatment planning. Caldwell et al. (2007) found that psychopathy scores did not predict poor treatment response, and that youths with psychopathic features showed significant response to treatment. Hawes and Dabbs (2005) aimed to examine the impact of callous-unemotional traits on treatment outcomes and processes in a ten-week behavioural parent-training intervention with children with conduct problems. Children with high callous-unemotional traits were less responsive to discipline with timeout than children without callous-unemotional traits and reacted to this discipline with less effect, whereas the effectiveness of reward strategies, such as descriptive praise, was not dependent on callous-unemotional traits. Therefore, for children with callous-unemotional traits problems may be reduced by teaching parents to use rewards, rather than punishment, to guide the child's behaviour. Both studies are methodologically flawed as they did not use a randomised treatment design. There still remains the need for well-controlled studies of treatment process and outcomes. A recent review of family-based interventions for conduct disorder found evidence that social-learning-based parent training can lead to durable positive change in callous-unemotional traits (Hawes et al., 2014).

Gene–environment interaction studies suggest that intervening to eliminate specific environmental factors, such as maltreatment, that interact with specific genes to increase risk for antisocial behaviour, would protect genetically vulnerable children from the consequences of the environmental factor. However, the alternative side to gene–environment interaction studies would be to suggest some form of gene therapy for violence. Common gene variants more than likely have multiple functions, some of which are desirable, others not. Therefore, a candidate gene may have many functions over and above increasing risk for a disease or disorder. Also, genes interact in a very complex system, with environmental risk factors; therefore, removing the effects of one gene via gene therapy is unlikely to be effective (Viding and Larsson, 2007).

Conclusions

We are still far from fully understanding the origins and nature of individual violence and yet individual violence inflicts high costs on health, criminal justice and social services and particularly for the victims and individuals directly involved. A number of developmental pathways to violence have been described but, based on current evidence, it cannot be said that any one is more valid than another. They are not mutually exclusive, but look at heterogeneity of pathways to antisocial behaviour/violence from different perspectives. Young people do not tend to fall neatly into the prototypes suggested by research, and therefore, such descriptions serve as hypotheses around which to organise assessment. Equally, our knowledge of biological and environmental origins of individual violence is not well understood. From current evidence, it appears that aggression and violence involve distributed processes within the brain and that a vast number of brain regions, genes and neurochemicals are involved.

Given the complexity of aggression and violence, that is, type, frequency, context, there cannot be one single origin for individual violence; neither can all the factors highlighted earlier be clearly separated from each other. However, research should still continue to highlight the specific neurobiological factors involved and how they interact, since this offers greater understanding of the relationship between the brain and individual violence and also can identify targeted interventions. Established and emerging treatment programmes should be robustly evaluated to develop an evidence base of 'what works', for whom, when and how.

References

Babcock, J. C., Tharp, A. L. T., Sharp, C. et al. (2014). Similarities and differences in impulsive/premeditated and reactive/proactive bimodal classifications of aggression. *Aggression and Violent Behavior*, **19**(3), 251–262.

Barker, E., Oliver, B. and Maughan, B. (2010). Co-occurring problems of early onset persistent, childhood limited and adolescent onset conduct problem youth. *Journal of Child Psychology and Psychiatry*, **51**, 1217–1226.

Blair, R. J. R. (2005). Applying a cognitive neuroscience perspective to the disorder of psychopathy. *Developmental Psychopathology*, **17**, 865–891.

Blair, R. J. R., Colledge, E., Murray, L. and Mitchell, D. G. (2001). A selective impairment in the processing of sad and fearful expressions in children with psychopathic tendencies. *Journal of Abnormal Child Psychology*, **29**, 491–498.

Caldwell, M. F., McCormick, D. J., Umstead, D. and Van Rybroek, G. J. (2007). Evidence of treatment progress and therapeutic outcomes among adolescents with psychopathic features. *Criminal Justice and Behavior*, **34**, 573–587.

Caspi, A., McClay, J., Moffitt, T. E. et al. (2002). Role of genotype in the cycle of violence in maltreated children. *Science*, **297**, 851–854.

Caspi, A., Langley, K., Milne, B. et al. (2008). A replicated molecular genetic basis for subtyping antisocial behavior in children with attention-deficit/hyperactivity disorder. *Archives of General Psychiatry*, **65**(2), 203–210.

Craig, I. W. (2007). The importance of stress and genetic variation in human aggression. *BioEssays*, **29**, 22–236.

Damasio, A. (1996). The somatic marker hypothesis and the possible functions of the prefrontal cortex. *Philosophical Transactions of the Royal Society: Biological Sciences*, **351**, 1413–1420.

Dolan, M. and Fullam, R. (2010). Emotional memory and psychopathic traits in conduct disordered adolescents. *Personality and Individual Differences*, **48**, 327–331.

Dolan, M., Lennox, C., Hayes, A. et al. (2010). An evaluation of Enhanced Thinking Skills (ETS) versus waiting list control group in offenders with antisocial personality disorder traits. Final Report submitted to the National Forensic Mental Health R&D Programme.

Drabick, D. A. G. and Kendall, P. C. (2010). Developmental psychopathology and the diagnosis of mental health problems among youth. *Clinical Psychology: Science and Practice*, **17**, 272–280.

Ellis, M. L., Weiss, B. and Lochman, J. E. (2009). Executive functions in children: associations with aggressive behaviour and appraisal processing. *Journal of Abnormal Child Psychology*, **37**, 945–956.

Fairchild, G., Van Goozen, S., Stollery, S. and Goodyer, I. M. (2008). Fear conditioning and affective modulation of the startle reflex in male adolescents with early-onset or adolescence-onset conduct disorder and healthy control subjects. *Biological Psychiatry*, **63**, 279–285.

Fairchild, G., Van Goozen, S., Stollery, S. et al. (2009). Decision making and executive function in male adolescents with early-onset or adolescence-onset conduct disorder and control subjects. *Biological Psychiatry*, **66**, 162–168.

Fairchild, G., Passamonti, L., Hurford, G. et al. (2011). Brain structure abnormalities in early-onset and adolescent-onset conduct disorder. *American Journal of Psychiatry*, **168**, 624–633.

Fergusson, D. M., Boden, J. M., Horwood, J. L. et al. (2011). MAOA, abuse exposure and antisocial behaviour: 30-year longitudinal study. *British Journal of Psychiatry*, **198**, 457–463

Frick, P. J. (2012). Developmental pathways to conduct disorder: implications for future directions in research, assessment and treatment. *Journal of Clinical Child and Adolescent Psychology*, **41**, 378–389.

Frick, P. J. and Viding, E. M. (2009). Antisocial behavior from a developmental psychopathology perspective. *Development and Psychopathology*, **21**, 1111–1131.

Hawes, D. J. and Dadds, M. R. (2005). The treatment of conduct problems in children with callous-unemotional traits. *Journal of Consulting and Clinical Psychology*, **73**(4), 737–741.

Hawes, D. J., Price, M. J. and Dadds, M. R. (2014). Callous-unemotional traits and the treatment of conduct problems in childhood and adolescence: a comprehensive review. *Clinical Child and Family Psychology Review*, **17**, 248–267.

Henggeler, S. W. (2011). Efficacy studies to large-scale transport: the development and validation of multisystemic therapy programs. *Annual Review of Clinical Psychology*, **7**, 351–381.

Huebner, T., Vloet, T. D., Marx, I. et al. (2008). Morphometric brain abnormalities in boys with conduct disorder. *Journal of the American Academy of Child and Adolescent Psychiatry*, **47**, 540–547.

Ishikawa, S. and Raine, A. (2003). Prefrontal deficits and antisocial behaviour: a causal model. In Lahey, B. B., Moffitt, T. E. and Caspi, A. Editors. *Causes of Conduct Disorder and Juvenile Delinquency*. New York: Guilford Press.

Jones, A., Laurens, K. R., Herba, C. M. et al. (2009). Amygdala hypoactivity to fearful faces in boys with conduct problems and callous-unemotional traits. *American Journal of Psychiatry*, **166**, 65–102.

Loeber, R. (1985). Patterns and development of antisocial child behaviour. *Annals of Child Development*, **2**, 77–116.

Loeber, R. and Burke, J. D. (2011). Developmental pathways in juvenile externalizing and internalizing problems. *Journal of Research on Adolescence*, **21**, 34–46.

Lynam, D. R. and Henry, B. (2001). The role of neuropsychological deficits in conduct disorders. In Hill, J. and Maughan, B. Editors. *Conduct Disorders in Childhood and Adolescence*. Cambridge: Cambridge University Press.

McMahon, R. J., Witkiewitz, K. and Kotler, J. S. (2010). Predictive validity of callous-unemotional traits measured in early adolescence with respect to multiple antisocial outcomes. *Journal of Abnormal Psychology*, **119**, 764–763.

Moffitt, T. E. (2003). Life-course persistent and adolescence-limited antisocial behaviour: a 10-year research review and a research agenda. In Lahey, B., Moffitt, T. E. and Caspi, A. Editors. *The Causes of Conduct Disorder and Serious Juvenile Delinquency*. New York: Guilford.

Moffitt, T. E. (2009). A review of research on the taxonomy of Life-Course Persistent versus Adolescence-Limited antisocial behaviour. In Cullen, F. T., Wright, J. P. and Blevins, K. R. Editors. *Taking Stock, The Status of Criminological Theory*. New Jersey: Transaction Publishers.

Moffitt, T. E. and Henry, B. (1991). Neuropsychological studies of juvenile delinquency and violence: a Review. In Miller, J. S. Editor. *Neuropsychology of Aggression*. Norwell: Kluwer Academic.

Morgan, A. B. and Lilienfeld, S. O. (2000). A meta-analytic review of the relation between antisocial behavior and neuropsychological measures of executive function. *Clinical Psychology Review*, **20**, 113–136.

National Institute for Health and Care Excellence. (2009). *Antisocial Personality Disorder (ASPD): Treatment, Management and Prevention*. NICE Clinical Guideline 77. London: National Collaborating Centre for Mental Health.

Newman, J. P. (1998). Psychopathic behaviour: an information processing perspective. In Cooke, D. J., Forth, A. E. and Hare, R. D. Editors. *Psychopathy: Theory, Research, and Implications for Society* (pp. 81–104). Dordrecht: Kluwer.

Passamonti, L., Fairchild, G., Goodyer, I. M. et al. (2010). Neural abnormalities in early-onset and adolescent-onset conduct disorder. *Archives of General Psychiatry*, **67**, 729–738.

Rhee, S. H. and Waldman, I. D. (2002). Genetic and environmental influences on antisocial behavior: a metaanalysis of twin and adoption studies. *Psychological Bulletin*, **128**, 490–529.

Rubia, K., Halari, R., Cubillo, A. et al. (2010). Disorder-specific inferior prefrontal hypofunction in boys with pure attention-deficit/hyperactivity disorder compared to boys with pure conduct disorder during cognitive flexibility. *Human Brain Mapping*, **31**, 1823–1833.

Salekin, R. (2002). Psychopathy and therapeutic pessimism: clinical lore or clinical reality. *Clinical Psychology Review*, **22**, 79–112.

Sarkar, S., Craig, M. C., Catani, M. et al. (2013). Frontotemporal white-matter microstructural abnormalities in adolescents with conduct disorder: a diffusion tensor imaging study. *Psychological Medicine*, **43**, 410–411.

Scott, S. (2008). An update on interventions for conduct disorder. *Advances in Psychiatric Treatment*, **14**, 61–70.

Séguin, J. R., Parent, S., Tremblay, R. E. et al. (2009). Different neurocognitive functions regulating physical aggression and hyperactivity in early childhood. *Journal of Child Psychology and Psychiatry*, **50**, 679–687.

Siever, L. J. (2008). Neurobiology of aggression and violence. *American Journal of Psychiatry*, **165**, 429–442.

Skardhamar, T. (2009). Reconsidering the theory on adolescent-limited and life-course persistent antisocial behaviour. *British Journal of Criminology*, **49**, 863–878.

Sterzer, P., Stadler, C., Krebs, A. et al. (2005). Abnormal neural responses to emotional visual stimuli in adolescents with conduct disorder. *Biological Psychiatry*, **57**, 7–15.

Tarrier, N., Dolan, M., Doyle, M. et al. (2010). Exploratory randomised control trial of schema model therapy in the personality disorder service at Ashworth hospital. Ministry of Justice Research Series 5/10. London: Ministry of Justice. Available from: www.justice.gov.uk/downloads/publications/research-and-analysis/moj-research/randomised-control-research.pdf. Accessed 01 December 2014.

Teichner, G. and Golden, C. J. (2000). Neuropsychological impairment in conduct-disordered adolescents: a conceptual review. *Aggressive and Violent Behavior*, **5**, 509–528.

Teichner, G., Golden, C. J., Crum, T. A. et al. (2000). Identification of neuropsychological subtypes in a sample of delinquent adolescents. *Journal of Psychiatric Research*, **34**, 129–132.

Tremblay, R. E. (2010). Developmental origins of disruptive behaviour problems: the original sin hypothesis, epigenetics and their consequences for prevention. *Journal of Child Psychology and Psychiatry*, **51**, 341–367.

Tuvblad, C., Grann, M. and Lichtenstein, P. (2006). Heritability for adolescent antisocial behaviour differs with socioeconomic status: gene–environment interaction. *Journal of Child Psychology and Psychology*, **47**, 734–743.

Vassos, E., Collier, D. A. and Fazel, S. (2014). Systematic meta-analyses and the field synopsis of genetic associations studies of violence and aggression. *Molecular Psychiatry*, **19**, 471–477.

Viding, E., Blair, R. J. R., Moffitt, T. E. et al. (2005). Evidence for substantial genetic risk for psychopathy in 7-year-olds. *Journal of Child Psychology and Psychiatry*, **46**, 592–597.

Viding, E. and Larsson, H. (2007). Aetiology of antisocial behaviour. *International Congress Series*, **1304**, 121–132.

Viding, E., Larsson, H. and Jones, A. (2008). Quantitative genetic studies of antisocial behaviour. *Philosophical Transactions of the Royal Society: Biological Sciences*, **363**, 2519–2527.

Viding, E., Hanscombe, K., Curtis, C. et al. (2010). In search of genes associated with risk for psychopathic tendencies in children: a two-stage genome-wide association study of pooled DNA. *Journal of Child Psychology and Psychiatry*, **51**, 780–788.

Viding, E., Sebastian, C. L., Dabbs, M. R. et al. (2012). Amygdala response to preattentive masked fear in children with conduct problems: the role of callous-unemotional traits. *American Journal of Psychiatry*, **169**, 1109–1116.

Vloet, T. D., Konrad, K., Huebner, T. et al. (2008). Structured and functional MRI – findings in children and adolescents with antisocial behaviour. *Behavior Science and the Law*, **26**, 99–111.

World Health Organisation. (2010). Preventing violence and knife crime in young people. Geneva: World Health Organisation. Available from: www.euro.who.int/__data/assets/pdf_file/0012/121314/E94277.pdf. Accessed 01 December 2014.

Youth Justice Board. (2016). Youth Justice Statistics 2014/2015. London: Youth Justice Board. Available from: www.gov.uk/government/uploads/system/uploads/attachment_data/file/495708/youth-justice-statistics-2014-to-2015.pdf. Accessed on 31 December 2016.

Childhood Predictors of Young Homicide Offenders and Victims and Their Implications for Interventions

Lia Ahonen, David P. Farrington, Rolf Loeber, Rebecca Stallings and Dustin Pardini

Introduction

One of the most serious and long-standing societal traumas is lethal violence involving young people either as offenders or victims. Firearm-related deaths as well as non-fatal shootings in the USA have decreased steadily since the massive peak in 1993. However, the decrease has slowed down from around 2001 and the homicide rate, with the exceptions of some local variations, has stayed relatively constant ever since (Pew Social Trends, 2013). Still, in 2013, the number of homicides in the USA was 16,121 (and the homicide rate was 5.1 per 100,000 citizens), many of which were committed by young people between the ages of 18 and 24 killing other young people. Farrington et al. (2004: 67–68) concluded that policy initiatives have not succeeded in lowering the homicide rates of (and by) young people in the USA to a level that is comparable to other developed Western countries. Because of the extensive burden of young homicide offenders and their victims on the justice system and social welfare systems, it is crucial to investigate not only who will become involved in homicide as either an offender or a victim but also how to apply this knowledge to practical interventions aimed at reducing homicide in particular and violence in general. The purpose of the current chapter is to fill this gap in knowledge by summarising and presenting longitudinal data on predictors of male homicide offenders and male homicide victims, and including two case studies. We will pay special attention to early dynamic factors, which potentially can be changed, and discuss the relevance of the results for prevention and intervention.

For decades the study of homicide and violence has taken many different directions, depending on a researcher's theoretical orientation. Some perspectives have been more dominant than others, reflecting different approaches to the explanation of serious violence and homicide offenders, and also representing different approaches to intervention other than incarceration. Table 7.1 shows five theoretical perspectives put forward to explain violence (and usually implicit homicide), each of which focused on a circumscribed set of risk factors. For example, the psychopathological perspective, originating from research on biosocial criminology and mental health factors, concentrates on callous-unemotional behaviours and hyperactivity/impulsivity. In contrast, the core element of the social learning perspective, stemming from the work by Bandura (1977) and Patterson et al. (1992), focuses on children's learning of aggression to exercise control over others. Table 7.1 also shows the sociological perspectives associated with strain theory (e.g. Agnew, 1992), developmental escalation pathways (e.g. Loeber et al., 1993) and life course developmental theories such as the integrated cognitive antisocial propensity theory (Farrington, 2005).

The different theoretical perspectives represented in Table 7.1 offer differing explanations for the same phenomenon, and rarely present a comprehensive, data-based picture of all explanatory factors of violence and homicide offending. Media reports focus more often than not on fatal incidents involving multiple victims like school and other mass shootings. This gives the impression of a larger number of incidents than is actually the case based on national statistics, and a sense that victims of homicide most often are random strangers, which is not true. Much more common is that the victims and the offenders are in some way known to one another. Further, media reports tend to be poor in explaining the full range of putative causal factors and processes underlying homicide offenders and their victims.

These are the reasons why we summarise in this chapter empirical knowledge from the longitudinal Pittsburgh Youth Study (PYS) on young homicide

Table 7.1 Five Theoretical Approaches to Violence and Homicide Offending

Perspective	Explanatory Level	Primary Focus	Examples of Studies
Psychopathology	Individual	Callous-unemotional behaviours, impulsivity, hyperactivity and attention problems.	Pardini and Loeber, 2008
Social learning	Family, peers	Learning and adopting aggression to exercise control over others.	Patterson, Reid, and Dishion, 1992
Sociological	Macro/community	Families' low socio-economic status, neighbourhood disadvantage, no collective control of young people in a neighbourhood.	Laub and Sampson, 2001
Escalation	Individual	Within-individual change, gradual development of aggression and violence, absence of de-escalation processes.	Loeber et al., 1993
Life course development	Individual	Long- and short-term changes in motivation, opportunities and situations.	Farrington, 2005

offenders and victims. Instead of adopting a particular theoretical perspective, we will include a large range of risk factors to better guide intervention science. We will also focus on street homicides rather than domestic violence or mass killings, because street violence characterises the majority of all homicides in the USA. In a second focus, we use findings on the predictors of homicide offenders and victims as a tool to suggest screening instruments to identify youths at a young age who are at risk of killing or being killed. At a time when voters are calling for cutting deficits and ensuring that taxpayers' money is used responsibly, these models offer a basis for cost-effective interventions.

Scientific Studies on Homicide Offenders and Homicide Victims

Although many studies have been conducted on homicide offending by young people, most have been restricted in scope and provide more information about prevalence rather than causes. However, the studies often provide good information on how often homicides committed by young people have varied nationally over decades (Federal Bureau of Investigation, 2003, 2008) and at the local level (Costantino et al., 1977; Dalton et al., 2009). A substantial body of knowledge also exists concerning the lives of individual homicide offenders (e.g. Bailey, 2000; Heide, 1999), but almost all these studies are based on arrests or court records only (e.g. Wolfgang,

1958). However, court records often provide incomplete information about possible risk factors. Moreover, many homicide studies have focused on retrospective reports of putative causes, which are known to have serious limitations (Goodman et al., 1988). Importantly, most homicide studies lack prospective data to identify predictors of homicide. In contrast, the longitudinal data from the PYS study presented in this chapter have overcome many of the drawbacks associated with previous homicide studies.

Are the findings from the Pittsburgh Youth Study comparable to the USA and the UK findings? Knowledge about homicide offenders and victims is dependent on the sources of information used and on the geographic location. Some critics may argue that the homicide cases in the PYS represent a relatively small land area and that the characteristics may not apply to state or national crime figures in the USA. To check this, we compared the extent to which murders in the PYS resembled those reported nationally in the USA. The results, detailed below, support the notion that homicide offenders and victims in the PYS constitute a microcosm of what happens elsewhere in the USA. Specifically, PYS data show that the conditions associated with homicide offences (such as the use of guns, involvement of gangs and drugs, male against male arguments, African American young males victimising other African American young males) are similar for Allegheny County in which Pittsburgh is situated, the Commonwealth of Pennsylvania and the rest of the USA. It should be noted that the comparisons between the PYS homicide offenders and victims and those in other locations have limitations, especially because of the low base rate. Nevertheless, conclusions from this research are likely to apply to young homicide offenders and victims in many locations in the USA, especially in large metropolitan areas of which Pittsburgh is one.

How do the PYS results compare with findings from the UK? First, the prevalence of homicide and the use of guns to kill are much higher in the USA than in the UK (Farrington et al., 2004). However, homicide offenders in both countries often are recidivist offenders, have substance abuse problems and are exposed to early risk factors such as family dysfunction and educational difficulties (for the UK, see e.g. Bailey, 1996; Rodway et al., 2011). Thus, conditions that are thought to foster homicide (and violence in general) in the UK overlap considerably with those observed in the USA, including predictive factors found in the PYS, which are reported in the present chapter.

Homicide Offenders and Victims: An Overview

Not all homicide incidents are the same. They may differ in terms of the type of victim, such as a relative, a friend or a stranger. The motivation also varies and may include conflict, alcohol use, robbery, revenge and retaliation, and drug deals that have gone badly. Homicides also take place in many different settings. In some cases, mental illness, such as antisocial personality or paranoia, also may play a role although evidence of the connection between mental health problems and violence, including homicide, is vastly different in different studies (e.g. Fazel et al., 2009; Swanson et al., 2015).

Homicide offenders. Cornell et al. (1987) classified young homicide offenders into three types: the psychotic offender, the conflict-driven, and the crime-driven homicide offender (such as robbery). Some research proposes that some offenders are over-controlled rather than impulsive and under-controlled (e.g. Hardwick and Rowton-Lee, 1996), but many other typologies have also been proposed (e.g. Bijleveld and Smit, 2006; Roberts et al., 2007). The three types of homicide offenders, however, are likely to vary in different populations. For example, psychotic conditions tend to be less common among

young homicide offenders (American Psychiatric Association, 2013), as compared to older offenders, which means that fewer homicide offenders are psychotic. In addition, it may be that under-controlled young homicide offenders are more typical than over-controlled young homicide offenders.

It has been suggested that homicide offenders more often than not come from disadvantaged neighbourhoods, where more illegal activities tend to occur (e.g. Loeber and Farrington, 2011: 9; Piquero and Brame, 2008), and as a consequence lead to a higher rate of conflicts in which parties apply personal justice rather than turning to the law or the police. These conflicts are often settled by angry and sometimes impulsive individuals who also may have more access to guns in their neighbourhoods than do nondelinquent individuals. It is common that homicide offenders are characterised at a young age by a diagnosis of Disruptive Behaviour Disorder (DBD), which includes symptoms of aggression and theft (e.g. Loeber and Ahonen, 2013; Loeber and Farrington, 2011: 9). In sum, the majority of young homicide offenders are not likely to be characterised by mental illness, other than DBD, but tend to have been highly disruptive when young; have a long history of under-controlled behaviour; and carry guns and engage in illegal activities, such as robbery, drug dealing and gang activity. We did not find any validated screening instruments for risk of homicide offending.

Homicide victims. Compared to the number of studies on young homicide offenders, relatively few studies focus on young homicide victims (Lauritsen et al., 1992; Ezell and Tanner-Smith, 2009). There is a need to study victimisation in low- and high-risk populations to better understand the risk factors for homicide victimisation. Studies should also examine homicide victimisation in general populations based on longitudinal data, particularly in inner cities where crime victimisation rates are often high.

Another important issue is to determine the extent to which homicide offenders and homicide victims differ in their early behavioural development and their exposure to known risk factors associated with violence. A key question is whether the predictors of homicide victims are similar to or different from predictors of homicide offenders. A few studies have compared homicide offenders with victims of homicide (e.g. Brodie et al., 2006), showing that homicide offenders and homicide victims are drawn from the same population with similar life experiences. Other studies confirm that assault victims disproportionately tend to have committed violent offences (e.g. Rivara et al., 1995). There is a scarcity of studies on the prediction of homicide victimisation outside of intimate relationships. In addition, we have not found any validated screening instruments designed to identify youth at risk of homicide victimisation.

The Pittsburgh Youth Study (PYS)

Pittsburgh, Pennsylvania, is a largely blue-collar (working-class) city with mostly Caucasian and African American inhabitants. The city has a large number of different neighbourhoods, some of which are hyper-segregated, meaning that they comprise more than 90% of Caucasian or African American households. The PYS offers a unique opportunity to study the early development of homicide offenders and homicide victims, long before they became involved in homicidal incidents. The PYS was initiated in 1987. At the first assessment, the boys were in grades, 1, 4 and 7 (youngest, middle and oldest cohorts) in Pittsburgh public schools. Overall, the PYS team contacted 1,006 (grade 1), 1,004 (grade 4) and 998 (grade 7) families, and the participation rate of boys and their parents at the beginning of the study was 84.6%, 86.3% and 83.9%, respectively. Because of the high initial participation rate of families, we believe that the cohorts are representative of the populations from which they were drawn. Further screening to increase the number of high-risk males resulted in 30% of boys being identified as the most antisocial. They were included in the follow-up along with another 30% who were randomly selected from the remaining 70%. The final cohort consisted of 503, 508 and 506 boys in grades 1, 4 and 7 (average ages 6.7, 10.0 and 13.1, respectively), which was followed up with their parents.

In this chapter we use results based on self-reports and parent–teacher ratings together with official juvenile and criminal records. This chapter is primarily concerned with the 37 convicted homicide offenders, and the 39 homicide victims, both between the ages of 15 and 29, in the PYS (see Loeber and Farrington, 2011: 47). We focus on two different types of predictors in this chapter: explanatory and behavioural. Explanatory factors are factors that clearly do not measure problem or delinquent behaviour while behavioural factors are those that reflect such behaviours (Loeber and Farrington, 2011: 57).

Both explanatory and behavioural factors can have a causal effect on the outcome, but in either category, the factors can be either static (i.e. not changeable, such as coming from a single-parent household, or the child's past delinquent behaviour) or dynamic (i.e. potentially changeable, such as a parent's child-rearing practices, or the child's current delinquency), and therefore candidates for prevention or intervention.

Early Risk Factors for Homicide Offending in the PYS

African American males were more likely to become homicide offenders than Caucasian males. In the PYS, out of the 37 individuals convicted of homicide, 32 were African American (86%). The prevalence of convicted homicide offenders was 3.7% of the African American boys compared to 0.8% of Caucasian boys. Weighting back to the population of Pittsburgh public schools, 3.2% of African American boys became homicide offenders compared to 0.5% of the Caucasian boys. We compared 37 convicted homicide offenders with 1,406 control boys, excluding arrested but not convicted offenders. Of the 1,406 control boys, 765 were African American (54%). We examined 21 explanatory and 19 behavioural risk factors measured in childhood to predict homicide offenders in the analyses. For detailed information about all variables included in the original analyses, see Loeber and Farrington (2011: 51–65).

Explanatory predictors of homicide offending. Homicide offenders were more likely than controls to have had an unstable childhood. The significant predictors are shown in Table 7.2. Some of the strongest predictors were the following: a broken family, the family on welfare, growing up in a bad neighbourhood (as defined by US Census Bureau data on single-parent households, median income, public assistance, and unemployed adults) and having a young mother (for details of odds ratios, see Table 7.2). Environmental explanatory factors seemed to have stronger predictive power than individual factors. For example, while the odds ratios for lack of guilt and being held back in school (being old for the grade) were statistically significant, they were relatively small. In addition, the odds ratio for hyperactivity-impulsivity-attention deficit did not reach significance (and therefore was not shown in Table 7.2). The strongest predictor was living in a broken family (i.e. the biological parents are

Table 7.2 Explanatory Predictors of Convicted Homicide Offenders

	% of Controls (1,406)	% of Offenders (37)	Odds Ratio	Partial OR	p
Broken family	62	89	5.0*	–	–
Bad neighbourhood (C)	32	65	3.9*	3.2	0.004
Family on welfare	43	71	3.2*	–	–
Young mother	21	45	3.1*	2.5	0.016
Old for the grade	25	49	2.9*	–	–
Unemployed mother	25	45	2.6*	1.9	0.081
Lack of guilt	24	43	2.4*	–	–
Father's behaviour problems	17	32	2.4*	–	–
Low socio-economic status	26	43	2.2*	2.0	0.064

Note: C = Census, * $p < 0.05$, OR = Odds Ratio.
Source: Based on table 4.1 of Loeber and Farrington (2011).

separated/divorced): 89% of homicide offenders came from a broken home compared with 62% of the controls (OR = 5.0, CI 1.8–14.3). All in all, a much larger proportion of the homicide offenders were exposed to environmental and individual explanatory risk factors than the boys in the control group.

We carried out a stepwise logistic regression analysis to further investigate which of the significant explanatory factors were independent predictors of homicide offending. Four out of the nine explanatory factors independently predicted homicide offending (although unemployed mothers were on the borderline of significance): bad neighbourhood, having a young mother, low socio-economic status and an unemployed mother.

Behavioural predictors of homicide offending. Turning to behavioural predictors of homicide offending, Table 7.3 shows that 11 out of the 19 behavioural factors significantly distinguished homicide offenders from controls. These factors were: being suspended from school, having a high risk score at the initial assessment, a favourable attitude to delinquency (i.e. approval of law-breaking), a diagnosis of DBD, serious delinquency, peer delinquency, a positive attitude to substance use, covert or concealing behaviour (such as lying, and shoplifting), being cruel to people, having bad friends (parents disapproving of friends, and boys reporting that their friends behave badly), and truancy. The strongest predictor was being suspended from school: 78% of the convicted homicide offenders had been suspended, in comparison with 43% of the controls (OR = 4.9, CI 2.2–10.7).

As with the explanatory factors, we performed a logistic regression analysis to identify independent behavioural predictors of homicide offending. In a stepwise analysis we found that 4 out of the 11 behavioural predictors were independent predictors: having a positive attitude to delinquency, suspended from school, DBD and a high risk score at initial screening (marginally significant).

Early Risk Factors for Homicide Victimisation

As mentioned, it is not clear to what extent predictors of homicide offenders are similar to predictors of homicide victims. No previous longitudinal study has investigated this.

Not surprisingly, in light of national statistics, African American males were more likely than Caucasian males to be homicide victims in Pittsburgh. In the PYS, 37 of the 39 victims (95%) were African American, compared with 765 of the 1,406 controls (54%). Weighting back to the population of Pittsburgh public schools, 3.7% of African American males were killed compared with 0.3% of Caucasian males. To identify the explanatory predictors of homicide victims, we compared the 39 homicide victims with the 1,406 control boys. The same 21 explanatory and 19 behavioural risk factors that were used to predict homicide offenders are included in these analyses of homicide victims.

Explanatory predictors of homicide victimisation. Table 7.4 shows that 11 of the 21 explanatory factors

Table 7.3 Behavioural Predictors of Convicted Homicide Offenders

	% of Controls (1,406)	% of Offenders (37)	Odds Ratio	Partial OR	p
Suspended	43	78	4.9*	2.9	0.012
High-risk score	49	81	4.4*	2.2	0.076
Positive attitude to delinquency	23	54	3.9*	2.9	0.002
Disruptive Behaviour Disorder	23	51	3.5*	2.1	0.038
Serious delinquency	29	57	3.3*	–	–
Peer delinquency	24	49	3.0*	–	–
Positive attitude to substance use	24	46	2.7*	–	–
Covert behaviour	24	46	2.7*	–	–
Cruel to people	24	43	2.4*	–	–
Bad friends	25	41	2.0*	–	–
Truant	38	54	1.9*	–	–

Note: * p < 0.05; OR = Odds ratio.
Source: Based on table 4.2 of Loeber and Farrington (2011).

Table 7.4 Explanatory Predictors of Homicide Victims

	% of Controls (1,406)	% of Victims (39)	Odds Ratio	Partial OR	P
Lack of guilt	24	62	5.0*	4.5	0.0001
Broken family	62	87	4.1*	3.1	0.035
Low achievement (CAT)	24	51	3.4*	2.3	0.016
HIA	17	36	2.7*	–	–
Old for the grade	25	46	2.6*	–	–
Low achievement (PT)	24	44	2.5*	–	–
Father's behaviour problems	17	33	2.5*	–	–
Large family size	21	38	2.3*	2.3	0.023
Family on welfare	43	62	2.2*	–	–
Bad neighbourhood (P)	24	41	2.2*	–	–
Bad neighbourhood (C)	32	49	2.0*	–	–

Note: CAT = California Achievement Test, HIA = Hyperactivity-impulsivity-attention deficit P = Parent; T = Teacher; C = Census, * = p < 0.05; OR = Odds ratio.
Source: Based on table 6.2 of Loeber and Farrington (2011).

Table 7.5 Behavioural Predictors of Homicide Victims

	% of Controls (1,406)	% of Victims (39)	Odds Ratio	Partial OR	P
Serious delinquency	29	67	5.0*	3.5	0.0006
Physical aggression	26	56	3.6*	2.0	0.050
Nonphysical aggression	25	54	3.5*	–	–
Bad relationship with parent	24	51	3.3*	2.2	0.024
Covert behaviour	24	50	3.1*	–	–
High risk score	49	74	3.0*	–	–
Bad relationship with peers	26	49	2.7*	–	–
Suspension from school	43	66	2.6*	–	–
Bad friends	25	46	2.6*	–	–
Low school motivation	37	59	2.5*	–	–
Cruel to people	24	44	2.4*	–	–
Peer delinquency	24	41	2.2*	–	–
Truancy	38	56	2.1*	–	–
Disruptive Behaviour Disorder	23	37	2.0*	–	–
–	–	–	–	–	–

Note * = p< 0.05; OR = Odds Ratio.
Source: Based on table 6.3 of Loeber and Farrington (2011).

significantly predicted homicide victims: lack of guilt, broken home, low achievement in school, hyperactivity-impulsivity-attention deficit, old for the grade (meaning that the boy repeated a year that he had failed academically), fathers' behaviour problems, large family size, family on welfare, and two measures (based on parent and census ratings) of bad neighbourhood. In addition, callous-unemotional behaviour was almost significant as a predictor. The strongest predictor was lack of guilt: 62% of homicide victims had low guilt compared with 24% of controls (OR = 5.0, CI 2.6–9.6).

A logistic regression investigated which of the 11 significant explanatory predictors of homicide victims were independent predictors of homicide victims. Four variables were significant: low guilt, low achievement on the California Achievement Test (CAT; which is a standardised academic test for students),

a broken home and a large family. The results suggest that individual, family and school factors contributed to the explanation and prediction of homicide victims.

Behavioural predictors of homicide victimisation. As shown in Table 7.5, 14 of the 19 behavioural factors significantly predicted homicide victims: serious delinquency, physical and nonphysical aggression, a bad relationship with a parent, covert behaviour, a high screening risk score for behavioural problems at the beginning of the study, a bad relationship with peers, suspension from school, bad friends, low school motivation, cruel to people, peer delinquency, truancy and DBD. The strongest predictor was serious delinquency: 67% of homicide victims had been serious delinquents compared with 29% of controls (OR = 5.0, CI 2.5–9.8).

A logistic regression analysis showed that three variables independently predicted homicide victims in a stepwise analysis: serious delinquency, a bad relationship with a parent and physical aggression.

The Issue of Race

Studies show that African American males are over-represented among both homicide offenders and homicide victims in the USA (e.g. Pope and Snyder, 2003; Strom and MacDonald, 2007). The increase in homicide offending that took place in the early 1990s in the USA was largely driven by an increase in homicides by and of African American males (Harms and Snyder, 2004). Likewise, the PYS found that the majority of homicide offenders and homicide victims were African Americans (Loeber et al., 1999; Farrington et al., 2003). Yet results reported elsewhere show that race did not predict violent offenders in multivariate analyses after controlling for other risk factors (Loeber et al., 2008). On the other hand, race did independently predict homicide victimisation when controlling for other risk factors. Altogether, it is still likely that African American boys are exposed to more deprivation and more risk factors than are Caucasian boys (Loeber and Farrington, 2011). We believe that race is a predictor of both homicide offending and victimisation primarily because it is associated with risk factors such as broken families and living in the most deprived neighbourhoods.

Comparing Explanatory and Behavioural Predictors of Homicide Offenders and Homicide Victims

Homicide offenders and victims were more alike than different on the explanatory factors, and homicide offenders were not more extreme than homicide victims on these factors. Homicide offenders and homicide victims shared five explanatory factors: old for the grade in school, low guilt, coming from a broken family, a family on welfare, and growing up in a disadvantaged neighbourhood ('bad neighbourhood', as measured by census data). Nine behavioural factors significantly predicted both homicide offenders and homicide victims: a high screening risk score, truancy, serious delinquency, covert (concealing) behaviour, suspension from school, cruel to people, peer delinquency, bad friends and DBD. Homicide offenders were not more extreme than victims, and the results

suggest that young homicide offenders were not more antisocial than homicide victims. Although homicide offenders and victims, compared to controls, engaged in later delinquent behaviours – such as carrying a gun, belonging to gangs and selling drugs – these antisocial behaviours are not studied here as risk factors because the focus in this chapter is on early childhood predictors.

Is There a Dose-Response Relationship between the Number of Risk Factors and Homicide Offending or Victimisation?

We found that for homicide offenders and homicide victims, the higher the number of risk factors, the more likely it was that the individual would become involved in a homicidal incident. This conclusion applies to both the explanatory and behavioural risk scores. Only 0.7% of boys with none of the explanatory and behavioural risk factors became homicide offenders, compared to 10.3% of the boys with four explanatory factors and 17.1% of the boys with four behavioural factors.

A similar cumulative risk score applied to homicide victims: 0.6% of the boys with none of the four explanatory factors or three behavioural factors became homicide victims, compared with 8.9% of the boys with all four explanatory factors and 9.5% of the boys with all three behavioural risk factors. Overall, the behavioural prediction of homicide victims was as accurate as the behavioural prediction of homicide offenders.

Two Case Studies

Many scientific studies focus on empirical results, which do not always translate well into knowledge applicable to clinical settings and practice guidelines. In this section we present two cases, Boxes 7.1 and 7.2, from the PYS, one homicide offender and one homicide victim, from a prevention/intervention perspective. The information in the case of the homicide offender derives from a face-to face-interview, and the information on the homicide victim derives from official records and longitudinal data collected in the PYS. The names of the individuals have been changed in both cases to preserve confidentiality.

Sean's case reflects several of the risk factors which predicted homicide offenders. He was exposed to

---

BOX 7.1 Case Example 1: Sean

Homicide Offender Case Example

Sean was age 18 when he and some friends robbed and shot the victim, to avoid being later identified as the robbers. Sean has shown disruptive problem behaviours from at least age 7 onwards, including frequent lying, shoplifting, fighting, and disobedience at home and in school before age 11. Sean was born to a single, drug using mother and came from a family of five, and did not have contact with his biological father. At age 6, Sean and the other children, because of the bad situation in the home, were placed in foster care. Sean did poorly in school and could not read at age 14. His first act of serious delinquency (breaking and entering) took place when he was 11 and then he offended again at age 12, when he was first arrested. He was first placed in a detention home (secure children's home) at the age of 12, and again at ages 15 and 18. A psychiatric diagnosis at age 13 included conduct disorder and learning disability. He had repeated run-ins with the law for a variety of delinquent acts, including drug possession, before being arrested for homicide.

BOX 7.2 Case Example 2: Carl

Homicide Victim Case Example

Carl was shot at point-blank range outside a garage. He had a lengthy arrest history dating back to his early childhood years; he had been arrested 12 times by the age of 14. The majority of his arrests were for possession or sale of drugs. However, he also had been arrested for theft, auto theft, disorderly conduct and aggravated assault. Early in his life, he lived with his mother, but the whereabouts of his father were not known. He completed high school and two years of college but quit and became unemployed. At the time of his death at age 21, he had three children by his girlfriend.

---

several explanatory risk factors; he came from an environment with a broken family, and the whereabouts of the father was unknown, so it is not clear whether the father had behavioural problems or not. Sean and his siblings were placed outside the home early in life. It is reasonable to speculate that many of the factors described in the above summary can be directly related to the high risk factors identified in our analyses.

Turning to behavioural factors, several factors applied to Sean's situation; Sean's problematic behaviour was already in evidence from age seven onwards, which indicates that he may have lacked a sense of guilt, and acted callously towards other individuals. He showed academic problems in school (which may have been enhanced by learning disabilities), a positive attitude to delinquency and substance use, a high risk score, DBD, peer delinquency, covert behaviour, being cruel to people, having bad friends and truancy.

In summary, Sean was exposed to a high level of both explanatory and behavioural risk factors, based on our statistical models.

We examined the extent to which *explanatory factors* from the regression model (lack of guilt, low achievement on the CAT, a broken home and large family) may have applied to Carl. He grew up in a broken home, with only one caregiver. From an intervention point of view, there is reason to believe that Carl, in agreement with his versatile arrest record, may have had a problem with lack of guilt, but he did reasonably well in school, since he graduated from high school and finished two years in college. However, he became unemployed and started a family early, having three children by age 21.

Carl engaged in serious delinquency from an early age, with multiple arrests on a variety of charges, and since he was arrested for assault, it is appropriate to suggest that Carl had some problems with physical aggression. We were not able to draw conclusions about the quality of Carl's relationship with his mother. Carl seemed to be at high risk to become involved in homicide, and to become a homicide victim.

Prevention and Intervention for Young Persons at an Elevated Risk for Involvement in Homicide Offending or Victimisation

We have demonstrated that homicide offenders and their victims in the PYS were more similar then different in terms of their exposure to certain types of risk factors, and in the accumulation of risk factors. This risk pattern is also very similar to the risk of becoming a serious and violent offender, excluding homicide (Ahonen et al., 2015), and of becoming a shooting victim (Loeber and Farrington, 2011:107). We briefly discussed explanatory and behavioural factors that predicted homicide offenders and homicide victims. We also noted that some of these factors are potentially changeable. We hypothesise that once individual exposure to known risk factors is reduced, the probability of becoming a homicide offender or victim will be reduced as well.

Some of the risk factors highlighted in this chapter have been incorporated in prevention and intervention programmes to reduce disruptive and delinquent behaviour in young people. We will illustrate this by discussing two intervention programmes identified as validated and evidence-based according to the Blueprints Program (www.blueprintsprograms.com), each of which addresses several of the explanatory and behavioural factors which we identified as predictors of homicide offenders and homicide victims. First we focus on a universal school-based intervention and then we present an example of a targeted intervention for more serious and established problem behaviours.

Universal prevention. First, at early ages and in elementary school it is appropriate to focus on universal prevention that includes all children. One example of a promising programme is the Good Behavior Game (GBG) which focuses on children between 5 and 11 years. This is a school- and classroom-based early programme for preventing alcohol, drug and tobacco use; disruptive and aggressive behaviour; internalisation of mental health problems; and suicidal thoughts or suicide. The programme consists of a behaviour management game performed by elementary teachers, integrated with the standard school curriculum, to reduce children's disruptive and aggressive behaviours. The game is played in teams several times a week in the classroom and builds upon the notion that the students

help each other to follow classroom rules, especially at times when the students are working independently with less structure in the room. This programme is predictable at first, in that the children know when the game will start and end. However, over time, the programme becomes more random and can occur at any time and in any part of the day in school. Early evaluations have shown a significant reduction in aggressive behaviour both for males and females as rated by teachers (Dolan et al., 1993). Later evaluations showed that treated males compared to controls had lower rates of antisocial personality disorder and violent and criminal behaviour by young adulthood (Petras et al., 2008).

Targeted intervention. When problem behaviours are already established, a more targeted intervention is appropriate, and also programmes that are designed for older children and adolescents. One example is multisystemic therapy (MST) for ages 12–17. MST is a family- and community-based intervention programme aimed to reduce recidivism rates in the juvenile justice systems, reduce delinquency and especially violence, improve relationships with parents and reduce alcohol/drug use and improve prosocial behaviour. MST focuses on enhancing parenting skills and provides extensive family work for juveniles with severe behavioural problems. It also focuses on peer, school and neighbourhood factors that may be difficult for the young person to deal with. Evaluations have shown improvements in behavioural functioning over time in three settings (in school, at home, at work) and in moods and emotions (Timmons-Mitchell et al., 2006). Other evaluations showed a decrease in both externalising and internalising symptoms, and in the number of out-of-home placements (Ogden and Halliday-Boykins, 2004; Ogden and Hagen, 2006).

Treatment evaluation studies have shown that MST has long-term beneficial effects. Sawyer and Borduin (2011) followed up an experiment from age 14 to age 37, and found that the MST group had fewer felony arrests (33% versus 55%) and fewer years incarcerated (mean 5.3 versus 7.9) compared with a control group who received individual therapy.

Another way of examining possible treatment effects is to simulate interventions using longitudinal population data. Ebel et al. (2011) have investigated the effects on the US homicide rate, through a simulation study, of implementing three programmes sequentially. The first was the nurse–family partnership programme (Olds et al., 1998), in which nurses visit mothers during pregnancy and the first two years of a child's life, providing primarily low-income, first-time parents with advice about infant development, child-rearing and avoiding substance use. The second was the Perry Preschool intellectual enrichment programme (Schweinhart et al., 2005), which consists of a programme in the preschool years focusing on developing cognitive skills such as independence, curiosity, decision-making, cooperation, persistence, creativity, and problem solving. The third programme was MST (as described above) in the teenage years. They estimated that those programmes would reduce homicide offending by one third, save 4,205 lives annually and cause a 5.2 billion dollar reduction in the lifetime costs of incarceration.

Conclusions

In this chapter, we have demonstrated that explanatory and behavioural factors for homicide offenders and homicide victims in the longitudinal data from the PYS to a large degree were similar. The results show that there is no simple or single factor explaining homicide offending or homicide victimisation. As a rule of thumb, the larger the number of risk factors, and the greater the magnitude of them, the higher the risk that an individual will live in environments that are crime ridden, disadvantaged and marked by conflict. This combination will further contribute to the level of risk. We have also presented two case studies (Sean and Carl). Ideally, empirical findings should always guide interventions. However, it is important to keep in mind that scientific findings on aggregated longitudinal data of populations of offenders, including homicide offenders and homicide victims, need to be applied with caution in clinical and other intervention settings. Empirical group-based findings can never replace clinical judgement for the evaluation and treatment of individuals. Although many specific factors significantly predict homicide offending and victimisation, it is crucial not to have a too narrow focus on intervention targets alone but to consider all levels and stages of people's lives, and their functioning in their families, schools and communities.

It is currently impossible to say for certain whether evidence-based programmes known to reduce delinquency and violence will also reduce homicide offending and victimisation. We have described some examples of effective prevention and treatment programmes from the USA that have shown to reduce delinquency and violence. However, we are optimistic that the programmes described here, and several other evidence-based programmes, would also prove to be effective in preventing homicide offending and homicide victimisation, both in the USA and the UK.

Acknowledgements

The first author is grateful to the Swedish National Research Council [Vetenskapsrådet] for supporting her work. We are very grateful to Springer for giving permission to reproduce Tables 7.2, 7.3, 7.4 and 7.5 from the book by Loeber and Farrington (2011).

References

Agnew, R. (1992). Foundations for a general strain theory of crime and delinquency. *Criminology*, **30**(1), 47–87.

Ahonen, L., Loeber, R. and Pardini, D. (2015). The prediction of young homicide and violent offenders, *Justice Quarterly*, **10**, 1–28.

American Psychiatric Association. (2013). *Diagnostic and Statistical Manual of Mental Disorders*. 5th Edition. Washington, DC: American Psychiatric Association.

Bailey, S. (1996). Adolescents who murder. *Journal of Adolescence*, **19**, 19–36.

Bailey, S. (2000). Juvenile homicide. *Criminal Behaviour and Mental Health*, **10**, 149–154.

Bandura, A. (1977). *Social Learning Theory*. Englewood Cliffs, NJ: Prentice-Hall.

Bijleveld, C. and Smit, P. (2006). Homicide in the Netherlands: on the structuring of homicide typologies. *Homicide Studies*, **10**, 195–216.

Brodie, L.M., Daday, J. K., Crandall, C. S., Sklar, D. P. and Jost, P. F. (2006). Exploring demographic, structural, and behavioral overlap among homicide offenders and victims. *Homicide Studies*, **10**, 155–180.

Cornell, D. G., Benedek, E. P. and Benedek, D. M. (1987). Youth homicide: prior adjustment and a proposed typology. *American Journal of Orthopsychiatry*, **57**, 383–392.

Costantino, J. P., Kuller, L. H., Perper, J. A. and Cypess, R. H. (1977). An epidemiologic study of homicides in Allegheny County, Pennsylvania. *American Journal of Epidemiology*, **106**, 314–324.

Dalton, E., Yonas, M., Warren, L. and Sturman, E. (2009). Research Report: Violence in Allegheny County and Pittsburgh. Pittsburgh: Allegheny County Department of Health, unpublished report.

Dolan, L. J., Kellam, S. G., Brown, C. H., Werthamer-Larsson, L., Rebok, G. W., Mayer, L. S., Laudolff, J., Turkkan, J. S.,

Ford, C. and Wheeler, L. (1993). The short-term impact of two classroom-based preventive interventions on aggressive and shy behaviors and poor achievement. *Journal of Applied Developmental Psychology*, **14**, 317–345.

Ebel, B. E., Rivera, F. P., Loeber, R. and Pardini, D. A. (2011). Modeling the impact of preventive interventions on the national homicide rate. In Loeber, R. and Farrington, D. Editors. *Young Homicide Offenders and Victims. Risk Factors, Prediction and Prevention from Childhood* (pp. 123–136). New York, NY: Springer.

Ezell, M. E. and Tanner-Smith, E. E. (2009). Examining the role of lifestyle and criminal history variables on the risk of homicide victimization. *Homicide Studies*, **13**, 144–173.

Farrington, D. P. Editor. (2005). *Integrated Developmental and Life-Course Theories of Offending*. New Brunswick, NJ: Transaction.

Farrington, D. P., Loeber, R. and Stouthamer-Loeber, M. (2003). How can the relationship between race and violence be explained? In Hawkins, D. F. Editor. *Violent Crimes: Assessing Race and Ethnic Differences* (pp. 213–237). Cambridge, UK: Cambridge University Press.

Farrington, D. P., Langan, P. A. and Tonry, M. (2004). *Cross-National Studies in Crime and Justice*. Washington, DC: US Bureau of Justice Statistics.

Fazel, S., Gulati, G., Linsell, L., Geddes, J. R. and Grann, M. (2009). Schizophrenia and violence: systematic review and meta-analysis. *PloS Med*, **6**(8), e1000120. doi: 10.1371/journal.pmed.1000120.

Federal Bureau of Investigation (2003). *Crime in the United States, 2001*. Washington, DC: Federal Bureau of Investigation.

Federal Bureau of Investigation (2008). *FBI, Supplementary Homicide Reports, 1990–2008*. Washington, DC: Federal Bureau of Investigation.

Goodman, R. A., Mercy, J. A., Layde, P. M. and Thacker, S. B. (1988). Case-control studies: design issues for criminological applications. *Journal of Quantitative Criminology*, **4**, 71–84.

Hardwick, P. J. and Rowton-Lee, M. A. (1996). Adolescent homicide: towards assessment of risk. *Journal of Adolescence*, **19**, 263–276.

Harms, P. D. and Snyder, H. N. (2004). *Trends in Murder of Juveniles: 1980–2000. Juvenile Justice Bulletin*. Washington, DC: Office of Juvenile Justice and Delinquency Prevention.

Heide, K. M. (1999). *Young Killers: The Challenge of Juvenile Homicide*. Thousand Oaks, CA: Sage.

Laub, J. H. and Sampson, R. J. (2001). Understanding desistance from crime. *Crime and Justice*, **28**, 1–69.

Lauritsen, J. L., Laub, J. H. and Sampson, R. J. (1992). Conventional and delinquent activities: implications for the prevention of violent victimization among adolescents. Violence and Victims, 7, 91–108

Loeber, R., Wung, P., Keenan, K., Giroux, B., Stouthamer-Loeber, M., Van Kammen, W. B. and Maughan, B. (1993). Developmental pathways in disruptive child behavior. *Development and Psychopathology*, **5**, 101–132.

Loeber, R., DeLamatre, M., Tita, G., Cohen, J., Stouthamer-Loeber, M. and Farrington, D. P. (1999). Gun injury and mortality: the delinquent backgrounds of juvenile victims. *Violence and Victims*, **14**, 339–352.

Loeber, R., Farrington, D. P., Stouthamer-Loeber, M. and White, H. R. (2008). *Violence and Serious Theft: Development and Prediction from Childhood to Adulthood*. New York: Routledge.

Loeber, R. and Farrington, D. P. (2011). *Young Homicide Offenders and Victims: Risk Factors, Prediction and Prevention from Childhood*. New York, NY: Springer.

Loeber, R. and Ahonen, L. (2013). Street killings: prediction of homicide offenders and their victims. *Journal of Youth and Adolescence*, **42**(11), 1640–1650.

Ogden, T. and Hagen, K. A. (2006). Multisystemic therapy of serious behaviour problems in youth: sustainability of therapy effectiveness two years after intake. *Journal of Child and Adolescent Mental Health*, **11**, 142–149.

Ogden, T. and Halliday-Boykins, C. A. (2004). Multisystemic treatment of antisocial adolescents in Norway: replication of clinical outcomes outside of the US. *Journal of Child and Adolescent Mental Health*, **9**(2), 77–83.

Olds, D., Henderson, C. P., Cole, R., Eckenrode, J., Kitzman, H., Luckey, D. and Powers, J. (1998). Long-term effects of nurse home visitation on children's criminal and antisocial behavior: 15-year follow-up of a randomized controlled trial. *Journal of the American Medical Association*, **280**(14), 1238–1244.

Pardini, D. and Loeber, R. (2008). Interpersonal callousness trajectories across adolescence: early social influences and adult outcomes. *Criminal Justice and Behavior*, **35**, 173–196.

Patterson, G., Reid, J. and Dishion, T. (1992). *Antisocial Boys*. Eugene, OR: Castalia.

Petras, H., Kellam, S. G., Brown, C. H., Muthen, B. O., Ialongo, N. S. and Poduska, J. M. (2008). Developmental epidemiological courses leading to antisocial personality disorder and violent criminal behavior: effects by young adulthood of a universal preventive intervention in first- and second-grade classrooms. *Drug and Alcohol Dependence*, **95**(Suppl. 1), 45–59.

Pew Charitable Trust (2015). *Gun Homicide Rate Down 49% Since 1993 Peak; Public Unaware*. Available from: www.pewsocialtrends.org/2013/05/07/gun-homicide-rate-down-49-since-1993-peak-public-unaware/. Accessed 22 November 2015.

Piquero, A. R. and Brame, R. W. (2008). Assessing the race–crime and ethnicity–crime relationship in a sample of serious adolescent delinquents. *Crime and Delinquency*, **54**(3), 390–422.

Pope, C. E. and Snyder, H. N. (2003). *Race as a Factor in Juvenile Arrests.* Washington, DC: Office of Juvenile Justice and Delinquency Prevention.

Rivara, F. P., Shepherd, J. P., Farrington, D. P., Richmond, P. W. and Cannon, P. (1995). Victim as offender in youth violence. *Annals of Emergency Medicine,* **26**, 609–614.

Roberts, A. R., Zgoba, K. M. and Shahidullah, S. M. (2007). Recidivism among four types of homicide offenders: an exploratory analysis of 336 homicide offenders in New Jersey. *Aggression and Violent Behavior,* **12**, 493–507.

Rodway, C., Norrington-Moore, V., While, D., Hunt, I. M., Flynn, S., Swinson, N., Roscoe, A., Appleby, L. and Shaw, J. (2011). A population-based study of juvenile perpetrators of homicide in England and Wales. *Journal of Adolescence,* **34**, 19–28.

Sawyer, A. M. and Borduin, C. M. (2011). Effects of multisystemic therapy through midlife: a 21.9-year follow-up to a randomized clinical trial with serious and violent juvenile offenders. *Journal of Consulting and Clinical Psychology,* **79**(5), 643–652.

Schweinhart, L. J., Montie, J., Zongping, X., Barnett, W. S., Belfield, C. R. and Nares, M. (2005). *Lifetime Effects: The High/Scope Perry Preschool Study Through Age 40.* Ypsilanti, MI: High/Scope Press.

Strom, K. J. and MacDonald, J. M. (2007). The influence of social and economic disadvantage on racial patterns in youth homicide over time. *Homicide Studies,* **11**, 50–69.

Swanson, J. W., McGinty, E. E., Fazel, S. and Mays, V. M. (2015). Mental illness and reduction of gun violence and suicide: bringing epidemiological research to policy. *Annals of Epidemiology,* **25**, 366–376.

Timmons-Mitchell, J., Bender, M., Kishna, M. A. and Mitchell, C. (2006). An independent effectiveness trial of multisystemic therapy with juvenile justice youth. *Journal of Clinical Child and Adolescent Psychology,* **35**(2), 227–236.

Wolfgang, M. (1958). *Patterns of Criminal Homicide.* Philadelphia, PA: University of Pennsylvania Press.

Group Violence and Youth Gangs

Heather Law, Lorraine Khan and Sally Zlotowitz

Introduction

Despite the relatively recent surge in political, public and media attention, adolescent group violence is not a new phenomenon; it is generally agreed that violent youth gangs have existed since at least the Middle Ages (Pearson, 1983). There is emerging evidence that young people in gangs (and particularly young women) have higher levels of mental health needs, as well as multiple physical health and social needs (Coid et al., 2013: 988; Khan et al., 2013: 30–31).

This chapter looks at what we know about youth gang membership, examining their mental health, well-being and broader needs, their patterns of help seeking and implications for commissioning of services. It also considers the future of youth gangs, including the recent interest in 'girl gangs' and 'internet gangs', and the problems associated with these new phenomena. Finally, the chapter concludes with ways of working with violent youth gangs and how we can intervene and perhaps prevent young people engaging in violent youth gangs.

Definitions of Gangs

Since the early research of Frederick Thrasher in the 1920s (see Dimitriadis, 2006, for summary), a variety of collective titles, including 'youth gangs', 'street gangs', 'delinquent youth groups' and 'troublesome youth groups', have been afforded to clusters of young people who engage in violent or delinquent behaviours. Historically, defining 'gangs' has been an area of contention and often a source of frustration for those looking to work with or study these young people.

To resolve this contention and establish a single definition which can guide approaches to tackling violent youth groups, the Ending Gangs and Youth Violence report (2011) proposes the following definition of a street gang (taken from the Centre for Social Justice's 2009 report, Dying to Belong (Centre for Social Justice, 2009: 21)):

A relatively durable, predominantly street-based group of young people who:

(1) See themselves (and are seen by others) as a discernible group;
(2) Engage in criminal activity and violence;
(3) Lay claim over territory (this is not necessary geographical territory but can include an illegal economy territory);
(4) Have some form of identifying structural feature; and
(5) Are in conflict with other, similar gangs.

It should be noted that labelling youth gangs can be considered contentious. Definitions can appear circular when addressing the problem of group violence and delinquency. If we are to define the 'gang' by its delinquency, then how can we expect to intervene unless we attempt the seemingly impossible task of eradicating the presence of youth gangs completely?

As suggested by Klein (1971), we should also exercise caution when labelling the 'gang' because this may serve to strengthen the group. Sullivan (2005) recommends caution when using the term 'gang', partly because of the subjective nature of the term but also because the interest in gangs is perhaps 'overly romantic' and can 'cloud our view' of the important issue of group violence. It should also be considered that the 'gang' label itself evokes considerable concern and anxiety amongst the general public.

There is often a discrepancy between accepted definitions of gangs and the way young people see themselves, which is often simply as part of a group of friends or peers. Additionally, young people may have their own language and labels, such as 'on road' for gang involvement or 'off road' when moving away from gang activity (Hallsworth and Young, 2004).

The Scale of the Problem: Political and Policy Context

It seems that youth gangs are a global phenomenon; they are present in different cultures and have been found to exist throughout history. Many of us are aware of the presence of youth gangs, perhaps through first-hand encounters in our local area but almost certainly through media coverage of violence perpetrated by groups of young people. In the UK, most people will be aware of the gang-connected murder of Gary Newlove, and the shootings of Jesse James in Manchester (2006) and Rhys Jones in Liverpool (2007). Incidents like these and extensive media coverage influence public perceptions and political agendas within our society. Similarly, the riots of 2011 were a turning point in the UK (even though it is generally accepted now that gang activity was not a major underpinning actor). Before this, there was no unified definition of what was meant by a gang. Following the riots, the Home Secretary made a commitment to put gangs on the political agenda and a virtual team of peer reviewers were commissioned to explore the key factors driving gang activity. Mental health issues and sexual exploitation came out as common themes during this review (Home Office, 2011: 6).

The 2004 Offending, Crime and Justice Survey (OCJS) found that 6% of all young people (aged 10–19) would be classified as belonging to a gang (Home Office, 2006: v). Based on self-definition of gang involvement, that is, when the young person is asked directly whether they view their group of friends as a gang, one in ten young people would be classified as belonging to a gang. About 40% of the young people who were classed as belonging to a delinquent youth group said that their group had 'frightened' or threatened people, and 29% has used force or violence.

The Youth Justice Board (YJB) report Groups, Gangs and Weapons (2007) found that two-thirds of youth offending team (YOT) practitioners were aware of gangs in their area and half said that they had a specific local problem, manifesting itself in high levels of group antisocial behaviour, fighting and carrying weapons. The YJB highlighted that there is still a need for a national assessment of the extent of youth group violence, and more work is needed to ensure police reporting includes details of whether an offence was committed by an individual or by a group.

Whilst gang membership is in itself not a measure of the problem of adolescent group violence, it does appear to be both a risk factor for group violence and an indicator of the extent of the problem. Understanding what makes the gang so appealing to adolescents, and why these groups of youths often engage in violent activity, is of central importance.

Profile of a Youth Gang Member: Myths, Realities and Risk Factors

It is essential to dispel the myths of gang life depicted in the media. From the romanticised gangs in 'West Side Story' to the glamorised lifestyles of hip-hop artists such as '50 cent', there is the common misconception that gang life is about a culture of money, strong group allegiances and respect earned through violence. The reality of life for young gang members is often far from this. It is firstly important to understand young people in gangs as individuals, and consider their developmental histories and risk factors, in order to comprehend their motivation for becoming involved in youth gangs.

Age: 'Elders, Youngers and Tinys'

The US Office of Juvenile Justice and Delinquency (OJJD) reported that the average age of youth gang member was between 12 and 24 (Office of Juvenile Justice and Deliquency, 1996). Similarly, the UK Offending, Crime and Justice Survey found that children as young as 10 reported being involved with gangs, although the most common self-reported age of involvement in gangs was 14–15 (Home Office, 2006: 3–4). Research into the Waltham Forest gang members included reports of some children aged 7–8 years claiming affiliation, and gang-related disputes in some primary schools (Pitts, 2007: 39–40). This paper also describes the hierarchical structure of youth gang members: including 'elders', 'youngers' or 'soldiers' and 'tinys'. 'Elders' usually consist of youths aged in their late teens and early twenties, 'youngers' usually in their mid teens and 'tinys' are as young as ten years old.

Ethnicity

Another common myth is that gangs are a predominantly black phenomenon. Whilst it is true that a higher proportion of gang members are black, this is likely to reflect the disproportionate number of black communities living in deprived inner city areas where gangs are more prevalent.

Research suggests that the general ethnic make-up of gangs is dependent on the ethnicities of the residents in the local area. It is also a common misconception that gangs are made up of a single ethnicity. Research conducted in the UK found that very few gangs are made up of just one ethnicity (Pitts, 2007: 40), although the majority of respondents to the OCJS 2006 (Home Office, 2006: 20) reported their gangs were predominantly homogenous in ethnicity, with only a third reporting a mix of ethnic groups.

Gender

Another widely held belief is that youth gangs are predominantly male. Even academic research reflects this assumption, with a lack of studies investigating the prevalence and nature of female involvement in gangs. It is true that police statistics, ethnographic data and often anecdotal evidence report that youth gangs are made up of mostly males, however recent research using self-report surveys seems to suggest an equal level of male and female gang membership (Home Office, 2006: 20). Data from the OCJS 2004 (Home Office, 2006: 20) reports 6% of males, and an equal 6% of females aged 10–19 would be classified as belonging to a gang. Other studies have also reported higher rates of female gang involvement than previously reported (see Esbensen and Deschenes, 1998: 799–827 for review).

The literature on young women in gangs details family histories characterised by exposure to violence, maltreatment and abuse. Sexual abuse is a common theme (Moore and Hagedorn, 1996; Miller, 2001; Fleisher and Krienert, 2004) as is a range of behavioural difficulties, which are seen as attempts to escape chaotic family backgrounds and blot out trauma. Persistent problematic behaviour is often a significant marker of young people's internal distress; behavioural problems most commonly associated with females in gangs included:

- a history of running away;
- a fourfold increase in risk of school expulsion;
- a fourfold greater risk of involvement in fights;
- early and risky sexual activity;
- teenage pregnancies;
- involvement in substance abuse;
- involvement in violence;
- offending.

(Miller, 1998: 443–447; Wingood et al., 2002; St. Cyr and Decker, 2003; Snethen and Van Puymbroeck, 2008: 350; Chesney-Lind and Shelden, 2013).

Over the years, there has been increasing female involvement in gangs and heterogeneity in the roles they adopt (Esbensen and Deschenes, 1998: 799; Thornberry and Krohn, 2004; Archer and Grascia, 2006: 38; Centre for Social Justice, 2009: 73; National Gang Intelligence Center, 2009), including increasing parity in the prevalence of male and female acts of violence (Wang, 2000: 618). Regardless of these shifts, there is still overwhelming evidence in the literature suggesting exploitation, vulnerability and victimisation of women affiliated with gangs (Archer and Grascia, 2006: 38–39; Vigil, 2008: 70; Young, 2009; Berelowitz et al., 2012; Khan et al., 2013: 30–31).

Qualitative research also highlights a range of other drivers for gang involvement including:

- The need to feel protected and to feel safe;
- The need to build and maintain status or to boost young people's reputation;
- Using gangs as a substitute family unit;
- Deprivation, inequalities and marginalisation.

Over half of female gang members identified problems at home as a motivator for involvement (Wang, 2000: 624; Vigil, 2008: 56). Girls were more likely to describe experiences of membership in terms of providing an alternative and compensatory family structure (Molidor, 1996; Esbensen and Deschenes, 1998: 820; Snethen and Van Puymbroeck, 2008: 348). Although many young women join gangs to get protection, they ironically experience increased risk through membership of such groups (Curry, 1998; Miller, 1998: 438–440). Furthermore, girls experiencing exploitation don't always see themselves as victims or as needing help, and for many young women, exiting gangs can also carry high risks for their future safety; these safeguarding risks have been noted to be higher among young women than among young males exiting gangs (Peterson, 2009: 18–21).

Developmental Pathways

Studies which track children's development and circumstances over time identify many risk factors for poor outcomes in later life such as poverty, a lack of positive parenting, family conflict, maltreatment, school failure and lack of positive opportunities or adult role models as well as individual factors (early behavioural difficulties and neurodevelopmental disorders). The more risks a child accumulates, the greater the probability of persistent offending, poor mental health, poor educational attainment, violence and poor physical health including lower life expectancy (Centre for Community Child Health, 2000). A stepping-stone pattern of risk is commonly observed; risks during infancy increase the chance of antisocial behaviour and health and social inequalities during mid-childhood, which in turn amplify the likelihood of convictions during adolescence.

There is an association between the number of risk factors experienced by young people and gang membership; Hill (Hill et al., 1999; Hill et al., 2001) noted that youth exposed to seven or more risk factors were observed to be 13 times more likely to join and become embedded in gangs. However, increased likelihood of gang affiliation was not just dependent on a simple multiplication of risk but also dependent on the extent to which these risks spanned five broad developmental domains: (see National Gang Centre: www.nationalgangcenter.gov/SPT/Risk-Factors/Research-Review-Criteria). Many of these risk factors are mirrored in broader international literature (see www.ojjdp.gov/jjbulletin/9808/chart.html).

Mental Health Needs

There is a lack of robust data on mental health needs among gang-affiliated young people. Two recent studies have provided an emerging indication of the extent of need among this group in the UK (Coid et al., 2013: 989; Khan et al., 2013: 30–31). These findings mirror US research (Corcoran and Washington, 2005; Madan et al., 2011; Harris et al., 2013). However, more robust research is still required to confirm initial indications of need.

Coid et al.'s research(2013: 987), which focused on males aged 18–34 years, suggests that gang members had significantly higher levels of mental illness. After controlling for demographic and other key factors, gang membership was associated with an increased risk of all conditions except depression. Khan et al.'s (2013: 31) study suggested that almost 40% of young gang members present with conduct problems before the age of 12, compared with 13% of general youth justice entrants. Around a quarter had a suspected mental health diagnosis and over a quarter were suffering sleeping or eating problems (compared with less than 10% for general entrants). A third of gang-involved females and one in ten males were considered at risk of suicide or self-harm. Both girls and boys in this sample presented with more child development risk factors associated with poor mental health and social outcomes (including histories of maltreatment, school exclusions, sexual abuse and

severe parental difficulties) than other youth justice entrants. Despite small sample sizes (particularly in the case of the young women), almost all differences between gang involved and non-gang-involved youth were statistically significant.

Neurodevelopmental Needs

Associations between neurodevelopmental difficulties, such as ADHD and autism, and gang membership have rarely been explored in gang-related literature. More analysis does exist of associations between ADHD and risks of offending, but this appears to be primarily explained through the coexistence of conduct disorder(Khong, 2014). As with most neurodevelopmental disorders, general prevalence studies suggest that boys with ADHD outnumber girls (3:1) (Heptinstall and Taylor, 2002). Although some prevalence studies of young people in the justice system observe similar patterns of ADHD prevalence by gender (Chitsabesan et al., 2006), others suggest a higher rate of ADHD in girls. For example, Fazel's international meta-analysis (Fazel et al., 2008) identified around 19% of young women screening positively for ADHD compared with 12% of young men in youth custody. Similarly, a study focusing on young people screened at the point of arrest identified broadly equal numbers of young men and young women aged 10–18 presenting with suspected 'developmental' difficulties (e.g. ADHD or autism), although the validity of the screening methodology has been raised (Khan et al., 2013: 11). The study found that suspected developmental difficulties were more closely associated with young women's gang involvement whereas such conditions were not as strongly associated with male gang activity compared with other vulnerabilities such as poor sleeping or eating habits and drug misuse. Girls in gangs in this study were also as likely as boys in gangs to have histories of early starting behavioural difficulties (the most common childhood mental health condition and a risk factor for very poor adult outcomes) whereas general prevalence studies suggest that boys with early conduct problems outnumber girls by around 3:1. All these observations should be viewed cautiously and merit further in-depth and robust investigation to understand better gender-specific trajectories towards risky behaviour.

Garbarino (1991, 1995) noted similarities between children living in warzones and children living in inner cities. This research highlighted that prolonged exposure to dangerous and high-risk environments and communities can result in borderline post-traumatic stress symptoms and behaviours.

Poor mental health not only drives gang involvement but gang involvement also undermines young people's mental health. Gang-involved young people are at increased risk of violence as victims, perpetrators and witnesses (Decker et al., 2008; Gover and Tewksbury, 2009). Exposure to and witnessing violence can be traumatising, and repetitive exposure is particularly detrimental.

The Impact of Traumatic Experiences

Experiences of trauma, particularly if severe or persistent during early life, can have a long-lasting impact. We are all programmed to protect ourselves from potential threats with 'fight or flight' responses. The more threatening or dangerous the experiences we are exposed to, the more sensitive we become to perceived threat and possible danger. In children and young people exposed to repeated threats, long-term physical and psychological changes can affect the brain, leading to hypersensitivity towards perceived threatening events or situations (Bloom, 1999). In order to survive, young people often develop self-destructive, antisocial or dissociative responses. Flannery and Singer (1998) note the impact of violence and 'stored' trauma on young people's brains. Traumatic experiences and responses can get buried in the amygdala – the more primitive part of the brain. Further trauma can reawaken these buried memories and exaggerated, impulsive and hyper-vigilant responses which bypass more rational brain processes.

Violence is a common response to traumatic experiences during early years. Memories of traumatic events are fragmented and can return as physical sensations, flashbacks, nightmares and even behavioural re-enactment (Van der Kolk, 1989). A major cause of violence in young people is believed to be this re-enactment of victimisation, where the victim becomes the victimiser, and research indicates that the majority of violent offenders have been physically or sexually abused as children (Van der Kolk, 1989). It is important to note that, whilst research has shown that the majority of violent offenders will have experienced traumatic events during childhood, not all victims will go on to be violent. It appears to be a combination of risk factors, such as when traumatic experiences are compounded by the lack of a secure attachment relationship during childhood, that create a pathway for violence in adolescence and adulthood.

Substance Misuse

Young people in gangs frequently resort to the drugs trade in order to secure an income. Fringe members of gangs are expected to become 'runners' to secure their place within the gang and the income to support the lifestyle they desire. Huge amounts of money can be earned by the key players in a drugs trade; some reports estimate an elder will earn around £130,000 - per year and even the foot soldiers can earn £26,000 - per year (Pitts, 2007: 28).

As well as trading in drugs, young people in gangs are also more likely to use illegal substances: almost half of youth gang members had used drugs within the last 12 months (Home Office, 2006: 7) and binge drinking was also common. Alcohol and drug use certainly seem to be associated with violence and are likely to play a key role in fuelling group violence. It is unclear whether drug use itself or involvement in the drugs trade are the greater risk factors for violence, however it is likely that both can have a detrimental effect.

Socio-economic Factors
Socio-economic Status

Gangs usually exist in deprived communities, where social exclusion, inequality and poverty are commonplace. In these areas, young people lack the opportunities to achieve aspirations and progress socially and economically, resulting in frustration. Whilst not every young person in this situation becomes affiliated to gangs, it is apparent that gang membership often seems to be the only way out for these young people. Opportunities to join gangs in the first place are more common in disadvantaged neighbourhoods where the environment is more conducive to groups congregating (in abandoned buildings for example), and social disorganisation allows for less control over the behaviour of groups of youths. Social inequality is prevalent in inner city areas, leading to a greater sense of exclusion and disempowerment.

All of these social, economic and community-based factors can impact upon the likelihood of young people becoming involved in gangs. Deprivation and social inequality are also linked to criminal activities and could contribute to the occurrence of group violence. Young people become involved in criminal activity, such as drugs trade, to generate income and inevitably become involved in the violence between rival traders. Feelings of exclusion and disempowerment only serve to strengthen gang cohesion, with members uniting to fight poverty and social exclusion.

Education and Employment

Research consistently points to young gang members having been failed by the education system. Most have few or very poor qualifications and are either excluded from school or do not attend regularly (Pitts, 2007: 41). Lack of educational attendance, attainment or employment opportunities can be significant risk factors for involvement in gang activity.

Whether formally excluded or simply not attending school, many young people lack basic qualifications, and some cannot read or write. With few if any qualifications or skills, these young people face the seemingly impossible task of gaining employment. Without these opportunities for social progression via employment, young people will seek an alternative way of establishing a secure and profitable lifestyle for themselves, one which often centres around gang and criminal activity (Pitts, 2007: 18–19; Centre for Social Justice, 2009: 88).

The Role of the Family

Parents play a significant role in the development of the child but are also hugely important in supporting young people through their adolescence. Many parents are unaware that there are two key periods of brain development: the first, as expected, is between birth and two years old and the second is during adolescence. Interactions during adolescence shape the way the young person will view the world, themselves and others throughout their lives and inevitably influence the way they react and interact within that world. Absent parents can create a sense of rejection during childhood, and living with this 'toxic shame' appears to be a common risk factor for violence during adolescence. Many academics and professionals alike agree that disruptions to attachment relationships and abandonment experiences in early life, in particular separation from the mother, can be significant risk factors for violence and delinquency in adolescence. The gang offers an opportunity to feel safe and protected within a substitute family unit.

Other Factors

Weapons

Increasing use of weapons is a growing concern among the public and health professionals alike, although it is difficult to evidence a significant upwards trend in the possession and use of weapons. Police crime data does not require a note on offending in gangs, and as noted by the YJB there is also no requirement to document the weapons used in an offence. Advances in data recording are being made in an attempt to address the problem, and police forces in the UK now document knife crime.

Despite the lack of comprehensive data, available evidence does seem to indicate an increase in the use of weapons by gangs. The OCJS (Home Office, 2006: 6) found that young people were three times more likely to carry a knife if they were members of a gang. The main reason for carrying a knife or gun is for protection. Increasing levels of group violence and ease of access to weapons can only result in more young people feeling they have to resort to carrying and using weapons. The fight against gun and knife crime has received much attention in the media in recent years, and whilst it may be possible to target those possessing weapons, it is also imperative to tackle the causes of group violence and weapon use.

The Impact of Technology

The internet has been one of the most significant technological advances of the modern world, allowing us to communicate thoughts, opinions and information to a global audience in just seconds. However, the internet can also be an uncensored, unmonitored environment and there is a growing concern about young people's activities online. There is very little research on the impact of internet usage by young people in gangs, although an initial survey in 2007 in the USA indicates that a quarter of gang members use the internet for four hours per week and almost three quarters of gang members had set up a website to show or gain respect for their group or gang (cited in King et al., 2007).

The internet allows youth gang members to express themselves, publicise their group and beliefs, and provides a fast method of communication. This could impact on planning and organisation of group violence and intergroup conflicts. Gang members can post photographs and videos of themselves engaging in antisocial acts and sometimes violent acts. Social networking sites strengthen group cohesiveness by improving communication, organisation and sharing. The internet is now being recognised as a potential source of evidence for police investigations of gangs (O'Deane, 2011) and should also be acknowledged as a potential means of intervention via a medium which is accessible and favoured by young people.

Mobile phones have also been a major development in technology and most young people now have access to a phone at all times. Most phones have access to the internet for social networking and blogging, and a camera for photos and videos which can be uploaded instantaneously to the internet. Use of mobile phones by gang members allows instant communication of group meetings, locations of rival groups and uploading of photos and videos of gang activities. They can increase social cohesion between group members and act as a medium for communicating abusive messages to others or organising group violence. Health professionals, schools and families are becoming increasingly aware of the impact of these modern forms of communication, and further research into online gang activity is imperative.

The Challenge of Supporting the Emotional Well-being of Young People Involved in Gangs

It is well established that young people engaged in gang-related activity have multiple health and social needs (Khan et al., 2013: 30–31) with much higher levels of poor mental health than other young people engaged in offending and antisocial behaviour (Coid et al., 2013: 987–990; Khan et al., 2013: 30–31). Mental health services for young people reach only the minority of those needing help (Green, 2004: 28). Furthermore, poor mental health in young people presents differently: problems are either identified by chance or are overlooked until young people drift into crisis as adults (Khan et al., 2013: 17). Young people involved in gangs are even less likely to be identified with mental health problems as they function in a world where disclosing vulnerability is problematic and perceived as 'weakness'. As a result they tend to be non-help seeking, avoiding early opportunities to receive help at school or through primary care services.

What Works

To be most effective, strategies for intervention of youth group violence have to happen across the entire life course to reduce the chances of risk factors accumulating and thus affecting multiple areas of young people's lives. To make significant changes to the lives of young people attracted to gang involvement is not an easy task but one that would have far-reaching effects on communities and future generations. To achieve such an enormous task requires whole system vigilance to support children's assets from birth and address risks early. It requires the involvement of early years workers, health professionals, schools, voluntary and social care workers, housing and employment providers and the justice system to work together, acknowledging that accomplishing even small changes with individual young people could have a huge impact on families and the wider community. There needs to be recognition of similarities and differences in risk factors for boys and girls. For example, girls are more likely to end up in gangs due to family or friends' involvement or to gain access to boys, whilst young men are more likely to cite excitement, territoriality, and belonging as drivers for entry. Both genders said they joined gangs to get protection, status and to have fun (Maxson and Whitlock, 2002).

The evidence base for gang-involved interventions is still evolving. The US National Gang Centre has identified a range of age-appropriate promising and effective interventions which tend to focus on multiple risk factors affecting the young person or in the systems around the young person (e.g. Aggressive Behavioral Control Program Intervention; Ages 18–35 Risk Factors; Operation New Hope Intervention; Ages 16–22 Risk Factors). Most of these interventions are US developed (and therefore possibly more adapted to the US gang context). Many are designed for males rather than females. Very few of these interventions build in systematic help to address young people's mental health problems.

One promising programme which mobilises multi-agency support and draws in resources to address mental health issues is Project Safe Neighbourhoods Prevention (Lowell, Massachusetts); (see here for evidence and risk factors targeted www.nationalgangcenter.gov/SPT/Programs/3588).

Emerging Approaches in the UK Supporting the Emotional Health and Well-being of Young People in Gangs

The charity MAC-UK has a vision to radically transform mental health services for excluded young people in the UK. It started its journey when a clinical psychologist asked for help from young people involved in a gang, who she met whilst working on a deprived estate in London, to co-produce a project alongside her. The project they developed together was called 'Music & Change' and was a youth-led intervention putting evidence-based mental health practice at the heart of the approach. Early evaluations suggested it had psychological benefits at personal, relational and community levels for young people (Zlotowitz, 2010). Benefits included young people feeling safe with staff and in the project spaces; the development and opportunity to practise skills, both emotional and professional; to help others; and to increase connections with the community. This led to the development of the 'Integrate' approach.

The MAC-UK Integrate approach is delivered as an adaptive, flexible intervention which is created with, by and for groups of young people who do not otherwise easily access support from professionals. The hope is to transform services to more effectively address the health and social inequalities of excluded young people. As an approach, it is driven by a set of emerging principles, which are evolving with practice- and evidence-based learning (Zlotowitz et al., 2015). These principles include:

- Co-production – working in partnership with young people who are experts by experience, asking for their help to develop services and employing them in these services.
- Taking services to young people – professionals spend time and proactively go to where young people are, whether that's the streets or community spaces.
- Working at multiple levels – supporting individuals with their emotional well-being or mental ill-health through 'street therapy' to working in partnership with young people to address the social, community and economic conditions that create risk factors for gang involvement and poor mental health.
- Responsivity – creating adaptive and flexible services with the enabling governance that meet the multiple needs of excluded young people.
- Relationship-focused services – recognising that there is a need for excluded young people to have experiences of consistent and attuned relationships with professionals who can support them with both practical (e.g. social care needs) and emotional support.

- Wrapping mental health support around relationships and activities excluded young people already engage with and making it relevant to their everyday lives.
- Working with the whole peer group and utilising a peer-referral approach which brokers trust and gives ownership to young people.
- Developing authentic partnerships with multiple agencies to meet the needs of excluded young people. This involves taking an assets-based approach to local community resources and building pathways and links between agencies or realigning workers to services.

These principles have emerged from the four Integrate projects that MAC-UK has piloted in partnership with multiple agencies across different communities within Inner London, including the original Music & Change project. The projects are being evaluated by the Centre for Mental Health and there are promising early outcomes for young people and the wider community. These Integrate projects are named by young people; are highly intensive, lasting for up to three years; and use a multiagency approach, reconfiguring staff from health, local authority and the voluntary sector to work in partnership with excluded young people within their local community. Local adaptations are encouraged to meet local need and draw on local community assets and resources. Generally the projects have implemented the following phases:

Phase 1 – Engagement and 'hanging out'. Integrate practitioners spend time in the community and build relationships with the young people. Joining alongside community gatekeepers and employing young people from the area is of key importance. This initial engagement phase will vary with each young person, but the model estimates that it will take a minimum of six months. Integrate practitioners build partnerships with local agencies that can support them with targeting the appropriate young people and risk management. However, the projects are unique in using a peer-to-peer referral approach, rather than professional referrals. This system of referral means that there are no formal barriers to who can access the support but ensures that practitioners always work within the dynamic of the gang.

Phase 2 – Youth-led activities. The young people involved in the project are asked for their help to set up activities that interest them. This could be anything from music production through to campaigns or website building. These youth-led activities allow Integrate practitioners to engage with young people and to build relationships. Young people learn skills, opportunities and experiences through having roles in setting up these activities and projects. They may be employed as staff on these projects and activities.

Phase 3 – Street therapy. This is a therapeutic method developed by MAC-UK to work with the young people in a highly adaptive and flexible way but drawing on evidence-based practice. The young people dictate the pace and location of the work; for example, MAC-UK staff spoke to one anxious young man, who had been the victim of a stabbing, through his letterbox for three months using a highly adapted cognitive behavioural therapy (CBT) approach.

Phase 4 – Building bridges. Integrate practitioners, from health, local authority and voluntary sectors, support young people to access other services that can support them. Pathways and progress forward are entirely shaped by young people, who are focused on the wider determinants of well-being and are goal orientated (e.g. focusing on securing employment). Some young people become peer mentors and youth experts leading and supporting other areas in co-production, youth engagement and thinking differently about how services are made available to children and young people from vulnerable groups.

Phase 5 – Changing wider systems. The approach looks to create wider systemic change for excluded young people. For example, making education, training and employment services more aware of the needs of young people and making these services more accessible. Where possible, this is done in partnership with young people who may work to transform local or national policy, speak at conferences, meet with their Member of Parliament or local councillors to support young people to have a voice in their wider community and to facilitate changes in other agencies.

The Integrate approach has now become widely acclaimed by national governments and is recommended as an approach for other agencies and services to take up more effectively to meet the needs of excluded young people (e.g. Department of Health, 2015; Home Office, 2011). The Integrate Movement is a sister organisation to MAC-UK, which is facilitating change to statutory services through 'change labs' to more effectively meet the holistic needs of excluded young people. The aim is transfer the Integrate principles and learning such as 'street therapy', employment of young people and co-production practice to other mental health or general youth services and practitioners.

Supporting Young Women in Gangs

As noted earlier in this chapter, young women involved in gangs frequently have severe, multiple and long-standing risk factors – even when compared with other girls in the Youth Justice System (Khan et al., 2013: 30–31). These young women often don't see themselves as victims or needing help, and exiting gangs can also carry high risks for their safety (Peterson, 2009: 18–21).

Interventions supporting young women need to first and foremost prioritise their safety when seeking to exit gangs. They should also provide alternatives to gang activity, access to caring adults, an alternative meaningful role (including education and employment), and importantly offer respect, care and consistency. Female-specific components should be included into effective programmes including (Peterson, 2009: 22–24):

- Attention to issues of sexual abuse/assault and particularly addressing trauma and Post-Traumatic Stress Disorder;
- Attachment disorders and explosive anger;
- School commitment, school success, aspiration/expectations;
- Raising self-esteem and supporting empowerment;
- Exploring the impact of gender-related media images and messages;
- Empowerment to make decisions.

Delivering Effective Programmes to Support Young People in Gangs

Research studies suggest that young people in gangs don't access services, instead preferring to 'stay under the radar'. Young people may wish to avoid showing vulnerability and admitting emotional mental health distress; additionally, they may be offered services that aren't attractive or accessible to them. Many of these young people have experienced events (for example, school failure, school exclusion, lack of academic skills to match their 'street skills' and status, unemployment etc.) which cumulatively increase marginalisation from mainstream society and embed gang involvement. All of this makes help seeking with this group complex and challenging. Services have to change but there also has to be some work to change their help-seeking behaviours.

The style of delivery of these programmes is as important as the content. The literature on effective

---

BOX 8.1 Case Example 1: A Young Person's Journey through an Integrate Project

Background

Nathan at 17 years old was identified by the local police and community safety team as a young man on a path to prison with a gradual increase in his offending since age 15, both in frequency and severity. Nathan grew up with his mum and three younger siblings in a socially deprived and under-resourced community. His mother struggled with low mood after surviving many years of domestic violence perpetrated by Nathan's father, but she worked very long hours. Nathan's father was now in prison. Nathan's interests were music and sports. He was really good at sports but had been excluded from school. Nathan was now smoking and dealing skunk regularly. His mother's house was often raided and he was regularly stopped and searched which made him furious with the police. He took part in some burglaries with his gang elders and had witnessed several fights and stabbings.

Assessment/Formulation

The local Integrate project clinical psychologists became aware of Nathan through their engagement with his peers in his local youth centre. Through gradual interactions with him over a year during youth-led activities, and through conversations with a youth worker who knew Nathan and his family well, they pieced together an informal understanding of his needs and drew up a shared formulation. Nathan was clearly mistrustful of professional 'help', perhaps due to difficulties in Nathan's early attachment experiences and learning from his father to reject professionals. The staff hypothesised that his cannabis use helped him manage the high levels of threat in his environment as he looked calmer after smoking. He sold cannabis to make money for his family, which also provided him with a sense of purpose and connection to his peer group. His experiences of violence both past and present led Nathan to relate aggressively with others as a means of protecting himself. This made it difficult for him to access services and resources, including employment.

Intervention

After many months and with support from the youth worker he knew, Nathan trusted Integrate practitioners enough to ask for their support at court and to ask for a character reference. On the bus to court, Integrate practitioners used street therapy skills to open conversations with Nathan about the stress of court and his situation at home. He disclosed he was close to being kicked out of home. Despite many missed meetings, Integrate practitioners persisted and helped Nathan to understand and navigate the housing system, often acting as an advocate, as well as complete a passport application. Nathan spoke about his hopelessness, lack of sleep and his concerns for his younger siblings. Integrate practitioners drew on CBT and mentalization-based techniques (Bevington et al., 2012) to link his feelings, thoughts and behaviour and motivational interviewing to discuss his skunk use. Integrate practitioners' clinical approaches helped Nathan's emotional development and understanding of his own and other's mental states

Nathan was asked for his help with sports activities for the Integrate project and first he was 'Head of Sport' until he was recruited for a paid position as 'Project Support Worker'. In this role, he met with local employers and community agencies to support a new football tournament for his younger peers and create apprenticeships for local young people. After meeting with an NHS substance misuse worker for his professional development, he also facilitated workshops about the impact of skunk use on physical and mental health and football performance before tournaments. To further create wider change, the local police agreed to play in the tournament and Nathan was encouraged by the local government to attend council meetings in which he could raise the issue of lack of funding for local sports centres.

---

diversionary models with children suggest that an effective child-centred model is one which maximises engagement, is family focused, is outreach in approach, founded on strong relationships, achieves better outcomes with longer contact and which links to evidence-based family and system-focused interventions. (Haines et al., 2012: 189–192; Schwalbe et al., 2012: 30–32). This means that traditional appointment and formal clinic-based approaches are often not attractive to these young people and consequently may not encourage disclosure and help seeking. These young people

BOX 8.2 Case Example 2

Background

Jodie lived in London in a family with a history of domestic violence. During early teenage years, she hung out with her brother and his friends. Her brother was involved in dealing drugs and after he was imprisoned, she continued to mix with his friends. One young man singled her out, started giving her gifts and taking her out, and she assumed they were girlfriend and boyfriend. One evening, when attending a party with him, her drink was spiked. She was persuaded into a 'line-up' (the term for a group of boys lining up for oral sex); sexually explicit photos were circulated, and shortly after she was seriously assaulted. All this activity was retaliation following suspicion that her brother had 'snitched' on another gang member. She became socially withdrawn and self-harmed – attempting suicide. On her brother's release, both were faced with the sexually explicit pictures. Her brother confronted her abusers and was stabbed in front of her ending up hospitalised in a coma. Police attending the hospital referred Jodie to the Safer London 'Safe and Secure' project.

Assessment/formulation

Safer London is a London-based charity working with vulnerable young people. A Safer London Support Worker quickly visited Jodie at home. By this time Jodie hardly left home, her school grades had deteriorated and there were signs of poor self-care and mental health including possible trauma. She wanted help. She was assessed as being high-risk in terms of her future safeguarding. In the worker's view, a history of witnessing and experiencing violence at home had led to poor self-esteem and a pattern of abusive relationships with males. Jodie had also grown up with a huge distrust of statutory services hindering engagement without significant additional support.

Intervention

The Support Worker and Jodie worked together to rehouse her in a new area away from her family and previous peer group (Safer London has a protocol with a large social housing provider in London providing a range of rehousing options for vulnerable young people). This move and how it might feel was discussed in detail and she was helped to make practical and emotional adjustments including getting new bank accounts; becoming familiar with her new area; developing life skills; re-engaging with education/training; linking with primary/secondary healthcare (particularly trauma-based services); forging new social relationships; completing job interviews; developing her self-esteem; and developing a better understanding of healthy relationships, consensual sex, female self-image and identity.

Jodie was helped to prosecute those who exploited her. They were successfully dealt with via the courts.

Following intervention, Jodie had new friends and was settled in her new home, in part-time employment and was back in college (destined to achieve the grades predicted before gang involvement). She had also ceased self-harming. Work was completed over 12 months with step-down support through volunteer mentors. Safer London's role involved supporting Jodie into services (brokering relationships, selling benefits to young people, talking them through practical arrangements, handholding to appointments and debriefing) – essentially taking on a role similar to a concerned family member.

infrequently attempt to access traditional services (until things reach a crisis and sometimes not even then). Young adults are particularly unlikely to disclose vulnerability and seek out help at this stage in their life. For this reason, it is vital for services to adopt approaches which maximise the chances of successful engagement, such as through activities including sport, music and through providing support for education and training, employment and accommodation. These assertive and proactive approaches that bring support to non-help-seeking populations are frequently more successful than traditional approaches. Evidence of this has emerged from Early Intervention in Psychosis (Mental Health Network NHS Confederation, 2011; NICE, 2014) and mental health Assertive Outreach (RETHINK, 2011).

Strong therapeutic relationships are critical to successful engagement with young people (Schwalbe et al., 2012: 30–32). Successful 'therapeutic alliances' require patient persistence, a willingness to listen and work alongside young people and are characterised by genuine warmth and empathy. There is emerging evidence that longer periods of contact with a significant worker or service is associated with better outcomes for young people (Haines et al., 2012: 15). Furthermore, positive adult role models can help build resilience particularly in vulnerable young people with previously inconsistent relationships in their lives (Lennox and Khan, 2013).

Young people are more likely to engage with holistic support tailored to a range of needs. Evidence indicates that effective models of care address risks and mobilise strengths both in the young person themselves and more importantly in the systems around them. For children this often means building family strengths; for young people and young adults the focus shifts to building educational and employment opportunities, peers, relationships, positive activities and community strengths. Wraparound services and multisystemic therapy (Henggeler et al., 2009) both provide evidence for the benefits of integrating and tailoring care to the young person, as does AMBIT (Adolescent Mentalization-Based Integrative Treatment), which brings integrated care to young people with multiple and complex needs (see Bevington et al., 2012). There is growing evidence from a variety of areas that mobilising 'experts by experience' and peer mentors supports engagement and a positive outlook on help-seeking. Evidence on this is emerging from Mental Health Recovery and the Through the Gate approach developed by St Giles Trust (St Giles Trust, 2009) amongst others.

Conclusions

Intervening in an integrated, proactive and engaging way and as early as possible is likely to create opportunities for successful lives and save public money. It is vital to ensure that interventions are consistently delivered (even when they are highly flexible in nature) by therapeutically capable and well-supervised staff to ensure that programmes have the best in helping young people and communities achieve successful outcomes.

Acknowledgement

The authors would like to thank Claire Hubberstey, Chief Executive of 'Safer London', for contributing Case Example 2.

References

Archer, L. and Grascia, A. M. (2006). Girls, gangs and crime: profile of the young female offender. *Journal of Gang Research*, **13**(2), 37.

Berelowitz, S., Firmin, C., Edwards, G. and Gulyurtlu, S. (2012). 'I thought I was the only one. The only one in the world': the Office of the Children's Commissioner's inquiry into child sexual exploitation in gangs and groups: Interim report.

Bevington, D., Fuggle, P., Fonagy, P., Asen, E. and Target, M. (2012). Adolescent mentalization-based integrative therapy (AMBIT): a new integrated approach to working with the most hard to reach adolescents with severe complex mental health needs. *CAMH Journal*. 2012; published electronically 4 May 2012.

Bloom, S. L. (1999). Trauma theory abbreviated. In *Final Action Plan: A Coordinated Community-Based Response to Family Violence*. Attorney General of Pennsylvania's Family Violence Task Force. Available from: www.dhs.vic.gov.au/__data/assets/pdf_file/0005/587966/trauma_theory_abbreviated_sandra_bloom.pdf.

Centre for Community Child Health. (2000). A review of early childhood literature: prepared for the Department of Family and Community Services as a background paper for the National Families Strategy. Canberra: Centre for Community Child Health.

Centre for Social Justice. (2009). Dying to Belong: An in-depth Review of Street Gangs in Britain. A Policy Report by the Gangs Working Group. London: Centre for Social Justice.

Chesney-Lind, M. and Shelden, R. G. (2013). *Girls, Delinquency, and Juvenile Justice*. 4th Edition. Chichester: John Wiley & Sons, Inc.

Chitsabesan, P., Kroll, L., Bailey, S., Kenning, C. A., Sneider, S. W. M. et al. (2006). Mental health needs of young offenders in custody and in the community. *British Journal of Psychiatry*, **188**, 534–548.

Coid, J. W., Ullrich, S., Keers, R. et al. (2013). Gang membership, violence, and psychiatric morbidity. *American Journal of Psychiatry*, **170**(9), 985–993.

Corcoran, K. and Washington, A. N. M. (2005). The impact of gang membership on mental health symptoms, behavior problems and antisocial criminality of incarcerated young men. *Journal of Gang Research*, **12**(4), 25–35.

Curry, G. D. (1998). Female gang involvement. *Journal of Research in Crime and Delinquency*, **35**(1), 100–118.

Decker, S. H., Katz, C. and Webb, V. (2008). Understanding the black box of gang organization: implications for involvement in violent crime, drug sales, and violent victimization. *Crime and Delinquency*, **54**(1), 153–172.

Department of Health, HM Government. (2015). Future in Mind: Promoting, Protecting and Improving Our Children and Young People's Mental Health and Wellbeing

[Electronic Version]. Available from: www.gov.uk/govern ment/uploads/system/uploads/attachment_data/file/41402 4/Childrens_Mental_Health.pdf. Accessed 06 July 2015.

Dimitriadis, G. (2006). The situation complex: revisiting Frederic Thrasher's The Gang: a study of 1,313 gangs in Chicago. *Cultural Studies / Critical Methodologies*, **6**(3), 335–353.

Esbensen, F-A. and Deschenes, E. P. (1998). A multisite examination of youth gang membership: Does gender matter? *Criminology*, **36**, 799–827.

Fazel, S., Doll, H. and Langstrom, N. (2008). Mental disorders among adolescents in juvenile detention and correctional facilities: a systematic review and metaregression analysis of 25 surveys. *Journal of the American Academy of Child & Adolescent Psychiatry* (September), **47**(9), 1010–1019. doi: 10.97/CHI. ObO13e31817eecf3.

Fixsen, D. L., Naoom, S. F., Blasé, K. A., Friedman, R. M. and Wallace, F. (2005). Implementation Research: A Synthesis of the Literature [Electronic Version]. Available from: http://ctndisseminationlibrary.org/PDF/nirnmono graph.pdf. Accessed 19 September 2015.

Flannery, D. J. and Singer, M. (1998). Adolescent violence exposure and victimization at home: coping and psychological trauma symptoms. *International Review of Victimology*, **6**(1), 29–48.

Fleisher, M. and Krienert, J. (2004). Life-course events, social networks, and the emergence of violence among female gang members. *Journal of Community Psychology*, **32**, 607–622.

Garbarino, J. (1995). *Raising Children in a Socially Toxic Environment*. San Francisco, CA: Jossey-Bass San Francisco.

Garbarino, J., Kostelny, K. and Dubrow, N. (1991). What children can tell us about living in danger. *American Psychologist*, **46**(4), 376.

Gover, A. J. W. and Tewksbury, R. (2009). Adolescent male and female gang members' experiences with violent victimization, dating violence, and sexual assault. *American Journal of Criminal Justice*, **34**(1–2), 103–115.

Green, H. (2004). *The Mental Health of Children and Young People in Great Britain*. Basingstoke, Hampshire: Palgrave.

Haines, A., Goldson, B., Haycox, A., Houten, R., Lane, S., McGuire, J., Nathan, T., Perkins, E., Richards, S. and Whittington, R. (2012). Evaluation of the Youth Justice Liaison and Diversion (YJLD) Pilot Scheme: Final Report [Electronic Version]. Available from: www.gov.uk/govern ment/uploads/system/uploads/attachment_data/file/21511 8/dh_133007.pdf. Accessed 20 January 2012.

Hallsworth, S. and Young, T. (2004). Getting real about gangs. *Criminal Justice Matters*, **55**, 68.

Harris, T. B., Elkins, S., Butler, A., Shelton, M., Robles, B., Kwok, S., Simpson, S., Young, D. W., Mayhew, A., Brown, A. and Sarg, A. J. (2013). Youth gang members: psychiatric disorders and substance use. *Laws*, **2**, 392–400.

Henggeler, S. W., Schoenwald, S. K., Borduin, C. M., Rowland, M. D. and Cunningham, P. B. (2009). *Multisystemic Therapy for Children and Adolescents*. 2nd Edition. London, New York: The Guildford Press.

Heptinstall, E. and Taylor, E. (2002). Sex differences and their significance. *Hyperactivity and Attention Disorders of Childhood*, 99–125.

Hill, K. G., Howell, J. C., Hawkins, J. D. and Battin-Pearson, S. R. (1999). Childhood risk factors for adolescent gang membership: results from the Seattle Social Development Project. *Journal of Research in Crime and Delinquency*, **36**(3), 300–322.

Hill, K. G., Lui, C. and Hawkins, J. D. (2001). *Early Precursors of Gang Membership: A Study of Seattle Youth*. Washington, DC: US Department of Justice, Office of Justice Programs, Office of Juvenile Justice and Delinquency Prevention.

Home Office. (2006). Delinquent Youth Groups and Offending Behaviour: Findings from the 2004 Offending, Crime and Justice Survey [Electronic Version]. Available from: http://library.npia.police.uk/docs/hordsolr/rdsol r1406.pdf. Accessed 7 April 2012.

Home Office. (2008). Young People and Crime: Findings from the 2006 Offending, Crime and Justice Survey [Electronic Version]. Available from: http://dera.ioe.ac.uk/ 9140/1/hosb0908.pdf. Accessed 7 April 2012.

Home Office. (2011). Ending Gang and Youth Violence: A Cross-Government Report [Electronic Version]. Available from: www.homeoffice.gov.uk/crime/knife-gungang-youth-violence/. Accessed 7 April 2012.

Khan, L., Helena, B., Saunders, A. and Plumtree, A. (2013). *A Need to Belong: What Leads Girls to Join Gangs*. London: Centre for Mental Health.

Khong, B. (2014). *The Lifetime Costs of Attention Deficit Hyperactivity Disorder (ADHD)*. London: Centre for Mental Health.

King, J., Walpole, C. and Lamon, K. (2007). Surf and turf wars online: growing implications of internet gang violence. *Journal of Adolescent Health*, **41**(6), 66–68.

Klein, M. W. (1971). *Street Gangs and Street Workers*. Englewood Cliffs, NJ: Prentice Hall.

Lennox, C. and Khan, L. (2013). Youth Justice Annual Report of the Chief Medical Officer 2012: Our Children Deserve Better: Prevention Pays. Chief Medical Officer's Report. London: Chief Medical Officer's Report.

Madan, A., Mrug, S. and Windle, M. (2011). Brief report: do delinquency and community violence exposure explain internalizing problems in early adolescent gang members?. *Journal of Adolescence*, **34**(5), 1093–1096.

Maxson, C. L. and Whitlock, M. L. (2002). Joining the gang: Gender differences in risk factors for gang membership. In Huff, C. R. Editor. *Gangs in America*. 3rd Edition (pp. 19–36). Thousand Oaks, CA: Sage Publications.

Mental Health Network NHS Confederation. (2011). Early intervention in psychosis services. [Electronic Version] NHS Confederation. Available from: www.iris-initiative.org.uk/silo/files/nhs-confederation-briefing-on-early-intervention-in-psychosis.pdf.

Miller, J. (1998). Gender and victimization risk among young women in gangs. *Journal of Research in Crime and Delinquency*, **35**, 429–453.

Miller, J. (2001). *One of the Guys: Girls, Gangs and Gender*. New York: Oxford University Press.

Molidor, C. E. (1996). Female gang members: a profile of aggression and victimization. *Social Work*, **41**(3), 251–257.

Moore, J. W. and Hagedorn, J. (1996). What happens to girls in the gang? In Huff, C. R. Editor. *Gangs in America*. 2nd Edition. Thousand Oaks, CA: Sage Publications.

National Gang Intelligence Center. (2009). National Gang Threat Assessment (Product No. 2009-M0335-001). Washington, DC: US. Department of Justice.

NICE. (2014). *Psychosis and Schizophrenia in Adults: Treatment and Management*. NICE Clinical Guideline 178. National Institute for Health and Care Excellence [Electronic Version]. Available from: www.nice.org.uk/guidance/cg178/evidence/cg178-psychosis-and-schizophrenia-in-adults-full-guideline3.

O'Deane, M. (2011). Combatting Gangsters Online [Electronic Version]. Available from: www.fbi.gov/stats-services/publications/law-enforcement-bulletin/april_2011/april-2011-leb.pdf. Accessed 7 April 2012.

Office of Juvenile Justice and Deliquency. (1996). Youth Gangs: An Overview [Electronic Version]. Available from: www.ncjrs.gov/pdffiles/167249.pdf. Accessed 7 April 2012.

Pearson, G. (1983). *Hooligan: A History of Respectable Fears*. London: Macmillan Education.

Peterson, D. (2009). Girls in Gangs and Implications for Gender-specific Programs [Electronic Version]. Available from: www.documentcloud.org/documents/605090-girls-in-gangs-and-implications-for-gender.html. Accessed 20 April 2015.

Pitts, J. (2007). Reluctant Gangsters: Youth Gangs in Waltham Forest [Electronic Version]. Available from: www.hillingdon.gov.uk/media/pdf/b/7/reluctant-gangsters.pdf. Accessed 7 April 2012.

RETHINK. (2011). Assertive Outreach Factsheet [Electronic Version]. Available from: www.rethink.org/resources/a/assertive-outreach-factsheet.

Schwalbe, C. S., Gearing, R. E., MacKenzie, M. J., Brewer, K. B. and Ibrahim, R. (2012). A meta-analysis of experimental studies of diversion programs for juvenile offenders. *Clinical Psychology Review*, **32**(1), 26–33.

Snethen, G. and Van Puymbroeck, M. (2008). Girls and physical aggression: causes, trends, and intervention guided by social learning theory. *Aggression and Violent Behavior*, **13**(5), 346–354.

St Giles Trust. (2009). Evaluation of Through the Gates [Electronic Version]. Available from: http://site.stgilestrust.org.uk/project/uploads/user_files/files/Evaluation%20into%20Through%20the%20gates%20summary.doc. Accessed 16 July 2015.

St. Cyr, J. L. and Decker, S. H. (2003). Girls, guys, and gangs: convergence or divergence in the gendered construction of gangs and groups. *Journal of Criminal Justice*, **31**(5), 423–433.

Sullivan, M. L. (2005). Maybe we shouldn't study gangs. *Journal of Contemporary Criminal Justice*, **21**(2), 170–190.

Thornberry, T. P. and Krohn, M. D. (2003). *Taking Stock of Delinquency: An Overview of Findings from Contemporary Longitudinal Studies*. Springer: Springer Science & Business Media.

Van der Kolk, B. (1989). The compulsion to repeat the trauma: re-enactment, revictimization, and masochism. *Psychiatric Clinics of North America*, **12**(2), 389–411.

Vigil, J. D. (2008). Female gang members from East Los Angeles. *International Journal of Social Inquiry*, **1**(1), 47–74.

Wang, J. Z. (2000). Female gang affiliation: knowledge and perceptions of at-risk girls. *International Journal of Offender Therapy and Comparative Criminology* (1 October), **44**(5), 618–632.

Wingood, G. M., DiClemente, R. J., Crosby, R., Harrington, K., Davies, S. L. and Hook, E. W. (2002). Gang involvement and the health of African American female adolescents. *Pediatrics* (1 November), **110**(5), e57.

Young, T. (2009). Girls and gangs: 'Shemale' gangsters in the UK? *Youth Justice*, **9**(3), 224–238.

Youth Justice Board. (2007). Groups, Gangs and Weapons [Electronic Version]. Available from: www.yjb.gov.uk/publications/Scripts/prodView.asp?idproduct=341&eP. Accessed 7 April 2012.

Zlotowitz, S. (2010). Grime not crime: the psychological impact of a community-based music project for marginalized young people. Doctoral Thesis, UCL: University College London.

Zlotowitz, S., Barker, C., Moloney, O. and Howard, C. (2015). *Service Users as the Key to Service Change? The Development of an Innovative Intervention for Excluded Young People*. Child and Adolescent Mental Health.

Sexually Harmful Behaviour in Young People

Maeve Murphy, Kenny Ross and Simon Hackett

Introduction

The problem of children and young people who sexually offend or harm others as a result of their sexual behaviour has been the subject of international commentary for over 50 years (Chaffin et al., 2002). Most current knowledge has emerged since the mid-1980s following the establishment in the USA of a number of early intervention programmes to address this issue. It was not until the early 1990s with the publication of the *Report of the Committee of Enquiry into Children and Young People Who Sexually Abuse Other Children* (NCH, 1992) that the existence of children and young people with harmful sexual behaviours was brought into the professional consciousness in the UK; progress in the development of practice responses to this issue since then has been steady. A range of specialist assessment and intervention services has been established in the voluntary, private and statutory sectors across the UK, though there are areas where significant gaps in service remain (Smith et al., 2013). Many Local Safeguarding Children Boards or Child Protection Committees across the four nations of the UK now acknowledge the issue of young people with harmful sexual behaviours in their interagency procedures and policy documents. There is, however, evidence to suggest that knowledge and awareness is not evenly distributed amongst professionals more generally (Criminal Justice Joint Inspection, 2013).

Research on the issue of sexual abuse perpetrated by children and young people has gathered pace in recent years. On the basis of few studies prior to the 1980s, Finkelhor et al. (2009) reported that well over 200 research articles had been published internationally. There is a developing body of UK publications (e.g., Erooga and Masson, 1999, 2006) but relatively little UK-based empirical research on the subject. It has been suggested that the state of research in the sexual abuse field consists of a mixture of developmental and clinical studies, which often use less rigorous methods than other areas of research (New et al., 1999). Nonetheless, understanding of the diversity of young people who sexually abuse others has increased with recognition that they do not comprise one homogenous group in terms of either their offending patterns or their psychosocial needs, alongside a recognition that subgroups of adolescent sex offenders exist including those with learning disability, Autistic Spectrum Disorders and female adolescent sex offenders. Research has led to the development of assessment tools and intervention models. However, to date, the effectiveness of different therapeutic approaches with sexually abusive children and young people has largely not been demonstrated (Seabloom et al., 2003).

Definitions

As a sensitive area of professional debate and a relatively recent field of empirical study, it is perhaps unsurprising that there is great variability and some ongoing uncertainty about the appropriateness of terminology and language to describe the issue of sexual abuse perpetrated by children and young people. An early, and frequently cited, definition developed by Ryan and Lane (1991) defines the juvenile sexual offender as someone who commits a sexual act with a person of any age: (i) against the victim's will; (ii) without consent; and/or (iii) in an aggressive, exploitative or threatening manner. Hackett (2014: 17) notes that, whilst this definition helpfully raises the important constructs of consent, equality and authority, it is hard to see how it would now extend to phenomena that have emerged in recent years – for example the downloading of child abuse imagery by young people.

In the UK, the (NCH) National Children's Home report (1992) debated a range of terms, such as 'adolescent sexual abuser' or 'adolescent sexual offender' before agreeing on the term 'children and young people who sexually abuse'. More recently, other labels such as 'young abuser' or 'young sexual abuser'

(Vizard, 2002) or 'young people who sexually harm' (NOTA, 2003) have been suggested. According to Hackett (2014: 16), in many cases the use of particular terms says more about the specific professional contexts and legal jurisdictions in which researchers, practitioners and policy makers are embedded than it does about the nature of the behaviours being researched or considered. As the issues that practitioners face are so diverse, it is likely that a range of terms is necessary to describe sexual behaviour problems exhibited by such children and young people; both 'abusive' and 'problematic' sexual behaviours are developmentally inappropriate and may cause developmental damage, a useful umbrella term is 'harmful sexual behaviours'.

Incidence

An overview of sexual offending in England and Wales published by the Ministry of Justice (2013) highlighted that of 5,977 offenders found guilty of sexual offences in 2011 in England and Wales, 491 were juveniles under the age of 18 (i.e. 8.2% of all convictions). This represents a decrease of 11.9% from the corresponding figure (20.1%) in 2005. Of the 491 juvenile sexual offenders, the overwhelming majority (80.9%) were given community sentences; only 13.8% were sentenced to immediate custody.

Hackett (2014: 15) argues that official criminal statistics record only the minority of cases involving sexual offences by young people that come to the attention of police and the courts, however, little is known about young people who display problematic sexual behaviours that do not reach the level where it is regarded as warranting action through the criminal justice system. The few general population surveys that have considered the issue suggest that a high level of sexual abuse of children and young people is perpetrated by peers. In their study of child maltreatment in the UK using a randomly generated postcode sample of over 6,000 individuals, Radford et al. (2011) found that 65.9% of the contact sexual abuse reported by children and young people was perpetrated by under 18-year-olds, although the overall rate of coerced sexual acts under the age of 16 fell between 1998 and 2009.

Hackett (2014: 15) says that although it is difficult to establish accurate figures, indicators suggest that harmful sexual behaviours perpetrated by children and young people are a considerable problem that impacts both the victims and the children and young people who display those behaviours, as well as their families.

Classification

There is no diagnostic category for paedophilia for those under the age of 16 in either the Diagnostic and Statistical Manual of Mental Disorders 4th Edition (DSM-IV) or International Classification of Diseases 10th version (ICD-10). Specialist practitioners and commentators alike believe that the creation of a new category of sexual behaviour disorders in childhood is necessary with appropriate operational criteria for the purpose of diagnosis, thus avoiding labelling the child or young person. It is to be hoped that the dynamic nature of DSM-5 will enable this development and that ICD-11(under construction) will address the classification issue.

Worling (2001) presented a cluster analysis of personality variables of adolescent male sex offenders and outlined four distinct typologies. There were no significant differences between the groups in terms of offender age, socio-economic status, history of child sexual victimisation or age and gender of victims. The four subtypes identified were the following:

Antisocial/Impulsive: Antisocial, impulsive, anxious and unhappy.

Unusual/Isolated: Unusual, undependable, isolated, controlled, trusting and spontaneous.

Over-controlled/Reserved: Emotionally over-controlled, responsible, reserved, reliable, suspicious of others and rigid.

Confident/Aggressive: Confident, self-centred, outgoing, aggressive, sociable, dependable, organised and optimistic.

Butler and Seto (2002) distinguished between two types of adolescent sexual abusers in terms of the persistency of their delinquent behaviours, proposing that life-course sexual offenders are antisocial and have a history of conduct problems that resemble other criminally versatile offenders. In comparison with sexual offenders whose antisocial behaviour does not persist beyond adolescence and non-offenders, those whose antisocial behaviour is more persistent showed greater levels of anger, hostility and endorsement of pro-criminal attitudes. The level of antisocial behaviour displayed by adolescent-only offenders was more similar to non-offenders than life-course persistent offenders.

Distinguishing between Appropriate and Inappropriate Sexual Behaviours in Children and Young People

The general lack of knowledge about childhood sexuality means that it is difficult to define harmful sexual behaviours demonstrated by children and young people. This is compounded by the fact that research has focused primarily on those young people who have committed serious sexual crimes and are referred to specialist services. Therefore little is known about those young people who display sexually harmful behaviours that have not crossed the threshold for being regarded as criminal.

Hackett (2010) describes the sexual behaviours of children and young people on a continuum which ranges, on the one hand, from normal and developmentally appropriate to highly abnormal and violent, on the other, as depicted in Figure 9.1.

Asessment of a child's sexual behaviour should occur within a developmental context, not only because of the differing status of pre-adolescents and adolescents within the criminal justice system but also because sexual behaviour may have substantially different motivations and different developmental

significance across these two developmental stages. As Ryan (2000) points out, some behaviours are normal if they are demonstrated in pre-adolescent children but concerning if they continue into adolescence. Others, by contrast, are considered a normal part of the development of adolescents but would be highly unusual in pre-adolescent children, thereby warranting referral for specialist help. Making distinctions in individual cases about where on this continuum any given behaviour fits is a complex process, not least because the perceived appropriateness of sexual behaviours is culturally influenced and varies substantially across time both between and within societies.

Various researchers have attempted to describe models that can locate children and young people's sexual behaviours at various levels of seriousness or concern. Ryan and Lane (1997) suggested a checklist distinguishing between normal behaviours; behaviours suggesting the need for assessment, and limited monitoring and behaviours warranting a legal response and treatment. Adapting the work of Barnett et al. (2007) provided the following definitions of age-appropriate and age-inappropriate adolescent sexual behaviours:

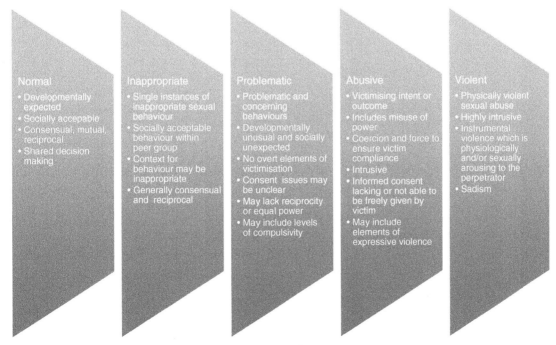

Normal
- Developmentally expected
- Socially acceable
- Consensual, mutual, reciprocal
- Shared decision making

Inappropriate
- Single instances of inappropriate sexual behaviour
- Socially acceptable behaviour within peer group
- Context for behaviour may be inappropriate
- Generally consensual and reciprocal

Problematic
- Problematic and concerning behaviours
- Developmentally unusual and socially unexpected
- No overt elements of victimisation
- Consent issues may be unclear
- May lack reciprocity or equal power
- May include levels of compulsivity

Abusive
- Victimising intent or outcome
- Includes misuse of power
- Coercion and force to ensure victim compliance
- Intrusive
- Informed consent lacking or not able to be freely given by victim
- May include elements of expressive violence

Violent
- Physically violent sexual abuse
- Highly intrusive
- Instrumental violence which is physiologically and/or sexually arousing to the perpetrator
- Sadism

Figure 9.1 A Continuum of Children and Young People's Sexual Behaviours
Source: Hackett (2010: 122).

Age-appropriate adolescent sexual behaviour

- Sexually explicit conversations with peers;
- Obscenities and jokes within the cultural norm;
- Sexual innuendo and flirting;
- Solitary masturbation;
- Kissing, hugging, holding hands;
- Foreplay with mutual informed consent and peer-aged partner;
- Sexual intercourse plus full range of sexual activity.

Concerning sexual behaviours

- Sexual preoccupation or anxiety;
- Pornographic interest (sources include the internet, pay TV, videos, DVDs and magazines);
- Promiscuity;
- Verbal sexually aggressive themes or obscenities;
- Invasion of others' body space.

Very concerning sexual behaviours

- Compulsive masturbation (especially chronic or public);
- Degradation/humiliation of self using sexual themes;
- Degradation/humiliation of others using sexual themes;
- Chronic preoccupation with sexually aggressive pornography (sources include the internet, pay TV, videos, DVDs and magazines), child pornography;
- Attempting to expose others' genitals;
- Touching others' genitals without permission;
- Sexually explicit threats (verbal or written);
- Obscene phone calls, exhibitionism, voyeurism, sexual harassment;
- Sexual contact with significantly younger people;
- Sexual contact with animals;
- Forced penetration.

In the UK the Sexual Offences Act (2003) defines the full range of sexual offences and describes disposal options including Sexual Offences Prevention Orders. Risk of Sexual Harm Orders do not apply to people under the age of 18.

According to Epps (2003) the research literature states that adolescent sexual offenders are not a homogenous group. In studying four matched groups of adolescent boys who had committed (i) sexual offences against children under the age of ten years; (ii) sexual offences against female peers and women; (iii) non-sexual violent offences and (iv) non-sexual and non-violent offences, three clusters of young people were identified, with sexually abusive young people represented to a greater or lesser extent in each group. The three groups displayed the following characteristics:

(1) Developmentally impaired group: more of child sex offenders, some sexual assaulters; higher levels of enuresis, encopresis, speech and language delay, learning difficulties; lower IQ, higher levels of victimisation through both intra-familial and extra-familial sexual abuse, emotional abuse and bullying; higher levels of sexually inappropriate behaviour in school and in the community, especially in children's homes; higher levels of social isolation and withdrawn behaviour.

(2) Violent, physically abused group: there were no child molesters in this group; some of the young people had committed sexual offences against peers and women; there were higher levels of violent non-sexual offending; higher levels of childhood physical abuse; higher levels of violence at school; failure to attend and expulsion; no social isolation or withdrawn behaviour at school; more foster and residential placements; more placement moves; more offending and convictions of any type; no property-only offenders; more substance misuse; more likely to blame criminal behaviour on mental or emotional instability; more likely to have relationship problems with father/father figure; more evidence of hyper-masculinity.

(3) Socialised delinquent group: most well-adjusted; higher number of sexual assaults on female peers and women; some child sex offenders; fewer with a history of emotional and behaviour problems, neglect, sexual and physical abuse, special educational needs, and peer relationship problems; lower number of foster and residential placements and fewer placement moves; higher Full-Scale IQ and verbal IQ; higher reading age; higher age at first recorded offence; less delinquency; fewer family and educational problems; and lower self-reported psychological problems.

Hunter et al. (1993) stated that young people who commit sexual offences against children show greater deficits in their psychosocial functioning compared to those who offend against pubescent females, display less aggression in their offending and are more likely to be related to their victims.

Specific Issues Related to Gender

The most strikingly consistent finding across studies of young people demonstrating harmful sexual behaviours is the gender bias towards boys and young men within overall samples. In Finkelhor et al.'s (2009) large sample, 93% of all juvenile sexual offenders were male. In the UK, Hackett et al. (2013) found that 97% (n = 676) of children and young people referred to nine UK services over a nine-year period as a result of their harmful sexual behaviours were male, with only 3% (n = 24) female. This compares to 92% of males in Taylor's research (2003) and 91% in that of Vizard et al. (2007). The evidence, therefore, strongly supports the view that the vast majority of adolescents engaging in sexually abusive behaviours are male, even taking into account under-reporting and the lack of services for young women with harmful sexual behaviours.

Matthews et al. (1997) studied 67 females and 70 males with a history of sexual offending and found that Post-Traumatic Stress Disorder, depression and anxiety were reported in over half the females. There was a higher frequency of family dysfunction in the females than the males (77.6% versus 44.3%). A higher proportion of the females had been victims of sexual abuse (64% versus 25.8%).

Masson et al. (2015) report on a sample of 24 young females aged 8–16 who were referred to specialist services in England during the 1990s because of harmful sexual behaviours, and compare them to young men in a larger sample. There were two peak ages for referral among the female group: 10–13 years. The youngest female at referral was eight years old and the oldest 16, with a mean age for referral of 12.3 years. Compared with the young men, females were likely to be referred at a younger age and much less likely to have any criminal convictions at the point of referral. They also had higher rates of sexual victimisation in their own histories and tended to have fewer victims drawn from a more narrow age range. However, young women displayed similar kinds of sexually abusive behaviours as young men. They were also quite likely to abuse male and female victims and, in most cases, their victims were known to them, whether related or not. Rates of sexual violence or the use of physical force during the commission of the abuse was relatively rare.

McCartan et al. (2010: 5–6) analysed 258 female referrals to a national community adolescent forensic service. Thirty-eight females had a history of sexually abusive behaviours but only in five cases was this mentioned in the referral letter; 20.5% of the sample demonstrated sexualised behaviour of any type. This included sexually abusive behaviours as well as promiscuity and prostitution. The authors found that 50% had been involved in indecent assault; 13% had made sexually inappropriate comments; 13% had incited inappropriate sexual behaviour; 11% had exposed themselves; 9% had made verbal sexual threats; and 4% reported thoughts of sexually abusing others. In those females who had sexually abusive behaviours 49% only perpetrated indecent assault; 11% made inappropriate sexualised comments; 8% incited sexually inappropriate behaviour; 5% only perpetrated indecent exposure; and 5% had made verbal sexualised threats. 22% of the sample had demonstrated at least two different types of sexually abusive behaviours.

Interestingly, McCartan and Murphy (2010: 6–8) found that those young women with sexually abusive behaviours displayed more cruelty to animals (13.2% versus 8.2%) and abduction (2.6% versus 1.4%) when compared with those without sexually abusive behaviours. However, they demonstrated lower levels of fire setting, acquisitive offending, criminal damage, violence and aggression, absconding and use of weapons. Those with sexually abusive behaviours displayed less self-harm, parasuicide and substance misuse compared to their non-abusing peers. Young women with sexually abusive behaviours also had more learning difficulties when compared with their non-abusive peers. When grouped together, conduct disorders was the most prevalent disorder evident in those females with sexually abusive behaviours.

Learning Disability

Young people with learning disability are over-represented in services for sexual offenders. There may be a number of reasons for this including that young people with learning disabilities who sexually offend may be more repetitive and habitual in their choice of victims and the location and frequency of their behaviour (O'Callaghan, 1998: 435); they may also be more impulsive in their offending and more naive when challenged (Thompson and Brown, 1997). The latter cautioned against concluding that young people with learning disabilities are more likely than their peers to sexually offend.

In their survey of the prevalence of sexually abusive behaviours amongst adolescents using services in England and Wales, Hackett, Masson and Phillips (2005: 42) found that adolescents with learning disability comprised 25% of the workload for 53% of Youth Offending Services with a further 18% of Youth Offending Services reporting higher rates. Similarly, of the young people referred to G-map (a specialist service for young people with sexually problematic behaviour in the North-West of England), approximately half had some form of learning disability (O'Callaghan, 1998: 437), and Vizard et al. (2003) reported similar findings when they looked at young people referred to another specialist service (42% had mild learning disability and 48% a Statement of Special Educational Needs).

There is some support for the view that the sexually abusive behaviours of young people with learning disabilities are often less sophisticated, involve fewer grooming strategies and are more opportunistic than those of young people without learning disabilities (O'Callaghan, 1998; Timms and Goreczny, 2002). Almond and Giles (2008) found that young people with learning disabilities engaged in 'nuisance' behaviours, such as indecent exposure, but they also engaged in a wide range of offence behaviours involving trickery and coercion. However, those without learning disabilities exhibited an even wider range of offence behaviours. Timms and Goreczny additionally suggested that young people with learning disabilities who commit sexually abusive acts are often unaware of the social taboos around sexual behaviours, and that empirical research about treatment options is absent. Fairbairn et al. (1995) suggested the concept of 'abuse without abuser' to describe sexual behaviours in which the person initiating the sexually abusive interaction does not understand the nature of consent or the impact of the behaviour on others. It is also important to highlight how the persistent lack of appropriate sex education, and the lack of appropriate opportunities for sexual relationships and sexual expression, may be important in the aetiology of sexual aggression in this group of young people. O'Callaghan (1998: 445) described a balanced approach to practice with this group that understands their differential life opportunities and developmental processes but also takes the abusive behaviours seriously.

Mental Health Needs

Professionals working with young people who have sexually abused others will be aware that these young people have multiple complex psychosocial and behavioural problems, with their sexually abusive behaviour being just one difficulty amongst many (Vizard, 2004). The Assessment, Intervention, and Moving On (AIM) model (AIM, 2001) identifies mental health concerns as risk factors, distinguishing between those with strong empirical support (high levels of trauma, e.g. own victimisation and witnessing domestic violence; a formal diagnosis of conduct disorder; poor social and intimacy skills; and highly compulsive/impulsive behaviours) and others based on practice consensus (diagnoses of Attention Deficit Hyperactivity Disorder, depression or other significant mental health problems). Conduct disorders are the most common DSM diagnosis in adolescent sexual offenders but it must be noted that inappropriate sexual behaviours per se can lead to this diagnosis. Post-Traumatic Stress Disorder and Reactive Attachment Disorder are also reported in this group.

Assessment of an adolescent sex offender should include a holistic assessment of needs and risks, including an assessment of mental health. These young people often have a history of involvement in other offending behaviours; have suffered traumas and losses; and suffer from a range of mental health disorders. Assessment and treatment of these disorders should be an integral part of the interventions addressing problematic sexual behaviours. It must be borne in mind by those undertaking both assessments and therapeutic interventions that the nature of the issues that need to be addressed can have an adverse impact on the mental health of the adolescent. It would not be unusual for the young person's mental health/emotional well-being to deteriorate and this is often accompanied by a deterioration in behaviour, which can be externalising and/or internalising in nature.

Autistic Spectrum Disorder (ASD)

Attwood (2005) stated that people with Asperger's Syndrome have sexual interests, issues and diversity that are no different to those which apply to the population as a whole. What matters is that adolescents with ASD may experience significant problems in regard to recognising and understanding the thoughts and feelings and actions of others, which may be both subtle and complex, and in expressing their own feelings. There are further complications: the adolescent peer group may not be the best source of role models or information and that the gullibility and uncertainty of the individual with ASD may be mischievously exploited by some peers (see Chapter 15 by Gralton and Baird).

Connor (2007: 3) quoted Griffiths (1999) in stating that adolescence is a time when individuals are driven by sexual interest and want to explore behaviours, but it is noted that there are additional factors which impact specifically on those adolescents with ASD:

(1) **Lack of socio-sexual knowledge and understanding** (an extension of the limited understanding of social conventions and of the notions of mutuality or consent) complicated by the discomfort amongst some parents or carers in dealing with sexuality and sex education such that a conflict arises because of the link between the sexual interests/drives and the observed denial of, or even punitive reactions towards, such features.

(2) **Segregation by gender**, either by attendance at single-sex schools or by participation in specialist support groups where there usually are many more males than females is common, so that opportunities available to boys for interaction with girls can be limited. Griffith believes that unsatisfactory or minimal contact with members of the opposite sex can be associated with lone sexual behaviours, such as masturbation, to a high, even intrusive, level.

(3) **Inconsistencies in formal and informal rules** can be unsettling and confusing leading to difficulties among young people with ASD to recognise which behaviours are acceptable and unacceptable. Therefore consistency when dealing with sexual matters with young people with ASD is crucial to try and avoid these difficulties.

(4) **Intimacy** (the opportunity for time with an individual partner) may be a rare experience for those with ASD, and there may be a risk (Aston, 2001) whereby unfulfilled sexual interest turns into an obsession reflected in fixed behaviours.

Henault (2005) highlights that masturbation is the most common sexual behaviour reported by male adolescents with ASD (and those without ASD). Self-stimulation is of itself not a problem if the context is appropriate (private). However, public masturbation is the most frequently reported form of inappropriate sexual behaviour. Such behaviour can become a compulsion or a source of distraction. Connor (2007: 4) states that children and young people with ASD do not set out to shock or embarrass other people but may be reacting to some anxiety or stressful situation which could involve some unexpected change in routine, negative interaction with a group of peers, excessive demands or uncertainty over what is expected.

Connor (2007: 8–9) concludes that in assessing behaviours that are thought to reflect inappropriate sexualisation among children and young people with ASD, it is:

> important constantly to keep in mind the context in respect of limited social communication, and delayed or disordered theory of mind involving difficulty in understanding the feelings of others and their likely reactions to given situations or approaches. However, this is not to belittle at all the significance of behaviours which appear motivated by sexual curiosity etc. and one needs to keep in mind the current public fears about the apparent incidence of sexual misbehaviour and the very hostile attitudes to anyone suspected or accused of sexual offences. This suggests the need to take concerns very seriously, especially given the 'hidden' nature of the ASD condition, in order to protect the individuals with ASD as much as, or as well as, anyone else.

The implication is for a clear (functional) assessment of the behaviours which have become the source of concern. What is the purpose of the behaviours? What outcome is sought? What seems clear from the literature is that young people with ASD require clear, consistent messages (including sex education) from the adults in their lives about what is, and what is not, acceptable sexual behaviour in different settings. Young people with ASD and problematic sexual behaviours require assessments and interventions that are tailored to their specific needs and difficulties.

Haracopos and Pederson (2012) stated that an adolescent with Asperger's Syndrome may have excellent language, analytical and other educational skills but at the same time find it harder to understand social mores, metaphors and abstract thinking. They are less adept than their peers at understanding body language and subtler cues that let people know what is, and what is not, appropriate socio-sexual behaviour. This can lead to inappropriate sexual behaviours such as public exposure of sexual organs, inappropriate touching of self or others, staring at sexual characteristics of other people and talking about sexual subjects around those not comfortable with it. These behaviours may not be driven by deviant objectives, as the adolescent may not be aware of the inappropriateness of the behaviours in the context he or she displays them.

In contrast with the rather slow social development and maturation, adolescents with ASD develop physiologically and sexually at the same pace as their peers without ASD. Adolescents with ASD may require an individualised assessment of sexuality and sex education tailored to their own needs. Behaviour modification techniques can be used to promote appropriate sexual behaviours and to discourage inappropriate sexual behaviours.

Gillberg (1983) mentions three main problems encountered in discussions about sexuality in persons with ASD:

(1) They tend to masturbate in public;
(2) They demonstrate inappropriate sexual behaviour towards other people;
(3) Many use a self-mutilating technique when they masturbate.

The core deficits seen in adolescents with ASD clearly have an adverse impact on their ability to express themselves sexually and to form intimate relationships. The lack of understanding of social norms and rules can lead adolescents to undress in public and masturbate. Difficulties in empathy can lead to adolescents trying to hug or kiss strangers. The desire for an intimate relationship can develop into an obsession.

Gillberg describes the following steps in assessing unresolved sexual problems:

(1) Determining whether sexual signs are present or not;
(2) Assessing whom the sexual desire is directed towards;
(3) Assessing what stimulates the sexual drive;
(4) Describing the behaviour that occurs when the person is sexually aroused;
(5) Assessing frequency, intensity and duration;
(6) Assessing how others react to the sexual behaviours;
(7) Assessing physical and physiological states after the sexual activity has ended.

Gillberg asserted that these steps should be used to target specific interventions to address problematic sexual behaviours. The Treatment, Education, of Autistic and Communication-Handicapped Children

(TEACHH) Report (www.autismuk.com) is clear that any interventions must be at a developmentally appropriate level, that is, matched to the person's level of functioning. It states that sex education needs to be highly structured and individualised, and uses concrete strategies whenever possible. The use of language needs to be carefully considered. It defines pertinent skills in stages as follows:

(1) Discriminative learning (e.g. knowing when and where to disrobe, masturbate, touch other people etc.);
(2) Personal hygiene;
(3) Body parts and their function;
(4) A programme of sex education.

The TEACCH Report is clear that depending on the level of functioning of an individual with ASD that he or she may or may not be able to complete all four stages.

Intervention Approaches

Hackett (2014: 82) charts how early intervention responses to young people with harmful sexual behaviours were largely based on adult sex offender models, with adaptations for use in work with young people. According to Longo (2003) this 'trickle down effect' has been highly destructive in the way it influenced work with children and young people. The call for approaches that are more child-focused and developmentally sensitive has grown substantially in recent years (Hackett, 2004) and appears to have contributed to a change in focus in working with adolescent sexual aggressors in the UK. There is now consensus about the necessity of child-focused and holistic work (Hackett et al., 2006), in both targeting harmful sexual behaviour and addressing more general areas of unmet need. The highly confrontational and punitive methods traditionally used in treating adult sex offenders have been rejected in the adolescent field. Along with this has come the realisation that it is as important to address issues within the young person's broader social existence, including family relationships and context, as it is to work individually with the young person (Masson and Hackett, 2003). Likewise, NICE (2016, rec 1.3.1) stresses that the cornerstone of effective intervention is a comprehensive assessment process with a 'Focus on the child or young person as an individual and not on the presenting behaviour' (see Box 9.1). Several tiers of intervention are likely to be required ranging

BOX 9.1 Case Example

Tommy is a 15-year-old white young man who lived with his biological parents and two younger sisters. He was diagnosed with Asperger's Syndrome and Attention Deficit Hyperactivity Disorder (ADHD). He was under the care of Child and Adolescent Mental Health Services (CAMHS) and was prescribed stimulant medication. He attends mainstream school. He was referred to a forensic CAMHS team for a risk assessment with a view to intervention following a number of incidents of inappropriate sexual behaviour including:

(1) Pulling down the trousers of a seven-year-old neighbour's son and asking him to kiss him.

(2) Two incidents of his attempting to touch girls' breasts in school.

(3) Hiding items of female underwear in his bedroom.

(4) Accessing pornography on the school computer.

The initial assessment involved a global assessment of needs and risks. The conclusion was that Tommy's inappropriate sexual behaviour arose from a combination of his inherent social communication difficulties; his ADHD; his social isolation including a lack of contact with peers. Gaps in his psychosexual knowledge and understanding were identified.

Following this Tommy was offered individual sessions with two therapists, one male and one female, over a period of 18 months, either weekly or twice-weekly (in school holidays).

Initial sessions focused on rapport building and engagement alongside establishing a clear understanding of the need for interventions with Tommy. Early areas addressed included psychosexual education (including both appropriate and inappropriate sexual behaviours) and formulation of timelines (both of significant life events and sexual development/behaviour). Specific attention was paid to the use of language, and concrete examples were used. Significant input covered enhancing his social skills in order to help Tommy form appropriate peer relationships. This included the use of role play.

Tommy's use of pornography formed another stream of work, including helping him consider how he could express his sexual feelings appropriately, and increase his understanding of how his use of pornography could negatively impact on his sexual behaviours.

Resources used included the Good Lives Model, cognitive-behavioural therapy, role play and social skills training resources developed for use with young people with Autistic Spectrum Disorders.

Regular review meetings were held and were attended by Tommy and his parents; the therapists; and representatives from CAMHS, Education, and Social Care. A number of joint sessions were held with Tommy and his parents towards the end of the intervention.

Challenges that were overcome included Tommy's poor concentration and his impulsivity, as well as his social isolation. Liaison with local CAMHS led to more effective medical treatment of his ADHD.

The last three sessions with Tommy focused on formulating a joint discharge letter to the referrer. Tommy was able to identify that he had improved his sexual knowledge and learnt how to make friends; he was able to identify situations that would increase the risk of his behaving in an inappropriate sexual manner; and that excessive use of pornography, spending time alone and not taking his stimulant medication increased his risk.

At the point of discharge Tommy had joined a local sports team and a youth club where he made two friends and became engaged in prosocial activities.

from parental supervision to treatment services provided in secure establishments.

Creeden (2004: 223–247) similarly describes a move towards a more 'developmental' or 'holistic' approach to understanding and addressing problematic sexual behaviour in children. He states that this move has generated increased interest in the relevance of attachment theory and the addressing of attachment deficits in interventions with young people with harmful sexual behaviours. Alongside this are the advances in brain imaging technology that have spurred research on the development of the human brain. One aspect of this research has been the impact of trauma on brain development with studies linking abuse and neglect in childhood with structural and functional consequences for neurodevelopment.

Creeden (2004: 232) indicates that 'an understanding of the developmental and processing obstacles experienced by many of our clients may refocus and refine not only how we make interventions but our understanding of the aetiology of the problem'; and that assessment and intervention protocol approaches need to be re-evaluated to ensure that they keep pace with neurodevelopmental research. With regards to assessment, he suggests that assessment of cognitive abilities should be more than merely assessing a patient's Full-Scale IQ but should also include an assessment of executive functioning. Alongside this enquiries should be made in the area of receptive/expressive language difficulties. Additionally he argues that given the impact that trauma can have on overall physiological arousal, cognitive functioning and social functioning, some assessment of a young person's current trauma symptoms need to be made. With regard to interventions, he argues that we often fail to address young people's experiences of early trauma and attachment difficulties. He suggests that a 'phase-orientated' approach is the most appropriate manner to undertake trauma-related interventions and follows van der Kolk et al. (1996) and suggests that this should include:

(1) Stabilisation, including (a) education and (b) identification of feelings through verbalising somatic states;

(2) Deconditioning of traumatic memories and responses;

(3) Restructuring of traumatic personal schemes;

(4) Re-establishment of secure social connections and interpersonal efficiency;

(5) Accumulation of restitutive emotional experiences.

The Good Lives Model

Along with shifts away from more adult-based approaches towards more developmentally sensitive and holistic approaches for young people has come an increased emphasis on strengths-based models of intervention for young people with harmful sexual behaviours. Perhaps the best known strengths-based model of intervention proposed to date is the 'Good Lives Model' proposed by Tony Ward and others (2007) and based on the principles of positive psychology. The model conceptualises that individuals are predisposed to seek a number of 'primary goods' – that is, states of mind, characteristics, activities or experiences – which, if achieved, will increase their well-being. Primary goods can include (but are not restricted to) healthy living and functioning,

knowledge, inner peace, autonomy and self-directedness, friendship, community, happiness and creativity. The assumption is that people are more likely to function well if they have access to these various types of goods.

In the Good Lives Model criminogenic needs are internal or external obstacles that frustrate and block the acquisition of primary human goods, that is, the individual involved lacks the ability to obtain important outcomes (i.e. goods) in their life and, in addition, is frequently unable to think about their life in a reflective manner. The authors suggest that there are four major types of difficulties often evident in offenders' life plans:

(1) The 'means' used to obtain goals, e.g. using inappropriate strategies to achieve the necessary primary goods needed for a good life such as a paedophile preferring to identify with and socialise with children in order to achieve the primary good of relatedness.

(2) A lack of 'scope' with a number of important goods being left out of the life plan, e.g. the good of work-related competence may be missing leaving the offender with chronic feelings of inadequacy and frustration.

(3) Some offenders may have 'conflict' (and a lack of coherence) among the goods being sought and therefore experience acute psychological stress and unhappiness, e.g. an offender who attempts to control and dominate a partner to attain the good of autonomy may be less likely to achieve the goods related to intimacy.

(4) An offender may lack the 'capabilities' (such as skills and knowledge) to form or implement a good lives plan in the environment that they live in, or to adjust a good lives plan to changing circumstances.

The Good Lives Model therefore proposes that the concept of psychological well-being should be central to interventions with sexual offenders, determining both the form and content of rehabilitation alongside that of risk management. Treatment of the offender is thus seen as an activity that should add to his or her skills and personal functioning, rather than one that simply removes a problem or is devoted to managing problems. The Good Lives Model therefore suggests that sex offender treatment should aim to return individuals to as normal a level of functioning as possible and only place restrictions on activities that are highly related to the problem behaviour.

Although originally proposed for adult sex offenders, the positive emphasis of the Good Lives Model approach has attracted significant interest among service providers working with young people, not least because the attainment of 'primary goods' is integral to the developmental tasks of adolescence.

Evidence for Effectiveness of Service Provision

Whittle et al. (2006) state that the lack of randomised control trials and the ethical issues of withholding treatment in this group of young people mean that it is not possible to conduct prospective studies into the effectiveness of treatment. They suggest that longitudinal studies are needed to measure the effectiveness of existing programmes with regards to recidivism rates, and how the programmes meet the psychosocial needs of these young people. They also raise the issue of dropout rates and suggest that these may be reduced by tailoring programmes to meet the individual needs of young people attending them.

The authors concur with the need for longitudinal research into the effectiveness of intervention programmes. Specialist intervention services within statutory agencies such as health, social care and youth justice should be further developed, possibly with the introduction of dedicated services for adolescent sex offenders with specific needs such as learning disability, Autistic Spectrum Disorders and mental health difficulties. Whether female adolescent sex offenders require gender-specific assessments and interventions is another area that requires further research.

Conclusions

The problem of children and young people who display harmful sexual behaviours has become increasingly apparent to professionals in the UK over the last two decades, and professional knowledge has increased considerably in that time. However, there continue to be gaps in policy and practice, particularly in the availability of post-assessment intervention services. The characteristics of children and young people with harmful sexual behaviours point to the need for a holistic approach, which considers all areas of the child's life. Adolescents who display harmful sexual behaviours share many characteristics with other young people who have a wide range of difficulties. It is important to address their broader problems, as well as dealing with their sexually abusive behaviours; and to remember that they are young people first, and 'sex offenders' second.

References

AIM. (2001). *Working with Children and Young People Who Sexually Abuse: Procedures and Assessment.* Manchester: The AIM Project.

Almond, L. and Giles, S. (2008). Young people with harmful sexual behaviour: Do those with learning disabilities form a distinct subgroup? *Journal of Sexual Aggression*, **14**(3), 227–239.

Aston, M. (2001). *The Other Half of Asperger Syndrome: A Guide to an Intimate Relationship with a Partner who has Asperger Syndrome.* London: The National Autistic Society.

Attwood, T. (2005). *Foreword.* In Henault, I. Editor. *Asperger's Syndrome and Sexuality from Adolescence through Adulthood.* London: Jessica Kingsley.

Barnett, M., Giaquinto, A. and Worth, C. (2007). *Age Appropriate Sexual Behaviour in Children and Young People: Information Booklet for Carers and Professionals.* Page 7. Melbourne: SECASA and Gatehouse Centre.

Butler, S. M. and Seto, M. C. (2002). Distinguishing two types of adolescent sex offenders. *Journal of the American Academy of Child and Adolescent Psychiatry*, **41**, 83–90.

Chaffin, M., Letourneau, E. and Silovsky, J. (2002). Adults, Adolescents and Children Who Sexually Abuse Children: A developmental perspective. In Myers, J., Berliner, L., Briere, J., Hendrix, C., Jenny, C. and Reid, T. Editors. *The APSAC Handbook on Child Maltreatment.* 2nd Edition. Thousand Oaks, CA: Sage.

Connor, M. J. (2007). *Inappropriate Sexual Behaviour and the Child with Asperger's Syndrome and Similar Conditions. Information Sheet.* Brockenhurst: OAASIS.

Creeden, K. (2004). The neurodevelopmental impact of early trauma and insecure attachment: Re-thinking our understanding and treatment of sexual behavior problems. *Sexual Addiction and Compulsivity*, **11**, 223–247.

Criminal Justice Joint Inspection (2013). *Examining Multi-Agency Responses to Children and Young People Who Sexually Offend: A Joint Inspection of the Effectiveness of Multi-Agency Work with Children and Young People in England and Wales Who Have Committed Sexual Offences and were Supervised in the Community.* London: HM Inspectorate of Probation.

Epps, K. (2003). Sexual aggression in adolescent offenders. Paper presented at the Home Office and DoH Conference on Young People who Sexually Abuse – 17 October 2003.

Erooga, M. and Masson, H. Editors. (1999) *Children and Young People Who Sexually Abuse Others: Challenges and Responses.* London: Routledge.

Erooga, M. and Masson, H. Editors. (2006). *Children and Young People Who Sexually Abuse Others: Current Developments and Practice Responses*. 2nd Edition. Abingdon, OX: Routledge.

Fairbairn, G., Rowley, D. and Bowen, M. (1995). *Sexuality, Learning Difficulties and Doing What's Right*. London: Fulton.

Finkelhor, D., Ormrod, R. and Chaffin, M. (2009). *Juveniles Who Commit Sex Offenses against Minors. Juvenile Justice Bulletin (December)*. Washington, DC: Office of Juvenile Justice and Delinquency Prevention, US Department of Justice.

Gerardin, P. and Thibaut, F. (2004). Epidemiology and treatment of Juvenile sexual offending. *Paediatric Drugs*, **6** (2), 79–91.

Gillberg, C. (1983). Adolescence in Autism. Awakening of sexual awareness. Paper presented at the 1983 Europe Autism Conference.

Griffiths, D. (1999). The sexuality of people presenting with a pervasive developmental disorder. Presentation at the Conference for Services for Persons with Pervasive Developmental Disorder. Montreal.

Grimshaw, R. and Salmon, S. (2000). *Adolescent Sexual Abusers and Offenders in Inner London: A review and audit of needs and provision*. Draft report for Inner London Youth Justice Services. October 2000, The Centre for Crime and Justice Studies. London: King's College.

Hackett, S. (2004). *What Works for Children and Young People with Harmful Sexual Behaviours?* Barkingside: Barnardos.

Hackett, S. (2010). Children, young people and sexual violence. In Barter, C. and Berridge, D. Editors. *Children Behaving Badly? Exploring Peer Violence between Children and Young People*. London: Blackwell Wiley.

Hackett, S. (2014). *Children and Young People with Harmful Sexual Behaviours*. Dartington: Research in Practice.

Hackett, S. and Masson, H. (2003). Mapping and exploring services for young people who have sexually abused others: Findings from a two-year research programme into policy, practice and services delivery across the UK and ROI. Paper presented at the Home Office and DoH Conference on Young People who Sexually Abuse – 17 October 2003.

Hackett, S., Masson, H. and Phillips, S. (2005). *Services for Young People Who Sexually Abuse*. London: Youth Justice Board for England and Wales.

Hackett, S., Masson, H. and Phillips, S. (2006). Exploring consensus in practice with youth who are sexually abusive: Findings from a Delphi study of practitioner views in the United Kingdom and the Republic of Ireland. *Child Maltreatment* 11(2), 146–156.

Hackett, S., Phillips, J., Masson, H. and Balfe, M. (2013). Individual, family and abuse characteristics of 700 British Child and Adolescent Sexual Abusers. *Child Abuse Review* 22(4), 232–245.

Haracopos and Pederson. (2012). *Sexuality and Autism Danish Report*. Available from: www.autismuk.com. Accessed January 2012.

Henault, I. (2005). *Asperger's Syndrome and Sexuality: From Adolescence through Adulthood*. London and Philadelphia: Jessica Kingsley Publications.

Home Office (2003). *The Sexual Offences Act*. London: HMSO.

Hunter, J., Lexier, L., Googwin, D., Browne, P. and Dennis, C. (1993). Psychosocial attitudinal and developmental characteristics of juvenile female sexual perpetrators in residential treatment setting. *Journal of Child and Family Studies*, **2**, 317–326.

Longo, R. (2003). Emerging issues, policy changes, and the future of treating children with sexual behavior problems. *Annals of the New York Academy of Sciences*, **989**, 502–514.

Lovell, E. (2002). '*I think I might need some more help with this problem . . .': Responding to Children and Young People Who Display Sexually Harmful Behaviour*. London: NSPCC.

Masson, H. and Hackett, S. (2003). A decade on from the NCH report (1992): adolescent sexual aggression policy, practice and service delivery across the UK and Republic of Ireland. *Journal of Sexual Aggression*, 9(2), 109–124.

Masson, H., Hackett, S., Phillips, J. and Balfe, M. (2015). Developmental markers of risk or vulnerability? Young females who sexually abuse – characteristics, backgrounds, behaviours and outcomes. *Child & Family Social Work*, **20**(1), 19–29

Matthews, R., Hunter, J. A. and Vuz, J. (1997). Juvenile female sexual offenders: clinical Characteristics and Treatment Issues. *Sexual Abuse: A Journal of Research and Treatment*, **9**(3), 187–199.

McCartan, F., Law, H., Murphy, M. and Bailey, S. (2010). Child and adolescent females who present with sexually abusive behaviours: a 10-year UK prevalence study. *The Journal of Sexual Aggression*, **17**(1), 4–14.

Ministry of Justice. (2013). *An Overview of Sexual Offending in England and Wales*. London: Ministry of Justice, Home Office and Office for National Statistics.

New, M., Stevenson, J. and Skuse, D. (1999). Characteristics of mothers of boys who sexually abuse'. *Child Maltreatment*, 4(1), 21–31.

NCH. (1992). *The Report of the Committee of Enquiry into Children and Young People Who Sexually Abuse Other Children*. London: NCH.

NICE. (2016). *Harmful Sexual Behaviour Among Children and Young People – NG55*. September. London: NICE.

NOTA. (2003). *Response to 'Protecting the Public – Strengthening Protection Against Sex Offenders and Reforming the Law on Sexual Offences (CM 5668)*. National Committee on Adolescents Who Sexually Harm.

O'Callaghan, D. (1998). Practice issues in working with young abusers who have learning disabilities. *Child Abuse Review*, 7, 435–448.

Radford L., Corral S., Bradley C., Fisher H., Bassett, C., Howat, N. and Collishaw, S. (2011). *Child Abuse and Neglect in the UK Today*. London: NSPCC.

Ryan, G. (2000). Childhood sexuality: a decade of study. Part 1- research and curriculum development. *Child Abuse and Neglect*, **24**(1), 33–48.

Ryan, G. and Lane, S. (1991). *Juvenile Sex Offending: Causes, Consequences, and Corrections*. Lexington, Massachusetts/ Toronto: Lexington Books.

Ryan, G. and Lane, S. Editors. (1997). *Juvenile Sexual Offending. Causes, Consequences and Corrections*. Lexington, Massachusetts/Toronto: Lexington Books.

Seabloom, W., Seabloom, M., Seabloom, E., Barron, R. and Hendrickson, S. (2003). A 14- to 24-year longitudinal study of a comprehensive sexual health model treatment program for adolescent sex offenders: predictors of successful completion and subsequent criminal recidivism. *International Journal of Offender Therapy and Comparative Criminology*, **47**(4), 468–481.

Smith, C., Bradbury-Jones, C., Lazenbatt, A. and Taylor, J. (2013). *Provision for Young People Who Have Displayed Harmful Sexual Behaviour: An Understanding of Contemporary Service Provision for Young People Displaying Harmful Sexual Behaviour in a UK Context*. London: NSPCC.

Taylor, J. (2003). Children and young people accused of child sexual abuse: A study within a community. *Journal of Sexual Aggression* **9**(1), 57–70.

TEACCH Report. (2012). Available from: www.autismuk .com. Accessed January 2012.

Thompson, D. and Brown, H. (1997). Men with intellectual disabilities who abuse: a review of the literature. *Journal of Applied Research in Intellectual Disabilities*, **10**, 140–158.

Timms, S. and Goreczny, A. (2002). Adolescent sex offenders with mental retardation. Literature review and assessment considerations. *Aggression and Violent Behavior* 7(1), 1–19.

van der Kolk, B. A., McFarlane, A. C., Weisaeth, L. Editors. (1996). *Traumatic Stress: The Effects of Overwhelming Experience on Mind, Body and Society*. New York: Guilford Press.

Vandiver, D. M. and Teske, R. (2006). Juvenile female and male sex offenders. *International Journal of Offender Therapy and Comparative Criminology*, **50**(2), 148–165.

Vizard, E. (2002). The assessment of young sexual abusers. In Calder, M. Editor. *Young People Who Sexually Abuse* (ch. 12, pp. 176–195). Lyme Regis: Russell House Publishing.

Vizard, E. (2004). Sexual offending in adolescence. In Bailey, S. and Dolan, M. Editors. *Forensic Adolescent Psychiatry* (ch. 17, pp. 228–246). London: Arnold Publishing.

Vizard, E., French, L., Hickey, N. and Bladon, E. (2003). Juvenile sexual offending: A developmental framework. Paper presented at the Home Office and DoH Conference on Young People Who Sexually Abuse – 17 October 2003.

Vizard, E., Hickey, N., French, L. and McCrory, E. (2007). Children and adolescents who present with sexually abusive behaviour: a U.K. descriptive study. *Journal of Forensic Psychology and Psychiatry*, **17**, 3.

Ward, T., Mann, R. E. and Gannon, T. A. (2007). The good lives model of offender rehabilitation: clinical implications. *Aggression and violent behavior*, **12**, 87–107.

Whittle, N., Bailey, S. and Kurtz, Z. (2006). *The Needs and Effective Treatment of Young People Who Sexually Abuse: Current Evidence*. London: Department of Health.

Worling, J. R. (2001). Personality-based typology of adolescent male sexual offenders: differences in recidivism rates, victim-selection characteristics and personal victimisation histories. *Sexual Abuse: A Journal of Research and Treatment*, **13**(3), 149–166.

Chapter

10

Depression, Self-Harm and Suicidal Behaviour in Young Offenders

Gemma Trainor, Justine Rothwell and Heidi Hales

Introduction

The primary focus of this chapter is depression, self-harm and suicide-related behaviour in young people across the criminal justice system; this includes those detained as well as those within the community. The chapter is divided into two main parts; first we consider depression and then, secondly, self-harm and suicide-related behaviour.

The two main sections will each initially describe the prevalence and issues around definitions, especially in respect of self-harm. Secondly, we will provide a clear presentation about what is known about risk, motivational factors and predictors in both the general population and in young offenders in custody. The current evidence base will be reviewed and good practice and promising treatments will be described.

The mental health needs of children and young people in local authority secure children's homes and in prisons are known to be considerable, severe and complex with rates of psychosis, self-harm and suicide well above those of other children in the general population (Department of Health, 2001). This population of secured young people often experience depression, anxiety disorders, and self-harm (Sukhodolsky and Ruchkin, 2006) and many present with significant levels of comorbidity such as depression (Axelson and Birmaher, 2001).

Depression

Definition and Diagnosis

The National Institute for Health and Care Excellence (NICE) (2005) guidelines on depression in children and young people describes depression as a cluster of symptoms and behaviours that focus on changes in mood, thinking and activity. The alterations significantly impact on personal, educational and social functioning. Typical changes in mood are characterised by sadness and/or irritability along with a loss of pleasure in a once-valued interest. Cognitive changes tend to result in poor concentration and attention, and problems making simple decisions leading to a loss of confidence in their abilities. In more severe cases they can report feeling guilty or so bad they feel they deserve to be punished. Some will have suicidal ideas and a small number of young people will experience delusions or hallucinations. Depression is characterised by low self-esteem which can lead to a sense of blame and hopelessness. Physical changes can result in the young person having low energy, poor nutrition and becoming less active; however, this can be masked by the presence of agitation and anxiety.

There are noticeable changes in appetite and weight gain or loss can be reported; sleep problems dominate with young people describing difficulties sleeping at night or needing to sleep in the day. Headaches, stomach aches, limb pain, tiredness and fatigue are regular complaints from young people with depression.

A proportion of young people will present with behavioural difficulties as this is a consequence of their internal mental states. The irritability experienced may result in regulation through externalising acts, for example, disruptive behaviour to others or property. Self-harm, disinterest in self-care, withdrawal and loss of interest all reflect an emerging depressive disorder. Additional non-specific behaviours include: a change in mental state, unexplained aggression, poor school performance and attendance and engaging in risk-taking behaviours, for example, substance misuse.

The symptoms can be classified as mild, moderate and severe depression; this classification is important as it determines the pathway of treatment offered. A young person with mild depression will experience two or three symptoms (low mood for two weeks, loss of pleasure and tiredness) but can function in other areas of life. A total of six symptoms of depression are required to fulfil the criteria for moderate depression and this will impact on the young person continuing with day-to-day activities. For severe depression the young person experiences marked symptoms, at least eight, that are distressing and impact significantly on their daily functioning in all areas of life (home, peers and education). Loss of self-esteem, guilt, worthlessness and suicidal thoughts and acts are common (WHO, 1993).

There are two main schedules used in generating a diagnosis of depression: a US manual for diagnostic criteria for depression, recently updated by the American Psychiatric Association (APA, 2013), and the current version of the International Classification of Diseases (ICD 10), a multiaxial classification framework for diagnosing a range of mental health disorders (WHO, 1993). The latter is the preferred system in the UK and most European countries. In both of these schemes a young person is required to score a number of features over an estimated period of time.

Prevalence and Risk Factors

The UK (ONS, 2005) and international studies (Sawyer et al., 2001; Angold et al., 2002) report that between 10 and 20% of adolescents in the general population have mental health difficulties. Depression in children and adolescents aged 11–16 years in the UK is estimated to be 1.4% (ONS, 2005). Depression is a significant risk factor in adolescents who complete suicide; up to 60% of adolescents had depression, and the increase in risk of suicide in comparison with non-depressed young people is between 11 and 27%.

A number of studies with adolescents within the criminal justice systems, both in the UK (Kroll et al., 2002; Chitsabesan et al., 2006) and internationally (Teplin et al., 2002; Vreugdenhil et al., 2004; Vermeiren et al., 2006), report disproportionally higher prevalence rates of depressive symptoms of between 11 and 26%. These adolescents are more likely to meet diagnostic criteria for a mood disorder compared to community-based adolescents. Moreover, the known number of deaths of adolescents in custody strongly indicates depression is present (NICE, 2004), and in the USA adolescents are three times more likely to die by suicide while in detention (Gallagher and Dobrin, 2006).

In a recent systematic review and meta-analysis of 25 studies of detained youth who met their inclusion criteria, 11 % boys and 29 % girls were diagnosed with major depression, evidencing that girls were more often diagnosed with depression than boys. This differs from the observations in prison and the general population (Fazel et al., 2008). In their sample, using 25 studies that met their inclusion criteria in assessing detained youth, the average age was 15 years. An important implication of these findings is that major depression is more prevalent in adolescents incarcerated than those in the general population. This suggests that there could be an association with a criminal history, the effect of being detained and/or the development of antisocial behaviour. Fazel et al. (2008) describes how the higher rates of depression could be a direct result of the difficulties faced within the system and the impact of detention, or indirectly through adverse life experiences; it is well documented that many of these young people have complex lifestyles and family histories.

The diagnosis of depression within this group of young people can be problematic; this has led to differences in reporting of prevalence figures within the group due to methodological differences between studies. Fazel et al. (2008) reports a disparity in prevalence rates between studies dependent on who has assessed the young person, for example researcher or clinician such as a psychiatrist. This needs to be considered when developing staff training within the different youth justice settings.

Risk Factors for Depression

It is rare that depressive episodes in children and adolescents will occur without preceding problems. Around 95% of major depressive episodes are in adolescents who experience a number of problems such as family breakdown, domestic violence, all forms of abuse, educational disruption, peer and social difficulties and social isolation. Few episodes of depression are experienced without the presence of previous difficulties (Rueter et al., 1999; Goodyer et al., 2000). Adolescents within the youth justice system experience high levels of psychosocial adversity and are significantly more at risk of developing depression due to both genetic and environmental factors. Dysfunctional families with criminal histories and parents experiencing a range of mental health needs increase the vulnerabilities of these adolescents (Kroll et al., 2002; Teplin et al., 2002, 2012; Chitsabesan et al., 2006). Furthermore, this vulnerable group is more likely to have contact with social care and around a third are 'looked after' by the care system (looked after child or LAC) (Chitsabesan et al., 2006). Other related difficulties within this group are low self-esteem, persistent academic problems, poor problem-solving skills and brain injury. Additionally, these adolescents are at greater risk of continued depression as they have fewer protective influences to compensate for the many adversities they face (Teplin et al., 2012).

Treatment and Management of Depression

Equity of access to treatments should be considered in young people in the secure care system. As part of the parity of esteem programme to improve resources for young people with depression and anxiety, the Children's and Young Peoples Improving Access to Psychological Therapies (CYP IAPT) in the UK was identified as a priority area. Collaborative working is an objective with mutual support and learning networks. NICE guidelines (NICE, 2005; updated March 2015) for treatment of depression in young people note that for those with mild to moderate depression, cognitive behavioural therapy (CBT), interpersonal therapy or family therapy for depression should be offered as a first-line treatment, for at least three months.

Cognitive Behavioural Therapy (CBT) for depression in adolescents is a structured intervention and has a strong evidence base (Rienecke and Shirk, 2005). A number of studies have reported its effectiveness within the offending population (McGuire, 1995). However, it has been recognised that some of these studies have limitations leading to problems with generaliseability. Central to this has been the criticism around inclusion criteria as many of the exclusions within the studies are common within the youth justice population, for example learning disability and comorbidity. (Curry et al., 2003; Vermeiren et al., 2006).

Interpersonal Psychotherapy for Adolescents (IPT-A) is an effective treatment option for depression in adolescents. When adolescents in the criminal justice system report depression, interpersonal treatment approaches such as interpersonal psychotherapy (Mufson et al., 2011) or other approaches with a focus on interpersonal relationships (such as those that teach social skills or skills for coping with interpersonal stressors) may be helpful. For adolescents in the youth justice system, interpersonal relationships both within family and peers, can be problematic.

Functional Family Therapy (FFT) and Systemic Family Practice (SFP) for conduct disorder and depression are interventions from a systemic perspective. SFP is part of the CYP IAPT and derives from functional family therapy (FFT) (Alexander and Parsons, 1982). Early studies demonstrated its effectiveness in reducing offending behaviour. It is thought that strengthening relationships may improve all outcomes for the young person, but particularly for those with depression. All these protocols might be adapted to focus more strongly on developing sibling and extended family support, which been important untapped resources in treating depression among these youth. Many of the promising treatments are discussed later in the text as there is significant overlap with the treatment of self-harm and suicidal behaviour with incarcerated youths.

Medication

For those who remain depressed with this treatment or who have severe depression, fluoxetine antidepressant (selective serotonin reuptake inhibitors or SSRI) can be prescribed alongside therapeutic treatment. As some antidepressants have been shown to increase risk of suicide-related behaviour, in the UK, it is recommended that fluoxetine should only be initiated by a psychiatrist to those under 18 years and that the young person be monitored weekly on initiation of medication (NICE, 2005). The risk of suicide-related behaviour may increase at the start of improvement in mood as they become more empowered but remain low in mood.

Self-Harm and Suicidal Behaviour

Similar to depression, assessing self-harm and suicidal behaviour in the youth criminal justice system is problematic. Much of the literature about suicidal behaviour is based on adults in the general population and there is a paucity of evidence for young people in the criminal justice system.

Within the UK, self-harm and suicide has been recognised as a matter of high concern. The National Suicide Prevention Strategy (Department of Health, 2002) recommends targeting specific groups perceived to be at a higher risk of self-harm or suicide and have identified those in the criminal justice system as a vulnerable group. It is recognised that rates of self-harm amongst this population are high and suicide is an increasing problem (Morgan and Hawton, 2004).

Strategies, policies and studies often report on the whole spectrum of self-harm and suicidal behaviour together, even though self-harm and suicide can be two distinctly different acts with differing end points. (Schreidman, 1993). Often self-harm is not about ending life, but is more about regulating emotions, surviving and coping with stress, whereas suicide is about ending one's life. It is our opinion that these behaviours can be understood as part of a continuum, from suicidal ideation at one end, moving through to non-fatal self-harm and attempted suicide, to death by suicide at the other end. Suicidal ideation is almost invariably a precursor to future suicide attempts (Kessler et al., 1999; Kuo et al., 2001), although many who have suicidal ideation do not act upon these thoughts, and many who self-harm do not die by suicide. However, entering the continuum is known to increase the risk of death by suicide (Social Care Institute for Excellence, 2005).

Definitions of Self-Harm and Suicidal Behaviour

Self-Harm

There is no single universal agreed definition of 'self-harm' and the term means different things to different people. The most commonly used explanation is the one offered by the NICE Guidelines (NICE, 2004) as intentional self poisoning or injury irrespective of the apparent purpose of the act.

In 2013 the updated American Psychiatric Association Diagnostic and Statistical Manual, DSM-5 (APA, 2013) (see also www.dsm5.org) identified and provided detailed definitions of two disorders not included in the previous edition of the manual (DSM-IV)

- Non-Suicidal Self Injury; and
- Non-Suicidal Self Injury, Not Otherwise Specified (NOS).

Two further definitions have been added to the literature which are also worth noting:

- Non Suicidal Self Injury (NSSI) is described as the direct, deliberate destruction of one's own body tissue in the absence of an intent to die (Nock et al., 2009).
- Non-suicidal self-injurious behavior (NSIB) is defined as "deliberate, direct destruction or alteration of body tissue, without conscious suicidal intent but resulting in injury severe

enough for tissue damage to occur" (Miller et al., 2007).

Given the complexities around definitions and the confusion with terminology, professionals should encourage the young person to provide their own definition of the event; each act may mean something different to that person. Appreciating the purpose of the self-harm is central to engagement, risk management and intervention to reduce further risk (Nock et al., 2009; Rodham et al., 2004).

Suicide-Related Behaviour

Based on the experience gained during the 15 years of the WHO/EURO Multicentre Study on Suicidal Behaviour, De Leo and colleagues (2006: 12) proposed the following unifying terminology for suicide-related behaviour, … 'A nonhabitual act with nonfatal outcome that the individual, expecting to, or taking the risk to die or to inflict bodily harm, initiated and carried out with the purpose of bringing about wanted changes'. Self-harming behaviour can be a common precursor to suicide; studies have shown that 10–25% young people who have self-harmed will repeat the act within a year (Owens et al., 2002), with the greatest risk within the first few weeks. In addition, suicidal thoughts may exist on their own and not necessarily be associated with suicidal behaviour (National Collaborating Centre for Women's and Children's Health, 2009).

Prevalence of Self-Harm and Suicidal Behaviour

In the general population there are no exact figures on the prevalence of self-harm as they vary significantly depending on the definitions used and timeframe covered. There are poor systems of recognition and recording this information and many young people do it in secret and do not present to services (McDougall et al., 2010). Recent studies in the UK, using a consistent definition, have reported that as many as one in ten 15- and 16-year-olds have engaged in self-harm, most having self-harmed in the previous year (Evans et al., 2005; ONS, 2006). Self-harm is increasing and rates of self-harm in the UK are higher than many European countries (Hawton and Harriss, 2008). Studies consistently report the prevalence of self-harm to be higher in girls than boys (Shaffer, 1974; Hawton and Fagg, 1992; ONS, 2006; Madge et al., 2008).

In young people suicide-related behaviour increases with age; it is more common after puberty and increases over the course of adolescence (Woodroffe et al., 1993). Suicide is the second biggest cause of death in male children (5–19 years of age), after road traffic accidents and was a leading cause of death for young men (20–34-year-olds) in the UK in 2012 (ONS, 2013). Self-harm in adolescence is associated with recurrent psychosocial problems (Kerfoot et al., 1996) and poor long-term outcomes (Fergusson et al., 1995).

The Scale of the Problem: Self-Harm in Young Offenders

Within the youth offending population it is difficult to understand the exact size of the problem as most of the research on self-harm in young offenders looks at custodial samples. This leads to limitations as many young offenders are managed in the community (POST, 2008). Penn et al. (2003) reviewed 289 adolescents admitted to a juvenile correction facility in the USA. The results of the study suggest that incarcerated youths have higher rates of suicide attempts and use more violent methods of attempt than adolescents in the general population.

Chitsabesan et al. (2006) found in a national study of 300 young people in the UK that about 10% of young people self-harmed within the last month with significantly increased rates reported by girls compared with boys, but no significant difference between custody or community sites. Of a sample of 200 children sentenced to custody, 20% were reported to have harmed themselves and 11% to have attempted suicide (at any previous point in their lives) (Jacobson et al., 2010).

Hawton and co-workers (2014) in the largest ever epidemiological study on self-harm in prisons in the UK found that over a four-year period (2006–2009) the annual prevalence of self-harm among female offenders was around five times higher than their male counterparts; occurring at 20–24% compared with rates of 5–6% among males. Self-harm was more common in younger inmates (aged 15–19). For those self-harming, females on average had twice as many self-harming incidents per individual as self-harming males.

Prevalence of Deaths by Suicide in Young Offenders

Within the general population, deaths by suicide represented almost 1% of all the deaths in the UK in those aged over 15 years of age (ONS, 2006, National Confidential Inquiry, 2001).

In England and Wales, the Prison and Probation Ombudsman (PPO) monitors, investigates and reports on all deaths (including suicides) that occur in custody. Most countries, similar to the UK, have an elevated rate of suicide in prisons compared with the general population (Daniel, 2006; Lohner and Konrad, 2006). The National Suicide and Homicide Inquiry has found that young people are particularly vulnerable in custody and there is an increase in suicide risk (Shaw et al., 2004). Since 1995 there have been 19 deaths by suicide of adolescents in custody in the UK. The last three young people died in 2011–2012 (about 0.1% of the youth population in custody at that time), but none since then.

The majority of deaths by suicide in custody occur within three months of reception into prison, most by self-strangulation or hanging (Dooley, 1990; Shaw et al., 2004). Dooley (1990) noted that although there was an over-representation of those on remand, young people who died by suicide, frequently had a history of previous convictions and detention. The method of self-strangulation relates to the most accessible method in custody, though care has been taken to remove ligature points in safer cells in the UK. Most incidents of suicide-related behaviour occur during lock up out of sight of prison officers and peers (Hales et al., 2003).

Risk and Motivational Factors

Risk Factors for Self-Harm and Completed Suicide

Adolescent self-harm is the result of complex interactions between interpersonal, social and psychiatric factors. There is no single risk factor associated with self-harm in young people, however a number of factors have been found to be associated with an increased risk of ongoing self-harm and completed suicide from research studies (see Table 10.1 for more details). It is more likely that the young person will experience a combination of external pressures, strong emotions and significant life events such as entry into secure estates. Self-harm can be a symptom of a more serious mental illness such as depression or psychosis. For others, it may be the result of experimentation and a part of adolescent identity and self-image (Anderson et al., 2004) and a means of communicating distress.

The Prison Reform Trust (2012) published a report, Fatally Flawed, in response to the rising

Table 10.1 Risk Factors Self-Harm and Completed Suicide

Factor	Youth in the General Population	Youth Involved with Criminal Justice System
Gender	Self-harming behaviour is more common in girls (Hawton et al., 2010). Young men are two to three times more likely than young women to complete suicide (ONS, 2006; Scrowcroft, 2014).	Over a third of 17-year-old girls in custodial care had self-harmed in the previous month (Douglas and Plugge, 2008). Young men in custodial units are 18 times more likely to commit suicide (Fazel et al., 2008).
Ethnicity	Suicide is the third-leading cause of death for adolescents between 15 and 24 years of age in the USA, and most studies show an overall higher risk for suicidal behaviour among Caucasian youth than any other ethnic group (Balis and Postolache, 2008). There is limited evidence in the UK on suicide risk and self-harm in different minority ethnic groups.	Black and Asian prisoners are less likely to have attempted suicide or self-harm during their present prison term. Most of those who committed suicide in prison in the UK were white (Coid et al., 2002; Shaw et al., 2004).
Social Factors	Suicide rates are greater in less-integrated and supported communities (Durkheim, 1897). Young people who are 'looked after' by the local authority often have a high degree of dysfunctional family relationships by nature of their 'looked after' status and have higher rates of family disruption, self-harm and suicidal behaviour (Brodie et al., 1997; Cousins et al., 2008). There is a two to sixfold increased rate of suicide-related behaviour in relatives of adolescent suicide victims and suicide attempters and family clustering of suicides. This may be partially transmitted through genetically inherited impulsivity and aggressive traits, but also through social modelling of behaviour (Roy et al., 1997; Qin et al., 2002; Bridge et al., 2006; Roy, 2006).	Suicidal behaviour in imprisoned people compared to those living at home was associated with factors such as being single, white, leaving school early, experiencing poor social support and significant social adversity. Loss and family breakdown contributing to chronic emptiness, loneliness and isolation may result in the young person being at greater risk of self-harm/suicide (Jenkins et al., 2005). Detention in custody separates a younger person from their normal network supports which can exacerbate mental health problems, symptoms and increase the risk of suicidal behaviour (Harrington, 2001). Reductions in staff, alongside overcrowding, which has led to longer time of being detained in cells and fewer staff to engage, is associated with a recent increase in suicide rates in UK prisons (HMIP, 2014).
Emotional, Physical and Sexual Abuse	Young people with a history of sexual abuse were at greater risk of becoming depressed or suicidal during their adolescence – cohort study (Brown et al., 1999).	There are high levels of sexual and emotional abuse in young people detained in prison (Lader et al., 2000).
Bullying	Bullying was the biggest single reason for young people resorting to self-harm and contacting Childline in 2007.	Young people in custody can be subjected to different forms of bullying (Utting, 1997; Bradley, 2009).
Anniversaries	A particular increased risk period can be anniversaries (Barker et al., 2014).	Suicidal ideation can increase around times of anniversaries, which is why the ACCT document (see section on ACCT) specifically

Table 10.1 (cont.)

Factor	Youth in the General Population	Youth Involved with Criminal Justice System
		notes high-risk times to provide increased monitoring and support (NCI, 2011; PPO, 2014).
Impulsivity	Higher levels of impulsive aggression are associated with suicidal behaviour and self-harm (Hawton et al., 1999; Ruchkin et al., 2003).	There are higher levels of impulsivity in young people detained in prison compared to those in the community (Chretien and Persinger, 2000).
Psychiatric Comorbidity	Psychiatric disorders are strongly associated with self-harm and suicide (Evans et al., 2004). Around two-thirds of children and adolescents engaging in self-harm also present with depression (Brent et al., 1993; Kerfoot, 1996; Burgess et al., 1998; Harrington et al., 2008). Anxiety disorders have been associated with self-harm and suicidal behaviour (Gould et al., 1998).	All psychiatric disorders are increased in youth in custody (Lader et al., 2000). Young women in custody have the highest rates of mental health problems, particularly depression, Post-Traumatic Stress Disorder and self-harm (Chitsabesan et al., 2006).
Prison Detention and Contact with the Criminal Justice System		Having shown that young offenders have higher rates of most risk factors for suicide-related behaviours, there is also evidence that prison detention itself is a risk factor (Gore, 1999; Blaauw et al., 2002; Daniel, 2006; Lohner and Konrad, 2006).

number of deaths of children and young people in custody. It was based on the experiences of 98 children and young people who died in secure settings between 2003 and 2010 (see Box 10.1 for summary findings from Prison Reform Trust, 2012: 7). Their detailed examination of factors associated with these deaths exposed systemic failings contributing to the risk of fatality and concluded that adult protocols had been applied to adolescent and young adults, without considering their individual and developmental needs. Furthermore, there had been inadequate institutional responses to the deaths in custody, such that investigations and inquests were subject to lengthy delays and inadequate reflective time to enable institutions and agencies to learn and prevent further deaths.

Imitation/Contagion

Suicide contagion is sometimes known as the 'Werther effect', a reference to Goethe's *The Sorrows of Young Werther*. Evidence for the mechanism of 'contagion' is not yet clear. It is thought to be related to the taboo against suicide being broken down by exposure to a first suicidal act (Sherman and Morschauser, 1989). Suicide contagion or 'copycat' imitation behaviour has been described in relation to clusters of adolescents who have heard about suicidal-related behaviour within their social network and then engaged in their own suicide-related behaviour (Brent et al., 1989; Taiminen et al., 1998). There are now media guidelines on how to report deaths by suicide, to prevent any such imitation (Pirkis and Machlin, 2013). Hales and colleagues (2003, 2014) found that those who had contact with another's suicide-related behaviour in a Young Offender Institution (YOI), had increased rates of own self-harm or suicide-related behaviour.

Protective Factors for Self-Harming Behaviour

When conducting assessments of risks it is essential to consider protective and resilient factors. These are the

---

BOX 10.1 Findings from the 'Fatally Flawed' Study (Prison Reform Trust, 2012)

Common themes identified by the report regarding young people who had died in custody:
- Were some of the most disadvantaged in society and had experienced problems with mental health, self-harm, alcohol and/or drugs;
- Had significant interaction with community agencies before entering prison yet in many cases there were failures in communication and information exchange between prisons and those agencies;
- Despite their vulnerability, they had not been diverted out of the criminal justice system at an early stage and had ended up remanded or sentenced to prison;
- Were placed in prisons with unsafe environments and cells;
- Experienced poor medical care and limited access to therapeutic services in prison;
- Had been exposed to bullying and treatment such as segregation and restraint;
- Were failed by the systems set up to safeguard them from harm.

BOX 10.2 Protective Factors

- Personal resources – emotional resilience
- Strong connections and supportive relationships with family and friends
- Evidence of ability to use problem-solving skills and coping strategies
- Restricted access to lethal means of self-harm and suicide
- Access to supportive mental health, care or therapeutic relationship
- Enjoyment and good involvement with education/vocational work
- A good sense of humour
- Life-affirming beliefs that discourage suicide and support self-preservation.

---

aspects of a person's life that may help to reduce the impact of the risks they are facing (McDougall et al., 2010). Protective factors can help facilitate positive outcomes, even when a young person is experiencing adverse life events and external stress, such as incarceration (see Box 10.2).

Box 10.3 presents a case example of a young person in the criminal justice system with self-harming and suicide-related behaviour.

Motivational Factors

A number of studies looking at self-harm in custodial settings reported that targeting individual psychological factors may be more valuable than population risk factors (Bonner and Rich, 1990).

It has been well documented that understanding the motives behind self-harm can prevent further self-harm episodes. (Nock et al., 2009; Rodham et al., 2004), but there has been little research into the reasons why young offenders engage in self-harm. The majority of a cohort (93%) of a sample of young women held in secure settings who had self-harmed in the previous month told researchers that they had cut themselves to relieve feelings of anger, tension, anxiety and depression rather than drawing attention to their situation (Douglas and Plugge, 2008).

Kircher et al. (2008) examined self-harming behaviour of young prisoners to identify, by means of coping typologies, prisoners at higher risk of self-harming behaviour. They found that it was possible to classify participants into four groups with lower and higher risk of self-harming behaviour. The group at greatest risk was the one that used more avoidance and less coping behaviours, for example poor problem-solving skills.

In comparing a group of young offenders in the community who had self-harmed with those who had not, Knowles and colleague (2011) found the most commonly reported motivations for self-harm were emotion regulation and expression, rather than external expression to affect others' behaviour towards them.

Screening and Assessment

Identifying Young People at Risk

Effective services should be able to identify and offer services to young people at specific risk, therefore screening and assessment are vital aspects of

BOX 10.3 Case Example

Jack is a 17-year-old boy who is currently on remand for possession of a weapon and resisting arrest. Jack is likely to be given a custodial sentence. His early formative years were characterised by emotional and physical abuse. His father committed suicide and was a well-known heroin addict. Jack is also impulsive and has abused street drugs. His chaotic behaviour contributed to the recent breakdown in his relationship with his long-term girlfriend.

Jack has a history of cutting and overdosing outside of prison and recently attempted to tie a ligature whilst in his cell. He made great efforts to avoid discovery of the act, by tying the ligature at night, in his cell, immediately after an officer had checked the cell. He was extremely disappointed when staff were alerted to his actions by the young man in the adjacent cell ringing his cell bell when he heard noises of difficulty in breathing.

Formulation

This suicide attempt is one of concern because Jack took care for it not to be discovered and used a method with high chance of a fatal outcome. His response to discovery is also suggestive of high suicidal intent. This attempt appears to have been precipitated by the recent breakdown in his relationship, in the context of him being on remand in prison and anticipating a custodial sentence. Jack has many risk factors for fatal suicide-related behaviour. The static factors include the fact that he suffered emotional and physical abuse as a child and his father committed suicide. He has also previously attempted self-harm and suicide, showing his lack of learning about how to manage stressful situations without self-harm. Dynamic factors, which can change, include his impulsiveness, his sense of loneliness, hopelessness and lack of social learning about how to manage stressful situations.

Treatment

Jack needs urgent support to reduce the risk of another imminent attempt at suicide. The healthcare in-reach team should liaise with the prison officers, in the immediate care planning for this young man, to consider what level of observations he needs in the immediate future, which can be monitored and reviewed within the ACCT document (see section on ACCT).

Having ensured that Jack is safe in the immediate future, care planning is needed to help him to gain psychological strength in the longer term. CBT would be helpful for him to find strategies to manage his emotions, which can be offered individually or in a group setting. He would also benefit from substance misuse work; his substance misuse and impulsive behaviour place him at high risk of impulsive suicide-related behaviour. A further assessment of impulsivity can consider whether Jack has Attention Deficit Hyperactivity Disorder (ADHD) and whether ADHD treatment would be appropriate. However, impulsive behaviour in victims of childhood abuse may be an avoidance of emotional turmoil. Interpersonal therapy could be considered to help Jack understand how his childhood experiences have impacted on his interpersonal relationships and to learn skills to manage relationships more effectively. Jack also needs help to return to prosocial daily activities, such as education and employment. This will help to build up his self-esteem and inner feelings of self-worth.

interventions and risk management programmes. However, these young people can be difficult to engage, often as a result of their childhood traumas and difficulties trusting adults and those in authority. Therefore, they are less likely to access services when needed. Recent NICE guidelines (2011) in the UK reviewed assessment for self-harm and suicide-related behaviour and stressed the importance of not relying solely on risk assessment tools, but noted that they could be used in conjunction with clinical judgement to aid assessment. There are some assessment tools used to assess future risk of suicide-related behaviour based on hopelessness and past behaviour. Below is a description of some of the tools used in the secure estates within the UK.

CHAT (Comprehensive Health Assessment Tool)

- Semi-structured tool assessing mental health needs and risk of self-harm. Currently used for all young people entering the secure estate within England (Offender Health Research Network, 2013; Chitsabesan et al., 2014).

Beck Hopelessness Scale (BHS)

- Self-reported 'actuarial' type scale comprising of 20 items (scored 0 or 1) assessing feelings about the future as hopelessness is high risk factor for completing suicide (Beck and Steer, 1988).

Beck Scale for Suicide Ideation (BSSI)

- A 19-item self-rating questionnaire measuring suicidal ideation, developed from the Scale for Suicidal Ideation (SSI) and rated on a three-point scale (0,1,2) (Beck et al., 1979; Beck and Steer 1988, 1991). Mainly used to differentiate between suicide ideators and non-ideators (Steer et al., 1993).

Risk Management Strategies

When a risk of self-harm or suicide-related behaviour has been identified, it is important that a care plan (risk management plan) is made to reduce the risk and distress that the young person is feeling. This involves considering how severe and imminent the risk is.

Place of Care

For those found to be at risk to themselves, the question arises about the most suitable place for their care. The decision for this should be based upon the underlying reasons for the risk of harm to self, where this would be most appropriately treated and the level of supervision required. Custodial settings may manage risk to self but some young people may benefit from transfer to hospital for treatment. Bradley (2009) recommended that offenders with mental health needs should be assessed to consider diversion from custody. For those with risks of self-harm or suicide-related behaviour associated with major mental illnesses such as psychosis or depression, it is accepted that hospital treatment is preferable to treatment during ongoing detention in a custodial setting.

Supervision and Restriction to Access of At-Risk Young People

For those at immediate risk, the clinician and carers need to consider how to keep the young person safe until their immediate risk reduces or their crisis ends. This may involve enhanced levels of supervision.

Restricting access to means of self-harm reduces opportunity for self-harm or suicide-related behaviour. However, primitive protective and punitive practices to manage risk, such as stripped cells, have been stopped in the UK, with those at risk of self-harm being managed in a more constructive and supportive manner.

Assessment, Care in Custody and Teamwork (ACCT)

The ACCT process is the way that UK prisons manage risk to self. It is managed by prison staff, but aims to bring all agencies working with the young person in the prison, together, to create a safe and caring environment, minimise distress and provide individual support for the person at risk.

Listeners and Support

In most prisons in the UK and secure placements, there are also 'listeners', peers trained by the Samaritans to listen to those at risk of harm to self.

Good Practice in Management of Self-Harm in the Criminal Justice System

The provision and providers of services to assist young people vary considerably across the secure estates and so the therapy offered can range from supportive counselling to a more in-depth psychodynamic approach. However, the following good practices should be noted:

- Working individually with the young person to understand their motivations, strengths and weaknesses.
- Developing treatment plans to focus on building up individual strengths, strengthening community support and reducing individual weaknesses.
- Matching the individual young person to therapies with which they would be able to engage.

Promising Interventions

Further research is required to develop robust therapeutic interventions in self-harm within the whole adolescent population. However, in recent years there has been an increase in a number of interventions that show potential. Ougrin et al. (2012) reported on the efficacy of randomised controlled trials (RCT) in reducing the repetition of self-harm in adolescents. The trials included in this review are listed in Table 10.2:

Dialectical Behavioural Therapy (DBT)

DBT focuses on several problems, including motivational issues, emotional reactivity, impulsivity and also on furnishing clients with improved behavioural skills through individual, family and group work.

Table 10.2 RCTs of Therapeutic Interventions in Self-Harm

Intervention	Reference
Specific problem-solving intervention designed to increase engagement	Spirito et al., 2002
Cognitive behaviour treatment (CBT) targeting problem solving and affect management skills	Donaldson et al., 2005
Home-based family therapy delivered by social workers	Harrington et al., 1998
Developmental group psychotherapy incorporating the techniques of problem solving and cognitive behavioural interventions, dialectical behaviour therapy (DBT) and psychodynamic group psychotherapy	Green et al., 2011; Hazell et al., 2009 and Wood et al., 2001;
Individual cognitive analytic therapy designed to prevent the development of borderline personality disorder	Chanen et al., 2008
Attachment-based family therapy	Diamond et al., 2010
Therapeutic assessment for self-harm	Ougrin et al., 2011
Emotion regulation group training	Schuppert et al., 2009
Issuing tokens allowing readmission	Cotgrove, et al., 1995
Youth-nominated support team	King et al., 2006, 2009

DBT has proved promising in adult populations (Linehan et al., 1999), and while prison and secure hospital-based DBT services for adults in the UK are developing rapidly, services for young offenders are in their infancy. A small number of community adolescent forensic services provide DBT as an 'in-reach' service, and a small number of YOIs offer DBT to young people in custody, particularly young women who self-harm (McDougall and Jones, 2007).

Cognitive Behavioural Therapy (CBT)

Engaging and retaining young people in CBT is acknowledged to be a common problem (Kazdin et al., 1997). Interventions typically rely on the participants' willingness to undertake homework tasks and assume competence in carrying these out and reporting back at subsequent sessions along with literacy skills and some capacity for reflection. These pose particular challenges working with young people in secure environments due to issues of trust (Reinecke and Shirk, 2005).

Multisystemic Therapy (MST)

This was originally designed as an intervention in the USA for the offending population and is now being adapted to meet the needs of various groups, including self-harm. It is so named because it addresses the different systems in a young person's life and is focused on intensive community- and family-based treatment. The goal is to reduce youth criminality and antisocial behaviours by decreasing rates of incarceration and out-of-home placements. The underlying principle is to empower youth and parents with skills and resources to address difficulties and cope with complex environmental and social problems. The treatment is targeted at improving the lives of juvenile offenders by professionals working creatively with the systems that the young person finds themselves in (Henggeler and Borduin, 1990).

Conclusions

It is of concern that despite the high prevalence of young people presenting with self-harming behaviours within the criminal justice system, little is known about effective interventions. There is no standard treatment in the UK or USA that has been found to be superior to another, even though there has been a significant increase in different treatment approaches for the wider general adolescent population over the past ten years (Hawton, 2010).

Self-harm is not an illness but a manifestation of significant unmet need and therefore underlying mental health disorders and coexisting problems that need to be addressed. Resilience is an essential component in protecting against risk and some children in adverse circumstances have less of these; therefore bolstering self-esteem, emotional well-being and promoting hope are imperative in the management of young people who have long since abandoned the notion of positive change

Many of the prison reform strategies are centred around early detection of young people at risk of developing depression, self-harming behaviour or attempting suicide. Terminology and definitions of the act can cause confusion. Therefore it is essential that professionals involved in caring for such young people reivew the need to consider every act of self-harm as a unique expression and ascertain the young person's intention at the time. Sound knowledge of the clinical features, course and treatment of depression, self-harm and suicide are essential skills when working with this uniquely challenging group of young people. One area that appears to be lacking in comparison to the advances in non-secured youths is the views and opinions of the young people themselves when planning, delivering or evaluating self-harm interventions in custody.

It is of concern that incarceration may increase the risk of self-harm or suicide-related behaviour. The shock and physical and emotional isolation of custody can leave young people feeling vulnerable. Additionally, in some custodial settings there are high rates of bullying (Utting, 1997, Bradley, 2009) which need to be addressed.

Interventions to reduce depression, self-harm and suicide-related behaviour require staff to support the young person, therapists to work alongside them and educational provision to help them develop their skills. Staff cuts have been seen in the prison establishment in the UK over austerity years, with associated increased rates of suicide. Investment in staff, embracing the concept of relational security and trauma informed care and support is required to ensure early detention of at-risk youths and strategies that are proactive in contrast to reactive.

References

Alexander, J. F. and Parsons, B. V. (1982). *Functional Family Therapy*. Monterey, CA: Brooks/Cole.

American Psychiatric Association (APA) (2013). *Diagnostic and Statistical Manual of Mental Disorders*. 5th Edition. Washington, DC: APA.

Anderson, M., Woodward, L. and Armstrong, M. (2004). Self harm in young people: a perspective for mental health nursing care. *International Nursing Review*, 51, 222–228.

Angold, A., Erkanli, A., Silberg, J., Eaves, L. and Costello, E. J. (2002). Depression scale scores in 8–17-year-olds: effects of age and gender. *Journal of Child Psychology and Psychiatry*, 43(8), 1052–1063.

Axelson, D. A. and Birmaher, B. (2001). Relation between anxiety and depressive disorders in childhood and adolescence. *Depress Anxiety*, 14(2), 67–78.

Balis, T. and Postolache, T. T. (2008). Ethnic differences in adolescent suicide in the United States. *International Journal of Child Health and Human Development*, 1, 281–296.

Barker, E., O'Gorman, J. and DeLeo, D. (2014). Suicide around anniversary times. Omega. *Journal of Death and Dying*, 69(3), 305–310.

Beck, A. T., Kovacs, M. and Weissman, A. (1979) Assessment of suicidal intention: the Scale for Suicide Ideation. *Journal of Consulting and Clinical Psychology*, 47(2), 343–352. Available from: http://dx.doi.org/10.1037/0022-006X.47.2.343. Accessed 31 October 2016.

Beck, A. T. and Steer, R. A. (1988). *Beck Hopelessness Scale Manual*. San Antonia: Tex Psychological Corporation.

Beck, A. T. and Steer, R. A. (1991). *Beck Scale for Suicide Ideation*. San Antonia: Tex Psychological Corporation.

Blaauw, E., Arensman, E., Kraaij, V., Winkel, F. W. and Bout, R. (2002). Traumatic life events and suicide risk among jail inmates: the influence of types of events, time period and significant others. *Journal of Traumatic Stress*, 15(1), 9–16.

Bonner, R. L. and Rich, A. R. (1990). Psychosocial vulnerability, life stress, and suicide ideation in a jail population: a cross-validation study. *Suicide and Life Threatening Behavior*, 20(3), 213–224.

Bradley, K. (2009). The Bradley Report: a Review of People with Mental Health Problems and Learning Disabilities in the Criminal Justice System. Available from: www.rcpsych.ac.uk/pdf/Bradley%20Report11.pdf. Accessed 19 October 2016.

Brent, D., Kerr, M., Goldstein, C., Bozigar, J., Wartella, M. and Allan, M. (1989). An outbreak of suicide and suicidal behaviour in a high school. *Journal of American Academy of Child Adolescent Psychiatry*, 28(6), 918–924.

Brent, D. A., Perper, J. A. and Moritz, G. et al. (1993). Bereavement of depression. The impact of the loss of a friend to suicide. *Journal of American Academy of Child and Adolescent Psychiatry*, 32, 1189–1197.

Bridge, J. A., Goldstein, T. R. and Brent, D. A. (2006). Adolescent suicide and suicidal behaviour. *Journal of Child Psychology and Psychiatry*, 47 (3), 372–494.

Brodie, I., Berridge, D. and Beckett, W. (1997). The health of children looked after by local authorities. *British Journal of Nursing*, 6(7), 386–390.

Brown, J., Cohen, P., Johnson, J. and Smaile, E. (1999). Childhood abuse and neglect: specificity of effects on adolescent and young adult depression and suicidality.

American Academy of Child and Adolescent Psychiatry, **38**(12), 1490–1496.

Chanen, A. M., Jackson, H. J., McCutcheon, L. K., Jovev, M., Dudgeon, P., Yuen, H. P., Germano, D., Nistico, H., McDougall, E., Weinstein, C., Clarkson, V. and McGorry, P. D. (2008). Early intervention for adolescents with borderline personality disorder using cognitive analytic therapy: randomised controlled trial. *British Journal of Psychiatry*, **193**(6), 477–484. doi: 10.1192/bjp.bp.107.048934.

Chitsabesan, P., Kroll, L., Bailey, S., Kenning, C., Sneider, S., MacDonald, W. and Theodosiou, L. (2006). Mental health needs of young offenders in custody and in the community. *British Journal of Psychiatry*, **188**, 534–540.

Chitsabesan, P., Lennox, C., Theodosiou, L., Law, H., Bailey, S. and Shaw, J. (2014). The development of the comprehensive health assessment tool for young offenders within the secure estate. *The Journal of Forensic Psychiatry & Psychology*, **25**(1), 1–25.

Chretien, R. D. and Persinger, M. A. (2000). 'Prefrontal Deficits' discriminate young offenders from age-matched controls: juvenile delinquency as an expected feature of the normal distribution of prefrontal cerebral development. *Psychological Reports*, **87**(3f), 1196–1202.

Coid, J., Petruckevitch, A., Bebbington, P., Bragha, T., Bhugra, D., Jenkins, R., Farren, M., Lewis, G. and Singleton, N. (2002). Ethnic differences in Prisoners. 1: criminality and psychiatric morbidity. *British Journal of Psychiatry*, **181**, 473–80

Cotgrove, A. J., Zirinsky, L., Black, D. and Weston, D. (1995). Secondary prevention of attempted suicide in adolescence. *Journal of Adolescence*, **18**, 569–577.

Cousins, W., McGowan, I. and Milner, S (2008). Self harm and attempted suicide in young people looked after in state care. *Journal of Children People's Nursing*, **2**(2), 51–54

Curry, J., Wells, K., Lochman, J., Craighead, E. and Nagy, P. (2003). Cognitive behavioral intervention for depressed, substance-abusing adolescents: development and pilot testing. *Journal of the American Academy for Child and Adolescent Psychiatry*, **42**, 656–665.

Daniel, A. (2006). Preventing suicide in prison: a collaborative responsibility of administrative, custodial, and clinical staff. *Journal of American Academy of Psychiatry and the Law*, **34**, 165–175.

De Leo, D., Burgis, S., Bertolote, J. M., Kerkhof, A. J. M. and Bille-Brahe, U. (2006). Definitions of suicidal behavior lessons learned from the WHO/EURO multicentre study, *Crisis*, **27**, 4–15.

Department of Health (2001). *Changing the Outlook – A Strategy for Developing and Modernizing Mental Health Services in Prisons*. London: HMSO.

Department of Health (2002). *National Suicide Prevention Strategy for England*. London: HMSO.

Diamond, G. S., Wintersteen, M. B., Brown, G. K., Diamond, G. M., Gallop, R., Shelef, K. and Levy, S. (2010). Attachment based family therapy for adolescents with suicidal ideation: a randomized controlled trial. *Journal of the American Academy of Child and Adolescent Psychiatry*, **49**, 122–131.

Donaldson, D., Spirito, A. and Eposito-Smithers, C. (2005). Treatment for adolescents following a suicide attempt: results of a pilot trial. *Journal of the American Academy of Child and Adolescent Psychiatry*, **44**(2), 113–120.

Dooley, E. (1990). Prison suicide in England and Wales, 1972–87. *British Journal of Psychiatry*, **156**, 40–45.

Douglas, N. and Plugge E. (2008). The health needs of imprisoned female juvenile offenders: the views of the young women prisoners and youth justice professionals. *International Journal of Prisoner Health*, **4**(2), 66–76. doi: 10.1080/17449200802038256.

Durkheim, E. (1897). Le Suicide: Etude de suicide: Etude de sociologie first published 1897, Paris. English edition 'Suicide' first published 1952 by Routledge & Kegan Paul Ld. Reprinted 2002 by London: Routledge & Kegan Paul Ltd.

Evans, E., Hawton, K. and Rodham, K. (2004). Factors associated with suicidal phenomena in adolescents: a systematic review of population-based studies. *Clinical Psychology Review*, **24**(8), 957–979.

Evans., E., Hawton, K. and Rodham, K. (2005). In what ways are adolescents who engage in self-harm or experience thoughts of self-harm different in terms of help-seeking, communication and coping strategies? *Journal of Adolescent*, **28**, 573–587.

Fazel, S., Doll, H. and Langastro, N. (2008). Mental disorders among adolescents in juvenile detention and correctional facilities: a systematic review and metaregression analysis of 25 surveys. *Journal of the American Academy for Child and Adolescent Psychiatry*, **47**, 1010–1019.

Fergusson, D. M., Horwood, L. J. and Lynskey, M. T. (1995). Maternal depressive symptoms and depressive symptoms in adolescents. *Journal of Child Psychology Psychiatry*, **36**, 1161–1178.

Gallagher, C. A. and Dobrin, A. (2006). Deaths in juvenile justice residential facilities. *Journal of Adolescent Health*, **38**(6), 662–668.

Goodyer, I. M., Herbert, J., Tamplin, A. and Altham, P. M. E. (2000). Recent life events, cortisol, dehydroepiandrosterone and the onset of major depression in high-risk adolescents. *British Journal of Psychiatry*, **177**, 499–504.

Gore, S. (1999). Suicide in prisons: reflection of the communities served, or exacerbated risk? *British Journal of Psychiatry*, **175**, 50–55.

Gould, M. S., King, R., Greenwald, S., Fisher, P., Schwab-Stone, M., Kramer, R., Flisher, A. J., Goodman, S., Canino, G. and Shaffer, D. (1998). Psychopathology associated with suicidal ideation and attempts among children and adolescents. *Journal of American Academy of Child Adolescent Psychiatry*, 37(9), 915–923.

Green, J. M., Wood, A. J., Kerfoot, M. J., Trainor, G., Roberts, C., Rothwell, J., Woodham, A., Ayodeji, E., Barrett, B., Byford, S. and Harrington, R. (2011). Group therapy for adolescents with repeated self harm: randomised controlled trial with economic evaluation. *British Medical Journal*, 342, d682. doi: 10.1136/bmj.d682.

Hales, H., Davison, S., Misch, P. and Taylor, P. J. (2003). Young male prisoners in a young offender institution: their experience of suicide attempts by others. *Journal of Adolescence*, 26, 667–685.

Hales, H., Edmondson, A., Davison, S., Maughan, B. and Taylor, P. J. (2014). The impact of contact with suicide-related behaviour in prison in young offenders. *CRISIS*, 31, 21–30.

Harrington, R. (2001). Depression, suicide and deliberate self-harm in adolescence. *British Medical Bulletin*, 57, 47–60.

Harrington, R. and Maskey, S. (2008). Behaviour disorders in children and adolescents. *Medicine*, 36, 482–485.

Harrington, R., Whittaker, J., Shoebridge, P. and Campbell, F. (1998). Systematic review of effectiveness of cognitive behaviour therapies in child and adolescent depressive disorder. *British Medical Journal*, 316, 57(1), 1559–1563.

Harrington, R., Bailey, S., Chitsabesan, P. D., Kroll, L., Macdonald, W. and Sneider, S. (2005). *Mental Health Needs and Effectiveness of Provision for Young Offenders in Custody and in the Community*. Youth Justice Board publication. Available from: www.mac-uk.org/wped/wp-content/uploads/2013/03/Youth-Justice-Board-MentalHealthNeeds-of-Young-Offenders.pdf. Accessed 19 October 2016.

Hawton, K. and Fagg, J. (1992). Deliberate self-poisoning and injury in adolescents: a study of characteristics and trends in Oxford 1976–89. *British Journal of Psychiatry*, 161, 816–823.

Hawton, K. and Harriss, L. (2008). Deliberate self harm by under 15 year olds: characteristics, trends and outcome. *Journal of Child Psychology and Psychiatry*, 49(4), 441–448.

Hawton, K., Simkin, S. and Deeks, J. (1999). Effects of a drug overdose in a television drama on presentations to hospital for self poisoning: time series and questionnaire study. *British Medical Journal*, 318, 972–977.

Hawton, K., Harriss, L. and Rodham, K. (2010). How adolescents who cut themselves differ from those who take overdoses. *European Child Adolescent Psychiatry*, 19, 513–523. doi: 10.1007/s00787-009-0065-0. Epub 26 September 2009.

Hawton, K., Linsell, L., Adeniji, T., Sariaslan, A. and Fazel, S. (2014). Self-harm in prisons in England and Wales: an epidemiological study of prevalence, risk factors, clustering, and subsequent suicide, *Lancet*. March 29, 383, 1147–1154. doi: 10.1016/S0140-6736(13)62118-2. Epub 16 December 2013.

Hazell, P. L., Martin, G., McGill, K., Kay, T., Wood, A., Trainor, G. and Harrington, R. (2009). Group therapy for repeated deliberate self-harm in adolescents: failure of replication of a randomized trial. *Journal of American Academy of Child Adolescent Psychiatry*, 48, 662–670. doi: 10.1097/CHI.0b013e3181aOacec.

Henggeler, S. W. and Borduin, C. M. (1990). *Family Therapy and Beyond: A Multisystemic approach to Treating the Behavior Problems of Children and Adolescents*. Pacific Grove, CA: Brooks/Cole.

HMIP (2014). HM Chief Inspector of Prisons for England and Wales Annual Report 2013–2014.

Jacobson, J., Bhardwa, B., Gyateng, T., Hunter, G. and Hough, M. (2010). *Punishing Disadvantage – A Profile of Children in Custody*. London: Prison Reform Trust.

Jenkins, R., Bhugra, D., Meltzer, H., Singleton, N., Bebbington, P., Brugha, T., Coid, J., Farrell, M., Lewis, G. and Paton, J. (2005). Psychiatric and social aspects of suicidal behaviour in prisions. *Psychological Medicine*, 35, 257–269.

Kazdin, A. E., Holland, L., Crowley, M. and Breton, S. (1997). Barriers to treatment participation scale: evaluation and validation in the context of child outpatient treatment. *Journal of Child Psychology and Psychiatry*, 38, 1051–1062.

Kerfoot, M., Dyer, E., Harrington, V., Woodham, A. and Harrington, R. (1996). Correlates and short-term course of self-poisoning in adolescents. *British Journal of Psychiatry*, 168, 38–42.

Kessler, R., Borges, G. and Walters, E. (1999). Prevalence of the risk factors for lifetime suicide attempts in the national comorbibity survey. *Archives of General Psychiatry*, 56, 617–626.

King, C. A., Kramer, A., Preuss L., Kerr, D. C., Weisse, L., Venkataraman, S. (2006). Youth-Nominated Support Team for Suicidal Adolescents (Version 1): a randomized controlled trial. *Journal of Consulting and Clinical Psychology*, 74(1), 199–206.

King, C. A., Klaus, N., Kramer, A., Venkataraman, S., Quinlan, P. and Gillespie, B. (2009). Youth-Nominated Support Team-Version II for suicidal adolescents: a randomized controlled intervention trail. *Journal of Consulting and Clinical Psychology*, 77(5), 880–893. doi: 10.1037/a0016552.

Kircher, T., Forns, M. and Mohiano, S. (2008). Identifying the risk of deliberate self-harm among young prisoners by means of coping typologies. *Suicide and Life-Threatening Behaviour*, 38(4), 442–448. First published online: 1 June 2011. doi:10.1521/suli.2008.38.4.442. 2008.

Knowles, S. E. and Townsend, E. (2011). Implicit and explicit attitudes toward self harm: Support for a functional model. *Journal of Behavior Therapy and Experimental Psychiatry*, 43(2), 730–736. doi: 10.1016/j.jbtep. 2011.10.007. Epub 2011.

Kroll, L., Rothwell, J., Bradley, D., Shah, P., Bailey, S. and Harrington, R. C. (2002). Mental health needs of boys in secure care for serious or persistent offending: a prospective, longitudinal study. *Lancet*, **359**, 1975–1979.

Kuo, W.-H., Gallo, J. J. and Tien, A. Y. (2001). Incidence of suicide ideation and attempts in adults: The 13-year follow-up of a community sample in Baltimore, Maryland. *Psychological Medicine*, **31**, 1181–1191.

Lader, D. Singleton, N. and Meltzer, H. (2000). *Psychiatric Morbidity Amongst Young Offenders in England and Wales*. London: Office for National Statistics.

Linehan, M. M., Schmidt, H., Dimeff, L. A., Kanter, J. W., Craft, J. C., Comtois, K. A. and Recknor, K. L. (1999). Dialectical Behavior Therapy for Patients with Borderline Personality Disorder and Drug-Dependence. *American Journal on Addiction*, **8**, 279–292.

Lohner, J. and Konrad, N. (2006). Deliberate self-harm and suicide attempt in custody: distinguishing features. *International Journal of Law Psychiatry*, Sepember–October **29**(5), 370–385. Epub 19 June 2006.

Madge., N., Hewitt, A., Hawton., K., de Wilde., E., Corcoran., P., Fekete, S., van Heeringen, K., De Leo, D. and Ystgaard, M. (2008). Deliberate self harm within an international community sample of young people: comparative findings from the Child and Adolescent Self Harm in Europe (CASE) study. *Journal of Child Psychology and Psychiatry*, **49**(6), 667–677.

McDougall, T. and Jones, C. (2007). Dialectical behavioural therapy for young offenders: lessons from the USA. Part 2. *Mental Health Practice*, **11**: 20–21.

McDougall, T., Armstrong, M. and Trainor, G. (2010). *Helping Children and Young People Who Self-harm: An Introduction to Self-harming and Suicidal Behaviours for Health Professionals*. Abingdon: Taylor and Francis Oxfordshire.

McGuire, J. E. (1995). *What Works: Reducing Reoffending: Guidelines from Research and Practice*. Chichester, UK: John Wiley & Sons.

Miller, A. Rathus, J. and Linehan, M. (2007). *Dialectic Behavior Therapy with Suicidal Adolescents*. New York: Guilford Press.

Morgan, J. and Hawton, K. (2004). Self-reported suicidal behaviour in juvenile offenders in custody: prevalence and associated factors. *Crisis*, **25**, 8–11.

Mufson, L., Dorta, K. P., Moreau, D. and Weissman, M. M. (2011). *Interpersonal Psychotherapy for Depressed Adolescents*. New York: Guilford Press.

National Collaborating Centre for Women's and Children's Health (2009). Available from: www.ncc-wch.org.uk/guidelines/. Accessed 19 October 2016.

National Confidential Inquiry (NCI) (2001). *Safety First: Five-Year Report of the National Confidential Inquiry into Suicide and Homicide by People with Mental Illness*. London: Department of Health.

National Confidential Inquiry (NCI) (2011). The National Confidential Inquiry into Suicide and Homicide by People with Mental Illness. A National Study of Self-Inflicted Deaths in Prison Custody in England and Wales from 1999 to 2007.

NICE (2005). *Depression in Children and Young People: Identification and Management in Primary, Community and Secondary Care*(Updated March 2015). National Institute for Health and Care Excellence. Available from: https://www.nice.org.uk/guidance/cg28. Accessed 19 October 2016.

NICE (2004). *Self-harm: The short-term physical and psychological management and secondary prevention of self-harm in primary and secondary care*. National Institute for Health and Social Care. Available from: www.nice.uk/guinance/cg16/resources/guidance-selfharm-pdf. Accessed 19 October 2016.

NICE (2011). NICE guidelines [CG133] *Self-harm: Longer term management*. Available from: www.nice.org.uk/guidance/cg133. Accessed 19 October 2016.

Nock, M., Joiner, T., Gordon, K., Lloyd-Richardson, E. and Prinstein, M. (2009). Non suicidal self injury among adolescents: diagnostic correlates and relation to suicide attempts. *Psychiatry Research*, **144**(1), 65–72.

Offender Health Research Network (OHRN) (2013). Manual for the Comprehensive Health Assessment Tool (CHAT): Young People in the Secure Estate. The Offender Health Research Network; Online. Available from: www.ohrn.nhs.uk/OHRNResearch/CHATManualSecure.pdf. Accessed 31 October 2016.

Office for National Statistics (ONS) (2005). *Mental Health in Children and Young People in Great Britain, 2004*. London: HMSO.

Office for National Statistics (ONS) (2006). *Suicide Trends and Geographical Variations in the United Kingdom, 1991–2004*. London: HMSO.

Office for National Statistics (ONS) (2013). What are the top causes of death by age and gender? Part of Mortality Statistics: Deaths Registered in England and Wales, 2012 release. Available from: http://webarchive.nationalarchives.gov.uk/20160105160709/; www.ons.gov.uk/ons/rel/vsob1/mortality-statistics–deaths-registered-in-england-and-wales–series-dr-/2012/sty-causes-of-death.html. Accessed 19 October 2016.

Ougrin, D., Zundel, T., Ng, A., Banarsee, R., Bottle, A., Taylor, E. (2011). Trial of therapeutic assessment in London: randomised controlled trial of therapeutic assessment versus standard psychosocial assessment in adolescents presenting with self-harm. *Arch Dis Child*, **96**(2), 148–153. doi: 10.1136/adc.2010.188755. Epub 27 October 2010.

Ougrin, D., Tranah, T., Leigh, E., Taylor, L. and Asarnow, J. R. (2012). Practitioner review: Self-harm in adolescents. *Journal of Child Psychology and Psychiatry*, **53**, 337–350. doi: 10.1111/j.1469–7610.2012.02525.x.

Owens, D., Horrocks, J. and House, A. (2002). Fatal and non fatal repetition of self harm. *British Journal of Psychiatry*, **181**, 193–199.

Parliamentary Office of Science and Technology (POST) (2008). Alternatives to custodial sentencing, May 2008. POST note 08/308.

Penn, J. V., Esposito, C. L., Schaeffer, L. E., Fritz, G. K. and Spirito, A. (2003). Suicide attempts and self-mutilative behavior in a juvenile correctional facility. *Journal of the American Academy of Child and Adolescent Psychiatry*, **42**, 762–769.

Pirkis, J. and Machlin, A. (2013). Differing perspectives on what is important in media reporting of suicide. *British Journal of Psychiatry*, Sepember, **203**(3), 168–169. doi: 10.1192/bjp.bp.112.124396.

Prisons and Probation Ombudsman for England and Wales (PPO) (2014). Learning from PPO investigations: Self-inflicted deaths of prisoners on ACCT April 2014. Available from: www.ppo.gov.uk/wp-content/uploads/2014/07/ACCT_thematic_final_web.pdf#view=FitH. Accessed 19 October 2016.

Prison Reform Trust (2012). Fatally Flawed: Has the State Learned Lessons from the Deaths of Children and Young People in Prison? London.

Qin, P., Agerbo, E. and Bio Mortensen, P. (2002). *Suicide Risk Management Strategy*. Edinburgh: Scottish Prison Service Occasional Paper Services 01/2003.

Reinecke, M. A. and Shirk., S. R. (2005). Psychotherapy with adolescents. In Gabbard, G. O., Beck, J. S. and Holmes, J. Editors. *Oxford Textbook of Psychotherapy* (ch. 30, pp. 353–366). Oxford: Oxford University Press.

Rodham, K., Hawton, K. and Evans, E. (2004). Reasons for deliberate self-harm: Comparison of self-poisoners and self-cutters in a community sample of adolescents. *Journal of American Academy of Child Adolescent Psychiatry*, **43**(1), 80–87.

Roy, A. (2006). Family history of suicide and impulsivity. *Archives of Suicide Research*, **10**, 347–352.

Roy, A., Rylander, G. and Sarchapone, M. (1997). Genetics of suicide. Family studies and molecular genetics. *Annals of New York Academy of Sciences*, **836**, 135–157.

Ruchkin, V. V., Schwab-Stone, M., Koposov, R. A., Vermeiren, R. and King, R. A. (2003). Suicidal ideations and attempts in juvenile delinquents. *Journal of Child Psychology and Psychiatry*, October, **44**(7), 1058–1066.

Rueter, M. A., Scaramella, L., Wallace, L. E. and Conger, R. D. (1999). First onset of depressive or anxiety disorders predicted by the longitudinal course of internalizing symptoms and parent-adolescent disagreements. *Archives of General Psychiatry*, **56**(8), 726–732.

Sawyer, M. G., Arney, F. M., Baghurst, P. A., Clark, J. J., Graetz, B. W., Kosky, R. J., Nurcombe, B., Patton, G. C., Prior, M. R., Raphael, B. and Rey, J. M. (2001). The mental health of young people in Australia: key findings from the child and adolescent component of the national survey of mental health and well-being. *Australian and New Zealand Journal of Psychiatry*, **35**(6), 806–814.

Schreidman, E. (1993). *Suicide as Psychache*. New York: Wiley.

Schuppert, H. M., Giesen-Bloo, J., Van Gemert, T. G., Wiersema, H. M., Minderaa, R. B., Emmelkamp, P. M. and Nauta, M. H. (2009). Effectiveness of an emotion regulation group training for adolescents – a randomized controlled pilot study. *Clinical Psychology and Psychotherapy*, **16**, 467–478.

Scrowcroft, E. (2014). Samaritans Suicide Statistics Report 2014: Including Data for 2010–2012. Available from: www.samaritans.org/sites/default/files/kcfinder/files/research/Samaritans%20Suicide%20Statics%20Report%202014.pdf. Accessed 19 October 2016.

Shaffer, D. (1974). Suicide in childhood and early adolescence. *Journal of Child Psychology and Psychiatry*, **15**: 275–291.

Shaw, J., Appleby, L. and Baker, D. (2003). Safer Prisons. A National Study of Prison Suicides 1999–2000 by the National Confidential Inquiry into Suicides and Homicides by People with Mental Illness. Department of Health.

Shaw, J., Baker, D., Hunt, I. M., Moloney, A. and Appleby, L. (2004). Suicide by prisoners: national clinical survey. *British Journal of Psychiatry*, **184**: 263–267.

Sherman, L. G. and Morschauser, P. C. (1989). Screening for suicide risk in inmates. *Psychiatric Quarterly*, **60**(2), 119–138.

Social Care Institute for Excellence (2005). SCIE Research briefing 16: Deliberate self-harm (DSH) among children and adolescents: Who is at risk and how is it recognised? Available from: www.scie.org.uk/publications/briefings/briefing16/. Accessed 19 October 2016.

Spirito, A., Boergers, J., Donaldson, D., Bishop, D. and Lewander, W. (2002). An intervention trial to improve adherence to community treatment by adolescents after a suicide attempt. *Journal of American Academy of Child Adolescent Psychiatry*, April, **41**(4), 435–442.

Stallard, P., Thomason, J. and Churchyard, S. (2003). The mental health of young people attending a youth offending team: a descriptive study. *Journal of Adolescence*, February, **26**(1), 33–43.

Steer, R. A., Beck, A. T., Brown, G. K. and Beck, J. S. (1993). Classification of suicidal and nonsuicidal outpatients: a cluster-analytic approach. *Journal of Clinical Psychology*, **49**(5), 603–614.

Sukhodolsky, D. G. and Ruchkin, V. (2006). Evidence-based psychosocial treatments in the juvenile justice system. *Child Adolescent Psychiatric Clinics of North America*, **15**, 501–516.

Taiminen, T., Kallio-Soukainen, K., Nokso-Koivisto, H., Kalijonen, A. and Helenius, H. (1998). Contagion of deliberate self-harm among adolescent inpatients. *Journal of*

American Academy of Child Adolescent Psychiatry, **37**(2), 211–217.

Teplin, L. A., Abram, K. M., McClelland, G. M., Dulcan, M. K. and Mericle, A. A. (2002). Psychiatric disorders in youth in juvenile detention. *Archives of General Psychiatry*, **59**, 1133–1143.

Teplin, A., Welty, L., Abram, K., Dulcan, M. and Washburn, J. (2012). Prevealence and persistence of psychiatric disorders in youth after detention: a prospective longitudinal study. *Archives of General Psychiatry*, **69**(10), 1031–1043.

Townsend, E., Walker, D. M., Sargeant, S., Vostanis, P., Hawton, K., Stocker, O. and Sithole, J. (2010). Systematic review and meta-analysis of interventions relevant for young offenders with mood disorders, anxiety disorders, or self-harm. *Journal of Adolescent*, **33** (1), 9–20. doi: 10.1016/j.adolescence.2009.05.015. Epub 27 June 2009. Review.

Utting, W. B. and Department of Health. (1997). *People Like Us: Report of the Review of the Safeguards for Children Living Away from Home*. London: Stationary Office Books.

Vermeiren, R., Jespers, I. and Moffitt, T. (2006). Mental health problems in juvenile justice populations. *Child and Adolescent Psychiatric Clinics of North America*, **15**(2), 333–351.

Vreugdenhil, C., Doreleijers, T. A. H., Vermeiren, R., Wouters, L. F. J. M. and van den Brink, W. (2004). Psychiatric disorders in a representative sample of incarcerated boys in the Netherlands. *Journal of the American Academy of Child and Adolescent Psychiatry*, **43**, 97–110.

Wood, A., Trainor, G., Rothwell, J., Moore, A. and Harrington, R. (2001). A randomized controlled trial of group therapy for repeated deliberate self-harm in adolescents. *Journal of the American Academy for Child and Adolescent Psychiatry*, **40**, 1246–1253.

Woodroffe, C., Glickman, M., Barker, M. and Power, C. (1993). *Young Persons, Teenagers and Health: Key Data*. Buckingham: Open University Press.

World Health Organisation (WHO) (1993). International Classification of Disease ICD-10 Geneva. Available from: www.who.int/classifications/icd/en/. Accessed 19 October 2016.

Post-Traumatic Stress Disorder, Adjustment Disorder and Complex Trauma in Young People at Risk of Entering the Criminal Justice System

Shreeta Raja and Andrew Rogers

Introduction

Childhood exposure to trauma is common, with 39.7% of an inner-city sample of over 16-year-olds in the UK reporting exposure to childhood trauma (Frissa et al., 2013) and 25.1% of young people in the USA reporting having experienced a significant trauma before the age of 16 years (Costello et al., 2002). Such traumatic experience can include physical and sexual abuse, neglect, accidents, war, traumatic loss and exposure to domestic or community violence. Young people involved in the criminal justice system appear to experience disproportionally high levels of trauma, with between 33% and 92% of young people entering custody in the UK having experienced some form of past maltreatment (Day et al., 2008).

It is important to recognise that not all of those who experience a traumatic event will necessarily experience long-term consequences, with some young people displaying high levels of resilience and ability to adapt and cope with their experiences (DuMont et al., 2007). However, the negative impact of trauma particularly that experienced in childhood can be pervasive and significantly increase the risk of long-term psychological, physiological and behavioural consequences. These risks may include the following: impaired brain development and difficulties with emotional regulation; cognitive and social functioning; substance misuse difficulties and high-risk behaviour to name but a few (e.g. van der Kolk, 1987; Bloom, 1999; Perry, 2008; Clark et al., 2010). Traumatised individuals may also present with high levels of distress, flashbacks, hypervigilance, avoidance behaviours and other symptoms that are associated with a diagnosis of Post-Traumatic Stress Disorder (PTSD).

The chapter begins with a summary of the key features of PTSD and Adjustment Disorder (AD) including the ongoing debate surrounding the clinical utility of AD and PTSD diagnoses, particularly in relation to youth within the criminal justice system. National Institute for Health and Care Excellence (NICE) recommendations for intervention are discussed and approaches including trauma-focused cognitive behaviour therapy (CBT) and eye-movement desensitisation reprocessing (EMDR) are highlighted.

The chapter then focuses on understanding complex trauma from a developmental perspective and how such understanding may better inform an integrated, psychologically informed approach to assessment and intervention with young people within criminal justice settings. A brief illustrative case example is used to highlight the importance of adopting a developmental, multisystemic formulation approach to addressing the needs of young people with complex trauma presentations. The chapter will conclude with a summary of the challenges for such management approaches and ideas for further development in the area.

Post-Traumatic Stress Disorder and Adjustment Disorder

PTSD and AD are both diagnoses that focus on an individual's response to a specific stressor or event. The 5th edition of the *Diagnostic and Statistical Manual of Mental Disorders* (DSM-5 – American Psychiatric Association, 2013) presents both PTSD and AD within the new chapter 'Trauma and Stressor Related Disorders'.

PTSD Diagnosis and Prevalence

A diagnosis of PTSD requires the person to have been exposed to a significant 'traumatic' stressor such as death, threatened death, actual or threatened serious injury, or actual or threatened sexual violence. In addition, the individual must also present with symptoms from each of the four clusters; intrusion (e.g. memories, nightmares, flashbacks), avoidance, negative alterations in cognitions and mood and alterations in arousal and reactivity. The symptoms must be persistent for one month, with a significant impairment in functioning and must not be attributable to any substance or co-occurring medical condition (APA, 2013). The International Classification of Diseases 10 (ICD-10 – World Health Organisation, 1992: 120) suggests that the stressor should be of an 'exceptionally threatening or catastrophic nature ... likely to cause distress in almost anyone'. Symptoms include persistent 'reliving' through flashbacks, memories, dreams or distress when exposed to situations resembling the stressor. The criteria also highlight avoidance of situations that are associated or resemble the stressor. The criteria for a diagnosis also define the presence of either an inability to recall all or some important aspects of the period of exposure to the stressor or the presence of persistent symptoms of increased psychological arousal and sensitivity. The following symptoms are listed under this category:

- difficulty in falling or staying asleep;
- irritability or outbursts of anger;
- difficulty in concentrating;
- hypervigilance;
- exaggerated startle response.

Within ICD-10 criteria, symptoms usually present themselves within six months of experiencing the stressor. It is possible to diagnose PTSD after six months of exposure to the stressor, however, only if symptoms are atypical and do not meet the criteria for any other disorders (World Health Organisation, 1992).

While many children over the age of ten may display reactions closely similar to those manifested by adults (NICE, 2005), 'PTSD is diagnosed less often in young people, among whom co-occurring chronic trauma and adversity are more commonly experienced' (Rahim, 2014: 2). Clinical practice with adolescents supports this view and indicates that many present with atypical presentations including somatisation and dissociative experiences that are complicated by the developmental nature of childhood. Indeed, Gerson and Rappaport (2013: 138) highlight that 'Children and adolescents who

have experienced trauma can manifest severe disturbances in mood, behavior, attention, attachment, and impulse control, which may mimic other psychiatric disorders, such as bipolar disorder and ADHD.' The impact of this may mean that a young person's experience of trauma is missed, misinterpreted and/or misdiagnosed, reducing the chance of the young person receiving the most appropriate intervention.

Estimates of the prevalence of PTSD are varied and wide ranging depending on the methodology, thresholds, timeframes and diagnostic criteria used in each study. Epidemiological studies often use samples of adults or older young people. In the US National Comorbidity Survey, the lifetime prevalence of PTSD in adults and older young people was 10% (Kessler et al., 1995). In the UK, a national survey of children and young people found that 0.4% of young people aged 11–15 years had received a diagnosis of PTSD, whilst very few children under the age of ten had received this diagnosis (Meltzer et al., 2000). It should be borne in mind that this study illustrates point prevalence, rather than lifetime prevalence, which is likely to be higher.

PTSD is even more prevalent within the juvenile offender population, with estimates in the USA varying between 2% and as high as 32% (Abram et al., 2004). In the UK, as many as one in ten young offenders report symptoms of anxiety or PTSD, with significantly more young people from black and minority ethnic groups reporting PTSD symptoms (Chitsabesan et al., 2006). The Annual Report of the Chief Medical Officer stated that 9% of 13–18 -year-olds in custody have a diagnosis of PTSD (Lennox and Khan, 2013).

Trauma Theory and PTSD

There are a number of theories in relation to the aetiology of PTSD, with the traumatic experience itself being clearly implicated as a major cause of the symptoms of PTSD (NICE, 2005). Ehlers and Clark (2000) describe a cognitive model of PTSD that implicates an individual's perception and interpretation of the event and its consequences as important in its development. It is also suggested that some coping strategies such as excessive rumination, suppression of trauma memories and emotion, dissociation, avoidance, substance misuse and social withdrawal, may serve to reinforce the symptoms (NICE, 2005).

Distortions in the initial processing of the traumatic memory may also be implicated in the development of PTSD. This may be particularly relevant during childhood and adolescence as the brain is developing. Indeed, there is 'growing evidence for "critical windows" of vulnerability to traumatic stress in brain development' (Gerson and Rappaport, 2013: 138). In simple terms, when we experience threat, our preprogrammed alarm system prepares us for 'fight or flight' (or freeze). This process impacts on our brains, focusing attention on survival, rather than effective processing of memory. In effect, when our brains are overwhelmed with fear, our capacity for processing coherent memories is reduced and the resultant stored information becomes fragmented. It is these fragmented memories that are hypothesised to return as physical sensations, flashbacks, nightmares or behavioural reenactments (intrusion). In addition, experience of trauma increases our sensitivity to threat and this hypersensitivity results in even mild threats or objectively 'harmless' triggers invoking significant fight–flight responses (for more in-depth information see De Bellis and Zisk, 2014; Bloom, 1999).

A number of vulnerability factors have been highlighted in relation to PTSD in children and adolescents. Trickey et al. (2012) conducted a meta-analysis of 64 studies (N = 32,238) that investigated potential risk factors for PTSD in young people. Results indicated 'a small effect size for race and younger age as risk factors for PTSD. A small to medium-sized effect was observed for: female gender, low intelligence, low socio-economic status, pre- and post-trauma life events, pre-trauma psychological problems in the individual and parent, pre-trauma low self-esteem, post-trauma parental psychological problems, bereavement, trauma severity, and exposure to the event by media; whilst a large effect was observed for low social support, peri-trauma fear, perceived life threat, social withdrawal, comorbid psychological problem, poor family functioning, distraction, PTSD at time 1, and thought suppression' (Trickey et al., 2012: 134).

Adjustment Disorder: Diagnosis, Complexities and Prevalence

The presence of emotional or behavioural symptoms in response to an identifiable stressor is the key feature of an AD diagnosis and includes consideration of six subtypes based on symptoms including the following: depressed mood, anxiety, mixed depression and anxiety, disturbance of conduct, mixed disturbance of emotions and conduct and 'unspecified'. DSM-5 specifies that AD is diagnosed when:

- the symptoms occur within three months of the onset of stressor(s);
- there is either marked distress in excess of what would be expected from exposure to the stressor or significant impairment in social or occupational/academic functioning;
- the symptoms do not meet the criteria for another Axis 1 disorder;
- the symptoms do not represent bereavement;
- the symptoms do not persist for over six months after the stressor(s) has terminated.

Symptoms associated with a diagnosis of PTSD may seem similar to those experienced with AD, as they are both linked to distress that develops after exposure to a stressor. They are suggested to be distinct in that for PTSD, the stressor is considered a traumatic event and PTSD symptoms must be present for at least a month, compared to AD where the stressor is considered as less severe or within 'normal human experience'. ICD-10 describes similar criteria for AD as DSM-5, highlighting the greater role of vulnerability and personal disposition in the occurrence and manifestation of AD than in other disorders. ICD-10 suggests that onset of AD is usually within one month of the stressor (and not exceeding six months) and also that the symptoms are not sufficient enough to warrant a more specific diagnosis.

In a study of adolescent detainees in Sweden, AD was one of the top five most common diagnoses with 19% of the sample having been diagnosed (Gisin et al., 2012). In a sample of 11- to 22-year-old non-psychotic outpatients in Finland, Pelkonen et al. (2007) found AD to be the second most common diagnosis after mood disorders.

Any discussion concerning the diagnosis of AD requires acknowledgement of the controversy that surrounds it. There is a significant body of literature that highlights criticism relating to the conceptual underpinning and diagnostic difficulties associated with AD (Baumeister and Kufner, 2009; Casey, 2009; Casey and Bailey, 2011).

Baumeister and Kufner (2009) refer to the lack of evidence for a distinct diagnosis of AD, few prevalence studies and little in the way of evidence-based treatment strategies. In the late 1970s, the diagnosis of AD had been referred to as a 'waste-basket diagnosis, used in such a vague and all-encompassing manner as to be useless' (Fard et al., 1979: 279).

Casey (2009) summarises the specific debates about the distinction between AD and other disorders and between AD and normal responses. The symptom overlap between AD and Axis 1 disorders such as major depression implies that symptoms could be misdiagnosed as AD and failure to recognise the needs of someone with major depression may have serious clinical implications. Conversely, if rigid diagnostic criteria are applied and the threshold for any other disorder is reached, the diagnosis of AD cannot be made and this, as suggested by Casey (2009; 933), means that prescription medications are often used 'even when spontaneous recovery is likely'. Finally, the lack of distinction between pathological and non-pathological responses to stressors demonstrates the crucial role of clinical judgement to minimise the danger of misdiagnosing 'normal' responses as AD. In relation to this, Casey and Bailey (2011: 12) recommended that 'future classifications should accord weight to culture, context and personal circumstances in differentiating normal from pathological distress'.

Despite the complexities surrounding the diagnosis, there is some data supporting AD as a diagnosis of clinical utility, albeit in adult populations. Although there is a lack of large-scale epidemiological studies that include the diagnosis of AD, especially for young people, there are some that highlight the prevalence within adults in different settings (Shear et al., 2000; Koran et al., 2003).

Strain and Diefenbacher (2008) refer to AD as a possible 'wild card' diagnosis, highlighting the opportunity for the diagnosis to be given to those who are clearly at risk of further deterioration if treatment is not offered. In a situation in which there are high levels of mental health need amongst young offenders, it could be argued that the use of an AD diagnosis may well, in some of these cases, ensure recognition that the young person is in need of a service. This is especially important given that for children and adolescents a diagnosis of AD has a relatively poor prognosis and a more significant impact on functioning than with adults (including increased likelihood of attracting a diagnosis of mental illness in the future) (Andreasen and Hoenk, 1982; Hill, 2002).

While it may be argued that the recognition of some symptoms may highlight clinical need and could ensure a referral for mental health support, it may also be argued that the potential risks of pathologising what may be a 'typical' human response to experience may outweigh any clinical utility.

Management and Treatment of PTSD and AD

Psychological Interventions for PTSD

NICE guidelines for the management and treatment of PTSD (2005) suggest a range of interventions, depending on the level and duration of symptoms following a traumatic experience. At the early intervention stage, where symptoms are mild and in cases where symptoms have been present for less than four weeks, 'watchful waiting' is advised. Parental warmth, high intelligence, family support and low family conflict are all protective factors likely to minimise the negative impact of the traumatic experience for children (Piquero et al., 2007). For children and young people who present with severe PTSD symptoms within the first month, trauma-focused CBT is advised.

Cognitive therapy was initially developed in the 1970s (Beck, 1976) for the treatment of depression and later for the treatment of anxiety (Clark, 1999). This model focuses on the relationship between thoughts, emotions and behaviours. Therapeutic work aims to support an individual to reduce the level of emotional distress by adapting to their thoughts, beliefs and their behaviours. More specifically for PTSD, there is an added focus on psychoeducation around trauma and responses to it, in order to help normalise the difficulties. Therapeutic techniques can include graded exposure to 'safe' situations that the individual has come to perceive as threatening due to their traumatic memory and hypervigilance. This may also include graded exposure to the distressing memory itself and related thoughts and feelings. Cognitive techniques include testing out the individual's predictions and interpretations about what is safe/unsafe, whilst encouraging less dependence on rumination or avoidance, which typically serves to maintain the difficulties. These techniques support the individual to arrive at more adaptive solutions, which aim to improve their level of related emotional distress. Stress management techniques are another aspect of CBT. In the treatment of PTSD, these techniques aim to improve the individual's coping skills.

For chronic PTSD where severe trauma symptoms present within three months of a single traumatic incident and may have been present for a number of months or even years, NICE guidelines recommend that trauma-focused cognitive behavioural therapy or EMDR should be offered regularly, by the same therapist for 8–12 sessions, with each one lasting approximately 90 minutes.

EMDR is a protocol-based therapy and was developed in the late 1980s by Francine Shapiro (Shapiro, 1989). It is based on an information-processing model that hypothesises that improper processing and storage of traumatic memories are linked to the symptoms of re-experiencing associated with PTSD. It proposes that during a traumatic event, the level of emotional arousal is so strong that it interferes with the individual's ability to process the experience in order to then form cohesive, contextualised memories. Due to this difficulty at the processing stage, recalling the memory becomes fragmented and very distressing, with the individual often feeling that they are reliving the experience. Also, as the memory had not been properly processed, it can be triggered 'out of the blue' by experiences in the present. During therapy, the individual is supported to develop coping strategies and a 'safe place' in order to help manage symptoms related to recalling the traumatic event. They are then asked to identify and recall a specific image from the traumatic event, after also identifying the negative beliefs related to this memory. Whilst they are recalling the memory, the therapist guides the client through a series of rapid eye movements (or other 'dual attention' processes such as bilateral sounds or tapping). It is hypothesised that this dual-processing task allows more effective reprocessing of the original traumatic experience and desensitisation of the negative beliefs related to it.

If there have been a number of traumatic experiences or comorbid diagnoses, NICE guidelines recommend that there may be more than 12 individual trauma-focused sessions required and that a trauma-focused approach is integrated in the overall treatment plan. Prior to any individual trauma-focused therapeutic work, it is recommended that professionals devote sessions to building a trusting therapeutic relationship and ensuring emotional stabilisation.

Pharmacotherapy for PTSD

While some previous research has highlighted limited evidence for the use of selective serotonin reuptake inhibitors in children as an adjunct to psychological therapy (Seedat et al., 2002; Cohen et al., 2007), NICE guidelines (2005) clearly state that medication should not be used routinely for children and adolescents to address symptoms of PTSD. A recent review of research findings by Gerson and Rappaport (2013: 141) support this view, indicating little evidence for the effectiveness of pharmacotherapy for post-traumatic symptoms in children and stating 'while selective serotonin reuptake inhibitors (SSRIs) are first-line pharmacotherapy for adult PTSD, evidence is lacking for their use in adolescents'. However, while cautioning against the use of pharmacotherapy for PTSD in adolescents, Gerson and Rappaport do suggest that the use of medication to address comorbid presentations (such as depression) could be considered, as clinically indicated.

Interventions for AD

Casey (2009) highlights that within clinical practice, psychological approaches are the most widely used interventions for young people with a diagnosis of AD. Brief psychological interventions appear to be considered the most appropriate intervention for AD (Casey and Bailey, 2011) and there are three main aspects of psychological treatment identified:

(1) reduction or removal of the stressor;
(2) facilitating adaptation;
(3) supporting behavioural change.

These broad categories can include therapeutic techniques such as problem solving, psycho-education, cognitive restructuring and relaxation techniques. Despite this, the evidence base for management of AD is limited (Casey, 2009). However, studies in a young population with a diagnosis of AD in relation to work stress and among army conscripts showed that participants benefitted from cognitive therapy (Nardi et al., 1994; van der Klink et al., 2003).

Complex Trauma

Many young people within the criminal justice system who present with pervasive and complex presentations often have an extensive history of repeated, continuous interpersonal traumatic experiences (Ford et al., 2013). Such interpersonal traumas include abuse/neglect, family breakdown, social and emotional deprivation and trauma related to their offences. In addition, they also have disrupted and chaotic early attachment experiences. Though many of these young people may meet the criteria for PTSD along with other comorbid conditions, it is argued strongly that such diagnoses oversimplify the complexity of their difficulties. Rahim (2014: 3) points out that 'the existing diagnosis of PTSD does not account for disturbance related to affect or attachment, nor for somatic difficulties', and van der Kolk and Courtois (2005: 387) recognise the overly simplistic nature of such diagnoses, stating that 'For a substantial proportion of traumatized patients, PTSD symptoms capture but a small part of their difficulties.'

Furthermore, offering individual psychological therapy (as recommended for PTSD by NICE) in isolation, without a comprehensive psychological formulation, often fails to recognise and integrate the systemic complexities and developmental nature of the trauma experience. Such 'prescribed' interventions based on 'simple' diagnoses, delivered in the absence of a clear psychologically informed formulation (which takes into account complexity, developmental timing, pace and 'dosage' of the intervention), can in our experience often be ineffective and at worst, may be, harmful. Indeed, van der Kolk and Courtois (2005: 386) highlight that 'By diagnosing traumatized patients with complicated clinical presentations with a simple diagnosis of PTSD, clinicians run the grave risk of applying treatments that may not only be irrelevant to them, but may, in fact, be harmful.'

To address these concerns, van der Kolk (2005) amongst others had called for a new diagnostic category of 'developmental trauma disorder', which was an attempt to recognise the complexity of responses to early childhood trauma. It was conceptualised as stemming from 'multiple and/or chronic and prolonged, developmentally adverse traumatic events, most often of an interpersonal nature (e.g. sexual or physical abuse, war, community violence) and early-life onset' (van der Kolk et al., 2005: 2). The proposed diagnostic category was not included in DSM-5 (Bremness and Polzin, 2014). Instead, within the new category, Trauma and Stressor-Related Disorders, subtypes such as developmental PTSD, complex PTSD, disorders of extreme stress, not otherwise specified (DESNOS) and relational trauma are included to reflect the complex nature of trauma and to introduce the developmental perspective. Although

ICD-11 has not been published at the time of writing, there is a renewed proposal for a separate diagnosis incorporating 'complex trauma' to be included (Cloitre et al., 2013). Whatever the outcome of the proposal, the clinical presentation remains highly clinically relevant when working in forensic settings with young people.

Early Interpersonal Trauma, Attachment and Brain Development

An understanding of the role of early interpersonal trauma on neurological and psychological development is fundamental in informing assessment and intervention with young people who have experienced 'developmental' or 'complex' trauma and may be presenting with high-need and high-risk behaviour.

The experience of early relationships provides a foundation for future social, emotional and cognitive development. Bowlby (1988) suggested that early attachment relationships lead to an internal working model, which strongly influences how the child learns, understands and interacts with the world. Since the 1970s there has been increased recognition and understanding of the influence of evolution and early experience on the development of the brain. In very simple terms, there are three key areas of the brain that have developed through evolution (MacLean, 1990). In order of development, the 'old' brain is responsible for basic bodily functions such as regulating breathing and body temperature. The 'emotional brain' (which includes the hypothalamus and the amygdala) is responsible for fear and self-defence systems such as the fight, flight or freeze responses. Finally, there is the development of the cortex, the 'thinking' or the 'social' part of the brain that is responsible for higher-level processes such as sense making, problem solving and regulating emotions. This part of the brain is particularly underdeveloped at birth, and its development is highly influenced by experience.

A 'good enough' relationship with the primary caregiver, based on warmth, attunement and co-regulation particularly within the first three years of life experience, has been linked to a secure attachment style in which the child develops a positive working model of the self and others and the assumption that the world is generally safe and can be approached with confidence (Golding et al., 2006). Such a model increases the chance that they are able to either seek support or regulate their own emotions (Perry, 2000) when faced with relational or environmental stress (Bowlby, 1988).

Disruption to the early attachment process through interpersonal trauma (parental inconsistency, neglect and abuse, for example) has a direct impact on the development of a child's brain, attachment style and emotional regulation systems (e.g. Schore, 2001). Over time, the brain can become hardwired to danger, and the child is more likely to have developed structures and connections between the parts of the brain based on recognising and interpreting threat (Sunderland, 2006). The child is therefore more likely to react in a survival way (flight or fight) and is less able to regulate their behavioural and emotional response to that situation.

Such young people tend to present with poor emotional regulation skills, 'anger management' difficulties, utilise illicit substances as a method of self-medication, have poor understanding of boundaries, negative or hostile attribution bias and associate with antisocial peers who often have similar difficulties. This is highly relevant to young people within the criminal justice system, particularly those in the secure estate, where many have a history of early attachment disruption, neglect and trauma (Crighton and Towl, 2008). Van der Kolk (2005) and Cook et al. (2005) describe characteristics and symptoms of complex trauma in children and adolescents as falling into seven domains: attachment (highlighting relational difficulties); biology (highlighting sensorimotor difficulties and higher levels of medical problems); emotional regulation (highlighting poor affect regulation and difficulties in expressing emotional states, needs and wishes); dissociation (including memory difficulties for state-based events); behavioural control (highlighting problems with impulse control and aggression); cognition (indicating attentional difficulties, difficulties processing new information and difficulties understanding 'cause-affect'); self-concept (highlighting low self-esteem and negative working models of self).

Despite the growing recognition of the importance of understanding these complex trauma presentations, the use of PTSD and AD as relevant diagnoses and the resulting 'prescribed therapy' is often observed in clinical practice with young people with complex presentations. We would argue that if CBT (or other trauma-focused therapies) is offered in isolation, without a broader multisystemic and multifactorial formulation, therapy can be mistimed and risk may increase. Indeed, we must be open to the notion that a focus on trauma experiences too early in the intervention process can serve to trigger traumatic re-enactment and re-traumatise individuals. Howe (2005) suggests delivering cognitive therapies prematurely is likely to result in traumatised children going into survival mode and the process coming to a halt because the cortex is unable to manage the demands of the emotional limbic system.

For young people already displaying high-risk behaviour, the consequences of this unregulated 'fight, flight or freeze' response may be severe, including placement breakdown, an increase in offending behaviour and/or an increase in self-destructive behaviours that at worst may place life at risk. In these circumstances, the importance of a risk management plan underpinned by a clear multifactorial and multisystemic formulation of needs is essential.

Understanding Integrated Management of Complex Trauma-Related Presentations

With a developmental perspective of trauma, it is argued that stand-alone treatment options such as those highlighted in guidelines for PTSD are likely to be less efficacious for this complex group of young people. Emphasis should therefore be on integrated multifactorial interventions (of which individual therapy may be a component), underpinned by psychological formulation. These interventions should both target the environment (in particular the system of care) and provide individual trauma-focused intervention.

It is recognised that PTSD symptoms are highly reactive to ongoing stresses and threats within the social environment (Duncan et al., 2002). To address this, trauma systems therapy (Saxe et al., 2007) places emphasis on intervening with the system around the young person. It focuses on addressing both a child's trauma-related symptoms and factors in the social environment that may contribute to the difficulties. Trauma systems therapy aims to increase the capacity of others to help the young person more effectively manage emotional and behavioural responses to the distress they are experiencing. All too often, clinic-based and 'prescribed' interventions can be far removed from the social–environmental factors that drive young people's traumatic stress symptoms, and have been found to be less efficacious (Dulcan, 2000).

Rogers et al. (2011) postulate the notion of 'redefining therapy', with more emphasis placed on addressing the emotional and relational environment of the individual and their 'system' and less on direct interventions with the individual.

Specifically in relation to complex cases, Briere and Scott (2006) highlight the importance of positive regard, respect and hope in the treatment of young people who have experienced trauma before highlighting a number of basic principles to consider when working with this client group. The principles imply that intervention should initially be preparatory in nature and involve the wider system of care at the same time as, if not before, engaging in individual trauma-focused work. The principles are highlighted below.

Providing and ensuring safety and stability – both physically/environmentally and psychologically. This links with the need to minimise hypervigilance and hyperarousal over time to a point that the client is and feels safe and stable enough to address past trauma. Without this as the foundation, addressing the traumatic memory directly may overwhelm the client's ability to regulate themself and lead to crisis, including disengagement from therapy, increased risk and overall dysfunction.

Maintaining a positive and consistent therapeutic relationship – a variety of benefits of a positive therapeutic relationship include greater treatment adherence, increased engagement and openness and an increased capacity to tolerate distress during exposure work.

Tailoring the therapy to suit the client – Briere and Scott (2006) highlight variables that should be considered when providing specific evidence-based interventions, including trauma therapy. This highlights the need to tailor the timing of trauma processing to the affect-regulation capacity of the client within any given session.

Taking gender and socio-cultural issues into account – possible additional victimisation due to social status or cultural/ethnic group should be considered, as should the expectations of those from diverse backgrounds about the format and content of therapeutic intervention.

Monitoring and controlling counter-transference – this highlights the need for the therapist to be aware of and to manage the activation of certain cognitive/emotional responses within themselves based on their own past experiences, but triggered by aspects of their relationship with the client. If left unacknowledged and unaddressed (e.g. without effective clinical supervision), it could impact on the therapist's ability to provide emotionally attuned care.

In addressing these principles, three broad areas of intervention are outlined: Firstly, psycho-education both for the individual and for the wider treatment (care-giving) system. Secondly, regulating distress and building coping skills both for the client and the care-giving system. Rogers and Law (2010) suggest that the experience of the youth justice system (and in particular secure provision) can itself be an additional source of trauma for both staff and young people due to witnessing and experiencing violence, extreme self-harm behaviours and restraint. Within a care-giving system that is often highly anxious and hypervigilant, and the possibility of an increased risk for prison officers experiencing PTSD (e.g. Wright et al., 2006), the need for these two areas of intervention with the system is emphasised. The third area of intervention is focused on reprocessing the trauma, and this would be in line with the specific treatment outlined in NICE guidelines, for example trauma-focused CBT or EMDR. A case example is presented in Box 11.1 using attachment theory.

Formulation

Callum's case was formulated with attachment theory and complex trauma in mind. It is presented diagrammatically in Figure 11.1. This diagrammatic approach was also used with Callum in sessions and with the staff team to make it more accessible.

Intervention

The following highlights the main principles in working with a case similar to that of Callum's.

Phase 1: Work with the Care System – A Shared Understanding

The first broad area of work is aimed at bringing together everyone that is involved in the care of the young person in order to provide training and psycho-education about complex trauma, attachment theory, brain development and the fight/flight system. All staff should be supported to contribute to a shared formulation, including the identification of possible maintaining factors within the environment that might increase the young person's threat system. Staff reported that Callum was especially hostile in the mornings. Through discussion, it was discovered that the morning routine involved a loud

BOX 11.1 Case Example

All assessment and intervention is undertaken following a full risk assessment and management plan that should be shared with all relevant professionals within the system. This case illustrates how the overall trauma intervention was focused on the system and the individual within it, rather than just on the individual.

Background Information

Callum is 16 years old and has three younger siblings. Callum's father left the family home when Callum was one year old. When Callum was three years old, his mother started a new relationship. This relationship was volatile with periods of separation. All of the children were taken into Local Authority care and placed on a full care order amidst concerns that they were continuing to witness domestic violence, were being neglected and exposed to drug use and sexualised behaviour. A social care report highlighted that Callum had witnessed his mother being dragged out of the house and threatened with a knife by her partner. Callum had intervened and was physically assaulted as a result.

Callum had been in a series of foster care placements and residential homes from the age of 12, each one breaking down due to Callum's absconding, failure to comply with rules and increasing involvement in criminal damage, local gangs and threats of violence. He became known to the Youth Offending Service (YOS) at the age of 14 and received various community orders. He was with a friend when they had to flee due to threats from another gang. His friend was stabbed and later died of his injuries. Callum's most recent index offence involved violent assault with a weapon on a member of staff at his care home – for which he was serving a two-year custodial sentence.

Presenting Difficulties

Once in a secure setting, Callum reported recurring thoughts of violence and paranoia in relation to peers and members of staff wanting to assault him. He had sleep difficulties, reported regular nightmares and presented as anxious and agitated in communal settings. Staff reported that he often placed himself at the centre of social interactions, which would often become increasingly hostile. He refused to engage in education within the establishment, reporting that he would be made to look 'stupid'. He had a number of fights with other young people and often found himself losing privileges and spending time on the care and separation unit. He was especially agitated in the period before returning to his room for the night and after waking in the mornings.

As a result, Callum was referred to the mental health service. His past experience of support services included school counselling, Tier 3 CAMHS and YOS, and he had attracted a number of diagnoses historically including ADHD, PTSD, conduct disorder and most recently 'psychosis'. At most, he had engaged superficially with some of these services and professionals.

Assessment

Callum was seen in a room on the prison wing, as he had refused to come to the unit. He had needed much reassurance from the caseworker about the type of support that the mental health team provided and that it was not a service for 'people who are mental'. He initially presented as guarded, agitated and hostile. He was sensitive to any movement outside the room window. He was initially reassured by explaining how the team worked, explaining the safety of the room that we were in and as standard, the limits of confidentiality. He was engaged in some non-problem-focused discussion before he appeared more relaxed and engaged.

Callum reported that he was constantly 'watching his back' and 'waiting for something bad to happen'. He described daily flashbacks of his friend being killed. He described that he forced himself to be in social situations so that others knew that he 'wasn't soft' and that he would quickly get into fights, which he later does not remember well. He was worried that he may inflict serious injuries on others, as with his previous worker in the care home. He reported that he had avoided supervised contact with his mother for approximately 12 months, as he found it difficult to be reminded that she is still with her partner. He reported that prior to prison, drugs and alcohol helped him to forget his problems for a while. He said that he was often filled with regret about the incidents he has been involved in.

As part of the assessment, typical staff responses to his risks and behaviours were acknowledged. Callum was also asked to complete a TSCC: Trauma Symptom Checklist for Children (Briere and Runtz, 1989). In diagnostic terms, he met the threshold for PTSD with the measure and clinical interview indicating that he was experiencing heightened sensitivity to threat, avoidance, traumatic re-enactment and replay (flashbacks).

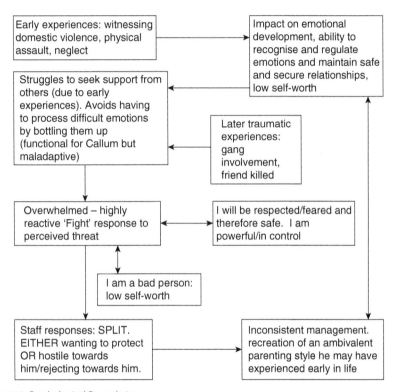

Figure 11.1 Diagrammatic Psychological Formulation

bang on the cell door and a loud wake-up call along the corridor, which reminded him of the shouting experienced when he witnessed his mother being assaulted by her partner. The shared insight allowed staff to alter their morning wake up routine to ensure that there was a knock on Callum's door five minutes before the wake-up call was made in the corridor, thus allowing him time to re-orientate himself to this environment.

Giving staff the opportunity to verbalise their feelings towards Callum allowed identification of the inconsistency in management approaches to his behaviour, as well as naming difficult emotions that were evoked through their work with Callum. This information could then be included in the formulation. A lack of a shared understanding about the nature of Callum's difficulties had led to different interpretations of his difficult behaviours and therefore different ways of managing them. This inconsistency often played out within each shift, providing at best an ambivalent care environment for Callum.

Phase 2: Individual Work – A Shared Understanding and Enhancing Skills

The early stages of work with Callum involved engagement through regular, predictable and consistent sessions. The initial work focused on psycho-education about trauma and basic fight–flight responses to threat. His difficulties with getting into fights and experiencing paranoid thoughts were explained in the context of witnessing and experiencing violence and seeing violence as a way of coping and surviving. This highlighted that at one time the coping strategy was functional, albeit 'high-risk' and having certain negative consequences, but now was proving maladaptive. As highlighted earlier, a shared decision was made not to explore his traumatic memories and flashbacks at this point, as he did not yet feel able to cope with the emotional distress that he perceived this would evoke.

In liaison with Callum's personal officer, a safety plan was drawn up. This was a collaborative plan that allowed Callum and others to identify triggers to increased emotional arousal, recognise changes in his physical and emotional state and agree on what would be either helpful or unhelpful in each scenario. By this time, Callum had started to talk more openly and make links between the times that he felt threatened, his thinking and his behaviour. He also started to develop insight into the fact that he used violence, but that it was linked to fear in relation to his early experiences. The safety plan aimed to support Callum to develop some basic emotional recognition and regulation through predictable and 'co-regulated' support from staff, and gradually over time to develop his own strategies. In essence, this was creating a plan that allowed staff to offer attuned care-giving – a type of care that Callum had not received in his early developmental years.

Specific sessions were used to help Callum develop 'grounding techniques' – specific coping strategies to regulate his emotions through orientating himself to his environment at times that he was distressed and experiencing flashbacks. On one occasion, the opportunity was taken to guide him through his techniques during an 'in-vivo' incident on the wing that occurred in the presence of the clinician. He was taken through relaxed breathing techniques that had been practised in session and he was supported to go to the 'safe place' he had developed in his mind. This also modelled for staff how Callum could be supported, and his distress de-escalated when in crisis. Such incidents were followed up with staff through ongoing psychological consultation with the staff team to support shared skills and understanding.

Phase 3: Individual Trauma-Focused Work

Over a period of 12 months, Callum's symptoms and incidents on the wing gradually decreased, as he developed skills to regulate himself and to reappraise situations that he originally perceived as threatening. He still continued to have flashbacks of the incident in which his friend was killed but he described them as less intense and more manageable. His levels of hypervigilance and avoidance had reduced and his confidence in managing difficulties as they arose had improved.

In agreement with the staff team, individual trauma-focused CBT work then began with Callum, in line with NICE guidelines previously described. With the continued use of the safety plan, different, more consistent dynamics amongst the staff team (caregivers) on any one shift and ongoing staff support in the form of psychological consultation and supervision, Callum's difficulties reduced. He made contact with his mother during this time, engaging in shared sense-making of some of their past experiences.

After 18 months, direct intervention with Callum came to an end. He was more able to regulate his emotions, seek support when required and noticeably more open about his day-to-day difficulties. Staff's observations and Callum's self-report (supported by psychometric measures exploring trauma symptomatology) evidenced improvements in PTSD symptoms, and the staff team around him had an understanding of how to help him maintain his well-being as well as request additional support or advice if they required.

Conclusions

Clinical experience and research indicate that high numbers of young people within forensic mental health settings present with an array of behavioural and psychological symptoms of traumatic stress – sometimes related to relatively mild stressors in the form of AD, more extreme, but discrete traumatic experiences as with PTSD, but all too often having experienced multiple and chronic traumatic events and attachment disruption throughout childhood. Many of these young people are likely to have found themselves in the criminal justice system as a consequence of their physiological, psychological and behavioural response to these experiences.

Once they have entered the system, they can often receive multiple diagnoses from health professionals, including AD and PTSD, in an attempt to understand

and communicate the difficulties they experience and to guide intervention. While such diagnoses can at times be useful to highlight need, from our experience they often do not capture the complexity of the experiences of many young people within forensic settings. We would therefore argue that a diagnostic approach alone is often too simplistic in understanding the complex needs of young people in forensic settings, and that this often leads to an oversimplification and a 'prescribed' approach to the intervention required. We would suggest that a developmentally informed, multifactorial formulation-based approach, underpinned by psychological theory, should at least supplement any diagnosis. This is deemed particularly important for those who have experienced multiple and complex trauma, often in conjunction with early chaotic life experiences. In our view, in order to truly understand the complexity of a young person's presentation and to provide multisystemic interventions pitched at the appropriate level and pace, it is essential to incorporate an awareness of the context of a young person's developmental experiences (including early attachment experiences and trauma), and their impact on brain development, emotional regulation skills and strategies for forming and maintaining relationships.

At a national level, it is necessary to use this growing perspective to inform and influence ongoing research and ultimately to shape recommendations for service provision: for instance, the provision of training for frontline professionals within youth justice services that includes an underpinning psychological framework addressing attachment and complex trauma, which aims to support clinicians to be more 'trauma aware' and facilitate the development of more psychologically informed therapeutic environments and interventions for those who have experienced complex trauma.

References

Abram, K. M., Teplin, L. A., Charles, D. R., Longworth, S. L., McClelland, G. M. and Dulcan, M. K. (2004). Posttraumatic stress disorder and trauma in youth in juvenile detention. *Archives of General Psychiatry*, **61**, 403–410.

American Psychiatric Association (APA) (2013). *Diagnostic and Statistical Manual of Mental Disorders*. 5th edition. Text rev. (DSM-5). Washington, DC: APA.

Andreasen, N. C. and Hoenk, P. R. (1982). The predictive value of adjustment disorders: A follow-up study. *American Journal of Psychiatry*, **139**(5), 584–590.

Baumeister, H. and Kufner, K. (2009). It is time to adjust the adjustment disorder category. *Current Opinion in Psychiatry*, **22**(4), 409–412.

Beck, A. T. (1976). *Cognitive Therapy for the Emotional Disorders*. New York: International Universities Press.

Bloom, S. L. (1999). Trauma Theory Abbreviated. Final Action Plan: A Coordinated Community-Based Response to Family Violence. Attorney General of Pennsylvania's Family Violence Task Force. Available from www.dhs.vic .gov.au/__data/assets/pdf_file/0005/587966/trauma_theor y_abbreviated_sandra_bloom.pdf. Accessed 31 October 2016.

Bowlby, J. (1988). *A Secure Base: Parent-Child Attachment and Healthy Human Development*. New York: Basic Books.

Bremness, A. and Polzin, W. (2014). Commentary: Developmental Trauma Disorder: A Missed Opportunity in DSM V. *Journal of the Canadian Academy of Child and Adolescent Psychiatry*, **23**(2), 142–145.

Briere, J. and Runtz, M. (1989). The trauma symptom checklist (TSC- 33): Early data on a new scale, *Journal of Interpersonal Violence*, **4**, 151–163.

Briere, J. and Scott, C. (2006). *Principles of Trauma Therapy: A Guide to Symptoms, Evaluation, and Treatment*. Thousand Oaks, CA: Sage Publications.

Casey, P. (2009). Adjustment disorder: Epidemiology, diagnosis and treatment. *CNS Drugs*, **23**(11), 927–938.

Casey, P. and Bailey, S. (2011). Adjustment disorders: The state of the art. *World Psychiatry*, **10**(1), 11–18.

Chitsabesan, P. and Bailey, S. (2006). Mental health, educational and social needs of young offenders in custody and in the community. *Current Opinion in Psychiatry*, **19**, 355–360.

Chitsabesan, P., Kroll, L., Bailey, S., Kenning, C., Sneider, S., MacDonald, W. and Theodosiou, L. (2006). Mental health needs of young offenders in custody and in the community. *British Journal of Psychiatry*, **188**, 534–540.

Clark, D. M. (1999). Anxiety disorders: Why they persist and how to treat them. *Behaviour Research and Therapy*, **37**, s5–s27.

Clark, D. B., Thatcher, D. L. and Martin, C. S. (2010). Child abuse and other traumatic experiences, alcohol use disorders, and health problems in adolescence and young adulthood. *Journal of Pediatric Psychology*, **35**(5), 499–510.

Cloitre, M., Garvert, D. W., Brewin, C. R., Bryant, R. A. and Maercker, A. (2013). Evidence for proposed ICD-11 PTSD and complex PTSD: A latent profile analysis. *European Journal of Psychotraumatology*, **4**, doi:10.3402/ejpt.v4i0.20706.

Cohen, J. A., Mannarino, A. P., Perel, J. M. and Staron, V. (2007). A pilot randomized controlled trial of combined trauma-focused CBT and sertraline for childhood PTSD symptoms. *Journal of the American Academy of Child and Adolescent Psychiatry*, **46**(7), 811–819.

Cook, A., Spinazzola, J., Ford, J., Lanktree, C., Blaustein, M., Cloitre, M., DeRosa, R., Hubbard, R., Kagan, R., Liautaud, J., Mallah, K., Olafson, E. and van der Kolk, B.

(2005). Complex trauma in children and adolescents. *Psychiatric Annals*, **35**, 390–398.

Costello, E. J., Erkanli, A., Fairbank, J. A. and Angold, A. (2002). The prevalence of potentially traumatic events in childhood and adolescence. *Journal of Traumatic Stress*, **15**, 99–112.

Crighton, D. A. and Towl, G. J. (2008). *Psychology in Prisons*. 2nd edition. Oxford: Wiley Blackwell.

Day, C., Hibbert, P. and Cadman, S. (2008). *A Literature Review into Children Abused and/or Neglected Prior to Custody*. London: Youth Justice Board.

De Bellis, M. D. and Zisk, A. (2014). The biological effects of childhood trauma. *Child and Adolescent Psychiatric Clinics of North America* **23**, 185–222.

Dulcan, M. (2000). Does community mental health treatment of children and adolescents help? *Journal American Academy of Child and Adolescent Psychiatry*, **39**, 153–154.

Duncan, S. C., Strycker, L. A., Duncan, T. E. and Okut, H. (2002). A multilevel contextual model of family conflict and deviance. *Journal of Psychopathology and Behavioural Assessment*, **24**, 169–175.

DuMont, K. A., Widom, C. and Czaja, S. J. (2007). Predictors of resilience in abused and neglected children grown-up: The role of individual and neighborhood characteristics. *Child Abuse & Neglect*, **31**(3), 255–274.

Ehlers, A. and Clark, D. M. (2000). A cognitive model of posttraumatic stress disorder. *Behaviour Research and Therapy*, **38**, 319–345.

Fard, F., Hudgens, R. W. and Welner, A. (1979). Undiagnosed psychiatric illness in adolescents. *A prospective and seven year follow up. Archives of General Psychiatry*, **35**, 279–281.

Ford, J. D., Grasso, D. J., Hawke, J. and Chapman, J. F. (2013). Poly-victimization among juvenile justice-involved youths. *Child Abuse & Neglect*, **37**(10), 788–800.

Frissa, S., Hatch, S. L., Gazard, B., SELCoH study team, Fear, N. T., Hotopf, M. (2013). Trauma and current symptoms of PTSD in a South East London community. *Social Psychiatry and Psychiatric Epidemiology*, **48**(8), 1199–1209.

Gerson, R. and Rappaport, N. (2013). Traumatic stress and posttraumatic stress disorder in youth: Recent research findings on clinical impact, assessment, and treatment. *Journal of Adolescent Health*, **52**(2), 137–143.

Gisin, D., Hallar, D., Cerutti, B., Wolff, H., Bertrand, D., Sebo, P., Heller, P., Niveau, G. and Eytan, A. (2012). Mental health of young offenders in Switzerland: Recognizing psychiatric symptoms during detention. *Journal of Forensic and Legal Medicine*, **19**(6), 332–336.

Golding, K., Dent, H. R., Nissim, R. and Stott, E. (2006). *Thinking Psychologically about Children Who are Looked after and Adopted: Space for Reflection*. Chichester: John Wiley & Sons.

Hill, P. (2002). Adjustment disorder. In M. Rutter, E. A. Taylor Editors. *Child and Adolescent Psychiatry*. Oxford: Blackwell, pp. 510–519.

Howe, D. (2005). *Child Abuse and Neglect: Attachment, Development and Intervention*. Basingstoke: Palgrave MacMillan.

Kessler, R. C., Sonnega, A., Bromet, E., Hughes, M. and Nelson, C. B. (1995). Posttraumatic stress disorder in the National Comorbidity Survey. *Archives of General Psychiatry*, **52**, 1048–1060.

Koran, L. M., Sheline, Y., Imai, K., Kelsey, T. G., Freedland, K. E., Mathews, J. and Moore, M. (2003). Medical disorders among patients admitted to a public sector psychiatric in-patient unit. *Psychiatric Services*, **53**, 1623–1625.

Lennox, C. and Khan, L. (2013). Youth justice. In Annual Report of the Chief Medical Officer 2012. *Our Children Deserve Better: Prevention Pays*. London: Chief Medical Officer's Report, pp. 200–214.

MacLean, P. D. (1990) *The Triune Brain in Evolution: Role in Paleocerebral Functions*. New York: Plenum Press.

Meltzer, H., Gatward, R., Goodman, R. and Ford, T. (2000) *Mental Health of Children and Adolescents in Great Britain*. London: Stationery Office.

National Institute for Health and Care Excellence (NICE) (2005) *Post-Traumatic Stress Disorder (PTSD): The Management of PTSD in Adults and Children in Primary and Secondary Care*. Available from: www.nice.org.uk/C G26. Accessed 12 May 2016.

Nardi, C., Lichtenberg, P. and Kaplan, Z. (1994). Adjustment disorder of conscripts as a military phobia. *Military Medicine*, **159**, 612–616.

Pelkonen, M., Marttunen, M., Henriksson, M. and Lonnqvist, J. (2007). Adolescent adjustment disorder: Precipitant stressors and distress symptoms of 89 out-patients. *European Psychiatry*, **22**, 288–295.

Perry, B. D. (2000). Traumatized children: How childhood trauma influences brain development. *The Journal of California Alliance for the Mentally Ill*, **11**(1), 48–51.

Perry, B. D. (2008). Child maltreatment: The role of abuse and neglect in developmental psychopathology. In Theodore P. Beauchaine and Stephen P. Hinshaw Editors. *Textbook of Child and Adolescent Psychopathology*. New York: Wiley, pp. 93–128.

Piquero, A. R., Farrington, D. P. and Blumstein, A. (2007). *Key Issues in Criminal Career Research: New Analyses of the Cambridge Study in Delinquent Development*. Cambridge: Cambridge University Press.

Rahim, M. (2014). Developmental trauma disorder: An attachment-based perspective. *Clin Child Psychol Psychiatry*, **19**(4), 548–560.

Rogers, A. and Law, H. (2010). Working with trauma in a prison etting. In J. Harvey and K. Smedley Editors. *Psychological Therapy in Prison and Other Settings*. London: Willan, pp. 150–175.

Rogers, A., McMahon, J. and Law, D. (2011). Expanding therapy: Challenging the dominant discourse of individual therapy when working with vulnerable young people. A discussion paper. *Clinical Psychology Forum*, 222, 9–14.

Saxe, G. N., Ellis, B. H. and Kaplow, J. B. (2007). *Collaborative Treatment of Traumatized Children and Teens: The Trauma Systems Therapy Approach*. New York: Guilford Press.

Schore, A. N. (2001). Effects of a secure attachment relationship on right brain development, affect regulation, and infant mental health. *Infant Mental Health Journal*, 22, 7–66.

Seedat, S., Stein, D. J., Ziervogel, C., Middleton, T., Kaminer, D., Emsley, R. A. and Rossouw, W. (2002). Comparison of a response to a selective serotonin reuptake inhibitor in children, adolescents and adults with PTSD. *Journal of Child and Adolescent Psychopharmacology*, 12(1), 37–46.

Shapiro, F. (1989). Eye movement desensitisation procedure: A new treatment for post-traumatic stress disorder. *Journal of Behaviour Therapy and Experimental Psychiatry*, 20, 211–217.

Shear, K. M., Greeno, C., Kang, J., Ludewig, D., Frank, E., Swartz, H. A. and Hanekamp, M. (2000). Diagnosis of non-psychotic patients in community clinics. *American Journal of Psychiatry*, 157, 581–587.

Strain, J. J. and Diefenbacher, A. (2008). The adjustment disorders: The conundrums of the diagnoses. *Comprehensive Psychiatry*, 49, 121–130.

Sunderland, M. (2006). *The Science of Parenting*. London: Dorling Kindersley.

Trickey, D., Siddaway, A. P., Meiser-Stedman, R., Serpell, L. and Field, A. P. (2012). A meta-analysis of risk factors for post-traumatic stress disorder in children and adolescents. *Clinical Psychology Review*, 32(2), 122–138.

van der Klink, J. J., Blonk, R. W., Schene, A. H., van Dijk, F. J. H. (2003). Reducing long term sickness absence by an activating intervention in adjustment disorders: A cluster randomised design. *Occupational and Environmental Medicine*, 60, 429–437.

van der Kolk, B. A. (1987). *Psychological Trauma*. Washington, D.C.: American Psychiatric Press, Inc.

van der Kolk, B. A. (2005). Developmental trauma disorder: Toward a rational diagnosis for children with complex trauma histories. *Psychiatric Annals*, 35(5), 401–408.

van der Kolk, B. A. and Courtois, C. A. (2005). Editorial comments: Complex developmental trauma. *Journal of Traumatic Stress*, 18, 385–388.

van der Kolk, B. A., Roth, S., Pelcovitz, D., Sunday, S. and Spinazzola, J. (2005). Disorders of extreme stress: The empirical foundation of a complex adaptation to trauma, *Journal of Traumatic Stress*, 18(5), 389–399.

World Health Organization. (1992). *The ICD-10 Classification of Mental and Behavioural Disorders: Clinical Descriptions and Diagnostic Guidelines*. Geneva: World Health Organization.

Wright, L., Borrill, J., Teers, R. and Cassidy, T. (2006). The mental health consequences of dealing with self-inflicted death in custody. *Counselling Psychology Quarterly*, 19(2), 165–180.

Young People with Schizophrenia in Forensic Settings

Enys Delmage

Introduction

Schizophrenia is a mental illness characterised by cognitive disruption, delusions (fixed, false beliefs), hallucinations, social dysfunction and a blurring of the boundaries between the internal and external worlds. The onset is normally in late adolescence or early adulthood. Sufferers frequently have elements of comorbidity including depression, anxiety and substance misuse. Social problems include time away from school, longer-term unemployment, disenfranchisement from friends and family, poverty and homelessness. There is also an association with increased risk of suicide and higher rates of physical health problems. The presentation in young people can be influenced by the developmental stage that the individual has reached, as well as by the social milieu in which they find themselves.

The estimated prevalence of schizophrenia worldwide varies between 0.3 and 3% with an average of 1.07% (Piccinelli et al., 1997). A report from the Office for National Statistics (2003) showed prevalence rates for any functional psychosis in the previous year of 8% for male-remanded young offenders and of 10% for male-sentenced young offenders (Lader et al., 2003). The numbers were too small to produce a meaningful analysis for female young offenders, though one study recorded prevalence rates of schizophrenia in incarcerated males as 6% and in females as 9% (Lader et al., 1997). These prevalence percentages are significantly higher than the rates reported in 16–19-year-olds living in private households (0.2%) (Meltzer et al., 1995). The disrupted social and cognitive development which may be a marked feature of the lives of many young offenders is compounded by the impact of the illness itself on the developing young mind which is associated with a poorer prognosis than those with adult-onset schizophrenia (Rabinowitz et al., 2006). A number of social factors common to this group can predict those who are more likely to show persistence and worsening of the symptoms of

childhood schizophrenia, including social deprivation, drug use, absence of a parent and childhood abuse or neglect (Kirkbridge et al., 2010; Kuepper et al., 2011).

In mentally disordered young offenders, schizophrenia is often complicated by substance misuse associated with psychosis, mixed disorders of conduct and emotions presenting with what can appear to be hallucinatory experiences, complex comorbidity and associated polypharmacy, social segregation as the underpinning of paranoid ideas, and a plethora of stressful life experiences including abusive experiences. When externally imposed separation from family and friends is added to this picture, through the criminal justice and/or welfare system, it is perhaps unsurprising that rates of schizophrenia are higher for young people in secure settings than that of the average young person in the community.

Diagnosis

Features of schizophrenia can be broadly divided into negative (deficit) and positive symptoms. Negative symptoms commonly include blunted emotions and mood, social withdrawal, reduced amount of speech, a lack of motivation, reduced interests and poor self-care. Normal rhythms can also be disrupted, including the sleep-wake cycle and appetite. These symptoms often represent a departure from normal habits and are usually more severe than that which would be ascribed to normal teenage behaviour. Positive symptoms can include delusions; hallucinations; disordered thoughts and speech; and feelings that other agencies may be controlling thoughts, emotion and volition.

Diagnosis is most frequently made by reference to either the *Diagnostic and Statistical Manual* or the World Health Organisation's *International Classification of Diseases*. Both classification systems periodically undergo review but are likely to continue to rely upon the presence of delusional perceptions (normal sensory experiences interpreted bizarrely), hallucinations and experiences of false external control of thought. In terms of the diagnostic criteria for research, the ICD-10 diagnosis is made on the basis of some of the following symptoms over a period of at least a month:

At least one of the following:

(1) Thought echo (hearing one's thoughts repeated back) or insertion (thoughts being added which do not belong to the patient) or withdrawal (thoughts being taken out of one's head), or thought broadcasting (beliefs that others can detect or overhear the thoughts of the patient);

(2) Delusions of control or influence linked to body movements or particular thoughts, actions or sensations, or delusional perceptions;

(3) Hallucinatory 'voices' giving a running commentary on the patient's behaviour, or discussing the patient between themselves, or other types of 'voice' coming from a part of the body;

(4) Persistent delusions of other kinds that are culturally inappropriate and impossible;

OR at least two of the following:

(1) Persistent hallucinations in any modality (for example touch or vision), when occurring every day for at least one month, when accompanied by delusions without clear mood content, or when accompanied by persistent over-valued ideas;

(2) Neologisms (use of fictitious words), breaks or interpolations in the train of thought, resulting in incoherence or irrelevant speech;

(3) Catatonic behaviour, such as excitement, posturing or waxy flexibility; negativism (reduction in normal functioning with opposition or no response to instructions or external stimuli); mutism; and stupor;

(4) 'Negative' symptoms such as marked apathy, paucity of speech and blunting or incongruity of emotional responses.

The Diagnostic and Statistical Manual of Mental Disorders Version 5 has raised the symptom threshold with a requirement for at least two defined symptoms as opposed to their previous requirement of one, and has removed the subtype descriptions on the basis that many patients will display characteristics of different subtypes simultaneously or across time, which can cause diagnostic confusion and is perhaps an unhelpful distinction.

Early-onset schizophrenia is associated with consistent symptom profiles to those reported in the adult literature, but are more severe in quality (Frazier et al., 2007). The picture can be significantly masked by a range of other factors which can make diagnosis challenging where there are other possible explanations for certain behaviours such as social communication difficulties, which is often the case for other mental disorders in this group (NICE Guidelines for Autism, 2011).

It is important to delineate that psychosis, which can present with all of the above features, does not always signify schizophrenia. A first psychotic episode may have multiple causes including drugs, brain injury or other physical illnesses which can produce identical symptoms. For those experiencing a first episode of psychosis, one study found that approximately 20% experienced full recovery at the two-year mark, with a suggestion that longer-term recovery results would be higher – half the patients showed symptom remission and a quarter showed functional remission (Wunderlink et al., 2009).

Epidemiology

The prevalence of childhood schizophrenia may be 1.6–1.9 per 100,000 child population (Burd and Kerbeshian, 1987; Hellgren et al., 1987; Gillberg, 2001) from the available research. Young people in the secure estate are approximately 10 times more likely to suffer from psychosis than the general adolescent population (Fazel et al., 2008). Mortality was found in one study of almost 3,000 young offenders, to be higher than in equivalent age groups with schizophrenia in the community (Coffey et al., 2003). The authors also concluded that young male offenders were nine times more likely and female offenders 40 times more likely to die than young people in the general population over an 11-year period – the mortality of 8.5/1,000 person years of observation in young offenders contrasted with a mortality of 1.1/1,000 for the matched specified age group in the general population (Coffey et al., 2003).

This rate is not dissimilar to a large study conducted in Finland where 3,743 young male and 89 young female offenders (aged 15–21) were followed up over a 20-year period which highlighted a standardised mortality ratio of 7.4, and which concluded that the high mortality was associated with psychiatric disorders (Sailas et al., 2006). The high prevalence of cannabis use in young offenders is concerning in the light of the strong association between cannabis use and onset of psychosis and schizophrenia in adult life (Arseneault et al., 2002).

Links with Aggression

Conduct problems (aggression, truancy and fire setting) may be a feature of early-onset schizophrenia (Russell et al., 1989). Young adults (up to the age of 21) meeting the diagnostic criteria for a schizophrenia-spectrum disorder in a birth cohort study were found in one study to be 3.8 times more likely than control subjects to be violent (Arseneault et al., 2000). In a study by Nolan et al. (1999), rates of comorbidity of schizophrenia with psychopathy (as defined by use of the Psychopathy Checklist – Shortened Version) were found to be higher in violent than non-violent patients, again raising the question as to whether violent patients with schizophrenia who score highly on measures of psychopathy have a personality disorder which precedes the schizophrenia or whether they might constitute a previously unclassified subtype of schizophrenia characterised by conduct disorder symptoms.

Violent and aggressive behaviour in adolescents who later develop schizophrenia has been described in a number of studies (Arseneault et al., 2003) and one such study found that a conviction of violence in late adolescence was significantly associated with a future diagnosis of schizophrenia (Gosden, 2005). The relationship between psychotic illnesses and violence in adolescence is clearly a complex one, and it is important to emphasise that there are other potential underpinnings for violence including a history of emotional and physical abuse, drug use and other developmental and social factors (Clare et al., 2000).

Findings from the Aetiology and Ethnicity in Schizophrenia and Other Psychoses (AESOP) First Episode Psychosis Study highlighted that of their study group, almost 40% ($n = 194$) were aggressive at first contact with services, and approximately half of these were physically violent (Dean et al., 2007), and younger age was significantly associated with aggression. A meta-analysis in 2009 (Douglas et al., 2009) showed that psychosis was significantly associated with a 49–68% increase in the odds of violence. However, there was substantial dispersion among effect sizes due to methodological factors, definition and measurement of psychosis.

Presentation to Services

Box 12.1 gives a description of an early presentation of a psychotic episode in a young person who is already hard to reach. In terms of likely presentations to mental health services it is worth commenting on the challenges to recognition of mental illnesses such as schizophrenia in young offenders. The challenges may include the following:

- Lack of engagement with school, social services and health practitioners (General Practice, community mental health services, health workers allied to Youth Offending Teams, early intervention provisions and so forth) meaning that recognition becomes more challenging. In addition, physical healthcare of children and young people with schizophrenia can suffer resulting in a reduced life expectancy (Parks, 2006; Brown et al., 2010);
- Frequent changes of geographical location common in both young offenders and their families;
- Inherent suspicion of a wide range of support services due to negative past experiences (for example local authority removal of a sibling, or perceptions of punitive sanctions imposed by Youth Offending Teams) combined with resistance to advice from authority figures such as members of the judiciary;

BOX 12.1 Case Example 1 – First Presentation

Amanda is a 15-year-old girl with a history of violence, repeated theft of items from shops and school non-attendance. She has become increasingly isolated and recently has seriously assaulted her mother. There is a family history of schizophrenia. She is known to the local Youth Offending Team who state that she has been very hard to engage and has been distancing herself from others. She has refused to have any contact with the local Child and Adolescent Mental Health Service (CAMHS) or social services team, stating, 'you just want to lock me away'. More recently the police have been called to the house on a daily basis as she has made threats to kill family members and she is now in a police cell awaiting assessment following a further arrest at home when she damaged various items of property and again made threats to kill others.

- Comorbidity reducing the chances of follow-up and likelihood of compliance with medication;
- High educational needs increasing the chances of a lack of understanding regarding links between, for instance, cannabis use and psychosis;
- Lack of clarity regarding which service is best placed to meet their needs;
- Abuse acting as a block to access external help;
- Lack of interested parties monitoring the well-being and advocating on behalf of the child;
- Lack of holistic assessments in settings such as social services units, Secure Children's Homes, Secure Training Centres and Young Offender Institutions.

Common presentations such as the so-called negative symptoms of schizophrenia (which often precede the 'positive' symptoms such as hallucinations and delusions) may be masked by other difficulties. For example, social withdrawal, loss of skills and poor self-care may be attributed to drug use, conduct disorder, the consequences of offending and general social decline.

Young offenders with schizophrenia may be diagnosed and treated via a number of routes including:

(1) General Practice;
(2) Mental health workers allied to Youth Offending Teams and Court Diversion Schemes;
(3) Inreach services to Secure Children's Homes, Secure Training Centres and Young Offender Institutions;
(4) Community and inpatient CAMHS Teams;
(5) Early Intervention in Psychosis services;
(6) Forensic CAMHS teams;
(7) Forensic adolescent consultation and treatment services;
(8) Adolescent forensic inpatient services;
(9) Assessments on behalf of the courts.

This list is not definitive – it is also worth mentioning that there is a considerable amount of heterogeneity internationally, but in general most jurisdictions will have a framework for mental healthcare, physical healthcare, social services and criminal justice resources focused on young people. Some locations in each country have comprehensive services whilst others may have a lack of local services and may need to access expert opinion from farther afield. In the UK, there are moves to make the provision within Young Offender Institutions and Secure Children's Homes standardised in terms of the inreach services.

The recommendations from other sources including the reports of Lord Bradley (2009) and Lord Darzi (2008) with their emphasis on early assessment and treatment of mental health problems, and the Youth Crime Action Plan (2008), would seem to suggest that regional community forensic CAMHS teams are an important part of providing holistic assessment and treatment of mentally disordered young offenders.

Assessment of Mentally Disordered Young Offenders

Methods for the assessment of the mental health of young offenders include clinical assessment and identification via screening tools. The mentally disordered offender may be recognised by friends or family as having mental health needs, or by a variety of professionals involved with their management, which may include the police, the courts, solicitors, educational or vocational services, the Youth Offending Team, staff in secure settings such as Young Offender Institutions, Secure Training Centres, Local Authority Secure Children's Homes, generic local authority services, GPs and other health services and so forth, any of whom may contact a local mental health service for advice.

Many UK services use the Asset assessment tool (2006), which has now been upgraded to the AssetPlus Tool (2014), which is commonly used in community settings (for instance by Youth Offending Teams). In addition, the Comprehensive Health Assessment Tool (CHAT) has been introduced to secure estates within England to assess all health needs in young people in custody (Chitsabesan et al., 2014). Following an initial reception screen to identify any urgent health needs, all young people have a mental health assessment which includes assessment of symptoms that may be indicative of a psychotic illness within three days of admission. Further urgent assessment may be requested as clinically indicated. A community version of the CHAT is available for use within community-based youth offending teams and is administered by the health worker (www.ohrn.nhs.uk/OHRNResearch/CHAT/).

It is important to highlight that these tools are for screening purposes, and where problems are identified, specialist assessment would then take place since the symptoms described may have a variety of underpinnings. It is also crucial not to miss comorbid conditions like autism, and information exists in relation to the assessment and treatment of this condition in the form of a National Institute for Health and Care Excellence (NICE) guideline (NICE Guidelines for Autism, 2011).

Treatment of Schizophrenia in Young Offenders

The principles of treatment for schizophrenia in adolescents are set out in NICE guidelines published in January 2013 (NICE, 2013). The recommended approach is to consider the patient's needs holistically – whilst medication has historically formed the mainstay of treatment, consideration of psychological and social treatment is now commonplace. Research related to the neurobiological models of early-onset schizophrenia, coupled with research in developmental psychology, give support to multidimensional treatment of adolescents with such illnesses (Eggers, 1999).

Medication

Research has illustrated that there are differences in potency and side-effect profiles between first- and second-generation antipsychotics, but there is no single class with superior efficacy (Leucht et al., 2009) nor any that is generally superior on other indices (Sikich et al., 2004; Armanteros and Davies, 2006; Kennedy, 2007). The current evidence base would seem to point towards individualised treatment based upon side-effect profile, specific drug features and previous treatment response. Various types of medication are available including the so-called typical antipsychotics (for instance Chlorpromazine and Haloperidol) and the newer atypical antipsychotics (for instance Olanzapine, Quetiapine and Risperidone). Side effects from the typical drugs can include dizziness and drowsiness, hypersalivation, weight gain, Parkinsonian symptoms including tremor and gait abnormalities, skin rashes and hormonal changes. The atypical drugs can cause similar problems in terms of weight gain, dizziness and drowsiness. While they tend to cause less Parkinsonian symptoms, they can cause blood sugar changes and diabetes in the longer term.

Clinician choice of antipsychotic is likely to be influenced by a number of factors including efficacy, tolerability and cost. Treatment should be guided by previous response to medication (if present) and other individual factors such as weight, a past history

of medical problems and, last but not least, service user choice – the potential weight gain and sexual side effects may dissuade many teenagers who are beginning to explore their sexuality. There are other health risks specifically pertinent to young offenders (Dolan et al., 1999). Those in secure settings may have limited access to exercise (especially if requiring regular seclusion or isolation from others) and dietary advice (this tends to be less of a problem in hospital settings where dieticians can be helpful in regulating dietary intake). There is emerging evidence to suggest that exercise can be useful in improving the mental health of young people (Ekeland et al., 2009), with obvious beneficial physical effects in addition, and this features as part of the treatment programme in most psychiatric units. NICE recommend the following: monitoring for the emergence of any movement disorders; weight to be measured weekly for the first 6 weeks, then at 12 weeks and then every 6 months; height to be factored in to growth plotting; regular monitoring of pulse and blood pressure (at 12 weeks and then every 6 months) and of fasting blood glucose, HbA1 C, blood lipid; and prolactin levels to be tested at 12 weeks and then every 6 months.

Those in the community may be involved in behaviour which puts them at greater health risk, such as smoking (itself an activity which causes liver enzyme induction and therefore sometimes greater doses of medication are needed for the same effect). Further challenges in this group may include poor dietary advice and health monitoring in their early years and a proclivity for unhealthy food, as well as underactive lifestyles, heavy alcohol use and other drugs which also pose a cardiac risk. Another challenge in the youth justice secure estate is that depot medication cannot be given, meaning that clinicians are often dependent on the patient complying with oral medication. Antipsychotic preparations do exist which dissolve on the tongue, if compliance is an issue, and these can be helpful especially in circumstances where the patient experiences paranoid thoughts about medication being poisoned, for instance, and may try to hide their tablets instead of swallowing them.

Dosing modification may be necessary since the side effects such as weight gain and prolactin elevation may be greater in adolescents, and arguably the psychological effects of the physical manifestations may have a greater impact in youth (Mattai et al., 2010). Most antipsychotics are not licensed for use in children; any prescription of an antipsychotic medication for those under 18 should take place only under specialist supervision, and the young person should, where possible, indicate that they understand that the medication is being used off-license where this is the case.

Treatment of schizophrenia in adolescents has been largely extrapolated from adult studies and there is little data available regarding the longer-term effects of antipsychotic medication on the developing nervous system. However, long-term treatment with a young person with a definitive diagnosis of schizophrenia should be considered even after a single episode in order to prevent the symptoms of the chronic illness. All drugs have specific licensing conditions for use with young people and it is advisable to consult the British National Formulary for Children (2016–17) – most antipsychotics are used off-license in children so it is important to ensure that the young person and their families/carers are aware of this.

Psychological Interventions

Psychological therapies have been used in combination with pharmacotherapy for some time – the evidence would suggest that social skills training, psycho-educational interventions with families and relatives, as well as cognitive behavioural therapy for persistent positive symptoms are efficacious. Family interventions in particular have been seen to be helpful (Leff et al., 1982) and can reduce relapse and hospitalisation rates (Pfammatter et al., 2006). Cognitive behavioural therapy can usefully focus on coping skills enhancement and challenging the basis of abnormal perceptions or beliefs, as well as addressing general symptomatology, depression and the negative symptoms interfering with social functioning (Garety and Kuipers, 1995). Compliance therapy can also be of use in terms of adherence to medication (Kemp et al., 1996), and cognitive remediation therapy has also shown some success in this group (Wykes et al., 2011) but is not widely available. The importance of supporting and delivering therapy to parents/carers has also been highlighted (Kuipers, 1993; Zhang, 1994; Tarrier and Barrowclough, 1995). Arts therapies have been recommended as part of the NICE guidelines for treatment of schizophrenia in adults (NICE, 2009), and ongoing research aims to examine the clinical effect and cost-effectiveness of this treatment via large-scale randomised controlled trials (Crawford et al., 2010).

Obvious challenges in the mentally disordered young offender group include disengagement from families, or rejection, fear and anger, especially where offending has been towards family members. In addition, for inpatient adolescent forensic settings, Young Offender Institutions, Secure Training Centres and Local Authority Secure Children's Homes, distance of travel can also prove to be a factor for interventions such as family therapy, but modern technology (for instance secure video conferencing) can provide some solutions where distances are prohibitive.

Other Therapeutic Approaches

The duration of untreated psychosis may be prolonged by poor engagement with services, mobility of the group and difficulties with recognition within the criminal justice system or welfare system, combined with poor supervision from family members in groups with challenging family dynamics. Recognition may be further hampered by comorbidity including drug misuse, hyperkinetic disorders and learning disability. Early intervention is crucial for this group, and the timely recognition of such disorders is likely to prove efficacious in the longer term – this may be achieved by training of non-mental health agencies to improve rates of detection and by implication early access to treatment. There are mental health service divisions with regard to those aged 15 and above who could be managed within an Early Interventions in Psychosis Service and/or a CAMH Service depending on local provision and availability. This may drive assessment of each case on its individual needs so that the most appropriate service may be utilised.

Early Intervention Services arose from the National Service Framework for Mental Health and they aim to deliver intensive therapeutic services for those aged 15–35, including a range of modalities and a focus on various aspects of functioning including meeting the mental health needs, addressing vocational/educational issues and providing the appropriate social support. This intensive input may be mirrored by the locality CAMHS team (though this degree of input is less likely to be available for those over 18) so the referral route should be considered on an individual basis and in the context of the availability of local services.

The difficulties in continuation of care for mentally disordered young offenders is an indicator that this group is particularly suited to a comprehensive package

---

BOX 12.2 Case Example 2 – Management

Background

Steve is a 17-year-old boy who is approaching his 18th birthday, and is placed in a Young Offender Institution. He is due for release one week before he is 18, and during his time in the custodial setting he has suffered with a psychotic illness which has been effectively treated by the inreach team using antipsychotic medication. Steve has used cannabis extensively in the community and states that although he understands it has made him unwell, he is planning to start again on release as he feels it helps him with his anxiety. His community social worker is planning to close his case when he reaches 18 and the local CAMHS team are not aware of him as he became unwell just prior to incarceration.

Formulation

It is likely that he is using cannabis as a form of self-medication and may mistrust the evidence that it is worsening his psychotic illness.

Assessment

Whilst the diagnosis is not debated, there are a number of concerning factors – firstly, his case will soon be closed to social services and in all likelihood to any Youth Offending Team that is involved, when he reaches 18; secondly, he is unlikely to continue to comply with his antipsychotic medication without support and education; and thirdly, there are no locality mental health teams that are aware of him.

Treatment

The crucial factor is comprehensive handover to the community mental health team and general practitioner. He will need the involvement of the adult mental health service and ideally will need an assertive outreach approach to build on the progress he has made in the Young Offender Institution. Early intervention teams and transition services can be highly effective in managing such cases and ensuring that risk is minimised.

---

including multidisciplinary and multiagency factions – typically, this would need to include mental health, the local authority and educational/vocational support, as well as close liaison with other agencies, for instance Multi-Agency Public Protection Arrangements (MAPPA) and the Youth Offending Teams. Where an individual has been detained in hospital under a treatment section, it may be that the provisions of the Mental Health Act's Section 117 aftercare (which places a statutory duty on health services and the local authority to provide support) are not adequate to manage the risk associated with the disorder and the speed of deterioration, so Supervised Community Treatment or a Conditional Discharge may be viable options to consider.

Challenges with Care and Rehabilitation

In the UK, the Care Programme Approach (CPA) forms a vital part of the care package and brings together the professionals involved with the young person's management, both current and future. The CPA is a method of including the patient and collaborating with all professionals involved with a patient's care – they operate both in community and inpatient settings and allow for regular communication between all disciplines and agencies working with the young person.

These meetings are vital in producing a cohesive approach to meeting the needs of mentally disordered young offenders and provide an arena to discuss risk, warning signs of relapse, treatment options and methods of managing problems appropriately, through mutual agreements and transparent communication between disciplines and agencies. CPAs also provide a means of checking that areas of unmet need can be addressed and that the global care package is providing adequate scaffolding to allow the young person to make good progress in whichever setting they find themselves.

Box 12.2 provides an example of some of the challenges faced by services, and some potential solutions. Mentally disordered young offenders require highly specialised input in order to safely manage the mental disorder and any associated risk to self and/or others. There may be specific problems where the individual's mental illness has been treated in a setting located some distance from the region where the young person will finally reside. Aspects of transition from one service to another can impair compliance with treatment and mentally disordered young offenders are especially prone to such transitions.

Solutions Lie in the Following Areas

(1) Effective inreach services that are able to alert the relevant CAMHS or adult team about a young person's mental health needs;

(2) Early intervention and proactive engagement prior to discharge or release by multiple agencies (social services and health are normally crucial to engage at an early juncture);

(3) A low threshold for consideration of the use of Community Treatment Orders on discharge from hospital which may provide the necessary scaffolding to support the young person in the area that they are returning to;

(4) Where on a treatment section of the Mental Health Act, use of Section 117 of the Mental Health Act 1983 places a statutory obligation on the local authority and health services to meet the needs of the individual – ideally local authority involvement should occur prior to discharge to enable a robust transition;

(5) Good communication with services, most often via CPA meetings (GPs, locality CAMHS and/or forensic adolescent community services, Early Intervention in Psychosis services, MAPPA, Youth Offending Teams, social services and non-statutory organisations that may be providing support to the young person);

(6) Clear consideration of educational/vocational elements to aid with structuring the day of the individual recovering from an episode of psychosis – children with schizophrenia may be considered to have special educational needs and this needs to be taken into account when planning education and requesting additional educational support;

(7) Incremental steps for the young person to make – this may lie in high levels of support on discharge from hospital/release from custody/discharge from care, which can be reduced as the young person progresses;

(8) Multidisciplinary and multiagency support with a high degree of transparency between teams – the Early Intervention in Psychosis services can provide care for those aged 14–35 and can work in tandem with other services to mitigate against the impact of transitions from childhood to adulthood;

(9) Systems of rapid response where a problem indicating relapse has arisen (to take into account the potentially grave risks) which again must involve clear lines of communication between multiple agencies;

(10) Nominated individuals within dedicated teams who are responsible for overseeing the care of the individual and to whom any concerns can be escalated.

The importance of a suitable activity to occupy the newly discharged mentally disordered young offender cannot be overstated – this could be educational via local college or school, or vocational on either a voluntary or paid basis – the utility lies in the engagement of the individual with gainful activities which provide an ongoing motivation as well as a deterrent from antisocial behaviour (including drug use) which may result in disengagement from treatment and support.

Longer-term solutions for mentally disordered young offenders suffering with schizophrenia should include further development of regional adolescent forensic community services which would aid in bridging the large gap between secure services (be it adolescent forensic inpatient care, incarceration within the youth justice secure estate or placement in a Local Authority Secure Children's Home) and the community.

Conclusions

Measuring the outcomes of young offenders treated for episodes of schizophrenia represents an important area of future research. Firstly it is necessary to define what is relevant to measure – this could encompass reoffending rates, further presentation to services, decline in educational/occupational abilities, compliance with medication, self-reported remission or relapse and quality of life reports. Mentally disordered young offenders are a group of adolescents with high unmet needs spanning a wide variety of domains and frequently in need of effective and timely treatment.

As stated, the diagnostic picture is frequently muddied which can make research challenging, but it is arguably an extremely important area: secure care is expensive not just in terms of direct financial cost but also in terms of aftercare packages, not counting the emotional cost to the individual of separation from the social milieu.

Whilst there will always be individuals whose risk dictates that they require secure care, this should be minimised where possible since it can often involve separation from family, friends and professional links which not only make the process of treatment more challenging but hampers the process of rehabilitation once the acute phase of the illness has been managed. Early intervention services and intensive input from locality community and inpatient CAMHS teams, in combination with a multitude of other agencies, can make a difference in the lives of this most disenfranchised group.

One source of optimism is the development of regional community adolescent forensic services who can offer the early treatment of such young people and also consultation and advice to the plethora of other agencies who are equally striving to manage both the mental disorder of the young person and the associated risks. It is widely hoped that these teams will continue to develop across the UK and provide access to specialist support to help meet the needs of these young people.

References

Armanteros, J. and Davies, M. (2006). Antipsychotics in early onset schizophrenia: Systematic review and meta-analysis. *European Child and Adolescent Psychiatry*, **15**, 141–148.

Arseneault, L., Cannon, M. and Poulton, R. (2002). Cannabis use in adolescence and risk for adult psychosis: Longitudinal prospective study. *British Medical Journal*, **325**, 1212–1213.

Arseneault, L., Cannon, M., Murray, R., Poulton, R., Caspi, A. and Moffitt, T. (2003). Childhood origins of violent behaviour in adults with schizophreniform disorder. *British Journal of Psychiatry*, **183**, 520–525.

Arseneault, L., Moffitt, T., Caspi, A., Taylor, P. and Silva, P. (2000). Mental disorders and violence in a total birth cohort. *Archives of General Psychiatry*, **57**(10), 979–986.

Asset- Young Offender Assessment TOOL. (2000). Youth Justice Board for England and Wales.

AssetPlus; Assessment and Planning in the Youth Justice System. (2014). Youth Justice Board for England and Wales.

British National Formulary for Children. (2016–2017). BMJ Group, the Royal Pharmaceutical Society of Great Britain, and Royal College of Paediatrics and Child Health Publications Limited.

Brown, S., Kim, M. and Mitchell, C. (2010). Twenty-five year mortality of a community cohort with schizophrenia. *The British Journal of Psychiatry*, **196**, 116–121.

Burd, L. and Kerbeshian, J. (1987). A North Dakota prevalence study of schizophrenia presenting in childhood. *Journal of the American Academy of Child and Adolescent Psychiatry*, **26**, 347–350.

Chitsabesan, P., Lennox, C., Theodosiou, L., Law, H., Bailey, S. and Shaw, J. (2014). The development of the comprehensive health assessment tool for young offenders within the secure estate. *Journal of Forensic Psychiatry and Psychology*, **25**(1), 1–25.

Clare, P., Clarke, A. and Bailey, S. (2000). Relationship between psychotic disorders in adolescence and criminally violent behaviour. *British Journal of Psychiatry*, **177**, 275–279.

Coffey, C., Veit, F., Wolfe, R., Cini, E. and Patten, G. (2003). Mortality in young offenders: Retrospective cohort study. *British Medical Journal*, **326**, 1064.

Crawford, M., Killaspy, H., Kalaitzaki, E., Barrett, B., Byford, S., Patterson, S., Soteriou, T. O., Neill, F., Clayton, K., Maratos, A., Barnes, T., Osborn, D., Johnson, T., King, M., Tyrer, P. and Waller, D. (2010). Study protocol: The MATISSE study: A randomised trial of group art therapy for people with schizophrenia. *BioMed Central Psychiatry*, **10**, 1–9.

Dean, K., Walsh, E., Morgan, C., Demjaha, A., Dazzan, P., Morgan, K., Lloyd, T., Fearon, P., Jones, P. and Murray, R. (2007). Aggressive behaviour at first contact with services: Findings from the AESOP first episode psychosis study. *Psychological Medicine*, **37**(4), 547–557.

Dolan, M., Holloway, J., Bailey, S. and Smith, C. (1999). Health status of juvenile offenders: A survey of young offenders appearing before the juvenile courts. *Journal of Adolescence*, **22**(1), 137–144.

Douglas, K., Guy, L. and Hart, S. (2009). Psychosis as a risk factor for violence to others: A meta-analysis. *Psychological Bulletin*, **135**(5), 679–706.

Eggers, C. (1999). Some remarks on etiological aspects of early-onset schizophrenia. *European Child & Adolescent Psychiatry*, **8**(Sup 1), S1–S4.

Ekeland, E., Heian, F., Hagen, K., Abbott, J. and Nordheim, L. (2009). Exercise to improve self-esteem in children and young people. *The Cochrane Library*, (1), 1–38.

Fazel, S., Doll, H. and Langstrom, N. (2008). Mental disorders among adolescents in juvenile detention and correctional facilities: A systematic review and metaregression analysis of 25 surveys. *Journal of the American Academy of Child & Adolescent Psychiatry*, **47**(9), 1010–1019.

Frazier, J., McClellan, J., Findling, R., Vitiello, B., Anderson, R., Zablotsky, B., Williams, E., McNamara, N.,

Jackson, J., Ritz, L., Hlastala, S., Pierson, L., Varley, J., Puglia, M., Maloney, A., Ambler, D., Hunt-Harrison, T., Hamer, R., Noyes, N., Lieberman, J. and Sikich, L. (2007). Treatment of early-onset schizophrenia spectrum disorders: Demographic and clinical characteristics. *Journal of the American Academy of Child & Adolescent Psychiatry*, **46**(8), 979–988.

Garety, P. and Kuipers, L. (1995). *Cognitive Behaviour Therapy for People with Psychosis: A Clinical Handbook*. Chichester: Wiley and Sons.

Gillberg, C. (2001). Epidemiology of early onset schizophrenia. In Remschmidt, H. Editor. *Schizophrenia in Children and Adolescents*. Cambridge: Cambridge University Press, 43–59.

Gosden, N., Kramp, P., Gorm, G., Andersen, T. and Dorte, S. (2005). Violence of young criminals predicts schizophrenia: A 9-year register-based follow-up of 15- to 19-year-old criminals. *Schizophrenia Bulletin*, **31**(3), 759–768.

Hellgren, L., Gillberg, C. and Enerskog, I. (1987). Antecedents of adolescent psychoses: A population-based study of school health problems in children who develop psychosis in adolescence. *Journal of the American Academy of Child and Adolescent Psychiatry*, **26**, 351–355.

Kemp, R., Hayward, P., Applewhaite, G., Everitt, B. and David, A. (1996). Compliance therapy in psychotic patients: Randomised controlled trial. *British Medical Journal*, **312**, 345–349.

Kennedy, E., Kumar, A. and Datta, S. (2007). Antipsychotic medication for childhood-onset schizophrenia. (updated 2012) *Cochrane Database of Systematic Reviews*, **3**, Article Number CD004027. 1–28.

Kirkbridge, J., Coid, J. and Morgan, C. (2010). Translating the epidemiology of psychosis into public mental health: Evidence, challenges and future prospects. *Journal of Public Mental Health*, 4–14.

Kuepper, R., Van Os, J. and Lieb, R. (2011). Do cannabis and urbanicity co-participate in causing psychosis? Evidence from a 10-year follow-up cohort study. *Psychological Medicine*, **41**, 2121–2129.

Kuipers, L. (1993). Family burden in schizophrenia: Implications for services. *Social Psychiatry and Psychiatric Epidemiology*, **28**, 207–210.

Lader, D., Singleton, N. and Meltzer, H. (1997). *Psychiatric Morbidity among Young Offenders in England and Wales*. London: Office for National Statistics.

Lader, D., Singleton, N. and Meltzer, H. (2003). *Psychiatric Morbidity among Young Offenders in England and Wales: Further Analysis of Data from the ONS Survey of Psychiatric Morbidity among Prisoners*. London: Office for National Statistics.

Leff, J., Kuipers, L. and Berkowitz, R. (1982). A controlled trial of social interventions in the families of schizophrenic patients. *The British Journal Of Psychiatry*, **141**, 121–134.

Leucht, S., Corves, C., Arbter, D., Engel, R., Li, C. and Davis, J. (2009). Second-generation versus first-generation antipsychotic drugs for schizophrenia: A meta-analysis. *Lancet*, **3**(373) (9657), 31–41.

Lobban, F. and Barrowclough, C. (2007). *A Casebook of Family Interventions for Psychosis*. Chichester: Wiley and Sons.

Lord Bradley (2009). Review of people with mental health problems or learning disabilities in the criminal justice system, Department of Health Publication (Copyright Crown), April.

Lord Darzi (2008). High quality care for all: NHS Next Stage Review final report, Department of Health Publication (Copyright Crown), June.

Mattai, A., Hill, J. and Lenroot, R. (2010). Treatment of early-onset schizophrenia. *Current Opinion in Psychiatry*, **23**(4), 304–310.

Meltzer, H., Gill, B., Petticrew, M. and Hinds, K. (1995). *OPCS Surveys of Psychiatric Morbidity in Great Britain, Report 1: The Prevalence of Psychiatric Morbidity among Adults Living in Private Households*. HMSO: London.

NICE (National Institute for Health and Care Excellence) (2011). *Guidelines on Psychosis with Coexisting Substance Misuse: Assessment and Management in Adults and Young People* (CG120). March. London: NICE publications.

NICE (National Institute for Health and Care Excellence) (2009). *Schizophrenia: Core Interventions in the Treatment and Management of Schizophrenia in Adults in Primary and Secondary Care*. London: NICE publications.

NICE (National Institute for Health and Care Excellence) (2011). *Guidelines for Autism (Recognition, Referral and Diagnosis of Children and Young People on the Autistic Spectrum)*. (September) Paragraph 1.5.12. London: NICE publications.

NICE (National Institute for Health and Care Excellence) (2013). *Guidelines on Psychosis and Schizophrenia in Children and Young People: Recognition and Management* (CG155). January. London: NICE publications.

Nolan, K., Volavka, J., Mohr, P. and Czobor, P. (1999). Psychopathy and violent behaviour among patients with schizophrenia or schizoaffective disorder. *American Psychiatric Association*, **50**, 787–792.

Parks, J., Svendsen, D. and Singer, P. (2006). *Morbidity and Mortality in People with Serious Mental Illness*. 13th Technical Report, Alexandria: National Association of State Mental Health Program Directors.

Pfammatter, M., Junghan, U. and Brenner, H. (2006). Efficacy of psychological therapy in schizophrenia: Conclusions from meta-analyses. *Schizophrenia Bulletin*, **32** (Supplement 1), S64–S80.

Piccinelli, M. and Gomez Homan, F. (1997). *Gender Differences in the Epidemiology of Affective Disorders and*

Schizophrenia. Geneva: World Health Organisation Publications.

Rabinowitz, J., Levine, S. and Hafner, H. (2006). A population based elaboration of the role of age of onset on the course of schizophrenia. *Schizophrenia Research*, **88**, 96–101.

Russell, A., Bott, L. and Sammons, C. (1989). The phenomenon of schizophrenia occurring in childhood. *Journal of the American Academy of Child and Adolescent Psychiatry*, **28**, 399–407.

Sailas, E., Feodoroff, B., Lindberg, N., Virkkunen, M., Sund, R. and Wahlbeck, K. (2006). The mortality of young offenders sentenced to prison and its association with psychiatric disorders: A register study. *European Journal of Public Health*, **16**, 193–197.

Sikich, L., Hamer, R. and Bashford, R. (2004). A pilot study of risperidone, olanzapine, and haloperidol in psychotic youth: A double-blind, randomised, 8-week trial. *Neuropsychopharmacology*, **29**, 133–145.

Tarrier, N. and Barrowclough, C. (1995). Family Interventions in schizophrenia and their long term outcomes. *International Journal of Mental Health*, **24**(3), 38–53.

Wunderlink, L., Sytema, S., Nienhuis, F. and Wiersma, D. (2009). Clinical recovery in first-episode psychosis. *Schizophrenia Bulletin*, **35**(2), 362–369.

Wykes, T., Huddy, V. and Cellard, C. (2011). A Meta-analysis of cognitive remediation for schizophrenia: Methodology and effect sizes. *The American Journal of Psychiatry*, **168**, 472–485.

Youth Crime Action Plan. (2008). Home Office Publications (Copyright Crown).

Zhang, M., Wang, M., Li, J. and Phillips, M. (1994). Randomised control trial of family intervention for 78 first episode male schizophrenic patients: An 18 month study in Suzhou, Jiangsu. *British Journal of Psychiatry*, **165**, 96–102.

Chapter 13

Substance Misuse in Young People with Antisocial Behaviour

Louise Theodosiou

Introduction

The World Health Organisation (2014a) uses the term 'psychoactive substance misuse' to describe the use of a substance for a purpose other than the legal or medical guidelines, for example, the non-medical use of prescription medications. The term is perceived as less judgemental than drug abuse. The National Institute for Health and Care Excellence (NICE, 2007: 22) defines substance misuse as 'intoxication by – or regular excessive consumption of and/or dependence on – psychoactive substances, leading to social, psychological, physical or legal problems. It includes problematic use of both legal and illegal drugs (including alcohol when used in combination with other substances)'.

Many works of fiction depict the potent combination of youth and intoxicants. Adolescence can be a time of risk-taking, particularly for young people with additional vulnerabilities. Experimentation with alcohol and drugs such as cannabinoids is associated with later dependence and abuse (Casey and Jones, 2010). Alcohol and drugs are associated with acquisitive crime and violence (Mulvey et al., 2010). Furthermore, the World Health Organisation (2014b) reports that 25% of deaths in the 20–39 age range were linked to alcohol. This cocktail of disinhibiting substances and vulnerable adolescents must be examined further.

The US Department of Justice (Mulvey et al., 2010) notes that serious or chronic young offenders are the most likely to have substance use disorders, and that substance use and serious offending fluctuate across parallel patterns. Within the UK, youth offending teams and professionals in other youth justice settings (including residential) continue to be the highest single referral source of children into community-based substance misuse specialist treatment services. The evidence indicates that over 60% of adolescents in residential youth offending settings had often used illegal drugs to relieve anxiety, stress or depression, indicating a link between mental health needs and substance misuse (Youth Justice Board, 2009).

The Department of Health (2011: 9) lists psychoactive substances including alcohol, and defines psychoactive drugs as 'substances that, when ingested, affect mental processes e.g. cognition or affect'. While sharing this broad definition, psychoactive drugs have key differences with regard to their individual legal status and their relationship with the Youth Justice System (YJS). Furthermore, while alcohol and cigarettes can be legitimately bought, by adults, there are restrictions in the age at which adolescents are allowed to access them. The sale, purchase and consumption of any illegal drug is a criminal offence, as is the retail of prescription drugs when not dispensed to complete a prescription.

In addition to addressing the complex relationship between offending and substance use, there is a need to improve health outcomes and reduce drug-related morbidity and mortality. The Health and Social Care Information Centre (2013) notes the correlation between the age at which adolescents start using drugs and the drugs they use; younger children typically start using solvents, while older children typically start using cannabis. The Office of National Statistics (2013) reports that during 2012 in England, there were 1,496 drug-related deaths, while 46 deaths in the UK were associated with volatile substance abuse (International Centre for Drug Policy, 2012). Looking at the risks of alcohol intoxication, it is important to note that in the USA, drivers aged between 16–19 years old were three times as likely to die in a car crash (Insurance Institute for Highway Safety, 2012), and that 23% of 15- to 20-year-olds in fatal car accidents in the USA had been drinking (National Highway Traffic Safety Administration, 2012).

McArdle and Angom (2012) note that substance use became a relatively common phenomenon among adolescents towards the end of the twentieth century, a timescale that parallels an increase in behavioural problems. Levels of parental supervision and family support have been linked to initiation and ongoing use of cigarettes, drugs and alcohol. The European Monitoring Centre for Drugs and Drug Addiction (2009a) distilled data from 22 European countries and found that between 22% and 32% of adolescents using the widest range of drugs had parents who did not know where they were in the evening.

A common theme emerging internationally is the recognition that polydrug use is associated with poorer outcomes for adolescents. This is concerning in view of the fact that the European Monitoring Centre for Drugs and Drug Addiction (2009b) notes that the range of drugs available have increased in the past decade and that European adolescent drug use has increased. Furthermore, patterns and demographics of adolescent drug use are becoming more complex (Australian Institute of Health and Welfare Canberra, 2007). The European Monitoring Centre for Drugs and Drug Addiction (2009b) notes that the use of alcohol by adolescents in the context of other drugs can lead to misjudgement in the pharmacological combinations ingested and increase risks. The report made use of school population surveys and juxtaposed this data with information regarding young adults drawn from European population surveys. While direct comparison cannot happen between the two data sets, the report demonstrates that adolescents are more likely than young adults to be using more than one drug.

The Crime Survey for England and Wales provides an insight into UK drug use. In 2010–2011 roughly one in five people between 16 and 25 years reported using some form of illegal drug in the preceding year (Home Office, 2014), although the use of heroin in the under-18 population is decreasing (Public Health England, 2013). However, in the USA, opioid use is seen to be increasing in all ages, including adolescents and adults between 12 and 25 years (Greenfield et al., 2014).

In Australia, Kelly et al. (2014) identified that adolescents who use a range of intoxicating substances were less likely to finish high school. Meanwhile, in Turkey, Evren et al. (2015) found that male students with lifetime use of alcohol, tobacco or street drugs were at high risk of behavioural and psychological problems. Finally, looking at data from the Global Burden of Disease Study (Lozano et al., 2012) it can be seen that although life expectancy has increased across the world, lives lost through HIV/AIDS and drug use disorders have also increased.

Young people's substance misuse differs from that of adult substance misusing offenders who tend to present with class A dependent use and associated offending. Cannabis and alcohol are the main substances of choice reported by adolescents alongside the reports of increasing polydrug use. This difference in presenting need has resulted in services for adolescents prioritising the provision of psychosocial, 'talking therapies' which encourage the development of alternate coping strategies and different choices, building resilience in order to prevent adolescents from becoming dependent substance misusers in adulthood. Because of the multiple vulnerabilities often apparent in this cohort, the focus should be on a holistic response to need, and substance misuse service providers are encouraged to adopt a joint care planned, multiagency response to individual need in order to improve outcomes.

Definition

The American Psychiatric Association (2013) notes that the category of substance-related disorders addresses ten separate classes of drugs: including alcohol; caffeine; cannabis; hallucinogens; inhalants; opioids; sedatives, hypnotics and anxiolytics; tobacco and finally stimulants including the amphetamine family and cocaine. All are noted to have in common, the direct activation of the brain reward system when taken in excess and to activate this pathway with an intensity that may cause the neglect of normal activities. Substance-related disorders are divided into two groups, specifically substance use disorders and substance-induced disorders. The latter includes subdivisions such as intoxication, withdrawal, psychotic and anxiety disorder. The American Psychiatric Association (2013) offers guidance on the coding of substance use disorders. Substance use disorders can be described as a spectrum from mild to severe states of chronically relapsing and compulsive drug taking.

Developmental Pathways

The European Monitoring Centre for Drugs and Drug Addiction (2009a) examines the neurobiology of addiction and emphasises the role of the reward system in the brain formally known as the cerebral mesolimbic dopaminergic system. The report notes that dopamine is the neurotransmitter which appears to play a key role in the regulation of mood and affect, and that adolescent brains appear particularly sensitised to dopamine. The report addresses the mechanism of action of different drugs of abuse, noting that nicotine and amphetamine directly stimulate dopamine release, alcohol indirectly stimulates the release of dopamine, the tetrahydrocannabinol within cannabis binds directly to receptors within the reward system, while cocaine and methylphenidate inhibit the reuptake of naturally produced dopamine. Having previously established that young offenders are more likely to experience neglect, poverty and stressors, and less likely to experience adequate parental supervision, it is concerning to note that they are more sensitive than adults to mood-enhancing neurotransmitters.

Mulvey et al. (2010) found that adolescents who struggle to regulate their affect and experience high levels of stress may use alcohol to manage their distress. Varlinskaya and Spear (2012) note that adolescent rats, unlike adult rats demonstrate a reduction in anxiety after ethanol, while Doremus et al. (2003) report that adolescent rats do not demonstrate anxiety during the withdrawal phase from ethanol. Furthermore, Spear and Varlinskaya (2005) note that adolescent rats are less likely than their adult counterparts to experience 'hangover'-type effects.

While regulations exist regarding the sale of alcohol and cigarettes to adolescents, the sale of illegal drugs is by its very nature unregulated; thus adolescents who are experiencing stress and whose experience of parental supervision may be limited may be drawn to the use of illegal drugs. The World Health Organisation (2006) notes that the use of alcohol can reduce parental inhibition and supervision and increase the risk of violence; this in turn increases the likelihood of neglect and abuse. Generations of people can thus experience childhoods impacted by alcohol and in turn use alcohol to manage their experiences.

In addition to supervising school attendance, behaviour at home and monitoring a child's presentation and development, parents also play a role in mediating peer relationships. The European Monitoring Centre for Drugs and Drug Addiction (2009a) examines psychosocial and familial risk factors in studies from Switzerland to the USA and notes that peer relationships play a key role in both experimentation with and ongoing use of alcohol, cigarettes and cannabis.

Childhood exposure to violence and abuse increases the likelihood of violence and problematic substance misuse in adulthood. McArdle and Angom (2012) note that early difficulties with behaviour are connected to adult drug use. Frisher et al (2007) identified that the more drugs adolescents used, the lower their self-esteem was and their levels of parental supervision and the higher their likelihood of engaging in delinquent behaviour.

Prevalence

Measham et al. (2011) and Mulvey et al. (2010) report that the disinhibiting effects of drugs such as alcohol can increase the risk of violent or risk-taking behaviour. Substance use has also been associated with indirect involvement in criminal activities, including risky activities such as sex working and gang involvement. Within the USA about 2.3 million adolescents were arrested in 2002 (Snyder, 2004). Of these young people, one in five are believed to have had significant mental health problems, often with comorbid substance misuse problems (Cocozza and Skowyra, 2000). Barton and Husk (2012) identify that roughly two-thirds of 17- to 30-year-olds arrested in a UK city claimed to have drunk alcohol prior to going out of the evening (pre-loaded). Finally, the Arrestee Survey (Boreham et al., 2007) reported that 16% of people arrested in the UK had been in Local Authority care at some point in their lives, while 52% of all people arrested had tried drugs, and nearly 50% of people arrested were under the age of 25.

Although not specific to adolescents within the UK youth justice system, Public Health England collate data submitted to the National Drug Treatment Monitoring System regarding young people's community-based specialist treatment services. A drop in the overall number of adolescents engaging in specialist interventions has been recorded and a change noted in the nature of the substances used by adolescents over time. Specifically Public Health England (2013: 1) noted that '20,032 young people accessed specialist substance misuse services in 2012–13. This is a decrease of 656 (3.2%) since 2011–12 and 1,923 (8.8%) since 2010–2011'. The majority of adolescents accessing specialist services did so with problems for cannabis (68%) or alcohol (24%) as their primary substance.'

Young people's substance use and offending appear to be associated (Mulvey et al., 2010). For example, a study from Australia found that prior to their arrest, 75% of adolescents reported using cannabis and 39% reported using amphetamines (Pritchard and Payne, 2005). Vreugdenhil et al. (2003) examined drug use in a cohort of Dutch incarcerated young offenders and identified that 92% reported alcohol use prior to admission, 86% reported cannabis use and 33% reported the use of other substances.

The phenomenon of novel psychoactive substances 'legal highs' presents a healthcare challenge. The European Monitoring Centre for Drugs and Drug Addiction (2011; 95) describes novel psychoactive substances, as a 'broad category of unregulated psychoactive compounds'. Novel psychoactive substances are associated with a number of deaths. For example, Fraser (2014) notes that between 2009 and 2013, novel psychoactive substances were implicated in 132 deaths in Scotland in all ages.

In conclusion, evidence from a number of countries suggests that drug use is higher among adolescents within the youth justice system (YJS) than the general adolescent population (Measham et al., 2011). A Home Office report found that 44% of the victims of violent crime report the perpetrator was affected by alcohol at the time of the offence (Office for National Statistics, 2012). Finally, Coffey et al. (2003) identified increased mortality rates for young offenders in Australia (crude mortality of 8.5/1,000 person years among young offenders compared to 1.1/1,000 among age equivalents), which were comparable to mortality rates for adolescents who misuse substances, highlighting significant health implications for this subgroup.

Comorbidity and Wider Health Needs

There is increasing awareness of the relationship between mental health needs and substance use and misuse. In the UK, Green et al. (2004) undertook a national survey of 5- to 16-year-olds and identified that adolescents with emotional disorders, conduct disorders and hyperkinetic disorders were more likely to drink, smoke and take drugs than their peers, and more likely to have parents who were widowed, separated or divorced. In this context it is worth noting that a survey of 582 excluded young people in the UK (User Voice, 2011), identified that 9% had never lived with either parent, less than a third had only lived entirely with both parents during their childhood, 71% had been excluded from school, 45% reported a drink or drug problem, 43% had been

incarcerated young offenders and 16% reported a mental health problem.

Overall offenders are known to experience a high level of mental health needs; Golzari et al. (2006) suggest between 60% and 80% of young offenders have psychiatric comorbidity, while Tolou-Shams et al. (2014) conclude that the co-occurrence of mental health problems and substance misuse is a key predictor of reoffending. A recent case control study by Bussing et al. (2010) suggests that symptoms of Attention Deficit Hyperactivity Disorder (ADHD) are as much of a risk factor for adult substance misuse as a family history of substance misuse. This is of concern given the increased rates of ADHD in young people in the criminal justice system (please refer to Chapter 14 by Young, Greer and White). A systematic review of the prevalence rate of ADHD in young offenders found a rate of 11.7% in males and 18.5% in females, compared with 3–5% of the general population (Fazel et al., 2008). Vreugdenhil et al. (2003) found that substance use was related to psychosis and to re-offending, although not violent re-offending.

Swogger et al. (2011) noted that among adult offenders, ongoing anxiety and depression exacerbated the link between childhood sexual abuse and adult substance misuse.

Substance use can impact on physical health such as lung damage through inhaling nicotine and cannabis, liver damage through ingesting alcohol and blood-borne diseases through unsafe injecting practices. Golzari et al. (2006) found that 37% of adolescents in a US prison had evidence of hepatitis, while 16% had respiratory infections and 13% had genitourinary infections. This is echoed in the work from the New Zealand Ministry of Health (2011) who noted that 16% of young offenders in an institute in South Auckland were found to have untreated physical health problems. Teplin et al. (2005) note that young offenders who misuse substances are at increased risk for the acquisition of HIV.

Links have been identified between parental substance use, reduced parental supervision and increased rates of substance use in young people (Neiderhiser et al., 2013). Reduced parental supervision can also lead to reduced maintenance of children's health, starting with missed inoculations and a nutritionally limited diet, and culminate in missed appointments for asthma care and dental care. However, the needs of this population, by their very nature may not be fully documented.

To summarise, young offenders are known to have higher than average rates of mental health and developmental needs (Fazel et al., 2008). They are more likely to have grown up in reconstituted or single-parent families with higher rates of poverty (User Voice, 2011). They are more likely to have left school early and more likely to be not in education, employment or training (User Voice, 2011). All of these risk factors are independently associated with increased risk of substance use. Furthermore, the stress of court proceedings, exposure to trauma and challenging family relationships and situations can further exacerbate mental health needs and the likelihood of managing anxiety through the use of substances. To quote from the User Voice study (2011: 28), 'I didn't have anyone to talk to, there was a lot of violence at home and I couldn't stop it or tell anyone. I was smoking weed and drinking with my friends, maybe if someone had helped me, I would not be here now'.

The need to systematically screen young offenders to routinely identify all outstanding health needs is a growing global concern, addressed in policy from the USA (Grisso and Underwood, 2004), the New Zealand Ministry of Health (2011) and England (Royal College of Paediatrics and Child Health, 2013). Conditions such as depression and ADHD both respond to treatment. Furthermore helping adolescents, their families and the professionals working with them to understand their developmental and learning needs can enable behaviour and treatment to be modified. Having established the link between treating comorbid conditions and enhancing a range of outcomes for young offenders who are misusing substances, there is a clear need to ensure that mental health service providers are adequately trained and resourced to meet the needs of this population.

Assessment and Screening

A key barrier to assessing any needs that any young person may have is the opportunity to meet with and engage a young person. A common theme emerging from the literature is the lack of resources for universal screening. When this is coupled with the fact that many young offenders come from families with multiple needs and limited supervision and advocacy, it becomes clear that contact with the youth justice system can represent an important opportunity to assess needs.

The New Zealand Ministry of Health (2011) notes the need for comprehensive screening of the health needs of young offenders. This need is echoed in the USA with the juvenile drug court programs (US Department of Justice, 2001). The Juvenile Drug Courts were developed in 1989 and represent a multiagency approach to young offenders with substance misuse problems. Within England, the Comprehensive Health Assessment Tool (CHAT) is now used to assess all young offenders entering custodial care (Offender Health Research Network, 2013; Chitsabesan et al., 2014). The CHAT has five parts: an initial screening tool, and four other parts that systematically assess physical, mental, developmental and substance misuse needs.

Guidance is available regarding the use of the CHAT which advises that young people are screened within hours of reception for needs that must be addressed immediately, for example drug withdrawal or acute suicidal ideation. Adolescents may have previously been managing anxiety or distress with alcohol or drugs, and this may first come to light during the early stages of incarceration (Kroll et al., 2002). The tool recommends that young people be screened to identify substance-related need within five days of admission. Figure 13.1 depicts the pathway recommended for adolescents with English youth custodial settings and offers guidance for good practice globally.

The American Academy of Child and Adolescent Psychiatry (2005) notes that adolescents are more likely to disclose an accurate picture of their substance use if they believe their information will not be shared. The document emphasises the need to explain what will happen to information gained during assessment and the need to observe confidentiality wherever possible.

In the UK, the Royal College of Psychiatrists produced Practice Standards for Young People with Substance Misuse Problems (2012). The themes in this document are echoed in the New Zealand document 'Youth forensic services development' (Ministry of Health, 2011), the US 'Practice parameter for the assessment and treatment of children and adolescents with substance use disorders' (American Academy of Child and Adolescent Psychiatry, 2005), and the US juvenile drug court programme (Hayden, 2012).

Factors that are known to increase young offenders' vulnerability to substance use include disengagement from education, limited parental supervision, mental health problems in parents and young

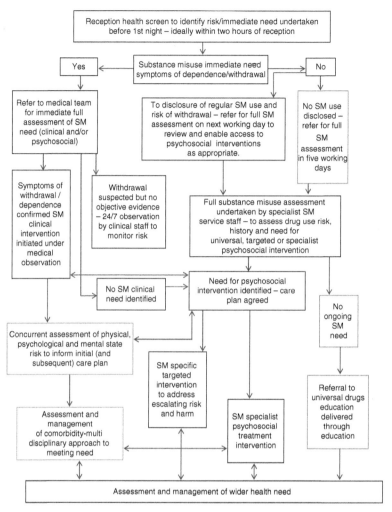

Figure 13.1 Substance Misuse Need/diagnosis Flow Chart: Mapping the SM Pathway in Secure Settings
Source: Based on the Offender Health Research Network CHAT pathway in the secure manual (2013)

offenders (Kelly et al., 2014; User Voice, 2011). All of these risk factors are further exacerbated by limited structured daytime activities, reduced self-esteem and social isolation leading to interaction with peers who may habitually use drugs and alcohol in a way that becomes socially sanctioned. All documents advise that detailed assessment should always precede treatment. This allows comorbidity and other issues to be identified and subsequently treated along with the substance use and also allows the development of tailored, age-appropriate care plans which can be coordinated across services whilst involving adolescents and families. The care plan can also ensure transition into adulthood is addressed. A recurring theme is that atypical developmental experiences,

including trauma, can affect presentation at assessment and subsequent engagement by young offenders. This may be further compounded by communication difficulties (Bryan et al., 2007) including problems with speech, language and hearing which significantly impact on an individual's functioning and ability to engage.

While healthcare staff perform an important but specific role in the support of young offenders, the custodial staff managing other aspects of the placement often spend many hours with young people. Thus, there is clear need to offer training to these staff about the way in which developmental and mental health and substance misuse disorders can present and impact on future propensity to offend.

Toxicology Screening

A way of examining the success of programmes supporting adolescents to manage their substance misuse is the use of toxicology screens. The American Academy of Child and Adolescent Psychiatry (2005) advises that the testing clinician should offer a clear explanation about the screening process, the potential impact of a positive result and the parameters of confidentiality as a precursor to testing. In the USA, urine drug screens have been used to elucidate both the successes and the areas needing development in the juvenile drug courts (Hayden, 2012). The New Zealand Department of Corrections (2016) advocates drug and alcohol testing to prevent the supply of drugs into prison environments. The document details a process of general random testing, testing after temporary release and testing when there are reasonable grounds to suspect substance use. In the UK, the random Mandatory Drug Testing programme detailed in Prison Service Order 3601 (2007) seeks to enable prisoners to resist peer pressure when offered drugs, to identify prisoners using drugs and to send a clear message that drug users will be punished. A clear theme throughout all guidance is the fact that positive test results should also provide a pathway into appropriate support.

Courts have the opportunity to impose drug testing for young offenders who are made subject to a community-based Youth Rehabilitation Order within England. The purpose of the drug testing requirement is to assist the young person in remaining drug-free and as such is used to sustain engagement in appropriate treatment, not just to monitor drug use. It can be enforced only with a concurrent drug treatment requirement. Consent to treatment is required for the latter, as is confirmation that drug use is a substantive contributory factor in the offending and an assessment of suitability for treatment by the substance misuse service provider.

Treatment and Management Approaches

The value of early intervention for health needs is widely acknowledged. Opportunities for intervening with substance misusing young offenders interface on several key axes: chronological, environmental and in terms of intrinsic difficulties and needs. The European Monitoring Centre for Drugs and Drug Addiction (2009a; 12) details the difficulties inherent when trying to develop prevention strategies, noting the complexity in differentiating between universal prevention which involves entire populations, selective prevention which addresses population subsets and indicated prevention which targets at risk individuals. They note that in 'a time of dwindling resources' this lack of clarity about thresholds and eligibility can lead to adolescents falling between, or outside services.

On a more positive note, Castellanos-Ryan et al. (2013) worked with boys in Montreal from the age of six who had been recruited to a study on the basis of teacher-rated disruptiveness. These boys were offered social and problem-solving skills training, while parents were offered training reinforcing appropriate behaviour and encouraged to supervise homework. Eight years on, the rates of substance use within this cohort were noted to be reduced. Furthermore, Riggs et al. (2009) offered a programme of teacher-led 'resistance skills' to adolescents. The course ran for about a year with an accompanying parent programme and significant reductions in drug using behaviour were found to persist beyond the age of 17.

However, Harrington and Bailey (2005) and Mulvey et al. (2010) have identified limitations in the provision of services and continuity of care for young offenders. Within England, the Health Care Standards for Children and Young People in Secure Settings (2013) emphasise the importance of a holistic approach to health, with joint care planning and appropriate sequencing of interventions supported by appropriate information sharing agreements. The standards also outline the importance of effective discharge planning in order to sustain gains made in the secure environment. Effective communication between different agencies and across geographical settings is important in order to reduce re-offending.

The Practice Parameters from the American Academy of Child and Adolescent Psychiatry (2005: 613) note that 'treatment is better than no treatment'. In an era of limited resources and high need, treatment needs to be pragmatic and systematic and clinicians are encouraged to examine the services they offer, audit them and share good practice. Treatment needs to be considered in terms of physical and psychological components. Very few young people entering custody are likely to need immediate clinical management to counteract physically threatening withdrawal symptoms as young people in the main do not tend to use opioid-based drugs. However, there are indications of psychological dependence in this cohort and in view of the comorbidities and multiple problem presentations in young offenders, the importance of multidisciplinary assessment and subsequent care planning cannot be overstated. In the rare cases where young people report dependent opioid use, the National Institute for Health and Care Excellence (2007b) offers clear guidance on the need to confirm the presence and severity of opioid dependence in adolescents before starting any pharmacological intervention. 'Guidance for the pharmacological management of substance misuse among young people in secure environments' (2009) sets out best practice in the delivery of interventions of this nature to those whose substance misuse places them at greatest risk and vulnerability.

The American Academy of Child and Adolescent Psychiatry (2005) notes that the primary goal of treatment is achieving and maintaining abstinence. However, harm reduction is seen as a pragmatic starting point. This concept involves reducing the intensity of use, the damage caused and an enhancement in the young person's functioning. As noted earlier in the chapter, the journey from experimental to problematic use does not happen in a vacuum. Thus, the guidance notes that treatment will be enhanced by a joined-up approach to need, addressing mental health needs, family functioning, peer relationships and academic performance, thereby building the young person's resilience and ability to resist substance use in the future.

The Practice Standards for Young People with Substance Misuse Problems (2012) emphasise the need to ascertain the severity of the substance use. Once this has been elucidated, decisions can be made regarding the need for intervention. The guidance specifies treatment for different forms of dependence; for example adolescents with opiate dependence should be offered methadone or buprenorphine in the detoxification and stabilisation phase with concurrent psychosocial interventions and family work leading towards abstinence. For adolescents judged to be at risk but not dependent, staff with training in substance misuse can offer developmentally appropriate interventions designed to increase motivation to stop substance use and offer relevant health education. For adolescents who meet the criteria for substance use disorders, there is a need to achieve and maintain reductions in substance misuse. Frye et al. (2008) note that

living with substance misuse impacts significantly on other family members. This emphasises the importance of involving families in therapeutic work. A family-based model multidimensional family therapy (Liddle et al., 2008) comprises individual work with the young person and family-based work. This has produced positive results in a large study of adolescents misusing cannabis (Phan et al., 2011). However, as noted previously, substance use must be addressed holistically alongside mental health, physical health and social needs (American Academy of Child and Adolescent Psychiatry, 2005; National Institute for Health and Care Excellence, 2007a).

In the USA, the Pathways to Desistance study is a multidisciplinary examination of the way in which adolescent offenders transition into adult roles (Mulvey et al., 2010). It is worth noting that preliminary findings reveal that individual therapy was effective in treating cannabis use, while cigarette smoking responded best to family and individual work.

Looking at the trajectories of young offenders through criminal justice processes in different countries, it can be seen that in many places adolescents have both custodial and community-based components to their sentences. Spending time in a secure setting may mean leaving the geographical location that a young person has been residing in. This can result in one healthcare team commencing a treatment programme and a second healthcare team being required to maintain the programme. Once again this requires clear communication and appropriate information sharing.

Finally, Mulvey et al. (2010) note the challenge faced by young offenders as they reach adulthood and face the demands of work, relationships and parenthood, emphasising the need for communication between different agencies. This is echoed by the Royal College of Paediatrics and Child Health (2013) and the Practice Standards for Young People with Substance Misuse Problems (2012) which detail the need for adolescents to be involved in discharge planning and to be advised on pathways to access community-based treatment services (whether adult or young people, for substance misuse or mental health need). Culturally there is a significant transition both in terms of identity and societal expectations as young people transition into adulthood. In practical terms this often means that young people move from more nurturing children's services into the recovery-based

BOX 13.1 Case Example

Background

Chelsey is a 17-year-old young offender who is admitted into custodial care. Community-based care home staff report that she is impulsive and struggles to sit still. She struggles to engage in talking therapy and damaged the waiting room in her local mental health service when a clinician was late to see her. Her grandmother remains involved in her life and reports that as a child Chelsey was similar to her father and uncle; her uncle has now been assessed and treated for ADHD. Community care home staff report that Chelsey's 19-year-old boyfriend Richard continues to supply her with cannabis. Richard is living with an older man who has previously used heroin. Custodial staff report that Chelsey has a dental abscess, she requests analgesia, but refuses to see a dentist. Staff are concerned that Chelsey is subdued and low in mood.

Assessment

Chelsey is found to be low in mood with fleeting thoughts of wanting to die. She is also noted to have a short attention span, to be restless and impulsive. She is found to have a dental abscess and to be very thin. She reports the use of cannabis and cigarettes, she does not appear distressed when she is unable to access nicotine and cannabis, but continues to complain of boredom. She receives developmentally appropriate information to enable her to consent to a pregnancy test and hepatitis screen, both of which come back negative.

Formulation/Diagnosis

Chelsey is a 17-year-old girl who displays evidence of ADHD and moderate depression. She has a dental abscess and may be in an intimate relationship with an older male which places her at risk of sexually transmitted diseases. She is using cannabis and cigarettes, but does not display evidence of dependence. There is a clear need to obtain consent to gather a developmental history and to assess Chelsey for ADHD.

Focus of Treatment

Addressing Chelsey's physical pain is a clear priority. Having addressed this through an appointment with a primary care physician, cognitive behavioural therapy should be initiated to address her low mood. An initial screen for ADHD should also be completed, including obtaining informant information; this can then form the basis of a referral to a clinician trained to diagnose and treat ADHD. In parallel with this referral, developmentally appropriate psychoeducation should be offered to address Chelsey's nicotine and cannabis use. Guidance regarding safer sex and contraception should also be offered.

model of adult substance misuse and mental health provision. It is important that clinicians prepare adolescents for this process. The case example (Box 13.1) illustrates the complexity of young people's lives, and the multiagency solutions needed.

Conclusions

Substance use disorders represent a global challenge. They impact on the quality of life of affected adolescents, their families and their communities. Further work is needed to fully understand the societal and developmental vulnerabilities that lead young people to journey from adolescent experimentation into problematic misuse and into dependence. This work will need to

elucidate the relationship between mental illness and substance use disorders. Understanding such dynamics may help to reduce associated comorbid needs.

Looking at developments globally, it is clear that adolescents who are not in employment, education or training are over-represented in the secure estate, and also that substance misuse is associated with offending behaviour and mental health problems. An emerging theme is therefore the importance of multiagency coordinated work.

What is also apparent is that the evidence base is limited in terms of longitudinal studies and also in the evaluation of the available therapies. Thus, a final recommendation for this chapter is that clinicians and researchers are encouraged to undertake further work to address the gaps in the evidence base for this vulnerable population. User Voice (2011) notes that many excluded young people feel that services have failed them, but also express a view that little more could be done to help them. 'The danger is with such a publicly unpopular and challenging group is that we all begin to agree with them' (User Voice, 2011: 37).

Acknowledgements

I would like to thank Sam Cox (Programme Manager, Alcohol, Drugs and Tobacco Division, Public Health England) for her contribution. Sam's specialist knowledge has played a valuable role in the development of this chapter.

References

American Academy of Child and Adolescent Psychiatry. (2005). Practice parameter for the assessment and treatment of children and adolescents with substance use disorders. *Journal of the American Academy of Child and Adolescent Psychiatry*, 44(6). 608–621.

American Psychiatric Association. (2013). *Desk Reference to the Diagnostic Criteria from DSM-5*. Arlington, VA: American Psychiatric Publishing.

Australian Institute of Health and Welfare Canberra. (2007). Statistics on drug use in Australia 2006 [online]. Available from: www.aihw.gov.au/WorkArea/DownloadAs set.aspx?id=6442459808. Accessed 28 October 2016.

Barton, A. and Husk, K. (2012). Controlling pre-loaders: alcohol related violence in an English night time economy, *Drugs and Alcohol Today*, 12(2): 89–97.

Boreham, R. Cronberg, A., Dollin, L., and Pudney, S. (2007). The Arrestee Survey 2003–2006. *Home Office Statistical Bulletin* [online]. Available from: http://webarchive.nationa larchives.gov.uk/20110218135832/rds.homeoffice.gov.uk/rds/pdfs07/hosb1207.pdf. Accessed 28 October 2016.

Bryan, K., Freer, J., and Furlong. C. (2007). Language and communication difficulties in juvenile offenders. *International Journal of language and communication difficulties*, 42: 505–520.

Bussing, R., Mason, D., Bell, L., Porter, P., and Garvan C. (2010). Adolescent outcomes of childhood attention-deficit/hyperactivity disorder in a diverse community sample. *Journal of the American Academy of Child and Adolescent Psychiatry*, 49(6): 595–605.

Casey, B. and Jones, R. (2010). Neurobiology of the adolescent brain and behaviour: implications for substance use disorders. *Journal of the American Academy of Child and Adolescent Psychiatry*, 49(12): 1189–1201.

Castellanos-Ryan, N., Séguin, J., Vitaro, F., Parent, S., and Tremblay R. (2013). Impact of a 2-year multimodal intervention for disruptive 6-year-olds on substance use in adolescence: randomised controlled trial. *British Journal of Psychiatry*, 203(3): 188–195.

Chitsabesan, P., Lennox, C., Theodosiou, L., Law, H., Bailey, S., and Shaw, J. (2014). The development of the comprehensive health assessment tool for young offenders within the secure estate. *The Journal of Forensic Psychiatry & Psychology*, 25(1): 1–25.

Cocozza, J. and Skowyra, K. (2000). Youth with mental health disorders: issues and emerging responses. *Office of Juvenile Justice and Delinquency Prevention Journal*, 7(1): 3–13.

Coffey, C., Veit, F., Wolfe, R., Cini, E., and Patton G. (2003). Mortality in young offenders: retrospective cohort study. *British Medical Journal*, 326(7398): 1064.

Crime Survey for England and Wales. (2011–2012) [online]. Available from: www.ons.gov.uk/ons/guide-method/sur veys/list-of-surveys/survey.html?survey= Crime+Survey+for+England+and+Wales. Accessed 28 October 2016.

Department of Corrections. (2016). Prison operations manual [online]. Available from: www.corrections.govt.nz/resources/policy_and_legislation/Prison-Operations-Manual/Security/S.html. Accessed 28 October 2016.

Department of Health (2009). Guidance for the pharmacological management of substance misuse among young people in secure environments [online]. Available from: www.nta.nhs.uk/uploads/guidance_for_the_pharmaco logical_management_of_substance_misuse_among_young_ people_in_secure_environments1009.pdf. Accessed 28 October 2016.

Department of Health. (2011). A summary of the health harms of drugs [online]. Available from: www.gov.uk/gov ernment/publications/a-summary-of-the-health-harms-of-drugs. Accessed 28 October 2016.

Doremus, T., Brunell, S., Varlinskaya, E., and Spear, L. (2003). Anxiogenic effects during withdrawal from acute ethanol in adolescent and adult rats. *Pharmacology Biochemistry and Behaviour*, 75(2): 411–418.

European Monitoring Centre for Drugs and Drug Addiction. (2009a). Preventing later substance use disorders in at-risk children and adolescents [online]. Available from: www.emcdda.europa.eu/system/files/publications/562/EM CDDA-TB-indicated_prevention_130796.pdf. Accessed 28 October 2016.

European Monitoring Centre for Drugs and Drug Addiction. (2009b). Polydrug use: patterns and responses [online]. Available from: www.emcdda.europa.eu/attache ments.cfm/att_93217_EN_EMCDDA_SI09_polydrug%20u se.pdf. Accessed 28 October 2016.

European Monitoring Centre for Drugs and Drug Addiction. (2011). The State of the Drugs Problem in Europe [online]. Available from: www.emcdda.europa.eu/s ystem/files/publications/969/EMCDDA_AR2011_EN.pdf. Accessed 28 October 2016.

Evren, C., Evren, B., Bozkurt, M., and Ciftci-Demirci, A. (2015). Effects of lifetime tobacco, alcohol and drug use on psychological and behavioral problems among 10th grade students in Istanbul. *International Journal of Adolescent Medicine and Health*, 27(4): 405–413.

Fazel, S., Khosla, V., Doll, H., and Geddes, J. (2008). The prevalence of mental disorders among the homeless in Western countries: Systematic review and meta-regression analysis. *PLoS Medicine*, 5(12): e225.

Fraser, F. (2014). New psychoactive substances – evidence review. *Safer Communities Analytical Unit, Scottish Government* [online]. Available from: www.scotland.gov.uk/Resource/0045/00457682.pdf. Accessed 28 October 2016.

Frisher, M., Crome, I., Macleod, J., et al. (2007). Home Office Online Report 05/07 Predictive factors for illicit drug use among young people: a literature review. [Online]. Available from: http://dera.ioe.ac.uk/6903/1/rdsolr0507.pdf. Accessed 28 October 2016.

Frye, S., Dawe, S., Harnett, P., Sascha Kowalenko, S and Harlen, M (2008). Supporting the families of young people with problematic drug use investigating support options [online]. Available from: www.atoda.org.au/wp-content/uploads/rp15_supporting_families.pdf. Accessed 28 October 2016.

Golzari, M., Hunt, S., and Anushiravani, A. (2006). The health status of youth in juvenile detention facilities. *Journal of Adolescent Health*, 38: 776–782.

Green, H., McGinnity, A., Meltzer, H., Ford, T., and Goodman, R. (2004). Mental health of children and young people in Great Britain [online]. Available from: www.hscic.gov.uk/catalogue/PUB06116/ment-heal-chil-youn-peop-gb-2004-rep2.pdf. Accessed 28 October 2016.

Greenfield, B., Owens, M., and Ley, D. (2014). Opioid use in Albuquerque, New Mexico: a needs assessment of recent changes and treatment availability. *Addiction Science & Clinical Practice*, 9: 10.

Grisso, T. and Underwood, L. (2004). Screening and assessing mental health and substance use disorders among youth in the juvenile justice system [online]. Available from: http://files.eric.ed.gov/fulltext/ED484681.pdf. Accessed 28 October 2016.

Harrington, R. and Bailey, S. (2005). *Mental Health Needs and Effectiveness of Provision for Young Offenders in Custody and in the Community*. London: Youth Justice Board [online]. Available from: www.mac-uk.org/wped/wp-content/uploads/2013/03/Youth-Justice-Board-MentalHealthNeeds-of-Young-Offenders.pdf. Accessed 28 October 2016.

Hayden, A. (2012). Evaluation of the Lexington (Fayette County) Kentucky Juvenile Drug Court Program. *Internet Journal of Criminology* [online]. Available from: www.internetjournalofcriminology.com/Hayden_Evaluation_of_Fayette_County_Kentucky_Juvenile_Drug_Court_Program_IJC_May_2012.pdf. Accessed 28 October 2016.

Health and Social Care Information Centre. (2013). Smoking, drinking and drug use among young people in England in 2012 [online]. Available from: http://content.digital.nhs.uk/catalogue/PUB14579. Accessed 28 October 2016.

Hibell, B., Guttormsson, U., Ahlström, S. et al. (2012). The 2011 ESPAD Report Substance Use Among Students in 36 European Countries [online]. Available from: www.espad.org/Uploads/ESPAD_reports/2011/The_2011_ESPAD_Report_FULL_2012_10_29.pdf. Accessed 02 October 2016.

Home Office (2014) Drug Misuse: Findings from the 2013/14 Crime Survey for England and Wales [online]. Available from: www.gov.uk/government/uploads/system/uploads/attachment_data/file/335989/drug_misuse_201314.pdf. Accessed 05 October 2016.

Insurance Institute for Highway Safety. (2012). Fatality facts: teenagers 2012 [online]. Available from: www.iihs.org/iihs/topics/t/teenagers/fatalityfacts/teenagers#cite-text-0-0. Accessed 28 October 2016.

International Centre for Drug Policy (2012). Trends in UK deaths associated with abuse of volatile substances 1971–2009 [online]. Available from: www.communityforrecovery.org/VSA-annual-report-no24.pdf. Accessed 03 October 2016.

Kelly, A., Evans-Whipp, T., Smith, R., Chan, G. C. K., Toumbourou, J. W., Patton, G. C., Hemphill, S. A., Hall, W. D. and Catalano, R. F. (2014). A longitudinal study of the association of adolescent polydrug use, alcohol use, and high school non-completion. *Addiction* [online]. Available from: http://onlinelibrary.wiley.com/doi/10.1111/add.12829/pdf. Accessed 28 October 2016.

Kroll, L., Rothwell, J., Bradley, D., Shah P, Bailey S and Harrington RC (2002). Mental health needs of boys in secure care for serious or persistent offending: a prospective, longitudinal study. *Lancet*, 359: 1975–1979.

Liddle, H., Dakota, G., Turner, R., Henderson, C., and Greenbaum, P. (2008). Treating adolescent drug abuse: a randomised trial comparing multi-dimensional family therapy and cognitive behavioural therapy. *Addiction*, 103: 1660–1670.

Lozano, R., et al. (2012). Global and regional mortality from 235 causes of death for 20 age groups in 1990 and 2010: a systematic analysis for the Global Burden of Disease Study 2010. *The Lancet*, 380(9859): 2095–2128.

McArdle, P. and Angom, B. (2012). Adolescent substance misuse: an update on behaviours and treatments. *Advances in Psychiatric Treatment*, 18: 299–307.

Measham, F., Moore, K., and Østergaard, J. (2011). Emerging drug trends in Lancashire: Night time economy surveys phase one report [online]. Available from: www.clubresearch.org/wp-content/uploads/2014/05/LDAAT-Phase-1-report.pdf. Accessed 28 October 2016.

Ministry of Health. (2011). Youth forensic services development [online]. Available from: www.health.govt.nz

/system/files/documents/publications/youth-forensicdevelopment-services-dec2011.pdf. Accessed 28 October 2016.

Mulvey, E., Schubert, C., and Chassin, L. (2010). Substance use and delinquent behaviour among serious adolescent offenders. *Juvenile Justice Bulletin. Office of Justice Programs* [online]. Available from: www.ncjrs.gov/pdffiles1/ojjdp/23 2790.pdf. Accessed 28 October 2016.

National Highway Traffic Safety Administration. (2012). Dept. of Transportation (US). Traffic safety facts 2012: Young Drivers [online] Available from: https://crashstats .nhtsa.dot.gov/Api/Public/ViewPublication/812019. Accessed 28 October 2016.

National Institute for Health and Care Excellence. (2007a). Substance misuse interventions for vulnerable under 25s. nice.org.uk/guidance/ph4 [online]. Available from: www .nice.org.uk/guidance/ph4/resources/substance-misuse-interventions-for-vulnerable-under-25s-55454156485. Accessed 28 October 2016.

National Institute for Health and Care Excellence. (2007b) Drug misuse in over 16s: opioid detoxification [online]. Available from: www.nice.org.uk/guidance/CG52. Accessed 28 October 2016.

National Institute for Health and Care Excellence. (2009). Reducing differences in the uptake of immunisations [online]. Available from: www.nice.org.uk/guidance/ph21. Accessed 28 October 2016.

Neiderhiser, J., Marceau, K., and Reiss, D. (2013). Four factors for the initiation of substance use by young adulthood: A 10-year follow-up twin and sibling study of marital conflict, monitoring, siblings, and peers. *Development and Psychopathology*, 25(1): 133–149.

Offender Health Research Network. (2013). Manual for the Comprehensive Health Assessment Tool (CHAT): Young People in the Secure Estate [online]. www.ohrn.nhs.uk/O HRNResearch/CHATManualSecure.pdf. Accessed 28 October 2016.

Office for National Statistics. (2012). Crime in England and Wales, year ending September 2012 [online]. Available from: www.ons.gov.uk/ons/dcp171778_296191.pdf. Accessed 28 October 2016.

Office for National Statistics. (2013) Deaths related to drug poisoning in England and Wales 2012 [online]. Available from: www.ons.gov.uk/peoplepopulationandcommunity/bi rthsdeathsandmarriages/deaths/bulletins/deathsrelatedto drugpoisoninginenglandandwales/2013-08-28. Accessed 28 October 2016.

Phan, O., Henderson, C., Angelidis, T., Weil, P., van Toorn, M., Rigter, R, Soria, C. and Rigter, H. (2011). European youth centre sites serve different populations of adults with cannabis use disorder. Baseline and referral data from the INCANT trial. *BMC Psychiatry*, 11: 110.

Pritchard, J. and Payne, J. (2005). Alcohol, drugs and crime: a study of juveniles in detention [online]. Available from: www.aic.gov.au/media_library/publications/rpp/67/rpp067 .pdf. Accessed 28 October 2016.

Prison Service Order 3601. (2007). Mandatory drug testing [online]. Available from: www.justice.gov.uk/offenders/ psos. Accessed 28 October 2016.

Public Health England. (2013). Young People's Statistics from the National Drug Treatment Monitoring System 1 April 2012 to 31 March 2013 [online]. Available from: www.nta.nhs.uk/uploads/young-peoples-statistics-from-the-national-drug-treatment-monitoring-system.pdf. Accessed 28 October 2016.

Riggs, N., Chou, C., and Pentz, M. (2009). Preventing growth in amphetamine use: long term effects of the Midwestern Prevention Project (MPP) from early adolescence to early adulthood. *Addiction*, 104: 1691–1699.

Royal College of Paediatrics and Child Health. (2013). Healthcare Standards for Children and Young People in Secure Settings [online]. Available from: www.rcpch.ac.uk/ CYPSS. Accessed 28 October 2016.

Royal College of Psychiatrists. (2012). Practice standards for young people with substance misuse problems [online]. Available from: www.rcpsych.ac.uk/pdf/Practice%20stan dards%20for%20young%20people%20with%20substance% 20misuse%20problems.pdf. Accessed 28 October 2016.

Snyder, H. N. (2004). Juvenile Arrests 2004 US Department of Justice [online]. J. Robert Flores, Administrator. Available from: www.ncjrs.gov/pdffiles1/ojjdp/214563.pdf. Accessed 28 October 2016.

Spear, L. and Varlinskaya, E. (2005). Adolescence. Alcohol sensitivity, tolerance, and intake. *Recent Developments in Alcoholism*, 17: 143–159.

Swogger, M., Conner, K., Walsh, Z., and Maisto S. (2011). Childhood abuse and harmful substance use among criminal offenders. *Addictive Behaviour*, 36(12): 1205–1212.

Teplin, L., Elkington, B., McClelland, G. Dulcan, M. K. and Mericle, A. A. (2005) Major mental disorders, substance use disorders, comorbidity, and HIV-AIDS risk behaviors in juvenile detainees. *Psychiatry Online*, 56(7): 823–828.

Tolou-Shams, M., Rizzo, C., Selby, M., Conrad, S., Johnson, S, Oliveira, C. and Brown, L. K. (2014). Predictors of detention among juveniles referred for a court clinic forensic evaluation. *Journal of the American Academy of Psychiatry and the Law*, 42(1): 56–65.

User Voice. (2011). What's Your Story? Summary of young offenders' insights into tackling youth crime and its causes [online]. Available from: www.uservoice.org/wp-content/ uploads/2011/03/User-Voice-Whats-Your-Story.pdf. Accessed 28 October 2016.

US Department of Justice. (2001). Juvenile Drug Court Programs [online]. Available from: www.ncjrs.gov/pdffile s1/ojjdp/184744.pdf. Accessed 28 October 2016.

Varlinskaya, E. and Spear, L. (2012). Increases in anxiety-like behavior induced by acute stress are reversed by ethanol in adolescent but not adult rats. *Pharmacology Biochemistry and Behaviour*, **100**(3): 440–450.

Vreugdenhil, C., Van Den Brink, W., Wouters, L., and Doreleijers, T. (2003). Substance use, substance use disorders, and comorbidity patterns in a representative sample of incarcerated male Dutch adolescents. *The Journal of Nervous and Mental Disease*, **191** (6): 372–378.

World Health Organisation. (2006). Child maltreatment and alcohol [online]. Available from: www.who.int/violence_injury_prevention/violence/world_report/factsheets/ft_child.pdf. Accessed 28 October 2016.

World Health Organisation. (2007). Health in prisons [online]. Available from: www.euro.who.int/__data/assets/pdf_file/0009/99018/E90174.pdf. Accessed 28 October 2016.

World Health Organisation. (2014a). Management of substance abuse [online]. Available from: www.who.int/substance_abuse/terminology/abuse/en/. Accessed 28 October 2016.

World Health Organisation. (2014b). Alcohol World Health Organisation [online]. Available from: www.who.int/mediacentre/factsheets/fs349/en/. Accessed 28 October 2016.

Youth Justice Board. (2009). Substance misuse services in secure settings [online]. Available from: http://yjbpublications.justice.gov.uk/Resources/Downloads/Substance%20misuse%20services%20in%20the%20secure%20estate_fullreport.pdf. Accessed 3 October 2016.

Attention Deficit Hyperactivity Disorder and Antisocial Behaviour

Susan Young, Ben Greer and Oliver White

Introduction

Attention-Deficit Hyperactivity Disorder (ADHD) is a neurodevelopmental disorder with onset in early childhood and an estimated global prevalence in young people under the age of 18 years of 5.3% (Polanczyk et al., 2007). Rates of ADHD in both young and adult offenders are considerably higher than general population estimates (Young et al., 2015a), with evidence to implicate the role of ADHD in earlier onset of offending and greater behavioural disturbance whilst incarcerated. Despite the complex presentation and vulnerability of young offenders with ADHD, diagnosis is often missed and appropriate treatment is not provided, to the detriment of the individual and society.

This chapter will describe the relationship between ADHD and young offenders, including overall prevalence, associated criminogenic and comorbid factors, and assessment and treatment of this population. A case example is also included which demonstrates assessment and treatment approaches in clinical practice with young people in the criminal justice system.

Prevalence in Offending Populations

ADHD is over-represented in youth prison populations, although estimates of prevalence vary as a result of differing methodologies and a frequent reliance on retrospective accounts to establish the presence of childhood ADHD. A meta-analysis of 42 international studies, utilising diagnostic interviews, indicated an ADHD prevalence rate of 30% for incarcerated young offenders, representing a fivefold increase compared to estimated prevalence in the general population (Young et al., 2015a). Markedly high rates of childhood ADHD have also been reported among individuals detained in police custody (32%; Young et al., 2013a), probation services (45%; Young et al., 2014) and secure care facilities (43%; Young et al., 2010). Of particular significance

is that probation staff significantly under-detect the number of young people with ADHD on their caseloads, estimating this to be 7.6% compared to the 45% detected by diagnostic screens. What is clear is that there are high rates of undiagnosed ADHD among young offenders (Young et al., 2014) and in turn this means that they are not receiving treatments that best meet their needs.

ADHD is a risk for antisocial outcomes. Adolescents with ADHD are up to five times more likely to be arrested and convicted compared to non-ADHD peers (Lambert, 1989; Mannuzza et al., 1989; Satterfield et al., 1994), and longitudinal data have indicated that ADHD symptoms in childhood are significantly associated with engagement in criminal activity (Fletcher and Wolfe, 2009) and incarceration (Satterfield et al., 2007; Klein et al., 2012) in adulthood. In a sample of approximately 300 male students, Gudjonsson et al. (2013) observed ADHD to be a significant independent predictor of self-reported offending. There is therefore robust evidence indicating an association between ADHD and offending behaviours, although there is also evidence that this may be mediated by conduct disorder (CD) (Gudjonsson et al., 2014).

Criminogenic Factors

The development of antisocial behaviour involves a complex interaction of intrinsic and psychosocial factors (please refer to Chapter 1 by Maughan); thus it should be borne in mind that ADHD is associated with a number of factors that may increase the likelihood of offending behaviour. This is of particular importance with regard to rehabilitation efforts, as these criminogenic factors will likely still be present in the young person's life following their contact with the justice system.

In addition to the core symptoms of the disorder, young people with ADHD may also experience deficits in intellectual functioning, executive function, emotion regulation, social skills and problem solving (Moffitt, 1990). These deficits may persist throughout the life course, with evidence from birth cohort studies indicating that genetic polymorphisms in dopaminergic genes are significantly associated with observed heterogeneity in intellectual functioning (Mill et al., 2006). Such deficits may affect the young person's ability to regulate their behaviours, plan and generate alternative strategies, thus potentially heightening the risk of the young person's involvement in situations and activities in which they may come into conflict with the law (please refer to Chapter 5 by Hughes, Williams and Chitsabesan). These deficits may also cause problems in an academic context, with evidence to indicate increased behavioural and disciplinary problems, and lower academic attainment (Mannuzza and Klein, 2000). Biederman (2006) reported that the suspension rate for school-age children with ADHD was significantly higher than those without the disorder (71% versus 21%), with a UK Audit Commission report (1996) indicating that children excluded from school are twice as likely to commit crime. Poor school achievement is an independent risk factor for violence among adolescents (Farrington, 1989; Denno, 1990) and education commitment is therefore an important protective factor (Farrington et al., 2008; Frey et al., 2009). For young people already incarcerated, these deficits may also serve to limit their capacity for meaningful engagement in rehabilitative services.

Adolescents with ADHD present an increased risk of experiencing peer rejection (Grygiel et al., 2014), which has also been associated with violence in youth (Coie et al., 1992). In a longitudinal study of peer rejection in childhood and adolescent delinquency, Miller-Johnson et al. (1999) reported that peer rejection in boys, in addition to aggression, was a significant predictor of serious delinquency. Peer rejection may also lead to low self-esteem and a gravitation to an antisocial peer group, strongly associated with delinquent behaviour (Keenan et al., 1995; Laird et al., 2001; Leve and Chamberlain, 2005; Piquero et al., 2005).

Comorbidity

Young people with ADHD frequently exhibit comorbidity with other disorders (Barkley, 2006; Takeda et al., 2012). Among non-offending youths, up to 44% present with at least one comorbid diagnosis (Szatmari et al., 1989), including anxiety disorders

(10–40%; Barkley, 2006), mood disorders (20–30%; Barkley, 2006) and neurodevelopmental disorders such as Autism Spectrum Disorder (ASD) (20–50%; Rommelse et al., 2010). Among a sample of over 1,800 young offenders, Abram et al. (2003) reported similar patterns of comorbidity to those seen in non-offending youth populations with regard to anxiety disorders (40% female, 35% male) and mood disorders (32% female, 28% male).

Among young offenders with ADHD, CD is one of the most prevalent comorbid diagnoses, affecting between 61% (Young et al., 2011a) and 75% (Satterfield et al., 1987). CD has been shown to be a robust antecedent of antisocial personality disorder and criminality, with a substantial proportion of youth and adult prison populations demonstrating one of these diagnoses (Fazel and Danesh, 2002; Sørland and Kjelsberg, 2009); therefore, it can be difficult to distinguish between the role of ADHD and CD in criminality among young offenders (Mannuzza et al., 2008). Indeed, a longitudinal investigation of lifetime criminality indicated that CD was strongly associated with increased criminality both alone and when comorbid with ADHD (Mordre et al., 2011). There is evidence that comorbid ADHD/CD are clinically and genetically more severe variants of their independent disorders (Thapar et al., 2001); therefore this comorbidity may represent a 'double dose' of risk. Moreover, it has been shown that the synergistic effect of conduct problems and ADHD in terms of delinquent behaviour is apparent even when the criteria for CD are not met (Loeber et al., 1995).

The co-occurrence of ADHD and substance misuse is also high (Young and Sedgwick, 2015), with 74% of males and 65% of females presenting with a comorbid substance use disorder (SUD) (Abram et al., 2003). A cross-sectional study of over 10,000 Icelandic adolescents indicated a significantly greater level of polysubstance misuse among those who were ADHD symptomatic versus non-symptomatic, in addition to a linear relationship between ADHD symptoms and polysubstance misuse (Gudjonsson et al., 2012a). In a sample of university students, severity of ADHD symptoms was noted to be proportionally associated with the use of alcohol, tobacco and marijuana (Upadhyaya and Carpenter, 2008). Young and Sedgwick (2015) reviewed the evidence pertaining to the key mechanisms underlying substance misuse in ADHD, concluding that the combined role of self-medication, behavioural disinhibition and comorbidity contributes to this highly prevalent behaviour.

Substance misuse is an important factor in understanding the association between ADHD and offending behaviours, as there exists a strong link between substance misuse and violence in adolescents (Loeber and Dishion, 1983), and criminal recidivism (Dembo et al., 1998). The association between comorbid ADHD/SUD and recidivism is perhaps unsurprising, given the criminalised status of substances in many countries worldwide. The dealing of substances and acquisitive offending to fund their substance misuse may also provide an explanation of increased levels of criminality among comorbid ADHD/SUD youths (Barkley et al., 2004; Young et al., 2011a). Suggested association between ADHD, comorbid disorders other than CD and criminality can be complicated by the high prevalence of CD in this population. Nevertheless, Mannuzza et al. (2008) reported significantly greater levels of criminality in comorbid ADHD/SUD youths free from CD.

Interface with the Criminal Justice System

Police and Court Issues

Adolescents with ADHD are likely to be less able to cope with arrest, police interviews and the court process. Attention deficits may impair their ability to sustain concentration during lengthy questioning under pressure; this is exacerbated should they concurrently be asked to look at exhibits. Young people are also more susceptible to interrogative pressure than adults (irrespective of whether they have ADHD or not) and are more likely to accept or comply with the suggestions of authority figures (Gudjonsson and Singh, 1984; Richardson et al., 1995). In a study of over 10,000 Icelandic students, 12% reported having given a false confession to the police, a finding which was significantly predicted by ADHD symptoms and negative life events (Gudjonsson et al., 2012b). To counteract the low levels of self-esteem expressed in youth with ADHD (Mazzone et al., 2013), individuals may exaggerate their role in situations, thereby potentially implicating themselves in accounts of criminal activities when they in fact played little or no part.

Recidivism and ADHD

Whilst it has been reported that youths with ADHD come into contact with the criminal justice system at a younger age compared with their non-ADHD peers, and have a greater number of convictions (Young et al., 2009, 2011b), other research has suggested that ADHD is not a predictor of recidivism when other variables such as CD and substance dependence are controlled for (Grieger and Hosser, 2012). However, Grieger and Hosser (2012) found that offenders diagnosed with ADHD re-offended sooner after release. Similar findings were reported by van der Put et al. (2012) in that of approximately 4,000 juvenile offenders, comorbid ADHD/conduct problems were a stronger predictor of recidivism than ADHD alone. Nevertheless, recidivism in the ADHD alone group was still significantly higher than young offenders without ADHD or conduct problems. As previously discussed criminogenic factors may still be present following the individual's release from incarceration, and the influence of unmet clinical needs may still be strong.

Behaviour in Custodial Settings

Individuals with ADHD in custody may present with behaviours which can lead to negative outcomes. These behaviours include increased demands on custody staff (Young et al., 2013a), and increased frequency and severity of institutional behavioural disturbances (Young et al., 2009, 2011a). These behaviours increase the risk of interpersonal conflict with peers and custodial staff, and may delay their progress by increasing the risk of adjudications during the individual's time in custody and, in turn, reducing the likelihood of early release. Such behaviours are most likely associated with emotional lability, and highlight that individuals with ADHD in custodial settings present a significant management problem. However, the core symptomatology of ADHD may also contribute to these behaviours, with hyperactive/impulsive symptoms in particular being associated with both violent and non-violent breaches of discipline (Gordon et al., 2012).

Assessment

A diagnosis of ADHD in youths (irrespective of offending status) should include the following core assessments (National Institute for Health and Care Excellence, 2013a):

- Clinical interview, both with the child/young person and a parent/carer;
- Standardised rating scales, including specific ADHD rating scales;
- Educational and occupational adjustment;
- Medical assessment;
- Psychological and psychometric assessment.

In addition to assessing core symptoms, the clinical interview should include details regarding pregnancy, birth, early neurodevelopment, medical history and an assessment of the level of global impairment at school, home and in a social context. The Children's Global Assessment Scale (Shaffer et al., 1983) may aid functional assessment.

Standardised rating scales can provide a measure of current ADHD symptoms in children, adolescents and adults. They have utility in clinical work to assist assessment and treatment planning, and help to ensure accountability in practice (Collett et al., 2003). Examples include the Conners' scales for young people (Conners, 1997), the Brown Attention Deficit Disorder Scale (Brown, 1996) and the SNAP-IV (Swanson, 1995). One of the most recently developed assessment tools is the ADHD Child Evaluation (ACE), developed by Young (2015). ACE is a semi-structured clinical interview designed for use in children aged 5–16 years and it is currently being translated into over 15 languages.

Given the high rates of comorbidity observed in individuals with ADHD, distinguishing between symptoms of ADHD and other disorders is an important part of the assessment process. This can be complicated by symptom overlap between ADHD and other disorders, requiring a systematic evaluation of the formal diagnostic criteria of ADHD. One of the key discriminants between ADHD and comorbid disorders is the chronic and trait-like nature of ADHD symptoms, present since childhood, as compared to a change from premorbid state. Where an individual may present with a comorbid neurodevelopmental disorder such as Autism Spectrum Disorders (ASD), it is important to take into account the potentially chronic impairments arising from this disorder, in addition to those arising from ADHD.

Assessing a young offender for ADHD will also require the use of offender-specific tools. Given the risk of under-/misdiagnosis of ADHD in this population (Young et al., 2014), all young offenders entering the criminal justice system should be screened for ADHD, an example within England is the use of the Comprehensive Health Assessment Tool or CHAT (Offender Health Research Network, 2013). It is also important to consider the most appropriate rater when assessing for ADHD, with Young et al. (2010) indicating that ratings obtained from teachers are the most sensitive and specific source of information for young offenders. Risk of violence and protective factors are also pertinent characteristics among young offenders for which youth-specific risk assessments have been developed (please refer to Chapter 4 by Millington and Lennox). These include the EARL-20B (Augimeri et al., 1998), SAVRY (Bartel et al., 2002) and SAPROF-YV (de Vries Robbé, 2014).

More recently, objective measures have been developed and are in increasing clinical use within community child and adolescent mental health services within the UK. QbTest (Bergfalk, 2003) combines a simultaneous high-resolution motion tracking system with continuous performance testing, and has FDA approval to supplement standard clinical assessment and treatment, and augment clinical decision making (FDA; Ref-k133382). It demonstrates good psychometric properties (see Hall et al., 2014 for overview). Individual performance is compared with a normative sample matched for both age and gender. One small study within the UK found that QbTest used with clinical judgement provided better reliability of diagnosis in comparison to clinical judgement alone (Vogt and Shameli, 2011), although further research is still required (AQUA Trial; Hall et al., 2014). Quality of care can be inconsistent as clinicians may sometimes be cautious to diagnose ADHD if symptoms are not pervasive across settings or comorbid needs are present (Vogt and Shameli, 2011). It must be borne in mind however, that the use of objective measures such as QbTest can only be used as an aid to assessment, and that previously mentioned core assessments must be utilised for a diagnosis of ADHD to be made.

Treatment

Studies concerning the treatment of young offenders with ADHD are limited. The UK Adult ADHD Network (UKAAN) produced a consensus statement concerning the effective management of offenders with ADHD (Young et al., 2011c), in which it was agreed that treatment should follow a Risk-Needs-Responsivity model, comprising three key areas of treatment:

(1) The alleviation of ADHD symptoms through pharmacological intervention;

(2) Psychosocial interventions targeting an individual's antisocial behaviours, cognitions and self-control;

(3) Treatment of comorbid disorders.

There is variation between different countries in the degree to which psychosocial interventions are prioritised compared with prescription of medication. The ADHD guidelines in the UK, which are broadly similar to the European and US guidelines, recommend medication be offered in combination with psychosocial interventions in children who are aged six years and older (NICE, 2013a; Taylor et al., 2004).

Psychosocial Interventions

Cognitive training and cognitive behavioural therapy (CBT) includes the use of practical strategies and instructions that aim to improve executive functioning such as time management, organisation and planning. In the past few years evidence has been accumulating for a CBT-based treatment programme that has been specifically adapted for antisocial youths and adults with ADHD, Reasoning & Rehabilitation 2 for ADHD Youths and Adults (R&R2ADHD; Young and Ross, 2007). R&R2ADHD is a cognitive skills programme from the internationally accredited Reasoning and Rehabilitation prosocial competence programme (Ross et al., 1988), developed for young people who experience problems associated with ADHD, and who have impairments in cognitive ability and social skills which serve as barriers to their effective and meaningful engagement in rehabilitative treatment. The programme targets five key areas of functioning: neurocognitive impairments, problem-solving skills, emotional control, social skills and critical reasoning. R&R2 has been delivered in a randomised controlled trial among adult community samples in receipt of ADHD medication, yielding large treatment effects at outcome (Emilsson et al., 2011; Young et al., 2015b). Small to medium treatment effects were also reported in a small controlled trial among personality disordered offenders detained in high security who were not receiving ADHD medication (Young et al., 2013b). The programme is currently being delivered in large-scale studies conducted in the UK, Sweden and Denmark, and was quoted in the Mayor's Office for Policing and Crime report as an example of good practice (King and Gieve, 2013).

Medication

Medication can improve the symptoms of ADHD (National Institute for Health and Care Excellence, 2013a). However, this is considered to be via short-term performance enhancement rather than indicative of the treatment of underlying psychopathology, as improvements in attention have also been shown when children without ADHD are prescribed ADHD medication (Del Campo et al., 2013). In the UK, atomoxetine, dexamfetamine and methylphenidate are licensed for the management of ADHD in children and young people. NICE concluded that these medications are effective in controlling the symptoms of ADHD (NICE, 2013a).

NICE recommends (based on effectiveness, side effect profile and cost) methylphenidate as first line treatment for severe ADHD, followed by atomoxetine and then dexamphetamine (NICE, 2006). Other medications, including atypical antipsychotics, bupropion, nicotine, clonidine, modafinil, tricyclic and other antidepressants are occasionally prescribed off-label to patients who do not respond to licensed medications although effect sizes are smaller. More recently guanfacine prolonged-release is also available and licensed for the treatment of ADHD in children and young people aged 6–17 years old for whom stimulants are not suitable, not tolerated or have been shown to be ineffective (NICE, 2016). Medications should be initiated only by an appropriately qualified healthcare professional with expertise in ADHD after a comprehensive assessment. There should be clinical follow-up to monitor the psychological and behavioural effects of drugs after each change in dose, then at three months and routinely every six months, when height, weight, heart rate and blood pressure should also be recorded. The use of rating scales can effectively monitor clinical and behavioural change.

Evidence for the efficacy of pharmacological interventions in young offenders with ADHD is lacking. However. Lichtenstein et al. (2012) utilised Swedish national register data to compare the rate of criminality of over 25,000 adults with a diagnosis of ADHD during periods of medication and non-medication. When in receipt of medication, irrespective of whether this was stimulant or non-stimulant, significant reductions in criminality were observed in both

BOX 14.1 Case Example – 'Michael'

Background

Michael is a 13-year-old boy who lives with his mother and two younger siblings. The home environment was described as chaotic and characterised by significant aggression between Michael and his brother, who is aged 11. Michael had sustained various minor injuries when he was younger, including a broken arm after falling from a tree. Social Care Children Services had been involved in the past.

Michael had a history of behavioural difficulties at nursery and primary school, where he was described by teachers as being 'always on the go, fidgety, unable to focus on specific tasks', requiring additional support in class. Difficulties continued at secondary school, where he received a number of short-term exclusions and had poor educational attainment.

Michael has been assessed by CAMHS in the past, where ADHD was considered but not formally diagnosed due to him and the family not attending follow-up assessment appointments. Michael was charged with assault occasioning actual bodily harm (ABH) following a fight with a peer outside of school. He was due to appear at Youth Court.

Assessment

Concern regarding Michael's mental health was raised by the police due to his apparent difficulties in concentrating during the police interview. The CAMHS Liaison and Diversion Team undertook a brief assessment in police custody, and significant difficulties regarding impulsivity and inattention were noted. Discussion with the Community Forensic CAMHS team resulted in an urgent assessment by local CAMHS. Information gathered from his mother and school, including the Conners' Rating Scale, supplemented a clinical assessment and Michael's self-rated Conners' Rating Scale score. Michael also completed a QbTest assessment at CAMHS. The collation of the assessment information resulted in Michael being diagnosed with ADHD.

Concern was raised about Michael's ability to effectively engage in the criminal justice proceedings in the context of his ADHD. A formal psychiatric report was commissioned by the Court for the purpose of assessing Michael's fitness to plead. This concluded that he was fit to plead, provided the Court adopted special measures, including ensuring that regular breaks were taken.

Formulation

Michael's ADHD resulted in various difficulties throughout his childhood, including a number of minor accidents due to him impulsively and hyperactively climbing trees. At the age of eight there was a near miss when he ran across a road.

Michael's ADHD had contributed to him exhibiting challenging behaviour in the home, in the form of fighting with his siblings, and at school, by disrupting class when he would impulsively shout out. His poor concentration during lessons resulted in educational underachievement. His impulsivity contributed to him being involved in frequent conflict with peers, including a fight in which a peer sustained significant bruising and a fractured nose, resulting in the current criminal charge.

Treatment

Following a medical assessment, Michael was prescribed long-acting methylphenidate medication. His blood pressure and weight were monitored, and his response to medication was assessed via further standardised assessments. This resulted in a significant reduction in his impulsivity and an improvement in his ability to concentrate and focus on individual tasks.

Michael pleaded guilty to the offence of ABH and received a community sentence. This resulted in twice-weekly input from the Youth Offending Team (YOT), which included specific sessions related to anger management. His mother was encouraged to attend some of these sessions so that Michael could be supported in utilising techniques learnt in the home environment. CAMHS and YOT also liaised with Michael's school, and a behavioural management plan was agreed, which included Michael being able to request 'timeout' from lessons and a consistent approach to negative behaviours.

males and females (32% and 41%, respectively). These findings appear to oppose those of Grieger and Hosser (2012) and Gudjonsson et al. (2014), that criminality is driven by comorbid difficulties rather than ADHD symptoms; however, it could be that these periods of medication served to ameliorate associated problems such as CD and substance misuse.

The case example of Michael (Box 14.1) will illustrate some of the key aspects regarding clinical assessment and management approaches outlined within this chapter.

Cost-benefit

The cost of treating ADHD among offenders is considerable (Young and Goodwin, 2010). Using a conservative estimate of the prevalence of ADHD among adult prisoners (25.5%; Young et al., 2015a) and an estimated average reduction in criminality of 36.5% following medication (Lichtenstein et al., 2012), treatment of ADHD among the total UK prison population may have the capacity to reduce this population by 7,767 (based on 2013 figures of 85,120 prisoners in the UK; Ministry of Justice, 2013). With an average cost per prisoner of £34,766 (Ministry of Justice, 2013), treating ADHD in the prison population of the UK alone has the potential to save £270 million annually. These figures clearly support an economic case for early intervention, as they imply that even relatively modest improvements in outcomes would yield significant financial returns. However, these figures do not include an imputed value for the adverse impact of this condition on the quality of life of the individuals affected and their families (Khong, 2014). Arguably this is the most important cost of ADHD, but not one which can readily be given a monetary value. From a welfare perspective, providing effective treatment will improve the quality of life of individuals with ADHD, their carers and their families, and at the same time may reduce the financial implications and psychological burden of ADHD on society (NICE, 2013b).

Conclusions

ADHD is over-represented among young offenders and is associated with a range of deleterious outcomes including criminogenic activities, comorbid psychiatric difficulties and institutional behavioural disturbance. It is also a costly disorder to the criminal justice system, society and the individual, yet it is treatable through a combination of pharmacological and psychosocial interventions.

Recommendations for future care and research for young people with neurodisabilities in contact with the justice system have been provided by Hughes et al. (2012). Chief among these are the importance of ensuring an early identification and intervention of the specific needs exhibited by this vulnerable population, and an overall reform of the juvenile justice system, in order to ensure that, where possible and appropriate, criminalisation of the young person is avoided, with referrals instead made to specialist services (please refer to Chapter 5 by Hughes, Williams and Chitsabesan). Where criminalisation does occur, training for those in the justice system is required in order to ensure an understanding of the specific needs and vulnerabilities of this population, appropriate sentencing, and that the young person has capacity to engage in the legal process.

Further cost-benefit analysis of early interventions for at-risk youths may assist in the development of a health economics model for the treatment of ADHD in the juvenile justice system. Moreover, future research is required in order to identify and evaluate efficacious rehabilitative strategies, ensuring continual understanding of developmental pathways for young persons with ADHD.

References

Abram, K. M., Teplin, L. A., McClelland, G. M. and Dulcan, M. K. (2003). Comorbid psychiatric disorders in youth in juvenile detention. *Archives of General Psychiatry*, **60**(11), 1097–1108.

Audit Commission (1996). *Misspent Youth: Young People and Crime*. London: Audit Commission.

Augimeri, L. K., Webster, C. D., Koegl, C. J. and Levene, K. S. (1998). *Early Assessment Risk List for Boys. Version 1. Consultation Edition*. Ontario: Earls Court Child and Family Centre.

Barkley, R. A. (2006). *Attention-Deficit Hyperactivity Disorder: A Handbook for Diagnosis and Treatment*. 3rd Edition. New York: Guilford Press.

Barkley, R. A., Fischer, M., Smallish, L. and Fletcher, K. (2004). Young adult follow-up of hyperactive children: Antisocial activities and drug use. *Journal of child psychology and psychiatry*, **45**(2), 195–211.

Bartel, P., Borum, R. and Forth, A. (2002). *Structured Assessment for Violence Risk in Youth (SAVRY)*. Tampa: University of South Florida.

Bergfalk, H. (2003). *QbTest User Manual*. Gothenburg, Sweden: Qbtech AB.

Biederman, J. (2006). Functional impairments in adults with self-reports of diagnosed ADHD: A controlled study of 1001 adults in the community. *Journal of Clinical Psychiatry*, **67**(4), 524–540.

Brown, T. E. (1996). *Brown Attention-Deficit Disorder Scales: Adolescents and Adults*. San Antonio, TX: Psychological Corporation.

Coie, J. D., Lochman, J. E., Terry, R. and Hyman, C. (1992). Predicting early adolescent disorder from childhood aggression and peer rejection. *Journal of Consulting and Clinical Psychology*, **60**(5), 783–792.

Collett, B. R., Ohan, J. L. and Myers, K. M. (2003). Ten-year review of rating scales. V: Scales assessing attention-deficit/hyperactivity disorder. *Journal of the American Academy of Child & Adolescent Psychiatry*, **42**(9), 1015–1037.

Conners, C. K. (1997). *Conners' Rating Scales-Revised: User's Manual*. North Tonawanda, NY: Multi-Health Systems, Incorporated.

de Vries Robbé, M. (2014). *Protective Factors. Validation of the Structured Assessment of Protective Factors for Violence Risk in Forensic Psychiatry*. Utrecht, NL: Van der Hoeven Kliniek.

del Campo, N., Fryer, T. D., Hong, Y. T., Smith, R., Brichard, L., Acosta-Cabronero, J., Chamberlain, S. R., Tait, R., Izquierdo, D., Regenthal, R., Dowson, J., Suckling, J., Baron, J. C., Aigbirhio, F. I., Robbins, T. W., Sahakian, B. J. and Müller, U. (2013). A positron emission tomography study of nigro-striatal dopaminergic mechanisms underlying attention: implications for ADHD and its treatment. *Brain*, **136**(11), 3252–3270.

Dembo, R., Schmeidler, J., Nini-Gough, B., Sue, C. C., Borden, P. and Manning, D. (1998). Predictors of recidivism to a juvenile assessment center: A three year study. *Journal of Child & Adolescent Substance Abuse*, **7**(3), 57–77.

Denno, D. W. (1990). *Biology and Violence: From Birth to Adulthood*. Cambridge: Cambridge University Press.

Durlak, J. A., Fuhrman, T. and Lampman, C. (1991). Effectiveness of cognitive-behavior therapy for maladapting children: A meta-analysis. *Psychological Bulletin*, **110**(2), 204–214.

Emilsson, B., Gudjonsson, G., Sigurdsson, J. F., Baldursson, G., Einarsson, E., Olafsdottir, H. and Young, S. (2011). Cognitive behaviour therapy in medication-treated adults with ADHD and persistent symptoms: A randomized controlled trial. *BMC Psychiatry*, **11**(1), 116.

Farrington, D. P. (1989). Early predictors of adolescent aggression and adult violence. *Violence and Victims*, **4**(2), 79–100.

Farrington, D. P., Loeber, R., Jolliffe, D. and Pardini, D. A. (2008). Promotive and risk processes at different life stages. In Loeber, R., Farrington, D. P., Stouthamer-Loeber, M. and White, H. R. Editors. *Violence and Serious Theft: Development and Prediction from Childhood to Adulthood*. New York: Taylor & Francis.

Fazel, S. and Danesh, J. (2002). Serious mental disorder in 23 000 prisoners: A systematic review of 62 surveys. *The Lancet*, **359**(9306), 545–550.

Fletcher, J. and Wolfe, B. (2009). Long-term consequences of childhood ADHD on criminal activities. *The Journal of Mental Health Policy and Economics*, **12**(3), 119–138.

Frey, A., Ruchkin, V., Martin, A. and Schwab-Stone, M. (2009). Adolescents in transition: School and family characteristics in the development of violent behaviors entering high school. *Child Psychiatry and Human Development*, **40**(1), 1–13.

Froelich, J., Doepfner, M. and Lehmkuhl, G. (2002). Effects of combined cognitive behavioural treatment with parent management training in ADHD. *Behavioural and Cognitive Psychotherapy*, **30**(1), 111–115.

Gordon, V., Williams, D. J. and Donnelly, P. D. (2012). Exploring the relationship between ADHD symptoms and prison breaches of discipline amongst youths in four Scottish prisons. *Public Health*, **126**(4), 343–348.

Grieger, L. and Hosser, D. (2012). Attention deficit hyperactivity disorder does not predict criminal recidivism in young adult offenders: Results from a prospective study. *International Journal of Law and Psychiatry*, **35**(1), 27–34.

Grygiel, P., Humenny, G., Rębisz, S., Bajcar, E. and Świtaj, P. (2014). Peer rejection and perceived quality of relations with schoolmates among children with ADHD. *Journal of Attention Disorders*. doi: 10.1177/1087054714563791.

Gudjonsson, G. H. and Singh, K. K. (1984). Interrogative suggestibility and delinquent boys: An empirical validation study. *Personality and Individual Differences*, **5**, 425–430.

Gudjonsson, G. H., Sigurdsson, J. F., Sigfusdottir, I. D. and Young, S. (2012a). An epidemiological study of ADHD symptoms among young persons and the relationship with cigarette smoking, alcohol consumption, and illicit drug use. *Journal of Child Psychology and Psychiatry*, **53**(3), 304–312.

Gudjonsson, G. H., Sigurdsson, J. F., Sigfusdottir, I. D. and Young, S. (2012b). False confessions to police and their relationship with conduct disorder, ADHD, and life adversity. *Personality and Individual Differences*, **52**(6), 696–701.

Gudjonsson, G. H., Sigurdsson, J. F., Adalsteinsson, T. F. and Young, S. (2013). The relationship between ADHD symptoms, mood instability, and self-reported offending. *Journal of Attention Disorders*, **17**(4), 339–346.

Gudjonsson, G. H., Sigurdsson, J. F., Sigfusdottir, I. D. and Young, S. (2014). A national epidemiological study of offending and its relationship with ADHD symptoms and associated risk factors. *Journal of Attention Disorders*, **18**(1), 3–13.

Hall, C., Walker, G. M., Valentine, A. Z., Guo, B., Kaylor-Hughes, C., James, M., Daley, D., Sayal, K. and Hollis, C.

(2014). Protocol investigating the clinical utility of an objective measure of activity and attention (Qbtest) on diagnostic and treatment decision-making in children and young people with ADHD (AQUA); a randomised controlled trial. *BMJ Open Access*, 4(12), e006838.

Hughes, N., Williams, H., Chitsabesan, P., Davies, R. and Mounce, L. (2012). *Nobody Made the Connection: The Prevalence of Neurodisability in Young People Who Offend*. London, UK: Office of the Children's Commissioner.

Keenan, K., Loeber, R., Zhang, Q., Stouthamer-Loeber, M. and Van Kammen, W. B. (1995). The influence of deviant peers on the development of boys' disruptive and delinquent behavior: A temporal analysis. *Development and Psychopathology*, 7(4), 715–726.

Khong, B. (2014). The lifetime costs of attention deficit hyperactivity disorder (ADHD). [Online] Available from: www.centreformentalhealth.org.uk/costs-of-adhd. Accessed 23 July 2015.

King, S. and Gieve, M. (2013). *Evaluation of a Pilot to Deliver Forensic Mental Health Interventions to Young People at Risk of Violent Offending*. London: The Tavistock Institute.

Klein, R. G., Mannuzza, S., Olazagasti, M. A., Roizen, E., Hutchison, J. A., Lashua, E. C. and Castellanos, F. X. (2012). Clinical and functional outcome of childhood attention-deficit/hyperactivity disorder 33 years later. *Archives of General Psychiatry*, 196, 235–240.

Laird, R. D., Jordan, K. Y., Dodge, K. A., Pettit, G. S. and Bates, J. E. (2001). Peer rejection in childhood, involvement with antisocial peers in early adolescence, and the development of externalizing behavior problems. *Development and Psychopathology*, 13(2), 337–354.

Lambert, N. M. (1989). Adolescent outcomes for hyperactive children: Perspectives on general and specific patterns of childhood risk for adolescent educational, social and mental health problems. *American Psychologist*, 43, 786–799.

Leve, L. D. and Chamberlain, P. (2005). Association with delinquent peers: Intervention effects for youth in the juvenile justice system. *Journal of Abnormal Child Psychology*, 33(3), 339–347.

Lichtenstein, P, Halldner, L., Zetterqvist, J., Sjolander, A., Serlachius, E., Fazel, S., Långström, N. and Larsson, H. (2012). Medication for attention deficit–hyperactivity disorder and criminality. *New England Journal of Medicine*, 367(21), 2006–2014.

Loeber, R. and Dishion, T. (1983). Early predictors of male delinquency: A review. *Psychological Bulletin*, 94(1), 68–69.

Loeber, R., Green, S. M., Keenan, K. and Lahey, B. B. (1995). Which boys will fare worse? Early predictors of the onset of conduct disorder in a six-year longitudinal study. *Journal of the American Academy of Child & Adolescent Psychiatry*, 34(4), 499–509.

Mannuzza, S. and Klein, R. G. (2000). Long-term prognosis in attention-deficit/hyperactivity disorder. *Child and Adolescent Psychiatric Clinics of North America*, 9(3), 711–726.

Mannuzza, S., Klein, R. G., Konig, P. H. and Giampino, T. L. (1989). Hyperactive boys almost grown up. Criminality and its relationship to psychiatric status. *Archives of General Psychiatry*, 46, 1073–1079.

Mannuzza, S., Klein, R. G. and Moulton, J. L. (2008). Lifetime criminality among boys with attention deficit hyperactivity disorder: A prospective follow-up study into adulthood using official arrest records. *Psychiatry Research*, 160(3), 237–246.

Mazzone, L. Postorino, V., Reale, L., Guarnera, M., Mannino, V., Armando, M., Fatto, L., De Peppo, L. and, Vicari, S. (2013). Self-esteem evaluation in children and adolescents suffering from ADHD. *Clinical Practice and Epidemiology in Mental Health*, 9, 96–102.

Mill, J., Caspi, A., Williams, B. S., Craig, I., Taylor, A., Polo-Tomas, M., Berridge, C. W., Poulton, R. and Moffitt, T. E. (2006). Prediction of heterogeneity in intelligence and adult prognosis by genetic polymorphisms in the dopamine system among children with attention-deficit/hyperactivity disorder: Evidence from 2 birth cohorts. *Archives of general psychiatry*, 63(4), 462–469.

Miller-Johnson, S., Coie, J. D., Maumary-Gremaud, A., Lochman, J. and Terry, R. (1999). Relationship between childhood peer rejection and aggression and adolescent delinquency severity and type among African American youth. *Journal of Emotional and Behavioral Disorders*, 7(3), 137–146.

Ministry of Justice (2013). Prison Population Figures: 2013. [Online] Available from: www.gov.uk/government/statistics/prison-population-figures. Accessed 14 August 2015.

Ministry of Justice (2013). Costs per place and costs per prisoner. [Online] Available from: www.gov.uk/government/uploads/system/uploads/attachment_data/file/251272/prison-costs-summary-12–13.pdf. Accessed 14 August 2015.

Mordre, M. et al. (2011). The impact of ADHD and conduct disorder in childhood on adult delinquency: A 30 years follow-up study using official crime records. *BMC Psychiatry*, 11(1), 57.

Moffitt, T. E. (1990). Juvenile delinquency and attention deficit disorder: Boys' developmental trajectories from age 3 to 15. *Child Development*, 61, 893–910.

National Institute for Health and Care Excellence (NICE) (2006). *Methylphenidate, atomoxetine and dexamfetamine for the treatment of attention deficit hyperactivity disorder in children and adolescents. Technology Appraisal 98*. London: NICE.

National Institute for Health and Care Excellence (NICE) (2013a). CG72 *Attention deficit hyperactivity disorder (ADHD)*: NICE guideline, modified 2013. [Online]

Available from: www.nice.org.uk/guidance/cg72. Accessed 15 September 2015.

National Institute for Health and Care Excellence (NICE) (2013b). CG158 *Antisocial behaviour and conduct disorders in children and young people: recognition, intervention and management.* [Online] Available from: www.nice.org.uk/guidance/cg158. Accessed 15 September 2015.

National Institute for Health and Care Excellence (NICE) (2016). *Attention deficit hyperactivity disorder in children and young people; guanfacine prolonged release.* London: NICE.

Offender Health Research Network. (2013). *The Comprehensive Health Assessment Tool (CHAT): Young People in the Secure Estate – Version 3.* Manchester: University of Manchester.

Piquero, N. L., Gover, A. R., MacDonald, J. M. and Piquero, A. R. (2005). The influence of delinquent peers on delinquency. Does gender matter? *Youth & Society,* **36**(3), 251–275.

Polanczyk, G., de Lima, M. S., Horta, B. L., Biederman, J. and Rohde, L. A. (2007). The worldwide prevalence of ADHD: A systematic review and metaregression analysis. *The American Journal of Psychiatry,* **164**(6), 942–948.

Richardson, G., Gudjonsson, G. H. and Kelly, T. P. (1995). Interrogative suggestibility in an adolescent forensic population. *Journal of Adolescence,* **18**, 211–216.

Rommelse, N. N., Franke, B., Geurts, H. M., Hartman, C. A. and Buitelaar, J. K. (2010). Shared heritability of attention-deficit/hyperactivity disorder and autism spectrum disorder. *European Child & Adolescent Psychiatry,* **19**(3), 281–295.

Ross, R. R., Fabiano, E. A. and Ewles, C. D. (1988). Reasoning and rehabilitation. *International Journal of Offender Therapy and Comparative Criminology,* **32**, 29–35.

Satterfield, J. H., Satterfield, B. T. and Schell, A. M. (1987). Therapeutic interventions to prevent delinquency in hyperactive boys. *Journal of the American Academy of Child & Adolescent Psychiatry,* **26**(1), 56–64.

Satterfield, J., Swanson, J., Schell, A. and Lee, F. (1994). Prediction of antisocial behavior in attention-deficit hyperactivity disorder boys from aggression/defiance scores. *Journal of the American Academy of Child & Adolescent Psychiatry,* **33**(2), 185–190.

Satterfield, J. H., Faller, K. J., Crinella, F. M., Schell, A. M., Swanson, J. M. and Homer, L. D. (2007). A 30-year prospective follow-up study of hyperactive boys with conduct problems: Adult criminality. *Journal of the American Academy of Child & Adolescent Psychiatry,* **46**(5), 601–610.

Shaffer, D., Gould, M. S., Brasic, J., Ambrosini, P., Fisher, P., Bird, H. and Aluwahlia, S. (1983). A children's global assessment scale (CGAS). *Archives of General Psychiatry,* **40**(11), 1228–1231.

Sørland, T. O. and Kjelsberg, E. (2009). Mental health among teenage boys remanded to prisoner. *Journal of the Norwegian Medical Association: Journal of Practical Medicine,* **129**(23), 2472–2475.

Swanson, J. M., 1995. *SNAP-IV Scale.* Irvine, CA: University of California Child Development Center.

Szatmari, P., Offord, D. R. and Boyle, M. H. (1989). Correlates, associated impairments, and patterns of service utilization of children with attention deficit disorders: Findings from the Ontario Child Health Study. *Journal of Clinical Psychology and Psychiatry,* **30**, 205–217.

Takeda, T., Ambrosini, P. J. and Elia, J. (2012). What can ADHD without comorbidity teach us about comorbidity? *Research in Developmental Disabilities,* **33**(2), 419–425.

Taylor, E., Döpfner, M., Sergeant, J., Asherson, P., Banaschewski, T., Buitelaar, J., Coghill, D., Danckaerts, M., Rothenberger, A., Sonuga-Barke, E., Steinhausen, H. C. and Zuddas, A. (2004). European clinical guidelines for hyperkinetic disorder–first upgrade. *European Child & Adolescent Psychiatry,* **13**(1), i7–i30.

Thapar, A., Harrington, R. and McGuffin, P. (2001). Examining the comorbidity of ADHD-related behaviours and conduct problems using a twin study design. *The British Journal of Psychiatry,* **179**(3), 224–229.

Upadhyaya, H. P. and Carpenter, M. J. (2008). Is attention deficit hyperactivity disorder (ADHD) symptom severity associated with tobacco use? *American Journal on Addictions,* **17**(3), 195–198.

van der Put, C. E., Asscher, J. J. and Stams, G. J. J. (2012). Differences between juvenile offenders with and without AD(H)D in recidivism rates and risk and protective factors for recidivism. *Journal of Attention Disorders.* doi: 10.1177/1087054712466140.

Vogt, C. and Shameli, A. (2011). Assessments for attention-deficit hyperactivity disorder: Use of objective measurements. *The Psychiatrist,* **35**(10), 380–383.

Young, S. (2015). *ADHD Child Evaluation (ACE).* [Online] Available from: www.psychology-services.uk.com/resources.htm#resource-14. Accessed 10 October 2016.

Young, S. J. and Ross, R. R. (2007). *R&R2 for ADHD Youths and Adults: A Prosocial Competence Training Program.* Ottawa: Cognitive Centre of Canada.

Young, S. and Goodwin, E. (2010). Attention-deficit /hyperactivity disorder in persistent criminal offenders: The need for specialist treatment programs. *Expert Review of Neurotherapeutics,* **10**(10), 1497–1500.

Young, S. and Sedgwick, O. (2015). Attention deficit hyperactivity disorder and substance misuse: An evaluation of causal hypotheses and treatment considerations. *Expert Review of Neurotherapeutics,* **15**(9), 1005–1014.

Young, S., Gudjonsson, G., Wells, J., Asherson, P., Theobald, D., Oliver, B., Scott, C. and Mooney, A. (2009). Attention deficit hyperactivity disorder and critical incidents in a Scottish prison population. *Personality and Individual Differences*, **46**(3), 265–269.

Young, S., Gudjonsson, G., Misch, P., Collins, P., Carter, P., Redfern, J. and Goodwin, E. (2010). Prevalence of ADHD symptoms among youth in a secure facility: The consistency and accuracy of self-and informant-report ratings. *The Journal of Forensic Psychiatry & Psychology*, **21**(2), 238–246.

Young, S., Misch, P., Collins, P. and Gudjonsson, G. H. (2011a). Predictors of institutional behavioural disturbance and offending in the community among young offenders. *Journal of Forensic Psychiatry and Psychology*, **22**(1), 72–78.

Young, S., Wells, J. and Gudjonsson, G. H. (2011b). Predictors of offending among prisoners: The role of attention-deficit hyperactivity disorder and substance use. *Journal of Psychopharmacology*, **25**(11), 1524–1532.

Young, S. J., Adamou M., Bolea, B., Gudjonsson G., Miller U., Pitts M., Thome J. and Asherson P. (2011c). The identification and management of ADHD offenders within the criminal justice system: A consensus statement from the UK Adult ADHD Network and criminal justice agencies. *BMC Psychiatry*, **11**(1), 32.

Young, S., Goodwin, E. J., Sedgwick, O. and Gudjonsson, G. H. (2013a). The effectiveness of police

custody assessments in identifying suspects with intellectual disabilities and attention deficit hyperactivity disorder. *BMC Medicine*, **11**(1), 248.

Young, S., Hopkin, G., Perkins, D., Farr, C., Doidge, A. and Gudjonsson, G. (2013b). A controlled trial of a cognitive skills program for personality-disordered offenders. *Journal of Attention Disorders*, **17**(7), 598–607.

Young, S., Gudjonsson, G., Goodwin, E., Jotangia, A., Farooq, R., Haddrick, D. and Adamou, M. (2014). Beyond the gates: Identifying and managing offenders with attention deficit hyperactivity disorder in community probation services. *AIMS Public Health*, **1**(1), 33–42.

Young, S., Moss, D., Sedgwick, O., Fridman, M. and Hodgkins, P. (2015a). A meta-analysis of the prevalence of attention deficit hyperactivity disorder in incarcerated populations. *Psychological Medicine*, **45**(2), 247–258.

Young, S., Khondoker, M., Emilsson, B., Sigurdsson, J. F., Philipp-Wiegmann, F., Baldursson, G., Olafsdottir, H. and Gudjonsson, G. (2015b). Cognitive–behavioural therapy in medication-treated adults with attention-deficit /hyperactivity disorder and co-morbid psychopathology: a randomized controlled trial using multi-level analysis. *Psychological Medicine*, **45**(13), 2793–2804.

Chapter 15

Autism Spectrum Disorders in Young People in the Criminal Justice System

Ernest Gralton and Gillian Baird

Introduction, Definition and Aetiology

Autism spectrum disorder (ASD) is a neurodevelopmental disorder characterised by impairment in reciprocal social interaction and communication combined with restricted, often repetitive, stereotyped interests and behaviours (Lai et al., 2014) that significantly impact on the individual's function, and for many, has a significant lifetime cost for the individual, family and society (Buescher et al., 2014). Previous diagnostic classification systems (ICD-10: WHO, 1992; DSM-IV-TR: APA, 2000) used the terminology 'pervasive developmental disorders' and had a sub-classification structure including childhood autism (ICD-10)/autistic disorder (DSM-IV), Asperger's Syndrome/disorder, pervasive developmental disorder – unspecified/not otherwise specified (PDD-NOS). In the most recent revision of DSM (DSM-5: APA, 2013) and the forthcoming revision to ICD (ICD-11: WHO, due 2017) these sub-classifications have been removed and are unified under the broader diagnostic category 'autism spectrum disorder'. This follows research that had shown that the various sub-classifications had little scientific justification and were used unreliably, even across specialist teams (Lord et al., 2012). DSM-5 describes two domains rather than the previous three: (i) social and communication deficits which combines the previous social interaction and social communication domains; and (ii) restricted and repetitive interests and behaviours, including atypical sensory behaviour. Current impairment in function is essential; symptoms can be current or by history (see Box 15.1 for diagnostic criteria).

Prevalence of ASD

Recent prevalence estimates suggest that a minimum estimate is that 1% of children and young people have ASD (Baird et al., 2006; Kim et al., 2011; Centre for Disease Prevention, 2014), with an approximately four times higher rate in males than females. A similar prevalence figure has been found in adults in the UK (Brugha et al., 2011). There is little known about possible differences in the presentation of ASD in males and females and there is concern that many girls with ASD may go unrecognised. Clinical reports suggest that girls are better at 'apparent' sociability and though their interests may be intense and over-focused, they are not so abnormal in topic (Lai et al., 2011).

Causes of ASD

ASD is a biologically based disorder with differences in brain function from typical development, although the precise mechanism of causation is unknown. There is no specific biomarker or diagnostic test for ASD. Diagnosis is made on the basis of the presence of characteristic behaviours.

Genetic and environmental aetiological factors result in disruptions to early brain development that ultimately underlie the behavioural and developmental characteristics that define the disorder (Lai et al., 2014). There are differences in the function and structure of brain regions including the 'empathy circuit' (amygdala, ventromedial prefrontal cortex, temporo-parietal junction, orbitofrontal cortex, anterior cingulate (Lombardo et al., 2011). There are also differences in functional connectivity between different brain regions, although the particular patterns reported have varied across different research studies and include both possible under-connectivity and over-connectivity (Lai et al., 2014).

Estimates of the frequency of underlying medical causes vary widely but these probably occur in fewer than 10% of individuals with ASD. At least 60 different metabolic, neurological disorders and complex chromosome abnormalities, including Fragile X Syndrome and Tuberous Sclerosis Complex (TSC) (Murdoch and State, 2013), have been reported to be associated with increased risk of ASD. There is evidence of a substantial genetic basis with strong heritability; but current thinking

---

BOX 15.1 Diagnostic Criteria for Autism Spectrum Disorder (DSM-5)

1. Persistent deficits in social communication and social interaction across multiple contexts, manifested by the following, currently or by history (examples are illustrative, not exhaustive; see text):

   a. Deficits in social-emotional reciprocity; ranging, for example, from abnormal social approach and failure of normal back-and-forth conversation; to reduced sharing of interests, emotions, or affect; to failure to initiate or respond to social interactions.

   b. Deficits in nonverbal communicative behaviors used for social interaction, ranging, for example, from poorly integrated verbal and nonverbal communication; to abnormalities in eye contact and body language or deficits in understanding and use of gestures; to a total lack of facial expressions and nonverbal communication.

   c. Deficits in developing, maintaining, and understanding relationships, ranging, for example, from difficulties adjusting behavior to suit various social contexts; to difficulties in sharing imaginative play or in making friends, to absence of interest in peers.

2. Restricted, repetitive patterns of behavior, interests, or activities, as manifested by at least two of the following, currently or by history (examples are illustrative, not exhaustive; see text):

   a. Stereotyped or repetitive motor movements, use of objects, or speech (e.g., simple motor stereotypies, lining up toys or flipping objects, echolalia, idiosyncratic phrases).

   b. Insistence on sameness, inflexible adherence to routines, or ritualized patterns of verbal or nonverbal behavior (e.g., extreme distress at small changes, difficulties with transitions, rigid thinking patterns, greeting rituals need to take same route or eat same food every day).

   c. Highly restricted, fixated interests that are abnormal in intensity or focus (e.g., strong attachment to or preoccupation with unusual objects, excessively circumscribed or perseverative interests).

   d. Hyper- or hyporeactivity to sensory input or unusual interest in sensory aspects of the environment (e.g., apparent indifference to pain/temperature, adverse response to specific sounds or textures, excessive smelling or touching of objects, visual fascination with lights or movement).

3. Symptoms must be present in the early developmental period (but may not become fully manifest until social demands exceed limited capacities; or may be masked by learned strategies in later life).

4. Symptoms cause clinically significant impairment in social, occupational, or other important areas of current functioning.

5. These disturbances are not better explained by intellectual disability (intellectual developmental disorder) or global developmental delay. Intellectual disability and autism spectrum disorder frequently co-occur; to make comorbid diagnoses of autism spectrum disorder and intellectual disability, social communication should be below that expected for general developmental level.

---

is of a genetically heterogeneous disorder producing phenotypic heterogeneity (differing physical and behavioural characteristics). Candidate genes are emerging from the advances in molecular-genetic techniques (State and Levitt, 2011). Rare (occurring in ~1/1,000 affected individuals) micro-duplications and micro-deletions (referred to as copy number variants or CNVs) have been identified in up to 10% of individuals with so-called idiopathic ASD (Murdoch and State, 2013). Subgroups of genes have been linked to common underlying mechanisms such as synaptogenesis and cell-to-cell adhesion, as well as converging on different aspects of several common, underlying molecular signalling pathways. For families with a child with a diagnosis of ASD the likelihood of having another child with ASD is greatly increased.

The possible contribution of environmental factors, such as maternal infection and exposure to teratogens, has received increasing attention, prompted in part by the dramatic increase in prevalence estimates for ASD over the past few decades (Rutter, 2009), although the rise is likely largely due to increased recognition and enlarging diagnostic criteria. To date, few firm links to specific environmental factors have been established; maternal anticonvulsant use of sodium valproate is one example. A variety of non-specific risk factors including advanced parental age, maternal infection during pregnancy, prematurity, low birth weight, and early onset epilepsy and brain injury are factors that contribute to the risk of ASD.

Coexisting Conditions (Comorbidities)

Autism is strongly associated with a number of coexisting conditions which are not part of the diagnostic criteria but have an impact on the well-being of the child or young person and family. Recent studies suggest that approximately 70% of individuals with autism also meet diagnostic criteria for at least one other (often unrecognised) mental and behavioural disorder and 40% meet diagnostic criteria for at least two disorders, mainly anxiety, ADHD and oppositional defiant disorder (Simonoff et al., 2008; Hofvander et al., 2009), that further impair psychosocial functioning. Challenging behaviours including aggression to the environment or people, destructiveness and self-injury (e.g. head banging, hand or wrist biting, or skin picking) are more common in autism than in other conditions with similar levels of intellectual impairment). Intellectual disability (IQ<70) occurs in approximately 50% of young people with autism (Charman et al., 2011). Characteristic of autism is the gap between intellectual and adaptive skills, the latter usually more impaired, which has a significant impact on everyday functioning (Charman et al., 2011). Language disorders and specific learning difficulties (literacy and numeracy and other academic skills) are common (Jones et al., 2009). Developmental coordination disorder (DCD) also commonly co-occurs with autism manifesting as general clumsiness or an unusual gait and fine motor problems which can affect self-help skills and include slow, laboured handwriting leading to frustration at school. Epilepsy occurs in between one-quarter and one-third of children with ASD, most commonly in those with intellectual disability (Francis et al., 2013). Functional problems are common and have a major impact on the child and family such as sleeping problems and eating difficulties (restricted and rigid food choices, which may be the presenting feature of autism). Gastrointestinal problems are frequently reported, particularly diarrhoea, abdominal pain and constipation.

Recognising ASD

Impairments in reciprocal social interaction and social communication in ASD can be manifest in many different ways, and the profile of difficulties can differ widely from one person to another. No individual feature is either sufficient or necessary for diagnosis. Commonly, the first symptoms noticed by parents are those of language delay, lack of social interest and/or unusual, repetitive interests in the second or third years of life; together with behavioural challenges possibly related to sensory sensitivities, for example dislike of foods, or a dislike of change.

Symptoms and signs of ASD vary at different ages, and most individuals change with maturity. For example, early language delays may improve at around four to six years; sensory sensitivities often wane over time; and children who are initially socially very withdrawn or aloof may become much more socially interactive with age. On the other hand, motor mannerisms can become more obvious with age and although special interests can change, the repetitive or intense quality remains. A profile of marked strengths and weaknesses of skills both cognitive and neurodevelopmental is common in ASD. Symptoms vary with the demands of the environment and the presence of any coexisting conditions, as well as the severity of the core impairments. Thus in some young people with average or above-average intellectual ability, presentation may be through behavioural difficulties in school (see Box 15.2 for symptoms and signs from NICE Guideline 2011: 128).

Puberty, as with all children, can bring more challenging behaviour and increased awareness of difference from the peer group, which may be a factor in low mood and self-esteem. Symptoms such as rigidity and inflexibility of thinking, literal understanding of language and situations, sensory sensitivities, reactivity to change and a need for sameness may be features of autism first recognised in the criminal justice system as many individuals reach court without their ASD being recognised.

Diagnosis of ASD

Diagnosis is by history-taking focusing on the developmental story from those who know the child/young person well (which may be unavailable particularly in young people who have gone into care at an early age), systematically enquiring for core behaviours and by observation of social interactive and communicative behaviour in a number of settings. Standardised instruments for history taking and for observation are available (including ADI, DISCO, 3Di, ADOS; Lord, 2000; Wing et al., 2002; Leekam et al., 2002;

BOX 15.2 Signs and Symptoms of Possible Autism: Secondary School Children (over 11 years or equivalent mental age) (NICE Guideline, 2011)

Social Interaction and Reciprocal Communication Behaviours

Spoken Language

- Spoken language may be unusual in several ways:
  - very limited use
  - monotonous tone
  - repetitive speech, frequent use of stereotyped (learnt) phrases, content dominated by excessive information on topics of own interest
  - talking 'at' others rather than sharing a two-way conversation
  - responses to others can seem rude or inappropriate

Interacting with Others

- Reduced or absent awareness of personal space, or unusually intolerant of people entering their personal space
- Long-standing difficulties in reciprocal social communication and interaction: few close friends or reciprocal relationships
- Reduced or absent understanding of friendship; often an unsuccessful desire to have friends (although may find it easier with adults or younger children)
- Social isolation and apparent preference for aloneness
- Reduced or absent greeting and farewell behaviours
- Lack of awareness and understanding of socially expected behaviour
- Problems losing at games, turn-taking and understanding 'changing the rules'
- May appear unaware or uninterested in what other young people his or her age are interested in
- Unable to adapt style of communication to social situations, for example may be overly formal or inappropriately familiar
- Subtle difficulties in understanding other's intentions; may take things literally and misunderstand sarcasm or metaphor
- Makes comments without awareness of social niceties or hierarchies
- Unusually negative response to the requests of others (demand avoidant behaviour)

Eye Contact, Pointing and Other Gestures

- Poorly integrated gestures, facial expressions, body orientation, eye contact (looking at people's eyes when speaking) assuming adequate vision, and spoken language used in social communication

Ideas and Imagination

- History of a lack of flexible social imaginative play and creativity, although scenes seen on visual media (for example, television) may be re-enacted

Unusual or Restricted Interests and/or Rigid and Repetitive Behaviours

- Repetitive 'stereotypical' movements such as hand flapping, body rocking while standing, spinning, finger flicking
- Preference for highly specific interests or hobbies
- A strong adherence to rules or fairness that leads to argument
- Highly repetitive behaviours or rituals that negatively affect the young person's daily activities
- Excessive emotional distress at what seems trivial to others, for example change in routine
- Dislike of change, which often leads to anxiety or other forms of distress including aggression
- Over or under reaction to sensory stimuli, for example textures, sounds, smells
- Excessive reaction to taste, smell, texture or appearance of food and/or extreme food fads

Other Factors That May Support a Concern about Autism
- Unusual profile of skills and deficits (for example, social or motor coordination skills poorly developed, while particular areas of knowledge, reading or vocabulary skills are advanced for chronological or mental age)
- Social and emotional development more immature than other areas of development, excessive trusting (naivety), lack of common sense, less independent than peers

Skuse et al., 2004; Rutter et al., 2003). Relying on one instrument alone is not recommended (e.g. the ADOS can give false positives), particularly where the social impairment is due to another disorder (Mazefsky and Oswald, 2006).

The core behaviours follow a continuum between atypical and typical development; thus diagnostic cut-offs for ASD have been hard to define and diagnosis ultimately depends upon clinical judgement taking all sources of information into account. Functional impairment from symptoms is essential for diagnosis of a disorder.

ASD and the Criminal Justice System

Persons with ASD may be involved in the justice system as individuals through their own actions or as victims due to vulnerability or in the family courts, for example in relation to child protection cases. Within the criminal justice system, lack of empathy of a person with autism is prone to be interpreted as malign intent (e.g. criminal *mens rea*) unless expert evidence is provided to the contrary (Freckelton, 2013b). Questions involving hypothetical situations in legal contexts will be particularly difficult for patients with autism as a result of their cognitive rigidity (Clare and Woodbury-Smith, 2009). Practitioners need to be aware that adolescents who present to forensic services may require a specific assessment for ASD including assessment of social and communication needs in order to appropriately address and manage risk behaviour (Tiffin et al., 2007).

There is still limited epidemiological evidence linking adolescents with ASD and increased offending, as the majority of the studies relate to adult populations. The literature in adults is difficult to interpret; although the prevalence is higher than expected in forensic populations, this does not appear to be associated with an increased rate of offending or convictions (Dein and Woodbury-

Smith, 2010) and overall individuals with ASD are probably not over-represented in the criminal justice system (King and Murphy, 2014). However, there is some evidence that there is an over-representation of adults with ASD in English High Secure Special Hospitals (Hare et al., 1999). There was a surprisingly low rate of recognition (less than one-fifth of cases) and in some cases a diagnoses had been made, only to be subsequently lost. Diagnosis of autism was recognised as being more difficult in female patients and there was often confusion with schizophrenia. The issue of a diagnostic gender bias is still unresolved (Rivet and Matson, 2011).

A systematic review of people with autism and the criminal justice system was undertaken (King and Murphy 2014), and overall the evidence for increased offending among autistic individuals was poor and complicated by comorbid conditions.

There has, however, been concern about the possible links between autism and particular types of offending in adults since the 1980s (Mawson et al., 1985; Baron-Cohen, 1988; and Tantam, 1988a). There have been a number of very high-profile cases involving young people with ASD that has raised issues around the relationship between autism and some types of serious offending (Freckelton, 2013a). Certain types of offences may raise the suspicion of ASD, particularly obsessive harassment (stalking), arson, sexual offences, inexplicable violence, computer crime and offences arising out of the misjudgement of social relationships (Berney, 2004; Freckelton, 2013a). Individuals with ASD are more likely to adopt either a consistently conforming or nonconforming strategy (Bowler and Worley, 1994) and lack adaptive flexibility. Comparisons between offenders admitted to a learning disability forensic hospital with and without autism demonstrated that autistic offenders were significantly less likely to have an obvious gain or appear overtly instrumental in their offences and less likely to involve drugs or alcohol (O'Brien and Bell, 2004).

BOX 15.3 Reasons for Offending and Types of Offending

The reasons for offending by individuals with autism have been modified for adolescents from earlier authors (Wing, 1997; Berney, 2004).

(1) Aggression resulting from the disruption of routines. This includes a lack of motivation to change or adapt behaviour.

(2) Crimes resulting from social naivety (including various types of sexual offending).

(3) Pursuit of a special interest, e.g. weapons, militaria, poisons, fire, sadistic interests.

(4) Experiences of bullying, teasing, rejection and a desire for revenge or retribution. This may lead to an assault on the perpetrator or displacement onto another, often completely innocent, person.

(5) Hostility towards family members (often parents) representing long-standing complex dynamics due to the dependency of the individual with autism.

(6) Sensory sensitivities leading to high levels of arousal and violent behaviour.

(7) Passively following the lead of a stronger personality and committing an offence under their direction. More commonly in adolescents this takes the form of wanting to maintain membership of an antisocial peer group and being prepared to do anything to achieve this. A 'cry for help', in which violence is seen as the only way to obtain appropriate intervention.

(8) A lack of awareness of wrongdoing, or an assumption that the individual's own needs supersede all other considerations.

(9) Deficits in empathy or lack of recognition of fearful emotions in others may lead to indifference to the wider consequences of actions on others.

(10) An inability to see the consequences of actions due to poor central coherence or executive function impairment.

(11) Comorbid mental illness, including affective and psychotic illness.

(12) Any combinations of the above.

Autistic symptoms have been positively associated with delinquent behaviour in childhood arrestees, even after adjustment for externalising disorders (Geluk et al., 2012) (see Box 15.3 for reasons for offending). In one US survey, youths with ASD had higher rates of crimes against persons and lower rates of crimes against property when compared to youth without ASD (Cheely et al., 2012). Families often bear the brunt of violence and disruptive behaviour in autistic young people, and often do so without reporting it to support agencies or the police (O'Brien and Bell, 2004).

There is some limited evidence that sexual offending is more common in juvenile cases in the Family Court system in Japan (Kumagami and Matsuura, 2009). Significantly higher levels of ASD symptoms were found in a Dutch study of juvenile sex offenders in comparison to healthy controls ('t Hart-Kerkhoffs et al., 2009). Relatively high rates of autism have been found in adolescents in the USA who have been convicted of sexual offences, who had previously been undiagnosed (Sutton et al., 2013).

There is increasing concern about adolescents accessing sexual material on the internet (McColgan and Giardino, 2005). Many young people with ASD are highly interested in and motivated by computers (Oberleitner and Laxminarayan, 2004) and can spend significant periods of time on the internet where they are exposed to sexual material. Unsurprisingly young people with ASD and other developmental disorders appear more vulnerable to misinterpreting sexual material and misapplying it in real life. They can fail to contextualise sexual behaviour, misinterpret behavioural cues and often have an impaired understanding of issues around consent and legality. The understanding of consent may be impaired (particularly around the subtle consent negotiations that precede sexual activity) due to difficulties that many autistic people have interpreting facial expression and body language cues (Clare and Woodbury-Smith, 2009). Individuals with autism can develop a range of paraphilias, (Kellaher, 2015) including sexual attraction to much younger children. Adolescents with histories of sexual offending frequently have significant deficits in sexual knowledge and understanding (please refer to Chapter 9 by Murphy, Ross and Hackett for further information). Studies of adolescents and young adults with ASD in community group homes have shown a significant need for interventions to address sexual development and behaviour (Hellemans et al., 2007). However, there are no standardised instruments to formally assess this in adolescents with autism, and currently the most appropriate options are resources developed for adults with learning disabilities (Dodd et al., 2007). Therefore young people with autism are at increased risk of exposure to a variety of harmful sexual experiences both in real life and, virtually, via material from the internet. Images and films or self-generated material (sexting) communicated via personal devices like mobile phones appear to be particularly difficult for parents or carers to regulate or control (Livingstone and Smith, 2014).

Adolescent transitions are particularly problematic for young people with ASD and in particular the transition from primary to secondary school (Dillon and Underwood, 2012). Unsuccessful transitions may precipitate significant de-compensation in young people, potentially leading to antisocial and offending behaviour. A relatively high-functioning adolescent with autism may cope with whole class teaching from a single teacher and a relatively stable peer group but may not be able to manage the combined stress of navigating a complex new environment with multiple teaching staff. They are also particularly vulnerable to bullying and manipulation by more able peers (Schroeder et al., 2014). This can lead to a variety of disruptive aggressive and antisocial behaviours including school refusal and truancy.

Sensory sensitivities can occur in a range of sensory modalities and are common features of autism (Bogdashina, 2003). Environmental stimuli can lead to an elevation in arousal and an increased likelihood of physical aggression (Mazurek et al., 2013). Subsequently, unusual and inexplicable offences perpetrated by adolescents with autism may have their roots in a previously unrecognised sensory issue.

The Importance of Comorbidities with ASD

ASD as a vulnerability factor for delinquent or criminal behaviour is increased by the presence of other comorbid disorders and social factors (Palermo, 2004; Långström et al., 2009). A number of researchers have shown that many of these developmental disorders, including those of academic attainment, tend to cluster together. A number of psychiatric, motor and behavioural dyscontrol syndromes are associated with ASD (Gillberg and Billstedt, 2000). ADHD and autism are common comorbidities with Tourette's disorder (Kadesjö and Gillberg, 2000). Children with ADHD and motor disorders are more likely to have severe ADHD-combined type and other neurodevelopmental and behavioural problems (Tervo et al., 2002). Children with Developmental Coordination Disorder (DCD), obtained significantly poorer scores on measures of attention and learning (reading, writing and spelling) than comparison children, and were found to have a relatively high level of social problems (Dewey et al., 2002). Sudden outbursts of rage and aggression are associated with increasing numbers of comorbid developmental disorders (Budman et al., 2000).

How these developmental disorders influence developing personality and behaviour is a complex and difficult question. Childhood-onset neuropsychiatric disorders including learning disability, ADHD and ASD form complex comorbid patterns with adult personality disorders including psychopathic traits, mood disorders and substance abuse and support the notion that childhood-onset social and behavioural problems form a highly relevant psychiatric symptom cluster in relation to pervasive adult violent behaviour (Vizard et al., 2004). Significant social impairment and hyperactivity can also be features of Foetal Alcohol Spectrum Disorder that is probably distinct from ASD (Gralton, 2014). It has been recognised for some time that children who become persistently antisocial have neuropsychological deficits particularly in verbal ability and executive function (Moffitt, 1993), and both these areas can be significantly adversely affected in individuals with autism (please refer to Chapter 5 by Hughes, Williams and Chitsabesan).

There is strong evidence for links between offending behaviour and ADHD (Lundström et al., 2014), and this comorbid disorder is a significantly greater risk factor than autism alone. Psychosis, comorbid substance misuse and psychotic illness have been found to be associated with serious offending with ASD (Langstrom et al., 2008, Newman and Ghaziuddin, 2008).

BOX 15.4 Management Approaches

For individuals with autism who come in contact with the criminal justice system it is important to recognise the potential impact of the disorder at various stages and bear in mind the effect of their disability including:

- Difficulties coping with unfamiliar environments including sensory issues
- Problems understanding subtext in communications, e.g. may be verbally fluent but not fully understand implications
- Slow speed of processing information
- Desire to say the right thing and conform to authority expectations
- Wish to terminate interactions including interviews
- Difficulties giving evidence and false confessions, e.g. suggestible,
- Belief that others are truthful; undue compliance with authority
- Confusion and panic under stress
- Getting over-detailed and losing sight of what is important; cannot hold key points in head and think in an organised structured way

There is also the issue of overlap between high-functioning autism and personality disorder (Tantam, 1988b). However callous unemotional traits do not appear to be related to severity of autism or to core cognitive deficits in adolescent boys with ASD. Although both adolescents with psychopathic traits and adolescents with autism can appear uncaring, the affective and information processing correlates of psychopathy and autism appear different (please refer to Chapter 16 by Johnstone for further information). Psychopathic tendencies are associated with difficulties in resonating with other people's distress, whereas autism is characterised by difficulties in knowing what other people think (Jones et al., 2010). It is also possible that individuals with high-functioning ASD are less able to recognise fear in others that might be a factor in some types of offending (Woodbury-Smith et al., 2005). Individuals without autism with conduct problems and high levels of callous-unemotional traits appear to show intact theory of mind but reduced affective reactivity to others' emotions (O'Nions et al., 2014). This may suggest that young people with autism who commit overtly callous and psychopathic acts may have additional deficits that are unrelated to their core autism (Rogers et al., 2006).

Individuals with ASD are at greater risk of experiencing abuse and sexual trauma (Sevlever et al., 2013). Neglect and abuse in this population is significantly correlated with later offending behaviour (Kawakami et al., 2012). Trauma can exacerbate pre-existing social impairment and arousal control in young people with autism and therefore has specific implications for forensic adolescent services (Gralton et al., 2008).

Regardless of the offence committed there is unfortunately rarely a single responsible factor. It is the unique combination of multiple impairments interacting with the environment that determines specific risk behaviour in a particular individual with autism (Murphy, 2010).

There is concern from the National Autistic Society that it is difficult to substantiate an increased risk from the current literature due to the small sample sizes of existing studies and consequently large-scale longitudinal prospective studies are required (Gomez de la Cuesta, 2010).

We believe that the issue of whether autism increases overall rates of offending is especially difficult to discern because autism is a spectrum disorder with a high degree of variability between individuals, with respect to specific strengths and disabilities. The measurement of offending (like conviction rates) can be significantly influenced by factors like policies for the diversion for individuals with developmental disorders in specific jurisdictions. The issue of autism and offending is therefore probably best examined ideographically, rather than nomothetically, due to this inherent heterogeneity.

These impairments will affect issues such as fitness to plead and criminal responsibility (*mens rea*) (Dein and Woodbury-Smith, 2010), containment in the secure estate and assessment for parole in a system that depends on insight, self-reflection and understanding of the perspectives of others (McKay, 2012) (see Box 15.4 for management approaches).

Young people with ASD have difficulty adjusting and coping in custodial environments where change can be rapid and without warning, environments noisy and rules unyielding. In custodial settings adolescents with ASD are even more vulnerable to bullying and exploitation by antisocial peers. They are more likely to spend significant periods in isolation or segregation (Cashin and Newman, 2009) and are at risk of engaging in self harm.

Therapeutic Strategies

An essential part of treatment is recognition of the disorder and the complex comorbidities that are frequently present. An offence that may appear 'motiveless' or 'psychopathic' may be explicable once the young person's disabilities are understood in the context of the environment where the offence occurred. Forensic services may struggle to adapt to the very individual needs of patients with autistic disorders, particularly around obsessional or sensory problems that affect day-to-day function (Murphy, 2010). Emotional dysregulation and rigidity of thinking may also influence how a young person with ASD presents and relates to staff within secure settings.

Any treatment programme needs to be adapted for each individual because of their unique patterns of strengths and deficits. In terms of day-to-day management the SPELL principles advocated by the National Autistic Society (Structure, a Positive approach, Empathy, Low arousal, and Links with other professionals) are helpful approaches (Murphy, 2010).

The recognition and treatment of comorbid mental illness (particularly affective and anxiety disorders) is important. Comorbid mental illness may be difficult to recognise in young people with pre-existing developmental disorders as a result of the phenomenon of diagnostic overshadowing (Gralton, 2011). The individual may require areas of skill building or education in specific areas around arousal control, sexual understanding and social skills training. Sometimes an obsessional interest in a high-risk area like weapons or poisons can be adopted and focused onto a less harmful interest.

Managing arousal is a key task for many young people with ASD, as chronic high levels of physiological arousal can lead to physical aggression (McDonnell et al., 2015). Strategies to teach arousal control using progressive muscular relaxation augmented by biofeedback or sensory tools can be helpful. Other strategies like the use of structured eastern traditions including Tai Chi, Mindfulness and Yoga can also prove useful (Spek et al., 2013).

Pharmacotherapy

There is very limited evidence for the effectiveness of any pharmacological intervention on core autistic behaviours of social communications and restricted repetitive interests. NICE guidance (2013; autism in children and YP support and management) states not to use the following interventions for the management of core features of autism in children and young people:

- antipsychotics;
- antidepressants;
- anticonvulsants;
- exclusion diets (such as gluten- or casein-free diets).

However, NICE (2013) makes a number of recommendations about recognising common co-existing conditions in the diagnosis and management of those with ASD including those affecting mental health, making modifications to the environment and processes of care, the assessment of risk and training to all professionals involved in the care of those with autism.

In any situation where there is challenging behaviour, NICE guidance (2013) recommends assessment of factors that may increase the risk of behaviour that challenges in routine assessment and care planning, including:

- impairments in communication that may result in difficulty understanding situations or in expressing needs and wishes;
- coexisting physical disorders, such as pain or gastrointestinal disorders;
- coexisting mental health problems such as anxiety or depression and other neurodevelopmental conditions such as ADHD;
- the physical environment, such as lighting and noise levels;
- the social environment, including home, school and leisure activities;
- changes to routines or personal circumstances;

- developmental change, including puberty;
- exploitation or abuse by others;
- inadvertent reinforcement of behaviour that challenges;
- the absence of predictability and structure.

Only when psychosocial or other interventions are insufficient or cannot be delivered because of the severity of the behaviour should pharmacological intervention be used. There is evidence for efficacy of antipsychotic medication in reducing challenging behaviour, but there are also significant side effects. Medication should be prescribed and monitored by a suitable specialist who should:

- identify the target behaviour;
- decide on an appropriate measure to monitor effectiveness, including frequency and severity of the behaviour and a measure of global impact;
- review the effectiveness and any side effects of the medication after three to four weeks;
- stop treatment if there is no indication of a clinically important response at six weeks;
- start with a low dose;
- use the minimum effective dose needed;
- regularly review the benefits of the antipsychotic medication and any adverse events;
- the proposed duration of treatment;
- plans for stopping treatment.

If any coexisting mental or behavioural or medical problems are identified, NICE recommends psychosocial and pharmacological interventions in line with NICE guidance for children and young people, including:

- Attention Deficit Hyperactivity Disorder (ADHD) (NICE clinical guideline 72);
- Conduct disorders in children and young people (NICE clinical guideline 158);
- Constipation in children and young people (NICE clinical guideline 99);
- Depression in children and young people (NICE clinical guideline 28);
- Epilepsy (NICE clinical guideline 137);
- Obsessive-Compulsive Disorder (OCD) and Body Dysmorphic Disorder (BDD) (NICE clinical guideline 31);
- Post-Traumatic Stress Disorder (PTSD) (NICE clinical guideline 26).

The efficacy and tolerability of risperidone and aripiprazole for the treatment of irritability in autism have been established in multisite, randomised, controlled trials. Studies supporting the use of other atypical antipsychotics are either limited in scope or less robust in their findings, though newer agents such as ziprasidone and paliperidone show promise (Politte and McDougle, 2014). Low-dose risperidone has shown to be effective in reducing arousal and aggression in children with ASD (Canitano and Scandurra, 2008), while aripiprazole has shown to be effective in reducing irritability (Marcus et al., 2009). Propranolol appears to improve social functioning in autistic adults (Beversdorf et al., 2014) possibly as a result of anxiety reduction. Benzodiazepines are likely to be less useful due to issues around tolerance and dependence with longer-term use.

Group offence-related work may not be possible in some individuals whose social impairment means they are unable to function in groups or maintain confidentiality. Seeking significant changes in empathy in autistic individuals may be unrealistic. Small gains in a range of life skills can make a significant difference overall to the young persons' ability to function in a structured supported setting in the community. Successful management approaches on return to the community should focus on environmental support in ensuring that issues like social skills deficits and sensory sensitivities are not exacerbated leading to de-compensation. Importantly, staff working with a young person with autism must understand the nature of long-term risk issues as well as exacerbating and environmental factors and avoid complacency.

For adolescent sexual offenders with autism, modifying the traditional treatment programmes to match their learning styles (e.g. using visual learning, modelling with practice and feedback) as well as restricting contact with neurotypical sexual offenders is recommended (Sutton et al., 2013). (Please refer to Chapter 9 by Murphy, Ross and Hackett for further information).

The case example provided (Box 15.5) highlights how assessment and management principles outlined within the chapter may be used in clinical practice.

Conclusions

Young people with ASD who offend are likely to be a complex group with comorbid developmental disorders, like ADHD as well as comorbid mental illness that may require a combination of treatment

---

BOX 15.5 Case Example

Background

Tom, a 14-year-old, boy was referred from a Secure Training Centre where he was on remand following an armed robbery on a community post office. Tom had entered the shop wearing a balaclava and wielding a knife but his distinctive gait and speech impairment had been immediately recognised by the shop assistant. When he was challenged Tom ran away but was apprehended at his foster parents' the same day. Tom had been in foster care for the previous two years after he suffered physical abuse at the hands of his stepfather. Tom had recently been permanently excluded from school following a series of incidents where he had become aggressive in break times, getting in fights with other students who were 'baiting' him. He had been noted by his teachers to have difficulty tolerating bell alarms and other loud noises in class. His foster parents reported that Tom ate a very restricted diet at home and would not allow different food groups to touch each other on his plate. They could not do the vacuuming at home without him becoming agitated and physically aggressive. Since his exclusion from school Tom had been associating with a group of more able older boys who were hanging around on the street in a gang. It had been the suggestion of one of these antisocial peers that he should rob the shop in order to get them cigarettes. Tom who had been desperate to become a member of the 'gang' had therefore complied.

Assessment

An ADI-R (Le Couteur et al., 2003) completed with Tom's biological mother was diagnostic for autism, and he was also above the threshold for autism on module 4 of the ADOS 1 (Lord et al., 1994). He was 'sensation avoiding' on the Adolescent Adult Sensory Profile (Brown and Dunn, 2002) particularly for auditory stimuli.

He had a wide range of skills deficits as assessed by the MOHOST (Parkinson et al., 2006) particularly around communication, interaction and social skills, and met criteria for Developmental Dyspraxia on the QNST II (Mutti et al., 1998). He has articulation problems and a significant pragmatic deficit on specific speech and language assessment using the CASL (Carrow-Woolfolk, 1999).

Formulation

Tom had a combination of an ASD and Developmental Dyspraxia and specific sensory sensitivities around noise. He had chronic high levels of anxiety and arousal that had been exacerbated by his exposure to developmental trauma from domestic violence. Tom was vulnerable to influence from more able peers, and his social impairment was significantly exacerbated by his pragmatic language deficits and gross and fine motor dyspraxia.

Management

Tom's chronic anxiety and arousal was treated with a combination of propranolol and relaxation training with biofeedback and a mindfulness programme. He had a vitamin D and iron deficiency which was treated with comprehensive multivitamin supplementation. He was also given specific psychoeducation around his diagnosis of autism. Tom had specific social skills training in a group setting augmented by a computer-based programme. He engaged in life story work around his trauma history. Tom had specific adapted offence–related work focusing on his vulnerability and the adverse consequences for him around reoffending. Specific speech and language therapy was used to focus on his articulation and pragmatic language deficits. He had a tailored physiotherapy programme to improve his dyspraxia, and environmental modifications were made to reduce his exposure to noise as well as using an MP3 player with relaxation music to reduce external auditory input. An occupational therapy programme was provided to improve a range of personal and life skills.

---

interventions. The pharmacological treatments for core ASD are currently limited. This population are a particularly challenging group to research as there are complex ethical issues and problems with parental consent, difficulties with control groups and a lack of appropriate specific tools and outcome measures.

The research basis on which to develop treatments for adolescents with developmental disorders with forensic needs has historically been limited (Hall, 2000), and much evidence for interventions is therefore still extrapolated from mainstream adolescent or adult developmentally disabled populations.

Currently, there is still no body of evidence to suppose that people, including adolescents with ASD are statistically more prone to commit offences than anyone else. However, a smaller number of serious crimes can be linked to the core features of ASD and comorbid psychiatric disorders are important risk factors for offending (Mouridsen, 2012).

It is essential to remember that every adolescent with ASD who has offended is unique and requires a comprehensive multidisciplinary assessment prior to planning treatment interventions. All children in secure settings should have a neurodisability assessment to screen for developmental conditions, including ASD (Royal College of Paediatrics and Child Health, 2013).

References

American Psychiatric Association. (2000). *Diagnostic and Statistical Manual of Mental Disorders*. 4th Edition. Text Revision (DSM-IV-TR). Washington, DC: American Psychiatric Association.

American Psychiatric Association. (2013). *Diagnostic and Statistical Manual of Mental Disorders*. 5th Edition. Arlington, VA: American Psychiatric Publishing.

Baird, G., Simonoff, E., Pickles, A., Chandler, S., Loucas, T., Meldrum, D., and Charman, T. (2006). Prevalence of disorders of the autism spectrum in a population cohort of children in South Tham10 = es: the Special Needs and Autism Project (SNAP). *Lancet*, **368**(9531): 210–215.

Baron-Cohen, S. (1988). An assessment of violence in a young man with Asperger's syndrome, *Journal of Child Psychology and Psychiatry*, **29**(3): 351–360.

Berney, T. (2004). Asperger syndrome from childhood into adulthood. *Advances in Psychiatric Treatment*, **10**(5): 341.

Beversdorf, D., Zamzow, R., Ferguson, B., Martin, T., Lewis, M., and Stichter, J. (2014). Predictors of response to propranolol for social functioning in autism spectrum disorder (I4-1.002). *Neurology*, **82**(10 Supplement): I4–1.

Bogdashina, O. (2003). Editor. *Sensory Perception Issues in Autism and Asperger Syndrome*. London: Jessica Kingsley.

Bowler, D. and Worley, K. (1994). Susceptibility to social influence in adults with Asperger's syndrome: a research note. *Journal of Child Psychology and Psychiatry*, **35**(4): 689–697.

Brown, C. and Dunn, W. (2002). *Adult/Adolescent Sensory Profile: User's Manual*. San Antonio, TX: Psychological Corporation.

Brugha, T. S., McManus, S., Bankart, J., Scott, F., Purdon, S., Smith, J., . . . Meltzer, H. (2011). Epidemiology of autism spectrum disorders in adults in the community in England. *Archives of General Psychiatry*, **68**(5), 459–466.

Budman, C., Bruun, R., Park, K., Lesser, M., and Olson, M. (2000). Explosive outbursts in children with Tourette's disorder. *Journal of American Academy of Child Adolescent Psychiatry*, **39**(10): 1270–1276.

Buescher, A. V. S., Cidav, Z., Knapp, M., and Mandell, D. S. (2014). Costs of autism spectrum disorders in the United Kingdom and the United States. *JAMA Pediatrics*, **168**(8): 721–728. doi: 10.1001/jamapediatrics.2014.210.

Canitano, R. and Scandurra, V. (2008). Risperidone in the treatment of behavioral disorders associated with autism in children and adolescents. *Neuropsychiatric Disease and Treatment*, **4**(4): 723–730.

Carrow-Woolfolk, E. (1999). *Comprehensive Assessment of Spoken Language*. Circle Pines, MN: American Guidance Service.

Cashin, A. and Newman, C. (2009). Autism in the criminal justice detention system: a review of the literature. *Journal of Forensic Nursing*, **5**(2): 70–75.

Centre for Disease Prevention (CDC). (2014). Prevalence of autism spectrum disorder among children aged 8 years – Autism and Developmental Disabilities monitoring network. 11 Sites. United States 2010 MMWR Surveillance Summaries. 63, 1–21.

Charman, T., Pickles, A., Simonoff, E., Chandler, S., Loucas, T., and Baird, G. (2011). IQ in children with autism spectrum disorders: data from the Special Needs and Autism Project (SNAP). *Psychological Medicine*, **41**(3): 619–627. doi: 10.1017/s0033291710000991.

Cheely, C. A., Carpenter, L. A., Letourneau, E. J., Nicholas, J. S., Charles, J., and King, L. B. (2012). The prevalence of youth with autism spectrum disorders in the criminal justice system. *Journal of Autism and Developmental Disorders*, **42**(9): 1856–1862.

Clare, I. C. H. and Woodbury-Smith, M. (2009). Chapter 5 Autism spectrum conditions. In Susan Young, Michael Kopelman, and Gisli Gudjonsson, Editors. *Forensic Neuropsychology in Practice* (pp. 109–134). Oxford: Oxford University Press.

Dein, K. and Woodbury-Smith, M. (2010). Asperger syndrome and criminal behaviour. *Advances in Psychiatric Treatment*, **16**(1): 37–43.

Dewey, D., Kaplan, B., Crawford, S. and Wilson, B. (2002). Developmental coordination disorder: associated problems in attention, learning, and psychosocial adjustment. *Human Movement Science*, **21**(5–6): 905–918.

Dillon, G. V. and Underwood, J. D. (2012). Parental perspectives of students with autism spectrum disorders transitioning from primary to secondary school in the United Kingdom. *Focus on Autism and Other Developmental Disabilities*, **27**(2): 111–121.

Dodd K., Jones K., Liddiard H., and Stroud J. (2007). *Exploring Sexual and Social Understanding*. Kidderminster: British Institute of Learning Disabilities, ISBN 1-905218-01-X.

Francis, A., Msall, M., Obringer, E., and Kelley, K. (2013). Children with autism spectrum disorder and epilepsy. *Pediatric Annals*, **42**(12), E264–E269. doi: 10.3928/00904481-20131122-10.

Freckelton, I. (2013a). Autism spectrum disorder: Forensic issues and challenges for mental health professionals and courts. *Journal of Applied Research in Intellectual Disabilities* 2013, **26**: 420–434.

Freckelton, I. (2013b). *Forensic Issues in Autism Spectrum Disorder: Learning from Court Decisions*. INTECH Open Access Publisher. Available from: http://dx.doi.org/10.5772/55400. Accessed 03 October 2016.

Geluk, C. A., Jansen, L., Vermeiren, R., Doreleijers, T. A., van Domburgh, L., de Bildt, A., . . . and Hartman, C. A. (2012). Autistic symptoms in childhood arrestees: longitudinal association with delinquent behavior. *Journal of Child Psychology and Psychiatry*, **53**(2): 160–167.

Gillberg, C. and Billstedt, E. (2000). Autism and Asperger syndrome: coexistence with other clinical disorders. *Acta Psychiatrica Scandinavica*, **102**(5): 321–330.

Gomez de la Cuesta, G. (2010). A selective review of offending behaviour in individuals with autism spectrum disorders. *Journal of Learning Disabilities and Offending Behaviour*, **1**(2): 47–58.

Gralton, E. (2011). Mental Illness in Adolescents with Developmental Disabilities Who Require Secure Care In Forensic Issues in Adolescents with Developmental Disabilities. Gralton, E. Editor. London: Jessica Kingsley.

Gralton, E. (2014). Foetal alcohol spectrum disorder-its relevance to forensic adolescent services. *Journal of Intellectual Disabilities and Offending Behaviour*, **5**(3): 124–137.

Hall, I. (2000). Young offenders with a learning disability. *Advances in Psychiatric Treatment*, **6** (4): 278.

Hare, D. J., Gould, J., Mills, R., and Wing, L. A. (1999). A preliminary study of individuals with autistic spectrum disorders in three special hospitals in England. Available from: http://nas.live.clearpeople.net/~/media/F6C03DB687454477AF51EC0285B11209.ashx. [Accessed 25 December 2010].

Hellemans, H., Colson, K., Verbraeken, C., Vermeiren, R., and Deboutte, D. (2007). Sexual behavior in high-functioning male adolescents and young adults with autism spectrum disorder. *Journal of Autism and Developmental Disorders*, **37**(2): 260–269.

Hofvander, B., Delorme, R., Chaste, P., Nyden, A., Wentz, E., Stahlberg, O., . . . Leboyer, M. (2009). Psychiatric and psychosocial problems in adults with normal-intelligence autism spectrum disorders. *BioMedical Central Psychiatry*, **9**. doi: 10.1186/1471-244x-9-35.

Jones, C. R. G., Happe, F., Golden, H., Marsden, A. J. S., Tregay, J., Simonoff, E., . . . Charman, T. (2009). Reading and arithmetic in adolescents with autism spectrum disorders: Peaks and dips in attainment. *Neuropsychology*, **23**(6): 718–728. doi: 10.1037/a0016360.

Jones, A. P., Happé, F. G., Gilbert, F., Burnett, S., and Viding, E. (2010). Feeling, caring, knowing: different types of empathy deficit in boys with psychopathic tendencies and autism spectrum disorder. *Journal of Child Psychology and Psychiatry*, **51**(11): 1188–1197.

Kadesjö, B. and Gillberg, C. (2000). Tourette's disorder: epidemiology and comorbidity in primary school children. *Journal of American Academy of Child Adolescent Psychiatry*, **39**(5): 548–555.

Kawakami, C., Ohnishi, M., Sugiyama, T., Someki, F., Nakamura, K., and Tsujii, M. (2012). The risk factors for criminal behaviour in high-functioning autism spectrum disorders (HFASDs): A comparison of childhood adversities between individuals with HFASDs who exhibit criminal behaviour and those with HFASD and no criminal histories. *Research in Autism Spectrum Disorders*, **6**(2): 949–957.

Kellaher, D. C. (2015). Sexual behavior and autism spectrum disorders: an update and discussion. *Current Psychiatry Reports*, **17**(4): 1–8.

Kim, Y. S., Leventhal, B. L., Koh, Y. J., Fombonne, E., Laska, E., Lim, E. C., . . . Grinker, R. R. (2011). Prevalence of autism spectrum disorders in a total population sample. *American Journal of Psychiatry*, **168** (9): 904–912. doi: 10.1176/appi.ajp.2011.10101532.

King, C. and Murphy, G. H. (2014). A systematic review of people with autism spectrum disorder and the criminal justice system. *Journal of Autism and Developmental Disorders*, **44**(11), 2717–2733.

Kumagami, T. and Matsuura, N. (2009). Prevalence of pervasive developmental disorder in juvenile court cases in Japan. *The Journal of Forensic Psychiatry & Psychology*, **20** (6): 974–987.

Lai, M. C., Lombardo, M. V., and Baron-Cohen, S. (2014). Autism. *Lancet*, **383**(9920): 896–910. doi: 10.1016/s0140-6736(13)61539-1.

Lai, M. C., Lombardo, M. V., Pasco, G., Ruigrok, A. N. V., Wheelwright, S. J., Sadek, S. A., . . . Consortium, M. A. (2011). A behavioral comparison of male and female adults with high functioning autism spectrum conditions. *Plos One*, **6**(6). doi: 10.1371/journal.pone.0020835.

Långström, N., Grann, M., Ruchkin, V., Sjöstedt, G., and Fazel, S. (2008). Risk factors for violent offending in autism spectrum disorder: a national study of hospitalized individuals, *Journal of Interpersonal Violence*, **24**(8): 1358–1370.

Le Couteur, A., Lord, C., & Rutter, M. (2003). The autism diagnostic interview-revised (ADI-R). Los Angeles, CA: Western Psychological Services.

Leekam, S. R., Libby, S. J., Wing, L., Gould, J., and Taylor, C. (2002). The diagnostic interview for social and communication disorders: algorithms for ICD-10 childhood autism and wing and Gould autistic spectrum disorder. *Journal of Child Psychology and Psychiatry and Allied Disciplines*, **43**(3): 327–342. doi: 10.1111/1469-7610.00024.

Livingstone, S. and Smith, P. K. (2014). Annual research review: harms experienced by child users of online and mobile technologies: the nature, prevalence and management of sexual and aggressive risks in the digital age. *Journal of Child Psychology and Psychiatry*, **55**(6): 635–654.

Lombardo, M. V., Chakrabarti, B., Bullmore, E. T., Baron-Cohen, S., and Consortium, M. A. (2011). Specialization of right temporo-parietal junction for mentalizing and its relation to social impairments in autism. *Neuroimage*, **56** (3): 1832–1838. doi: 10.1016/j.neuroimage.2011.02.067.

Lord, C., Petkova, E., Hus, V., Gan, W. J., Lu, F. H., Martin, D. M., . . . Risi, S. (2012). A multisite study of the clinical diagnosis of different autism spectrum disorders. *Archives of General Psychiatry*, **69**(3): 306–313. doi: 10.1001/archgenpsychiatry.2011.148.

Lord, C., Risi, S., Lambrecht, L., Cook, E. H., Leventhal, B. L., DiLavore, P. C., Pickles, A., and Rutter, M. (2000). The autism diagnostic observation schedule – generic: a standard measure of social and communication deficits associated with the spectrum of autism. *Journal of Autism and Developmental Disorders*, **30** (3): 205–223.

Lord, C., Rutter, M., and Le, C. (1994). Autism diagnostic interview-revised: a revised version of a diagnostic interview for caregivers of individuals with possible pervasive developmental disorders. *Journal of Autism and Developmental Disorders*, **24**(5): 659–685.

Lundström, S., Forsman, M., Larsson, H., Kerekes, N., Serlachius, E., Långström, N., and Lichtenstein, P. (2014). Childhood neurodevelopmental disorders and violent criminality: a sibling control study. *Journal of Autism and Developmental Disorders*, **44**(11): 2707–2716.

Marcus, R. N., Owen, R., Kamen, L., Manos, G., McQuade, R. D., Carson, W. H., and Aman, M. G. (2009). A placebo-controlled, fixed-dose study of aripiprazole in children and adolescents with irritability associated with autistic disorder. *Journal of the American Academy of Child & Adolescent Psychiatry*, **48**(11): 1110–1119.

Mawson, D., Grounds, A., and Tantam, D., (1985). Violence and Asperger's syndrome: a case study. *British Journal of Psychiatry*, **147**: 566–569.

Mazefsky, C. A., and Oswald, D. P. (2006). The discriminative ability and diagnostic utility of the ADOS-G, ADI-R, and GARS for children in a clinical setting. *Autism*, **10**(6): 533–549.

Mazurek, M. O., Kanne, S. M., and Wodka, E. L. (2013). Physical aggression in children and adolescents with autism spectrum disorders. *Research in Autism Spectrum Disorders*, **7**(3): 455–465.

McColgan, M. and Giardino, A. (2005). Internet poses multiple risks to children and adolescents. *Pediatric Annals*, **34**(5): 405–414.

McDonnell, A., McCreadie, M., Mills, R., Deveau, R., Anker, R., and Hayden, J. (2015). The role of physiological arousal in the management of challenging behaviours in individuals with autistic spectrum disorders. *Research in Developmental Disabilities*, **36**: 311–322.

McKay, T. (2012). Criminal and Forensic Issues in Autistic Spectrum Disorders. Conference Paper Presented at the National Autistic Society's Professional Conference, 'Working together for better outcomes'. Manchester Central Convention Complex, 28–29 February 2012. National Autistic Society. UK.

Moffitt, T. (1993). Adolescence-limited and life-course-persistent antisocial behavior: a developmental taxonomy. *Psychological Review*, **100**(4): 674–701.

Mouridsen, S. E. (2012). Current status of research on autism spectrum disorders and offending. *Research in Autism Spectrum Disorders*, **6**(1): 79–86.

Murdoch, J. D. and State, M. W. (2013). Recent developments in the genetics of autism spectrum disorders. *Current Opinion in Genetics & Development*, **23**(3): 310–315. doi: 10.1016/j.gde.2013.02.003.

Murphy, D. (2010). Understanding offenders with autism-spectrum disorders: what can forensic services do? *Advances in Psychiatric Treatment*, **16**(1): 44–46.

Mutti, M., Sterling, H. M., Norma, V., and Salding, J. (1998). *Quick Neurological Screening Test Revised*. Michigan: Ann Arbor Publishers.

National Institute for Health and Care Excellence (NICE). (2011). *Recognition, Referral and Diagnosis of Children and Young People on the Autism Spectrum* (Clinical Guideline 128). London, UK: NICE.

National Institute for Health and Care Excellence (NICE). (2013). *Autism: The Management and Support of Children and Young People on the Autism Spectrum* (Clinical Guideline 170). London, UK: NICE.

Newman, S. S. and Ghaziuddin, M. (2008). Violent crime in Asperger syndrome: the role of psychiatric comorbidity. *Journal of Autism and Developmental Disorders*, **38**(10), 1848–1852.

O'Brien, G. and Bell, G. (2004). Learning disability autism and offending behaviour. In Bailey, S. and Dolan M. Editors. *Adolescent Forensic Psychiatry* (pp. 144–150). London: Arnold.

O'Nions, E., Sebastian, C. L., McCrory, E., Chantiluke, K., Happé, F., and Viding, E. (2014). Neural bases of theory of mind in children with autism spectrum disorders and children with conduct problems and callous-unemotional traits. *Developmental Science*, **17**(5): 786–796.

Oberleitner, R. and Laxminarayan, S. (2004). Information technology and behavioral medicine: impact on autism treatment & research. *Studies in Healthcare Technology and Informatics*, 103: 215–222.

Palermo, M. (2004). Pervasive developmental disorders, psychiatric comorbidities, and the law. *International Journal of Offender Therapy and Comparative Criminology*, 48(1): 40–48.

Parkinson, S., Forsyth, K., and Kielhofner, G. (2006). *The Model of Human Occupation Screening Tool (MOHOST) Version 2.0*. Chicago: Model of Human Occupation Clearinghouse, The University of Illinois.

Politte, L. C., and McDougle, C. J. (2014). Atypical antipsychotics in the treatment of children and adolescents with pervasive developmental disorders. *Psychopharmacology*, 231(6): 1023–1036.

Rivet, T. T. and Matson, J. L. (2011). Review of gender differences in core symptomatology in autism spectrum disorders. *Research in Autism Spectrum Disorders*, 5(3): 957–976.

Rogers, J., Viding, E., Blair, R., Frith, U., and Happé, F. (2006). Autism spectrum disorder and psychopathy: shared cognitive underpinnings or double hit? *Psychological Medicine*, 36(12): 1789–1798.

Royal College of Paediatrics and Child Health. (2013). Healthcare Standards for Young People in Secure Settings 2013 London. Available from: www.rcgp.org.uk/~/media/F iles/CIRC/Child-and-Adolescent-Health/RCGP-Healthcare-Standards-Secure-Settings-Report-June-13 .ashx [Accessed 22 May 2015].

Rutter, M. (2009). Commentary: Fact and artefact in the secular increase in the rate of autism. *International Journal of Epidemiology*, 38(5): 1238–1239. doi: 10.1093/ije/dyp257.

Rutter, M., LeCouteur, A., and Lord, C. (2003). *The Autism Diagnostic Interview-Revised (ADI-R)*. Los Angeles, CA: Western Psychological Services.

Schroeder, J. H., Cappadocia, M. C., Bebko, J. M., Pepler, D. J., and Weiss, J. A. (2014). Shedding light on a pervasive problem: A review of research on bullying experiences among children with autism spectrum disorders. *Journal of Autism and Developmental Disorders*, 44(7): 1520–1534.

Sevlever, M., Roth, M. E., and Gillis, J. M. (2013). Sexual abuse and offending in autism spectrum disorders. *Sexuality and Disability*, 31(2): 189–200.

Simonoff, E., Pickles, A., Charman, T., Chandler, S., Loucas, T., and Baird, G. (2008). Psychiatric disorders in children with autism spectrum disorders: Prevalence, comorbidity, and associated factors in a population-derived sample. *Journal of the American Academy of Child and Adolescent Psychiatry*, 47(8): 921–929. doi: 10.1097/CHI.0b013e318179964 f.

Skuse, D., Warrington, R., Bishop, D., Chowdhury, U., Lau, J., Mandy, W., and Place, M. (2004). The developmental, dimensional and diagnostic interview (3di): A novel computerized assessment for autism spectrum disorders. *Journal of the American Academy of Child and Adolescent Psychiatry*, 43(5): 548–558. doi: 10.1097/00004583-200405000-00008.

Spek, A. A., van Ham, N. C., and Nyklíček, I. (2013). Mindfulness-based therapy in adults with an autism spectrum disorder: a randomized controlled trial. *Research in Developmental Disabilities*, 34(1): 246–253.

State, M.W. and Levitt, P. (2011). The conundrums of understanding genetic risks for autism spectrum disorders. *Nature Neuroscience*. 30 October 2011; 14(12): 1499–1506.

Sutton, L. R., Hughes, T. L., Huang, A., Lehman, C., Paserba, D., Talkington, V., . . . and Marshall, S. (2013). Identifying individuals with autism in a state facility for adolescents adjudicated as sexual offenders a pilot study. *Focus on Autism and Other Developmental Disabilities*, 28 (3): 175–183.

't Hart-Kerkhoffs, L. A., Jansen, L. M., Doreleijers, T. A., Vermeiren, R., Minderaa, R. B., and Hartman, C. A. (2009). Autism spectrum disorder symptoms in juvenile suspects of sex offenses. *The Journal of Clinical Psychiatry*, 70(2): 266–272.

Tantam, D. (1988a). Lifelong eccentricity and social isolation. I. Psychiatric, social, and forensic aspects. *British Journal of Psychiatry*, 153(6): 777–782.

Tantam, D. (1988b). Lifelong eccentricity and social isolation. II: Asperger's syndrome or schizoid personality disorder? *British Journal of Psychiatry*, 783–791.

Tervo, R., Azuma, S., Fogas, B., and Fiechtner, H. (2002) Children with ADHD and motor dysfunction compared with children with ADHD only. *Developmental Medicine and Child Neurology*, 44(6): 383–390.

Tiffin, P., Shah, P., and le Couteur, A. (2007). Diagnosing pervasive developmental disorders in a forensic adolescent mental health setting. *British Journal of Forensic Practice*, 9 (3): 31–40.

Vizard, E., French, L., Hickey, N., and Bladon, E. (2004). Severe personality disorder emerging in childhood: a proposal for a new developmental disorder. *Criminal Behaviour and Mental Health*, 14(1): 17–28.

Wing, L. (1997). Asperger's Syndrome: management requires diagnosis. *Journal of Forensic Psychiatry & Psychology*, 8(2): 253–257.

Wing, L., Leekam, S., Libby, S., Gould, J., and Larcombe, M. (2002). The diagnostic interview for social and communication disorders: background, inter-rater reliability and clinical use. *Journal of Child Psychology and Psychiatry*, **43**(3): 307–325.

Woodbury-Smith, M., Clare, I., Holland, A., Kearns, A., Staufenberg, E., and Watson, P. (2005). A case-control study of offenders with high functioning autistic spectrum disorders. *Journal of Forensic Psychiatry & Psychology*, **16**(4): 747–763.

World Health Organisation. (1992). *The ICD-10 Classification of Mental and Behavioural Disorders: Clinical Descriptions and Diagnostic Guidelines*. Geneva, Switzerland: World Health Organisation.

Youth Psychopathy: a Developmental Perspective

Lorraine Johnstone

Introduction

One of the most abhorrent events to confront any civilised society is an act of seemingly gratuitous violence perpetrated by a child. The names Jamie Bulger, Columbine, Brian Blackwell, Daniel Bartlam, Elliot Turner and Will Cornick require no explanation. The media frenzy in the wake of such incidents might lead one to conclude that serious violence by a child is among the rarest of the rare events. This is not so. All forms of violence – sexual, stalking, interpersonal, extremism, familial and intimate partner can manifest in children just as it does in adults. Indeed, according to the World Health Organization, youth homicide is responsible for 42% of premature deaths (Krug et al., 2002). A long tradition of research has consistently shown a range of factors underpin youth violence. These are complex, varied and fall across the individual, familial, parenting, school, individual and community domains (Borum et al., 2003). The focus of this chapter is on one particular variable: 'psychopathy'.

Modern conceptualisations of the construct of psychopathy owe much to the early work of Hervey Cleckley. In 1941, he published his seminal works in which he described the hallmarks of this disorder. The foundations were therefore set for considerable evolution in the knowledge base. Psychopathy is considered to be a severe form of personality dysfunction characterised by a unique cluster of traits. Interpersonally, the psychopath can be a highly engaging and entertaining conversationalist but, when examined closely, it is apparent that they are both glib and superficial. They can also show a remarkable, almost palpable, omnipotence: grandiosity is a defining trait. Psychopaths also show a proclivity to deception. They are remarkably adept at manipulating and deceiving other people. They are master manipulators utilising their false affect for their own ends. Emotionally, they are shallow, cold and callous, and harm and exploit others without compunction, and behaviourally, they are impulsive, irresponsible, have poor behavioural controls and have an unusual need for stimulation and proneness to boredom. They are unable or unwilling to accept responsibility for their actions, and they are poorly regulated whereby their behavioural controls are limited.

Building on Cleckley's early and astute clinical observations, Robert Hare and his colleagues went on to pioneer several decades of research. Their work has provided an important framework for understanding this disorder by making available a commonly used measurement tool known as the Psychopathy Checklist Revised(PCL-R) (1991, 2003). The PCL-R is a 20-item rating scale completed by an expert rater on the basis of a multimodal, multi-informant data set. Cut-off scores are used to categorise the individual in terms of their level of psychopathy and these numbers have been used to group offenders into psychopathic and non-psychopathic groups.

Since the advent of the PCL-R, a voluminous body of research has been published which underscores the utility of this disorder. Findings converge to reveal that psychopathy, as it is conceptualised in the PCL-R, affects less than 1% of the population but around 15–25% in criminal justice populations, and the association between scores on the PCL-R and antisocial behaviour is well-established. Psychopathy predicts violence (Salekin et al., 1996; Hart, 1998; Hemphill et al., 1998), substance use (Hemphill et al., 1994), institutional misconduct (Hobson et al., 2000) and poor treatment responsivity (Seto and Barbaree, 1999; Salekin, 2002; Skeem et al., 2003). Such has been the influence of this work that PCL-R scores have been used in some jurisdictions to determine different legal disposals and access to treatment and rehabilitation. Notwithstanding, influential theorists and experts take the view that these outcomes are consequential to the core disorder (See Skeem and Cooke, 2007 for a discussion) and concerns have been expressed whereby it has been argued that the PCL-R conflates the clinical construct of psychopathy with criminality and therefore results in a tautological reasoning process. In response to this, Cooke and his colleagues have developed an alternative, arguably purer, method of conceptualising psychopathy. The Comprehensive Assessment of Psychopathic Personality Disorder (CAPP) presents a hierarchical conceptual model of psychopathy with six different dimensions: attachment, behavioural, cognitive, dominance, emotional, and self-styles of functioning. As well as being an attempt to encapsulate the 'clinical' construct, the CAPP is also able to capture change. This model provides a sophisticated conceptualisation of psychopathy and, whilst still in its early stages of validation, has been welcomed as an important contribution to the field, and an international body of research is beginning to support this approach as a viable way forward.

Whilst psychopathy is a construct most commonly applied to the adult field, it has been widely acknowledged by both early commentators such as Cleckley (1941) and Karpman (1948) and contemporary theorists that 'child psychopathy' is a viable construct. Indeed, Hare stated, 'Psychopathy does not suddenly spring, unannounced, into existence in adulthood. The precursors . . . first reveal themselves early in life' (Hare, 1993: 191). Given the importance of the research literature coupled with the prospect of early intervention and prevention, it is unsurprising that the construct of psychopathy has found its way into the parlance of practitioners working with young offenders. There is no shortage of cases which illustrate

how and why 'youth psychopathy' may be accepted as the most likely hypothesis. Two such examples are presented below (see Boxes 16.1 and 16.2).

But is 'Psychopathy' Really the Best Fit for Understanding these Types of Youth Violence?

Benjamin and Colleen certainly resemble psychopathy. But, the construct of youth psychopathy is controversial, a position not *de novo*. It has been argued before, and by several authors, that the importation of ad hoc models of adult psychopathology into children is replete with challenges from both a developmental and empirical perspective (Johnstone and Cooke, 2004). Despite early calls for the need to establish the construct as a coherent syndrome and thereafter the testing of relevant causal processes, the extant literature has continued to focus on establishing the nomological net with regard to models mirroring Hare's conceptualisations of psychopathy. In order to illustrate the position, the key issues are restated particularly with regard to the 'developmentalists' dilemmas' (Richters, 1997) that remain to be resolved and at the outset, it can be stated that little progress has been made. Thus, as the discussion unfolds, it will be clear as to why some may take the view that psychopathy is a construct that should *never* be applied to youth (Ells, 2005). Nonetheless, it is argued herein that, in the real-world

---

BOX 16.1 Case Example 1: Benjamin

Benjamin has been found guilty of raping his sister, sodomising his six-year-old nephew, beating his father and stabbing his mother. These offences are the most recent in a long list of severe behavioural disturbances that began in toddlerhood. He was aggressive in nursery and his conduct problems in primary school were excessive. He was excluded regularly. He is now aged 14 years and has been arrested by police for over 90 offences involving fire setting, gang fighting, assault and robbery, theft, shoplifting and supplying drugs to school children. In the last year, his violence diversified with the focus moving from peer-related fighting to family-based violence. As a result, his sister went to live with her grandparents and it was at a family gathering at Christmas that he assaulted his nephew when out for a walk with him, and, on his return, isolated his sister and raped her. When challenged by his uncle and father, he assaulted his dad causing him to suffer a broken wrist and pneumothorax. When Benjamin's mother tried to intervene, he stabbed her in the shoulder. Several months later, Benjamin remains in secure care. He is boastful about his actions, describes his family as 'pathetic' and claims they have made 'a mountain from a molehill'. Benjamin has been extensively assessed by child and adolescent mental health services. He does not suffer from Attention Deficit Hyperactivity Disorder, although his impulsivity is of note. He is not on the Autistic Spectrum, although he lacks empathy and remorse. His neurological functioning is normal and he has a high level of intellect (Full-Scale IQ = 123). He is described as 'very articulate' with a knack of explaining-away his behaviour in a highly plausible and convincing manner. He is a gifted artist, a talented sportsman, and his care-staff describe him as a 'loveable rogue' who is both witty and charming.

BOX 16.2 Case Example 2: Colleen

Colleen has been convicted of murder. She has just turned 16 years of age. In her local community, she was known as the 'Pied Piperette' because of her ability to influence others to follow her. Her victim was a 38 -year-old learning-disabled man. He was well known in the local village. He was provided with support from local residents following the death of his mother who had prided herself in having cared for him without the assistance of agencies: friends and neighbours wished to continue her legacy. After moving into a residential children's unit nearby, Colleen and a group of age-related peers started to 'visit' their victim. They used his house for parties, took his benefits and food and plied him with alcohol. The victim was not willing (or able) to follow advice from anyone or agencies as he saw Colleen and her peers as 'his friends'. Before formal procedures could be implemented, Colleen arranged via social media to host a party at his house. A group of youths arrived and took over the premises for three full days. As the crowds dwindled and time passed, Colleen began to tease and taunt her victim encouraging her peers to join in. After a prolonged, severe and unusually brutal attack, her victim was killed as a result of multiple wounds. There was evidence of sexual assault and the victim's body was found in the bath after being set alight. Colleen has a long history of trauma and distress. She was a Looked After and Accommodated Child. She was in foster care for 12 years. Throughout that time, she had long-standing oppositional and conduct disorder problems. Aggression was a particular problem: she would harm and kill family pets. She also self-harmed but this was superficial although she claimed suicidal intent – often quite dramatically. Her carers were very attached to her but despite their best attempts could not elicit a reciprocal bond. Her placement ended when she made an allegation of ritualistic and sadistic sexual abuse against her foster father; her method of disclosure was also via social media. Colleen's allegations were investigated and adjudged to be fantastical. Some years later, after learning that her foster mother had suffered a stroke, Colleen admitted that she had created this story for attention and laughingly acknowledged that her foster carers had been 'nothing but nice' to her.

setting, when it comes to understanding and managing youth who commit serious crimes and who resemble adult psychopaths, an *either-or* position is likely to be both futile and limiting. Similarly, it is recognised that it is simply impractical to await what, in fact, may actually be unachievable; that is unequivocal conceptual clarity, absolute precision in measurement processes and unquestionable and irrefutable causal processes to explain the phenomenon of psychopathic traits in children and young people. Eager to avoid a polarised view, a pragmatic approach is proposed here. The penultimate section of this chapter argues that to make sense of psychopathic-like traits in youth, formulation is an essential part of understanding the possible trajectories that result in a developmental process with psychopathy as its outcome. Formulation is presented as the most viable method of reaching an individualised, meaningful and relevant understanding of the individual youth; the chapter concludes with some practice principles that should guide the use of the construct to youth whilst models become refined and validity research accrues.

'Youth psychopathy: forensic and developmental perspectives' expanding on the work of Hare, there now exists several protocols purporting to provide a method assessing 'youth psychopathy' including: the Youth Psychopathy Inventory (YPI) (Andershed et al., 2002); the Child Psychopathy Scale (CPS) (Lynam, 1997); the Psychopathy Checklist Youth Version (PCL:YV) (Forth et al., 2003), the Antisocial Processes Screening Device (APSD) (Frick and Hare, 2001) and the Comprehensive Assessment of Psychopathic Personality, Youth Version (CAPP). Two of these protocols – the PCL:YV and APSD – have been subject to the most empirical research, are commercially available and are marketed for use in applied settings, and research using the CAPP is beginning to emerge. As such, the focus of the discussion is confined to these three approaches.

The PCL:YV, APSD and CAPP

Modelled on the PCL-R, the PCL:YV was developed to provide a standardised and systematic method of assessing psychopathic-like traits in youth, male and female, ranging in age from 12 to 17 years. The content was adapted to capture developmentally appropriate symptoms of psychopathy. The PCL:YV follows the same assessment format but no explicit cut-off score is recommended; the relevance of scores is considered according to which percentile they belong and clinical inferences drawn from that basis. In other words, it is permissible to express the assessment results as follows: 'John's score on the PCL:YV places him in the top 10th percentile for psychopathic traits. Expressed differently, out of 100 of his peers, only 10 would be more psychopathic than him.' Factor analysis has revealed a structure that parallels that which is found in adults with respect to the three- or four-factor model, reliability and item homogeneity (e.g. Forth et al., 2003; Salekin et al., 2006).

Also modelled on the PCL-R, the APSD was developed to assess psychopathic-like traits in youth ranging from 6 to 13 years. The APSD is a 20-item rating scale with parallel versions for parents, teachers and self-report. Like the PCL:YV, no explicit cut-off score has been proposed and a range of different approaches including (i) categorising groups above and below a specific cut-off score, (ii) grouping children in terms of whether they scored above or below the mean and (iii) using the upper quartile measures of Callous–Unemotional (CU) traits, have been used to identify children 'high' versus 'low' on psychopathic-like traits. However, the manual suggests using T-scores and percentiles to assist in understanding the level of psychopathic-like traits in the child. As with the PCL:YV, research using the APSD has resulted in data confirming a three-factor model that is, a Narcissism (Nar) subscale (seven items), Impulsivity (I/CP) subscale (five items) and Callous-Unemotional (CU) subscale (six items), and these factors have been taken to represent the interpersonal, socially deviant and emotional features of the disorder, the term 'CU traits' is used to categorise those children who most closely resemble the adult psychopath with respect to their lack of empathy and remorse being defining features.

The CAPP model has also been extended downwards and Corrado and colleagues have been using the protocol with youth since 2005. It follows the same scoring procedure as the adult version.

Evidencing the 'Forensic' Nomological Net

For the forensic practitioner, the utility of these models will be adjudged against whether or not there is evidence of the nomological net. On that basis, some would conclude that there are grounds for optimism. Considering the PCL:YV, a sizeable literature exists which shows key points of convergence with the adult field. Put briefly, the factor structure is similar; the PCL:YV identifies a discrete subgroup of delinquent youth (while most young offenders meet diagnostic criteria for conduct disorder, only a small proportion will show significant psychopathic-like traits: estimates range from 20 to 30% for institutionalised offenders and 10% for those on probation); and on some studies, the PCL-YV has shown predictive validity across a range of variables including criminal and violent recidivism – a finding that has held even when subject to meta-analysis (Edens et al., 2007) – institutional misconduct (Edens and Campbell, 2007), substance misuse problems (Corrado et al., 2004; Murrie et al., 2004), personality disorders (Myers et al., 1995). Similar to the adult field, research has also found a negative correlation between PCL:YV total scores and anxiety and depression in adolescent offenders (Salekin et al., 2005).

The presence of CU traits as identified by the APSD has been shown to identify a discrete group of conduct-disordered children. CU traits have been found to predict more severe conduct problems (Christian et al., 1997; Moran et al., 2008, 2009; McMahon et al., 2010), the use of both reactive and proactive aggression (Fanti et al., 2009), number of sexual offence victims, level of violence and sexual offence planning among detained adolescents (Lawing et al., 2010), and substance use (Wymbs et al., 2012).

Considering etiology, whilst there is no definitive theory accounting for the development of CU traits, as with adults, the research suggests a biological basis to the disorder. It has been argued that children who develop CU traits have unique neural mechanisms characterised by low cortisol and under arousal. This is thought to result in a distinct temperamental style which has a reward dominant orientation, low emotional reactivity to aversive stimuli, low fearfulness to threatening or novel stimuli, a poor responsiveness to cues to punishment and impaired ability to attend to attachment figures (Frick and Ellis, 1999; Frick et al., 2003; Hawes et al., 2009; Frick et al., 2014) leading Frick and others (e.g. Wotton et al., 1997; Frick et al., 2003) to theorise that this type of temperament could render the child relatively immune from the effects of parental socialisation thus underscoring the biological basis of the disorder.

Research using the CAPP model in youth has also shown parallels with the adult field. Clercx and colleagues reported good content validity (Clercx et al., 2012) and case-study analysis has also indicated that it enables a broader and more in-depth analysis of personality functioning (Dawson et al., 2012). The model has also been viewed as having considerable utility in terms of improving knowledge regarding the specificity of causal mechanisms underlying chronic, serious and violent offending (Corrado et al., 2015).

In sum, there is an emerging research base showing the presence of a coherent syndrome, reliability, construct validity and evidence of a diathesis and associations with fundamental abnormalities of a psychological or biological nature. Such has been the strength of these findings that CU traits are now included as a diagnostic specifier for conduct disorder in the Diagnostic and Statistical Manual of Mental Disorders, fifth edition (American Psychiatric Associaiton, 2013). Notwithstanding, closer inspection of the literature reveals significant areas of divergence from the adult field. These are summarised below.

Exceptions to the 'Forensic' Nomological Net

Considering the PCL:YV, effect sizes demonstrating an association between psychopathy scores and both general and violent recidivism in the research have been markedly smaller to those observed in adults, and some of the variability was accounted for by ethnicity and gender (Edens and Campbell, 2007). Furthermore, using a different methodology (i.e. longitudinal research), Edens and Cahill reported that, over a 10-year period, PCL:YV scores did not predict violent reconvictions (Edens and Cahill, 2007). Similarly, the strength of the association between the PCL:YV and institutional misconduct was small, unlike the results reported for adults. Furthermore, some research has produced contradictory results. For example, Schmidt et al. (2006) reported that scores on the PCL:YV demonstrated a positive association with axis one disorders, a finding not observed in the adult literature.

Exploring the APSD, a number of significant concerns have been noted. As Johnstone and Cooke (2004) observed, the actual structural properties of the APSD remain unclear. Notwithstanding the three-factor model, it is not immediately apparent which label maps to which trait, and the items load in a different way. 'Emotions seem shallow', which is a core symptom of psychopathy, loads on the affective factor in adolescents and in adults is associated with

Narcissism in the three-factor model of the APSD. In addition, the pathological nature of some of the items, for example 'Is concerned about school-work', and 'Keeps the same friends', are highly questionable and with respect to inter-rater reliability, some studies have reported low ratings even between raters in the same settings (Blair et al., 2001). Perhaps more fundamentally, as research has been progressed in an attempt to establish the PCL-R construct in youth, the credibility of Hare's model has been subject to serious criticism. It is beyond the scope of this chapter to discuss this issue extensively, but as indicated above, a key theme relates to the fact that the scales have been criticised for their over-reliance on criminality (Skeem and Cooke, 2007). Whilst this may not initially seem a serious concern – it most certainly is. Because it is possible to reach diagnostic threshold by only showing primarily behavioural features – not the core components of the disorder per se it is possible that the scores are contributing to misdiagnosis. This tautological reasoning leads to a phenomenon referred to as 'criterion contamination' whereby predictor and outcome variables overlap and are inflating (Vincent and Hart, 2002). In addition, when the stability of different dimensions of functioning is tracked across time, behavioural features show less stability (Lynam and Gudonis, 2005). Thus, any diagnosis or decision based primarily on behaviour may not, in fact, be reliable.

A further source of error is rater-bias. Adversarial allegiance was found to be present in a statewide sample of sexually violent predator evaluations (Boccaccini et al., 2008) and in another study, individual differences in the rater's personality were relevant to scores (Miller et al., 2011). This is associated with fears that the term 'psychopathy' might result in more punitive sanctions, limit access to treatment and other interventions and ultimately function in a more prejudicial than probative manner. The relevance of these concerns cannot be understated. Where the death penalty or full life-sentences are influenced by a score on the PCL-R, one or two point differences *really* start to count. Edens and colleagues found that mock jurors in the USA who perceived an accused as having psychopathy were more likely to vote for the death penalty than when the offender appeared less psychopathic (see Petrilla and Skeem, 2003; Edens et al., 2005; Jones and Cauffman, 2008). Alongside these concerns, the predictive validity with respect to violence and criminality may not, in fact, be as strong as once thought. Finally, other associated and very serious concerns relating to attempts to undermine the peer-review process by suppressing publications that challenge the construct have been raised (see Poythress and Petrilla, 2010). Thus, whilst the PCL-R derived models have given a template for extending the disorder into youth, this approach has not been without serious controversy. Furthermore, these conceptual and measurement concerns reflect a rather narrow lens of analysis. The 'developmentalists' remain to be convinced; this is the focus of the next section.

Developmental Dilemmas on Youth Psychopathy

Nearly two decades ago, Richters (1997) explained that for any psychopathological construct to be valid at the developmental level, key issues need to be resolved. These include:

- *Change and Stability*. The extent to which an individual's personality functioning as measured at any point in time is deterministic of their future is questionable. This is particularly so when it comes to adolescents. This is a key developmental phase associated with considerable change and flux. It is a period of experimentation where the evolving child may 'try out' different identities, roles and behaviours, some of which may be impulsive, risk-taking and antisocial. Adolescence is also a time dominated by egocentric thinking and linking this to psychopathy, Seagrave and Grisso (2002) spoke about the problem of 'transient developmental phenomenon' being erroneously interpreted as 'psychopathic-like traits' when in fact they may simply be exaggerated features of typical adolescent development.
- *Homotypic versus Heterotypic Continuity*. In the psychological literature, the term 'Homotypic Continuity' means that there is an identical expression of a disorder across different developmental stages – this is very rare. Heterotypic Continuity is more common. 'Heterotypic Continuity' is the term that is used to describe the changing manifestation of a disorder across time that allows for the influence of biological, cognitive, emotional, moral, representational and social–cognitive domains on the expression of the disorder.

- *Equifinality versus Multi-Finality*. The question of causality is also key. The term 'Equifinality' refers to the process whereby different causal pathways and processes lead to the same endpoint. Expressed differently, it is the process whereby different conditions, events or experiences lead to the same outcome. In contrast, 'Multi-Finality' is the term used to account for the circumstances whereby the same casual process actually leads to different endpoints and outcomes.

Reviewing the available literature on psychopathy, it is clear that whilst these issues have been discussed extensively before (see Johnstone and Cooke, 2004), none has been satisfactorily addressed with regards to youth (or indeed adults). In a short chapter such as this, it is impossible to explore each of these in-depth. But, to illustrate the point, the concept of 'equifinality' is explored more fully below using attachment and trauma theory to illustrate some key concerns.

Equifinality, Attachment and Trauma

While biology may be relevant, indeed highly relevant to the development of psychopathic personality, the literature has not yet provided a fail-safe developmental model for explaining psychopathy. There is a dearth of literature testing alternative etiological models and explanations. It seems that the research that does exist is focused on confirmatory rather than exploratory work with a bias towards demonstrating findings that concur with the Hare model, not necessarily the disorder itself. Day-to-day experience across all clinical populations underscores the importance of other variables such as childhood experiences in understanding personality development and practitioners working with children, and increasingly those working with adults are acutely aware that attachment and trauma-based theories also provide a viable model of explaining psychopathic-like traits. Raja and Rogers, (please refer to Chapter 11), provide a comprehensive overview of the extant literature. For the purposes of this chapter, some relevant themes are used to illustrate this below.

Attachment Theory. In brief, attachment theory posits that a person's ability to function in the social world and how they relate to self and others stems from our early relational experiences (Bowlby, 1969, 1973; Ainsworth et al., 1978; Main and Solomon, 1986; Schore, 1994). Infants are egocentric beings with little notion and lack of skills to navigate the social world. They are able only to experience the

---

BOX 16.3 Overview of Attachment Styles

Secure

According to attachment theory, the securely attached child benefits from sensitive and consistent care and nurture from their primary attachment figure. They are more likely to be positive, prosocial, emotionally regulated, able to enjoy autonomy and reciprocity in their relationships and to enjoy better psychosocial outcomes. They can empathise, show moral emotions, are regulated, affiliative and have a stable sense of self.

Insecure-Ambivalent

This attachment style develops from parenting that is inconsistent, unpredictable and insensitive and where parents are poorly attuned to the child. The child seeks to ensure consistency. This can manifest in distressing behaviours that mirror the unpredictability, for example, helplessness and aggressiveness to secure another's attention. The child will have low self-esteem, lack of self-worth and core schemas that see the world and others as unreliable.

Avoidant-Attachment

This evolves from caregiving where parents are rejecting, hostile, intrusive, over-bearing. This child will learn to be over-controlled, suppress its emotion and expect the world and others to act in the same manner as their primary attachment figure.

Disorganised

This attachment style refers to behaviour that is disconnected, extreme and unusual. Children are unable to tolerate stress; they behave in an unpredictable and irrational manner and can be controlling, aggressive and unable to self-sooth. They can be labile and show inappropriate or bizarre affect and tend to be lacking in control.

---

primary emotions (such as surprise, anger, fear, etc.), and the secondary (or socio-moral) emotions (such as love, shame, empathy, guilt etc. and those that are missing from the psychopathic profile) come later and are largely dependent on the presence of a safe and secure attachment figure and inductive parenting practices. Attachment theory shows that nurture is vital for a child to learn to regulate their emotion, develop trust, show reciprocity and feel a sense of safety and predictability. It has long been held that the early caregiving experience will lead to different attachment styles whereby the process of these early interactions result in the child adopting a style most suited to their survival. See Box 16.3 above for an overview of the key themes of Ainsworth's descriptions of the dominant styles.

According to theory, it is this child with a disorganised attachment who may be most at risk of being perceived later in life as a psychopath. This idea is not new: John Bowlby and Patricia Crittenden in their various writings accept that a severely impaired attachment could lead to a 'psychopathic presentation' (e.g. Bowlby, 1969; Crittenden, 2008). As indicated above, disorganised attachment refers to a style of behaviour that is disconnected, extreme and unusual and one where there is a lack of coherency in the internal working model and where the child is unable to tolerate stress. It has been noted that adolescents with a disorganised attachment style can be controlling, aggressive and unable to self-soothe (Holmes, 2004), and Hilburn-Cobb (2004) noted that this subgroup of children can be labile, show inappropriate or bizarre affect that is entirely mismatched to the situation and display a lack of control appropriate for their age and stage and Fonagy (2001, 2004) has linked this attachment style to controlling and violent behaviours in adults.

Whilst there are various ways in which attachment can be threatened, such as neurodevelopmental difficulties, contextual factors, toxicity, etc., a major source of disruption for the child and a variable commonly observed in violent youth is the experience of complex trauma. It is important that this is borne in mind when considering the psychopathic presentation in young people especially because it is a theory that is compatible with the biological vulnerability and merely expands the explanatory framework rather than undermines or challenges it.

Whilst no single accepted definition of trauma exists, for the purposes of this chapter, 'childhood trauma' is considered as an effect that can follow from exposure to events such as neglect; sexual, physical and emotional abuse; traumatic loss; betrayal or disruption of attachment relationships; and chronic dysregulation of caregivers (van der Kolk, 2005; Sarr, 2011). It is well documented that for infants and children who experience multiple and/or prolonged trauma, the risk of developing a disorganised attachment style is increased. Repeated incidents of trauma leave a child in a highly contradictory and confusing world. This frightening and frightened model of relating to others becomes imprinted and presents an intolerable and fragmented sense of the self and world and places the child in a flight or fight state of mind. According to van der Kolk's (2005) model of developmental trauma, a child, who has experienced multiple and complex traumas, shows impairments in several domains. These are summarised below and, for the purposes of the argument made herein reveal striking similarities with the writings on psychopathy. Firstly, the child may show a developmental delay leading to potential 'cognitive impairment' consequent to their focus on survival through either avoiding or being over-reliant on caregiver relationships. Being in a state of hypervigilance is the style that evolves so that the youngster has a pervasive readiness and preparedness to respond to any potential threat. This could explain the poor behavioural controls observed in this psychopathology. It has also been suggested that childhood trauma leads to a 'poor self-concept' and 'a sense of the world as a dangerous place' where help is unavailable. Whilst for some children, this may lead to a sense of helplessness, self-blame and guilt (Cook et al., 2005), it could, as the individual develops, account for the apparent narcissism and sense of omnipotence observed in psychopathy. This self-concept may have developed as a defence against early experience of ineptness, shame and guilt. Pathological narcissism is a fragile sense of self extremely vulnerable to any sense of rejection or threat, so much so, that a narcissistic rage can manifest itself in response to even minor slights. It could also explain why the child 'learns' not to seek or trust interpersonal affiliation and attachments with others. It has also been explained that the traumatised child lives in a paradoxical universe. They must be prepared to maintain proximity to the carer and abuser for their safety. They are the same person. This is thought to lead to what Crittenden describes as 'false cognitions' and 'false affect'. Being socialised by a caregiver who also poses a threat, when internalised, is thought to lead to inconsistent emotional learning and expression and may be relevant to the use of charm and manipulation as a survival mechanism. Thirdly, children with trauma histories also show 'dissociation and fragmented consciousness'. It is accepted that dissociation can develop as a psychic defense against intolerable anxiety associated with fear, terror, helplessness and an awareness of a carer's potential dangerousness. Dissociation could therefore lead to a numbing or apparent absence of affect where painful emotions and memories are managed via disconnecting and defending oneself from an awareness of feelings. Taking this into account, the presence of shallow affect, lack of empathy and lack of remorse becomes understandable and explicable as disconnect from, as opposed to absence of, emotion. The blunted affect and lack of attachment, remorse and secondary emotions observed in the psychopathy may actually reflect an overdeveloped system of adaptation that enables the divorce between event and emotion observed in this condition. Furthermore, it has been hypothesised that this fragmented consciousness may drive behavioural re-enactments of trauma and the divorce from emotion explains the lack of internal and anticipatory negative affect and the lack of punishing self-affect following an event. Another common effect of trauma is 'affect dysregulation'. Once triggered via internal or external stimuli, the child can react with highly aggressive and externalising behaviours, but as well as numbing and dissociation (van der Kolk, 2005; Bailey et al., 2007). Furthermore, children with backgrounds of trauma can have a sense of a foreshortened future and 'impaired world view'. This could explain the link between trauma and lack of planfulness and the risk taking that is observed in psychopathy.

It is also important to note that, with advances in neuroscience, a growing body of research has shown that brain abnormalities can occur as a result of adversity and abuse and these can parallel the deficits observed in the 'psychopathic' brain. Biological findings indicate that trauma interferes with the integration of the right and left hemispheres leaving the individual unable to access rational thought. This results in increased vulnerability to stress and arousal

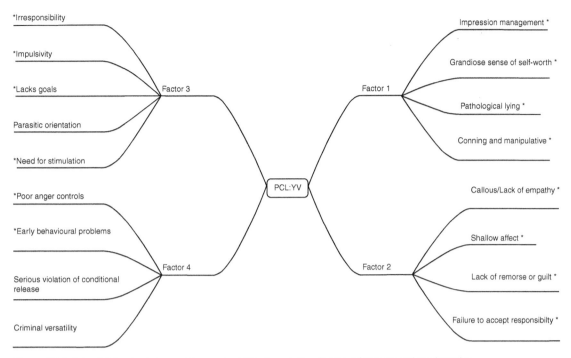

*Irresponsibility

*Impulsivity

*Lacks goals — Factor 3

Parasitic orientation

*Need for stimulation

*Poor anger controls

*Early behavioural problems

Serious violation of conditional release — Factor 4

Criminal versatility

PCL:YV

Factor 1 — Impression management *

Grandiose sense of self-worth *

Pathological lying *

Conning and manipulative *

Factor 2 — Callous/Lack of empathy *

Shallow affect *

Lack of remorse or guilt *

Failure to accept responsibilty *

Figure 16.1 Potential Overlap between Disorganised Attachment, Developmental Trauma and Psychopathy

modulation. It has been suggested that such experiences and over-focus on threat can actually lead to structural changes in brain development and manifest as impaired attention, learning and memory capacities (Ford, 2005), abstract reasoning and problem solving (Cook et al., 2005; van der Kolk, 2005). Thus, these findings underscore the risk that focusing on neurological anomalies to explain the causal basis of psychopathy in the absence of studies where trauma and attachment are properly controlled for could lead to a highly misleading conclusion. To illustrate the overlap between attachment, trauma and psychopathy, the symptoms of the PCL:YV that are also found in traumatised children are asterisked in Figure 16.1 above.

As it stands at the present time, and against this background, it is perhaps surprising that the link between childhood events and psychopathy has been little explored. But, there are some important findings.

From a forensic perspective, Marshall and Cooke (1996) found that the early childhood experiences of adults who scored highly on the PCL-R were more likely to involve adverse childhood experiences, and Kimonis et al. (2012) explored psychopathy and emotional processing in a sample of juvenile offenders and

suggested that there seemed to be different variants of youth psychopathy that may have different etiological pathways – one with a deficit in emotional processing and the other whose difficulties seemed more likely to be related to histories of abuse. Similarly, Pasalich et al. (2012) investigated the relevance of attachment, CU traits and conduct problems and found that high levels of CU traits were associated with more insecure attachment, and this finding held independent of conduct problems. They found that children with higher levels of CU are at higher risk of experiencing disruptions in parent–child attachment therefore underscoring this as an important area for treatment and prevention efforts. In addition, a warm parenting style has been noted to mediate the role of CU traits over time. Maternal emotional responsiveness has been associated with a moderating effect on children with high CU traits (Pardini et al., 2007). Similarly, concerned that environmental factors such as exposure to negative life events and Post-Traumatic Stress Disorder (PTSD) are often overlooked in research involving youth with CU traits, Sharf and colleagues (2014) found that CU traits are significantly positively associated with both the experience of negative life events as well as PTSD symptomatology. They, like others, have called for further exploration of how

225

trauma might impact or maintain the development of CU traits.

Furthermore, when the developmental literature is examined, there exists a sizeable literature denoting the association between the development of moral affect and inductive parenting techniques. Induction has been described as the process whereby parents use their children's acts of inappropriate or unacceptable social behaviour as an opportunity to teach, inform and reason with the child. These involve other-orientated inductive messages that also provide teaching about the feelings of others. These parents/caregivers engage in 'mind-mindedness' and are interested in what their children are thinking and feeling, seek to share this understanding and are good at translating psychological processes into conversations where children can link feelings and words. Mind-minded interactions facilitate emotional competence where the development of social emotions (love, empathy, remorse, shame, etc.) is strongly related to these parenting practices. And, encouragingly, there is evidence of such thinking being applied. Rogers (2014) produced the DART Model (Developmentally informed Attachment, Risk and Trauma) to provide a comprehensive intervention framework for adolescents in secure settings whereby he emphasises the applied value of this approach. DART is a sophisticated multi-theoretical model that draws from attachment theory, Crittenden's dynamic maturational model of attachment, trauma theory, conceptualisations of developmental trauma, mentalisation and trauma systems theory to provide interventions for vulnerable and violent youth.

Thus, from a developmental point of view, theories and research which emphasise the biological primacy of psychopathy as operationalised by the PCL-R – to the exclusion of other risk factors, may deliberately or inadvertently reinforce a belief that this condition is immune from (or at least more resistant to) the effects of environment. Consequently, the field is vulnerable to accepting highly misleading and very harmful lines of enquiry. The ethics of assigning a somewhat narrow label (or diagnosis) of psychopathic personality disorder which implies a certain inevitability to their trajectory, to an individual who has in fact experienced considerable adversity and abuse and whose brain structure is the result of complex trauma falls well outwith the realms of what many practitioners would consider acceptable. But,

trauma and attachment is not the only mechanism that might exist. For example, within the last few years, there is a growing recognition of the prevalence and relevance of the range of neurodevelopmental disorders and, as yet, the nature and existence of associations between neurodevelopmental disorders and psychopathy have been little explored. This is of concern. For example, anecdotal evidence suggests that practitioners, parents, and policy makers may actually favour a label of Autism Spectrum Disorder to explain a young person's lack of empathic responding when it is coupled with violence and may find ways of explaining their inconsistent features such as superficial charm and theory of mind capacities. It is likely that there are many possible etiological pathways worth exploring.

Reflecting on the above discussion, key themes have emerged. Firstly, models of 'Youth Psychopathy' are based on a fallible measure of the construct, the PCL:YV. It is a cause for concern that where psychopathic-like traits may be identified, practitioners could engage in a process of confirmatory diagnosis, in other words, determining a percentile on a psychopathy protocol and leaving it at that. It is the position of the author that a score or percentile should not dictate a child's future any more than it should dictate their past. Numbers can be highly misleading. Secondly, since current nosology, including the psychopathy models, are almost entirely descriptive and symptom focused and because no single etiological theory for the development of psychopathy exists, any attempts to properly understand the what, why and wherefores of any given child's difficulties will require a broad-based examination. Taking a narrow biologically based perspective on causality is problematic. As this chapter demonstrates, the root cause may be less relevant than the developmental process (i.e. impaired attachment) that accounts for the psychopathic profile. Linked to this, there are many developmental challenges associated with extending the construct of psychopathy to youth. It is necessary to give very careful consideration on how to use this construct in a meaningful way. Erroneous conclusions whether they are false positive or negatives could have catastrophic consequences. As such, it is argued in the section to follow that formulation provides a key process when a child or young person displays 'psychopathic-like' traits.

Formulating 'Psychopathic-Like Traits in Youth': What, Why and How

'Formulation' is neither a new nor novel concept. It is a term that occurs in many professions and, put most simply, can be thought of as a method of integrating information into some sort of structure or 'formula' so the information has *meaning*. Formulation is ubiquitous in psychotherapy. It is a method of using theory, empirical and practice-based knowledge to integrate and thereafter make inferences about predisposing vulnerabilities, proximal or distal, regarding biological, genetic, family, care-giving, learning, cultural and contextual factors to explain the person's presenting problems and difficulties. Most, if not all, models have a preferred format for organising assessment information into a specific type of formulation; models vary with regard to which particular aspect is considered more or less relevant. For instance, the cognitive behavioural therapy requires information to be organised according to thought processes, thinking errors and behaviours that maintain a problem and how these have been developed through early experiences and the development of core schema about the self, world and others.

Formulation requires the assessor to propose a mechanism, identified from theoretical, research or clinical practice, by which to explain the link between what has gone before (the past) and what is observed just now (the present). In other words, it can test the diathesis-stress framework advanced by the clinician. It can also help speculate what is likely to occur in the future. It also ensures that interventions, whilst nomothetically informed, are idiographic in practice. Furthermore, formulation is open to verification and testing and thus provides scope for collaboration and problem-specific interventions. Notwithstanding, in the forensic field, formulation is a practice that seems to have lain dormant for a while and even although Johnstone and Cooke (2004) argued for its use in assessing children presenting with psychopathic-like traits, there exists no particular practice guidelines to aid this exercise. Thus, in an attempt to ensure this chapter has practical utility and to promote a balanced position, a possible model by which formulation can be applied when psychopathic-like traits in youth are observed is proposed. The model draws heavily on the principles espoused in Alan Carr's (1999) textbook on clinical psychology as well as other principles espoused in the forensic literatures.

The first step and essential standard is to conduct a *biopsychosocial, multimodal, multi-informant, multi-level assessment*; this is a minimum standard. Interviews, questionnaires, rating scales, observations should be completed with multi-informants including the young person, parents/carers, school and siblings, etc. Records should be reviewed, especially any health or developmental records, school reports and social work notes. Triangulation of measures should take place. It is also recommended that different protocols, developed by different stables of researchers, be used to enhance the prospect of a broad and reliable coverage of the phenomena of interest. When it comes to assessing children, the evaluation should address their developmental history; educational functioning; family composition and functioning; peer relationships; attachment and trauma history; medical history; substance use; parental factors including mental health; attachment; physical health; attitudes; parenting style and any contextual factors such as living in an area of deprivation, poverty, subcultural criminality. And, of course, individual factors relating to temperament, attitudes, activity levels, developmental disorders, stress and coping skills, etc. should be thoroughly assessed.

Step two should involve a *topographical analysis of the problem*. In order to reach a formulation, it is necessary to move beyond a simple listing of problems. It is insufficient to merely list the violent incidents or immoral acts perpetrated by a child. A topographical analysis of the behaviour is required. Key questions are: what occurred; where was it; who was involved; how intense, prolonged and severe was the behaviour; what triggered the incident; and what was the immediate outcome? In the absence of such a detailed analysis, 'psychopathic-like traits' may become the catch-all explanation for all unacceptable acts and result in a tautological reasoning process – and perhaps a self-fulfilling prophecy. Whilst covariation between psychopathic-like traits has been established, it is impossible to ascertain causality in the absence of reliable temporal precedence of one variable over the other (Haynes, 1992).

The third stage should involve a *temporal sequencing of the problem development mapped with significant attachment or trauma events*. It is suggested that once a comprehensive data set is obtained, a useful method of understanding potentially relevant causal processes and influences on problem development and expression is to complete a temporal ordering of difficulties and associated events. Formulation, provides a potentially acceptable method of delineating the diachronic nature of a disorder whilst linking presenting problems (e.g. violence) to the range of variables that might be related to the onset and persistence of a problem and thereby also revealing targets for intervention and thereby scope for change. This also helps build the basis of the formulation framework with reference to the diathesis-stress requirement.

Step four involves a *pragmatic formulation*. Once an in-depth assessment and analysis is completed, the presenting problem(s) should be considered with reference to a diathesis-stress framework where mechanisms are proposed to account for the onset and development of a problem. When it comes to understanding children and adolescents, a pragmatic approach is preferred. An analysis of the relevant predisposing, precipitating, perpetuating and any protective factors is drawn together to build a case-specific narrative.

- *Predisposing Factors*. These are factors that place the child 'at risk' of developing psychopathic-like traits. These could be one or more vulnerabilities relating to biological, prenatal and perinatal, cognitive, temperamental, family, parenting and parental factors.
- *Precipitating Factors*. These are variables that may evoke or trigger the problem manifesting itself. When it comes to psychopathy, this may be an actual or perceived attack on the person's identity, having their needs and goals refused or obstructed in some way, taking pleasure from experiences affording them ego-gratification, opportunistic and impulsive acts, etc.
- *Perpetuating Factors*. As above, these too can involve features of the individual and their context such as biological, cognitive, temperamental, family and parenting factors as well as learning experiences and whether these have been pathogenic. In this section, the existence of defence mechanisms, dysfunctional coping, problematic attitudes and schema etc. would also be relevant.
- *Protective Factors*. Any factors that might mitigate any vulnerabilities are identified. For example, the presence of a stable attachment figure, escape from an abusive environment, etc.

After identifying the various 'P' factors, the assessor should then intertwine the findings into an individualised narrative that provides a coherent explanation of what, why and how problems have come to be. This process is referred to as producing a 'narrative formulation with postulated causal mechanisms'. This is an important step as it ensures the shift from the nomothetic data to the idiopathic level.

It is also necessary to conduct a 'reliability and validity check'. While the child and their wider care systems may well be the best judge of accuracy of a formulation, when it comes to a disorder associated with adverse outcomes, it may be sensibly denied. Similarly, where there is a history of trauma and abuse that may or may not be remembered, admitted or disclosed, an over-reliance on any one data source is to be avoided. Hart and colleagues (2011) have indicated that other steps can be taken to ensure that the formulation is meaningful and proposes that the following criteria are used to ensure utility. They recommend that assessors should address the following questions: Is the formulation consistent with theory (external coherence)? Is the formulation consistent with the data (factual foundation)? Does the formulation tie together the multiple facets and features of the person's presentation (explanatory breadth)? Is the formulation consistent, compatible and not contradictory (internal coherence)? Does the formulation knit together information relevant to the person's past, present and future (diachronicity)? Is the formulation free from unnecessary information (simplicity)? Is it consistent with formulations generated by others (reliability)? Are the hypotheses correct (accuracy)? And is the content acceptable to others (acceptability)? Because a formulation is a set of hypothesis, it is necessary to ensure that it can be *revised and reformulated*.

When working with youth, one of the most appealing facets of formulation (as opposed to diagnosis or the use of a score) is that it can remain a 'hypothesis' to be tested and proved. It is not necessarily definitive or prognostic of adult outcomes, and the use of such a highly pejorative label such as 'psychopathy', a formulaic approach, is far more preferable. Scope for change is always seen as a viable possibility. Finally, the formulation should provide the basis upon which any and all interventions are delivered. Because there is no specific treatment for psychopathic-like traits, a multilevel, multisystems, multimodal intervention should be devised which aims to address all the component parts of problem development and maintenance identified in the formulation. It has been argued elsewhere (Forensic Mental Health Matrix Group, 2011; Chapter 11 by Raja and Rogers) that interventions with complex cases should follow an eclectic, multi-theoretical, multisystemic and sequenced intervention.

To illustrate the contribution of formulation to achieving more confident hypothesis about a young person's difficulties, the above process is illustrated for Benjamin and Colleen. A brief case formulation for each is presented in Boxes 16.4 and 16.5.

BOX 16.4 Case Formulation – Benjamin

Biopsychosocial, multimodal, multi-informant, multilevel assessment

Interviews Conducted:

- Mother
- Father
- Adult siblings
- Grandparents
- Teachers
- Care providers (key workers).

Observations

- Within the unit (daily logs)
- Educational settings
- At contact with family
- Any other observations in the unit, at home and in the community.

Specialist Assessments/ Psychometrics for

- Temperament
- Psychopathy
- Emotional functioning
- Behaviour
- Trauma history
- Child attachment
- Adult attachment
- Parenting styles.

Topographical Analysis

- Nature: Sexual, interpersonal and verbal violence. Lack of remorse, empathy and guilt. High recklessness
- Victim–perpetrator: Family members (adult and child), peers
- Onset: Pre-school
- Duration: Across each developmental stage
- Frequency: Highly frequent
- Motivations: Not clear but reactive aggression is relevant

Temporal Sequencing

0–2	Healthy pregnancy and labour, good physical health, achieved developmental milestones within normal or above average limits but noted to be 'into everything', restless and 'on the go'.	Planned baby. Mother (teacher), father (engineer). Stable family in the first 6 months but maternal grandmother died in a RTA and Benjamin's mother suffered a severe reactive depression/grief. She admitted to consuming alcohol for around 6 months, as a coping mechanism but was able to benefit from counselling and made a good recovery. She has little memory of Benjamin at this time.
2–3	Aggressive towards mother and new sibling, cruel to the dog. Took pleasure in inflicting pain. Showed no response to others' distress.	Paediatric assessment completed; conclusion was the presentation of 'terrible twos' and nothing to worry about.
6	Disrespectful and demeaning to teachers. He would not comply with instructions. Bullying peers. Known as 'Walter Mitty'. But also described as having huge potential academically and as a young person who was able to engage in highly prosocial and charming behaviour.	Benjamin's father had attempted to engage him in various extra-curricular activities in order to motivate him to channel his intelligence and energy and to afford him the opportunity to meet new peers. The parents maintained regular contact with experts and attended parent training programmes and

229

| 11 | Started puberty. Would bypass parental controls on IT systems, including television and leave pornography running so that his sister and other family members would unwittingly be exposed to highly sexual images. He found this funny and ridiculed his parents and others for being 'prudish' when they attempted to give him guidance against this. |

sourced self-help and educational events in order to help them 'be better parents'. School commented on Benjamin's poor peer relationships and his inability to read and respond to other's emotions and social-communication needs. School also commented that his mother compared him unfavourably to his sister and described her as being 'so much easier' than he ever was. Benjamin had been presented and assessed by CAMHS, had independent health assessments completed and an array of educational assessments were completed. At that time, there was no diagnosis although his lack of empathy and impulsivity were noted. His parents were encouraged to maintain consistent boundaries and be vigilant with supervision. Benjamin was offered some 1:1 therapy sessions but when he attended, he was highly demeaning to the therapist and about the other people using the service.

| 12 | Benjamin kicked the family dog; the animal later died. When this happened, he wore a smirk and ridiculed his sister for being 'hysterical'. Around this time, he also started to assault his sister in a manner that was beyond sibling rivalry. He was emotionally abusive towards her – indeed the school described him as 'terrorising' her. He would talk of the future and repeatedly claim he would be wealthy, famous and powerful and would dissociate himself from his family. This period coincided with him intimidating his mother and, on occasion, approaching her from behind, throttling her and pulling her to the ground, for, what he described as, 'a joke'. He started to watch inappropriate films, became preoccupied with weapons and began to hide weapons under his bed. He harassed his parents to let him join cadets because he wanted to learn to shoot firearms. |

The family moved house around this time to ensure that Benjamin could travel to school for a short period of time. He had been complaining that he needed to commute for 30 minutes. This coincided with his brothers moving away from home and being in contact less often. They had both graduated from university – one in medicine and the other in law. His mother and sister were with Benjamin more often now. It was noted by the paternal grandmother who had accompanied Benjamin on a school trip that academic performance 'was everything' in their family and that she and the wider system were 'at their wits end' with Benjamin because he 'could not recognise this for himself'. The family was encouraged to refrain from putting pressure to achieve on Benjamin but they were dismissive of this and instead suggested he apply for a scholarship in the USA.

Pragmatic Formulation

Predisposing	Precipitating	Perpetuating	Protective
Difficult temperament	At interview, he indicated that when at the family gathering, he was being compared unfavourably to	Benjamin is highly defended and claims to have little feelings towards his family or	Intelligent
Maternal attachment style and mental			Family Support

health impacted on bonding

Esteem and sense of worth dependent on academic prowess

Pressure to achieve

Scapegoating

Indulging parenting

his siblings and younger cousin and felt intense anger towards his parents. He had consumed alcohol and new psychoactive substances when he went for a walk and when he returned felt 'out of control'.

behaviour. He is unable or unwilling to recognise his wrongdoing. He has achieved status and recognition among his family for his conduct.

Narrative Formulation

Benjamin's early life was characterised by maternal trauma, loss and poor coping in the form of alcohol use which may have impacted on her ability to bond and attune with him. His mother acknowledges a different 'bonding' process with Benjamin. She described feeling 'overwhelmed by him' and that he could outwit and outsmart her from an early age. She remembered feeling angry towards him even as a young infant. This was noticed by her and by her husband so they tended to compensate by indulging Benjamin materially and, at times, took a very lax approach to their discipline. As the years progressed, Benjamin, who is a highly intelligent child, struggled to gain recognition in the family. He was restless and could not concentrate and so was not able to achieve well academically. His family seemed unable to provide alternative outlets that were met with equal value. As time progressed, he was compared unfavourably to his siblings, and his sister always had a 'special status' as the only girl. It seems aggression offered him a sense of control and a means by which to regulate himself. The problematic mother–infant attachment and maternal-child relationship may have impacted upon Benjamin's ability to empathise and contributed to his fragile sense of self whereby he tends to feel extreme narcissistic rage in response to slights.

BOX 16.5 Case Formulation – Coleen

Biopsychosocial, multimodal, multi-informant, multilevel assessment

Interviews Conducted:

- Foster carers
- Social workers
- Teachers
- Adult acquaintances
- Care providers (key workers).

Observations

- Within the unit (daily logs)
- Educational settings
- Any other observations in the unit, at home and in the community.

Specialist Assessments/ Psychometrics for

- Temperament
- Psychopathy
- Emotional functioning
- Behaviour
- Trauma history
- Child attachment
- Adult attachment
- Parenting styles.

Topographical Analysis

- Nature: Interpersonal, exploitation/bullying, fire setting, sexual, harassment coupled with a lack of remorse, empathy and guilt. High recklessness
- Victim–perpetrator: Vulnerable individuals – older adults, adults with incapacity, carers
- Onset: Pre-school
- Duration: Across each developmental stage
- Frequency: Highly frequent
- Motivations: Unclear – seem intrinsic or possibly as a way of achieving affiliation with 'group'

Temporal Sequencing

0–2	Low birth weight, difficulties feeding, special care for 4 days, infant withdrawal syndrome, difficulty to soothe and regulate, slightly below average achieving milestones.	Child conceived as a result of rape Mother abused heroin throughout pregnancy and ongoing intermittent substance use Mother ambivalent about child during pregnancy – had been a concealed pregnancy for 5 months. Neglect concerns raised by midwife and health visitor. Child Protection Order in situ.
3	Aggressive towards mother – biting, spitting, hissing, scratching and showing this behaviour towards other children; excluded from mainstream nursery due to poor behavioural regulation and peer difficulties; noted to become highly distressed and hypervigilant. Noted as being entirely indifferent to her mother's presence or absence.	Mother had new relationship and was severely assaulted in the presence of Colleen. Her partner was incarcerated due to these offences but mother remained in relationship and regularly took Colleen to visit him in prison and insisted she referred to him as 'dad'. She was in three different foster placements – all short-term and her grandparents provided weekend respite care.
6	Colleen was viewed as dysregulated and aggressive for mainstream school. She was described as 'paranoid' and as seeing everyone and every situation as a potential threat to her integrity but also being able to 'be charm personified'. She was also described as having a propensity to tell fantastical stories about herself and her life. She was placed in a special educational provision although was deemed to be academically able. She showed a complete inability to form and maintain relationships with peers. Aggression continued to be a problem and she exhibited sexualised behaviour. However, her relationship with her mother was slightly more settled.	After her mother had successfully opposed a permanence plan after which Colleen had been rehabilitated to her full-time care, her mother gave up her rights to care for her and returned her to social work services. She presented her to her local office with a black bin bag full of her possessions and said she could no longer look after her.
11	Colleen was accused of attempting to have sexual intercourse with a local child in a play park where he was allowed to play unsupervised. She had also been witnessed masturbating and medical examination revealed a ruptured anus. She disclosed sexual abuse by her mother's partner. She was noted to be entirely forthright and numb during the disclosure and showed no apparent emotional distress in relation to this or the allegations against her.	It transpired that, during the time Colleen had been in her mother's care, she had formed a relationship with an older male. The male had used an alias to keep secret his past which involved a series of historical offences involving child sexual abuse. Her mother attempted suicide and was treated as an inpatient for 4 months. Colleen was made aware of this, her foster placement broke down and she was placed in a children's unit.
14	Colleen along with a male adult broke into a sheltered housing complex for older adults.	Colleen's mother committed suicide.

	The adult was convicted of robbing the 87-year-old female. The victim was struck across the head and suffered serious injuries as a result of her attack. He justified his conduct by saying he needed money for drugs. He also rationalised his conduct by saying the age of the victim was relevant and 'she had had a good life'. Colleen was charged and convicted with aiding and abetting the offender and attempting to pervert the course of justice.		
15	Whilst in foster care, she made allegation of ritualistic and sadistic sexual abuse against her foster father – her method of disclosure was via social media.	Her carers were very attached to her but despite their best attempts could not elicit a reciprocal bond. Colleen's allegations were investigated and adjudged to be fantastical and untrue.	

Predisposing	Precipitating	Perpetuating	Protective
Biological factors – substance use	At 14 years of age, Colleen's mother ended her life. As she was maturing, she left a prosocial foster placement and began to associate with antisocial peers.	Lacking in interpersonal connections, empathy, social and moral emotions, remorse and regret. Seems to experience intrinsic reward from harming and controlling others.	Lack of significant protective factors
Neurocognitive difficulties			
Difficult temperament			
Early caregiver disruption			
Domestic violence/ trauma (possibly child sexual abuse)			
Accommodated			
Lack of attachment			
Poor peer relationships			

Narrative Formulation

Colleen was disadvantaged in utero whereby she was exposed to neurotoxins via maternal substance use. She was neglected and her health was poor at birth. She suffered withdrawal symptoms and it is likely that her psychological functioning has been impaired as a result. Thereafter, she experienced and witnessed trauma, poor parenting, neglect, caregiver disruption and frequent placements. She presents as a young person with a disorganised attachment and as showing the effects of cumulative developmental trauma. These events and experiences have resulted in her forming a style of relating to the world and others whereby she is unable or unwilling to engage in trusting, reciprocal, caring and nurturing relationships. She has learnt that others are likely to exploit her and this may justify her belief that she should, and is entitled to, exploit them.

Conclusions

Reflecting on the above, it is entirely understandable that any civilised society may seek to explain the reasons behind abhorrent events. Attaching a mental disorder label is one way of achieving this. Psychopathy, as it is conceptualised in adults, has made an unprecedented contribution to our understanding and knowledge base when it comes to serious offenders. For this reason, importing the construct downwards to youth is both logical and rationale. If the forensicist can demonstrate a good fit with the nomological net, he or she may be content with the model. However, as this chapter has shown, whilst there are key points of convergence between the adult and youth models, there are very important differences, not least that developmental models explaining 'how and why' seem rather narrow. It is likely that for a practitioner who has worked with abused, traumatised or attachment-impaired children, the notion that 'psychopathy' is the best fit for explaining the child who lacks social emotions and who has developed an attachment style that has allowed them to achieve skills in manipulating, deceiving and ultimately controlling others, may seem abhorrent. For some, it could lead to a position, perhaps justifiably, where the use of the psychopathy protocols are wholeheartedly dismissed as useful. However, polarisations such as this will only serve to split the field and impede its progress. As such, an appeal is made for the developmentalists and forensicists to join forces in the pursuit of understanding, assessing and intervening with young people on a trajectory that might make them vulnerable to being viewed through a psychopathy lens. This marriage is required to ensure appropriate theorising and research if the promise of early detection, intervention and prevention is to be realised. In the meantime, for the practitioner tasked with making sense of complex case presentations, formulation may provide the only viable framework within which this complexity can be contained, made meaningful and critically provide the map to follow if interventions are to have any prospect of success.

Acknowledgements

Thanks to Dr Leanne Gregory, Clinical Psychologist; Dan Johnson, Forensic Psychologist; Dr Lucie Mackinlay, Clinical Psychologist; Dr Andrew Rogers, Clinical Psychologist; and Euan Dawtrey, student for comments on previous drafts.

References

Ainsworth, M., Blehar, M., Waters, E. and Wall, S. (1978). *Patterns of Attachment*. Hillsdale, NJ: Erlbaum.

American Psychiatric Association (2013). *The Diagnostic and Statistical Manual of Mental Disorders*. Washington, DC: American Psychiatric Association.

Andershed, H., Kerr, M., Stattin, H. and Levander, S. (2002). Psychopathic traits in non-referred youths: A new assessment tool. In Blaauw, E. and Sheridan, L. Editors. *Psychopaths: Current International Perspectives* (pp. 131–158). The Hague: Elsevier.

Bailey, H. N., Moran, G. and Pederson, D. R. (2007). Childhood maltreatment, complex trauma symptoms, and unresolved attachment in an at-risk sample of adolescent mothers. *Attachment and Human Development*, **9**(2): 139–161.

Blair, R. J. R., Colledge, E., Murray, L. and Mitchell, D. G. V. (2001). A selective impairment in the processing of sad and fearful expressions in children with psychopathic tendencies. *Journal of Abnormal Child Psychology*, **29**: 491–498.

Boccaccini, M. T., Murrie, D. C. and Turner, D. B. (2008). Do some evaluations report consistently higher or lower PCL-R scores than others. Findings from a statewide sample of sexually violent predator evaluations. *Psychology, Public Policy, and Law*, **14**(4): 262–283.

Borum, R., Bartel, P. and Forth, A. (2003). *The Structured Assessment of Violence Risk in Youth*. Odessa, FL: Psychological Assessment Resources, PAR.

Bowlby, J. (1969). *Attachment and Loss, Volume 1, Attachment*. New York: Basic Books.

Bowlby, J. (1973). *Attachment and Loss, Volume 2, Separation*. New York: Basic Books.

Carr, A. (1999). The handbook of child and adolescent clinical psychology. *A Contextual Approach*. London: Routledge.

Christian, R., Frick, P., Hill, N., Tyler, L. A. and Frazer, D. (1997). Psychopathy and conduct problems in children: Subtyping children with conduct problems based on their interpersonal and affective style. *Journal of American Academy of Child and Adolescent Psychiatry*, **36**(2): 233–241.

Cleckley, H. (1941). *The Mask of Sanity*. St Louis: Mosby.

Clercx, M., Johnstone, L., Cooke, D. J. and de Ruiter, C. (2012, March). *The Concept of Psychopathy before Adulthood: A Study on the Content Validity of the CAPP in Adolescents*. Poster presented at the 3rd European Association for Forensic Child & Adolescent Psychiatry, Psychology & other involved professions (EFCAP) Congress: Berlin, Germany.

Cook, A., Balustein, M., Spinazzola, J. and van der Kolk, B. (2005). Complex Trauma in Children and Adolescents. White paper from the National Child Traumatic Stress Network, Complex Trauma Task Force. Available from: www.nctsnet.org/nctsn_assets/pdfs/edu_materials/ComplexTrauma_All.pdf. Accessed 10 August 2015.

Cooke, D. J., Hart, S. D., Logan, C. and Michie, C. (2004). The Comprehensive Assessment of Psychopathic Personality Disorder. Available from: www.gcu.ac.uk/capp2/whatisthecapp/thecappmodel/

Cooke, D. J., Hart, S. D., Logan, C. and Michie, C. (2012). Explicating the construct of psychopathy: Development and validation of a conceptual model, the comprehensive assessment of psychopathic personality (CAPP). *International Journal of Forensic Mental Health*, **11**(4): 242–252.

Corrado, R. R., DeLisi, M., Hart, S. D. and McCuish, E. C. (2015). Can the causal mechanisms underlying chronic, serious and violent offending trajectories be elucidated using the psychopathy construct? *Journal of Criminal Justice*. doi: 10.1016/j.jcrimjus.2015.04.006

Corrado, R. R., Vincent, G. M., Hart, S. D. and Cohen, I. M. (2004). Predictive validity of the psychopathy checklist: Youth version for general and violent recidivism. *Behavioral Sciences and the Law*, **21**: 829–846.

Crittenden, P. M. (2008). *Raising Parents: Attachment, Parenting and Child Safety*. Cullompton: Willan Publishing Ltd.

Dawson, S., McCuish, E., Hart, S. D. and Corrado, R. R. (2012). Critical issues in the assessment of adolescent psychopathy: An illustration using two case studies. *International Journal of Forensic Mental Health*, **11**(2): 63–79.

Edens, J. F. and Cahill, M.A., (2007). Identifying youths at risk for institutional misconduct: A meta-analytic investigation of the psychopathy measures. *Psychological Review*, **4**(1): 13–27.

Edens, J. F., Campbell, J. S. and Weir, J. M. (2007, February). Youth psychopathy and criminal recidivism: A meta-analysis of the psychopathy checklist measures *Law and Human Behavior*, **31**(1): 53–75.

Edens, J. F., Cowell, L. H., Desforges, D. M. and Fernandez, K. (2005). The impact of mental health evidence on support for capital punishment: Are defendants labeled psychopathic considered more deserving of death? *Behavioral Sciences and the Law*, **23**: 603–623.

Ells, L. (2005). Juvenile psychopathy: The hollow promise of prediction. *Columbia Law Review*, **105**(a): 158–208.

Fanti, K. A., Frick, P. J. and Georgio, S. (2009). Linking callous-unemotional traits to instrumental and non-instrumental forms of aggression. *Journal of Psychopathology and Behavioural Assessment*, **31**(4): 285–298.

Fonagy, P. (2001). *Attachment Theory and Psychoanalysis*. New York: Other Press.

Fonagy, P. (2004). Early life trauma and the psychogenesis and prevention of violence. *Annals of the New York Academy of Sciences*, **1036**: 1–20.

Ford, J. D. (2005). Treatment implications of altered affect regulation and information processing following child maltreatment. *Psychiatric Annals*, **35**: 410–419.

Forth, A. E., Kosson, D. S. and Hare, R. D. (2003). *The Hare Psychopathy Checklist: Youth Version*. Toronto, ON: Multi-Health Systems.

Frick, P., Bodin, S. and Barry, C. T. (2000). Psychopathic traits and conduct problems in clinic referred samples of children: Further development of the Psychopathy screening device. *Psychological Assessment*, **12**(4): 382–393.

Frick P. and Ellis, M. (1999). Callous-unemotional traits and subtypes of conduct disorder. *Clinical Child and Family Psychology Review*, **2**: 149–168.

Frick, P. and Hare, R. D. (2001). *The Antisocial Process Screening Device*. Toronto, ON: Multi Health Systems.

Frick, P. J., Cornell, A. H., Bodin, S. D., Dane, H. E., Barry, C. T. and Loney, B. R. (2003). Callous-unemotional traits and developmental pathways to severe conduct problems. *Developmental Psychology*, **39**(2): 246–260.

Frick, P. J., Ray, J. V., Thornton, L. C. and Kahn, R. E. (2014). Annual research review: A developmental psychopathology approach to understanding callous-unemotional traits in children and adolescents with serious conduct problems. *Journal of Child Psychology and Psychiatry*, **55**(6): 532–548.

Hare, R. D. (1991). *Manual for the Psychopathy Checklist Revised*. Toronto, ON: Multi Health Systems.

Hare, R. D. (1993). *Without Conscience: The Disturbing World of Psychopaths Among Us*. London: Warner Books.

Hare, R. D. (2003). *Manual for the Psychopathy Checklist Revised, 2nd Edition*. Toronto, ON: Multi-health systems.

Hart, S. D. (1998). The role of psychopathy in assessing risk for violence: Conceptual and methodological issues. *Legal and Criminological Psychology*, **3**: 121–137.

Hart, S. D., Sturmey, P., Logan, C. and McMurran, M. (2011). Forensic case formulation. *International Journal of Forensic Mental health*, **10**: 118–26.

Hawes, D. J., Brennan, J. and Dadds, M. R. (2009). Cortisol, callous-unemotional traits, and pathways to antisocial behaviour. *Current Opinion in Psychiatry*, **22**(4): 357–362.

Haynes, S. N. (1992). *Models of Causality in Psychopathology*. New York: Macmillan.

Hemphill, J. F., Hare, R. D. and Wong, S. (1998). Psychopathy and recidivism: A review. *Legal and Criminological Psychology*, **3**: 139–170.

Hemphill, J. F., Hart, S. D. and Hare, R. D. (1994). Psychopathy and substance use. *Journal of Personality Disorders*, **8**: 169–180.

Hilburn-Cobb, C. L. (2004). Adolescent-parent attachments family problem-solving styles. *Family Process*, **35**(1): 57–82.

Hobson, J., Shine, J. and Roberts, R. (2000). How do psychopaths behave in a therapeutic community. *Psychology, Crime and Law*, **6**: 139–154.

Holmes, J. (2004). Disorganized attachment and borderline personality disorder. A clinical perspective. *Attachment and Human Development*, **6**: 181–190.

Johnstone, L. and Cooke, D. J. (2004). Psychopathic-like traits in childhood: Conceptual and measurement concerns. *Behavioral Sciences and the Law*, **22**: 103–125.

Jones, S. and Cauffman, E. (2008). Juvenile psychopathy ad judicial decision making: An empirical analysis of an ethical dilemma. *Behavioral Sciences and the Law*, **26**: 151–165.

Karpman, B. (1948). The myth of psychopathic personality. *American Journal of Psychiatry*, **104**: 523–534.

Kimonis, E. R., Frick, P. J., Cauffman, E., Goldweber, A. and Skeem, J. (2012). Primary and secondary variants of juvenile psychopathy differ in emotional processing. *Development and Psychopathology*, **24**(3): 1091–1103.

Krug, E. G., Dahlberg, L. L., Mercy, J. A., Zwi, A. B. and Lozano, R. (2002). Editors. *World Health Report on Violence and Health*. Geneva: World Health Organization.

Lawing, K., Frick, P. J. and Cruise, K. R. (2010). Differences in offending patterns between adolescent sex offenders high or low in callous-unemotional traits. *Psychological Assessment*, **22**(2): 298–305.

Lynam, D. (1997). Childhood psychopath: Capturing the fledgling psychopath in a nomological net. *Journal of Abnormal Psychology*, **106**: 425–438.

Lynam, D. R. and Gudonis, L. (2005). The development of psychopathy. *Annual Review of Clinical Psychology*, **1**: 381–408.

Main, M. and Solomon, J. (1986). Discovery of a new, insecure-disorganized/disoriented attachment pattern. In Brazelton T. B. and Yogman M. Editors. *Affective Development in Infancy*. Norwood, NJ: Ablex, 95–124.

Marshall, L. M. and Cooke, D. J. (1996). The childhood experiences of psychopaths: A retrospective study of familial and societal factors. *Journal of Personality Disorders*. **13**(3): 211–225.

McMahon, R. J., Witkiewitz, K., Kotler, J. S. and The Conduct Problems research Group (2010). Predictive validity of callous-unemotional traits measured in early adolescence with respect to multiple antisocial outcomes. *Journal of Abnormal Psychology*, **119**(4): 752–763.

Miller, A. K., Rufino, K. A., Boccaccini, M. T., Jackson, R. L. and Murrie, D. C. (2011). On individual differences in person perception: Raters' personality traits relate to their psychopathy checklist-revised scoring tendencies. *Assessment*, **18**(2): 253–260.

Moran, P., Ford, T., Butler, G. and Goodman, R. (2008). Callous and unemotional traits in children and adolescents living in Great Britain. *The British Journal of Psychiatry*, **192**: 65–66.

Moran, P., Rowe, R., Flach, C., Briskman, C., Ford, T., Maughan, B., Scott, S. and Goodman, R. (2009). Predictive value of callous-unemotional traits in a large community sample. *Journal of the American Academy of Child and Adolescent Psychiatry*, **48**(11): 1079–1084.

Murrie, D. C., Cornell, D. G., Kaplan, S., McConville, D. and Levy-Eikon, A. (2004). Psychopathy scores and violence among juvenile offenders: A multi-measure study. *Behavioral Science and the Law*, **22**: 49–67.

Myers, W. C., Burkett, R. C. and Harris, H. E. (1995). Adolescent psychopathy in relation to delinquent behaviours, conduct disorders, and personality disorders. *Journal of Forensic Science*, **40**: 436–440.

Pardini, D. A., Lochman, J. E. and Powell, N. (2007). The development of callous-unemotional traits and antisocial behavior in children: Are there shared and/or unique predictors? *Journal of Clinical Child and Adolescent Psychology*, **36**(3): 319–333.

Pasalich, D. S., Dadds, M. R., Hawes, D. J. and Brennan, J. (2012). Attachment and callous-unemotional traits in children with early-onset conduct problems. *Journal of Child Psychology and Psychiatry*, **53**(80): 838–845.

Petrilla, J. and Skeem, J. (2003). An introduction to the special issues on juvenile psychopathy and some reflections on the current debate. *Behavioral Sciences and the Law*, **21**: 689–694.

Poythress, N. and Petrilla, J. (2010). PCL-R psychopathy: Threats to sue, peer review, and potential implications for science and law. A commentary. *International Journal of Forensic Mental Health*, **9**(1): 3–10.

Richters, J. E. (1997). The hubble hypothesis and the developmentalists' dilemmas. *Development and Psychopathology*, **9**: 193–229.

Rogers, A. (2014). DART Model. (personal communication)

Salekin, R. (2002). Psychopathy and therapeutic pessimism: Clinical lore or clinical reality? *Clinical Psychology Review*, **22**: 79–112.

Salekin, R. T., Rogers, R. and Sewell, K. W. (1996). A review and meta-analysis of the psychopathy checklist and psychopathy checklist revised: Predictive validity of dangerousness. *Clinical Psychology, Science and Practice*, **3**: 203–215.

Salekin, R. T. and Frick, P. J. (2005). Psychopathy in children and adolescence: The need for a developmental perspective. *Journal of Abnormal Child Psychology*, **33**: 403–409.

Salekin, R. T. (2006). Psychopathy in children and adolescents. In Patrck C. J. Editor. *Handbook of Psychopathy*. (pp. 389–414). New York, Guilford Press.

Sarr, V. (2011). Developmental trauma, complex PTSD, and the current proposal of the DSM-5. *European Journal of Psychotraumatology*, **2**: 5622–5631.

Schmidt, F., McKinnon, L., Chatta, H. K. and Brownlee, K. (2006). Concurrent and predictive validity of the psychopathy checklist: Youth version across gender and ethnicity. *Psychological Assessment*, **18**: 393–401.

Schore, A. N. (1994). *Affect Regulation and the Origin of the Self: The Neurobiology of Emotional Development*. Mahweh, NJ: Erlbaum.

Seagrave, D. and Grisso, T. (2002). Adolescent development and the measurement of juvenile psychopathy, *Law and Human Behaviour*, **26**(2): 219–239.

Seto, M. and Barbaree, H. E. (1999). Psychopathy, treatment, behaviour and sex offender recidivism. *Journal of Interpersonal Violence*, **14**: 1235–1248.

Sharf, A., Kimonis, E.R. and Howard, A. (2014). Negative life events and post traumatic stress disorder among incarcerated boys with callous-unemotional traits. *Journal of Psychopathology and Behavioural Assessment*, 36(3): 401–414.

Skeem, J. and Cooke, D. J. (2007). Is antisocial behaviour essential to psychopathy. Conceptual directions for resolving the debate. *Psychological Assessment*, **35**: 2007–2021.

Skeem, J., Monahan, J. and Mulvey, E. P. (2003). Psychopathy, treatment involvement, and subsequent violence among civil psychiatric patients. *Law and Human Behaviour*, **26**: 577–603.

Van der Kolk, B. A. (2005). Developmental trauma disorder: Towards a rational diagnosis for children with complex trauma histories. Available from: www.traumacenter.org/products/pdf_files/Preprint_Dev_Trauma_Disorder.pdf. Accessed 10 August 2015.

Vincent, G. M. and Hart, S. D. (2002). Psychopathy in childhood and adolescence: Implications for the assessment and management of multi-problem youths. In Corrado, R. R., Roesch, R., Hart, S. D. and Gierowski, J. K. Editors. *Multi-Problem Youth: A Foundation for Comparative Research on Needs, Interventions, and Outcomes* (pp. 150–163). Amsterdam: IOS Press.

Wootton, J. M., Frick, P., Shelton, K. K. and Silverthorn, P. (1997). Ineffective parenting and childhood conduct problems. The moderating role of callous-unemotional traits. *Journal of Consulting and Clinical Psychology*, **65**: 301–308.

Wymbs, B. T., McCarty, C. A., King, K. M., McCauley, E., Vander Stoep, A., Baer, J. S. and Waschbusch, D. A. (2012). Callous-unemotional traits as unique prospective risk factors for substance use in early adolescent boys and girls. *Journal of Abnormal Child Psychology*, **40**(7): 1099–1110.

17

Early Interventions in Conduct Disorder and Oppositional Defiant Disorder

Stephen Scott, Leena K. Augimeri and Justine Fifield

Introduction to Early Intervention

The subject of early intervention for children with serious behavioural issues such as conduct disorder (CD) and oppositional defiant disorder (ODD) is often a source of contention among researchers and practitioners alike. On the one hand, some researchers argue that disruptive behaviours in young children should not be pathologised, as aggressive, disruptive and defiant behaviours are often thought to be developmentally normative in the preschool period. Beyond this, some researchers feel that children falsely identified as having CD will be stigmatised, or that unnecessary referral for treatment will 'waste' healthcare resources.

However, CD and ODD are the two most prevalent mental health disorders diagnosed in childhood, affecting approximately 5% of children and adolescents (e.g. Baker, 2012). Contrary to what some researchers might believe, these children pose a great concern not only to their families, but also to society in general. Children with CD tend to be older and engage in repeated and persistent patterns of antisocial behaviour, including acts of theft, shoplifting, vandalism, assault, bullying and aggression that violate the rights of others (Scott, 2015). Children diagnosed with ODD tend to be younger and have recurring patterns of negativistic, defiant, disobedient and hostile behaviours towards authority figures (American Psychiatric Association [APA], 2013). CD and ODD share similar patterns of behaviour and predictive factors. Researchers have found that factors such as chaotic home environments, social/ economic disadvantage, family instability and parental mental health issues are strongly associated with both CD and ODD in children (e.g. Loeber and Farrington, 1998; Murray et al., 2010). In addition, these children have often been exposed to family violence, have experienced abuse (physically, sexually and emotionally), often associate with delinquent peers and struggle academically in school. Such children are susceptible to a number of negative life outcomes such as pervasive mental health issues, physical ailments, unemployment and criminality – all of which come at a very high cost to society (Cohen and Piquero, 2009). Thus, given the prevalence and high costs of childhood CD and ODD, it is important to intervene at an early age when problems have not yet become 'fixed'. This urgency is supported by Hawkins et al. (2005: 25), whose research found that 'preventive interventions in early childhood can have enduring outcomes in promoting positive adolescent and adult outcomes'. This chapter will highlight the importance of early intervention and will explore some of the best assessment and intervention practices for children with CD and/or ODD.

How Early Can a Diagnosis Be Made?

Evidence suggests that conduct problems often emerge in preschool-age children. It is also suggested that the youngest age of onset is associated with the poorest long-term prognosis, and that long-established conduct problems are more difficult to treat than those treated early on (Moffitt et al., 2002). This evidence has resulted in calls for intervention in preschool-age children to prevent early conduct problems from becoming chronic. Leading researchers (e.g. Tremblay and Nagin, 2005) have stated that it is critical to intervene at the preschool level, as this is when children learn how to interact positively with others.

If unsuccessful in catching children at the preschool level, the elementary school phase (middle years, 6–11) is a critical time to intervene. There is a consensus among empirical research findings clearly showing that children who engage in delinquent acts prior to the age of 12 are at risk of becoming tomorrow's chronic offenders. Research tells us that there are up to seven years of warning (between the ages of 7 and 14) before minor behaviour problems become serious delinquent behaviours (Loeber et al., 2003).

These are the critical years for prevention and intervention as they are the most successful years to teach children self-control and problem-solving skills (Piquero et al., 2010, 2016; Moffitt et al., 2011). In addition, vulnerable young children who begin to engage in delinquent behaviour at an early age warrant particular attention as they are at especially high risk for serious, violent and chronic delinquency (Howell et al., 2014: 8). Indeed, Scott et al. found that 'forty percent of 8 year old children with CD are repeatedly convicted of crimes such as theft, vandalism, and assault in adolescence', and that 90% of repeat juvenile offenders had CD in childhood (2001).

In order to intervene early in individual cases, valid assessment methods (e.g. standardised evidence-based measures and clinical risk assessment tools) must first be available to diagnose conduct problems in young children. The *Diagnostic and Statistical Manual* (DSM)-5 is one such assessment method used to diagnose CD in young children (American Psychiatric Association, 2013). In a study performed by Kim-Cohen et al. (2005), the validity of the DSM-IV was tested by applying it to screen a birth cohort of 2,200 four- to five-year-olds. The diagnosis successfully identified those children in the cohort who most needed treatment: they were aggressive and antisocial, had co-occurring cognitive deficits and Attention Deficit Hyperactivity Disorder (ADHD) symptoms, came from adverse family backgrounds and were likely to have experienced harsh parenting and physical maltreatment. After following up two years later at age seven, over half of the diagnosed children still met diagnostic criteria for CD. Even those children who were apparently remitted continued to display clinically significant behavioural and academic difficulties at school, suggesting that preschool intervention would not have been wasted on them.

Using Multiple Instruments and Multiple Informants to Enhance Diagnostic Validity

Research has shown that using a multimethod and multi-informant approach increases the probability of having reliable and valid clinical assessments (Lavigne et al., 2001; McMahon and Frick, 2005). In keeping with these findings, there are many different instruments used in the assessment of childhood conduct problems for research and clinical practice. As juvenile antisocial behaviour can be defined either in terms of diagnostic categories or continuous distributions of symptom behaviours, assessment tools typically reflect these two classifications. Interviews aim to operationalise the specific DSM and ICD (International Classification of Diseases) criteria to achieve a categorical diagnosis (Costello et al., 1996; Goodman et al., 2000). Alternatively, symptom checklists such as the Child Behavior Checklist (CBCL) and Teacher Report Form (TRF) (e.g. ASEBA; Achenbach and Rescorla, 2001) aim to broadly cover a variety of internalising (e.g. anxiety and depression), externalising (e.g. conduct and oppositional behaviour problems) and social competency (e.g. school functioning and extracurricular activities) issues, operating on the evidence-based principle that a variety of presenting factors (i.e. comorbidity) is the best indicator of a poor prognosis.

Whatever instruments are applied, information must be obtained from multiple cross-sector informants, including (if possible) parents, teachers, police officers, clinicians and the children themselves (Arseneault et al., 2005). Children who display conduct problems pervasively across multiple settings such as their home, school and neighbourhood often have a poorer prognosis (Rutter et al., 1970; Deater-Deckard et al., 1998). Multiple cross-sector informants are essential to obtaining a more complete picture, as no single reporter can observe all instances of a child's antisocial conduct across multiple settings.

Risk-assessment and Treatment-planning Approaches

Manuals such as the SAVRY (Structured Assessment of Violence Risk in Youth; Borum et al., 2002), the START:AV (Short-Term Assessment of Risk and Treatability: Adolescent Version; Viljoen et al., 2014), the EARL-20B (Early Assessment Risk List for Boys; Augimeri et al., 2001) and the EARL-21G (Early Assessment Risk List for Girls; Levene et al., 2001) are often described by clinicians as 'decision-enhancing' tools that support assessment and case planning. Grounded in scientific literature, these easy-to-use manuals provide operational definitions to assist clinicians in assessing a number of risk factors that serve as the most valid predictors of a child's poor antisocial prognosis. Scales are included for rating the severity of each risk factor, resulting in the creation of a risk summary. This summary guides the clinical risk management plan and acts as a prescription for treatment.

Over the past decade, such assessments have shown both reliability (e.g. Augimeri et al., 2010a) and long-term predictive validity (e.g. Enebrink et al., 2006; Koegl, 2011). Once assessed, each child's specific areas of risk and need are considered when developing the intervention plan, including responsivity items that focus on issues pertaining to child and family engagement.

Interventions

In their Interventions chapter, van Yperen and Boendermaker (2008: 197) remark 'the ultimate goal of interventions is to reduce disruptive behaviours to a more normal level and reduce the risk of a criminal career'. A number of interventions have been proven effective in treating childhood conduct problems. In order to be successful, interventions for children with CD and/or ODD must include a comprehensive, multicomponent and multifaceted intervention structure that is tailored to the unique risks and needs of the individual child and their family (Augimeri et al., 2011). In their 2010 study, Kimonis and Frick highlight four effective treatment modalities: behavioural management strategies, parenting interventions, cognitive-behavioural skill building programs and stimulant medication where there is comorbid ADHD. Eyberg et al. (2008) found that the most effective way to reduce child CD and/or ODD symptoms is to utilise interventions that draw on a cognitive-behavioural approach and focus on both parenting strategies and child behaviours. Such a combination has shown a positive generalisation of reduced levels of childhood aggression across multiple settings (Pepler et al., 2011). However, Kimonis and Frick also point out that a number of interventions have been proven to be *ineffective* – for example, placing high-risk youth in boot camps (thus increasing their exposure to antisocial role models) and general counselling lacking a skills element.

Principles of Intervention

Basing Treatment on the Assessment

As noted earlier, in order to be successful it is imperative that interventions be tailored to the particular risks, needs and strengths of the child and family in question as revealed by their unique risk-needs assessment. Structured assessment tools can serve as decision-enhancing guides by pinpointing various levels of risk and identifying critical risk factors (Augimeri et al., 2012). These tools should take into consideration all aspects of a child's environment and functioning – something that can be gleaned, for example, through the use of the ICD 10's multiaxial framework (World Health Organization, 1996) or structured professional judgement tools that enhance clinical risk assessments and management such as the EARLs. Given the complexity of issues faced by children experiencing disruptive behaviour problems and their families, such assessment tools help to determine effective clinical management strategies tailored to meet their unique risks and needs.

Choosing Which Treatment Modality to Use

A child's antisocial behaviour may occur predominantly in one setting (e.g. in the home, at school, with peers or in the community) or it may be pervasive across multiple settings. If possible, interventions should address each context specifically, rather than assuming that successful treatment in one area will generalise to another. For example, improvements in the home arising from a successful parent training programme will not necessarily lead to improved behaviour at school. Therefore, for cases with difficulties that are mainly at home where the child is performing reasonably at school and has a friend or two, parent training would be the first line of treatment. Alternatively, if classroom behaviour is a problem and a school visit shows that the teacher is not using successful child management strategies, then advice, consultation and/or support to the teacher and other school staff can be very effective. Where there are pervasive problems including fights with peers, then individual work on anger management and social skills should be added as, on its own, anger management is unlikely to be nearly as successful as when it is combined with other approaches. Use of medication is controversial and is generally best avoided, given that there is little evidence of its effectiveness for CD and ODD. Possible indications for the use of medication are discussed later in this chapter, for example where there is comorbid ADHD.

Developing Strengths

Identifying and developing the strengths of the young person and their family is crucial, as this aids with engagement and increases the chances of effective treatment. Encouraging prosocial activities helps the child spend more time behaving constructively and less time behaving destructively – for example, more time spent playing football is less time hanging around the streets looking for trouble. Encouraging a child's specific abilities – for example, completing a good drawing or learning to play a musical instrument well – also increases self-esteem and hope for the future. Stattin and Magnusson (1995) found that for children with antisocial behaviour living in high-risk areas (which the majority of these children do), those with strengths or skills ended up with far lower rates of criminality than those without. Augimeri et al. (2006) also found that high-risk CD boys who received a multicomponent intervention including mentoring and structured community activities showed a higher response rate to treatment than those who did not receive these additional strength-building components. Interestingly, for a similar sample of CD girls, it was the overall intensity of treatment versus any of the individual treatment components that predicted treatment outcomes (Pepler et al., 2011: 246).

Engaging the Family

Any family coming to a mental health service is likely to have some fears about being judged. Furthermore, families of children with conduct problems are more likely to be faced with other disadvantaged circumstances that often result in disorganised and chaotic lifestyles. Such families often face challenges when dealing with official agencies such as schools and welfare offices, which may lead to suspicion of officialdom. Additionally, certain family-related factors such as marital adjustment, maternal depression, paternal substance abuse and child comorbid anxiety/depression may influence treatment outcomes (Attride-Stirling et al., 2004; Johnson et al., 2008). Drop-out rates for families with conduct problems in treatment are high and often reach up to 60% (Kazdin, 1996a). However, enforcing practical treatment measures such as assisting with transportation, providing childcare and holding sessions at times that suit the family are all likely to facilitate retention. Engaging and developing a good alliance with the family is especially important; Prinz and Miller (1994) showed that adding engagement strategies during the assessment (e.g. showing parents that the therapist clearly understands their viewpoint) led to increased attendance at treatment sessions. Stern et al. (2015) found that incorporating a contextually responsive enhanced interview during an initial intake call for multistressed families

increased the odds that families attended their initial agency appointment and continued in treatment service. Once engaged, the quality of the therapist's alliance with the family greatly affects treatment success, accounting for 15% of the variance in outcome as shown in one meta-analysis by Shirk and Carver (2003).

Treating Comorbid Conditions

Childhood antisocial behaviour is often so attention-consuming that comorbid conditions can easily be missed. Yet in clinical referrals, comorbidity is the rule rather than the exception. Common accompaniments to childhood antisocial behaviour are anxiety (Granic, 2014), depression, ADHD and sometimes even PTSD (Post Traumatic Stress Disorder) for those children who suffered or witnessed violence within the home. In recent years, there has been an increased awareness of the overlap between childhood antisocial behaviour and Autism Spectrum Disorders (Gilmour et al., 2004; Farmer and Aman, 2011), with the understanding that a minority of these children will present with psychopathic traits. Each of these comorbid conditions requires appropriate management and treatment in their own right.

Promoting Social and Scholastic Learning

Treatment of childhood CD and/or ODD involves more than simply the reduction of antisocial behaviour. For example, while stopping tantrums and aggressive outbursts may be helpful in the moment, it will not lead to better overall functioning if the child lacks the skills to make friends or negotiate. Thus, positive behaviours and coping strategies must be taught and practised as well. In addition, specific learning disabilities such as reading delays (especially common in antisocial children; Trzesniewski et al., 2006) should be targeted, as well as more general difficulties such as the inability to complete homework.

Making Use of Guidelines

The American Academy of Child and Adolescent Psychiatry has published sensible practice parameters for the assessment and treatment of CD (AACAP, 1997). In addition, the UK National Institute for Health and Care Excellence (NICE, 2006) has published a 'technology appraisal' that establishes the clinical and cost-effective criteria for parent training programs (e.g. that the programme must be backed by evidence from randomised controlled trials).

Treating the Child in Their Natural Environment

Most of the interventions described here are intended for outpatient or community-based settings. Psychiatric hospitalisation is very rarely necessary, as there is no evidence to suggest that inpatient admissions lead to gains that are maintained after the child is returned to their family. The objective of treatment is to enable the child to cope with the environment he or she lives in, and to alter that environment wherever necessary. Where there is parenting breakdown or a total inability to manage the child, foster care may be necessary.

Family Interventions

Several studies have repeatedly found that family factors are strongly associated with antisocial behaviour and appear to have a causal role in many child cases (Farrington, 2011; Howell et al., 2014). Even when the antisocial behaviour appears to have arisen 'in a clear blue sky' without adverse family risk factors, living with a child with marked antisocial behaviour can, itself, lead to coercive parenting styles, which, in turn, may exacerbate the problem (O'Connor et al., 1998). Therefore, improving family risk factors such as coercive parenting is likely to be beneficial, whether or not they were originally implicated as a cause. Family interventions can be divided into two main types: those derived from Family Systems Theory, which tend to be more broad-based, and those derived from Social Learning Theory, which tend to be more specifically focused on training parents to improve moment-to-moment interactions with their children.

Family Systemic Therapies

Family systemic therapies typically involve the attendance of all family members. The goals of these therapies differ according to the style and underlying theory of the particular therapy; for example, structural family therapy, as pioneered by leaders such as Minuchin (1974), would try to restore a clear hierarchy of parent-over-child authority, as antisocial children often become domineering in their own homes. Alternatively, systemic therapies attempt to reveal and address relevant factors that impinge on the family system from both within and outside the family. Other forms of family therapy focus on improving negative patterns of communication. Unfortunately, a relatively small number of good quality evaluations exist to determine the effects of family or systemic therapies on childhood antisocial behaviour. However, one exception is Jim Alexander's functional family therapy (Barton and Alexander, 1981), which has several trials to support its effectiveness.

Parenting Therapies

Parent management training programs are designed to improve both parents' behaviour management skills and the quality of their relationship with their child. Most programs target parenting skills such as promoting play, using praise and rewards to increase desirable social behaviour, giving clear directions and rules, using calm and consistent consequences for unwanted behaviour, reorganising the child's day to prevent problems and developing a positive parent–child relationship (e.g. Kazdin, 2005). Parenting interventions may also address distal factors likely to inhibit change such as parental drug/alcohol abuse, maternal depression and relational violence between parents (Scott, 2008). Treatment can be delivered in individual parent–child appointments or in a parenting group, though individual approaches offer the advantages of 'in vivo' observation of the parent–child dyad, therapist coaching and therapist feedback regarding progress.

Examples of Good Practice

Three examples of well-validated individual programs that can be used for complex, comorbid cases are *Helping the Non-Compliant Child* (McMahon and Forehand, 2003), *Parent Child Interaction Therapy* (PCIT; Eyberg, 1988) and *Parent Management Training – Oregon* (PMT-O; Patterson et al., 2010). For uncomplicated cases, group treatment has been shown to be equally effective as it offers parents the opportunity to share their experiences with others also struggling with a disruptive child. Group treatments emphasise discussion between group leaders and parents, and may use videotaped vignettes of parent–child interactions that illustrate the 'right' and 'wrong' ways to handle situations. Two well-known group treatments are *The Incredible Years Program* (IY; Webster-Stratton, 1981) and *The Positive Parenting Program* - (Triple P; Sanders et al., 2000).

Effectiveness

Behavioural parent training is the most extensively studied treatment for childhood conduct problems, as there is considerable empirical support for its effectiveness (Weisz et al., 2004; Furlong et al., 2012). Several of these programs are considered to be 'well-established', according to American Psychological Association criteria, with multiple randomised trials (e.g. Patterson et al., 1982) and replications by independent research groups (e.g. Scott et al., 2001). There have also been a number of randomised trials showing the effectiveness of PCIT, PMT-O and Triple P (e.g. Bor et al., 2002; Ogden et al., 2009; Sanders et al., 2000: 629), and at least one independent replication of the PCIT model (Nixon et al., 2003). Studies have shown that behavioural parent training leads to short-term reductions in antisocial behaviour, with moderate to large effect sizes of $d = 0.5$ to 0.8 (NICE, 2013). Moreover, follow-up studies suggest enduring effects at up to six-years post-treatment (Hood and Eyberg, 2003; Reid et al., 2003). For the 25–33% of cases that do not improve, Scott and Dadds have suggested a number of theory-driven clinical strategies that can be applied (2009).

Recently, some programs have included the element of training parents to read with their children in addition to learning behaviour management strategies, with the idea of targeting multiple risk factors for antisocial behaviour at the same time. Although this has not always proven successful in the past, Scott et al. (2010) combined a 12-week behaviour management programme with a relatively intense detailed reading programme (ten two-hour sessions) for five- and six-year-olds. In a randomised controlled trial (RCT), this combination reduced the rate of ODD by one half, increased reading age by six months and reduced ADHD symptoms. This kind of approach is promising as it is relatively inexpensive (it uses parents as the only vehicle for treatment), yet still targets multiple risk factors (e.g. parenting strategies, ODD, ADHD symptoms, reading ability) for poor outcomes in treating antisocial behaviour.

Child Therapies

Cognitive-behavioural therapies (CBT) and social skills therapies can have several different targets: (i) to reduce children's aggressive behaviour such as shouting, pushing and arguing; (ii) to increase prosocial interactions such as entering a group, starting a conversation, participating in group activities,

sharing, cooperating, asking questions politely, listening and negotiating; (iii) to correct the cognitive distortions and inaccurate self-evaluations exhibited by many of these children; and (iv) to ameliorate emotional regulation and self-control issues so as to reduce emotional liability, impulsivity and explosiveness, thereby enabling the child to be more in control of how he or she responds to provoking situations. In practice, most programs aim to cover all four target areas to a greater or lesser extent. While child CBT approaches were originally used with children school-aged and older, more recently they have been successfully adapted for preschoolers. These interventions may be delivered in individual or group therapy formats. Though groups offer several advantages (e.g. opportunities to practise peer interactions), there is some research documenting iatrogenic effects, especially with adolescents (Dishion et al., 1999). This appears to be particularly problematic in larger adolescent groups (or in those with inadequate therapist supervision), as youth may learn deviant behaviour from their peers and may encourage each other to act in antisocial ways. Therefore, lower patient–therapist ratios are recommended for group work.

Examples of Good Practice

Two of the more popular treatment models are Kazdin's *Problem Solving Skills Training* (PSST-P; see Kazdin, 1996b for a review) and Lochman and Wells' (1996) *Coping Power Program*. In PSST-P (used with children aged seven and upwards), the child receives individual training in interpersonal cognitive problem-solving techniques in 12 to 20 one-hour sessions. The focus of these sessions is identifying problem situations, learning a series of problem-solving steps and applying these steps firstly in hypothetical situations, then in role-plays and, finally, in real-life situations. Therapeutic strategies include games, therapist modelling and role-plays with therapist feedback. A token system is used in sessions to reinforce children's efforts when practicing target skills. Parents are involved periodically for joint sessions and may receive behavioural parent training as an adjunctive treatment. The *Coping Power Program* (used with children aged eight and upwards) is fairly lengthy (comprised of 33 one- to one-and-a-half-hour group sessions), with monthly individual meetings. Training focuses on the interpretation of social cues, generating prosocial solutions to problems and learning anger management and arousal reduction strategies. Treatment is delivered in groups of five to seven by a therapist and co-therapist. Sessions include imagined scenarios, therapist modelling, role-plays with corrective feedback and assignments to practise learned skills outside of sessions. Parent and teacher training components have also been developed as adjunct treatments.

Specifically targeting younger children aged four to eight with conduct problems, Webster-Stratton et al. (2004) have added a child social skills training group component to their *Incredible Years Program* called *Dinosaur School*. The programme is comprised of 20–22 two-hour sessions, during which parents typically attend a corresponding parenting group. This programme covers interpersonal problem-solving for young children in a group format, with approximately six children at a time. Sessions include discussions of hypothetical situations and possible solutions, therapist modelling of prosocial responses and practicing skills through role-playing with therapist feedback. Puppets, child-friendly cue cards, colouring books and cartoons are used for interactive role-plays, and videotaped vignettes are used to present situations for discussion. *Dinosaur School* dovetails with other interventions in the *Incredible Years Program*, including parent training and a curriculum used to train teachers in classroom management skills.

Effectiveness

In two RCTs, Kazdin et al. (1987, 1989) found that PSST results in both significant decreases in deviant behaviour and increases in prosocial behaviour. The PSST outcomes were superior to those of other more client-centred, relationship-based treatments, and were maintained at one-year follow-up. Furthermore, the addition of both in vivo practices and a parent training component was found to enhance treatment outcomes. Evaluations of the *Coping Power Program* demonstrate reductions in aggression and substance use, improved social competence and treatment effects that were maintained at one-year follow-up – particularly for those children whose parents also received training components (Lochman and Wells, 2004). Now, replications by independent research groups are needed to test the external validity of these positive results. The *Dinosaur School* programme discussed earlier has been found to result in significant decreases in problem behaviours and increases in prosocial

behaviour, with treatment gains appearing to be maintained after one year. These findings have been independently replicated by Hutchings et al. in their 2004 study.

Though decisive studies have yet to be undertaken, scientific literature is generally unsupportive of the effectiveness of individual psychodynamic psychotherapies or drama and art therapies in this specific population, especially when used as sole treatment modalities. However, one or two studies (though methodologically limited) suggest that an attachment-based approach (Moretti et al., 1994) or a classical explorative approach (Fonagy and Target, 1993) might possibly be helpful, at least for a sub-set of antisocial children. Again, properly conducted RCTs are needed before any conclusions can be drawn.

Combined Family and Child Interventions

The leading child and parenting programs (e.g. those developed by Webster-Stratton and by Kazdin earlier) are often delivered in tandem. Furthermore, interventions that address impulse control are also showing promise in the treatment of childhood antisocial behaviour (e.g. Augimeri et al., 2007; Burke and Loeber, 2015, 2016).

Examples of Good Practice

One such programme that focuses on teaching children and parents effective emotion-regulation, self-control and problem-solving skills within a multifaceted modality is the SNAP® (Stop Now And Plan) programme developed in Toronto, Ontario. SNAP is a proven, evidence-based, gender-specific programme designed for young children under the age of 12 with serious disruptive behaviour problems and their families. SNAP teaches children with behavioural problems and their parents how to make better choices 'in the moment' by increasing emotion-regulation, self-control and problem-solving skills. For over 30 years, SNAP has helped to keep children in school and out of trouble by reducing aggression, anxiety and antisocial behaviour while increasing social competency and effective parent management skills, as well as preventing criminal justice contact (Augimeri et al., 2014, 2015). This programme has been noted as the leading evidence-based programme for aggressive children with serious, violent and chronic potential (Howell et al., 2014: 46) and the most fully developed intervention for child delinquents to date (Howell, 2001). Key strategies of this intervention are, first, teaching children (and their families) to become aware of their emotional and physiological responses to situations that may trigger aggressive behaviour and, second, training them to respond effectively by making choices that will reduce the severity of their problems.

From its onset, the SNAP model utilised components from a variety of established interventions (e.g. skills training, cognitive problem solving, self-control and anger management strategies, cognitive self-instruction, family management skills training and parent management training). Falling under the umbrella of social learning therapies, the SNAP technique is a cognitive-behavioural strategy intended to help children control impulsivity, think about the consequences of their behaviour, and develop a socially appropriate plan (Augimeri et al., 2015).

Effectiveness

Overall, both internal and external evaluations on the SNAP programme have yielded positive outcomes for children with conduct problems and their families. Published RCTs show immediate moderate to large treatment effects, with treatment gains maintained at follow-up (Burke and Loeber, 2015: 250; Pepler et al., 2011). Furthermore, long-term follow-up indicates that the SNAP programme may delay and/or prevent criminal justice involvement (Augimeri et al., 2010b; Burke and Loeber, 2015). In addition to decreases in the child's conduct problems, parents and children reported improved parental efficacy and decreases in punitive discipline strategies (Pepler et al., 2011: 236), as well as an increase in positive parent–child communications (Granic et al., 2007). More recently, innovative neurological research is showing discernible changes in the brain systems responsible for impulse control in those SNAP children who also show significant pre-post changes on standardised measures in just 13 weeks (Lewis et al., 2008; Woltering et al., 2011, 2013). Additionally, a stringent cost-benefit analysis showed that the monetary benefits of the SNAP programme greatly exceed its monetary costs, can reduce crime by 33% and saves money (Farrington and Koegl, 2015).

Interventions in School

School-based interventions are appealing in that they provide a cost-effective platform from which many children can be reached, thus allowing for universal targeting and the multiplier effect (Hawkins et al., 2005). Indeed, schools are important settings as they often serve as the 'hub' of the community and may be the only avenue through which some children can access services (Augimeri and Walsh, 2013). The school environment is also an important milieu for intervention, in that negative school experiences can increase the risk of antisocial behaviour. Difficulties with self-control such as poor emotion regulation and impulsivity (often displayed by children with conduct problems) may lead to peer rejection, aggressive social behaviour and academic difficulties when entering the school system. In turn, these experiences may heighten the risk of further conduct problems (Conduct Problems Prevention Group, 1999). Finally, research has indicated that though early intervention involving both parents and children may lead to behavioural improvements at home, these improvements do not always extend to gains within the classroom or school setting.

School-based Interventions That Promote Positive Behaviour

Typically, teachers are taught techniques that can be applied to all of their students, not only those exhibiting the most antisocial behaviour. Successful approaches use proactive strategies, include a focus on positive behaviour and group interventions, and combine effective instructional and behavioural management strategies. Typically, these interventions target four main areas of functioning: (i) they promote positive behaviours such as compliance and following established classroom rules and procedures; (ii) they prevent problem behaviours such as talking at inappropriate times and fighting with peers; (iii) they teach social and emotional skills such as conflict resolution, self-control and problem-solving; and (iv) they prevent the escalation of angry behaviour and acting out.

A number of these aforementioned targets can be met by training teachers to use techniques similar to the ones taught to parents when dealing with antisocial children. However, these techniques are often adapted to be classroom-specific; for example, establishing classroom policies and procedures often involves setting rules such as 'use a quiet voice', 'listen when others are speaking', 'keep your hands and feet to yourself' and 'use respectful words'. Note that these rules are all expressed positively and describe what the child *should* do, rather than prohibiting what they should *not* do. Striepling (1997) offers six 'rules for making rules': (i) make only a few rules (between three and six); (ii) negotiate them with the children; (iii) state rules behaviourally and positively; (iv) make a contract with the children to adhere to them; (v) post them in the classroom and (vi) send a copy home to parents. Crucial to all of this is a systematic and consistent response to children for following or *not* following the rules. Rewards can be social (e.g. teacher praise, peer recognition, notes home to parents), material (e.g. stickers, certificates, tokens to exchange for prizes), or in the form of privileges (e.g. extra break time, games, parties, computer time). Mild punishments include reprimands, response-costs procedures (e.g. losing privileges or points) and timeout (i.e. being sent to the corner of the room or to another boring place).

School-based Interventions to Promote Academic Engagement and Learning

Interventions that promote academic engagement and learning include self-management and self-reinforcement training programs, which, for example, help children spend more time on tasks and help them to complete written work more quickly and accurately. An older review of 16 studies found moderate to large treatment effects of such programs (Nelson et al., 1991), and subsequent trials uphold this (e.g. Levendoski and Cartledge, 2000).

A number of programs build on the evidence that antisocial, academically failing children often have parents who are not involved in their schoolwork, and who may not value the importance of academics. Often, these parents have negative and discouraging school-related memories of their own, and do not read with their children, encourage homework or attend school meetings. Approaches include removing barriers to home–school cooperation through training parents to approach teachers positively, training teachers to be constructive in solving children's difficulties and helping parents engage in academic activities with their children. Although there are good descriptions of programs such as these (e.g. Christenson and Buerkle, 1999), rigorous evaluations are currently lacking.

Medication

At present, there are no pharmacological interventions approved specifically for use with CD and/or ODD. Nonetheless, in the USA, medications are used frequently and increasingly with this population (Steiner et al., 2003; Turgay, 2004). In the UK, use of medication is not generally supported as well-replicated trials of its effectiveness are limited, particularly for those children without comorbid ADHD.

The best-studied pharmacological interventions for youth with CD are psychostimulants (methylphenidate and dexamfetamine), as used only with those children presenting with comorbid ADHD. In these circumstances, there is evidence that reduction in hyperactivity/impulsivity will also result in reduced conduct problems (Connor et al., 2002; Gerardin et al., 2002). However, there is insufficient reliable evidence to confirm that stimulants reduce aggression in the absence of ADHD.

Other pharmacological approaches for antisocial behaviour have tended to target reactive aggression and over-arousal, primarily in highly aggressive and psychiatrically hospitalised youth. Medications used in these conditions include mood stabilisers (e.g. lithium, carbamazepine), and those purported to target dysregulation (e.g. buspirone, clonidine). While Campbell and colleagues (1995) found that lithium reduced aggression and hostility in psychiatrically hospitalised youth (e.g. Malone et al., 2000), others have failed to show effectiveness in outpatient samples (e.g. Klein, 1991) and in studies of shorter treatment intervals (e.g. two weeks or less; Rifkin et al., 1997). Carbamazepine failed to outperform placebo in a double-blind, placebo-controlled study (Cueva et al., 1996). In a placebo-controlled, randomised trial of stimulants plus placebo versus stimulants plus clonidine, Hazell and Stuart (2003) found the latter to be more effective in children with aggression and hyperactivity. However, it should be noted that the use of polypharmacy treatment also carries the possibility of increased side effect risks (Impicciatore et al., 2001).

In the last few years, the use of antipsychotics such as risperidone, aripiprazole, clonidine and others in outpatient settings has been increasing. However, there is scant evidence for their effectiveness when treating CD and/or ODD in children with normal IQ scores who do not present with comorbid ADHD. The review by Pappadopoulos et al. (2006) found that effect sizes were larger where ADHD or intellectual disabilities were also present. In a small ($n = 10$ per group) double-blind, placebo-controlled study, Findling and colleagues (2000) found significant short-term reductions in aggression. Alternatively, the Risperidone Disruptive Behaviour Study Group used a placebo-controlled, double-blind design to study the effects of risperidone in 110 children with conduct problems and sub-average IQ scores. Results suggested that risperidone results in significant improvements in behaviour versus placebo (Aman et al., 2002; Snyder et al., 2002), but it remains unclear whether the same findings would apply to children with normal IQ scores. Recently, Gadow et al. (2014) conducted an open trial with children ages 6 to 12 with severe physical aggression, ADHD, and CD/ODD, and found that children receiving both risperidone and methylphenidate in combination with parent management training experienced a significant reduction in parent-rated ODD severity and peer aggression, and teacher-rated ADHD with small-moderate effect sizes.

Even newer antipsychotics, while not especially sedating, have substantial side effects. For example, risperidone typically leads to considerable weight gain, and the prevalence of long-term movement disorders, which may arise, is unknown. Clinical experience suggests that antipsychotics can lead to useful reductions in aggression in some cases, especially where there is poor emotional regulation characterised by prolonged rages. Prescribing antipsychotics for relatively short periods (e.g. up to four months) in lower doses (e.g. no more than 1 to 1.5 mg risperidone per day) can help families cope. However, during this time it is crucial to introduce more effective psychological management.

Conclusions

As our review of treatments has demonstrated, psychosocial therapies are the mainstay of treatment for CD and ODD. However, despite this strong evidence base, only a small number of children in the USA, Canada and the UK receive any treatment, and even fewer receive empirically supported interventions. Furthermore, the 'effectiveness' of these interventions as practised in community settings tends to lag behind documented 'efficacy' in controlled trials (e.g. Curtis et al., 2004).

The next generation of evidence-based treatments for CD and ODD will likely include much greater attention paid to implementation and dissemination, including strategies for ongoing training and supervision of practitioners to ensure treatment fidelity and integrity. It is clear that over the past

two decades of dissemination alone, the programme developers of SNAP have found that training and ongoing consultation and supervision activities are critical for successful implementation and sustainability. Such processes serve as a quality assurance mechanism that promotes support and feedback between the developers and practitioners, and helps to establish best practices with regard to children with CD and/or ODD. In addition, the SNAP developers further identified the need for replication standards and principles, licensing agreements, accreditation and ongoing evaluation activities that include fidelity frameworks to ensure treatment adherence. Of course, the ultimate goal must remain to ensure that children with CD and/or ODD have access to high-quality, evidence-based treatment that will lead to successful life outcomes.

References

Achenbach, T. M. and Rescorla, L. A. (2001). *Manual for the ASEBA School-aged Forms and Profiles.* Burlington: University of Vermont, Department of Psychiatry.

Aman, M. G., De Smedt, G., Derivan, A., Lyons, B. and Findling, R. L., and the Risperidone Disruptive Behavior Study Group. (2002). Double-blind, placebo-controlled study of risperidone for the treatment of disruptive behaviors in children with subaverage intelligence. *American Journal of Psychiatry,* **159**, 1337–1346.

American Academy of Child and Adolescent Psychiatry. (1997). Practice parameters for the assessment and treatment of children and adolescents with conduct disorder. *Journal of the American Academy of Child and Adolescent Psychiatry,* **36**, 122S–139S.

American Psychiatric Association. (2013). *Diagnostic and Statistical Manual of Mental Disorders.* 5th Edition. Arlington, VA: American Psychiatric Publishing.

Arseneault, L., Kim-Cohen, J., Taylor, A., Caspi, A. and Moffitt, T. E. (2005). Psychometric evaluation of 5- and 7-year-old children's self-reports of conduct problems. *Journal of Abnormal Child Psychology,* **33**, 537–550.

Attride-Stirling, J., Davis, H., Farrell, L., Groark, C. and Day, C. (2004). Factors influencing parental engagement in a community child and adolescent mental health service: a qualitative comparison of completers and non-completers. *Clinical Child Psychology and Psychiatry,* **9**, 347–361.

Augimeri, L. K., Enebrink, P., Walsh, M. and Jiang, D. (2010a). Gender-specific childhood risk assessment tools: early Assessment Risk Lists for Boys (EARL-20B) and Girls (EARL-21 G). In Otto, R. K. and Douglas, K. S. Editors. *Handbook of Violence Risk Assessment* (pp. 43–62). Oxford, UK: Routledge, Taylor and Francis.

Augimeri, L. K., Farrington, D. P., Koegl, C. J. and Day, D. M. (2007). The under 12 outreach project: Effects of a community based program for children with conduct problems. *Journal of Child and Family Studies*, 16, 799–807. [Online] doi: 10.1007/s10826-006-9126-x. Accessed 10 January 2007.

Augimeri, L. K., Jiang, D., Koegl, C. J. and Carey, J. (2006). Differential Effects of the SNAP® Under 12 Outreach Project (SNAP ORP) Associated with Client Risk and Treatment Intensity. Program Evaluation Report Submitted to the Centre of Excellence for Child and Youth Mental Health at CHEO.

Augimeri, L. K., Koegl, C. J., Webster, C. D. and Levene, K. (2001). *Early Assessment Risk List for Boys: EARL-20B, Version 2*. Toronto: Earlscourt Child and Family Centre.

Augimeri, L. K., Pepler, D., Walsh, M. M., Jiang, D., and Dassinger, C. (2010b). Aggressive and antisocial young children: Risk prediction, assessment and clinical risk management. Program Evaluation Report submitted to The Provincial Centre of Excellence for Child and Youth Mental Health at CHEO (Grant: # RG-976).

Augimeri, L. K. and Walsh, M. (2013). School-based interventions: Commentary. In Pepler, D. and Ferguson, B. Editors. *Understanding and Addressing Girls' Aggressive Behaviour Problems (A Focus on Relationships)*. Waterloo: Wilfred Laurier University Press.

Augimeri, L. K., Walsh, M., Jiang, D. and Woods, S. (2012). Risk-assessment and clinical risk management for young antisocial children: The forgotten group. *Universitas Psychologica*, 11(4), 1147–1156.

Augimeri, L. K., Walsh, M., Levene, K., Sewell, K. and Rajca, E. (2014). Stop Now And Plan (SNAP) model. *Encyclopedia of Criminology and Criminal Justice*, 5053–5063. New York, NY: Springer Science – Business Media.

Augimeri, L. K., Walsh, M., Levene, K., and Slater, N. (2015). Scaling Deeper: SNAP® model and implementation frameworks. In Corrado, R., Leschied, A., Lussier, P. and Watley, J. Editors. *Serious and Violent Young Offenders and Youth Criminal Justice: A Canadian Perspective*. British Columbia: Simon Fraser University Press.

Augimeri, L. K., Walsh, M. M., Liddon, A. D. and Dassinger, C. R. (2011). From risk identification to risk management: a comprehensive strategy for young children engaged in antisocial behavior. In Springer, D. W. and Roberts, A. Editors. *Juvenile Justice and Delinquency* (pp. 117–140). United States: Jones and Bartlett.

Baker, K. (2012). Conduct disorders in children and adolescents. *Paediatrics and Child Health*, 23(1), 24–29.

Barton, C. and Alexander, J. F. (1981). Functional family therapy. In Gurman, A. S. and Kniskern, D. P. Editors. *Handbook of Family Therapy* (pp. 403–443). New York: Brunner/Mazel.

Bor, W., Sanders, M. R., and Markie-Dadds, C. (2002). The effects of the Triple P-Positive Parenting Program on preschool children with co-occurring disruptive behavior and attentional/hyperactive difficulties. *Journal of Abnormal Child Psychology*, 30, 571–587.

Borum, R., Bartel, P. and Forth, A. (2002). *Manual for the Structured Assessment of Violence Risk in Youth (SAVRY), Version 1 Consultation Edition*. Tampa: University of South Florida.

Burke, J. and Loeber, R. (2015). The effectiveness of the Stop Now and Plan (SNAP) Program for boys at risk for violence and delinquency. *Prevention Science*, 16(2), 242–253 [Online] doi: 10.1007/s11121-014-0490-2. Accessed 24 April 2014.

Burke, J. and Loeber, R. (2016). Mechanisms of behavioral and affective treatment outcomes in a cognitive behavioral intervention for boys. *Journal of Abnormal Child Psychology*, 44, 179–189 [Online] doi: 10.1007/s10802-015-9975-0. Accessed 27 January 2015.

Campbell, M., Adams, P. B., Small, A. M., Kafantaris, V., Silva, R. R., Shell, J., Perry, R., and Overall, J. E. (1995). Lithium in hospitalized aggressive children with conduct disorder: a double-blind and placebo-controlled study. *Journal of the American Academy of Child & Adolescent Psychiatry*, 34, 445–453.

Christenson, S. L. and Buerkle, K. (1999). Families as educational partners for childrens' school success: Suggestions for school psychologists. In Reynolds, C. R. and Gutkin, T. B. Editors. *The Handbook of School Psychology*. 3rd Edition. (pp. 709–744). New York: Wiley.

Cohen, M. A. and Piquero, A. R. (2009). New evidence on the monetary value of saving a high risk youth. *Journal of Quantitative Criminology*, 25(1), 25–49.

Conduct Problems Prevention Group. (1999). Initial impact of the fast track prevention trial for conduct problems: I. The high risk sample. *Journal of Consulting and Clinical Psychology*, 67(5), 631–647.

Connor, D. F., Glatt, S. J., Lopez, I. D., Jackson, D., and Melloni, R. H. (2002). Psychopharmacology and aggression. I: a meta-analysis of stimulant effects on overt/covert aggression-related behaviors in ADHD. *Journal of the American Academy of Child & Adolescent Psychiatry*, 41, 253–261.

Costello, E. J., Angold, A., Burns, B. J., Stangl, D., Tweed, D. L., and Erkanli, A. (1996). The Great Smoky Mountains Study of youth: goals, designs, methods, and the prevalence of DSM-III-R disorders. *Archives of General Psychiatry*, 53(12), 1129–1136.

Cueva, J. E., Overall, J. E. Small, A. M., Armenteros, J. L., Perry, R., and Campbell, M. (1996). Carbamazepine in aggressive children with conduct disorder: a double-blind and placebo-controlled study. *Journal of the American Academy of Child & Adolescent Psychiatry*, 35, 480–490.

Curtis, N. M., Ronan, K. R., and Borduin, C. M. (2004). Multisystemic therapy: a meta-analysis of outcome studies. *Journal of Family Psychology*, 18, 411–419.

Deater-Deckard, K., Dodge, K. A., Bates, J. E. and Pettit, G. S. (1998). Multiple risk factors in the development of externalizing behavior problems: group and individual differences. *Developmental Psychopathology*, **10**, 469–493.

Dishion, T. J., McCord, J. and Poulin, F. (1999). When interventions harm: peer groups and problem behavior. *American Psychologist*, **54**, 755–764.

Enebrink, P., Långström, N. and Gumpert, C. H. (2006). Predicting aggressive and disruptive behavior in referred 6- to 12-year-old boys: prospective validation of the EARL-20B risk/needs checklist. *Assessment*, **13**, 356–367.

Eyberg, S. M. (1988). Parent-child interaction therapy: integration of traditional and behavioral concerns. *Child and Family Behavior Therapy*, **10**, 33–48.

Eyberg, S. M., Nelson, M. N. and Boggs, S. R. (2008). Evidence-based psychosocial treatments for children and adolescents with disruptive behavior. *Journal of Clinical Child & Adolescent Psychology*, **37**(1), 215–237.

Farmer, C. A. and Aman, M. G. (2011). Aggressive behavior in a sample of children with autism spectrum disorders. *Research in Autism Spectrum Disorders*, **5**(1), 317–323.

Farrington, D. (2011). Family influences on delinquency. In Springer, D. W. and Roberts, A. R. Editors. *Juvenile Justice and Delinquency* (pp. 203–222). United States: Jones and Bartlett.

Farrington, D. P. and Koegl, C. J. (2015). Monetary benefits and costs of the stop now and plan program for boys aged 6–11, based on the prevention of later offending. *Journal of Quantitative Criminology*, **31**(2), 263–287. [Online] doi: 10.1007/s10940-014-9240-7.

Findling, R. L., McNamara, N. K., Branicky, L. A., Schluchter, M. D., Lemon, E., and Blumer, J. L. (2000). A double-blind pilot study of risperidone in the treatment of conduct disorder. *Journal of the American Academy of Child & Adolescent Psychiatry*, **39**, 509–516.

Fonagy, P. and Target, M. (1993). The efficacy of psychoanalysis for children with disruptive disorders. *Journal of American Academy of Child & Adolescent Psychiatry*, **33**(1), 45–55.

Furlong, M., McGilloway, S., Bywater, T., Hutchings, J., Smith, S.M. and Donnelly, M. (2012). Behavioural and cognitive-behavioural group-based parenting programmes for early-onset conduct problems in children aged 3 to 12 years. *Cochrane Database of Systematic Reviews*, **2**, CD008225. doi: 10.1002/14651858.CD008225.pub2.

Gadow, K. S., Arnold, L. E., Monlina, B. S. G., Finding, R. L., Bukstein, O. G. and Brown, N. V. (2014). Risperidone Added to Parent Training and Stimulant Medication: Effects on Attention-Deficit/Hyperactivity Disorder, Oppositional Defiant Disorder, Conduct Disorder, and Peer Aggression. *Journal of American Academy of Child Adolescent Psychiatry*, **53**(9), 948–959.e1. doi: 10.1016/j.jaac.2014.05.008.

Gerardin, P., Cohen, D., Mazet, P., and Flament, M. F. (2002). Drug treatment of conduct disorder in young people. *European Neuropsychopharmacology*, **12**, 361–370.

Gilmour, J., Hill, B., Place, M., and Skuse, D. H. (2004). Social communication deficits in conduct disorder: A Clinical and community survey. *Journal of Child Psychology & Psychiatry*, **45**, 967–978.

Goodman, R., Ford, T., Richards, H., Gatward, R., and Meltzer, H. (2000). The development and well-being assessment: Description and initial validation of an integrated assessment of child and adolescent psychopathology. *Journal of Child Psychology and Psychiatry*, **41**(5), 645–655.

Granic, I. (2014). The role of anxiety in the development, maintenance, and treatment of childhood aggression. *Development and Psychopathology*, **26**, 1515–1530. [Online] doi: 10.1017/S0954579414001175.

Granic, I., O'Hara, A., Pepler, D., and Lewis, M. (2007). A dynamic system analysis of parent-child changes associated with successful 'real-world' interventions for aggressive children. *Journal of Abnormal Child Psychology*, **35**(5), 845–857. [Online] doi: 10.1007/s10802-007-9133-4.

Hawkins, D., Kosterman, R., Catalano, R. F., Hill, K. G. and Abbot, R. D. (2005). Promoting positive adult functioning through social development intervention in childhood: long term effects from the Seattle social development project. *Archives of Pediatric and Adolescent Medicine*, **159**, 25–31.

Hazell, P. L. and Stuart, J. E. (2003). A randomized controlled trial of clonidine added to psychostimulant medication for hyperactive and aggressive children. *Journal of the American Academy of Child & Adolescent Psychiatry*, **42**, 886–894.

Hood, K. and Eyberg, S. M. (2003). Outcomes of parent-child interaction therapy: mothers' reports on maintenance three to six years after treatment. *Journal of Clinical Child and Adolescent Psychology*, **32**, 419–429.

Howell, J. C. (2001). Juvenile justice: programs and strategies. In Loeber, R. and Farrington, D. P. Editors. *Child Delinquents: Development, Intervention and Service Needs* (pp. 305–321). Thousand Oaks, CA: Sage Publications.

Howell, J. C., Lipsey, M. W. and Wilson, J. J. (2014). *A Handbook for Evidence-Based Juvenile Justice Systems*. London, UK: Lexington Books.

Hutchings, J., Lane, E., Owen, R. E. and Gwyn, R. (2004). The introduction of the Webster-Stratton incredible years classroom dinosaur school programme in Gwynedd, North Wales: a pilot study. *Educational and Child Psychology*, **21**, 4–15.

Impicciatore, P., Choonara, I., Clarkson, A., Provasi, D., Pandolfini, C. and Bonati, M. (2001). Incidence of adverse drug reactions in paediatric in/out-patients: a systematic review and meta-analysis of prospective studies. *British Journal of Clinical Pharmacology*, **52**(1), 77–83.

Johnson, E., Mellor, D. and Brann, P. (2008). Differences in dropout between diagnoses in child and adolescent mental health services. *Clinical Child Psychology and Psychiatry*, **13**(4), 515–530.

Kazdin, A. E. (1996a). Dropping out of child therapy: issues for research and implications for practice. *Clinical Child Psychology and Psychiatry*, **1**, 133–156.

Kazdin, A. E. (1996b). Problem solving and parent management in treating aggressive and antisocial behavior. In Hibbs, E. S. and Jensen, P. S. Editors. *Psychosocial Treatments for Child and Adolescent Disorders: Empirically-based Strategies for Clinical Practice* (pp. 377–408). Washington, DC: American Psychological Association.

Kazdin, A. E. (2005). *Parent Management Training.* New York: Oxford University Press.

Kazdin, A. E., Bass, D., Siegel, T. and Thomas, C. (1989). Cognitive-behavioural treatment and relationship therapy in the treatment of children referred for antisocial behaviour. *Journal of Consulting and Clinical Psychology*, **57**, 522–535.

Kazdin, A. E., Esveldt-Dawson, K., French, N. H. and Unis, A. S. (1987). Problem-solving skills training and relationship therapy in the treatment of antisocial child behavior. *Journal of Consulting and Clinical Psychology*, **55**, 76–85.

Kim-Cohen, J., Arseneault, L., Caspi, A., Taylor, A., Polo-Tomas, M. and Moffitt, T. E. (2005). Validity of DSM-IV conduct disorder in 4.5–5 year old children: A longitudinal epidemiological study. *American Journal of Psychiatry*, **162**, 1108–1117.

Kimonis, E. R. and Frick, P. J. (2010). Oppositional defiant disorder and conduct disorder grown-up. *Journal of Developmental & Behavioral Pediatrics*, **31**(3), 244–254.

Klein, R. (1991). Preliminary results: lithium effects in conduct disorders. In: CME Syllabus and Proceedings Summary, 144th Annual Meeting of the American Psychiatric Association, New Orleans, pp. 119–120.

Koegl, C. J. (2011). High-risk antisocial children: predicting future criminal and health outcomes. Unpublished doctoral dissertation, University of Cambridge.

Lavigne, J. V., Cicchetti, C., Gibbons, R. D., Binns, H. J., Larsen, L. and Devito, C. (2001). Oppositional defiant disorder with onset in preschool years: longitudinal stability and pathways to other disorders. *Journal of American Child and Adolescent Psychiatry*, **40**(12), 1393–1400.

Levendoski, L. S. and Cartledge. G. (2000). Self-monitoring for elementary school children with serious emotional disturbances: Classsroom applications for increased academic responding. *Behavioral Disorders*, **25**, 211–224.

Levene, K. S., Augimeri, L. K., Pepler, D. J., Walsh, M. M., Webster, C. D. and Koegl, C. J. (2001). *Early Assessment Risk List for Girls: EARL-21 G, Version 1, Consultation Edition.* Toronto: Earlscourt Child and Family Centre.

Lewis, M. D., Granic, I., Lamm, C., Zelazo, P. D., Stieben, J., Todd, R. M., Moadab, I. and Pepler, D. (2008). Changes in the neural bases of emotion regulation associate with clinical improvement in children with behaviour problems. *Development and Psychopathology*, **20**, 913–939.

Lochman, J. E. and Wells, K. C. (1996). A social-cognitive intervention with aggressive children: Prevention effects and contextual implementation issues. In Peters, R. and McMahon, R. J. Editors. *Prevention and Early Intervention: Childhood Disorders, Substance Use and Delinquency* (pp. 111–143). Thousand Oaks, CA: Sage Publications.

Lochman, J. E. and Wells, K. C. (2004). The coping power program for preadolescent aggressive boys and their parents: outcome effects at the 1-year follow-up. *Journal of Consulting & Clinical Psychology*, **72**, 571–578.

Loeber, R. and Farrington, D. P. (1998). Never too early, never too late: risk factors and successful interventions for serious and violent juvenile offenders. *Studies on Crime and Crime Prevention*, **7**(1), 7–30.

Loeber, R., Farrington, D. and Petechuk, D. (2003). *Child Delinquency: Early Intervention and Prevention.* Child Delinquency Bulletin Series. Washington, DC: US Department of Justice, Office of Juvenile Justice and Delinquency Prevention.

Malone, R. P., Delaney, M. A., Luebbert, J. F., Cater, J. and Campbell, M. (2000). A double-blind placebo-controlled study of lithium in hospitalized aggressive children and adolescents with conduct disorder. *Archives of General Psychiatry*, **57**, 649–654.

McMahon, R. J. and Forehand, R. L. (2003). *Helping the Noncompliant Child Family-based treatment for Oppositional Behavior.* Second Edition. New York: The Guilford Press.

McMahon, R. J. and Frick, P. J. (2005). Evidence-based assessment of conduct problems in children and adolescents. *Journal of Clinical & Adolescent Psychology*, **34**(3), 477–505.

Minuchin, S. (1974). *Families and Family Therapy.* Cambridge, MA: Harvard University Press.

Moffitt, T. E., Arseneault, L., Belsky, D., Dickson, N., Hancox, R. J., Harrington, H., Houts, R., Poulton, R., Roberts, B. W., Ross, S., Sears, M. R., Thomson, W. M. and Caspi, A. (2011). A gradient of childhood self-control predicts health, wealth, and public safety. *Proceedings of the National Academy of Sciences of the United States of America*, **108**(7), 2693–2698. [Online] doi: 10.1073PNAS1010076108.

Moffitt, T., Caspi, A., Harrington, H. and Milne, B. (2002). Males on the life-course-persistent and adolescence-limited antisocial pathways: follow-up at age 26 years. *Development and Psychopathology*, **14**, 179–207.

Moretti, M., Holland, R. and Peterson, S. (1994). Long-term outcome of an attachment-based program for conduct disorder. *Canadian Journal of Psychiatry*, **39**(6), 360–370.

Murray, J., Phil, M. and Farrington, D. P. (2010). Risk factors for conduct disorders and delinquency: key findings from longitudinal studies. *Canadian Journal of Psychiatry*, **55**(10), 633–642.

National Institute of Health and Care Excellence. (2006). *Heath Technology Appraisal: Parent Training and Education Programmes for Childhood Conduct Disorder*. London: NICE.

National Institute for Health and Care Excellence. (2013). *Antisocial Behaviour and Conduct Disorders in Children and Young People: Recognition, Intervention and Management*. London: NICE.

Nelson, J. R., Smith, D. J., Young, R. K. and Dodd, J. M. (1991). A review of self-management outcome research conducted with students who exhibit behavioral disorders. *Behavioral Disorders*, **16**, 168–179.

Nixon, R. D., Sweeney, L., Erickson, D. B., and Touyz, S. W. (2003). Parent-child interaction therapy: a comparison of standard and abbreviated treatments for oppositional defiant preschoolers. *Journal of Consulting & Clinical Psychology*, **71**, 251–260.

O'Connor, T., Deater-Deckard, K., Fulker, D., Rutter, M., and Plomin, R. (1998). Genotype-environment correlations in late childhood and early adolescence: Antisocial behavioural problems and coercive parenting. *Developmental Psychology*, **34**, 970–981.

Ogden, T., Amlund Hagen, K., Askeland, E. and Christensen, B. (2009). Implementing and evaluating evidence-based treatments of conduct problems in children and youth in Norway. *Research on Social Work Practice*, **19** (5), 582–591.

Pappadopoulos, E., Woolston, S., Chait, A., Perkins M., Connor, D. F. and Jensen, P. S. (2006). Pharmacotherapy of aggression in children and adolescents: efficacy and effect size. *Journal of the Canadian Academy of Child and Adolescent Psychiatry*, **15**, 27–39.

Patterson, G. R., Chamberlain, P. and Reid, J. B. (1982). A comparative evaluation of a parent training program. *Behavior Therapy*, **13**, 638–650.

Patterson, G. R., Forgatch, M. S. and DeGarmo, D. S. (2010). Cascading effects following intervention. *Development and Psychopathology*, **22**, 949–970.

Pepler, D., Walsh, M., Yuile, A., Levene, K., Vaughan, A. and Webber, J. (2011). Bridging the gender gap: interventions with aggressive girls and their parents. *Prevention Science*, **11**, 229–238. [Online] doi: 10.1007/s11121-009-0167-4.

Piquero, A. R., Jennings, W. G. and Farrington, D. P. (2010). Self-control interventions for children under age 10 for improving self-control and delinquency and problem behaviors. *Campbell Systematic Reviews*, **2**. doi: 10.4073/csr.2010.2.

Piquero, A. R., Jennings, W. G., Farrington, D. P., Diamond, B. and Reingle Gonzalez, J. M. (2016). A meta-analysis update on the effectiveness of early self-control improvement programs to improve self-control and reduce delinquency. *Journal of Experimental Criminology*, **12**(2) 249–264.

Prinz, R. J. and Miller, G. E. (1994). Family-based treatment for childhood antisocial behavior: Experimental influences on dropout and engagement. *Journal of Consulting and Clinical Psychology*, **62**(3), 645–650.

Reid, M. J., Webster-Stratton, C. and Hammond, M. (2003). Follow-up of children who received the incredible years intervention for oppositional-defiant disorder: Maintenance and prediction of 2-year outcome. *Behavior Therapy*, **34**, 471–491.

Rifkin, A., Karajgi, B., Dicker, R., Perl, E., Boppana, V., Hasan, N. and Pollack, S. (1997). Lithium treatment of conduct disorders in adolescents. *American Journal of Psychiatry*, **154**, 554–555.

Rutter, M., Tizard, J. and Whitemore, K. (1970). *Education, Health, and Behaviour*. New York: Wiley.

Sanders, M. R., Markie-Dadds, C., Tully, L. A. and Bor, W. (2000). The Triple P-Positive Parenting Program: a comparison of enhanced, standard, and self-directed behavioral family intervention for parents of children with early onset conduct problems. *Journal of Consulting and Clinical Psychology*, **68**, 624–640.

Scott, S. (2008). Parenting programs. In Rutter, M., Bishop, D., Pine, D., Scott, S., Taylor, E., Stevenson, J. and Thapar, A. Editors. *Rutter's Child and Adolescent Psychiatry* (pp. 1046–1051). Oxford: Blackwell.

Scott, S. (2015). Oppositional and conduct disorders. In Thapar, A., Pine, D., Leckman, J., Scott, S., Snowling, M. and Taylor, E. Editors. *Rutter's Child and Adolescent's Psychiatry*. New York: Wiley.

Scott, S. and Dadds, M. (2009). When parent training doesn't work: theory-driven clinical strategies. *Journal of Child Psychology and Psychiatry*, **50**, 1441–1450.

Scott, S., Spender, Q., Doolan, M., Jacobs, B. and Aspland, H. (2001). Multicentre controlled trial of parenting groups for childhood antisocial behaviour in clinical practice. *British Medical Journal*, **323**, 1–7.

Scott, S., Sylva, K., Doolan, M., Price, J., Jacobs, B., Crook, C. and Landau, S. (2010). Randomized controlled trial of parent groups for child antisocial behaviour targeting multiple risk factors: the SPOKES project. *Journal of Child Psychology and Psychiatry* **51**, 48–57.

Shirk, S. R. and Carver, M. (2003). Prediction of treatment outcome from relationship variables in child and adolescent therapy: a meta-analytic review. *Journal of Consulting & Clinical Psychology*, **71**, 452–464.

Snyder, R., Turgay, A., Aman, M., Binder, C., Fisman, S. and Carroll, A., and the Risperidone Conduct Study Group. (2002). Effects of risperidone on conduct and disruptive behavior disorders in children with subaverage IQs. *Journal of the American Academy of Child and Adolescent Psychiatry*, **41**, 1026–1036.

Stattin, H. and Magnusson, D. (1995). Onset of official delinquency: its co-occurrence in time with educational, behavioural, and interpersonal problems. *British Journal of Criminology*, **35**, 417–449.

Steiner, H., Saxena, K. and Chang, K. (2003). Psychopharmacologic strategies for the treatment of aggression in juveniles. *CNS Spectrums*, **8**, 298–308.

Stern, S. B., Walsh, M., Mercado, M., Levene, K., Pepler, D. J., Carr, A., Heppell, A. and Lowe, E. (2015). When they call, will they come? A contextually responsive approach for engaging multistressed families in an urban child mental health center: a randomized clinical trial. *Research on Social Work Practice*, **25**(5), 549–563.

Striepling, S. H. (1997). The low-aggression classroom: A teacher's view. In Goldstein, A. P. and Conoley, J. C. Editors. *School Violence Intervention: A Practical Handbook* (pp. 23–45). New York: Guilford Press.

Tremblay, R. E. and Nagin, D. S. (2005). The developmental origins of physical aggression in humans. In Tremblay, R. E., Hartup, W. W. and Archer, J. Editors. *Developmental Origins of Aggression* (pp. 83–106). New York: Guilford Press.

Trzesniewski, K., Moffitt, T. E., Caspi, A., Taylor, A., and Maughan, B. (2006). Revisiting the association between reading achievement and antisocial behavior. *Child Development*, **77**, 72–88.

Turgay, A. (2004). Aggression and disruptive behavior disorders in children and adolescents. *Expert Review of Neurotherapeutics*, **4**, 623–632.

van Yperen, T. and Boendermaker, L. (2008). Interventions. In Loeber, R., Wim Slot, N., van der Laan, P. and Hoeve, M.

Editors. *Tomorrow's Criminals: The Development of Child Delinquency and Effective Interventions* (pp. 197–214). Burlington, VT: Ashgate Publishing Company.

Viljoen, J. L., Nicholls, T. L., Cruise, K. R., Desmarais, S. L. and Webster, C. D. (2014). *Short-Term Assessment of Risk and Treatablity: Adolescent Version (START:AV) User Guide*. Vancouver, BC: ProActive ReSolutions Inc.

Webster-Stratton, C. (1981). Modification of mothers' behaviors and attitudes through a videotape modeling group discussion program. *Behavior Therapy*, **12**, 634–642.

Webster-Stratton, C., Reid, M. J. and Hammond, M. (2004). Treating children with early-onset conduct problems: intervention outcomes for parent, child, and teacher training. *Journal of Clinical Child and Adolescent Psychology*, **33**, 105–124.

Weisz, J. R., Hawley, K. M. and Doss, A. J. (2004). Empirically-tested psychotherapies for youth internalizing and externalizing problems and disorders. *Child and Adolescent Psychiatric Clinics of North America*, **13**, 729–815.

Woltering, S., Granic, I., Lamm, C. and Lewis, M. D. (2011). Neural changes associated with treatment outcome in children with externalizing problems. *Journal of Biological Psychiatry*, **70**, 873–879.

Woltering, S. and Lewis, M. D. (2013). Changing the neural mechanism of emotion regulation in children with behavior problems. In Hermans, D., Rime, B. and Mesquita, B. Editors. *Changing Emotions* (pp. 37–43). New York, NY: Psychology Press.

World Health Organization. (1996). *Multiaxial Classification of Child and Adolescent Psychiatry Disorders*. Cambridge, UK: Cambridge University Press.

Chapter 18

Cognitive, Behavioural and Related Approaches in Young Offenders

Paul Mitchell and Charlotte Staniforth

Introduction

This chapter addresses the use of cognitive and related interventions for young people within youth justice contexts, and is broadly split into two parts: the first part covers clinical interventions (i.e. those delivered by mental health practitioners for unmet mental health needs), and the second part addresses the delivery of offence-related interventions by youth justice practitioners. Both sections are underpinned by the same theoretical principles, and it is acknowledged that there is a great deal of overlap between unmet mental health needs and offending behaviour. Throughout the chapter there is an emphasis on effective engagement and case management as a key element in working with young people with high-risk behaviours.

Cognitive and Related Approaches

Cognitive Behavioural Therapy

Cognitive behavioural therapy (CBT) is a structured psychological therapy which uses both behavioural and cognitive techniques to reduce psychological distress. Cognitive therapy (also known as cognitive behaviour therapy) was originally developed by Beck in the 1970s as an individual therapy for people suffering from depression. Beck highlighted the link between an individual's interpretation of a situation (thoughts and assumptions) and the link to emotions and consequent behaviour. The emphasis in therapy was on challenging faulty thinking patterns to improve associated emotions (Beck, 1979). Over the years cognitive therapy has incorporated behavioural techniques informed by behavioural theory which led to the development of the present-day concept of CBT which now has many different forms and adaptations.

It is now well accepted that CBT is an effective psychological intervention for a number of mental health difficulties. The National Institute for Health and Care Excellence (NICE) guidance recommends CBT as the evidence-based treatment of choice for a number of mental health problems in childhood and adolescence including depression (NICE, 2005a), social anxiety disorder (NICE, 2013a) and Post-Traumatic Stress Disorder (NICE, 2005b).

It is recommended that CBT should be delivered in a 50-minute session once per week for a defined number of weeks, often varying between 5 and 20 sessions for most mild to moderate conditions. For effectiveness, it requires the client to agree goals for treatment and be motivated to change, regularly attend treatment sessions and undertake homework exercises. There are obvious challenges to applying this model to young people with high-risk behaviours who can be difficult to engage. Adolescents rarely present to mental health services themselves, often being referred by parents (Piacentini and Bergman, 2001). Within a custodial, youth offending or psychiatric setting the person is also often not there through choice. This can mean that from the outset the young person does not recognise the need for and/or does not want intervention. There are also some potential clashes between the theoretical underpinning of CBT and young people's developmental phase. The premise behind more traditional CBT approaches is that the client has faulty thinking patterns. Adolescence is a time of increasing autonomy and there is a normalised push against authority. There may therefore be conflict between the adolescent perceiving that the therapist is in an expert role and telling them the way they are thinking and feeling is somehow wrong. One approach for the therapist is to encourage the young person to collaborate with the process by, for example, contributing to the session agenda and incorporating their interests into sessions (Kingery et al., 2006).

CBT with Young People in the Justice System

There is a lack of research relating to psychological interventions for mental health problems in young people who engage in high-risk behaviours (any behaviour that can put the young person or members of the public at risk of significant psychological or physical harm, whether or not this behaviour has resulted in a conviction) with few high-quality studies including randomised controlled trials (RCTs). There is a particular need for more research relating to interventions in young people in the community and female offenders (Townsend et al., 2010).

Studies that have been conducted with young people engaging in high-risk behaviours indicate that CBT may be useful. In a systematic review Townsend et al. (2010) concluded that CBT may help reduce symptoms of depression in young offenders. CBT group treatment was found to be effective for (non-incarcerated) young people with major depression and comorbid conduct disorder (Rohde et al., 2004). In a study exploring the effectiveness of CBT for young people with co-occurring depression and substance misuse (Hides et al., 2010), improvements were found in: depression, anxiety, substance use, coping skills, depressive and substance use cognitions and functioning mid- and post-intervention which were maintained at six-month follow-up.

Although some studies have shown promise this has not been without exception. Mitchell et al. (2011) conducted the first RCT of cognitively based intervention for mental health problems with young people in secure care. All young people had conduct disorder; however, many also had comorbid conditions including Attention Deficit Hyperactivity Disorder (ADHD), PTSD and emotional disorders. There was also a high level of learning disability in the sample. No significant differences were found on key measures assessing psychosocial need, risk of violence, coping and internalising/externalising problems between the group receiving CBT and the group receiving treatment as usual (TAU). Despite the non-significant results, the CBT group did show a decrease in the number of needs over time compared to the TAU group who showed an increase in need over time.

In reality there are many factors that may influence research results which are relevant for wider discussions about the applicability of CBT interventions for young people who engage in high-risk behaviours including: the research methodology and a potential lack of clinical influence/reality, exclusion criteria, drop-out rates, and whether cognitive and behavioural interventions are being targeted at

a specific mental health difficulty or a behavioural presentation. Young people who engage in high-risk behaviours often have a number of comorbid difficulties, including emotional regulation difficulties, depression, ADHD and conduct problems (Abram et al., 2003). CBT is a problem-focused intervention which emphasises different factors depending on the condition being targeted. For this reason it is important for the clinician to prioritise the most disabling condition and target that first.

There is also substantial evidence to suggest that young people who engage in high-risk behaviours have some neurocognitive deficits (Hughes et al., 2012). On average, scores on IQ tests are lower and there is a higher occurrence of traumatic brain injury. This was the case in the Mitchell et al. study (2011), where the mean IQ of the sample was 76 with a mean verbal IQ score of 68. Young offenders have also been found to have high levels of speech, language and communication difficulties (Bryan, 2004; Bryan et al., 2007). Cognitive and speech and language difficulties may make it more difficult for young people to engage in some of the tasks generally required for CBT to be effective, which indicates that CBT interventions may require significant adaptation. As a prerequisite for CBT the young person also has to be able to access thoughts; be able to recognise, label and communicate emotions; and have some capacity to access internal dialogue/capacity to reflect. If the young person does not have these basic skills then interventions aimed at developing these skills should be done first, for example emotional regulation and thinking skills work.

Other factors that may influence access to and efficacy of CBT interventions include: identification of mental health problems, access to trained professionals to deliver interventions, length of treatment and continuity between services (e.g. transition from a custodial to a community setting). Despite some of these challenges there is scope for CBT approaches to have great value in addressing both the mental health difficulties and high-risk behaviours of adolescents.

Adaptations for Treatment

The format and delivery of CBT may require adaptation taking into account the developmental phase of adolescence including the young person's level of cognitive, social and emotional development including neurodevelopmental impairment. In terms of

---

BOX 18.1 Key Elements in Delivering Cognitive Intervention

Key elements in delivering cognitive interventions to young people with serious conduct and behaviour problems:
- Be flexible on the times and location of the sessions, especially in the early stages
- Appropriate screening and assessment for mental health difficulties
- An initial focus on the behavioural elements of CBT
- Psychologists and other trained professionals supporting others to do CBT informed work/tasks
- Involve significant others in supporting the young person to aid skill generalisation
- Visual material should be provided wherever possible, including the session structure and content
- Use simplified language and ensure the young person knows what the words used mean
- Use concrete and age appropriate examples
- Sessions should be multimodal to enable the young people to practise the skills using different methods, e.g. written, role-play, discussion
- Make the sessions as fun and engaging as possible, ideally using the young person's interests where possible
- Reduce distractions as much as possible
- Develop clear rules and expectations for sessions, ideally with the young person's involvement
- Use positive reinforcement as much as possible, e.g. working towards a desired reinforcer, having fun review sessions after a series of positive sessions

---

delivery there are a number of adaptations that may aid learning, including making sessions fun and multi modal, for example presenting information visually, encourage verbal learning through games, reducing distractions and using simplified language (Kingery et al., 2006). In terms of the format, adapting how the young person accesses sessions may increase the likelihood of engagement, for example changing session location, involving others (friends, family, teachers) and using positive reinforcement. Multi-modal elements to help embed learning factors that may need considering when adapting CBT are included in Box 18.1.

Consideration should also be given to the appropriateness of the timing of CBT in the process of recovery. CBT can be a helpful theoretical concept to use at the start of engagement in terms of helping the young person build insight into their difficulties by understanding the link between thoughts, feelings and behaviours and the possibility of alternative interpretations, and behaviours. This process can aid collaborative formulation. The more cognitive elements of CBT may become particularly useful once the young person has gained some emotional and behavioural stabilisation, and they can start to reflect on thought processes and use alternative cognitive coping strategies. One of the benefits of cognitive behavioural approaches is the flexibility of techniques that can be used for a variety of difficulties. Future research should now focus on robust research methodologies with specific thought being given to measuring effectiveness and what is considered to be a positive outcome.

Compassion- and Mindfulness-based Approaches

In more recent years there has been a move away from the traditional CBT models and the need to change 'faulty thinking' to so-called third wave therapies. Therapies such as mindfulness-based cognitive therapy (MBCT), compassion-based therapy and acceptance and commitment therapy (ACT) focus more on the contextual and experiential change strategies required to improve mental well-being in addition to the more direct ones.

In the 1990s Professor Jon Kabat-Zinn developed mindfulness-based stress reduction (MBSR) (Kabat-Zinn, 2013), which drew upon Buddhist philosophy, specifically meditation to improve mental and physical well-being. MBCT was developed by Segal et al. (2002) and drew upon Kabat-Zinn's MBSR programme to aid the recovery of people with recurrent depression. Rather than focusing on changing the way you think, mindfulness-based approaches emphasise a focus on the present moment, recognising and accepting that certain thoughts are occurring without letting those thoughts take over emotions and cloud perceptions – becoming more aware of the present moment means noticing the sights, smells, sounds and tastes experienced, as well as the thoughts and feelings that occur from one moment to the next. Mindfulness can help us enjoy the world more and understand ourselves better, leading to better mental well-being.

A systematic review of the use of mindfulness with adults in correctional settings found that participants demonstrated significant improvements across five key criminogenic areas, including negative affect, substance use, anger and hostility, relaxation capacity, and self-esteem and optimism (Shonina et al., 2012). The authors highlighted quality issues with studies and suggested significant improvements are required in methodological factors.

For adolescents with behaviour problems there is an emerging literature relating to the effectiveness of mindfulness procedures. Van de Weijer-Bergsma et al. (2012) found that an eight-week group mindfulness training for adolescents with ADHD and behavioural problems and parallel mindful parenting training for parents were effective in reducing attention and behaviour problems and increasing executive functioning in adolescents. Fathers, but not mothers, reported reduced parenting stress. The authors suggested that maintenance strategies need to be developed in order for this approach to be effective in the longer term. Bögelsa et al., (2008) also used an eight-week group mindfulness programme to reduce attention and impulsivity problems in adolescents with a variety of different externalising disorders, including ADHD and oppositional defiant and/or conduct disorder. Improvements were noted in personal goals, internalising and externalising complaints, attention problems, happiness and mindful awareness. Young people also performed better on a sustained attention test, and these improvements were maintained at eight-week follow-up.

For adolescents in custodial settings, a ten-week group mindfulness-based intervention significantly decreased perceived stress and increased healthy self-regulation. No significant differences were found on self-reported mindfulness (Himelstein et al., 2012). In terms of applicability to young people with developmental disabilities, mindfulness meditation has been found to lessen anxiety, promote social skills and improve academic performance among adolescents with learning disabilities (Beauchemin et al., 2008). A study has also found that mindfulness-based procedures may also help young people with Asperger syndrome to control their aggressive behaviour (Singh et al., 2011).

Overall, the current research base provides support for the feasibility of mindfulness-based interventions with children and adolescents, and there is an emerging evidence base in relation to adolescence with behavioural problems and those in custodial settings; however, there is no generalised empirical evidence of the efficacy of these interventions at present (Burke, 2009).

The theory behind compassion-based approaches is that shame and self-criticism make it difficult for people to feel relieved, reassured or safe, and that there is a specific affect regulation system linked to these feelings. Training a person to develop a compassionate mind encourages people to develop and work with experiences of inner warmth, safeness and soothing (Gilbert, 2009). ACT uses acceptance and mindfulness strategies, together with commitment and behaviour change strategies, to increase psychological flexibility.

The Improving Access to Psychological Therapies positive practice guide for offenders (NHS England, 2013) states that clinicians at Step Four (specialist mental health services) have found MBCT, compassionate mind, ACT, integrative therapy and cognitive analytic therapy clinically beneficial when working with offenders. At Step Three (high-intensity primary care service), the traumatic experience can be directly addressed though trauma-focused CBT and or EMDR. Although these recommendations are made for adults it opens up the possibility of these approaches being useful for adolescents. Despite the evidence base for these interventions being limited with adolescents, compassion-based approaches hold promise for young offenders, particularly when considering that high levels of shame in young offenders have been linked with higher recidivism rates (Tangney et al., 2011) and that young offenders who convert shame into blaming of others have higher levels of violent delinquency (Gold et al., 2011).

Dialectical Behaviour Therapy (DBT)

Dialectical behaviour therapy (DBT) was developed by Marsha Linehan as a treatment for suicidal adults being treated in outpatient clinics (Linehan, 1993).

One of the main premises of DBT is that people who engage in life-threatening behaviours (to themselves or others) do not possess the skills to create a life worth living, and the main initial aim of treatment is to build these skills, specifically skills in mindfulness, emotional regulation, distress tolerance and interpersonal effectiveness. Although DBT is a cognitive behavioural approach there is increased emphasis on behavioural treatment targets and acceptance of issues that cannot be changed. The theory behind DBT is that individuals have been raised in invalidating environments where they have learnt not to trust their own emotions. This leads to difficulties with emotional regulation where difficulties are expressed through life-threatening behaviours either to the individual or to others. A full DBT programme incorporates both individual sessions and participation in a group skills programme. Therapists also have to attend a weekly group consultation to ensure that they are delivering high-quality therapy. For individuals to have completed the DBT skills programme they are generally expected to have gone through all of the skills training modules twice which takes a minimum of one year (Linehan, 1993).

There is a strong evidence base for the effectiveness of DBT with adults with borderline personality disorder (DeVylder, 2010). In relation to adolescents, Hjalmarsson et al. (2008) reported low drop-out rates and decreases on measures of psychological distress and para-suicidal behaviours following the use of DBT in a sample of Swedish adolescents and young adults in an outpatient setting.

It therefore may seem reasonable that the skills taught in DBT could be very useful for many young people engaging in high-risk behaviours who share similar skills deficits, particularly relating to emotional regulation and interpersonal effectiveness. Over recent years, DBT has been modified and adapted to meet the needs of individuals within forensic settings. McCann and Ball (2007) provide a comprehensive description of adaptions made to the standard DBT programme. This includes an addition to the Emotional Regulation module to include a module addressing emotional insensitivity, adaptations to the interpersonal effectiveness module aimed at targeting antisocial characteristics, the introduction of an anger management module and a crime review module to develop insight into the build-up prior to offences and develop relapse prevention plans using

DBT skills. McCann and Ball (2007) also discuss implementation difficulties, including difficulties training staff and adapting the material and model to meet the restrictions of the environment and the needs of the individuals.

In terms of adolescent-specific studies, Trupin et al. (2002) explored the use of DBT in an adolescent correctional facility and found a significant reduction in behaviour problems during the ten-month period of the study. The authors reported that staff's punitive actions were significantly lower and that there were significant decreases in serious behaviour problems including suicidal acts, aggressive behaviour and class disruption. An adolescent outpatient study (Nelson-Gray et al., 2006) reported statistical significance in improved functioning, increased interpersonal strength and reductions in externalising behaviour and Oppositional Defiant Disorder (ODD) symptoms in a sample of non-suicidal outpatients with ODD.

There are known associations between parental psychopathology, parenting strategies and children's emotional and mental health; yet few parenting programmes target parents' emotional regulation instead of teaching skills for managing their children's behaviour. Ben-Porath (2010) has suggested that there may be a place for DBT in parent skills training for difficult-to-reach parents. Applying DBT theory to parenting styles can help parents to understand how they may adopt opposing parenting styles and hold opposing views towards their child and try and find the synthesis between both positions. Supporting parents to manage their own emotions can also have far-reaching consequences on the child as the parents' ability to emotionally regulate may aid their generalisations of skills learnt in the clinic to real-life situations in the home.

Mentalisation-Based Treatments

Mentalisation is the capacity to understand our own and others' actions in terms of thoughts and feelings. It has been described as seeing ourselves from the outside and others from the inside. Enhanced mentalisation is associated with increased agency, and self-control in those with emotional dysregulation and difficulties controlling impulses. Two RCTs have demonstrated reductions in self-harm in adults following mentalisation-based treatments (Rossouw and Fonagy, 2012).

Mentalisation-based treatment for adolescents (MBT-A) is a year-long psychodynamic psychotherapy programme with roots in attachment theory. The programme aims to enhance the young person's capacity to represent their own and other's feelings accurately in emotionally challenging situations. The programme targets both young people and their families. MBT-A was found to be more effective than treatment as usual in reducing self-harm and depression in adolescents (Rossouw and Fonagy, 2012).

MBT-A has been influential in the development of a more systemic approach called adolescent mentalisation-based integrative therapy (AMBIT), specifically designed for 'hard to reach' adolescents with mental health problems who may be/or are at risk of offending and are residing in the community (Bevington et al., 2013; Fuggle et al., 2014). Bevington et al. (2013) describe the different settings in which AMBIT was developed. AMBIT uses mentalisation as an organising framework that is applied not only to the young person and/or their family, but also the multiagency networks involved. Emphasis is placed on the therapeutic relationship between the child and the key worker and then on the relationship between the key worker and others involved in the wider team.

The AMBIT philosophy has eight components designed to shape practice for professionals struggling to deliver interventions to a complex client group; these are: clinical governance (a system through which organisations are accountable for continuously improving the quality of their services and safeguarding high standards of care), intervening in multiple domains, key worker responsible for integration, respect local practice and expertise, respect for evidence, key worker well connected to the team, individual key worker relationship and scaffolding existing relationships. These guiding principles then support four key practice components which include: active planning, addressing disintegration, supervisory structures and wiki-manualisation (all the training materials are available on the web and can be individually tailored to the specific circumstances and client group of the specific service or team). Although an evidence base is yet to be developed at the time this paper was written, formal feedback from 150 professionals has been positive. To date, 40 UK- and Northern Ireland-based teams have been trained.

Cognitive Interventions for Behavioural Problems and Offending

This section will address assessment and interventions for offending and behavioural problems in community settings during adolescence; the management of behavioural problems among younger children is addressed in Chapter 17 by Scott, Augimeri and Fifield, as is the care and management of young people in secure residential settings (see Chapter 23 by Rose, Hibbert and Mitchell). Conduct disorder is defined in the ICD-10 classification of mental and behavioural disorders (World Health Organisation, 1994) by a repetitive and persistent pattern of dissocial, aggressive or defiant behaviour, which amounts to major violations of age-appropriate social expectations. The key characteristics are the persistence of problems and the degree to which they exceed social norms. This definition is the one used in the recent guidance from the National Institute for Health and Care Excellence (NICE, 2013b), although the title of the guidance also refers to antisocial behaviour – reflecting a broader concern regarding the impact of behavioural problems and the need for early intervention. Young people in contact with the justice system almost always meet the criteria for conduct disorder due to the persistence of their behavioural problems and the degree to which they exceed social expectations.

The cognitive behavioural model has long been acknowledged as a potentially effective intervention for addressing offending behaviour (McGuire, 1995), as it enables practitioners to address in a structured way the specific factors in people's thinking and behaviour that are associated with offending. Meta-analysis suggests that recidivism could be reduced by 10–12% (McGuire and Priestley, 1995). However, the authors noted that there was wide variation in the effectiveness of particular interventions; in fact some interventions were associated with increased recidivism.

Interventions for adult offenders have been much more extensively developed and evaluated than those for young people. Two of the most widely utilised interventions in the UK are the Reasoning and Rehabilitation programme (R&R), and Enhanced Thinking Skills (ETS). The Reasoning and Rehabilitation programme was first used in Canada in the 1970s (Ross and Fabiano, 1985; Porporino and Fabiano, 2000), and is delivered over 36 two-hour sessions. Enhanced Thinking Skills is based on R&R and was developed by HM Prison Service in 1993 for use with less serious offenders (Clarke, 2000); it is delivered over 20 two-hour sessions.

Cognitive Programmes for Young People Who Offend

Adult-based cognitive programmes such as R&R have been used with younger offenders (including adolescents) but with mixed results; some studies have reported positive outcomes, but they have been associated with an increase in recidivism in some studies (Pullen, 1996; Wilkinson, 2005). It has been suggested that this is due to neurodevelopmental differences (and therefore differences in learning styles) between adolescents and adults.

Both R&R and ETS have subsequently been adapted for use with adolescent offenders. R&R has been developed into the Reasoning and Reacting programme – R&R2, also known as the Ross programme (Ross and Hilborn, 2003). Key changes from the adult programme are shorter sessions, more activity-based learning and an acknowledgement that adolescents' moral values are less developed than adults. Elements such as problem solving, consequential thinking and emotional competence continue to be core elements of the programme. ETS has been developed into the Juvenile Enhanced Thinking Skills programme – JETS (Nichols and Mitchell, 2004). It contains core elements of the original programme, such as interpersonal problem solving, perspective taking and moral reasoning, but also includes more activity-based learning, greater emphasis on visual (rather than written) material and individual sessions to supplement the programme. A similar approach is taken in other programmes, such as the Juvenile Cognitive Intervention programme – JCIP (Smith et al., 2004 – quoted in Bogestad et al., 2010); in which key elements of cognitive programmes are re-packaged for younger participants. All three of these programmes have been evaluated and have demonstrated significant cognitive changes in the programme participants (Curran and Bull, 2009; Ministry of Justice, 2012; Bogestad et al., 2010). However, the studies were relatively small; only the Bogestad study exceeded 50 participants ($n = 165$). All the interventions were evaluated in secure or residential (rather than community) settings, and none of the studies reported recidivism or reconviction rates.

Effective Programmes and Matching Interventions to Needs

The lack of high-quality evidence to support the effectiveness of offence-related interventions remains a source of concern (National Audit Office, 2010), and understanding the elements or processes necessary for effectiveness remains a priority (National Association for the Care and Resettlement of Offenders, 2006). The most frequently quoted principles for understanding programme effectiveness are the McGuire principles (McGuire, 1995), and they remain helpful in understanding the elements of effectiveness for cognitive programmes.

The first principle is *risk classification*, which is targeting intensive programmes at high-risk young people and by definition *not* at low-risk young people. The potentially adverse effects of using adult programmes for adolescents have already been discussed. If this was simply an issue of 'the wrong learning style' then we could expect the programmes to be ineffective; however, they can be positively harmful which suggests that exposure to unnecessary material or concepts during a programme may have a toxic effect. There is also evidence that it is those at greatest risk of re-offending who derive the most benefit from programmes (Landenberger and Lipsey, 2005). *Dosage* is the principle of providing sufficient intervention to effect a meaningful change, and is directly analogous to the idea of medication being effective when taken at the right strength and for a sufficiently long period. This principle is further underpinned by evidence that people who complete programmes have lower recidivism than non-completers (Cann et al., 2005).

The third principle is that of *criminogenic need*, which means interventions that specifically target factors that contribute directly to offending behaviour. Some elements of cognitive interventions fit neatly into this principle, for instance work on consequential thinking for young people whose offending is impulsive or occurs under the influence of drugs or alcohol. However, there is also evidence that programmes that address the less direct or contextual factors (such as improving family interactions and skilling up parents/carers) are associated with greater effectiveness than programmes that focus exclusively on the young person (Greenwood, 2008). This point is further emphasised by the fourth principle, *intervention modality*, which suggests that programmes that are multimodal and address a wide

BOX 18.2 Key Elements in Delivering Effective Cognitive Offending Programmes

Key elements in delivering effective cognitive offending programmes with young people

- Comprehensive assessment of the young person's needs, not only factors associated with offending
- Ensure programme content is appropriate based on young person's risk level and is relevant based on young person's needs and risk factors
- Ensure programme delivery takes into account the young person's specific strengths and weaknesses – particularly in relation to their learning style and communication abilities
- If possible, locate programme delivery in a context that can offer ongoing support following completion of the programme
- Ensure programme delivery is by appropriately trained and supported staff and that programme fidelity is maintained by ongoing training/supervision for staff and quality audits

range of needs are more likely to be effective. Recent guidance (NICE, 2013b) has identified such interventions as the most effective, although it is acknowledged that they are very expensive and most suitable for high-risk young people.

Responsivity suggests that interventions are more likely to be effective if tailored to the learning styles or strategies of programme participants. Comparison of cognitively based programmes with other types of intervention generally show larger effect sizes for the cognitive interventions (Lipsey et al., 2001). It has already been noted that young people's learning styles differ from those of adults, and that this is one of the key factors in developing effective programmes for adolescents. Additionally, there is increasing awareness of the neurodevelopmental needs of young people in the justice system (Hughes et al., 2012), and programme delivery will have to take this into account if meaningful changes in young peoples' thinking and behaviour are to take place.

Meta-analysis has been used to identify the specific elements of cognitive programmes that are associated with reduced recidivism, and has identified interpersonal problem-solving and anger control elements as the most significant (Landenberger and Lipsey, 2005); victim impact and behaviour modification components were the least effective.

Programme integrity is the principle that effective programmes have a clear rationale and aims, and that they are delivered by well-trained and supported staff. Comparison of different cognitively based programmes suggests that 'generic' programmes are as effective as 'branded' programmes as long as they are effectively delivered and include problem-solving

and anger control elements (Landenberger and Lipsey, 2005). Systematic review has identified programme fidelity, high-quality training for the programme providers and low drop-out rates for participants as the key characteristics of effective programmes (Lipsey et al., 2007). The same review also noted that these features are more likely to be found in research and demonstration programmes than in routine practice.

The final principle is that of *community base*, the concept that programmes delivered close to the young person's home environment are more likely to be effective as they can draw on local resources and support networks, and therefore are more likely to have an effect beyond the end of the programme as these resources will continue to be available.

Consequently, reviewing the evidence base and also taking these principles into account suggest a number of key elements are required if programmes are to be delivered effectively. These key elements are outlined in Box 18.2 with a case example (Box 18.3) describing how these principles might be provided in clinical practice. The main challenge with a programme-based approach is to maintain programme fidelity while at the same time ensuring that delivery takes account of each young person's needs and risks.

Conclusions

Recently, greater consideration has been given to the wider social and interpersonal factors that are likely to influence the effectiveness of any intervention with a young person within a youth justice context (National Association for the Care and Resettlement

---

BOX 18.3 Community-based Case Example

Background

Michael was 14 years old and came from a disrupted family background. He lived with his mother with whom he had a close relationship. However, his mother suffered from episodes of depression and during these times she was not emotionally available for Michael. Michael had been involved with CAMHS from a young age due to behaviour problems, and he received a diagnosis of ADHD at the age of ten. He had been excluded from school due to aggression and was currently sporadically attending a pupil referral unit. Two years ago Michael's father had died and since this time he had been getting involved with antisocial peers. Over the last year in particular Michael had been coming to the attention of the police through shoplifting and antisocial behaviour. Michael was most recently referred to the youth offending service as he had been arrested for a violent assault against another young person. When Michael had been arrested the police had noticed that Michael had self-harming injuries across his chest. The local YOS had an in-reach psychologist attached to the team who conducted an initial assessment with Michael. The psychologist and the YOS worker went to do the assessment at Michael's home address. They considered that they would more likely to get see Michael this way and they could also speak with Michael's mother.

Assessment and Formulation

Michael's engagement with the assessment was initially poor; however, he began to talk more openly when the psychologist explained her understanding of how some of Michael's difficulties may have developed. Through the assessment the psychologist and Michael were able to develop a tentative formulation of his difficulties which centred around low self-esteem, negative thinking patterns and emotional regulation problems. The link between thoughts, feelings and behaviour was explained to Michael, who was provided with some sheets to aid reflection around any difficult feelings that had occurred throughout the day.

Intervention

Michael's mother was asked to complete a reflective account with Michael after any incident of aggression. Michael agreed that he would meet with the YOS worker weekly to review his reflective accounts and do some work around recognising, labelling and regulating emotions. This work would also look at the link between thoughts, feelings and behaviour to help Michael build reflective capacity. The psychologist agreed to attend these appointments once every three weeks to support delivery of the intervention and also met the YOS worker separately for supervision. The YOS worker also did some work with Michael's mother to help her with understanding Michael's difficulties and managing his behaviour.

In relation to self-harm, the team decided to take an approach of watchful waiting in terms of Michael's response to the interventions offered. The local CAMHS team did offer a DBT service which may become appropriate for Michael should he not respond to the interventions offered.

The psychologist also consulted with the school around behaviour management so that Michael was receiving a consistent approach.

---

of Offenders, 2007). There has been an increasing awareness of the importance of protective factors (as opposed to risk factors) in identifying those young people most at risk of further offending. Alongside this there has been a shift of focus onto the positive elements in a young person's life, perhaps best described as their 'social capital' (as opposed to the young person's perceived deficits) that may be utilised to promote social engagement and reduce the risk of reoffending. This approach ('desistance')

directly parallels the recent emphasis on 'recovery' (rather than concepts such as symptom severity) in mental healthcare delivery. It pays attention to a broader context than just programme delivery, and is increasingly influencing the approach to young people who offend. In particular, it acknowledges the importance of effective engagement and relationship building with the young person and their carers, and good case management (see Box 18.2).

There are also emerging models of service delivery that utilise recent improvements in communication technology and online resources. 'Tele-health' is a term used to refer to health-related services and information delivered via telecommunications technologies including the phone, video conferencing and the internet. One of the benefits of tele-mental health is that people can access a mental health professional or therapy group from their own home via the web. This makes access much easier for people in rural communities or those client groups who may be difficult to reach for other reasons such as physical disabilities and ill health, people without transport and carers. There is also the scope for a single therapist to access a much larger number of people at the same time potentially decreasing the waiting times for access to services. There is evidence to suggest the efficacy of internet interventions for depression and anxiety and alcohol abuse disorders in adults and somatic health problems in adolescents. Siemer et al. (2011) argue for the expansion of tele-mental health and web-based applications for children and adolescents.

There have been understandable concerns regarding the harmful influence of some online resources and websites, but it is increasingly acknowledged that young people participate in communication through social media and other internet resources. There are already some online resources available that promote positive mental health and well-being, and provide support for young people experiencing difficulties. Future developments in service delivery will have to take into account young people's preferences for accessing resources this way and be more creative in their use of such technology.

References

Abram, K. M., Teplin, L. A., McClelland, G. M. and Dulcan, M. K. (2003). Co-morbid psychiatric disorders in youth in juvenile detention. *Archives of General Psychiatry*, **60**, 11.

Beauchemin, J., Hutchins, T. and Patterson, F. (2008). Mindfulness meditation may lessen anxiety, promote social skills, and improve academic performance among adolescents with learning disabilities. *Complementary Health Practice Review*, **13**, 34–45.

Beck, A. T. (1979). *Cognitive Therapy and the Emotional Disorders*. New York: Penguin Books.

Ben-Porath, D. D. (2010). Dialectical behaviour therapy applied to parent skills training: Adjunctive treatment for parents with difficulties in affect regulation. *Cognitive and Behavioral Practice*, **17**, 458–465.

Bevington, D., Fuggle, P., Fonagy, P., Target, M. and Asen, E. (2013). Innovations in practice: Adolescent mentalization-based integrative therapy (AMBIT) – a new integrated approach to working with the most hard to reach adolescents with severe complex mental health needs. *Child and Adolescent Mental Health*, **18**, 46–51.

Bögelsa, S., Hoogstada, B., van Duna, L., de Schuttera, S. and Restifoa, K. (2008). Mindfulness training for adolescents with externalizing disorders and their parents. *Behavioural and Cognitive Psychotherapy*, **36**, 193–209.

Bogestad, A., Kettler, R. and Hagan, M. (2010). Evaluation of a cognitive intervention program for juvenile offenders. *International Journal of Offender Therapy and Comparative Criminology*, **54**(4), 552–565.

Bryan, K. (2004). Preliminary study of the prevalence of speech and language difficulties in young offenders. *International Journal of Language and Communication Disorders*, **39**, 391–400.

Bryan, K., Freer, J. and Furlong, C. (2007). Language and communication difficulties in juvenile offenders. *International Journal of Language and Communication Disorders*, **42**, 505–520.

Burke, C. (2009). Mindfulness-based approaches with children and adolescents: A preliminary review of current research in an emergent field. *Journal of Child and Family Studies*, **19**, 133–144.

Cann, J., Falshaw, L. and Friendship, C. (2005). Understanding 'what works': Accredited cognitive skills programmes for young offenders. *Youth Justice*, **5**(3), 165–179.

Clarke, D. (2000). *Theory Manual for Enhanced Thinking Skills. Prepared for the Joint Prison Probation Service Accreditation Panel*. London: Home office.

Curran, J. and Bull, R. (2009). Ross programme: Effectiveness with young people in residential childcare. *Psychiatry, Psychology and Law*, **16**, S1, S81–S89. doi: 10.1080/13218710802242029. Available from: http://dx.doi.org/10.1080/13218710802242029. Accessed 15 January 2015.

DeVylder, J. E. (2010). Dialectical behavior therapy for the treatment of borderline personality disorder: An evaluation of the evidence. *International Journal of Psychosocial Rehabilitation*, **15**, 61–70.

Fuggle, P., Hanley, J., Hare, S., Lincoln, J., Richardson, G., Stevens, N., Tovey, H. and Zlotowitz, S. (2015). The adolescent mentalization-based integrative treatment (AMBIT) approach to outcome evaluation and manualization: Adopting a learning organization approach. *Clinical Child Psychology and Psychiatry*, **20**(3), 419–435).

Gilbert, P. (2009). Introducing compassion-focussed therapy. *Advances in Psychiatric Treatment*, **15**, 199–208.

Gold, J., Wolan Sullivan, M. and Lewis, M. (2011). The relation between abuse and violent delinquency: The conversion of shame to blame in juvenile offenders. *Child Abuse and Neglect*, **35**, 459–467.

Greenwood, P. (2008). Prevention and intervention programs for juvenile offenders. *The Future of Children*, **18** (2), 185–210.

Hides, L., Cotton, S. M., Baker, A., Scaffidi, A. and Lubman, D. I. (2010). Outcomes of an integrated cognitive behaviour therapy (CBT) treatment program for co-occurring depression and substance misuse in young people. *Journal of Affective Disorders*, **121**, 269–174.

Himelstein, S., Hastings, A., Shapiro, S. and Heery, M. (2012). Mindfulness training for self-regulation and stress with incarcerated youth: A pilot study. *Probation Journal*, **59**, 151–165.

Hjalmarsson, E., Kåver, A., Perseius, K., Cederberg, K. and Ghaderi, A. (2008). Dialectical behaviour therapy for borderline personality disorder among adolescents and young adults: Pilot study, extending the research findings in new settings and cultures. *Clinical Psychologist*, **12**, 18–29.

Hughes, N., Williams, H., Chitsabesan, P., Davies, R. and Mounce, L. (2012). *Nobody Made the Connection: The Prevalence of Neurodisability in Young People Who Offend*. London: Office of the Children's Commissioner.

Kabat-Zinn, J. (2013). *Full Catastrophe Living: Using the Wisdom of Your Body to and Mind to Face Stress, Pain and Illness*. New York: Random House.

Kingery, J. N., Roblek, T. L., Suveg, C., Grover, R. L., Sherrill, J. T. and Bergman, R. L. (2006). They're not just 'little adults': developmental considerations for implementing cognitive-behavioral therapy with anxious youth. *Journal of Cognitive Psychotherapy: An International Quarterly*, **20**, 3.

Landenberger, N. A. and Lipsey, M. W. (2005). The positive effects of cognitive–behavioral programs for offenders: a meta-analysis of factors associated with effective treatment. *Journal of Experimental Criminology*, **1**, 451–476.

Linehan, M. M. (1993). *Cognitive-Behavioral Treatment of Borderline Personality Disorder*. New York: Guilford Press.

Lipsey, M. W., Chapman, G. L. and Landenberger, N. A. (2001). Cognitive-behavioural programs for offenders. *Annals of the American Academy of Political and Social Science*, **578**, 144–157.

Lipsey, M. W., Landenberger, N. A. and Wilson, S. J. (2007). Effects of cognitive-behavioral programs for criminal offenders. *Campbell Systematic Reviews*, **6**. doi: 10.4073/csr.2007.6.

McCann, R. and Ball, E. M. (2007). DBT with an inpatient forensic population. The CMHIP forensic model. *Cognitive and Behavioral Practice*, **7**, 447–456.

McGuire, J. (1995). *What Works: Reducing Reoffending, Guidelines from Research and Practice*. Chichester: John Wiley and Sons.

McGuire, J. and Priestley, P. (1995). Reviewing 'what works': Past, present and future. In McGuire, J. Editor. *What Works: Reducing reoffending–Guidelines From Research and Practice*. Chichester: John Wiley and Sons.

Ministry of Justice (2012). An evaluation of the effectiveness of the JETS programme. Available from: www.justice.gov.uk/youth-justice/effective-practice-library/the-jets-programme. Accessed 16 January 2015.

Mitchell, P., Mckee, A., Woods, D., Rennie, C. E., Bell, R. V., Aryamanesh, M. and Dolan, M. (2011). Cognitive behaviour therapy for adolescent offenders with mental health problems in custody. *Journal of Adolescence*, **34**, 433–443.

National Association for the Care and Resettlement of Offenders (2006). *Effective practice with children and young people – Part 1*, Youth crime briefing, September 2006. Available from: www.nacro.org.uk/data/files/nacro-2007061800–57.pdf. Accessed 16 January 2015.

National Association for the Care and Resettlement of Offenders (2007). *Effective practice with children and young people – Part 2*, Youth crime briefing, September 2006. Available from: www.nacro.org.uk/data/files/nacro-2008012503–546.pdf. Accessed 16 January 2015.

National Audit Office (2010). *The Youth Justice System in England and Wales: Reducing Offending by Young People*. Norwich: The Stationery Office.

National Institute for Health and Care Excellence (NICE) (2005a). *Depression in Children and Young People (Clinical Guideline 28)*. Manchester: National Institute for Health and Care Excellence.

National Institute for Health and Care Excellence (NICE) (2005b). *Post-Traumatic Stress Disorder (PTSD): The Management of PTSD in Adults and Children in Primary and Secondary Care (Clinical Guideline 26)*. Manchester: National Institute for Health and Care Excellence.

National Institute for Health and Care Excellence (NICE) (2013a). *Social Anxiety Disorder: Recognition, Assessment and Treatment (Clinical Guideline 159)*. Manchester: National Institute for Health and Care Excellence.

National Institute for Health and Care Excellence (NICE) (2013b). *Antisocial Behaviour and Conduct Disorder in Children and Young People: Recognition, Intervention and Management*. Manchester: National Institute for Health and Care Excellence.

Nelson-Gray, R. O., Mitchell, J. T., Warburton, J. B., Chok, J. T. and Cobb, A. R. (2006). A modified DBT skills training program for oppositional defiant adolescents: Promising preliminary findings. *Behavior Research and Therapy*, **44**, 1811–1820.

NHS England (2013). *IAPT: Improving Access to Psychological Therapies. Offenders; Positive practice guide*. Available from: www.iapt.nhs.uk/silo/files/offenders-positive-practice-guide.pdf. Accessed 15 January 2015.

Nichols, C. E. and Mitchell, J. (2004). *The JETS Living Skills Programme: An Integrated Cognitive Behavioural*

Programme for Juvenile Offenders. Theory Manual. London: HMPS Offending Behaviour Programmes Unit, Home Office.

Piacentini, J. and Bergman, R. L. (2001). Developmental issues in cognitive therapy for childhood anxiety disorders. *Journal of Cognitive Psychotherapy: An International Quarterly,* **i**5(3), 165–182.

Porporino, F. J. and Fabiano, E. A. (2000). *Theory Manual for Reasoning and Rehabilitation.* Prepared for the Joint Prison Probation Service Accreditation Panel. Ottawa: T3 Associates.

Pullen, S. (1996). *Evaluation of the Reasoning and Rehabilitation Cognitive Skills Development Program as Implemented in Juvenile ISP in Colorado.* Washington, DC: National Institute of Justice.

Rohde, P., Clarke, G. N., Mace, D. E., Jorgensen, J. S. and Seeley, J. R. (2004). An efficacy/effectiveness study of cognitive-behavioral treatment for adolescents with comorbid major depression and conduct disorder. *Journal of the American Academy of Child and Adolescent Psychiatry,* **43**, 660–668.

Ross, R. R. and Fabiano, E. A. (1985). *Time to Think: A Cognitive Model of Delinquency Prevention and Offender Rehabilitation.* Johnson City, TN: Institute of Social Science and Arts Inc.

Ross, R. R. and Hilborn, J. (2003). *The Ross Programme (R&R2) Short Version for Youths: A Handbook for Teaching Prosocial Competence.* Wales: Cognitive Centre Foundation.

Rossouw, T. I. and Fonagy, P. (2012). Mentalization-based treatment for self-harm in adolescents: A randomized controlled trial. *Journal of the American Academy of Child and Adolescent Psychiatry,* **51**, 1304–1313.

Segal, Z., Teasdale, J. and Williams, M. (2002). *Mindfulness-Based Cognitive Therapy for Depression.* New York: Guilford Press.

Shonina, E., Van Gordon, W., Sladea, K. and Griffiths, M. D. (2012). Mindfulness and other Buddhist-derived interventions in correctional settings: A systematic review. *Aggression and Violent Behavior,* **18**, 219–227.

Siemer, C. P., Fogel, J. and Van Voorhees, B. W. (2011). Telemental health and web-based applications in children and adolescents. *Child and Adolescent Psychiatric Clinics of North America,* **20**, 135–153.

Singh, N. N., Lancioni, G. E., Singh, A. A. A., Winton, A. S. W., Singh, A. N. A. and Singh, J. (2011). Adolescents with Asperger syndrome can use a mindfulness-based strategy to control their aggressive behaviour. *Research in Autism Spectrum Disorders,* **5**, 1103–1109.

Smith, D. L. et al. (2004). *Juvenile Cognitive Intervention Program Description.* Unpublished manuscript.

Tangney, J. P., Stuewig, J. and Hafez, L. (2011). Shame, guilt and remorse: Implications for offender populations. *Journal of Forensic Psychiatry and Psychology,* **22**, 706–723.

Townsend, E., Vostanis, P., Hawton, K., Stocker, O. and Sithole, J. (2010). Systemic review and meta-analysis of interventions relevant for young offenders with mood disorders, anxiety disorders, or self-harm. *Journal of Adolescence,* **33**, 9–20.

Trupin, E. W., Stewart, D. G., Beach, B. and Boesky, L. (2002). Effectiveness of a dialectical behaviour therapy program for incarcerated female juvenile offenders. *Child and Adolescent Mental Health,* **7**, 121–127.

van de Weijer-Bergsma, E., Formsma, A. R., de Bruin, E. I. and Bögels, S. M. (2012). The effectiveness of mindfulness training on behavioral problems and attentional functioning in adolescents with ADHD. *Journal of Child and Family Studies,* **21**, 775–787.

Wilkinson, J. (2005). Evaluating evidence for the effectiveness of the reasoning and rehabilitation programme. *Howard Journal of Criminal Justice,* **44**, 70–85.

World Health Organisation. (1994). *ICD-10 Classification of Mental and Behavioural Disorders.* Geneva: World Health Organisation.

Chapter 19

Systemic Treatment Approaches in Young People with Risky Behaviours

Simone Fox and Helen Jones

Introduction

Antisocial behaviour and offending in young people are viewed as serious and costly phenomena, with effects felt on an individual, familial, societal and financial level. Traditional interventions for this population have tended to focus on working either individually with the young person or delivering manualised interventions in a group setting (Ashmore and Fox, 2011). These approaches, including in detention settings, have several limitations and have been described as ineffective at best and harmful at worst (Tarolla et al., 2002). It has been noted that significant advances in treatment have been made over the years (Kazdin and Weisz, 1998), which have taken a more comprehensive approach to targeting the range of systemic and contextual risk factors associated with youth delinquency. This includes the development of multisystemic therapy (MST), functional family therapy (FFT), multidimensional family therapy (MDFT) and treatment foster care oregon (TFCO, previously known as multidimensional treatment foster care, MTFC).

This chapter will briefly review the various risk factors for the development of antisocial behaviour which go beyond the individual factors within the young person. These are expanded on further in the chapter on the origins of offending (please refer to Chapter 1 by Maughan). The traditional approaches that are offered will be summarised and the various limitations of these will be highlighted. Some of the evidence-based systemic approaches to working with young people with aggressive and antisocial behaviour will be covered, including the model of delivery and the research base. Case examples will be used to illustrate how some of the models work in practice. The chapter will conclude by drawing together some of the advantages of working with the

systems around the young person but will also cover some of the limitations of these models.

Risk Factors for Offending and Intervention

The risk factors for the development of conduct behaviour problems and antisocial behaviour range from the individual (e.g. poor problem-solving, self-regulation and skills deficits) to family and other contextual factors (such as harsh and inconsistent parenting practices, low supervision and monitoring and antisocial peers) (Loeber et al., 2000; Farrington and Welsh, 2003). Thus, for interventions to be effective they need to: target the multiple factors across the various domains, be individualised to the strengths and needs of each young person and their family, and be delivered in the naturally occurring systems in which the behaviours occur and implemented in 'ecologically valid' ways. Family and parenting interventions make the assumption that family interaction may cause, maintain or worsen conduct disorder and delinquency and that if family relationships are improved they can be a key therapeutic agent for reducing unwanted behaviours and prevent relapse (Diamond et al., 1996).

Summary of Traditional Interventions

The delivery of traditional interventions to young people with severe conduct problems has typically meant services delivered to individual young people in groups in custody or in the community with others who have offended or are behaving antisocially (Ashmore and Fox, 2011). Furthermore, the cultural context still considers therapy 'individual' and

---

Treatment Foster Care Oregon (TFCO, previously known as multidimensional treatment foster care, MTFC) will be used throughout the chapter.

targeted at the young person, rather than the systems within which they are embedded.

There are a number of child-focused interventions for young people with conduct problems and/or in contact with the criminal justice system because of antisocial behaviour. National Institute for Health and Care Excellence (NICE, 2013) guidelines recommend group social and cognitive problem-solving programmes, typically consisting of 10–18 weekly meetings that use modelling, rehearsal and feedback to improve skills based on a cognitive behavioural problem-solving approach. These interventions tend to adhere to a developer's manual.

Limitations of Traditional Interventions

There are a number of limitations to approaches that work solely with the young person. Firstly, the main target is the individual risk factors; the focus of the intervention is on the professional working directly with the young person and the risk factors in the wider system are not addressed in any meaningful way. Once the young person is engaged in individual treatment there is a worry that the caregiver may minimise their responsibility, or not attend to their role in maintaining their child's negative behaviours as they become more excluded from the target of treatment. For example, individual interventions in custody, such as enhanced thinking skills, will try and address specific thinking patterns that have contributed to offending, but unless there have been systemic interventions put in place, the family and environmental risk factors will remain unchanged.

With this approach, there is an onus on the young person to engage. This particular group of young people are typically hard to engage and they may have had numerous previous interventions, and a variety of professionals from health, social care and education working with them since early childhood. They often do not trust professionals and may not engage well with services.

A further concern is that many of the traditional approaches, particularly in the youth justice system, offer group interventions which bring the young person into contact with other delinquent peers. Peer interactions, especially association with deviant peers or rejection or neglect by peers, are well known to have a powerful effect on antisocial behaviour in adolescents (e.g. Lahey et al., 2003). Most young people commit criminal offences in the context of peer activities

(Howell, 2003). It is therefore not recommended that interventions bring antisocial peers in contact with each other, as one of the main aims of intervention should be to develop more prosocial peer involvement.

Furthermore, many of these programmes have been manualised on a particular population and have not been individualised. This means that offenders with specific needs, such as learning difficulties, severe mental health problems or pervasive developmental disorders, may not be suited to the intervention and may not achieve positive outcomes.

Traditional models, for example accredited group work programmes, start by selecting participants on the basis that they have identified needs which can be met by that particular programme, for example cognitive deficits, poor problem solving abilities, anger/violence management difficulties or sexual offending behaviours. There is less of a focus on the strengths within the young person.

Other limitations of traditional interventions include delivery at fixed times often limited to working hours, they are clinic-based and treatment is non-contextual. All of these factors may hinder engagement and contribute to young people dropping out of treatment.

Review of Systemic Approaches to Conduct Problems

Family-based systemic interventions have been shown to be effective for a proportion of childhood behaviour problems (or oppositional defiant disorder), pervasive adolescent conduct problems, substance misuse or Attention Deficit Hyperactivity Disorder (Carr, 2009).

Many meta-analyses and systematic reviews have found that behavioural parent training is particularly effective in reducing childhood behaviour problems, leading to an improvement in 60 to 70% of children (Barlow et al., 2002; Farrington and Welsh, 2003; Kazdin, 2007). Behavioural parent training is also more effective than individual therapy (McCart et al., 2006). However, while the evidence for parent training programmes is well established for children aged 11 years or younger, there is limited evidence for these programmes in older children despite the recognition that parenting difficulties continue to impact on the development and maintenance of conduct disorders (NICE, 2013).

About a third of children with childhood behaviour problems develop conduct disorder, which is a pervasive and persistent pattern of antisocial behaviour that extends beyond the family into other systems (WHO, 1992; APA, 2000). NICE (2013) recommend multi modal interventions for the treatment of conduct disorder in children and young people aged between 11 and 17 years. A meta-analysis of eight family-based treatment studies of adolescent conduct disorder found better outcomes for three family-based treatments: FFT, MST and TFCO compared to routine treatment (Woolfenden et al., 2002). These interventions will be discussed in more detail in the next section.

Multisystemic Therapy

MST is a systemic intervention for young people who exhibit aggressive or antisocial behaviour who are living with their biological parents or a permanent caregiver. It was developed in the USA in the 1970s with the aim of addressing the limitations of traditional services for juvenile offenders (Henggeler et al., 2009). Although it is the young person's behaviour that is likely to trigger a referral to MST, the intervention's focus is primarily working with the family and the systems around them. The main aim of MST is to provide parents and carers with the skills to tackle future difficulties and to reduce further antisocial behaviour in order to prevent the risk of out-of-home placements, either in custody or in care.

MST is based on the assumption that antisocial behaviour is multi-determined and is related not only to the characteristics of the individual, but also the risk factors in the wider ecology including the family, peer group, school and community (Henggeler et al., 2009). Thus, interventions need to be able to address the risk factors identified within these systems in the young person's ecology if they are going to be effective in reducing antisocial behaviour.

In MST, the majority of the intervention is carried out with the primary caregivers, who are seen as the main catalyst for change. The interventions are thus focused on empowering the caregivers through the acquisition of skills to manage their child's behaviour effectively (Henggeler et al., 2009). As such, the MST therapist works with the family to overcome barriers that prevent effective parenting and management of child behaviour (e.g. systematic monitoring, reward and discipline systems, prompting parents to communicate effectively and problem-solve day-to-day conflicts). The theory is that as the parents' effectiveness increases, so will their impact on the other systems

around the young person, thus reducing the risk of antisocial behaviour. See Box 19.1 for a case example of how MST may work with a family.

One MST team consists of a supervisor and two to four therapists who come from a range of different professional backgrounds including psychology, social work and family therapy. Supervision is provided weekly on-site by the MST team supervisor and an off-site MST expert consultant. There is a strong emphasis on drawing upon evidence-based psychological approaches to intervention development such as behavioural, cognitive and structural/strategic family therapy models. The therapist has a small caseload of four to six families and delivers all of the intervention with the family and the systems around the young person. The intervention lasts for three to five months. Although the intervention is relatively brief, the intervention process is intensive and involves multiple contacts each week between the therapist and the family. Families have access to an MST trained therapist 24 hours a day, seven days-a-week for several key purposes such as removing barriers to service access, enhancing therapeutic engagement and timely responding in times of crises.

The evidence base, especially from the USA, is strong (Borduin, 1999; Fonagy et al., 2002; Henggeler et al., 2009). However, MST has also been subject to some criticism including that the initial RCTs have been carried out by the programme developers in the USA and there were questions raised around the transportability of the intervention (Littell et al., 2005). Littell and colleagues reported that results were inconsistent across studies and there was a variation in quality and context. There are now an increasing number of RCTs outside the USA that have also shown good outcomes for MST (e.g. Ogden and Hagen, 2006; Butler et al., 2011). These studies have found that it is effective, both in the short and long term, in reducing 'out-of-home' placements and antisocial behaviour and improving family relationships (Schaeffer and Borduin, 2005).

There are various adaptations of the standard MST intervention that have been developed for specific populations, a couple of which are particularly suited to young offenders. Multisystemic therapy – problem sexual behaviour (MST-PSB) has been developed specifically for chronic and violent young offenders who engage in criminal sexual behaviour such as sexual abuse of younger children, rape and sexual assault. There is a focus on addressing components of the young person's environment that contributes to sexual delinquency; issues around denial by the

BOX 19.1 Case Example 1

MST Vignette – Korey, Aged 15 years

Korey was referred to the MST team by social care services. The family had come to the attention of social services as there had been a number of incidents of Korey being physically and verbally aggressive towards his mother, which included holding a knife against her throat, breaking furniture in the house, punching walls and swearing. There were also concerns that Korey was associating with a gang and he was not in any regular education or work placement.

The MST therapist initially met with Korey and his mother to discuss their desired goals for the intervention, get a comprehensive picture of the various system strengths and needs and a more in-depth understanding of the various referral behaviours (including frequency, intensity and duration of each). The therapist prioritised the aggression at home and developed a safety plan. A 'fit' of the aggressive behaviour was done, which included getting a good sequence of a recent incident. The main drivers for aggression were Korey's mother reacting to Korey's button pushing and inconsistent consequences for his negative behaviours. Work was done with both Korey and his mother (and occasionally stepfather) around identifying specific triggers and helping his mother to not react to button pushing, giving her alternative responses and helping her to walk away when Korey was starting to call her names. A clear behavioural plan was developed in conjunction with all family members and his mother was helped to ensure that this was followed through consistently.

As well as working on the aggression at home, the concerning behaviours outside the home were also a focus of the work. Korey made it clear that he did not wish to return to the pupil referral unit (PRU) as he was concerned about the negative peer influence there. The therapist worked with the family and education welfare services to identify a suitable work placement. A 'fit' was completed on Korey associating with negative peers, which highlighted the key drivers of 'gangs give Korey a sense of identity' and 'low supervision and monitoring'. Her mother was supported in getting a better understanding of Korey's friends and setting rules around whom he was allowed to associate with, where and what time he needed to be home. Several sessions were completed with Korey and his mother around the long-term and short-term costs and advantages of associating with gangs, with the aim of addressing the specific cognition around identity.

After 14 weeks of intervention there had been a sustained period of time with no incidents of physical aggression, Korey was regularly attending a suitable work placement and he was reportedly no longer associating with the specific negative peers. Although there were some minor incidents of verbal aggression, his mother felt better able to manage these. A maintenance plan was developed and the family were discharged from the service.

individual and family are also addressed. A second adaptation is Multisystemic therapy – substance abuse (MST-SA) that involves working with young people who are abusing drugs or alcohol.

Functional Family Therapy

FFT is a manualised systemic, cognitive behavioural model of therapy that targets 11- to 18-year-olds with antisocial and violent behaviour (Alexander et al., 2013). It is predominantly home-based, but can also be carried out in clinics, schools and other community settings.

There are distinct stages of engagement, motivation, relational assessment, behaviour change and generalisation. Engagement involves everything it takes to

get the family to attend sessions; it is the initial reach out to the family that allows the family to trust that the therapist can be a credible helper. There is an emphasis on forming a balanced therapeutic alliance with each family member.

The motivation phase seeks to help the family shift from an individual focus to a relational focus. An attempt is made to help families see the patterns of behaviours they are all involved in, in an attempt to make them less blaming on an individual level and shift to thinking about what is going on between them. Through the use of themes and reframes the family is also helped to begin to change the story they have about themselves. They are helped to see the positive intent

BOX 19.2 Case Example 2

FFT Vignette – Jane, Aged 14 years

Jane was referred by the social worker at A&E following her second paracetamol overdose. Her parents were reporting that they could not cope with her behaviours and did not want to take her home from hospital. Behaviours included not adhering to boundaries, verbal abuse, absconding, substance misuse and putting herself at risk of sexual exploitation. She was on the verge of being excluded from school. Jane was the subject of a child protection plan and at risk of becoming looked after.

Engagement – dad was initially reluctant to join the sessions, so the therapist worked on being flexible and highlighting his important role in the family. The therapist also called Jane to let her know the sessions would not be just focusing on her but would help the whole family with their struggles.

Motivation (3 sessions) – there were high levels of conflict and the family felt hopeless. Jane and dad frequently shouted at each other and walked out of sessions. Hopelessness was raised by acknowledging that whilst arguments were painful at least the family had not given up on trying to communicate with each other. The family had experienced a significant bereavement, and themes around loss and protectiveness were worked with. Jane's risk-taking behaviour was reframed as her way of expressing her distress and a way of alerting the outside world to the fact that the family needed help. The family were helped to look at patterns of interaction and shift the focus from the problem just being about Jane to seeing how they were all playing a part in what was going on.

Behaviour Change (8 sessions) – various skills were introduced to the family as a way of helping them all to manage their levels of distress and reactiveness. These included: emotional regulation/mindfulness skills, communication and negotiation skills, and psycho-education about substances and peer refusal skills.

Generalisation (4 sessions). The family was helped to identify the changes that they had made and how to maintain those changes. During generalisation there was a relapse; the therapist used this as an opportunity to help the family to identify what might have been the signs that they had stopped using the skills. They were also helped to generalise the skills to other settings; for example, Jane was able to use her negotiation skills at school to get time out of class when she was becoming stressed rather than being disruptive. The family was also helped to identify what other resources might be helpful as FFT was ending. Jane's mother said she was now able to seek individual counselling to address her bereavement.

At the end of FFT, there were significant changes in the levels of conflict in the house. There were no further overdoses, Jane was coming home when expected and she was attending school. She reported that she was no longer using illegal substances, although she did admit to drinking on occasion. She was also no longer the subject of a child protection plan.

behind each other's behaviour, and as they begin to think differently about themselves and each other, the negativity is reduced and there develops an increased motivation for change.

Before moving on to behaviour change, the therapist spends time assessing the relationship styles within the family in order to ensure that any behavioural interventions match the particular relational functions within the family. The behaviour change phase focuses on helping to build new skills that develop the protective factors and reduce the risk factors within the family. All family members have new skills to develop. In-session behavioural rehearsal with the whole family is an essential component of the behaviour change phase. The therapist

also works to ensure that the behavioural payoff that referral behaviours may be achieving are met in a way that is less harmful for the family.

Once new skills have been introduced and practised the therapist moves on to help the family to generalise the use of these skills on a multi-systemic level. The generalisation phase sees the therapist withdrawing from the more central position and working with the family to identify the skills they have learnt and the development of their own relapse prevention plans. The family are also supported to identify where else within the community they may get the support that they may need to sustain the changes they have made in the future. For a sample FFT case example, refer to Box 19.2.

The intervention uses a strength-based relational focus, with behavioural components, and is for three to six months in duration. Those with moderate need have 8–12 sessions compared to 26–30 sessions for those with high needs. All practitioners are trained family therapists, and there is a comprehensive system of training and supervision built into the model which ensures fidelity.

There is good evidence from outcome studies in the USA that suggest that FFT, when applied as intended, can reduce recidivism and/or the onset of offending from 25% to 73% compared to other routine interventions over follow-up periods of up to five years (Alexander et al., 2000). One recent study found that FFT, when used with juvenile offenders and their families in community justice settings in the USA, reduced the likelihood of violent crimes by 30% (Sexton and Turner, 2010). A reduction in conduct problems has also been demonstrated in siblings of those referred. There have been several RCTs conducted in the USA and Sweden (Hansson et al., 2000; Hansson et al., 2004), and there is one in the UK (Humayun et al., 2014). Cost savings in comparison to juvenile detention or residential treatment and a reduction in treatment drop-out (10%) compared to usual drop-out rates of 50–70% in routine community treatments have also been demonstrated (Sexton and Alexander, 2003). However, one UK RCT that evaluated the effectiveness of FFT compared to management as usual (MAU) found no evidence that FFT was more effective than existing services at reducing offending, improving a young person's mental health or family relationships (Humayun et al., 2014). The authors concluded that the discrepancy in findings with US trials may have been due to the use of superior MAU.

A meta-analysis of 24 studies of MST and FFT has provided additional evidence that these interventions had a significant and substantial effect on adolescent delinquency relative to control groups (Baldwin et al., 2012). However, these effects were smaller when MST and FFT are compared to alternative therapies (Baldwin et al., 2012).

Treatment Foster Care

Treatment Foster Care Oregon (TFCO) was originally designed as an intervention for young people in contact with youth justice services with a range of complex needs and behaviours. It has since been developed for young people who are looked after and for two younger age groups where the impact of abuse and neglect on developmental progress and behaviours are impacting on their functioning in a number of domains. These include attachment relationships, educational attainment and peer relationships and may lead to poor outcomes including placement disruption, conduct problems and offending. The intervention is for 6–12 months.

TFCO was developed by Dr Patricia Chamberlain and her colleagues at the Oregon Social Learning Centre in the USA. TFCO uses social learning theory, delivering intensive support through a very close 'team around the child' approach (Chamberlain, 2003). For adolescents it is a time-limited placement where the focus is on a supportive mentoring relationship with the foster carer, close supervision, clear, fair and consistent boundaries, minimal association with delinquent peers and the development of prosocial relationships. As the programme has developed for the two younger age groups (3–6 years and 7–11 years), particularly the former, the model has been informed by attachment theory and brain science in addition to social learning theory. The focus is on promoting positive child development, emotional regulation and learning skills where the child's difficulties may be impacting on the possibility of them finding permanence and if left untreated may lead to much greater difficulties.

The foster carer is supported by a role-stratified team around the carer and child, which provides skills training for the young person, behavioural interventions and support in school, weekly support groups for the foster carer, family therapy for the birth parent or other permanent carer and psychiatric consultation when needed.

For young people referred by youth justice services, the intervention is targeted at serious and persistent young offenders for whom the alternative to fostering would be custody or an Intensive Supervision and Surveillance Programme (ISSP) (Marshall and Smith, 2013). The intention is to ensure that the young person returns to an environment where they will receive a reasonable amount of consistent and authoritative care and support, and that desired behaviours will continue to be encouraged and reinforced in a positive manner. For the youth justice population about 85% of adolescents return to

BOX 19.3 Case Example 3

TFCO Vignette – Shara, Aged 16 years

Shara was sentenced to TFCO-A at Crown Court for possession with intent to supply class A drugs. She could have received a four-year prison sentence. Prior to being placed in TFCO-A Shara was engaging with antisocial peers and gangs. There were concerns about her daily use of drugs and alcohol and risk of sexual exploitation. She had stopped attending her college course due to drug use and had started to sleep through the day and use drugs in the evening and through the night. Shara had a poor relationship with her parents and had been verbally and physically aggressive towards them.

Shara participated in weekly drug counselling through a community drug treatment programme (that was separate to the TFCO team), focusing on drug-free lifestyle and identifying and managing triggers for drug use and harm minimisation. She has been substance-free since coming onto the TFCO programme and is very pleased and proud of her achievement.

Shara worked very hard with all professionals on the TFCO programme and showed herself to be a thoughtful and motivated young person. The work with her individual therapist involved utilising strategies to support herself through difficulties, expressing herself in an appropriate manner, dressing appropriately in different situations and identifying high-risk relationships. She practised strategies developed with her individual therapist for keeping herself safe by not engaging in lengthy conversations, revealing too much information about herself to strangers and informing males that she was not interested and walking away. Shara also worked well with her skills coach in identifying and attending positive activities such as kayaking, swimming and ice-skating. Shara successfully completed a motor mechanics course, participating in practical work, course work and group work. She achieved distinction marks for English and had positive feedback from the college for her behaviour.

At the beginning of the intervention the relationship between Shara and her mother was very poor. Her mother had a history of alcohol misuse and would be abusive towards her daughter. Her father had a sporadic relationship with his daughter and had another family. The birth family worker was involved with Shara's mother and later father, to improve levels of communication, stabilise the relationship and keep Shara safe. They looked at the risks of giving Shara money and how to work better with services as opposed to seeing them as a hindrance. Shara's relationships with her parents improved significantly while she was on the TFCO IF programme, and contact with them increased towards the end of her treatment placement.

The supervising social worker supported the aforementioned interventions by working with the foster family.

During her time on the TFCO IF programme Shara was questioned and cautioned by police regarding a matter prior to being placed. The matter was dropped because of the significant positive changes that she had made during her placement. This included removing herself from gang involvement.

their biological parents' home (Carr, 2009). See Box 19.3 for case example of TFCO.

There have been a number of RCTs of TFCO that have demonstrated the positive effect of the intervention on high-risk young people in foster care (e.g. Chamberlain et al., 2007; Fisher et al., 2005; Westermark et al., 2010; Westermark et al., 2011). Eddy and his colleagues (2004) found that adolescents who received MTFC services were less likely to commit violent offences (21%) than young people who lived in group homes (38%). They are also less likely to run away from placement and have lower re-arrest rates (Chamberlain and Smith, 2003).

However as with MST, there have been concerns that most of the trials have been conducted by the programme developers. In England a non-RCT study conducted on the intensive fostering (TFCO) programme for offending adolescents found that while the young people were in the foster home, re-offending rates dropped and they were more likely to be engaged in education and training and positive activities. However, re-offending resumed when they went home, pointing to the need for greater attention to after care (YJB, 2010). In the CaPE trial of TFCO for adolescents (TFCO-A) in child welfare, the findings were that in a sub-sample of young people with severely antisocial problems, for whom the programme is intended, those placed in TFCO-A showed reductions in their behaviour problems and improvements in their overall social adjustment over those in usual care placements (Biehal et al., 2012). However, for the sample as a whole, placement in TFCO-A showed no statistically significant benefit over usual care placements across all the outcomes studied. Girls in the sample faced particular issues. They were more likely to display the internalising of difficulties in addition to the externalising of (antisocial) behaviour. Subsequent adaptations to the programme for girls by the programme developers in the USA have included more CBT components to address issues of trauma and sexual abuse.

While the CaPE trial has been an important contribution to the difficult science of undertaking an RCT in a children's social care context, several concerns have been raised about the overall design and the conclusions drawn from the study (see Harold and DeGarmo, 2014). The randomising element of the project successfully managed to eliminate the differences between the TFCO-A and Treatment as Usual (TAU) groups. However, the numbers were too small to power up (12 received TFCO-A and 13 received TAU). Conversely, the observational arm contained a good size sample (92 in TFCO-A and 93 in TAU respectively) but the groups were noticeably different, making it difficult to compare them fairly. Given the early stage of development that the TFCO-A sites were at during the trial, it is reasonable to conclude that the fully accredited sites which now exist would be better suited for a trial of the efficacy of the intervention.

Multi-Dimensional Family Therapy

MDFT is an empirically supported family-focused therapy that specialises in the treatment of youth substance abuse and antisocial behaviour (Liddle, 2013). It has been developed by Howard Liddle and his colleagues in California in the 1980s to address antisocial behaviour problems with special attention paid to substance misuse issues. MDFT involves assessment and intervention in four domains: adolescent, parent, interactions within the family and the family interactions with other systems such as the

school and youth justice system. There are three distinct stages of MDFT: the first is around engagement, the second is working with themes central to recovery and the final stage is consolidating treatment advances and disengagement. The intervention is between 16 and 25 sessions over a period of four to six months. Sessions may involve the young person, the parent, the whole family and other professionals. They may also take place in the clinic, home, school, court or community settings.

Rowe and Liddle (2008) completed a review of the evidence base for MDFT, and they concluded that it is effective in reducing drug and alcohol use, behavioural problems, negative peer associations, emotional problems and improving school outcomes. Findings from Vaughn and Howard (2004), who looked at 24 treatments for adolescent substance abuse, indicate that MDFT and cognitive behavioural group treatment received the highest level of evidentiary support. However, results are mixed and study characteristics and outcomes are diverse (Van der Pol, 2014). Van der Pol (2014) completed a multilevel meta-analysis and concluded that MDFT has a small effect in comparison with other treatments and was more beneficial for adolescents with more severe drug use and more externalising psychiatric problems, including conduct disorder.

Other Interventions: Milieu Therapy and Therapeutic Communities

Milieu therapy can be used in group settings to create a supportive and nurturing interpersonal environment for both service users and staff. The concept of the therapeutic community and milieu therapy originated from Maxwell Jones at the Henderson Hospital. It has been used in psychiatric inpatient units and (secure) residential settings for adolescents (Trupin et al., 2011). Milieu therapy is a planned treatment environment in which everyday events and interactions are therapeutically designed for the purpose of enhancing social skills and building confidence. It also recognises the need for staff to have time for learning and reflection.

The core components are to teach, model and reinforce constructive interaction and promote strategies for symptom reduction, increasing adaptive behaviours and reducing subjective distress. As part of this it encourages service user participation in decision-making and collective responsibility for ward events. There is a focus on mindfulness, distress tolerance and emotional regulation and is based on dialectical behavioural therapy (DBT) principles.

In the context of work with adolescents, it is being used in a secure setting as part of one of the MST adaptations called Family Integrated Transitions (FIT) for young people returning to the community from a secure setting. In these settings, DBT is at the heart of the model which focuses on improving the skills of the young person who is separated from his/her family and removed from the community context in which his behaviour occurred. Assessment of the offending behaviour uses a behavioural analysis to identify the contextual variables and the function of the offending behaviour. Using basic behavioural change techniques of shaping, reinforcement, extinction and contingency management, the model engages the young person in the change process, targets behaviour using a hierarchy system and then teaches the young person specific behavioural skills to change his/her actions, thoughts or feelings.

The outcome evaluation and benefit cost analysis for MST-FIT undertaken by the Washington State's Institute for Public Policy Research (WSIPPR) found that FIT worked in reducing offending and was cost-effective (Aos, 2004; Trupin et al., 2011).

Advantages of the Evidence-based Systemic Interventions

The majority of the interventions described earlier have a number of general principles which were also highlighted in a report to the Department of Health and the Prime Minister's Strategy Unit in (2007) by Utting and his colleagues. These principles can be grouped into a number of common themes.

The first is around *flexibility and collaboration* with families and key stakeholders. This theme has a major impact on increasing engagement and reducing drop-out. Treatment goals are developed with key participants from the outset, and there is clear liaison with stakeholders throughout the intervention. In terms of flexibility, the majority of the programmes are delivered within the family home, school or the community. One of the advantages of providing a service out of the office is that the family does not have to travel to a clinic (reducing financial costs, childcare of other children and time for the caregiver). These practical barriers are frequently reported by parents as a reason for non-

engagement in therapy (Garvey et al., 2006). Furthermore, the clinicians are better able to understand the environment within which the problems are occurring (and are often able to witness the issues live during sessions such as how arguments might escalate); thus the interventions are more ecologically valid. Some of the interventions operate outside of office hours (e.g. MST and TFCO), enabling parents who work to attend sessions with minimal disruption. These are factors which families have reported to increase engagement (Tighe et al., 2012; Paradisopoulos et al., 2015).

The second theme is around *model of delivery*. The interventions are based on the theory of social ecology which suggests that human behaviour is multi-determined, and the young person is influenced by the multiple systems and contexts in which they exist (Bronfenbrenner, 1979). As such, they target both the individual and the contextual risk factors that have been shown to contribute to the development of conduct disorder and antisocial behaviour. All the models have a strong, coherent and clearly articulated theoretical basis. They are multimodal and multidimensional. They are delivered by professional, qualified and trained staff who provide a high level of face-to-face contact for a sustained, but time-limited, treatment period.

The final theme is around *evaluation and outcome*. Each intervention is monitored to ensure high levels of 'programme fidelity' (core elements of the intervention are consistently delivered). There are clearly defined, operationalised goals and a strong emphasis on outcome measurement (with clear definitions of outcome such as reduction in offending and substance misuse, and improvements in education). The evidence base for the interventions is also strong, especially from the USA but increasingly from other countries too.

A further advantage of these interventions is that the ultimate aim is to reduce offending and prevent the young person from entering or returning to expensive care or custodial placements. Significant cost savings have been found by Aos and his colleagues across several of the interventions (Aos, 2004; Aos et al., 2006).

Limitations of These Interventions

Each intervention has specific inclusion criteria and by definition some people are excluded. For example, the standard MST intervention does not target everyone who is at risk of going into custody. Where there is an insufficient evidence base that MST is effective, for example for young people with severe pervasive developmental delays or young people referred primarily for psychiatric service needs, then the intervention would not be offered. There may be specialised adaptations of the intervention, but these are not currently widely available.

There is a limited time frame to complete treatment, even if goals have not been achieved. An underlying assumption of these interventions is that change can occur quickly. Duration of treatment for MST and FFT is no more than six months, and TFCO is up to a year. There may be pressure by services to extend the intervention period but there is no research to suggest that extending would improve outcomes (Fox and Ashmore, 2014).

These interventions are usually seen as specialist and separate from mainstream services, such as CAMHS. This leads them to being vulnerable to closure at times of economic hardship. It is therefore vital to take a systems approach to implementation, which includes looking at budgets across services and agencies such as health, education, social care and youth justice.

Conclusions

Multiple agencies may be involved in the care and treatment of children and young people with conduct disorders, and this can present a major challenge for services in the effective coordination of care across agencies (NICE, 2013). Furthermore, practitioners require specific evidence-based statements about the types of family-based interventions that are most effective for particular types of problems and populations (Carr, 2009).

There is a global move towards evidence-based practice and increasing pressures across health and social care systems internationally to prioritise the provision of evidence-based interventions (Carr, 2009). It is essential that going forward, commissioners and provider organisations work together to ensure a secure and integrated funding stream for the long-term sustainability of these interventions.

Acknowledgements

The authors would like to thank Kate Friedman, Myles Taylor and Joanna Pearse for their help with developing FFT and TFCO case examples.

References

Alexander, J. F., Pugh, C, Parsons, B.F. and Sexton, T. (2000). Functional family therapy. In Elliott, D. S. Editor. *Blueprints for Violence Prevention*. 2nd Edition, Book 3. Boulder, CO: University of Colorado, Institute of Behavioral Science, Center for the Study and Prevention of Violence.

Alexander, J. F., Waldron, B. H., Robbins, M. S., and Neeb, A. A. (2013). *Functional Family Therapy for Adolescent Behaviour Problems*. Edition 1. Washington, DC: American Psychological Association.

American Psychiatric Association APA. (2000). *Diagnostic and Statistical Manual of the Mental Disorders*. 4th Edition – Text Revision, DSM-IV-TR. Washington, DC: American Psychological Association.

Aos, S. (2004) *Family Integrated Transitions Program for Juvenile Offenders: Outcome Evaluation and Benefit-Cost Analysis*. Olympia: Washington State Institute for Public Policy.

Aos, S., Miller, M., and Drake, E. (2006). *Evidence-Based Public Policy Options to Reduce Future Prison Construction, Criminal Justice Costs and Crime Rates*, Olympia: Washington State Institute for Public Policy.

Ashmore, Z. and Fox, S. (2011). How does the delivery of multisystemic therapy to adolescents and their families challenge practice in traditional services in the Criminal Justice System? *The British Journal of Forensic Practice*, **13**(1) 25–31.

Baldwin, S. A., Christian, S., Berkeljon, A., Shadish, W. R. and Bean, R. (2012). The effects of family therapies for adolescent delinquency and substance abuse: A meta-analysis. *Journal of Marital and Family Therapy*, **38**(1), 281–304.

Barlow, J., Parsons, J. and Stewart-Brown, S. (2002). *Systematic Review of the Effectiveness of Parenting Programmes in the Primary and Secondary Prevention of Mental Health Problems*. Oxford: Health Service Research Unit, University of Oxford.

Biehal, N., Dixon, J., Sinclair, E., Sinclair, I. and Green, J. (2012). The care placements evaluation (CaPE) evaluation of Multidimensional Treatment Foster Care for Adolescents (MTFC-A). ISBN 978-1-78105-069-9. Available from: www.york.ac.uk/inst/spru/pubs/pdf/MTFC.pdf. Accessed 12 February 2016.

Borduin, C. M. (1999). Multisystemic treatment of criminality and violence in adolescents. *Journal of the American Academy of Child and Adolescent Psychiatry*, **38**, 242–249.

Bronfenbrenner, U. (1979). *The Ecology of Human Development: Experiments by Nature and Design*. Cambridge, MA: Harvard University Press.

Butler, S., Baruch, G., Hickey, N. and Fonagy, P. (2011). A randomized control trial of multisystemic therapy and a statutory therapeutic intervention for young offenders.

Journal of the American Academy of Child and Adolescent Psychiatry, **50**(12), 1220–1235.

Carr, A. (2009). The effectiveness of family therapy and systemic interventions for child-focused problems. *Journal of Family Therapy*, **31**, 3–45.

Chamberlain, P. (2003). *Treating Chronic Juvenile Offenders: Advances Made Through the Oregon Multidimensional Treatment Foster Care Model*. Washington, DC: American Psychological Association.

Chamberlain, P., Leve, L. D. and Degarmo, D. S. (2007). Multidimensional foster care for girls in the juvenile justice system: 2 year follow-up of a randomized clinical trial. *Journal of Consulting and Clinical Psychology*, **75**(1), 187–193.

Chamberlain, P. and Smith, D. (2003). Antisocial behaviour in children and adolescents. The Oregon multidimensional treatment foster care model. In Kazdin, A. and Weisz, J. Editors. *Evidence Based Psychotherapies for Children and Adolescents* (pp. 282–300). New York: Guilford Press.

Diamond, G. S., Serrano, A. C., Dickey, M. and Sonis, W. A. (1996). Current status of family-based outcome and process research. *Journal of the American Academy of Child and Adolescent Psychiatry*, **35**(1), 6–16.

Eddy, J. M., Whaley, R. B. and Chamberlain, P. (2004). The prevention of violent behavior by chronic and serious male juvenile offenders: a 2-year follow-up of a randomized clinical trial. *Journal of Emotional and Behavioral Disorders*, **12**, 2–8. doi: 10.1177/10634266040120010101.

Farrington, D. and Welsh, B. (2003). Family-based prevention of offending: a meta-analysis. *Australian and New Zealand Journal of Criminology*, **36**, 127–151.

Fisher, P. A., Burraston, B. and Pears, K. (2005). The early intervention foster care program: permanent placement outcomes from a randomized trial. *Child Maltreatment*, **10**, 61–71.

Fonagy, P., Target, M., Cottrell, D., Phillips, J. and Kurtz, Z. (2002). *What Works for Whom? A Critical Review of Treatments for Children and Adolescents*. New York: Guildford Press.

Fox, S. and Ashmore, Z. (2014). Multisystemic therapy as an intervention for young people on the edge of care. *British Journal of Social Work*, 1–17. doi: 10.1093/bjsw/bcu054.

Garvey, C. Juilon, W., Fogg, L., Kratovil, A. and Gross, D. (2006). Measuring participation in a prevention trial with parents of young children. *Research in Nursing and Health*, **29**, 212–222.

Hansson, K., Cederblad, M. and Hook, B. (2000). Functional family therapy: A method for treating juvenile delinquents. *Socialvetenskaplig tidskrift*, **3**, 231–243.

Hansson, K. Johansson, P., Drott-Englen, G. and Benderix, Y. (2004). Funktionell familjeterapi I barnpsykiatrisk praxis: Om behandling av ungdomskriminaliet utanfor universitetsforskningen. *Nordisk Psykologi*, **56**(4), 304–320.

Harold, G. T. and Degarmon, S. (2014). Concerns regarding the evaluation of MTFC-A for adolescents in English care. *The British Journal of Psychiatry*, **205**(6), 498. doi: 10.1192/bjp.205.6.498a.

Henggeler, S. W., Schoenwald, S. K., Borduin, C. M., Rowland, M. D. and Cunningham, P. B. (2009). *Multisystemic Therapy for Children and Adolescents*. 2nd Edition. New York, London: The Guildford Press.

Howell, J. C. (2003). *Preventing and Reducing Juvenile Delinquency: A Comprehensive Framework*. Thousand Oaks, CA: Sage.

Humayun, S. (2014). A randomised controlled trial of functional family therapy for English young offenders. Paper presented at 4th EFCAP Congress.

Kazdin, A. (2007). Psychosocial treatments for conduct disorder in children and adolescents. In Nathan, P. and Gorman, J. Editors. *A Guide to Treatments that Work*. 3rd Edition (pp. 71–104). New York: Oxford University Press.

Kazdin, A. E. and Weisz, J. R. (1998). Identifying and developing empirically supported child and adolescent treatments. *Journal of Consulting and Clinical Psychology*, **66**(1), 19–36.

Lahey, B., Moffitt, T. E. and Caspi, A. (2003). *Causes of Conduct Disorder and Juvenile Delinquency*. New York: The Guildford Press.

Liddle, H. (2013). Multidimensional family therapy for adolescent substance abuse: a developmental approach. *Interventions for Addiction. Comprehensive Addictive Behaviors and Disorders*, **3**, 87–96.

Littell, J. H., Popa, M. and Forsythe, B. (2005). *Multisystemic Therapy for Social, Emotional, and Behavioural Problems in Youth Aged 10–17*. Campbell Systematic Reviews. The Campbell Collaboration. Issue 3. Chichester, UK: John Wiley and Sons, Ltd.

Loeber, R., Burke, J. D., Lahey, B. B., Winters, A. and Zera, M. (2000). Oppositional defiant and conduct disorder: a review of the past 10 years, Part 1. *Journal of the American Academy of Child and Adolescent Psychiatry*, **39**, 1468–1484.

Marshall, J. and Smith, P. (2013). Multi-dimensional Treatment Foster Care (MTFC): preventing and treating offending among looked after children. *Forensic Update*, **112**, 28–33.

Mccart, M., Priester, P., Davies, W. and Azen, R. (2006). Differential effectiveness of cognitive-behavioural therapy and behavioural parent-training for antisocial youth: a meta-analysis. *Journal of Abnormal Child Psychology*, **34**, 527–543.

National Institute for Health and Care Excellence (NICE). (2013). *Antisocial Behaviour and Conduct Disorders in Children and Young People: Recognition, Intervention and Management*. London, NICE Clinical Guidelines, 158.

Ogden, T. and Hagen, K. A. (2006). Multisystemic therapy of serious behaviour problems in youth: sustainability of therapy effectiveness two years after intake. *Journal of Child and Adolescent Mental Health*, **11**, 142–149.

Paradisopoulos, D., Pote, H., Fox, S. and Kaur, P. (2015). Developing a model of sustained change following multisystemic therapy: young people's perspectives. *Journal of Family Therapy*, doi: 10.1111/1467–12070.

Rowe, C. and Liddle, H. A. (2008). Multidimensional family therapy for adolescent alcohol abusers. *Alcoholism Treatment Quarterly*, **26**, 105–123.

Schaeffer, C. M. and Borduin, C. M. (2005). Long-term follow-up to a randomized clinical trial of multisystemic therapy with serious and violent juvenile offenders. *Consulting and Clinical Psychology*, **73**(3), 69–91.

Sexton, T. and Alexander, J. (2003). Functional family therapy; a mature clinical model for working with at-risk adolescents and their families. In Sexton, T., Weeks, G., and Robbins, M. Editors. *Handbook of Family Therapy* (pp. 323–350). New York: Brunner Routledge.

Sexton, T. L. and Turner, C. T. (2010). The effectiveness of functional family therapy for youth with behavioural problems in a community practice setting. *Journal of Family Psychology*, **24**(3), 339–348.

Tarolla, S. M. Wagner, E. F., Rabinowitz, J. and Tubman, J. G. (2002). Understanding and treating juvenile offenders: A review of current knowledge and future directions. *Aggression and Violent Behaviour*, **7**, 125–143.

Tighe, A. Pistrang, N., Casdagli, L., Baruch, G., and Butler, S. (2012). Multisystemic therapy for young offenders: Families' experiences of therapeutic processes and outcomes. *Journal of Family Psychology*, **26**(2), 187–197.

Trupin, E. J., Kerns, S. E. U., Cusworth Walker, S., DeRobertis, M. and Stewart, D. G. (2011). Family integrated transitions: A promising program for juvenile offenders

with co-occurring disorders. *Journal of Child and Adolescent Substance Abuse*, **20**, 421–436.

Utting, D., Monteiro, H. and Ghate, D. (2007). Interventions for children at risk of developing antisocial personality disorder. Department of Health: Policy Research Bureau.

Van Der Pol, T. (2014). The effectiveness of multidimensional family therapy in treating adolescents with behaviour problems: a meta-analysis. Paper presented at 4th EFCAP Congress 2014.

Vaughn, M. G. and Howard, M. O. (2004). Adolescent substance abuse treatment: a synthesis of controlled evaluations. *Research on Social Work Practice*, **14**, 325. doi: 10.1177/1049731504265834.

Westermark, P. K., Hansson, K. and Olsson, M. (2010). Multidimensional treatment foster care (MTFC): results from an independent replication. *Journal of Family Therapy*, **33**, 20–41.

Westermark, P. K., Hansson, K., and Olsson, M. (2011). Multidimensional Treatment Foster Care (MTFC): results from an independent replication. *Journal of Family Therapy*, **33**, 20–41. doi: 10.1111/j.1467–6427.2010.00515.

Woolfenden, S., Williams, K. and Peat, J. (2002). Family and parenting interventions for conduct disorder and delinquency: a meta-analysis of randomised controlled trials. *Archives of Diseases in Childhood*, **86**, 251–256.

World Health Organisation (WHO). (1992). *The ICD-10 Classification of Mental and Behavioural Disorders*. Geneva: WHO.

Youth Justice Board. (2010). A Report on the Intensive Fostering Pilot Programme. Available from: www.york.ac.uk/inst/spru/pubs/pdf/IFpilot.pdf. Accessed 11 February 2016.

Chapter 20

Sounding the Picture – Drawing Out the Sound

Music Therapy and Art Therapy with Young People Who Have Committed Serious Criminal Offences

Lynn Aulich and Joanna Holroyd

Introduction

Young people often struggle to engage with psychological therapies that depend on talking as the only form of communication. Enlightened services recognise the benefits of the Arts psychotherapies – art; dance movement; music and dramatherapy. The art and music therapy described here is offered to young people between 10 and 18 years of age who have mental health, emotional and behavioural problems and have committed serious offences. Some are residents of forensic mental health secure units; others live in local authority secure accommodation. Wherever the young people are art and music therapy interventions will occur alongside other approaches from forensic mental health practitioners.

Young people are not always diagnosed with formal mental disorders: they may have developmental disorders on the autistic spectrum and/or learning disabilities. Most of the young people will have attachment issues subsequent to difficulties in relationships in early childhood; these may include abandonment, neglect, rejection, loss; subjugation and abuse leading to Post-Traumatic Stress Disorder. The resulting mental and emotional distress may contribute to disabling difficulties in forming positive relationships with others; possible self-harm and offending behaviours. A number of young people may also have developed problems with substance misuse.

Origins of Psychopathology

Children who have experienced neglect, their basic physical needs remaining unmet, and without formative interactions with caregivers from an early age miss out on the opportunity to play. All their energy and resources are required to ensure survival from day to day. The behaviour between a baby and its caregivers

and vice versa is the central tenet of attachment theory (Bowlby, 1988). Bowlby maintained that a disturbed attachment will have consequences for the development of pathological attachment behaviour and also be detrimental to the development of the child's personality. Some children may experience social marginalisation through poverty – and be deprived of educational and everyday cultural opportunities. Young people who have experienced rejection in very early childhood may grow up very angry, disturbed and distressed, and may eventually commit serious criminal offences.

Young people in this predicament find it difficult to engage in and sustain long-term therapy. They are 'hard to reach' emotionally (Case, 2005) – difficult to communicate and build rapport with. Consent to treatment is ambivalent and provisional, rarely given wholeheartedly. Suffering from attachment disorders youngsters struggle to trust the therapist to provide a 'good-enough' therapeutic experience. The relationship is marked by transference and countertransference – both may have feelings of failure and fear that the therapy is in danger of collapsing. The therapist has to manage these feelings, survive persecution, and the youngster's attempts to annihilate the therapeutic relationship; it is easier for a young person to destroy the chance of change and reject therapy than it is to trust the therapist and maintain hope.

Traumatic experiences frequently impair the capacity for reflection necessary to developing a sense of self. A severely traumatised young person cannot play with ideas, identify preferences or access the mental and emotional activity that constitutes creativity. They can only describe or imagine themselves as empty, blank or 'no one'. Lacking a sense of self they cannot reflect on, identify or regulate mental states in themselves and as a consequence will struggle to differentiate themselves or understand that other people have separate minds and feelings. The process of mentalisation can be developed significantly through engagement in arts therapies, specifically in their capacity to aid the recognition and regulation of feelings (Fonagy, 2010).

Mentalisation

Art objects embody the process of mentalisation (Bat Or, 2010; Holmes, 2011). Art bridges the internal and external worlds; the act of manipulating materials with hands or tools engages the mind and brings attention to perceiving, feeling, thinking, making adjustments, changing a line, a shape or a colour. Art embodies and externalises aspects of our thought, feeling and experience; it is a real object and is available for other people to see and think about in their own terms. Encouraging young people to externalise and embody aspects of their inner world through making art objects helps them to reflect on themselves, and the feelings of other people. In music therapy interactive improvisation requires active listening and thinking about the other person's music and reciprocating, which are aspects of mentalising.

Art and music therapists share a common belief that meeting the psychological, emotional and social needs of clients requires more than the use of words and language alone. In addition to language both use a creative medium as the primary mode of communication and expression. Of the young people we work with in secure settings, a significant number cannot express themselves in a 'talking therapy' due to a number of potential inhibitors, such as limited cognitive ability, learning disability and speech and language difficulties. Their personal histories may have inhibited their abilities to express their experiences in words without diminishing emotional resonance; or they may simply, as part of adolescence, have difficulty in talking directly about their worries, thoughts and feelings. Both therapies are helpful to young people who dissociate or 'lose their memory' as a consequence of experiencing and inflicting traumatic violence because art and the music circumvent the need for words; giving access to different parts of the brain and memory (O'Brian, 2004).

Art and Music Therapies

Art and music therapies have at their core the requirement to establish a trusting therapeutic relationship, within which the client is able to develop a sense of self and to help repair difficulties in forming and maintaining relationships. Therapy is an opportunity to explore the emotional world with the aim of developing greater self-awareness. It builds on strengths, improves self-esteem and increases resilience to deal with life events in the future.

Music and art differ from other psychological therapies in that the medium of the music or art gives form to and contains the projection of feelings over and above the usual transference mechanism. There is a three-way process of communication between the client, the therapist and the sound or art object, although this works differently in aural and visual media.

Art and music therapists work to address the needs of victims and offenders. The experience of being a victim is often intricately interwoven, and unconsciously re-enacted in the young person's manner of relating to others and in the nature and detail of offence behaviour. The trauma issues they bring to therapy are linked to both victim and offender roles (Kolk, 1989, 1996; Zulueta, 2006). Both the case examples illustrate aspects of re-enactment (see Boxes 20.1 and 20.2).

Some young people, especially if they are victims and perpetrators of sexual abuse, find it difficult to tolerate the intimate nature of the sensory aspects of the artistic medium, the spontaneous creativity of improvised music and the tactile use of art materials in the therapeutic relationship. These sensual aspects can be so uncomfortable that they demonstrate a need to control this (Flower, 1993). The therapist needs to be mindful of where this may exacerbate distress. The use of musical structure, composition, songwriting and pre-composed material, is a means of establishing rapport without this level of intimacy, with the aim of working towards integration of a more spontaneous interplay as a therapeutic alliance develops. This process of structured play moving towards a more dynamic form is illustrated in Millie's music therapy (see Box 20.2).

Art and music making are about looking, hearing and touching combined with thinking processes; a sequence of decisions made and actions performed. When making art or music people often describe entering into a reverie, a transitional reflective space in the mind that contributes to being aware of oneself:

> It shall exist as a resting place for the individual engaged in the perpetual human task of keeping inner and outer reality separate yet interrelated.
>
> *(Winnicott, 1971)*

BOX 20.1 Art Therapy with Eliza

Eliza, aged 12, had an adolescent mother, whose family belief was that children over four should fend for themselves. Eliza's natural father left when she was very young, so she lived with mum, her stepfather and younger brother. Eliza was neglected, physically and emotionally abused by her parents. From when they got up Eliza and her brother were locked out of the house and went to school or were left to roam about all day and could return in the evening but were frequently out after dark. They begged for food by knocking on neighbour's doors. Eliza made dens and played in the scruffy hinterland of their housing estate, where she lured younger friends to play cruel games. On one occasion she attacked and injured a little girl so badly the child only just survived. Her history documented disruptive behaviour in school when she attended, cruelty to animals and fire setting. She was charged with attempted murder and placed in secure care. She came to art therapy for the first 18 months of her sentence to work through what had led to such a vicious attack.

Eliza was bright, lively and energetic, creating a chaotic atmosphere around her on the unit. In the art room she went through a period of being extremely messy. She might begin with the intention of making a picture but during the process of mixing secondary colours, the sensual pleasure of mixing took over until the mixture turned brown. She named the mixture 'shit', as she smeared and threw it around the art room. She layered it on paper so that the paper became so heavy and sodden that it disintegrated, occasionally splattering and smearing paint on herself and therapist alike. This was her way of expressing chaotic, angry feelings belonging to the pre-verbal child that she did not have the vocabulary to articulate. Without the words for expression a baby might use her own raw materials, her bodily substances to express anger. If the feelings she needed to express belonged to babyhood then art materials like clay, brown paint and water are excellent substitutes. Even if she was not expressing inchoate feelings from babyhood she might well be using the art materials to symbolise evacuating and dumping her present hateful and angry feelings. Sometimes the mess is just a way a young person demonstrates how they feel right now on their way to articulating their feelings verbally (Aldridge, 1998). Art therapists working with sexually abused children have identified this kind of mess making as being one of the ways the child can dispose of their own abusive feelings towards others safely (Sagar, 1990; Murphy, 1998). Mess, while revealing abuse, can also defend against allowing the experience to emerge into consciousness. This is not the shouting, banging, hitting rage of an adolescent but emerges from an earlier pre-verbal self. The art room and the art therapist can contain this mess; if it is contained it is possible to work towards giving it form.

The spectacular messes that spread out over the room lasted for many sessions. Gradually, Eliza began to make objects to contain mixtures and made several clay vessels with sealed lids, like pods or paint bombs filled with brown and red paint. They were to be kept safe and placed in a box in the cupboard and locked away. For her the contents were a secret. They were decorated like little jewel caskets: beautiful and organised on the outside but full of toxic sludge on the inside. Several weeks later she would decide it was time to cut open the pods and look inside them, examining the sticky contents. They served the purpose of containment of inarticulate feelings; cherished rather than discarded they were kept safe until she wanted them back. The objects could be symbolic in that the images of a jewel casket or a bomb may be standing in for sexual parts of her body; metaphorical in that they were containers, looking whole and integrated on the outside but undifferentiated and formless inside.

Eliza frequently used overt graphic, rather than symbolic, sexual imagery. In an early session she related to me as if I were a man. In a face painting session she painted me as Hitler. She painted a portrait of me with a penis on my head and made a clay penis which she took out of the session, parading around the nursing staff saying it was it was mine, ambiguous as to whether I made it (which would have been completely inappropriate and highly embarrassing for me!). Or, that it was part of me she had cut off and was parading as a trophy like a warrior. Aspects of her handling of clay and water, paint and glue were like re-enactments of sexual play and very uncomfortable to witness. Eliza never made a verbal disclosure of sexual abuse; the only way she could communicate about it was through art and play. The likelihood that she had been sexually abused or at least exposed to the sexual violence and humiliation between her mother and stepfather was revealed through the way she made her sculptures and the way she responded to me.

Eliza made a den under the table with cardboard boxes fixed with sticky tape; it was painted with earthy bodily colours. She hid in it and spoke from inside while she drew pictures, or she would just be there 'on her own' but with me outside. It was reminiscent of the den where she seriously injured her playmate. I was uneasy about her being secretive, and she both enjoyed and was furious that I peered into the den, calling me a 'nosy cow'. Towards the end of this phase she seemed to be re-enacting her offence symbolically (Bailey and Aulich, 1997) in an attempt to understand and come to terms with what she had done. Eliza placed her hands covered in red paint around my neck very quickly but very gently so it looked like I had been badly hurt and bloodied – analogous to the way she had attacked her victim.

When I first began working with Eliza it was a struggle to contain her within the art therapy room. She was not into routines or beginnings and endings of meetings with people, timetables and regular meal times. It was difficult for her to tolerate being with me in a relationship. In her art therapy session she would frequently run out of the room; sometimes she would scream, 'Help! She's killing me' so that one of the nursing staff would come in and save her. I was frequently cast as a murderer or abuser. In her anger and bitterness I was frequently splattered and smeared with paint and clay alongside the furniture, floor and ceiling; she saw me, the art room and materials as inseparable. After a few weeks of extreme mess and chaotic discharge she began to work interactively in the manner of early play between mother and child but where she would always spoil the art works. Art therapy sessions felt like a battle for survival. She was jealous of me, hated, loathed and envied me. It was a weekly struggle to persuade her to attend. When she attended she was verbally abusive and made nasty pictures of me. Once she ate a lump of black plastic modelling material, putting me into a panic making frantic phone calls to the special helpline for poisonous substances.

Later in therapy Eliza loved, admired and wanted to be like me. She drew pictures of herself and me together. We made images of food, picnic baskets of bread, pies, fruit, cakes and ice cream. These images are of feeding, nourishment, nurture and taking care. On many occasions she spoiled beautiful pictures. Her love-hate relationship with me with was indicative of ambivalent, if not hostile, attachment. The transference was powerful and painful to bear, to the degree that I did not want to continue with the work. I had the feeling of mentally preparing myself for a battle; I would come away feeling deskilled, useless, ineffectual and almost unable to think or articulate my predicament to colleagues. The only way to find a space to think was to write detailed notes and read them out loud in clinical supervision hoping that hearing an account would afford perspective. It did. Understanding my hateful feelings towards Eliza as part of the counter-transference helped me to continue to sustain her in therapy (Cantle, 1983).

Attachment theory was helpful in understanding her intense and sustained persecution, her attempts to discredit and destroy her sessions. Eliza found it almost impossible to tolerate feeling close to anyone and wanted to force me to give up. In 'Tam Lin' the English folk tale, Janet had to hold on tight to Tam Lin, the bewitched prince she loved as he fought to escape her in the form of an eel, an adder, a bear, a lion, a red hot iron, a bowl of milk, a bowl of water, a toad, a dove and a swan before he could resume the form of a human man. Forming a therapeutic relationship with Eliza was a struggle where I had to hold on to her fighting as she turned from being a feral creature to becoming a human child.

BOX 20.2 Music Therapy with Millie

When first admitted to the unit, Millie was a thin and pale young girl, her eyes suspicious and watchful from underneath a mass of mousy brown hair falling across her face. Around the unit she had a quiet and fragile demeanour but her unpredictability commanded a sense of wariness and unease from those around.

Millie had been sentenced to an 18-month Detention and Training Order for a violent assault on a police officer. She had previous convictions for street robbery, some involving the use of weapons. Prior to being referred for music therapy she had undertaken comprehensive psychiatric assessment and input from the multidisciplinary mental health team due to her prolific self-harming, hearing voices, multiple threats to carry out assaults on staff and an attempt at suicide by drowning herself in the bath.

Millie was referred because of issues of poor self-esteem, poor emotional self-regulation and an innate and compounded lack of trust in others. During psychiatric assessment to establish the cause of her behaviour, Millie suggested her 'voices' told her to do 'bad things' to others but didn't either fully understand this or wish to talk about it. The multidisciplinary team felt the non-directive, creative aspect of music therapy could help her to access these issues without the pressure of having to find words.

When I met Millie for the first time she appeared timid and frightened, seeming much younger than 16 with her slight and wiry frame. She was overly compliant and polite, contrary to reports as someone who was frequently violent and abusive to staff and peers. She wanted to be liked and approved of and was on her best behaviour. Music therapy offered Millie a safe creative space, in a medium that she was familiar with and enjoyed. Millie had previously written poetry and songs to express her feelings, and showed a distinct interest and enthusiasm for the sessions. From the outset she identified the areas she struggled with most as her desire to stop self-harming; worries about her past and how this prevented her from being able to return home; anger 'at something but not sure what', and a poor self-image combined with low self-worth. Mirroring the reasons for referral it was encouraging that Millie had sufficient insight to see that she had areas of difficulty she wished to address. A formative process in sessions is dealing with resistance and establishing engagement. A major part of the work is trying to get young people to acknowledge there is a problem to work with.

Millie was the third of five children, and had taken over role of main caregiver for her younger siblings when the older two were removed by the criminal justice system from the family. Her parents were recovering heroin users who, despite treatment, were suspected of still using street drugs, which impaired their ability to parent their children. A component of Millie's offending behaviour was that she stole basic provisions of food and clothing for herself and her siblings to survive. In early sessions Millie was eager to explore the musical equipment, yet was in trepidation of trying out the unfamiliar. Instead she preferred to ask about the different sounds and occasionally sought permission to play. During these first tentative sessions she was compliant but suspicious of the therapist and the boundaries of the session. When she eventually explored the instruments, she demonstrated a childlike eagerness indicative of a lack of opportunities to indulge in playful and spontaneous encounters until this point in her late teens. Millie spent the first few sessions 'sorting' and categorising the instruments into those she liked and felt comfortable with and those she took an instant aversion to.

Millie showed a distinct preference for familiar safe instruments such as the solidity of the keyboard and the gentle, soothing qualities offered by the guitar and metallophone. The more unusual, atmospheric sounds such as the ocean drum and thunder drum presented more of a challenge with Millie saying they sounded 'mad' or 'crazy' before deciding they were intolerable and avoiding them completely. The ocean drum in particular seemed to provoke a strong sense of frustration and irritation. She explained it was because it was unpredictable and 'hard to control'. Millie identified with its qualities and characteristics and as sessions progressed she reflected that they were similar to those she disliked in herself and others.

Millie made associations to sounds and used the music to elicit memories. In one of the earliest sessions she tried to pick out the classical Beethoven piano piece 'Fur Elise' on the keyboard, telling me that this was a tune she was once able to play 'as a kid'. This reference to her childhood memory was poignant, as at 16 she was still very much a child but felt much older than her years. She quickly angered and was frustrated at not being able to play the instrument as she had before, and was highly critical of her attempts rubbishing her tentative explorations and then, abandoning all hope, she gave up completely. When it was pointed out to Millie that the situation shared similarities to the way she approached other aspects of her daily functioning within the unit and education, she agreed. She wanted to remember how to play the piece; metaphorically it seemed to hold the possibility of returning to a time of play and childhood, to being a 'kid' again. Time was dedicated each week to re-learning the piece, breaking it down into more manageable sections she felt able to deal with, each time reviewing the small steps she was making towards playing it as a whole piece. It is tempting to suggest that the process was contributing to rebuilding some of Millie's younger self. Simultaneously, it helped provide a practical strategy of how to manage her seemingly insurmountable difficulties that when regarded en mass appeared impossible but when broken down could be tackled more successfully.

The structure of pre-composed music offered an outlet for making free associations around the music. This 'learning' aspect enabled Millie to talk with ease about her lack of any real sense of childhood and her feeling more like the parent in her family. Millie demonstrated her honesty and maturity in reflecting that she was enjoying the safety and, ironically, the freedom that she felt being in secure accommodation. She was insightful enough to see that this was a place where she knew others were 'in charge' in a parental capacity, absolving her from the weight of her previous role of caregiver and allowing her to experience being cared for. Millie admitted this was something she resisted as it was a new and uncomfortable feeling for her; she was also able to acknowledge not wanting to leave because she liked being looked after and enjoyed people showing interest in her.

The predominant themes expressed in the unprompted poetry Millie brought into sessions were parental neglect, being witness and victim to physical abuse, lack of interest from both her family and social care team, feeling unworthy of love or affection and the ultimate loss of her childhood. The poetry initiated the process of incorporating narrative structures into her sessions using rap. Rudimentary methods such as live percussion and keyboard samples provided a rhythmic and melodic structure for the amplified microphone which became the way she communicated her feelings most successfully. These basic musical constructs progressed to incorporate pre-recorded and downloaded instrumental breaks and loops which were used to create a more authentic backing for the raps. Millie selected these according to their emotive qualities and tempo corresponding to the theme or message she was trying to convey with her words.

The raps were often adrenalin-fuelled, fast-paced, punchy and sometimes aggressive commentaries on significant moments in her life. In them she assumed a toughened persona, displaying an outward carapace behind which lay desperate feelings of sadness, loneliness, anger and confusion. The lyrical performance was impressive, given the speed at which her words were delivered and the energy required to perform them. In her everyday speech, Millie had a pronounced stammer that was notably worse in moments of high arousal or anxiety. Yet she never once stammered during her performance, even when the content recalled highly stressful and emotive situations. The narratives addressed chaotic fragmentation in her life she tried to hold together, but had not been fully able to process at any level other than to grudgingly accept them as being her 'lot'.

The form and style of Millie's raps enabled the free flow of her ideas. Her reflections on these difficulties and the nature of this style allowed for the more vehement and destructive feelings being expressed to be safely contained within the boundaries of a musical form and structure she could relate to. Millie had ultimate control of this too, having often written the poetry that she based her raps around outside of the session from week to week; this enabled her to create predictability and decide upon what parts of her chaos she felt safe to reveal.

Millie identified that rapping about her more traumatic and risky experiences from childhood allowed her to re-experience some of the 'rush' of the original encounter – something she appeared to have tried to re-capture through the less socially acceptable means of offending. She was repeatedly putting herself into dangerous or threatening situations to provoke a sense of fear in herself and others to re-create this dynamic. Millie admitted she craved something in this experience that felt familiar to her. It was as if Millie wished to re-traumatise herself or re-live these same feelings that her early life trauma had brought her. This correlated with Millie's aggressive and threatening behaviour which kept people at bay. When this idea was brought from an unconsciously expressed level within the music to a more conscious one, she was stunned, although pleased that it had been recognised, agreeing it made sense of her behaviour. Couching her traumatic experiences in terms of re-experiencing the trauma via relationships and offending provided a sense of acceptance. Millie's belief that she must have been 'mad' or alone in her experiences was alleviated. This validated her behaviour and offered a way to make sense of her world. It was a significant point in the therapy from which Millie allowed herself to engage in music making more spontaneously.

Millie displayed a strong sense of family loyalty despite her deprived childhood and the multiple traumatic encounters she had been subjected to. Millie said she felt disloyal because of what had already been disclosed in her therapy. She described this as 'breaking the chain of trust' but would simultaneously allude to there being 'loads of secrets' never to be told. Millie was checking out the safety of sessions for disclosure and displayed ambivalence towards sharing details. The only way to do this legitimately was to put specific thoughts and feelings into rap format so specific details would remain hidden but allowed her to externalise and 'let the secret out' as she put it. At a certain point in therapy I suggested that she improvise a rap – or 'freestyle'. Previously Millie had always arrived with her raps or poetry already written, and she was initially hesitant to relinquish this control, fearful of what she may reveal. Despite her misgivings, the improvised rap she produced was an uninterrupted flow of enraged feelings about her life, her childhood and anger towards her parents. It was a pivotal moment because it provided a vehicle for her deep-rooted feelings of shame and the fear of finding one or both of her parents dead from a drug overdose. It was a cathartic experience. In the moments that immediately followed the improvisation she appeared physically shocked, yet simultaneously relieved. She described feeling 'lighter', saying 'it was like being sick . . . in a good way!' – a type of musical excretion. She had held onto these feelings and fears about her parents' lifestyle for many years but had never disclosed them before.

Subsequently Millie demonstrated a greater sense of trust in the sessions, and there was a more freedom to her musical exploration, with her adopting the more spontaneous 'freestyle' model of rapping in sessions and outside, because it felt more real. In letting go of this part of herself that had consumed her over many years, she was able to integrate these feelings and accept, tolerate and withstand their potential threat. They continued to be a part of her reality, but their hold over her was radically diminished as a result.

Based on the progress Millie attained in 13 sessions, music therapy was identified as good medium to provide future support. In order to reduce her risk of re-offending Millie's local Youth Offending Team agreed to fund this when she returned to the community.

Art and music inhabit the transitional space between the inner and outer world. Young people who are referred need not be skilled in art or music; the concern is not with making an aesthetic or diagnostic assessment but to open a space for imagination and expression.

Therapy in Custody

Secure units, hospitals and prison mental health services are challenging places to offer psychodynamic therapies. In institutions offering care to highly disturbed people there is a danger that collusion, ignorance and lack of empathy can become extreme. In an attempt to contain anxiety the behaviour of the management and staff group can mirror the disturbance of the patients and become persecutory. Pervasive anxiety is difficult to manage, more so when staff have little time or inclination to reflect on the impact on themselves of caring and in maintaining a safe environment (Menzies-Lyth, 1988). Therapeutic work frequently upsets young people; they need emotional support and understanding from within the milieu, so therapists need to make time to communicate with staff about the therapeutic process. Caring for people with mental illness, Emerging Emotionally Unstable Personality Disorder and dangerous behaviour puts staff under intense emotional strain. The slow, difficult and sometimes impossible task of trying to effect positive change makes staff feel ineffectual and useless (Maine, 1957). There is a tendency among staff through complex psychodynamic processes to absorb hostile angry and negative feelings prevalent among this particular client group. These feelings are hard for people in the caring professions to acknowledge to themselves and left unexamined can lead to insensitive and destructive acting out, under the guise of improving patient care, bullying and harassment of individual staff and denigration of professional groups (Scanlon, 2011).

Containment

There are multiple layers of containment within institutions – physically, by the locked doors and functionally, via the hierarchies and working systems. The institutional milieu is usually consistent and incorporates routine tasks and activities that provide containment: the routine filters out the excessively stimulating occurrences that were formally part of the everyday life, and which the young person endured in her/his previous environments. Nurses, residential care and teaching staff provide relational containment and security. This 'holding environment' (Winnicott, 1965) facilitates psychodynamic work with damaged and fragmented individuals; it is an essential component of successful working. If the therapist does not feel safe and supported in the holding environment s/he cannot adequately provide a safe environment for therapy (Cox, 1988). Regular supervision is an integral part of clinical practice within art therapies and provides an additional layer of containment for the therapist.

Containment is an essential component of the therapeutic process for any psychoanalytic modus operandi. Within the session the therapist performs a role similar to Bion's (1962) definition of the Mother as a 'psychic container', who is able to absorb the excess of stimuli and feelings that spill over from the child. The Mother is not overwhelmed by the child's feelings but holds onto them, tolerates and makes sense of them, and responds by returning them to the child in a digestible form. In this attunement the child's experience and feelings are acknowledged, which enables the child to observe that the Mother is not destroyed by the chaotic 'mess' of emotions presented to her – but is able to give a sense of form and shape to them. The art or music therapist performs a similar role. A parallel can be drawn between the early mother–infant relationship and the fundamental process of attunement.

The sensory nature of art and music in their tactile, visual and aural forms has an intensity and immediacy in the expression of conscious and unconscious projections. The boundaries and containment a therapist offers through reliability, consistency, predictability and recognition of limits are vital when the contents and subject matter of the therapy sessions – pain, despair, confusion and muddles of life – are given time and space to emerge.

Rooms and Space

A therapy room should be well lit, warm and airy with sufficient space for people and equipment. There should be privacy to enable the child or young person to play, create and talk without fear of disruption or interruption.

Rooms should be dedicated to art or music therapy alone. More often art therapies are conducted in multipurpose rooms, where the therapist has to 'create' a self-contained space to minimise distraction and increase privacy and confidentiality. This usually involves the therapist adopting the 'portable studio' model developed in war zones and refugee camps where there are restrictions on the methods and materials used. The art and music therapist has to create a familiar and consistent space by setting the materials, instruments and equipment up in exactly the same way in each session.

In music therapy decisions on the musical resources taken to sessions have to be scaled down to assist portability, detrimentally affecting the expressive and formal qualities of the sessions. This is a significant factor because the equipment offered needs to be able to produce a 'good-enough' sound, while also being able to withstand the often robust expressive play seen in adolescent clients. While compromises can be made on size, the quality of instruments provided should be maintained. Otherwise to reduce quality affects the essence of their intended expression, and may also not survive the threats of annihilation that more vigorous and sometimes destructive play can incur.

The way a young person uses the therapy room can be an indication of how s/he perceives therapy and the relationship with the therapist. The demeanour of the young person who retreats to the cushions in the corner and sprawls conveys a different message to the one who saunters slowly and insolently around the room, opening all the cupboards and fingering the contents; or one who whirls around in excitement wanting to try and do everything at once compared to one who sits frozen at the table.

Art Therapy

Art therapy materials are selected for the qualities and properties of each medium. For example drawing materials such as pencils, crayons, pastels, felt pens in all varieties and thicknesses, and fluid materials like paint and ink, are provided for the varying degrees of control needed to use them. A variety of brushes, rollers, sponges and spatulas and – of course, hands feet and fingers – are useful. Materials for modelling such as Plasticine, clay and cardboard boxes, and a scrap box full of anything you can possibly use to make things are essential. A sand tray is useful and a water supply is vital. It is important to have the opportunity to get physically involved with stuff, to get messy, sticky and dirty without worrying about the state of the furniture and carpet. As in music therapy, art therapy makes use of developments in digital technology and the familiarity and ease young people have with it. A growing number of art therapists are using computers to generate images, video and photography to make short films and animations.

There are infinite ways of using art materials and making marks to convey individual style. In art therapy the ways of using materials can be gathered into categories. 'Chaotic discharge' – spilling, splashing, pounding and ripping – is an essentially destructive approach in which there is loss of content and loss of control over the art materials; there is no artwork. Being stuck in a regressive and destructive use of art materials may be a defensive strategy to avoid communication through formed symbolic expression. This is often a feature of art therapy with children who have committed serious offences. The art therapy with Eliza (Box 20.1) is an example of this.

Art therapists have connected these activities to the disruption in brain development as a result of traumatic experiences in early life (O' Brian, 2004). Research (Kravits, 2008) suggests that art therapies have a distinct and verifiable effect on repair, restoration and development of neural pathways in the brain, and are effective in assisting children and young people with attachment difficulties and emerging personality disorders. Then there are positive, sensual, pleasurable and experimental 'pre-cursory activities' such as scribbling, smearing and colour-mixing that do not necessarily lead to a symbolic configuration but are not destructive.

Pictographs and diagrams replacing or supplementing words are used in art therapy, especially as an adjunct when using CAT (cognitive analytic therapy). Diagrams are frequently used by young people who have previously participated in talking therapies and communicate conscious feelings.

Another category of art usage is 'art in the service of defence', the use of stereotypical, idiomatic images such as love hearts, swastikas, gravestones and flowers. Repetition, tracing and copying deny the exclusion of personal content. Young people love 'gothic' imagery preoccupied with pain, injury and death. Imagery used in tattoos and heavy metal band logos with swords, daggers, snakes and bleeding pierced hearts is idiomatic of an alternative, underground culture that represents abject, dispossessed people excluded from the mainstream. Young people relate to imagery concerned with mortality and haunting, the undead, zombies, vampires, ogres, ghosts, gravestones, coffins, skulls and skeletons; the range of colours being associated with bruising and flesh wounds. This use of imagery is a short cut, an impersonal way to refer to feeling unhappy and disaffected. Many ordinary 'miserable' teenagers use the same idiomatic ready-made imagery to effectively alarm their elders.

Fully formed expression in art produces symbolic configurations that successfully convey self-expression and communication. These images embody unconscious and conscious material relating to the inner world of the artist and to the therapeutic context.

Artwork is stored in the art room. In art therapy young people want to know that you are looking after their work – that they and their products are safe. The artworks are evidence of process and progress, and are one of the most powerful aspects of art therapy. A body of work is a resource for reflection; the ideas the artist had at the beginning change over time; new found courage and trust allow a young person to be able to say out loud something that s/he was silent about when the object was created – new insights and meanings emerge. Clay objects, drying on the shelves, stimulate conversations about the other pieces on display, arousing feelings of rivalry and possessiveness that are an important part of working with the transference relationship. Such curiosity presents an opportunity to explain confidentiality when it comes to the details of who made what, and to see that others share concerns and ideas about levels of competence in handling materials.

The interplay between therapist and young person during sessions is an important part of the therapeutic relationship. Eliza had a controlling, dependent – almost symbiotic – relationship with the therapist – initiated and led by her. For young people who are dependent and unable to initiate artwork there are interactive games and exercises. Some come to the art room but behave as if they were alone, ignoring and excluding the therapist; others who are ambivalent towards the therapist attend inconsistently and always arrive late; finally, those who avoid therapy and are hostile use the sessions to attack and reject the therapist, refusing sessions but never stating clearly that they do not want them.

Music Therapy

The selection of instruments used in music therapy is usually personal to the individual therapist, but generally includes a piano or keyboard, an acoustic guitar, tuned and un-tuned percussion instruments such as drums, gongs, cymbals, cabasas, glockenspiels and hand chimes. Some therapists may include instruments chosen for their more evocative qualities such as ocean drums, thunder drums, swanee whistles, wind chimes and rain sticks. Instruments can provide a basis for relating by being an interesting talking point. They may offer a new sonic experience to the young person, or may trigger memories of when they may have played them before.

The sounds of instruments may be elements of a soundtrack to a narrative. Story-telling is favoured by some young people as a means of self-expression, as the music can enable the descriptive process, allow the imagination to unfurl and facilitate the creation of the person's story. The overarching purpose behind the instruments selected for music therapy is that they demand no specific skill to play and are therefore accessible to all for the process of creative, musical exploration.

The traditional core collection of music therapy instruments can be adapted for working with adolescents to include drum kits, electric guitars, recording equipment, microphones, amplifiers and digital media, for creating sound loops or backing tracks over which a young person can choose to sing or rap. The adolescent identity in the choice of equipment allows the young person to meet her/his musical self, which can be at a formative stage in the process of self-discovery. Adolescence is a time of exploration of different identities, an opportunity to adopt different guises – to try them on for size and find which fits – to get a sense of where the young person belongs in her/his peer group, society and the wider world.

In communicating musically with an adolescent the therapist senses entering the client's inner, dangerous or fragile world, and it is important for the therapist to know when they are invited in or being excluded. We can relate this to the stereotypical idiom of the adolescent who listens to the kind of music that adults deem to be 'loud, tuneless, chaotic', in an attempt to dis-engage from those around her/him; or to create an impenetrable wall of noise keeping those who 'don't understand' her/him at a distance. The adolescent is changing physically, subject to pubescent hormones and is mentally preoccupied – feeling misunderstood and experiencing uncertainty in relationships. Developmental factors need to be held in mind to avoid pathologising behaviours that are part of adolescence, rather than a direct reflection of something potentially destructive.

Pre-composed or pre-recorded music is used frequently with the adolescent client group. Young people who identify with a particular genre may feel that it represents something of who they are and may choose to bring recorded music to sessions. The therapist may join the young person in listening to the music, consider its musical and lyrical qualities and how it relates to the young person. There may be a particular song that s/he identifies with because of its associations. This can be a safe means of beginning a therapeutic relationship, especially for those who need something more concrete and familiar. Playing spontaneous improvised music can be too intimidating a prospect; pre-composed or recorded music brings with it a sense of structure and predictability that does not demand immediate involvement with the instruments on offer.

Ideas from a safe, familiar world can be used as a basis for more spontaneously created music when greater trust is established in the therapeutic relationship. Some may struggle in moving away from recorded music, or may choose to re-visit it throughout the therapy process. This can be revealing of the youngster's ability to tolerate – or not – the 'dynamic interplay' (Pavlicevic, 1990) as the therapeutic relationship is forged.

The basis for music therapy is 'clinical improvisation' – a term used to describe the process of shared musical interaction between therapist and client. The 'dynamic interplay' suggests a force, something in motion, a 'reciprocal, mutual musical interaction' of change or growth, and 'interplay' between the therapist and the client. Pavlicevic and many other music therapists assert that this musical discourse, this finely-attuned 'dance', can be compared to the early mother–infant interactions that form the basis for the development of secure attachment relationships.

Music therapists seek to identify and adapt to the needs of the young people they work with, using similar processes of intuition and attunement described by Stern et al. (1977). Attunement requires the music therapist to 'read' and digest the musical and non-musical expressions of the young person's inner world and make sense of them, without being 'destroyed' by them along the way. This enables the young person's more negative, destructive, harmful or frightening feelings to be made more manageable. The explosion or expulsion of difficult feelings is often expressed in music therapy through improvisation – although it may be alarming and disturbing to receive this information through sometimes highly emotive and even disturbing dynamics, it is the role of the therapist to provide the 'container'. This is done by maintaining safety within the shared musical space, by accompanying and shaping the original outburst to give it clarity, expression acceptance and a willingness to hear it and 'be in it' with the client. Jos De Backer (1993) encapsulates this concept in a use of metaphor that describes the actions of the therapist in managing the unbearable feeling – both with and for the client: 'He will, as it were, stretch a skin over the patient's experience – an acoustic skin – which binds and shapes the expression of chaos.'

Multimodal Approaches

Contemporary developments in art therapies ideas and research suggest that creative participation beyond the therapy room enables therapeutic relationship building. Embracing a blended, eclectic approach to practice (McFerran, 2010) that encompasses working flexibly with young people in order to best support the process of transition is fundamental, not only to the transition from adolescence to adulthood but also from the secure establishment back into the wider community.

Conclusions

The prevalence of disrupted attachment in adolescent offenders within secure settings highlights the need for arts therapies to be considered as core components of psychological therapies offered to them. Within this chapter the analogy of the relationship between pre-verbal stages of development and the ability to re-create this through the creative means of art and music therapies illustrates the arts therapies' capacity to identify, explore and change basal inter-human attachment behaviour. Therapists must be mindful of their roles in secure institutions as they build temporary relationships for nurturing and fostering basic trusting alliances and must remain aware of limitations in this.

References

Aldridge, F. (1998). Chocolate or shit, aesthetics and cultural poverty in art therapy with children. *Inscape: The Journal of the British Association of Art Therapists*, 3(1), P2–9.

Backer, de J. (1993). Containment in music therapy. In Heal, M. and Wigram, T. Editors. *Music Therapy in Health and Education*. London: Jessica Kingsley Press.

Bailey, S. and Aulich, L. (1997). Understanding murderous young people. In Welldon, E. V. and Van Velsen, C. Editors. *A Practical Guide to Forensic Psychotherapy*. London: Jessica Kingsley Press.

Bat Or, M. (2010). Clay sculpting of mother and child figures encourages mentalization. *The Arts in Psychotherapy* 37, 319–327.

Bion, W. (1962). *Learning from Experience*. London: Heinemann.

Bowlby, J. (1988). *A Secure Base: Clinical Applications of Attachment Theory*. London: Routledge.

Cantle, T. (1983). Hate in the helping relationship: the therapeutic use of an occupational hazard. *Inscape: Journal of the British Association of Art Therapists*, October, 2–10.

Case, C. (2005). *Imagining Animals: Art, Psychotherapy and Primitive States of Mind*. London: Routledge.

Cox, M. (1988). *Structuring the Therapeutic Process Compromise with Chaos*. London: Jessica Kingsley Press.

Crossley-Holland, K. (1987). 'Tam Lin' in 'British Folk Tales New Versions' London: Orchard Books.

Flower, C. (1993). Control and creativity. In Heal, M. and Wigram, T. Editors. *Music Therapy in Health and Education*. London: Jessica Kingsley Press.

Fonagy, P. (2010). *Conference Paper. What happens on an Attachment Level in the Arts. Attachment and the Arts*. London: Conway Hall.

Holmes, J. (2011). *Frames and Faces Art Psychotherapy and the Art of Psychotherapy. Conference paper at Attachment and the Arts*. London: Conway Hall.

Kolk, van der B. A. (1989). The compulsion to repeat the trauma. *Psychiatric Clinics of North America*, 12(2), 389–411.

Kolk, van der B. A. (1996). The body keeps the score: approaches to the psychobiology of post traumatic stress disorder. In Kolk, van der B. A., Mc Farlane, A. C. and Weisaeth, L. Editors. *Traumatic Stress: The Effects of Overwhelming Experiences on Mind, Body and Society*. New York: Guilford Press.

Kravits, K. (2008). The neurobiology of relatedness: Attachment. In Hass–Cohen, N. and Carr, R. Editors. *Art Therapy and Clinical Neuroscience*. London: Jessica Kingsley Press.

Maine, T. F. (1957). *The ailment* reprinted in collected papers edited by Adshead, G. and Jacob, C. 2009 *Personality Disorder: The Definitive Reader*. London: Jessica Kingsley Press.

McFerran, K. (2010). *Music and Music Therapy – Methods and Techniques for Clinicians, Educators and Students*. London: Jessica Kingsley Press.

Menzies–Lyth, I. (1988). *Containing Anxiety in Institutions: Selected Essays, Vol. 1*. London: Free Association Press.

Murphy, J. (1998). Art therapy with sexually abused children and young people. *Inscape: The Journal of the British Association of Art Therapists*, 3(1), 10–16.

O' Brian, F. (2004). The making of mess in art therapy: attachment, trauma and the brain. *Inscape: The Journal of The British Association of Art Therapists*, 9(1), 2–13.

Pavlicevic, M. (1990). Dynamic interplay in clinical improvisation. *Journal of British Music Therapy*, 4(2), 5–9.

Sagar, C. (1990). Working with cases of child sexual abuse. In Case, C. and Daley, T. Editors. *Working with Children in Art Therapy*. London: Tavistock/Routledge.

Scanlon, C. (2011). On the Dis-organising Effects of Traumatisation on Staff Teams and Organisations. Conference paper at the Forensic Arts Therapists Advisory Group, London.

Stern, D., Beebe, B., Jaffe, J. and Bennett, S. (1977). The Infant's stimulus world during social interaction: A study of caregiver behaviours with particular reference to repetition and timing. In Schaffer, H. Editor. *Studies in Mother-Infant Interaction*. London: Academic Press.

Winnicott, D. W. (1965). *The Maturational Process and the Facilitating Environment: Studies in the Theory of Emotional Development*. New York: International Universities Press.

Winnicott, D. W. (1971). *Playing and Reality*. London: Tavistock.

Zulueta, de F. (2006). *From Pain to Violence: The Traumatic Roots of Destructiveness*. London: Wiley-Blackwell.

Chapter

21

Children and the Law

Enys Delmage, Hannele Variend and Mike Shaw

Introduction

This chapter explores both civil and criminal law as they relate to young people within England and Wales, taking into account some of the statutory frameworks (The Mental Health Act, 1983; The Human Rights Act, 1998; The Children Act, 2004; The Mental Capacity Act, 2005) as well as relevant common law (parental responsibility and Gillick West Norfolk and Wisbech AHA, 1985 competency). The way that the various pieces of legislation relate to the age boundaries for those under 18 is described and practical guidance is provided as to which framework might apply in various circumstances.

Definitions of a Child or Young Person

A 'child' is defined by the Family Law Reform Act (1969), the Children Act (2004) Section 105(1) and the United Nations Convention on the Rights of the Child (1989) as 'any person under the age of 18'. However, this is not applied universally, for instance the General Medical Council's Good Medical Practice Guide (2013) states that we use the term "children" to refer to younger children who do not have the maturity and understanding to make important decisions for themselves. We use the term 'young people' to refer to older or more experienced children who are more likely to be able to make these decisions for themselves. One other noteworthy distinction comes from the Mental Capacity Act where a child is defined as someone under the age of 16 and a young person is someone aged 16 or 17. For the purposes of this chapter, the term 'child' or 'children' will refer to anyone under the age of 18.

Criminal Law

In British law the minimum age of criminal responsibility is set at ten years of age (The Children and Young Person's Act, 1963) and has been since 1963.

In 1997, the Crime (Sentences) Act (1997) abolished a protection for children called 'doli incapax' whereby a child aged 10–14 could previously be exculpated on the basis that he or she did not know that what they were doing was seriously wrong. There is mounting pressure (including from the United Nations Convention Committee, 2007) to raise the minimum age of criminal responsibility, especially in light of current knowledge about the state of child brain development as it pertains to emerging aptitudes and abilities. Whilst in England, Wales and Northern Ireland, criminal responsibility set at the age of ten is the youngest age level in Europe, and one of the youngest ages worldwide, the means of dealing with those young people found guilty of serious offences does differ from that of adults, but this does not escape the fact that the criminal law is in marked discord with science in this matter.

Brain development continues into the early twenties (Anderson et al., 2001; Sowell et al., 2001; Blakemore and Choudhury, 2006), with the frontal lobes of the brain playing a key part in various elements of cognition including judgement, consequential thinking, inhibition of impulses, empathy and coherent planning. This frontal lobe functioning increases over the course of adolescence (Anderson et al., 2001; Sowell et al., 2001).This has been linked with development of the brain's prefrontal cortex (Blakemore and Choudhury, 2006), commensurate with an emerging ability to engage in consequential thinking (Steinberg, 2009). As noted by the Royal Society (2011a) (Brain Waves Module 2), the frontal lobes of the brain are the slowest areas to develop (Gogtay, 2004), in contrast with the amygdala (the part of the brain responsible for reward and emotion-processing). This imbalance is thought to account for increased arousal and risk-taking behaviour in adolescence (The Royal Society, 2011b; Brain Waves Module 4). Adolescence represents a phase of increased impulsivity and sensation-seeking behaviour (Baird et al., 2005; Steinberg, 2007; van Leijenhorst et al., 2010), in tandem with a developing ability to empathise (Strayer, 1993) and a heightened vulnerability to peer influence (Steinberg and Monahan, 2007), all of which have an impact upon decision making. These normal developmental stages are important to consider when assessing and passing comment on a child's criminal responsibility.

Developmental level and associated aptitudes are important in the context of criminal liability (so-called *mens rea*, the ability to form a guilty mind), but it is also important to consider the position of the child subsequently in court. All of the above impact factors in terms of criminal responsibility also apply when it comes to standing trial. Young people are frequently assessed by mental health professionals in relation to their 'fitness to plead', which is a standard set in case law by the Pritchard (1836) case. 'Fitness to plead' in this context requires that the individual (whether adult or child):

(1)   Has the ability to understand the charge(s);
(2)   Has the ability to decide whether to plead guilty or not guilty;
(3)   Has the ability to follow the course of proceedings;
(4)   Has the ability to instruct a solicitor;
(5)   Has the ability to challenge a juror;
(6)   Has the ability to give evidence in his/her own defence.

The Pritchard Criteria are thus relatively narrow in aspect but a wider view can be taken, the so-called effective participation, which examines the ability of the accused to engage with the trial. The European Court examination of the Thompson and Venables (T and V v. The United Kingdom, 1999) case (both aged ten at the time of their offence, aged 11 at the time of trial) took the view that neither young person was able to effectively participate in their trial (though they were 'fit to plead' by Pritchard standards) and a violation of Article 6 of the European Convention on Human Rights (1950) (the right to a fair trial) was found.

The Scottish Law Commission has previously commented that developmental immaturity would not in itself be sufficient to make a trial unfair, where the accused had representation and proper adjustments were made to the trial to take into account the age of the accused (Scottish Law Commission, 2004), but the Law Commission for England and Wales has suggested a defence of developmental immaturity as distinct from a recognised medical condition defence in the past (Criminal Liability, 2013) and has also passed comment in an issues paper out for consultation at the time of writing that developmental immaturity is an important factor to be taken into consideration when considering effective participation(Unfitness To Plead, 2014).

The MacArthur Adjudicative Competence Study (Poythress et al., 1997) examined 927 youths and 446 adults in four locations across the USA, and found that trial competence-related abilities tended to improve with age; 11- to 13-year-olds showed less understanding, less reasoning and less recognition than 14- and 15-year-olds, who in turn performed significantly more poorly than 16- and 17-year-olds (who functioned as well as adults). Low IQ scores were particularly associated with deficits. Young people were more likely to waive their rights than adults, more likely to accept plea agreements (even 16- and 17-year-olds) and were more likely to make choices in compliance with authority figures. Risk perception and future orientation deficits were found, and young people often did not understand their right to remain silent, and would see rights as being conditional. Research has also demonstrated that young people are more likely to make false confessions than adults (Redlich and Goodman, 2003).

It is furthermore important to recognise that those identified as young offenders frequently meet the criteria for being classed as 'children in need' from a local authority perspective, but there exists no easy means to transfer cases from youth court (criminal) to family court (civil) which would allow the young person's overarching needs to be considered.

Children may be dealt with in various types of criminal court. The youth court is a special type of magistrates' court which is less formal and deals with cases like theft and burglary, antisocial behaviour and drugs offences. It can pass a range of sentences including community sentences and Detention and Training Orders. The court is adapted for young people; the public are not permitted to enter and defendants are called by their first names, video links can be used to reduce anxiety and regular breaks are permitted to allow young people to effectively participate. Serious crimes like murder or rape will be dealt with in youth court initially, but will be passed to a Crown Court after the initial hearing.

In terms of issues of disposal from court, those aged under 15 years can be detained under criminal legislation in secure children's homes if required (where they will occupy youth justice beds as opposed to welfare beds), and those aged 15 to 18 years are managed in either secure training centres (always the case for girls) or young offender institutions. Non-custodial sentences are further nuanced and can include a variety of community-based requirements and support, including involvement with local youth offending teams. These teams have proven highly effective in managing young people and custodial rates have been dropping since the late 1990s (youth offending teams came into being in the year 2000).

Civil Law

The Children Act 2004

The Children Act (2004) provides various statutory means of managing children, including Emergency Protection Orders, Interim Care Orders and Care Orders, which allow for emergency and longer-term protection of children at risk of harm. These powers can allow the Local Authority to exercise parental responsibility over a child, either in tandem with one or both parents or in isolation where neither parent is able to execute this function safely.

Secure Accommodation Orders can be authorised under The Children Act (2004) Section 25 and have the power to place young people in secure social services accommodation. Conveying at-risk children to Local Authority Secure Children's Homes using the Secure Accommodation Order should not be considered as a last resort, but as part of the range of positive options when planning to meet the needs of children and young people whose behaviour leads to high levels of concern. Where a child displays a high risk of absconding and a likelihood of the individual or others suffering serious harm, but the purpose of detention is not for treatment of mental disorder, the Secure Accommodation Order may be used to keep that child and others safe.

The Act also describes a person with parental responsibility as someone with the rights and responsibilities that parents have in law for their child. A mother automatically has parental responsibility for her child from birth, unless the child has been adopted. A father has parental responsibility if he was married to the child's mother at the time of the child's birth, or if he subsequently acquires it, through registration, court order, or subsequent marriage to the mother. If the child was born after 1 December 2013 (4 May 2006 in Scotland), the father will also have parental responsibility if named on the birth certificate. Step-parents may acquire parental responsibility through an agreement or court order.

Other individuals may acquire parental responsibility through a Residence Order (The Children Act (2004) Section 12(2)), by adoption, or by being appointed as a child's guardian. Under Section 31 of the Children Act (2004) (the Care Order), a local authority, by order of the court, acquires parental responsibility for a child (delineated under Section 33(3)(a)) which it shares with the parents for the duration of the Care Order. However, it can determine the extent to which a parent or guardian of the child may meet their parental responsibility in order to safeguard the child's welfare (Section 33(3)(b) of the Children Act (2004)). The Local Authority does not automatically acquire parental responsibility if the person with parental responsibility has chosen to voluntarily accommodate the child. Where a Special Guardianship Order is in place, the appointed special guardian (usually a social worker) will share parental responsibility with the child's parent.

Parents do not lose parental responsibility if they divorce, but they do lose parental responsibility if a child is adopted. Parental responsibility can also be restricted by a court order. Where more than one person has parental responsibility, each of them may act alone and without the other. However, where there are disagreements in relation to decisions about a child's mental healthcare, the Mental Health Act Code of Practice (2015) suggests that it is advisable to seek the advice of the court where feasible.

The Mental Capacity Act 2005 and Gillick Competence

Capacity and competence refer to the ability of a child to make independent decisions. The term 'capacity' can in theory be applied to any age group, but in practice the term 'competence' is preferable in children under the age of 16 since those under the age of 16 are not covered by the Mental Capacity Act. The test for competence in under 16- year-olds is the common law standard laid out in the Gillick case, whereas the test for capacity in 16- and 17-year-olds is laid out in the Mental Capacity Act. There is a presumption of capacity in 16- and 17-year-olds (as with adults) whereas the presumption is that a child under 16 lacks competence until proven otherwise.

Judgments about consent can only be made on a case-by-case basis, taking account of the individual, the type of decision and the particular circumstances. In complex cases it is best practice for a professional external to the case to advice on competence. It is vital to carefully document all the factors contributing to a judgement of competence or lack of capacity. Finally, it is important not to set a higher standard for a child's competence than would be expected for adults.

In relation to capacity in children aged 16 and 17, recommended factors to think about can be found in the Mental Health Act Code of Practice (2015) at paragraph 19.25 which states that '(p)ractitioners should consider the following three questions:

- Has the child or young person been given the relevant information in an appropriate manner (such as age appropriate language)?
- Have all practicable steps been taken to help the child or young person make the decision?
  The kind of support that might help the decision-making will vary, depending on the child or young person's circumstances. Examples include:
  - Steps to help the child or young person feel at ease;
  - Ensuring that those with parental responsibility are available to support their child (if that is what the child or young person would like);
  - Giving the child or young person time to absorb information at their own pace; and
  - Considering whether the child or young person has any specific communication needs (and if so, adapting accordingly).
- Can the child or young person decide whether to consent, or not to consent, to the proposed intervention?'

For those aged under 16 years, the notion of a level of competence that a child should achieve in order to allow them to make decisions for themselves was made concrete by the Gillick Case (1985). 'Gillick competence' refers to a child having 'sufficient understanding and intelligence to enable him or her to understand fully what is proposed'. The Mental Health Act Code of Practice (2015) at paragraph 19.36 states that '(w)hen considering whether the child has the competence to decide about the proposed intervention, the practitioner may find it helpful to consider the following questions:

- Does the child understand the information that is relevant to the decision that needs to be made?

- Can the child hold the information in their mind long enough so that they can use it to make the decision?
- Is the child able to weigh up that information and use it to arrive at a decision?
- Is the child able to communicate their decision (by talking, using sign language or any other means)?'

These stipulations do not differ considerably from those laid out in the Mental Capacity Act. The Mental Capacity Act sets out a two-stage test for capacity assessments for those aged 16 years and above. Section 2(1) of the Mental Capacity Act states that a person lacks capacity in relation to a matter if at the relevant time they are unable to make a decision for themselves in relation to the matter 'because of an impairment of, or a disturbance in the functioning of, the mind or brain'. Section 3 of the Mental Capacity Act then states that a person is unable to make a decision if they are unable to understand the information relevant to the decision, retain that information, use or weigh that information as part of the decision-making process or communicate their decision (whether by talking, sign language or any other means).

Other than in an emergency or in certain circumstances described in the Mental Health Act (1983), consent is a necessary prerequisite for the treatment of any child. A Gillick-competent child or a child with capacity has an independent right to consent to treatment. This means that parental consent should not be relied upon when the child is Gillick competent (for those under 16) or has capacity (for those aged 16 or 17 years) to make a particular decision.

Whilst it is usually best practice to additionally seek consent from a person with parental responsibility, the child may use their right to confidentiality to prevent the involvement of that person. An example of a situation in which it is reasonable not to consult a parent is highlighted in the Gillick case wording below.

In the past the courts have ruled that a person with parental responsibility can override the refusal of their Gillick-competent child or child with capacity (Re R and Re W, 1992). This was prior to the introduction of the Mental Capacity Act (2005), which has changed the position for 16- and 17-year-olds (who cannot now have their capacitated decision overruled by a person with parental responsibility) and the Human Rights Act, which has given more weight to the views of the Gillick-competent child.

The Department of Health Reference Guide to Consent for Examination of Treatment (2009) states that

(a)lthough in the past the courts have found that parents can consent to their competent child being treated even where the child/young person is refusing treatment ... there is no post-Human Rights Act 1998 authority for this proposition, and it would therefore be prudent to obtain a court declaration or decision if faced with a competent child or young person who is refusing to consent to treatment, to determine whether it is lawful to treat the child.

Where a child lacks capacity, there are circumstances where a person with parental responsibility can consent on their behalf. However, limits on the influence that person with parental responsibility has over a child's ability to consent were introduced in the 2007 amendment of the Mental Health Act 1983 and accompanying Code of Practice. Initially called the 'zone of parental control', these limits are now known as the 'scope of parental responsibility'. This will vary from case to case, meaning that the scope may be small or large depending on the circumstances. The Mental Health Act Code of Practice (2015) at paragraph 19.41 states the following (although this is not limited to those detained under statute):

First, is this a decision that a parent should reasonably be expected to make? If the decision goes beyond the kind of decisions parents routinely make in relation to the medical care of their child, clear reasons as to why it is acceptable to rely on parental consent to authorise this particular decision will be required. When considering this question, any relevant human rights decisions made by the courts should be taken into account. Significant factors in determining this question are likely to include:

- The type and invasiveness of the proposed intervention – the more extreme the intervention, the greater the justification that will be required. Relying on parental consent to authorise an intrusive form of treatment might be justified because it is necessary to prevent a serious deterioration of the child's health, but this would need to be balanced against other factors such as whether the child is resisting the treatment; whether the specific form of treatment is particularly invasive and/or controversial (e.g. careful consideration should be given to the appropriateness of relying on parental consent to authorise electro-convulsive therapy);

- Whether the child had expressed any views about the proposed intervention when they had the competence or capacity to make such decisions; for example, if they had expressed a willingness to receive one form of treatment but not another, it might not be appropriate to rely on parental consent to give the treatment that they had previously refused.

Secondly are there any factors that might undermine the validity of parental consent? Irrespective of the nature of the decision being proposed, there may be reasons why relying on the consent of a person with parental responsibility may be inappropriate; for example:

- The age, maturity and understanding of the child: the role of parents in decision-making should diminish as their child develops greater independence, with accordingly greater weight given to the views of the child.

- The extent to which the decision accords with the wishes of the child, and whether the child is resisting the decision; and

- Where the parent is not able to make the relevant decision; for example, this may arise if the parent lacks capacity as defined in the MCA, because of their own mental health problems or learning disabilities. In cases of doubt, the parent's capacity will need to be assessed in accordance with the MCA.

- Where the parent is not able to focus on what course of action is in the best interests of their child; for example, where the parents have gone through a particularly acrimonious divorce, they may find it difficult to separate the decision whether to consent to their child's admission to hospital from their own hostilities.

- Where the poor mental health of the child has led to significant distress and/or conflict between the parents, so that they feel unable to decide on what is best for their child and/or cannot agree on what action should be taken; and

- Where one parent agrees with the proposed decision but the other is opposed to it. Although parental consent is usually needed from only one person with parental responsibility, it may not be appropriate to rely on parental consent if another person with parental responsibility disagrees strongly with the decision to admit and/or treat their child, and is likely to take action to prevent the intervention, such as removing the child from hospital or challenging the decision in court.

In order to utilise the parental responsibility power, it must also be the case that there are no indications that the parent might not act in the best interests of their child, for instance during an acrimonious divorce where the child is caught between two parents who are not making the child's needs paramount, or where the child alleges abuse.

If the assessing clinicians do not feel sure that the person with parental responsibility is acting in the best interests of the child, it makes it more likely that the decision will fall outside of the scope, in which case parental responsibility should not be relied upon. A parent can consent to treatment if a Gillick-competent child under the age of 16 refuses such treatment, as long as the decision falls within the scope of Parental Responsibility, but for a 16- or 17-year-old, a capacitated decision should not be overruled using parental responsibility unless in extreme circumstances (death or serious injury).

There may also be circumstances under which no parent could be expected to make a decision due for instance to the complexity and gravity of the decision. One example might be psychosurgery. The need for nasogastric feeding for conditions such as anorexia nervosa arises regularly in inpatient child mental health services and each case must be judged on its merits and with due regard to the size of the scope, and whether the child's rights are better protected by using alternative legal mechanisms.

Where dealing with anorexia nervosa, it is suggested that forcible nasogastric feeding would fall outside of the scope of parental responsibility, and the Mental Health Act is likely to be used to authorise this treatment. Other legal mechanisms might include common law duty of care in cases of emergency or by order of the courts where resolution cannot be achieved by other means and no statute covers the situation.

Even where a child lacks capacity to consent, there are still compelling reasons to involve them in decision making. These reasons may include answering questions and helping the child to know what to expect, to help reduce anxiety, to help the child make sense of their experience, to warn about risks, to prevent misunderstanding or resentment, to promote confidence and courage and to increase compliance (Alderson, 1993).

The Mental Health Act 1983

In relation to mental disorders, children of any age can be detained in hospital under the Mental Health Act if the criteria are met, namely the presence of a mental disorder of a nature or degree to require assessment and/or treatment, associated with risk to the individual

or others. The Mental Health Act conveys powers of detention and treatment (including medication) and carries with it various protections of the child's rights including regular tribunals (with automatic ones occurring more frequently than those for adults) and the ability to apply for managers' hearings to test the authority of ongoing detention. The civil and criminal parts of the Mental Health Act apply to children in the same way that they would to adults. However, the Hybrid Order (The Mental Health Act, 1983), a means of combining hospitalisation with a prison sentence, cannot be used in those under the age of 21.

The 2007 amendments to the Mental Health Act gave young people the right to request that the nearest relative be displaced or not be consulted during the detention process and at other times, though subsequent case law placed a higher expectation of what constitutes 'practicable' efforts to consult. Approved Mental Health Practitioners and other Social Workers (as a statutory duty) will need to record efforts to consult and seek the nearest relative's views for Mental Health Act assessments, renewals and appeals.

Emergencies

There are circumstances where treatment may be given without consent in a life-threatening emergency. Conditions include circumstances where failure to treat would be likely to lead to the death or severe permanent injury of a child but it is not possible to rely on the consent of a child, or a person with parental responsibility.

It may be medically necessary, in an emergency situation, to override the refusal of a Gillick-competent child, or child with capacity or a person with parental responsibility where seeking use of the Mental Health Act or the advice of a court would unnecessarily endanger the life of the individual due to the time involved. Under these circumstances it will be necessary to act immediately to preserve life. In cases in which a child is refusing life-saving treatment, the courts will be required to consider the best interests of that child alongside their duty to take reasonable action to prevent the child's death. Thus, in many cases, the outcome is likely to be that said refusal is overridden (Parker, in press).

The Mental Health Act Code of Practice (2015) at paragraph 19.71 makes clear that

> ... the courts have stated that doubt should be resolved in favour of the preservation of life.

However, at paragraph 19.72 the Mental Health Act Code of Practice (2015) states that '...(t)he treatment given must be no more than necessary and in the best interests of the child. Once the child's condition is stabilised, legal authority for ongoing treatment must be established...' and goes on to reflect that this might occur either on a consensual basis, under Part 4 of the Mental Health Act 1983, or with the authority of the court.

The Inherent Jurisdiction of the Court

This refers to the High Court's power to resolve issues where no statutory provision exists. It cannot be used to override statute law. It is most commonly used in the context of treatment of children, and is only applicable where the child may suffer 'significant harm'. It can allow the court to gain parental responsibility, and is a form of 'parens patriae' legislation whereby the needs of the child are the paramount consideration for the court.

International Instruments

A number of international legislative instruments exist which have variable degrees of binding powers on the countries that have signed up to them. Due to the usual number of member states, the stipulations tend to be broad and relatively intuitive, and the principles are often found enshrined in member states' individual legislation.

The United Nations' Declaration on the Rights of the Child (1959) describes special safeguards and care for children including legal protection and focuses on healthy physical and mental development with a paramount consideration of the best interests of the child (subsequently found in many other legal instruments pertaining to children).

The United Nations Convention on the Rights of the Child (1989) focuses on four basic principles: participation by children in decisions affecting them; protection of children against discrimination, neglect and exploitation; prevention of harm to them; and provision of assistance to them to meet their basic needs. Article 40 of that Convention also enshrines a child-specific right to a fair trial.

The European Convention on Human Rights (1953) could be described as a transnational agreement and the stipulations are largely embodied in the United Kingdom's Human Rights Act (1998). The terminology used throughout the Convention describes 'everyone' or conversely 'no-one', meaning that children are afforded the same protections as adults under this legislature. Of specific relevance here, Article 5 (the right to freedom) indicates that member states may take such measures as are necessary in the interests of the children despite the notion of parental responsibility (European Convention on Human Rights, 1953). Article 6 (the right to a fair trial) has been dealt with above in relation to effective participation. The latter European Convention on the Exercise of Children's Rights (1996) again promotes the rights and best interests of children, promoting autonomy and the right to inclusion in proceedings concerning them, and the right to appoint their own representative.

Of further relevance, the Universal Declaration of Human Rights (1948) and the International Covenant on Economic, Social and Cultural Rights (1966) both contain specific reference to the importance of access to education, and the International Covenant on Civil and Political Rights (1966) highlights that any judgment rendered in a criminal case or law suit shall be made public, but that children are afforded extra rights to protection of anonymity. It also indicates that proceedings should take account of age and the desirability of promoting rehabilitation.

Finally, the Standard Minimum Rules for the Administration of Juvenile Justice (1985) (the 'Beijing Rules') were a resolution of the United Nations General Assembly in relation to juvenile prisoners and offenders and include fundamental perspectives of furthering the well-being of the child and his or her family, providing conditions to allow for a meaningful life in the community, promoting education, establishing a comprehensive juvenile justice framework and supporting staff working with such young people. It discusses and provides guidance on the age of criminal responsibility and the aims of juvenile justice systems, the rights of young offenders and the need to protect their privacy, as well as promoting principles of diversion, avoiding institutionalisation, special training within the police forces in relation to children and research into effective interventions.

Guidelines for Which Framework to Use

Boxes 21.1 and 21.2 delineate the frameworks which can be used under various circumstances. Whilst these guidelines describe options, they do not give advice

---

BOX 21.1 Admission/Treatment for Those Under 16

Gillick incompetent child but the parents consent:	*One can use Parental Responsibility if the treatment is in the scope of parental control, or the Inherent Jurisdiction could be used if the decision is outside the scope, or the Mental Health Act may be used if a mental disorder is present. The Mental Health Act should be used if liberty must be restricted, and the child meets the criteria for detention under this Act. There is no minimum age limit for Mental Health Act.*
Gillick incompetent child and the parents refuse:	*The Inherent Jurisdiction may be used, or the Children Act may be used so that Parental Responsibility is given to the Local Authority by the court under a Care Order. The Mental Health Act may be used if a mental disorder is present and the criteria are met for detention under this Act.*
Gillick competent child who consents, and the parents consent:	*All parties may legally consent and good practice would suggest that all consenting parties are accounted for in the documentation.*
Gillick competent child who consents, but the parents refuse:	*The child is Gillick competent, so the child may be admitted and/or treated (as long as the treatment is in the best interests of the child), though the parents can appeal to the court who may overrule the decision.[1]*
Gillick competent child who refuses, but the parents consent:	*Parental responsibility may be used if the decision is in the scope of parental control, but Lord Donaldson commented that the importance of the refusal increases with age. The Inherent Jurisdiction may be used to resolve the issue, or the Mental Health Act can be used where a mental disorder is present.*
Gillick competent child who refuses, and the parents refuse or are unavailable:	*The Inherent Jurisdiction may be used, or the Children Act may be used so that Parental Responsibility is given to the Local Authority, or the Mental Health Act may be used if a mental disorder is present and the child meets the criteria for detention under this Act.*
Gillick incompetent child and parents lack capacity, or parents are unavailable:	*The Inherent Jurisdiction may be used, or the Children Act may be used so that Parental Responsibility is given to the Local Authority, or the Mental Health Act may be used if a mental disorder is present, or treatment may occur under the common law principle of 'best interests'.*

[1] Although there is no lower age limit, it has been suggested that it would rarely be appropriate for a young person under the age of 13 years to consent to treatment without their parent's involvement – Bailey, S. and Harbour, A. (1999) The law and a child's consent to treatment (England and Wales) *Child Psychology and Psychiatry Review* 4: 30–34.

---

about the single correct framework to use in each circumstance since cases are often highly nuanced and require balanced consideration. The least restrictive option possible must be used (bearing in mind the risks posed), and clinicians must avoid stigmatisation; aim for the least degree of separation from family, friends and the local community; and wherever possible avoid disruption to education, as well as considering the rights to dignity and respect and the right to respect for privacy and confidentiality.

Research and Organ Donation

There is a presumption of a lack of capacity for 16- and 17-year-olds in relation to research, as well as organ donation (The Mental Capacity Act Code of Practice, 2015). This differs from the usual presumption that 16- and 17-year-olds have capacity until proven otherwise and is present in order to ensure that young people have appropriate safeguards for particularly serious decisions. Those under 16 years are presumed to lack competence for both research and organ donation.

Electroconvulsive Therapy (ECT)

No patient under 18 years of age can be given ECT without the certification of a Second Opinion Appointed Doctor, whether detained under the Mental Health Act or not. Consent must also be obtained if the patient is voluntary. This treatment is highly likely to fall outside the scope of parental responsibility due to its gravity and complexity.

BOX 21.2 Admission/Treatment for Those Aged 16 or 17

Young person has capacity and consents and the parents consent:

The child has legally consented; the parents' consent is not necessary. Capacitated 16- and 17-year-olds are able to consent to informal admission for treatment for mental disorder, under Section 131 of the Mental Health Act 1983.

The child has capacity and consents but the parents refuse:

The child can consent despite the parental refusal (Section 8 of the Family Law Reform Act 1989 and Section 131 of the Mental Health Act) though in some circumstances the consent can be over-ridden by court.

The child has capacity and refuses, but the parents consent:

The Mental Health Act may be used where a mental disorder is present and the child meets the criteria for detention, or the Inherent Jurisdiction of the court may be relied upon. In extreme circumstances (likely death or severe permanent injury) the Mental Health Act Code of Practice (2015) advises that "doubt should be resolved in favour of the preservation of life" for those under 18 meaning that common law principles of "best interests" could apply – Parental Responsibility has been used in the past but since the advent of the Mental Capacity Act it is unlikely that this route could now be used. The Mental Health Act should be used if the criteria for detention are met and the child's liberty needs to be restricted.

The child has capacity and refuses, and the parents refuse:

The Mental Health Act may be used where a mental disorder is present and the criteria for detention are met, or the Inherent Jurisdiction of the court may be relied upon. Common law principles would apply as above in extreme circumstances. The Mental Health Act should be used if the criteria are met and the child's liberty needs to be restricted.

The child lacks capacity due to a mental disorder, but the parents consent:

For Admission: Parental responsibility may be used, or the Mental Capacity Act if the conditions to which the child was being admitted did not amount to a deprivation of liberty.[1] The Mental Health Act could be used, or the Inherent Jurisdiction of the court may be relied upon. The Children Act may be used if the parents were deemed not to be acting in the best interests of the child.

For Treatment: In addition to the Mental Capacity Act and the Mental Health Act, Parental Responsibility (if in the scope of parental control) may be used to treat, or the Inherent Jurisdiction of the court or the Children Act may be used if the parents are deemed not to be acting in the best interests of the child or that decision is outside the zone of parental control. It is unlikely that the Mental Capacity Act would be used in this context where the treatment is likely to restore capacity since the child may then refuse the treatment

The child lacks capacity due to a mental disorder, and the parents refuse:

The Mental Capacity Act may be used, but where it is being used for admission, the conditions to which the child is being admitted must not amount to a deprivation of liberty. The Mental Health Act could be used, or the Inherent Jurisdiction of the court may be relied upon. The Children Act may be used if the parents were deemed not to be acting in the best interests of the child.

The child is unable to make a decision, but not because of impairment of, or a disturbance in functioning of, their mind or brain, and their parents consent[2]:

The Mental Health Act could be used, or the Inherent Jurisdiction of the court may be relied upon. It is possible that Parental Responsibility could be used where the decision lies within the scope of parental control, or common law "best interests" principles could be used.

The child is unable to make a decision, but not because of impairment of, or a disturbance in functioning of, their mind or brain, and their parents refuse:

The Mental Health Act could be used, or the Inherent Jurisdiction of the court may be relied upon. Common law "best interests" principles could also be used.

---

[1] Parental responsibility has been scrutinised in relation to deprivation of liberty for those under 16 and found to be sufficient authority to allow for management in conditions amounting to said deprivation of liberty.

[2] Paragraph 19.31 of the Mental Health Act Code of Practice, 2015.

Conclusions

Despite their different applications, a common theme runs through each form of civil legislation: the tension in ensuring that young people's rights are preserved and protected to the greatest extent possible, namely that they are afforded due autonomy, whilst also meeting their safety and welfare needs. Civil law manages this via recognition of developing competencies over the spectrum of childhood and by ensuring that the safety of the child is paramount. Whilst age cut-offs do feature as a matter of absolute protection for very young children, a spectrum approach does helpfully exist for older children which allows for clinical discretion in terms of assessment and treatment.

The side effect of this bespoke and nuanced approach to developmental levels is that various forms of legislation may overlap in certain circumstances meaning that different routes may be pursued to meet the same end. This is concordant with the neuroscientific understanding of the functioning of the brain which recognises that development at chronological ages can vary significantly between individuals. Consideration of the fundamental principles of least restriction, best protection in terms of due process and greatest empowerment of the child should be taken into account.

The criminal law in England and Wales has different aims and has a specific chronological cut-off for criminal responsibility which is out of keeping with both the average international position and that of developmental science. However, a nuanced approach is taken when it comes to matters of disposal, which includes tailored facilities, and an approach focused not on punishment but on the best interests of the child.

References

Alderson, P. (1993). *Children's Consent to Surgery*. Buckingham: Open University Press.

Anderson, V., Anderson, P., Northam, E., Jacobs, R. and Catroppa, C. (2001). Development of executive functions through late childhood and adolescence in an Australian sample. *Developmental Neuropsychology*, **20**(1), 385–406.

Baird, A., Fugelsang, J. and Bennett, C. (2005). 'What were you thinking?': an fMRI study of adolescent decision making. Poster presented at the annual meeting of the Cognitive Neuroscience Society, New York.

Blakemore, S-J. and Choudhury, S. (2006). Development of the adolescent brain: implications for executive function and social cognition. *Journal of Child Psychology and Psychiatry*, **47**(3), 296–312.

The Children Act. (2004). Section 2(7) (Parental Responsibility for Children).

The Children Act. (2004). Section 12(2) (Child Arrangements Orders and Parental Responsibility).

The Children Act. (2004). Section 25 (Use of Accommodation for Restricting Liberty).

The Children Act (2004) Section 33(3)(b) (Effect of Care Order)The Children Act (2004) Section 105(1) (Interpretation).

The Children and Young Person's Act (1963).

The Crime (Sentences) Act (1997).

Criminal Liability: Insanity and Automatism – A Discussion Paper: Chapter 9: A New Defence of 'Not Criminally Responsible by Reason of Developmental Immaturity' – Law Commission Publications, Crown Copyright July 2013.

Department of Health Reference Guide to Consent for Examination of Treatment, 2nd Edition. (2009), 34.

European Convention on Human Rights. (1953). Protocol Number 7 accompanying Article 5.

The European Convention on Human Rights. (1950). (The Convention for the Protection of Human Rights and Fundamental Freedoms). Council of Europe.

The European Convention on Human Rights. (1953).

The European Convention on the Exercise of Children's Rights. (1996).

The Family Law Reform Act. (1969).

The General Medical Council's Good Practice Guide. (2013).

Gillick v. West Norfolk and Wisbech AHA. (1985). 1 AC 112.

Gogtay, N. (2004). Dynamic mapping of human cortical development during childhood through early adulthood. *Proceedings of the National Academy of Sciences*, **101**, 8174–8179.

The Human Rights Act. (1998).

The International Covenant on Economic, Social and Cultural Rights. (1966).

The International Covenant on Civil and Political Rights. (1966).

The Mental Capacity Act. (2005).

The Mental Health Act. (1983).

The Mental Health Act. (1983). Section 45(A).

The Mental Health Act Code of Practice. (2015).

Parker, C. (in press). Treatment without consent. Child and Family Justice: a developmental view. In Shaw, M. and Bailey, S. Editors. Royal College of Psychiatrists.

Part IV of the Mental Health Act. (1983).

Poythress, N., Hoge, S., Bonnie, R., Monahan, J. and Eisenberg, M. (1997) MacArthur Adjudicative Competence Study, MacArthur Foundation Research Network on Adolescent Development and Juvenile Justice.

Pritchard, R. V. (1836) 7 C&P 303.

Re R (A Minor) (Wardship: Medical Treatment) [1992] 1 FLR 190 and Re W (A Minor) (Medical Treatment: Court's Jurisdiction) [1992] 4 All ER 627.

Redlich, A. and Goodman, G. (2003). Taking responsibility for an act not committed: the influence of age and suggestibility. *Law and Human Behavior*, **27**, 141–156.

The Royal Society. (2011a). Brain Waves Module 2: Neuroscience: implications for education and lifelong learning. Excellence in Science publications.

The Royal Society. (2011b). Neuroscience and the law: Brain Waves Module 4. Excellence in Science publications.

Scottish Law Commission. Report on Insanity and Diminished Responsibility (SE/2004/92, no. 195, 2004).

Sowell, E., Thompson, P., Tessner, K. and Toga, A. (2001). Mapping continued brain growth and gray matter density reduction in dorsal frontal cortex: inverse relationships during postadolescent brain maturation. *Journal of Neuroscience* **21**, 8819–8829.

Steinberg, L. (2007). Risk Taking in Adolescence: new Perspectives from Brain and Behavioral Science. *Association for Psychological Science*, **16**(2), 55–59.

Steinberg, L. (2009). Adolescent development and juvenilejustice. *Annual Review of Clinical Psychology*, **5**, 27–73.

Steinberg, L. and Monahan, K. (2007). Age differences in resistance to peer influence. *Developmental Psychology*, **43**(6), 1531–1543.

Strayer, J. (1993). Children's concordant emotions and cognitions in response to observed emotions. *Child Development*, **64**(1), 188–201.

T and V v. The United Kingdom (Application number 24888/94) European Court of Human Rights judgment, Strasbourg 16 December 1999.

Unfitness to Plead: An Issues Paper – Law Commission Publications, Crown Copyright May (2014).

The United Nations Committee General Comment. (2007). 'A minimum age of criminal responsibility below the age of 12 years is considered by the Committee not to be internationally acceptable', 'States Parties are encouraged to increase their lower minimum age of criminal responsibility to the age of 12 years as the absolute minimum age and to continue to increase it to a higher age level', and 'the minimum age of criminal responsibility in England and Wales is too low by a considerable degree'.

The United Nations Convention on the Rights of the Child. (1989).

The United Nations Convention on the Rights of the Child. (1989). (Article 1).

The United Nations Declaration on the Rights of the Child. (1959).

The United Nations Standard Minimum Rules for the Administration of Juvenile Justice. (1985).

The Universal Declaration of Human Rights. (1948).

van Leijenhorst, L., Moor, B., Op de Macks, Z., Rombouts, S., Westenberg, P. and Crone, E.(2010). Adolescent risky decision-making: neurocognitive development of reward and control regions. *Neuroimage*, **51**(1), 345–355.

Chapter 22

Youth Justice Services in England and Wales

Paul Tarbuck

Introduction

This chapter outlines several developments in the evolution of the youth justice system (YJS) which have generated new approaches in response to challenges. The historical summary highlights evidence for effectiveness, and contributions to success in assisting some children and young people to pursue alternative pathways to a criminal career.

In England and Wales adulthood commences at 18 years of age. The law asserts that children and young people become criminally responsible at 10 years of age. There has been a welcome reduction in the number of children and young people involved in youth justice proceedings (YJB, 2016: 5–8):

- in 2014–2015 10- to 17-year-olds accounted for about 10% of the total population of England and Wales and in the same year there were 94,960 arrests for notifiable offences in England and Wales by children and young people – which is proportionate at about 10% of all arrests. The number of arrests of young people has fallen dramatically by 73% since the peak in 2006–2007;
- in 2014–2015 there were 87,150 proven offences committed by young people that resulted in a caution or conviction, down by 70% since 2005;
- in 2014–2015 20,080 youth cautions were issued by the police, a decrease of 22% since 2013–2014 and a decrease of 81% since 2005;
- in 2014–2015 there were 20,544 first time entrants (FTEs), a decrease of 82% since 2007. Females accounted for 21% of FTEs, which is an 85% reduction since 2005;
- in 2014–2015 young people who were from a Black, Asian or other Minority Ethnic (BAME) groups accounted for 18% of all FTEs in the year ending March 2015 while White young people accounted for 75%. This compares to 15% BAME and 82% White in the year ending March 2010. Since 2010 the number of BAME young people entering the YJS has fallen by 61% but their

proportion amongst FTEs is increasing. About 31% of FTEs were aged 10–14 years. This group showed the biggest reduction (59%) in FTEs between 2010–2011 and 2013–2014(YJB, 2015a).

One single body, the Youth Justice Board for England and Wales, has been responsible for the direction, operation and commissioning of youth justice services.

The Youth Justice System in England and Wales

The Youth Justice Board for England and Wales (YJB) was established by Section 37 of the Crime and Disorder Act 1998. It is a non-departmental public body with responsibility for improving the YJS. The principal aim of the YJB is to prevent offending by children and young people. In pursuance of this the YJB:

- advises the Secretary of State for England and Wales on the operation of and standards for the YJS;
- monitors performance;
- commissions places for young people remanded or sentenced to custody;
- identifies, promotes and publishes effective practice information;
- makes grants to local authorities and other bodies; and
- commissions research.

A key characteristic of the new YJS was to provide a coordinated multidisciplinary and integrated multi-agency response to young people who engage in antisocial behaviour and/or offending behaviour – in particular to target the risk factors associated with such behaviours. In addressing risk factors partnerships between mainstream, specialist and 'wrap around' services were necessary to intervene and support young people and their families. Mainstream agencies include the Ministry of Justice, Home

Office, Department of Health, Department for Education and the Welsh Assembly Government. The independent and voluntary sectors also have essential parts to play in these partnerships.

Youth Offending Teams

The YJB and Youth Offending Teams (YOTs) were established following the Audit Commission (1996) *Misspent Youth* review. The review identified that local services and mainstream departments were failing to meet the complex needs of young people who offend. The requirement for local authorities to establish multidisciplinary, multiagency YOTs with representation from education, health, police, probation and social services was set out in Crime and Disorder Act 1998. The Act also gave authority for agencies to share personal information where it was necessary for the successful implementation of the Act.

In 2013–2014 there were 140 YOTs in England and 18 in Wales with mixed local and central government multi-sectoral sources of funding. About 14,300 people worked in YOTs, though not all were full time. YOT staffing establishments range from 20 to 500. YOTs form the backbone of the YJS in England and Wales; they support all prevention and intervention components including out-of-court interventions, community and custodial interventions. They 'wraparound' periods of custody to provide continuous support, and may be involved in helping young offenders and their families where the youngster is in transition to adult criminal justice services.

The Audit Commission (2004) found that the YJB and YOTs were working well. It was identified that young offenders were being dealt with more quickly with a 50% reduction in the time from arrest to sentence compared to 1997; young offenders were more likely to receive interventions, less likely to commit an offence on bail; and magistrates were very satisfied with the service they received from YOTs.

Asset

Underpinning the work of YOTs is an evidence-based personalised assessment of each young offender known as Asset, introduced in 2000. Asset was designed for the age group, and examines all areas of the young person's life and not just criminogenic factors. It identifies risk and protective factors, including indicators of the young person's risk to others and vulnerabilities. It provides a score that is predictive of reoffending. It is a dynamic tool that reflects change over time and highlights areas for further assessment (Baker, 2004). Asset contains a brief health screen that may indicate areas for further assessment. Asset documents are periodically updated with the latest version being made freely available (YJB, 2014a).

Safeguarding Children and Young People

Many of the children and young persons involved with the YJS are vulnerable or have been themselves victims of crime. The YJB (2015b, 2015c) takes a robust approach to safeguarding those at risk and to preventing child sexual exploitation, in concert with other public services.

International Perspectives

Neil (2008) on behalf of the YJB compared elements of youth justice in over 90 jurisdictions. Whilst able to find some common models of policy and practice, the conclusion drawn was that direct comparisons are unwise because each jurisdiction is dynamic and responsive to internal and external pressures. So there is constant tension between philosophical and political approaches. The age of criminal responsibility also varies between jurisdictions.

Components of the Youth Justice System

The YJB developed a three-part integrated YJS which includes:

- **Prevention and Out-of-Court Interventions**
  - Safer Schools Partnerships;
  - Youth Inclusion Support Panels;
  - Youth Inclusion Programmes;
  - Restorative Justice;
  - Youth Restorative Disposal.

- **Community Sentences**
  - Reparation Order;
  - Referral Order;
  - Youth Rehabilitation Order.

- **Custodial Sentences, Supported by Resettlement**
  - Commissioning of custodial services;
  - Intensive Resettlement and Aftercare Provision;
  - Resettlement consortia.

Safer School Partnerships

There were over 450 Safer Schools Partnerships (SSPs) created. Their primary focus is to attach police officers or police community support officers (PCSOs) to schools under the umbrella of neighbourhood policing to address antisocial behaviour and crime committed in and around schools. Wider benefits have been found to include a stronger sense of citizenship among children, great quality of school life and improved community cohesion. Police officers and PCSOs work with school staff and other agencies to establish a whole-school approach to behaviour and discipline; reduce victimisation, antisocial behaviour and offending; support the full-time education of pupils and create and maintain a safe learning environment and support young people through the transition from primary to secondary school.

Bowles et al. (2006) carried out a study which compared 300 SSP schools with 1,000 similar schools, and found that rises in GCSE attainment were higher in SSP schools and that truancy rates in SSP schools had improved at a higher rate than the non-SSP schools.

Youth Inclusion Support Panels (YISPs)

Youth Inclusion Support Panels (YISPs) are multi-agency forums that coordinate early intervention services based on assessed risks and needs of young people of 8–13 years old (up to 17 years in some cases). The aim of the YISP is to identify local children and young people who are likely to become involved in antisocial behaviour and offending, and to put in place an appropriate multiagency response that will divert them from entering the YJS. There are over 200 YISPs in England and Wales. Support to parents may also be offered as part of the range of interventions. Harrison (2005) found some early indicators of effectiveness for YISPs.

Youth Inclusion Programmes (YIPs) are being delivered in 110 of the most deprived and high-crime areas in England and Wales. They aim to reduce antisocial behaviour and youth crime and, particularly, to reduce the number of first-time entrants to the YJS. Young people are identified through information provided by a range of agencies including schools, Local Education Authorities, Children and Families Services, the police, neighbourhood wardens, Antisocial Behaviour Teams and the YOT.

YIPs generally deliver services to either the 8–12 age group (Junior YIPs) or 13–17 age group (Senior YIPs). Young people are given somewhere safe to go where they can experience positive role models through the work of the staff and volunteers, can take part in activities and learn new skills and get support with their education and careers advice. Among the YIPs aims are to address risk factors and enhance protective factors as identified by the YIP assessment; broker access to mainstream and specialist services and to work with the individuals, their families – especially parents and carers – and the community. An evaluation of YIPs (YJB, 2008a) found that

- arrest rates for the 50 young people considered to be most at risk of crime in each YIP had reduced by 65%;
- of those who offended before joining the programme 73% were arrested for fewer offences; and
- of those identified as at risk but had not previously offended 74% did not go on to be arrested after support from the YIP.

Restorative Justice

Restorative justice (RJ) was a key priority in the government's Green Paper *Breaking the Cycle* (2011). RJ enables victims to have their say and to talk about the full impact of a crime on their lives; and they may actively participate in the resolution of the offence. They can receive answers to questions they may have about the incident, and receive reparation for the harm caused. Offenders can talk about why they committed the crime and are given the opportunity to help put things right for the victim, for example by repairing the damage they have caused. Common types of RJ interventions, which may be direct (face-to-face) or indirect, include:

- victim–offender mediation – communication between a victim and offender facilitated by a trained mediator;
- restorative conferencing – where, in addition to the primary victim and offender, other people connected to the victim and offender (such as family members) also participate;
- family group conferencing – which includes members of the wider extended family (with a particular onus on the family to provide an acceptable solution); and
- a Referral Order – Youth Offender Panels where trained community volunteers work alongside a

member of the YOT to talk to the young person, parents and victim to agree a tailor-made contract aimed at putting things right.

The results of introducing RJ were published in four reports by the Home Office and the Ministry of Justice (2004–2008). The fourth report (Shapland et al., 2008) highlighted key findings with respect to the impact of RJ on reoffending and found that RJ does not stop offenders offending altogether (the previous, traditional measure) but they do offend less. Each of the trial sites on their own demonstrated a positive impact on the frequency of reoffending and, taking all the RJ conferencing trials together, there was a statistically significant fall in the frequency of reconviction; the research demonstrating that 27% fewer crimes were committed by offenders who had experienced RJ conferencing compared with those offenders who had not. There was evidence that RJ conferencing provided value for money.

Youth Restorative Disposal

Youth Restorative Disposal (YRD) is a summary disposal approach which was piloted in eight police forces and corresponding YOTs in 2008–2009. YRD was designed to improve public confidence and earlier identification of young people presenting risks of later, more serious reoffending.

The YRD utilises principles of RJ to provide an effective, meaningful and proportionate response to minor offending at the scene of the offence (or soon thereafter). It challenges minor offending and antisocial behaviour by holding young people to account and allows them to take responsibility for their actions, repair the harm and improve their behaviour in a positive way without unnecessarily forcing them into the formal criminal justice system (CJS) and an early criminal record. It is an additional option to existing methods of disposal for young people aged 10–17 years who are first-time minor offenders. Eligible offences are those with specific exceptions – such as no weapons, drugs or sexual offences – as defined by the Association of Chief Police Officers.

Through consent from all parties the YRD focuses on meeting the joint needs of the victim, community and young person who offended. YRDs are recorded locally against the young person's name to ensure that young people are not issued with a further YRD and to avoid disproportionate criminalisation that would result from being recorded on the police national computer. All YRDs issued are sent by police to YOTs, and

they act as a trigger to identify any underlying risk factors and provide intervention where necessary.

Rix et al. (2011) evaluated the use of YRD. They found that the average age of young people given a YRD was between 13 and 14 years for shoplifting (52%), assault (22%) and criminal damage (19%). About 75% of the YRDs were carried out immediately with the majority of outcomes involving a verbal or written apology, and saving police time. Positive satisfaction has been reported from victims who have been confident in how the police dealt with the offences and the outcomes using YRDs. Satisfaction levels have also been reported as high by police, YOTs, young people issued with YRDs and their parents/guardians.

Community Sentences

Reparation Order – sometimes known as a 'community reparation order' – may be applied to a juvenile who is convicted of an offence. The purpose of the order is to take into account the feelings and wishes of the victims of crime, to prevent further offending by confronting the young person with the consequences of their crime and to allow her/him to make some amends (YJB, archive 1).

Referral Order – Youth Offender Panels

A *Referral Order* (RO) may be used for young persons who plead guilty. Its primary aim is to prevent young people reoffending and provide a RJ approach within a community context. A RO must be given by a youth/magistrates' court where a young person is convicted of an offence for the first time and pleading guilty (where there is no other fixed sentence or custody). Following sentence with a RO a young person must appear before a Youth Offender Panel (YOP) made up of a YOT worker and two trained members of the community where a RO contract is agreed, with progress reviews every three months. There are over 5,000 trained volunteers who represent their local communities on a YOP.

Young persons on ROs have the lowest actual reoffending rates within the YJS. A 2008 cohort showed reoffending rates for ROs as 38%, compared to 65.7% for reparation orders and 71% for supervision orders (MoJ, 2008). Of the 184,850 disposals given in 2008–2009 ROs accounted for the highest number of court disposals with 25,865 given, compared to 4,702 reparation orders and 10,153 supervision orders.

Youth Rehabilitation Order

Introduced in 2008 the *Youth Rehabilitation Order* (YRO) is a generic community sentence for young people under the age of 18, which mirrors the adult generic community sentence. YROs are used with the *Scaled Approach*.

The *Scaled Approach*, developed by the YJB in partnership with four pilot YOTs, aims to reduce the likelihood of reoffending by tailoring the intensity of the intervention to the young person's assessed risks and needs identified using the Asset assessment tool, and by ensuring more effective management of risk of serious harm to others. The Scaled Approach applies to young people who are subject to a YOT intervention through either a RO or a YRO.

Custodial Sentences, Supported by Resettlement

The YJB commissions residential secure places for children and young people who require a period of detention. Such places are commissioned within:

- Her Majesty's Prison Youth Offender Institutions (YOIs);
- Local Authority Secure Children's Homes (LASCHs); and
- Secure Training Centres (STCs).

Generally speaking, the youngest detainees are placed in LASCHs and STCs which have a residential school ethos. Older detainees (15 years and above) are placed in YOIs which have an approach for young adults, designed to encourage responsibility. All these places of detention are subject to independent scrutiny by members of the UK national preventative mechanism (NPM, 2014: 69) with a substantial and cumulative volume of reports from many of the NPM's members.

In April, 2015, the custodial population of 10- to 17-year-olds was 999, a reduction of 106 from the previous year (YJB, 2015d). A remarkable achievement since, at its inception, the YJB commissioned over 3,000 custodial places annually. In fact:

> Over the last five years there has been a welcome drop in the number of children in custody and in response several young offender institutions (YOIs) have been decommissioned and girls are now only held in secure training centres (STCs) or secure children's homes. *(HMIP, 2014)*

With falling numbers of commissioned places the youth custody estate has contracted into just a few centres. This means that the families and carers of youngsters in custody have to travel farther to support their loved ones. The effects of this phenomenon are too early to generalise but do give cause for concern. Also young persons with the most challenging problems are concentrated in fewer YOIs intensifying the issues in managing them safely. For example Her Majesty's Inspectorate of Prisons (2015) found that levels of violence in male YOIs remained high and 'often involved multiple assailants and a single victim in a gang-related assault', and nearly a third of boys reported feeling unsafe in a YOI.

The Harris review (2015) investigated the self-inflicted deaths of 18- to 24-year-olds in adult prisons. Young offenders whose sentence takes them into their 18th year and beyond transfer into adult prisons, and this transitional phase is known to be challenging for offenders. The YJB has welcomed this review as the rate of self-inflicted deaths has been increasing across the adult custodial estate since 2012. Young people in transition to adult custodial services need to be optimally prepared for adult prisons to reduce risks to them.

Minimising and Managing Physical Restraint

Physical restraint of individuals who are violent to others is a vexatious area of practice in public services, and is rightly the subject of public concern (Willow, 2014). Minimising and managing physical restraint (MMPR) brought a new approach to such events in YOIs and STCs, and is the first training to be 'approved' by a multi-departmental working group (NOMS, 2012, 2014). The approach is designed to de-escalate violent and potentially violent situations so that physical restraint of the child or young person is unnecessary; or to ensure that if physical restraint is used it is reasonable, necessary and proportionate.

Members of the UK national preventative mechanism (NPM) are scrutinising the implementation of MMPR (NPM, 2014: 28). The YJB (2015e) is monitoring the use of MMPR and has commissioned work to evaluate MMPR techniques with a view to minimising the use of physical techniques or directing the use of those techniques which are least likely to cause injury and distress (2015f).

In the first (partial) year of reporting there were a total of 2,475 use of force incidents across five secure establishments for the year ending March 2015. This gives an average of 206 incidents per month or an average of 30 incidents per 100 young people per month. MMPR techniques were involved in 1,439 of the incidents (58%), which gives an average of 120 incidents per month (YJB, 2016: 53).

Intensive Resettlement Support

The YJB (2010b) widened the resettlement model from RAP to Intensive Resettlement Support (IRS). Building on the original RAP scheme, IRS was able to provide enhanced resettlement resources to a further 48 YOTs resulting in resettlement programmes being funded in 107 Local Authorities in England and Wales.

Resettlement Consortia

In 2009 the YJB began establishing three regional resettlement consortia. The consortia focused on developing strategic relationships across a number of local authorities to enable a comprehensive approach to resettlement. This included improved partnership working between the YJS, children's services and other key services important to effective resettlement including accommodation and education, training and employment providers. By 2013 eight resettlement consortia had been established and evaluated (YJB, 2013b) identifying critical success factors in supporting young persons and effective cross-sector working.

Health and Substance Misuse Care in Youth Justice Services

Inequalities in health are a known correlate of offending behaviour (see Chapter 3 by Chitsabesan and Khan). *Every Child Matters: Change for Children* (DfES, 2004) aimed to improve outcomes for all children in five key areas:

- being healthy;
- staying safe;
- enjoying and achieving;
- making a positive contribution;
- and achieving economic well-being.

The aim of the strategy was to narrow the gap in outcomes between those who do well and those who do not. As a result of the strategy the YJB put in place a performance indicator which expected that young people identified as having acute mental health needs should be seen by child and adolescent mental health services (CAMHSs) practitioners within five working days, and those with non-acute mental health needs within 15 working days. Positive progress occurred in achieving the performance indicator, with 85% of young people with acute needs and 89% with non-acute needs reported as being seen within the target times during 2005–2006 (YJB, 2006).

Lord Bradley (2009) reported into the situation of persons with mental health problems and learning disabilities in the criminal justice system; the report was quickly followed by *Improving Health, Supporting Justice*, a national delivery plan (DoH, 2009a). Apart from insisting that all YOTs should include a 'suitably qualified mental health professional' Bradley promulgated the twin ideas of creating liaison and diversion services and reducing the use of Section 136 of the Mental Health Act 1983 in police custody.

Healthy Children, Safer Communities (DoH, 2009b) was published following a cross-governmental programme board which included the YJB. Both this strategy and the Bradley report signalled an intent, endorsed by the government, to develop effective diversion away from the YJS for children and young people with mental health needs and/or learning difficulties and/or disabilities (DoH, 2015a).

Diversion from custody (into more appropriate pathways of care and supervision) was a key theme of the Justice Green Paper (2010) which acknowledged the extent to which the CJS is currently a default pathway for a significant number of young people and adults who would more appropriately be dealt with by other services – especially mental health. Subsequently, the YJB was involved in six Department of Health youth justice liaison and diversion pilots, 'triage' pilots and six Home Office-led alcohol arrest referral pilot schemes. Work was commissioned to identify a best practice model for diversion schemes drawing from the findings of all these pilots which resulted in NHS-England securing new funding to expand the coverage of police liaison and diversion schemes up to 2017.

Diversion at 'first contact' or point of arrest, which was integral to some of the experimental schemes, should help to improve current practice by increasing the identification of needs among children and young people at the earliest possible stage within the YJS. Initial empirical data, whilst unpublished, shows promise in diverting the most vulnerable – including children and young people – from the CJS. *Street triage* is being developed in several cities to offer

NHS mental health assessment at point of first contact with an apprehended alleged offender, and may determine the pathway that person will follow – either into healthcare or into arrest and police custody (CrisisCC, 2013).

In *Future in Mind: Promoting, Protecting and Improving Our Children and Young People's Mental Health and Wellbeing* (DoH, 2015a), the government sought to update its policy towards CAMHS. According to the Minister of State *'Future in mind* sets out a compelling moral, social and economic case for change'. The Minister noted that 75% of mental health problems in adults originate before the age of 18 years. The policy contains a strategic intent to address many issues that directly affect children and young people in the YJS, including:

- tackling stigma;
- creating a culture where young people and their families are not afraid to seek help;
- more access and waiting time standards for services so that children and young people can expect prompt treatment when they need it, just as they can for physical health problems;
- 'one-stop shop' support services in the community so that anyone needing support knows where to find it;
- improved access to support through named points of contact in specialist mental health services and schools;
- improved care for children and young people in crisis so they are treated in the right place at the right time, as close to home as possible; and
- improved access for children and young people who are particularly vulnerable, such as looked-after children and care leavers, and those in contact with the YJS.

Access to CAMHS in YJS mirrors closely what is happening in the community so that access to CAMHS is sometimes problematic on a geographical basis for both YOTs and custodial YJS. The notion of introducing targets for access to CAMHS, specifically for those in contact with the YJS, will be welcomed in the YJS services. The development of community 'one-stop shops', named points of contact in CAMHS, and a commitment to encourage multi-agency working (which underpins the policy) should ensure that children and young people in contact with YJS have similar levels of service to those in the general community.

Complementary to the new policy is guidance for service commissioning to promote the health and well-being of looked-after children (DoH, 2015b). This guidance reinforces the policy of 'money following the patient'. That is, looked-after children, wherever they may be in state services, should be able to access healthcare at the point of need – and not be subject to the whims of commissioning payment disputes.

Health services within YOTs. Health practitioners in YOTs are a significant resource, working directly with some of the most vulnerable and difficult-to-engage young people. They provide assessment, early intervention and appropriate referral into a range of primary and secondary healthcare services. YOTs, and health practitioners within these teams, play a vital role in the development of local comprehensive Tiers 1 and 2 CAMHS, with some senior CAMHS practitioners providing Tier 3-level interventions with appropriate supervision. YOT primary healthcare workers also make up a significant percentage of the YOT health workforce.

YOT workers complete an Asset assessment of each child or young person who enters the service. Following assessment, referral to appropriate services is made via the YOT health practitioner. The health practitioner may use further screening and assessment tools among which are Screening Interview for Adolescents and Screening Questionnaire Interview for Adolescents. These clinical materials were commissioned by the YJB to ensure more accurate identification of the mental health needs of young offenders.

Substance Misuse Services in YOTs

In England and Wales in 2012–2013 there were over 200 substance misuse workers deployed in YOTs. The YJB worked closely with the National Treatment Agency (and now the Department of Health) to improve access to substance misuse services (SMS) for young people under YOT supervision in England. YOTs were responsible for the highest number of referrals to SMS of all services working with young people. Data collected by the YJB in 2005–2006 showed that YOTs in England and Wales screened 79,027 young people for substance misuse needs; of these 15,414 required a further assessment and 12,874 received an intervention within 20 working days (Bailey and Kerslake, 2008).

Healthcare in Custodial Youth Justice Services

In April 2003 the Department of Health (DoH) took responsibility for commissioning health services within prison service establishments in England and Wales. Primary Care Trusts took on the commissioning role over the period 2004–2006. Additional funds were provided by DoH to improve health services in prisons, and HMPYOIs benefitted from the investment. Workers in the field credit this strategic change with transforming the standards of healthcare in custodial settings so that they attained NHS standards of care. In 2012–2013 NHS-England became the service commissioner of all prison health services (as part of their developing remit for commissioning health in all justice services) and, in partnership with Public Health England, substance misuse services.

The prevalence of physical illnesses, learning difficulties, mental health problems, traumatic brain injuries and substance misuse among detained children and young people is greater than in the general young population (see Chapter 5 by Hughes, Williams and Chitsabesan). Health and substance misuse services which are age appropriate are required to address the many unmet needs that are identified when youngsters enter custody.

Comprehensive Health Assessment Tool

All new detainees are screened and assessed using the Comprehensive Health Assessment Tool (CHAT), a purpose-designed health assessment tool for use with children and young people with the following components:

- 1st night/reception screen;
- physical health assessment;
- substance misuse assessment;
- mental health assessment;
- and neurodisability assessment.

Other specialist assessments may also be required such as assessments to determine the level of learning disability. The CHAT was commissioned by the DoH, YJB and NHS-England at various stages of its development and it is now the bedrock of the detainees' clinical health records in HMPYOIs (YJB, 2013a, 2013b).

The YJB funded the medical Royal Colleges and other partners to produce a set of intercollegiate service standards (RCPCH, 2013) which were designed to inform planning, delivery and quality assurance of health services for children and young people who are detained in secure settings. Key drivers from the intercollegiate standards were to:

- ensure recognition of safeguarding needs and the risk to others;
- take advantage of a window of opportunity to get it right at this crucial formative age;
- ensure continuity of care;
- take steps to hear the voice of the young person and develop services accordingly;
- work together so that the yield of multiagency approaches is greater than the sum of its parts;
- develop health promoting environments.

The intercollegiate standards have been influential in informing thinking about service developments and in constructing the content of commissioner quality assurance tools known as HJIPs (health and justice indicators of performance).

Each custodial facility provides health services appropriate to the assessed needs of the population. Population health needs assessments are provided by Public Health England. For example, in the LASCHs a school nursing and visiting GP service will often suffice to meet health needs. In YOIs it is necessary to have a more substantive service which includes a primary care centre on site and possibly, access to healthcare beds, also on site.

In a typical service, there would be access to CAMHs and substance misuse workers, and access to visiting specialists. The services provide equivalence with community health services and are age-appropriate in terms of screening programmes, immunisations and vaccinations, and the expertise of staff members. A more assertive approach to well-being is expected in custodial services for children and young people with a multi-departmental plan to ensure a good diet, encourage prosocial coping, education and skills, and balance between physical activity and rest. The service would prepare those at the end of their sentences for release, and liaise with appropriate community health services.

Substance Misuse Services in Custodial Youth Justice

Research shows that young people in the YJS are more likely to use drugs than other groups of young people, and are more likely to suffer substance misuse-related problems (see Chapter 13 by Theodosiou).

This includes poly-drug use and dual diagnosis of mental health and substance misuse issues.

The YJB led the development of improved SMS services in the custodial estate for under-18-year-olds in partnership with the prison service. Significant investment occurred in 2003–2006 to improve SMSs and resettlement for under-18-year-olds in the 37 custodial establishments holding young people at that time. This programme established substance misuse services in all YOIs and provision in STCs and LASCHs to deliver the YJB (2009) *National Specification for Substance Misuse for Juveniles in Custody* and subsequent revisions. The national specification drove change in five key areas of substance misuse intervention which included the following:

- identification and assessment;
- detoxification and clinical management;
- education and prevention;
- support and programmes;
- and through care and resettlement.

The SMS programme based on these key areas continues to date and is delivered in partnership with statutory agencies from other sectors and the providers of custodial services.

SMS – Intensive Resettlement and Aftercare Provision

To improve SMS and dual diagnosis services in custody the YJB (2006) developed resettlement and aftercare provision (RAP). RAP seeks to ensure that achievements made through SMS interventions in custody are built upon when young people leave custody; a critical time for risk of relapse and overdose. A key element of RAP is that participation in the programme is voluntary and not a condition of sentence. Fifty-nine YOTs have attached RAP schemes, providing intensive support to over 1,896 young people leaving custody and on community sentences.

RAP teams undertake detailed resettlement planning with young people whilst in custody, provide up to 25 hours intensive support during the community element of a custodial Detention and Training Order – and can provide up to six months ongoing support following the end of the sentence. The programme gives more time for young people to stabilise and engage with mainstream services. RAP ensures that young people have access to the ongoing specialist SMS and mental health provision they require, as well as access to education, training and employment

opportunities, and stable accommodation. RAP provides support to parents, works with peers and guidance to make better use of leisure time. Many schemes are supported by the voluntary sector and recruit mentors who provide their time on a voluntary basis.

RAP works with some of the most complex young people in the YJS and aims to impact on their substance misuse, mental health needs and history of repeat offending. A fundamental element of RAP is that it is individually tailored to a young person's needs and participation is voluntary.

RAP showed the potential to reduce the demand for custody by reducing the number of young people who return to custody. The RAP evaluation (YJB, 2010a) found that young people on RAP 'are more likely to reduce the severity of their substance misuse' including the frequency of using alcohol, amphetamines, cannabis and cocaine; 'have a lower level of drop out from this voluntary scheme; have fewer unmet needs; appear to value the relationship with their RAP worker (and by association with their YOT)'; and RAP impacted on reduced reoffending rates – '78% of young people on RAP were reconvicted within one year of their first offence, compared to 86% of those not on RAP' a reduction of 8%. Also engagement and compliance on court orders was higher among young people on RAP.

RAP staff felt 'the voluntary nature of RAP enhanced the appeal of the scheme to young people' and they felt that young people did not perceive the programme as a punishment but as something enjoyable, illustrated by a dropout rate of below 25% for the first nine months of 2007–2008.

Success in Providing a Youth Justice Service

The National Audit Office (NAO, 2010) reviewed the YJS in England and Wales. The report concluded that the YJB had

> put in place a coherent structure for youth justice which is capable of delivering value for money in positive directions. The Board has led on successful attempts to reduce the use of custody, the most expensive sentencing option, and implemented reforms to align interventions more effectively with young people most at risk of future offending.

Key Elements of Effective Practice

KEEPs (Key Elements of Effective Practice) were issued in 2008 and include the following ten subject areas:

- accommodation;
- assessment, interventions and supervision;
- education, training and employment;
- engaging young people who offend;
- mental health;
- offending behaviour programmes;
- parenting;
- restorative justice;
- substance misuse;
- and young people who sexually abuse.

KEEPs materials include a summary document setting out key practice points for practitioners, managers and commissioners, each supported by relevant evidence on that topic. For example see Assessment, Planning, Interventions and Support (YJB, 2008b). In partnership with the Open University the YJB has provided a virtual Youth Justice Integrative Learning platform (YJILs) which provides an online qualification framework based on the material provided through the KEEPs.

Conclusions

Since the creation of the YJB the operational administration of juvenile justice services has often been debated, and continues to be so at the time of writing. Despite this the work of the YJB for England and Wales marked an enlightened attempt to assist children and young people to avoid a criminal career pathway and to divert those with special needs to more suitable agencies for care. The YJB created new approaches to supervision of young offenders in the community and in custodial care. It was and remains a catalyst for harnessing energy from existing public, private and third sector agencies to benefit from their expertise and focus their energies on the needs of individual young offenders.

The reduction in demand for custodial places and reduction in reoffence rates with several forms of intervention demonstrate that the YJB approach, and sustained effort, has been effective in helping many children and young people to change. In demonstrating its effectiveness the YJB has consistently invited external parties to investigate its services and performance. This is to be commended, albeit that several studies are now substantially out-of-date and the operating environment has changed.

Without good health, children and young people are not able to take full advantage of opportunities available to them, and are likely to be more vulnerable than their peers. Health and substance misuse services are integral to the work of both YOTs and the custodial care of children and young people; and partnership working is known to be a key element in the effective coordination of care and support of young offenders. Changes to commissioning of health services in custodial settings, aligning the standards of health and substance misuse care similar to those in the community, have ensured that children and young people in custody are not deprived of the medical attention they need to be healthy and to begin to fulfil their potential.

Acknowledgements

I would like to thank Bill Kerslake (Safeguarding and Child Protection Manager, Youth Justice Board for England and Wales) for his substantial contribution. Bill's specialist knowledge and unique historical perspective played an essential role in the construction of this chapter.

References

Audit Commission (1996). *Misspent Youth*. London: Audit Commission for Local Authorities and the National Health Service in England and Wales.

Audit Commission (2004). *Youth Justice 2004: A Review of the Reformed Youth Justice System*. London: Audit Commission for Local Authorities and the National Health Service in England and Wales.

Bailey, S. and Kerslake, B. (2008). The processes and systems for juveniles and young persons. In Soothill, K., Rogers, P. and Dolan, M. Editors. *Handbook of Forensic Mental Health*. Cullompton: Willan Publishing.

Baker, K. (2004). Available from: www.cepprobation.org /uploaded_files/Kerry%20Baker.pdf.

Bowles, R., Pradiptyo, R. and Garcia Reyes, M. (2006). *Estimating the Impact of the Safer Schools Partnerships*. York: University of York.

CrisisCC (2013). Available from: www.crisiscareconcordat .org.uk/inspiration/get-inspired-2/.

DfES (2004). *Every Child Matters: Change for Children*. London: Department for Education and Science.

DoH (2009a). *Improving Health, Supporting Justice: The National Delivery Plan of the Health and Criminal Justice Programme Board*. London: Department of Health.

DoH (2009b). *Healthy Children, Safer Communities*. London: Department of Health.

DoH (2015a). *Future in Mind Promoting, Protecting and Improving Our Children and Young People's Mental Health and Wellbeing*. London: Department of Health.

DoH (2015b). *Promoting the Health and Wellbeing of Looked after Children: Statutory Guidance for Local Authorities, Clinical Commissioning Groups and NHS England*. London: Department of Health.

Harris Review (2015). *Changing Prisons, Saving Lives: Report of the Independent Review into Self-inflicted Deaths in Custody of 18–24 Year Olds*. London: Ministry of Justice, Cmnd 9087.

Harrison, A. (2005). *Evaluation of the Wakefield Youth Inclusion and Support Panel (YISP) Process*. Wakefield: Wakefield Children's Fund.

HMIP (2014). *Children in Custody 2013–14: An Analysis of 12–18-Year-Old's Perceptions of Their Experience in Secure Training Centres and Young Offender Institutions*. London: Her Majesty Inspectorate of Prisons.

HMIP (2015). *Annual Report 2014–15*. London: Her Majesty Inspectorate of Prisons.

HO (2008). *Youth Crime Action Plan*. London: Home Office.

HoJ (2015). Ministerial statement in the House of Commons. Available from: www.publications.parliament.uk/pa/cm201415/cmhansrd/cm150317/wmstext/150317m0001.htm. Accessed 17 March 2015: Column 65WS.

Lord Bradley (2009, April). *'The Bradley Report' Lord Bradley's Review of People with Mental Health Problems and Learning Disabilities in the Criminal Justice System: Executive Summary*. London: Department of Health.

MoJ (2008). Available from: http://data.gov.uk/dataset/reoffending_of_juveniles_england_and_wales.

MoJ (2010). *Green Paper Evidence Report Breaking the Cycle: Effective Punishment, Rehabilitation and Sentencing of Offenders*. London: Ministry of Justice.

MoJ (2011). *Breaking the Cycle: Government Response*. London: Ministry of Justice.

NAO (2010). *The Youth Justice System in England and Wales: Reducing Offending by Young People*. London: National Audit Office.

Neil, A. (2008). *Cross-National Comparison of Youth Justice*. London: Youth Justice Board.

NOMS (2012). *Minimising and Managing Physical Restraint*. London: National Offender Management Service.

NOMS (2014). *Minimising and Managing Physical Restraint – Volume 5: Physical Restraint*. London: National Offender Management Service.

NPM (2014). *Monitoring Places of Detention 5th Annual Report of the United Kingdom's National Preventative Mechanism 2013–14*. London: Ministry of Justice, CM8964, p. 28.

RCPCH (2013). *Healthcare Standards for Children and Young People in Secure Settings*. London: Royal College of Paediatrics and Child Health.

Rix, A., Skidmore, K., Self, R., Holt, T. and Raybould, S. (2011). *Youth Restorative Disposal Process Evaluation*. London: Youth Justice Board.

Shapland, J., Atkinson, J., Atkinson, H., Dignan, J., Edwards, L., Hibbert, J., Howes, M., Johnstone, J., Robinson, G. and Sorsby, A. (2008, June). *Restorative Justice: Does Restorative Justice Affect Reconviction? The Fourth Report from the Evaluation of Three Schemes*. Ministry of Justice Research, Series 10/08. London: Ministry of Justice.

Welsh Assembly (2014). *All Wales Youth Offending Strategy*. Cardiff: Welsh Assembly.

Willow, C. (2014). *Gareth Myatt died 10 Years Ago, but Restraint on Children Continues*. Available from: www.theguardian.com/commentisfree/2014/apr/19/gareth-myatt-died-prison-restraint-children-rainsbrook.

YJB (archive 1). Available from: http://web.archive.org/20070621173420/www.yjb.gov.uk/en-gb/practitioners/CourtsAndOrders/Disposals/ReparationOrder/.

YJB (2006). *Annual Statistical Bulletin 2005/06*. London: Youth Justice Board.

YJB (2006b). *Resettlement and Aftercare Provision: Referral Criteria and Form*. London: Youth Justice Board.

YJB (2008a). *Evaluation of the Youth |Inclusion Programme: Reports on Phase 2*. London: Youth Justice Board.

YJB (2008b). Available from: http://yjbpublications.justice.gov.uk/Resources/Downloads/KEEP_APIS.pdf.

YJB (2009). *Substance Misuse Services in the Secure Estate*. London: Youth Justice Board.

YJB (2010a). *Evaluation of Resettlement and Aftercare Provision*. London: Youth Justice Board.

YJB (2010b). *Integrated Resettlement Support: Management Guidance*. London: Youth Justice Board.

YJB (2011). *Sustaining the Success: Extending the Guidance: Establishing Youth Offending Teams*. London: Youth Justice Board.

YJB (2013a). *The Development and Pilot of the Comprehensive Health Assessment Tool (CHAT): Young People in the Secure Estate*. London: The Offender Health Research Network and Youth Justice Board August.

YJB (2013b). Available from: www.justice.gov.uk/youth-justice/effective-practice-library/resettlement-consortia-evaluations.

YJB (2014a). Available from: www.gov.uk/government/publications/asset-documents.

YJB (2014b). *Commitment to Safeguard*. London: Youth Justice Board.

YJB (2015a). *Youth Justice Statistics: England and Wales: 2013–2014*. London: Youth Justice Board.

YJB (2015b). *Commitment to Safeguard*. London: Youth Justice Board.

YJB (2015c). *The Role of the Youth Justice Board for England and Wales in Preventing Child Exploitation and Harmful Sexual Behaviour*. London: Youth Justice Board.

YJB (2015d). *Monthly Youth Custody Report April, 2015.* London: Youth Justice Board.

YJB (2015e). *Statistical Notice: Minimising and Managing Physical Restraint Data Collection: April, 2014 – September, 2014.* London: Youth Justice Board.

YJB (2015f). *The Physiological and Psychological Impacts of Head-Hold Restraint Techniques.* London: Youth Justice Board.

YJB (2016). *Youth Justice Statistics: England and Wales: 2014–2015.* London: Youth Justice Board.

Chapter 23

Working with Young People in a Secure Environment

Jim Rose, Pam Hibbert and Paul Mitchell

Introduction

The work with a number of young people in the youth justice system crosses the boundary between community and custodial settings. For the most part, community-based Youth Offending Teams (YOTs), working with other agencies in the health and education sectors, provide services for young offenders. However, for some young people the escalation or the seriousness of their offending behaviour results in a custodial sentence and their subsequent admission into the secure estate.

Young People in Custody

Over recent years the numbers of young people under the age of 18 years sentenced to custody have reduced significantly (see Chapter 22 by Tarbuck). The reduction in numbers of young people detained in secure settings has, by and large, served to remove young people without significant offending histories and those aged under15 years of age. However, the offending profiles of these young people showed a higher number of previous offences than previously recorded and with the types of offences clustering at the more serious and violent end of the offending spectrum. About 30% of the young men and 44% of the young women had experienced one or more episodes of being in care and other indicators of disadvantage included 75% with an absent parent; 51% living in deprived or unsuitable accommodation and 39% having been at some stage on the child protection register (YJB, 2012); and the profile of young people in secure accommodation shows a toxic mix of complex and multiple needs disproportionate to the general youth population.

Regarding health and education the picture is no brighter; as well as having considerably higher levels of diagnosable mental health problems, a review by Hughes et al. (2012) suggests that the prevalence of neuro-developmental disorders among young people in custody is generally higher than in the general youth population. In addition, young people in custody have disproportionately higher levels of substance use. In a self-report study of over 500 boys and girls aged 12–17 from across the secure estate, consumption of tobacco, alcohol and drugs far exceeded the average for the general population. Cannabis was the most commonly used drug, followed by ecstasy and cocaine (Galahad SMS Ltd., 2004).

Educational performance is equally unsatisfactory with, at the time of admission to secure accommodation, 50% of young people achieving entry level or below in literacy and in numeracy a slightly better 59% (this represents what would be expected of a group of children aged 7–11 years). Many of these young people have experienced a disrupted education with 88% of young men and 74% of young women having been suspended from school on at least one occasion. Truancy rates for this group are high with some 36% of young men saying they have not been in school after the age of 14 years.

The Provision of Mental Health Services

Children's mental health and emotional well-being has been consistently promoted in government policy over recent years through a number of initiatives, including developments in Child and Adolescent Mental Health Services (CAMHS). The remit for CAMHS includes children and young people involved in the youth justice system although the extent to which CAMHS are involved with local YOTs is variable, as is the level of service provided by CAMHS to the secure estate. Bailey and Harrington found in their research that within YOT teams,

> [t]he health workers with mental health training were valuable in the assessment and management of young offenders with mental health problems. However, they were at risk of being overwhelmed and

unsupported, and few health workers had any clinical supervision from mental health services, although those who did found it valuable.

(Bailey and Harrington, 2005: 5)

However, across the secure estate Bailey and Harrington found

[t]here were considerable differences in the models of mental health provision in secure establishments compared with YOTs. In many secure estate establishments, mental health provision was provided on a sessional basis by mental health professionals who had a personal interest in the area. Subsequently, continuing provision was vulnerable to changes in personnel and priorities. Unlike community CAMHS, multi-disciplinary input was rare. However, secure estate establishments with multi-disciplinary mental health teams reported comparatively high levels of well-co-ordinated input to young people. One YOI had implemented a multi-disciplinary 'in-reach' mental health service, following extensive discussion between the YOI and local CAMHS. The service is based in the YOI, and has links with staff at operational and strategic levels. (Ibid.: 22)

Following on from Bailey and Harrington's work the Department of Health engaged the Centre for Mental Health to review the provision of mental health services for young people in Young Offender Institutions (YOI), particularly in the light of the significant changes in service commissioning arrangements that had taken place to standardise this provision and the additional funding made available for this purpose. The subsequent report, *Reaching Out, Reaching In: Promoting Mental Health and Emotional Well-Being in Secure Settings*, concluded that whilst improvements had been made, many of the issues raised by Bailey and Harrington still applied, notably the variable levels of service available to the secure estate and the difficulty of embedding a culture that recognises the importance of promoting and supporting the well-being of children and young people in custody:

The introduction of specific funding to support CAMHS in-reach services in young offenders institutions has resulted in notable improvements in YOIs. We found evidence that young people with evident mental health difficulties are identified, assessed and supported much more quickly, whether directly within the secure settings or through liaison with multidisciplinary community-based services.

However:

We found evidence of practices in secure regimes that compromise rather than support the emotional well-being of young people in custody; a predominantly reactive approach to mental health problems rather than an early intervention and proactive approach to supporting mental health and well-being; variations in commissioning expertise and interest throughout the entire young people's secure estate and across primary and secondary care; fragmentation in the provision of comprehensive CAMHS services; problems with access to sufficiently intensive support services at the point of resettlement; problems more generally with continuity of care, and underdeveloped work with particular groups of young people who offend. (*Reaching Out, Reaching In* 2010: 66)

The publication in June 2013 of the *Healthcare Standards for Children and Young People in Secure Settings* sets out an explicit set of national standards for enhancing the mental health of young people in secure units.

The Standards also acknowledge the extent of the general healthcare needs of these young people over and above those of their peers in the community and recognises the opportunities provided by a period in secure accommodation.

Young people in secure settings have significantly greater physical, mental and emotional health needs than their peers in the non-secure community. Any time spent in a secure setting is an opportunity to reach out to this vulnerable population and a chance to improve their health outcomes.
(*Healthcare Standards for Children and Young People in Secure Settings*, 2013:4)

In all sectors of the secure estate, there are good examples of how the mental health needs of young people in custody can be effectively addressed. The following example shows how a review of the mental health needs of young men in a YOI (Young Offenders Institution) in the north west of England demonstrated that the current service model was not effectively meeting their needs; resources were focused on providing an inpatient service, which could not provide a service for the overall population.

Analysis of the needs of the young people on the inpatient unit demonstrated that most had complex unmet emotional and behavioural needs rather than mental illness. These young people often rapidly cycled between the inpatient unit, ordinary location and the Care and Separation unit, depending on which of their needs were seen as a priority at any given time.

The unit was staffed by prison officers with support from the mental health team. There was explicit collaboration between the YOI and the mental health provider at strategic, management and operational levels, which ensured that all staff felt supported in the care of young men with high-risk behaviours.

Key elements for the success of the unit were:

- A small and cohesive team of prison officers able to establish good relationships and provide stable and emotionally attuned care, and also act as positive role models (most of the officers were male);
- A robust interagency pathway into the unit, including joint assessment by prison officers and mental health nurses;
- Working to a clear model based on attachment theory, in which the officers took the role of 'therapeutic parents' with a high level of support from the mental health team – although mental health practitioners undertook direct work, it was understood from the outset that the officers' relationships with the young men was the key agency of change;
- Mental health practitioners 'embedded' in the unit to support the officers in the delivery of care – this included joint assessments, support with case management and goal setting, and training.

Key challenges for the unit were:

- 'Holding one's nerve' – ensuring both agencies agreed on a common strategy when faced with an exceptionally challenging situation;
- Avoiding dependency – providing intensive support designed to improve self-management skills and promote independence runs the risk of achieving the opposite;
- Providing sufficient support for the officers – small-scale and consistent staffing of the unit led to more intensive relationships between young men and officers, and resulted in a higher than normal level of staff exposure to intense emotional states and vicarious trauma.

The unit accepted and worked with young men with a wide range of complex needs, which included emotional difficulties usually arising from complex and persistent trauma histories, neuro-developmental difficulties and serious assaultive and self-harming behaviours. Many were likely to meet the criteria for a diagnosis of personality disorder in adulthood. In many respects the unit model anticipated the implementation of Psychologically Informed Planned Environments (PIPEs) within prison and other justice settings (DH and NOMS, 2011). Evaluation of the unit (Ryan and Mitchell, 2011) demonstrated significant reduction in the young men's unmet needs, and improvement in their behaviour and social reintegration.

The unit was part of a larger redesign of the mental health service model; the resources previously committed to the inpatient unit could be used to develop a more comprehensive service for the entire YOI community. This included universal mental health screening, provision of services on a day unit and assertive in-reach services onto the residential units to provide a more visible and accessible service.

Sentenced to Custody

Young people may have their liberty restricted as a result of their offending behaviour in a number of different types of unit managed by different agencies in both the public and private sectors. These include Young Offender Institutions (YOI), managed by the prison service; Secure Training Centres (STC), managed by private companies; and Local Authority Secure Children's Homes (LASCH), managed by various local authorities. There are also a relatively small number of young people detained in mental health settings in both NHS and private healthcare provision. In this chapter, 'secure unit' is used as a generic term for the above health and non-health secure settings.

Caring for young people in a secure unit poses staff with a range of problems that have to be addressed and overcome on a daily basis. The dynamics between staff and young people are the same irrespective of the organisational context of the secure unit, although the varying management arrangements are reflected in such issues as staffing levels, staff qualifications and regime programmes.

Managing Transitions

Managing transitions is a critical issue for young people with serious conduct problems; they are likely to have persistent, multifaceted mental health (Maughan and Kim-Cohen, 2005), personality (Harrington and Bailey, 2004; Coid et al., 2006) and behavioural (Rutter et al., 1998) problems into adulthood. The provision and availability of consistent adult support figures within the context of a stable living environment is increasingly recognised as a critical element in providing essential containment for these young people. This is extremely difficult to sustain in what are often chaotic and changing family circumstances coupled with irregular school attendance.

Coping with change is therefore difficult at every level, from the big transitions, for example from primary to secondary education or the move from children's to adult services, to the disruption of a daily routine caused by a member of staff having to take sick leave.

Transitions into and Out of Secure Units

Nowhere is the issue of transition more focused than when a young person arrives at the secure unit where they are to serve their sentence. Irrespective of any previously known vulnerability to mental health problems, even the apparently most hardened young offender will find their first night, locked away alone in a small, confined space, a daunting experience.

Managing the admission process requires a combination of administrative thoroughness with a caring and sensitive approach to individual need: for example, staff will need to ensure the availability of all relevant documentation and check its validity whilst at the same time offering food and drink, ensuring physical comfort and making an initial assessment of the young person's emotional state, looking for potential risks of self-harm.

A similar approach is required when planning a young person's release from custody. Preparing young people to leave and for successful resettlement into the community involves a series of practical tasks but also needs recognition of the emotional impact on the young person of 'saying goodbyes' and their anxiety about what might be waiting outside.

The transition from custody to community is an area where difficulties have persisted over many years and providing continuity of treatment for young people requiring ongoing mental health services post-release has proved particularly difficult to sustain. This is why, although the pressure on staff within the secure unit means attention is likely to be concentrated on immediate presenting behavioural challenges, the focus of case work and planned

interventions must remain on the longer-term outcomes to be achieved when the young person returns to their community. Similarly, the 'out-of-sight, out-of-mind' response of community practitioners when a young person, who has likely been difficult to manage, is finally 'put away' must be constantly challenged.

Given that the average length of stay in custody is of relatively short duration, it is essential that all professionals, whether working inside or outside the secure unit maintain clear communication and share in the vital planning tasks to achieve positive resettlement.

What Happens Inside?

As the example from the unit illustrates, in order to achieve the levels of containment and stability required to ensure a safe and secure environment for a volatile cohort of young people, the core residential staff team must be able to build and sustain a network of cohesive relationships across different professional teams and with the young people. In a secure unit these key relationships are developed primarily in the context of a consistently delivered regime of daily routines and activities that provide the basis for effective education, health and offending behaviour programmes.

The Extraordinary Ordinary

It is a key skill of a residential worker, whether prison officer, social worker or nurse, to infuse daily routines with meaning and significance relevant to the needs of the young people with whom they are working. A stable, predictable and caring living environment will not be familiar to most of the young people and may challenge their expectation of how the adult group around them is likely to behave. It is these ordinary, mundane experiences of getting up in the morning, sharing meal times and activities and then going to bed at night that lay the foundation for change through education or structured interventions. Sustaining staff's enthusiasm for the delivery of these ordinary routines demands acknowledgement by managers of their critical importance for achieving the longer-term outcomes set for the young people.

An important aspect of this approach is the ability of staff to establish clear expectations about what is acceptable and unacceptable behaviour and to maintain boundaries around these. This links to the importance of the experience of secure care for young people as being one in which they can be sure that the adults in the placement are able to tolerate their behaviour, hold on through difficult times to the material with which they are being presented and believe that change and growth are possible despite what has gone before.

The recognition that the 'ordinary is indeed extraordinary' ensures that the delivery of the daily routine addresses more than just the physical needs of the young people, as the relationships formed between staff and young people begin to provide the necessary containment for the work of the secure unit as a whole.

Thinking Matters

In order for residential staff to do their work properly they require a coherent framework of ideas which they can use to inform their practice. This framework must be supported by managers who are able to stimulate staff thinking through the course of their day-to-day activities and offer professional supervision that combines professional accountability with opportunities for reflective thinking about the processes of the work.

In a television documentary about Feltham, one of the largest YOIs in the UK a relative of a young person who had tragically hanged himself whilst on remand in the prison made a most telling comment in a very simple and moving way: 'Nobody thought about him.' This wasn't just a comment about busy staff who were under so much pressure because of the numbers of young people they had to 'process', although it was clear from the documentary that this was a feature of the institution's functioning. It was an insight into a system in which the demands on staff were not being managed in a way that recognised their need for time and space to think about an individual young person and through thinking to embark on a course of action that literally might have saved his life.

The ability of the adult group to contain young people in a secure unit is always dependent on the provision of high levels of adult attention to the particular and individual needs of each young person in the group. It is critically important for each young person to know that at some level they are being thought about positively and 'held in mind' by the group of adults responsible for their care and in particular in the minds of those key adult figures involved in their daily programme.

Safe and Secure

There is no doubt that the general climate of a secure unit either promotes sound mental health and well-being or exacerbates the problems that young people already have. For some young people the mental health problems they are experiencing predate their admission and may have contributed to their offending and subsequent custodial sentence. Placement in a secure unit may serve to emphasise or highlight these problems and immediate treatment will be required. For others, the experience of being locked up may make them feel so depressed or anxious they too will need specific help. The creation of a positive culture in which staff pay attention to the needs of the young people in their care, get to know them, and in which everyone feels safe and secure goes a long way towards alleviating mental health problems and provides a much better environment for the assessment and diagnosis of more serious problems.

The particular dynamics of work in a secure environment mainly arise from the close proximity of the adult staff to a group of highly delinquent and often traumatised young people. Presented with what often seem inescapable situations, staff have to respond to the intense feelings of the young people and the processes that arise from the acting-out of these feelings within the day-to-day activities of the unit. When staff are encouraged in their work to engage with the young people, rather than just 'watch and respond' in a detached way, then it is inevitable that their reactions will generate levels of both individual and group anxiety that have to be managed and processed.

> These (secure units) are intense environments where, however strong the resistance and denial may be, there is no real escape from the conflict and pain that inevitably surface. (Rose, 2014: 49)

The Work of Managers in a Secure Unit

There is sometimes a debate about whether management is an art or a science. Many definitions of art include the idea that, at least in part, a work of art in any form should invite its audience to stand apart from daily routine and reflect on wider meanings. To create such opportunities for thinking within what is a busy and frenetic world, whilst at the same time looking after highly delinquent and severely damaged young people must be considered an art indeed! (Ibid.: 147)

To be effective, managers must combine the performance of those aspects of management that might be designated the 'hard' side of things with those 'softer' elements of the task that take into account the particular dynamics of working with young people in a secure environment.

As Pascale and Athos put it:

> The inherent preferences of organisations are clarity, certainty and perfection. The inherent nature of human relationships involves ambiguity, uncertainty and imperfection. How one honours, balances and integrates the needs of both is the real trick of management.
>
> (Pascale and Athos, 1981: 105)

So, whilst it is important to ensure that the routine tasks of management are carried our effectively and efficiently, managers must also provide appropriate levels of support that enable staff to have space for the reflection and thinking that is required to sustain their complex work with young people.

For example, one of the reoccurring features of work in a secure unit is a shared sense of helplessness that can overwhelm staff and managers alike:

> Staff blame managers for the fact that nothing seems to change, and managers blame their managers, right up to the point where the chain goes outside of the unit to 'them out there'. It is useful to be able to think that this sense of helplessness may reflect something of the powerlessness of young people locked up in secure units, but managers have to be able to do something about it as well.   (Rose, 2014: 153)

The ways in which managers deal with issues such as staff absence and lateness are telling indicators as to whether this balance has been achieved. High levels of sickness and absence are often a sign of high levels of stress in a staff group. However, it is important that managers not only provide some understanding about the underlying causes of this (perhaps there has been some serious self-harming behaviour in the young people's group) but are also able to confront individual staff about their response to the situation and the consequences of their 'acting out' behaviour on the capacity of the unit to safely contain the young people.

An Integrated Approach

One of the main challenges for secure units is to integrate the different strands of their regime into a coherent programme for each young person, so that their individual needs are accommodated but at the same time they also benefit from the experience of group life through the course of routine daily activities. Research indicates that interventions which are targeted on the assessed and identifiable needs of each young person are more likely to be effective than those which simply take a 'scatter gun' approach and spray young people with an uncoordinated range of disparate activities, however worthwhile or interesting these may appear.

(Rose, 2014: 198)

Whilst the daily routines of residential living provide the context for the all-important relationships between staff and young people, there are other activities that contribute to the intended outcomes for young people sentenced to custody and which also require a relational base. These include family contact, education and training and offending behaviour programmes. These activities are all coordinated through structured case management meetings involving professionals from the secure unit and from community agencies previously involved with the young person, coordinated by the YOT.

As the number of young people in all types of secure unit continues to decrease, capacity in the secure estate exponentially decreases as well. This means more young people are being placed at considerable distances from their homes, making visits by family even more difficult. This has, pretty much, always been the case for young women in custody but now the impact is wider. The challenge for secure units will be to develop more flexible arrangements for family visiting and to make more consistent attempts to include families in the series of meetings that mark a young person's progress through their sentence.

Maintaining contact between young people and their families or carers is a vital aspect of work in secure units, as is establishing a positive relationship between staff and families. Whilst this may be acknowledged in formal descriptions of an institution's work, the reality is often different! As with so many things it is the attitude and approach of staff that matter; when staff are friendly, welcoming and respectful, offer refreshments and create opportunities for families to meet their child in a more homely and private space, then a positive relationship will be possible. When concerns and suspicions about security dominate from the outset of a visit, then relationship building is inevitably more difficult.

Much of a young person's day in custody is spent in structured programmes of education or vocational training. With the rising average age of young people sentenced to custody the emphasis on work-related programmes is likely to increase.

Prison education and work-related experiences are often subject to criticism in formal inspection reports. There are, however, notable exceptions which are usually the result of efforts by particular groups of staff and by individual units taking more imaginative approaches to the delivery of programmes.

Ensuring continuity with mainstream curricula and providing work that has direct relevance to credible employment opportunities in the community is critical. But again, it is the ability of staff to engage positively with young people to gain their trust and inspire motivation to participate that makes the real difference.

The same principles apply in the assessment and implementation of offending behaviour programmes. Since the inception of the juvenile secure estate, surprisingly little progress has been made in the development of effective offending programmes for young people, either in the community or in secure settings. Other chapters look at this issue in more detail, but in this context it is worth re-emphasising the significance of positive adult–young people relationships and how the most powerful influences for shaping young people's behaviour and attitudes are located in the culture of routine daily events and activities.

The Use of Physical Restraint

It is a sobering fact that in the period between April 2000 and January 2012 16 children (under the age of 18 years) died in custody. This figure includes two 15-year-olds and a 14-year-old who died in a Secure Training Centre (STC) following an episode of restraint.

How conflict is managed is a telling indicator of the culture of any residential establishment and of staff attitudes towards the young people in their care. Staff working directly and closely, day in day out, with challenging young people experience high levels of anxiety, so

> [r]ather than allowing maladaptive ways of managing stress in secure units to become institutionalised in pointless routines and oppressive structures, there has to be a shared acknowledgement of its origins and nature. Fear of being alone and of being attacked, with a consequent breakdown of order, is shared by both adults and young people. A full understanding of what this actually

means is essential for the proper management and care of the young people and as a basis for providing sufficient and appropriate support systems for staff. These issues are brought into sharp relief when the question is considered as to how conflict and differences get dealt with in secure units.

> (Rose, 2014: 108)

In 2008 the Government commissioned a review by Peter Smallridge and Andrew Williamson to review the use of physical restraint in juvenile secure settings and in 2011 a Restraint Advisory Board (RAB) was appointed to assess a new restraint system to be used in YOIs and STCs. Subsequently the Independent Restraint Advisory Panel (IRAP) also undertook a review of the use of restraint in Local Authority Secure Children's Homes.

Neither the RAB nor the IRAP are now extant but both took the view that any system which allows the use of physical force against children and young people has to be underpinned by child-centred principles and a strong ethical framework. The full text of this work can be found in the RAB report to government (2011).

The RAB adopted the following principles, which were also carried forward to underpin the work done by IRAP

First Principle – the Status of the Child

- All young people aged under 18 and detained by the state are children and, as a matter of law, retain the same protection provided by domestic and international legal frameworks which is otherwise accorded to children who are not in custody.
- The welfare of the child is of paramount importance, and this principle must remain at the forefront in caring for and managing the behaviour of children detained by the state.
- Children and young people should have a say in how their behaviour is managed, and be able to voice their concerns over restraint confidentially and independently.

Second Principle – Use of Restraint

- The use of force should always be necessary, proportionate and in accordance with law.
- The use of force always carries an inherent and unavoidable risk to a child or young person being restrained and must be developed and employed as part of an effective overall behaviour management strategy.

Third Principle – Restraint of Children Involves Special Considerations

- Physical restraint is not deployed as a punishment but arises from a need to protect.
- Its use should not be understood and applied from a purely adult perspective but taught in the context of what we know about child and adolescent development, including:
  - The physical and psychological attributes of children and young people as immature, still developing human beings.
  - The wide differences that arise in how children and young people understand their circumstances, what is happening to them and what is being asked of them.
  - The wide variations that arise in children's behaviour and in their emotional responses from the impact of their past experiences and personal life narratives prior to custody, and the needs these give rise to.

Fourth Principle – Training is Critical to Safe Restraint

- The quality and frequency of training is vital to safe restraint.
- Training should be child focused, built upon these principles and should enhance staff skills in de-escalation and diversion to minimise the recourse to physical restraint.

Fifth Principle – Accreditation and Effective Governance

- Each establishment using physical restraint should demonstrate robust governance arrangements that ensure all elements of the accredited programme (the appropriate application of techniques, staff training, incident management and reporting and data capture) are subject to effective risk management.

A Systematic Approach to Decisions about Restraint in the Best Interests of Children

Making judgements and taking decisions in conflictual situations involves complex processes to assess situations quickly, taking account of divergent views and using risk/benefit analyses.

Many people who are involved in high anxiety/conflict situations say afterwards that they acted on 'instinct'. However, instinct is not an inherent attribute – it is learned behaviour that is probably based on prior knowledge, previous experiences and assessments (sometimes unconscious) of the situation.

Making decisions in someone's 'best interests', a concept established in law and professional practice, is complex, as is the balance between the interests of individual persons and groups of people. The RAB recommends that the following guidelines could assist staff in ascertaining the child or young person's best interests.

Decision makers must:

- *Take into account all relevant factors* that would be reasonable to consider, not just those that *they* think are important, or that reflect what they would prefer to happen.
- *Make every reasonable effort* to involve and enable the young person to take part in the decision making.
- Not be acting on preconceived ideas or negative assumptions.
- Not be acting on or making decisions based on *what they would want to do* if they were the person about whom the decision was being made.
- *Be able to explain the decisions* they've taken about the young person's best interests, giving their reasons for reaching those decisions and identifying the particular factors they have taken into account.

Not a Conclusion, but the Place to Begin

There can only ever be one answer to the question, what is the most valuable asset in a secure unit? It is the staff. Of course attention must be paid to the standard of the residential accommodation, the availability of resources for education and training, access to relevant materials to provide challenging offending behaviour programmes and facilities for physical and other kinds of leisure activities. However, to make the full use of these, in a purposeful way and for the benefit of young people, requires the presence on a regular and consistent basis of highly motivated and multi-skilled groups of competent staff who are committed to delivering the regime. (Rose, 2014: 179)

Residential staff often receive little by way of formal acknowledgement of the critical contribution their work makes to the outcomes for young people sentenced to custody and yet it is arguable that the work that they carry out on a daily basis is the most influential in any progress a young person may make during their time in a secure unit.

The distinguished American psychotherapist Irving Yalom is well known for his work with individual groups of patients. However, what he has to say is relevant to the task of a secure unit and to the importance of the work of residential staff and their relationships with young people:

> [A] therapist helps a patient not by sifting through the past but by being lovingly present with that person; by being trustworthy, interested, and by believing that their joint activity will ultimately be redemptive and healing. The drama of age regression and incest recapitulation (or for that matter any therapeutic cathartic or intellectual project) is healing only because it provides therapist and patient with some interesting shared activity while the real therapeutic force – the relationship – is ripening on the tree. So I devoted myself to being present and faithful.   (Yalom, 1989: 227)

Present and faithful: a good way to describe the qualities required for working with young people in a secure environment.

References

Bailey, S. and Harrington, R. (2005). *Mental Health Needs and Effectiveness of Provision for Young Offenders in Custody and in the Community*. London: The Youth Justice Board.

Coid, J., Yang, M., Tyrer, P., Roberts, A., and Ullrich, S. (2006). Prevalence and correlates of personality disorder in Great Britain. *The British Journal of Psychiatry*, **188**: 423–431.

Department of Health and National Offender Management Service. (2011). *Managing the Offender PD Pathway*. London: Department of Health & National Offender Management Service.

Galahad SMS Ltd. (2004). *Substance Misuse and Juvenile Offenders*. London: Youth Justice Board.

Harrington, R. and Bailey, S. (2004). Presentation of antisocial personality disorder: Mounting evidence on optimal timing and methods. *Criminal Behaviour and Mental Health*, **14**: 75–81.

HM Inspectorate of Prisons. The Youth Justice Board. (2012). *Children and Young People in Custody 2011–12: An Analysis of the Experiences of 15–18-year-olds in Prison*. London: The Youth Justice Board.

Hughes, N., Williams, H., Chitsabesan, P., Davies, R., and Mounce, L. (2012). *Nobody Made the Connection: The Prevalence of Neurodisability in Young People Who Offend*. London: Children's Commissioner.

Khan, L. (2010). *Reaching Out, Reaching In: Promoting Mental Health and Emotional Well-being in Secure Settings*. London: Centre for Mental Health.

Maughan, B. and Kim-Cohen, J. (2005). Continuities between childhood and adult life. *British Journal of Psychiatry*, **187**: 605–617.

Pascale, R. G. and Athos, A. G. (1981). *The Art of Japanese Management*. New York: Simm & Schuster.

Restraint Advisory Board. (2011) *Assessment of Minimising and Managing Physical Restraint (MMPR) for Children in the Secure Estate*. Available from: www.justice.gov.uk /downloads/youth-justice/custody/mmpr/mmpr-restraint-advisory-board-report.pdf. Accessed on 26 October 2011.

Rose, J. (2014). *Working with Young People in Secure Accommodation – From Chaos to Culture*. 2nd Edition. London: Routledge.

Royal College of Paediatrics and Child Health. (2013). *Healthcare Standards for Children and Young People in Secure Settings*. London: Royal College of Paediatrics and Child Health.

Rutter, M., Giller, H., and Hagell, A. (1998). *Antisocial Behaviour by Young People*. Cambridge: Cambridge University Press.

Ryan, T. and Mitchell, P. (2011, June). A collaborative approach to meeting the needs of adolescent offenders with complex needs in custodial settings: An 18-month cohort study. *The Journal of Forensic Psychiatry & Psychology*, **22**(3): 437–454.

Smallridge, P. and Williamson, A. (2008). *Independent Review of Restraint in Juvenile Secure Settings*. London: Ministry of Justice and the Department for children, schools and families.

Yalom, I. (1989). *Love's Executioner and Other Tales of Psychotherapy*. New York: Basic Books.

Youth Justice Board. (2012). *Managing the Behaviour of Children and Young People in the Secure Estate*. London: Youth Justice Board.

Epilogue

Maggie Atkinson

This book has proved a fascinating read. At times it has been a haunting and harrowing one to boot. I am not a practitioner in either the youth justice or mental health systems. I was once a teacher, and then a trainer, inspector, service and school improver, before becoming a Director of Children's Services in local government, in anything other than the target professions whose members will read this book. I have spent my career since 1979 working with, trying to understand and equally striving to bring to light the voices, views, experiences and contributions of children and young people. Some of the faces I have encountered came into my mind's eye as I read the case examples in some chapters in this text, leaving me wiser about why they were as they were, and sadder still that I could do so little for them when I taught them so many years ago.

I write this Epilogue having been deeply struck by the commonalities across the different chapters I have just read. I write it from two perspectives. Firstly, my personal career and long interest in how well or otherwise particularly challenged children and young people fare as they grow up and are schooled, protected, kept healthy and safe. Secondly, as the former Children's Commissioner for England whose remit in law for five years was to promote and protect the rights of the child, and to bring their voices to the hearing of those with the power to make their lives better.

I know many readers will approach this collection as one might any textbook: to find the particular issue one is studying or interrogating, and read that chapter, then turn to another source on the same topic. But I urge that when you have read my musings, when you have done the assignment for which you read that chapter alone, you go back to the start, and read all of it. This book is full of lively, engaging, challenging as well as rigorous and academically sound writing, supposedly with each chapter about something different. But read it again. The common threads are

remarkable, whatever the angle from which authors have approached their subjects and given us their wisdom about our most troubled and troubling young people.

This book reiterates what we already knew about the turbulent years we call adolescence, but it does so with a kaleidoscopic richness that bears close reading, and inter- as well as intra-professional reflection and discussion. There is a remarkable degree of agreement in its pages, chapter by chapter. Whichever professional background the reader may come from the content of this book resonates with what the reader sees in live day-to-day practice and, moreover, offers helpful solutions and ways forward.

What we see here, study after study and chapter by chapter, is a child or young person who, whatever their circumstances of birth, has all too often been neglected, unloved, sidelined, mistreated, ignored. All too often they have not been identified as early as necessary as a struggler or an outsider, whether at school or elsewhere. We are looking at children who have often been exposed, some of them since before birth, to sustained adult violence of thought, word and deed. These are children who have been made somehow immune to, even devoid of, the emotions you or I might feel when subjected to physically, emotionally or sexually abusive behaviour from those whose role should have been to care for them. They are children who have all too often been given little affection in their very earliest days and then cannot access it throughout their childhoods; whose siblings may have tried to protect them but then left the family home to escape elsewhere, leaving them unguarded to fend for themselves. They are children who may have witnessed, or been subject to, drink or drug-abused violence directed at one set of the people they love, by another. The incidence of language and other delay in their development, of speech and language difficulties, of neurological delays and related learning difficulties, of an inability to empathise or sympathise with others consistently or coherently, link the chapters of this book like a red thread. The case examples recording traumatic brain injuries sustained either in early life or at that crucial stage of brain plasticity and maturation between age 12 and 18 are remarkable unless you have met and worked with some of the children described.

The stories and case examples that so richly illustrate these contributors' accounts are never presented as excuses for criminal behaviours on these children's parts. The descriptions are quiet, dispassionate, observant, reflective. They are made all the more powerful to the reader because of these academically rigorous qualities. Each chapter is referenced so that it rests on a body of literature, a cannon of evidence that shows there is a minority of this nation's children who are somehow lost: both to us, and still more tragically, to themselves and what should, in adolescence and poised on the edge of the adventures of adulthood, surely be a growing sense of self-worth. Authors attend scrupulously to what we therefore need to do to help, support, contain and heal these damaged young people, to give them a fighting chance to come through not just coping, but resilient and healed.

That we have some children who commit crimes, some of them deeply disturbing and horrific, is not in question. A minority do so. We are, rightly, sent reeling in shock and disbelief. However, many of those who commit crimes, some seeming emotionally unaffected by what they have done, are deeply damaged and in need of expert treatment as well as containment, which is richly illustrated in this book. It is equally clear from these pages that we need a workforce, in schools and communities, in child mental health services and the criminal justice system, which is better trained to deal with these difficulties; peopled by those who are both better prepared and better able to address the reasons for the behaviour, not just to condemn or challenge it.

The purpose of a text such as this, backed as it is by years of professional expertise, knowledge and wisdom, by a depth and breadth of research and literature, and by accounts of the lived experiences of some deeply troubled and offending young people, is to play its part in that workforce development. We must, together, find ways to make key therapeutic differences with these young people, so as to positively change the lives of our most damaged and hurt.

The United Nations Convention on the Rights of the Child says loud and clear that ratifying nation states like the UK must first seek the reasons for children's offending, and start the journey to rehabilitation. This book lays out how we might go about doing that most difficult work, in a society that is mystified when children and young people do dreadful things to others. I could not be more pleased to contribute this Epilogue to this book, or more moved, challenged and informed by the content of every chapter in it.

Index

academic problems, 48, 247
acceptance and commitment therapy (ACT), 257
actuarial risk assessments, 55
ADHD Child Evaluation (ACE), 193
Adjustment Disorder (AD)
  conclusion, 162–163
  interventions, 156
  introduction, 152
  overview, 154–155
adolescence
  brain development, 3–4
  challenging stereotypes of, 3
  development stages of, 2
  early intervention, 9
  family reaction to conflict/consequences, 5
  illness during, 5
  in-born vs. acquired obstacles, 4–5
  introduction, 1
  possession charges during adolescence, 6–7
  reparative experience in therapy, 9–10
  repercussions for relationships, 8–9
  rival perspectives, 1–2
  serious situations during, 5–7
  sexual prowess in, 4
  shop-lifting charges during, 6
  sleep patterns in, 3
  soliciting charges during, 6–7
  stages of development, 2
  turmoil, normal vs. pathological, 4
  undermined by early deprivation, 7–8
adolescence-limited offending, 83
Adolescent Adult Sensory Profile, 211
adolescent mentalisation-based integrative therapy (AMBIT), 259
Adult Mental Health Team, 6
adult role models, 109
AESOP First Episode Psychosis Study, 168
affect dysregulation, 224
affective disorders, 42
aggression
  amygdala dysfunction, 88
  anger management difficulties, 158
  attachment security, 17
  information processing, 14
  integrated model of aggression and violence, 86
  neurodevelopmental impairment and youth crime, 70
  physical aggression, 12
  schizophrenia links with, 168
Aggressive Behavioral Control Program Intervention, 113
AIM assessment model, 126
alcohol misuse, 111, 178, 179
AMBIT (Adolescent Mentalization-Based Integrative Treatment), 118
American Psychiatric Association (APA), 136, 138, 178
American Psychological Association (APA), 26, 244
antipsychotic medication, 170–171, 248
antisocial behavior
  adolescent onset/risks, 19–20
  attachment security, 17
  autonomic reactivity, 13
  childhood-onset conduct disorder, 84
  conclusions, 20
  'covert' antisocial behaviours, 12
  early developmental pathways, 19
  family-level factors, 14–18
  heritable influences, 14–15
  heterogeneity of, 11–12
  individual factors, 12–14
  information processing and social cognition, 14
  intervention programs, 90
  introduction, 11
  maltreatment, 17
  neighborhood influences, 19
  neurodevelopmental impairment and youth crime, 70
  neuropsychological desficits, 13, 14, 15
  parenting influences, 16–17
  peer deviance, 18
  pregnancy/prenatal influences, 15–16
  psychopathy and, 217
  psychophysiological correlates, 14
  schooling and education, 18
  temperament concerns, 11, 12–13
  in twins, 88
antisocial parents, 15
Antisocial Personality Disorder (APD), 84
Antisocial Processes Screening Device (APSD), 219–220
anxiety disorders, 42
Arrestee Survey, 179
arson, 7
arts psychotherapies
  art therapy, 285–286
  case example, 280–284
  chaotic discharge in art therapy, 285
  conclusion, 287–288
  containment within institutions, 284–285
  in custody, 284
  introduction, 278
  learning disabilities, 278
  mentalization process, 279
  multimodal approach, 287
  music therapy, 279–284, 286–287
  psychopathology, origins, 278–279
  rooms and space, 285
Asperger's Syndrome, 127, 129
Assessment and Care in Custody Teamwork (ACCT), 58, 144
assessment of young offenders. See also risk assessment/formulation; screening and assessment
  ADHD, 192–193, 195
  Asset assessment tool, 46, 169, 306
  Autistic Spectrum Disorder, 211
  basing treatment on, 241
  biopsychosocial assessment, 13, 227, 229–233t
  case example, 116, 117
  child centred approach, 51
  cognitive and related interventions, 262
  complex trauma, 160–161
  criminal justice pathway, 51
  diagnosis/symptom-focused approaches, 45
  educational needs, 48–49
  gender and ethnicity differences, 49–50
  implications for practice, 50–51
  introduction, 41–42
  mental health screenings, 42–46, 43–44t, 47f

needs assessment approaches, 45–46
neurodevelopmental impairment, 77, 78
physical needs, 46–48
post-assessment intervention services, 131
risk and resilience approach, 46, 47f
schizophrenia, 169–170, 172
in secure environments, 318
self-harm, 141–142
sexually harmful behavior, 128
shared accountability, 52
social needs, 46
substance misuse, 181–182, 182f, 185
suicide concerns, 142–144
Asset assessment tool, 46, 169, 306
attachment
    arts psychotherapies, 281
    avoidant-ambivalent attachment style, 223
    case example, 159, 161f
    custodial youth, 314
    DART Model, 226
    defined, 222–223
    disorganized attachment style, 223
    early attachment process, 158
    harmful sexual behaviours, 129
    insecure-ambivalent attachment style, 223
    reactive attachment disorder, 126
    secure attachment style, 223
    security and aggression, 17
    trauma and, 222–226, 225f
attention deficit hyperactivity disorder (ADHD)
    assessment of, 192–193, 195
    case example, 195
    comorbidity, 42, 191–192, 203, 247
    cognitive behavioral therapy, 255
    cognitive empathy and, 71
    conclusions, 196
    cost-benefit, 196
    criminal justice system and, 192
    criminogenic factors, 190–191
    in custodial settings, 192
    diagnosing symptoms, 240
    emotional regulation, 72
    individual violence and, 84, 87
    introduction, 190
    medication, 194–196
    mindfulness approach, 257
    as neurodevelopmental impairment, 68
    police and court issues, 192
    prevalence among offenders, 190
    psychosocial interventions, 194
    recidivism and, 192
    sexually harmful behavior, 129

substance misuse, 180
support guidelines, 77
treatment, 193–196
youth gangs, 110–111
Audit Commission (2004), 301
autism spectrum disorder (ASD)
    adolescence, 5
    arts psychotherapies, 278
    assessment, 211
    case example, 211
    causes of, 201–203
    co-existing conditions, 203
    cognitive empathy and, 71
    comorbidities, 191, 203, 207–208
    conclusion, 210–212
    criminal justice system and, 205–207
    defined, 42–44, 203, 204–205t
    diagnosis, 202, 203–205
    empathic response lack, 226
    environmental influences and, 201
    formulation, 211
    introduction, 68, 201
    management approaches, 208, 211
    offenders and, 206
    pharmacotherapy, 209–210
    prevalence of, 201
    sexually abusive behavior, 126–128
    support guidelines, 77
    therapeutic strategies, 209
Autism Spectrum Quotient (AQ), 45
autonomic nervous system (ANS), 13

BARO assessment, 46
Beck Hopelessness Scale (BHS), 144
Beck Scale for Suicide Ideation (BSSI), 144
behavior pattern deficits, 202
behavioral parenting training, 90, 244, 267
binge drinking, 111
biopsychosocial assessment, 13, 227, 229–233t
borderline personality disorder, 258
brain. See also traumatic brain injury
    abnormalities from trauma, 224–225
    amygdala activity, 14, 88
    cortex and individual violence, 86–88
    development of, 3–4, 157–158, 289–290
    dopamine, 3, 178–179
    emotional brain, 157
    imaging technology, 129
    left cerebral hemisphere, 86
    prefrontal cortex, 3, 72, 86–88
    receptive plasticity state of brain, 3
    response with trauma, 158
British National Formulary for Children, 171

Brown Attention Deficit Disorder Scale, 193
building-bridges approach, 115
bullying concerns, 65

callous-unemotional (CU) traits
    evidence of, 14
    genetic influences, 14–15
    in homicide victimization, 100
    impact of, 89
    individual violence and, 85, 88
    'low reactive' pathway, 19
    overview, 11, 12
    parental discipline, 17
    subscale, 220
    trauma and, 225–226
CALMER model of PFA, 35
cannabis misuse, 178, 179
care-giving system, 159–161
Care Programme Approach (CPA), 172
change in personality functioning, 222
Child and Adolescent Intellectual Disability Screening Questionnaire (CAIDS-Q), 49
Child and Adolescent Mental Health Services (CAMHS), 6, 8, 129, 195, 305, 306, 307, 312–313
Child Behavior Checklist (CBCL), 240
child centred screening/assessment, 51
Child Protection Committees, 121
Child Psychopathy Scale (CPS), 219
Children Act (2004), 289, 291
children and young people (CYP). See law/laws for children and young people; psychosocial resilience
Children's Communication Checklist Questionnaire (CCC-2), 49
Children's Global Assessment Scale, 193
chronic PTSD, 156
Cleckley, Hervey, 217
client-focused therapy, 159
comorbidity
    attention deficit hyperactivity disorder, 42, 191–192, 203, 247
    autism spectrum disorder, 191, 203, 207–208
    conduct disorder, 42, 191
    early interventions, 242
    neurodevelopmental impairment, 191
    Oppositional Defiant Disorder, 203, 247
    substance misuse, 42, 180–181
co-production principles, 114
'coercive family process' model, 16
cognitive analytic therapy (CAT), 257, 286
cognitive and related interventions

behavioral problems and offending, 259–260
case example, 262
compassion approach, 256–257
conclusion, 261–263
effective programs, 260–261
introduction, 254
key elements, 261
mentalisation based treatments, 258–259
young offenders, 260
cognitive behavioral therapy (CBT)
adaptations for treatment, 255–256
ADHD, 194
brain response with trauma, 158
defined, 137
as early intervention, 244
effectiveness of, 259
formulation of psychopathic-like traits, 227
multimodal elements, 256
overview, 254–256
for PTSD, 155–156
risk management strategies, 145
schizophrenia, 171
trauma focus and, 152
young people in justice system, 254–255
cognitive emotional regulation framework, 28
cognitive empathy, 71–72
cognitive impairment, 224
cognitive remediation therapy, 171
collateral information in risk assessment, 57–59
collective psychosocial resilience, 29
communication disorders, 48, 68
community sentences, 303
community treatment orders, 173
community violence, 152
compassion approach, 256–257
compassionate mind therapy, 257
complex trauma. See also trauma
case example, 159–162
characteristics of, 158
conclusion, 162–163
developmental trauma disorder, 157
early interpersonal trauma, 157–158
integrated management, 158–159
intervention, 159–162
introduction, 152
overview, 156–157
compliance therapy, 171
Comprehensive Assessment of Psychopathic Personality (CAPP), 218, 219–220
Comprehensive Health Assessment Tool (CHAT), 50, 143, 169, 181, 193, 307
concerning sexual behaviors, 124

conduct disorder (CD)
comorbidity, 42, 191
defined, 259
early interventions, 239, 241
introduction, 12
sexually harmful behavior, 126
substance misuse, 180
conflict and homicide, 96
Cook County Juvenile Temporary Detention Centre, 42
Coping Power Program, 244, 245
coping responses, 4, 28, 35, 142
cortex and individual violence, 86–88
counter-transference, 159, 278
covert behaviours, 12, 85
Crime and Disorder Act (1998), 301
Crime Survey for England and Wales, 178
criminal justice system, 205–207
criminalisation, 74–75, 289–291
criminogenic factors in ADHD, 190–191
crimogenic need principle, 260
custodial healthcare, 307
custodial youth justice, 307–308

DART Model (Developmentally informed Attachment, Risk and Trauma), 226
Deliberate Self-Harm (DSH), 58
delusions with depression, 135
depression
alcohol misuse, 180
cognitive behavioral therapy, 254–256
definition and diagnosis, 135–136
delusions with, 135
early detection, 146
hallucinations with, 135
introduction, 135
medication for, 137
prevalence of, 136
risk factors for, 136–137
treatment and management of, 137
detachment from school, 48
development stages of adolescence, 2, 4, 19
developmental coordination disorder (DCD), 203, 207
developmental pathways, 19, 109–110, 178–179
developmental trauma disorder, 157, 224
developmentalists, 218
developmentally impaired groups, 124
Diagnosis Interview Schedule for Children-Version 2.3 (DISC-2.3), 42, 49
Diagnostic and Statistical Manual, DSM-5 (APA), 138, 167, 240

diagnostic validity, 240
dialectical behavioural therapy (DBT), 144–145, 257–258, 274
Dinosaur School program, 245
disability-adjusted life-years (DALYs), 83
discrimination and neurodevelopmental impairment, 74–75
disorders and psychosocial resilience, 31
disorganized attachment style, 223
disruptive disorders
behaviors in childhood, 11, 19
conflicts and, 96
homicide offending and, 98
rates of, 42
dissociation consciousness, 224
distress and psychosocial resilience, 31
'doli incapax' protection, 289
domestic violence, 126, 152
dopamine, 3, 178–179
dorsolateral prefrontal cortex, 71, 86
dosage principle, 260
dose-response relationship, 101
dynamic interplay in music therapy, 287
dysregulation of caregivers, 224

Early Assessment Risk List for Boys (EARL-20B), 56, 193, 240
Early Assessment Risk List for Girls (EARL-21 G), 240
early attachment process, 158
early deprivation concerns, 7–8
early developmental pathways, 19
early interpersonal trauma, 157–158
early interventions. See also interventions
academic engagement and learning, 247
basing treatment on assessment, 241
child therapies, 244
combined family and child, 245–246
comorbid conditions, 242
diagnostic validity, 240
effectiveness, 245
engaging the family, 242
family interventions, 243
family systemic therapies, 243
flexibility of approach, 9
goal of, 241
good practice examples, 244–245
guidelines for, 242–243
identification and development of strengths, 241–242
introduction, 239
medication as, 247–248
parenting therapies, 243–244
positive behavior and, 246–247

principles of, 241–243
in school, 246–247
social and scholastic learning, 242
summary, 248
treatment in natural
environment, 243
when to make diagnosis, 239–240
education
aggression in school, 18
antisocial behavior influence, 18
of custodial youth, 318
disengagement from, 18, 72–73
impact on youth gangs, 112
intervention in neurodevelopmental
impairment, 75–76
needs and assessment, 48–49
neurodevelopmental impairment
and, 72–73
'effective participation,' 290
electroconvulsive therapy (ECT), 296
emotional brain, 157
emotional disorders, 180, 255
emotional regulation, 72
empathy levels, 13
employment impact on youth
gangs, 112
engagement approach, 114
engagement theory, 28
Enhanced Thinking Skills (ETS),
259, 260
epidemiology of psychosocial
resilience, 29–31
epigenetic mechanisms, 15
equifinality and trauma, 222–223
equifinality vs. multi-equifinality, 222
ethnicity differences of young
offenders, 49–50, 108–109
European Convention on Human
Rights, 290, 295
European Monitoring Centre for
Drugs and Drug Addiction, 178,
179, 183
Every Child Matters: Change for
Children (DfES), 305–306
executive function deficits
individual violence, 86–87
meta-analysis of, 87
mindfulness approach, 257
neurodevelopmental impairment
and youth crime, 70–71
types of, 14, 48
externalizing behaviours, 15
eye-movement desensitisation
reprocessing (EMDR), 152, 156

false confessions, 290
Family Court system in Japan, 206
Family Integrated Transitions
(FIT), 274
family interventions, 243

Family Law Reform Act, 289
family-level influences
antisocial behavior, 18
as depression risk factors, 136
domestic violence, 126
group conferencing, 302
interventions, 243
systemic therapies, 243
youth gangs, 112
Family Systems Theory, 243
fight or flight response, 111, 154,
159, 162
firearm related deaths, 94
'5Ps' model in youth psychopathy, 61
foetal alcohol syndrome disorders
(FASD), 68, 71, 73
forensic mental healthcare, 33–34, 34f
formal operations thinking, 2
formulation. See also risk assessment/
formulation
autism spectrum disorder, 211
pragmatic formulation, 227
psychopathic traits, 227–229
substance misuse diagnosis, 185
suicide attempt concerns, 143
Fragile X Syndrome, 201
fragmented consciousness, 224
Full-Scale IQ assessment, 130
functional family therapy (FFT)
case example, 270
defined, 137
effectiveness trials, 243
family-based treatments, 268
overview, 269–271
risk factors, 266
functional literacy, 34
Future in mind: Promoting, protecting
and improving our children and
young people's mental health and
wellbeing (DoH), 306

gang violence. See group violence and
youth gangs
gender differences
assessment of young offenders,
49–50
issues with trauma, 159
sexually harmful behavior, 125
youth gangs, 109, 113
gene-environment interactions
(GxE), 15
General Medical Council's Good
Medical Practice Guide, 289
genetic influences
on antisocial behavior, 14–15
Autistic Spectrum Disorder, 201
delinquency studies, 20
gene-environment interactions, 15
individual violence, 88–89, 90
introduction, 12

Gilliam Autism Rating Scale – Second
Edition (GARS-2), 45
Gillick Case (1985), 292, 294
girl gangs, 107
Global Burden of Disease Study, 178
G-map service, 126
Good Behavior Game (GBG), 103
good-enough parenting, 5, 8
good-enough relationship with
caregiver, 157–158
Good Lives Model, 130–131
grandiosity trait, 217
group behavior, 29
group violence and youth gangs
average age, 108
case example, 116, 117
conclusions, 115–118
developmental pathways,
109–110
education and employment, 112
emotional well-being, support,
113–115
ethnicity, 108–109
gangs, defined, 107
gender differences, 109
girl gangs, 107
impact of trauma, 111
individual violence vs., 83
initiation rights of, 1
internet gangs, 107, 112–113
intervention strategies, 113
introduction, 107
member profile, 108
mental health needs, 110
neurodevelopmental impairment,
110–111
role of the family, 112
scale of problem, 108
socio economic status, 111–112
street gangs, 107
substance misuse, 111
technology impact, 112–113
Waltham Forest gang members, 108
weapons and, 112
women, support for, 115

hallucinations with depression, 135
hardiness in psychosocial resilience,
28, 31
Hayes Ability Screening Index
(HASI), 49
Health Care Standards for Children and
Young People in Secure Settings
(RCPCH), 183, 313
'Healthy Children, Safer Communities'
(DoH), 305
Helping the Non-Compliant Child
(McMahon, Forehand), 243
Her Majesty's Prison Youth Offender
Institutions (YOIs), 304

heritable influences as risk factor for youth offending, 14–15
heterotypic *vs.* homotopic continuity, 222
health and justice indicators of performance(HJIPs), 307
homicide offenders and victims
behavioral predictors, offending, 98, 99t
behavioral predictors, victimization, 100t, 100–101
case example, offender, 101–102
case example, victim, 102
classification of, 96
comparing predictors, 101
conclusion, 103
conflict and, 96
disruptive disorders, 98
dose-response relationship between, 101
early risk factors for offending, 97–98, 98t, 99t
early risk factors for victimization, 98–101, 99t, 100t
explanatory predictors, offending, 97–98, 98t
explanatory predictors, victimization, 98–100, 99t
homicide offending, 97–98, 98t
homicide victimization, 98–100, 99t
introduction, 94–95, 95t
overview, 96–97
prevention and intervention, 103–104
race issues, 101
racial concerns, 101
scientific studies on, 95–96
targeted intervention, 103
universal prevention, 103
victim overview, 96–97
homotypic *vs.* heterotypic continuity, 222
horizontal epidemiology, 29–31
human development stages, 4
hyper-segregated neighborhoods, 97
hyperkinetic disorders, 180. *See also* Attention Deficit Hyperactivity Disorder
hypothalamic-pituitary-adrenal (HPA) axis, 13

identity crisis, 4
Improving Access to Psychological Therapies positive practice guide, 257
Improving Health, Supporting Justice plan, 305
Impulsivity (I/CP) subscale, 220
The Incredible Years Program (IY), 243, 245

Independent Restraint Advisory Panel (IRAP), 318
individual trauma focused work, 162
individual work, 161–162
infant anger-proneness, 13
information processing, 14
initiation rights of gangs, 1
Integrate projects at MAC-UK, 114–115, 116
integrated approach in secure environments, 317–318
Integrated Emotional System (IES), 88
integrated management of complex trauma, 158–159
integrated model of aggression and violence, 86
integrative therapy, 257
intellectual functioning deficits, 190. *See also* learning disabilities
intelligence (IQ) assessments/scores, 48, 255, 290
Intensive Fostering (MTFC) programme, 272
intensive resettlement, 305
Intensive Supervision and Surveillance Programme (ISSP), 271
International Classification of Diseases (ICD)
categorical diagnosis, 240
conduct disorder, 259
defined, 136
early intervention, 241
PTSD, 153, 154
schizophrenia, 167
International Covenant on Civil and Political Rights, 295
International Covenant on Economic, Social and Cultural Rights, 295
internet gangs, 107, 112–113
interpersonal psychotherapy for adolescents (IPT-A), 137
interpersonal traumas, 156
interrogative pressure, 192
interventions. *See also* cognitive and related interventions; early interventions
Adjustment Disorder, 156
case example, 117
child therapies, 244
cognitive and related interventions, 262
complex trauma, 159–162
limitations of, 267
modality principle, 260–261
post-assessment intervention services, 131
psychological interventions for PTSD, 155–156
psychosocial interventions for ADHD, 194

risk assessment management, 63
sexually harmful behavior, 128–130
summary of, 266–267
for young women in gangs, 115
youth gangs, 113, 116
youth justice interventions, 76–77
interviews in risk assessment, 57

jurisdiction of court, 295
Justice Green Paper (2010), 305
Juvenile Cognitive Intervention programme (JCIP), 260
Juvenile Enhanced Thinking Skills programme (JETS), 260
juvenile sexual offender, 121, 122

KEEPs (Key Elements of Effective Practice), 308–309

language disorders, 41, 48, 72
lateralisation of cerebral hemispheres, 86
Law Commission for England and Wales, 290
law/laws for children and young people (CYP)
child/young person, defined, 289
civil law, 291
conclusions, 298
criminal law, 289–291
'doli incapax' protection, 289
electroconvulsive therapy, 296
emergency circumstances, 294–295
'fitness to plead,' 290
guidelines for choosing frameworks, 295–296
inherent jurisdiction of court, 295
international instruments, 295
introduction, 289
jurisdiction of court, 295
Mental Capacity Act, 289, 291–294
Mental Health Act (1983), 294
research and organ donation, 296
learning disabilities
academic underachievement and, 48
cognitive behavioral therapy, 255
cognitive empathy and, 71
emotional regulation, 72
introduction, 32–33, 68
neurodevelopmental impairment and youth crime, 74–75
rates of, 32–33, 41
sexually harmful behavior, 125–126
left cerebral hemisphere, 86
life-course-persistent offenders, 83
life expectancy with drug misuse, 178
life plans of offenders, 130
limited prosocial emotions, 12
Linehan, Marsha, 257

Local Authority Secure Children's Homes (LASCHs), 169, 304, 307, 314, 318
Local Safeguarding Children Boards, 121

MacArthur Adjudicative Competence Study, 290
maladaptive responses, 4
maltreatment, 17
managerial work in secure environments, 316–317
Mandatory Drug Testing programme, 183
MAOA genotype, 13, 15
MAPPA (Multi-Agency Public Protection Arrangements), 173
Massachusetts Youth Screening Instrument (Version 2), 45
masturbation behavior, 127, 128
maternal depression, 19
maternal emotional well-being during pregnancy, 16
maternal smoking in pregnancy, 15
maturity gap, 19–20
medication
    for ADHD, 194–196
    antipsychotic medication, 170–171, 248
    depression, 137
    as early interventions, 247–248
    pharmacotherapy, 156, 209–210
    schizophrenia, 170–171
melatonin, 3
Mental Capacity Act (2005), 289, 291–294
mental health
    assessment of young offenders, 42–44, 43t
    forensic mental healthcare, 33–34, 34f
    provisions for custodial youth, 312–314
    screenings, 44–46, 47f
    sexually harmful behavior, 126
    youth gangs, 110, 113
Mental Health Act (1983), 173, 294
Mental Health Act Code of Practice (2015), 291, 292, 293, 294–295
Mental Health Foundation, 180
Mental Health In-reach Team, 58
mentalization based treatment for adolescents (MBT-A), 259
mentalisation process, 279
meta-analysis of associations, 17
milieu therapy, 273–274
mindfulness approach, 226, 256–257
mindfulness-based cognitive yherapy (MBCT), 256, 257

mindfulness-based stress reduction (MBSR), 256
minimising and managing physical restraint (MMPR), 304
Misspent Youth review, 301
mobile phone use by youth gangs, 113
Moffitt, Terrie, 83, 84
monitoring in risk assessment management, 63
monoamine oxidase A (MAO-A), 89
mortality and schizophrenia, 167
motivational factors in suicide, 142
multi-dimensional family therapy (MDFT), 184, 266
multidimensional treatment foster care (MTFC), 266, 268, 271–272
multidimensional treatment foster care-Adolescents (MTFC-A), 273
multi-equifinality vs. equifinality, 222
multi-factorial interventions, 158
multi-informant assessment, 227, 229–233t
multi-level assessment, 227, 229–233t
multimodal assessment, 227, 229–233t
multi-stressed families, 242
multisystemic therapy (MST)
    benefits of, 118
    case example, 269
    defined, 90
    overview, 268–269, 273
    risk management strategies, 145
    for risky behaviours, 266
    as targeted intervention, 103
multisystemic therapy-problem sexual behaviour (MST-PSB), 268
'Music & Change' project, 113–115
music therapy. See also arts psychotherapies
    clinical improvisation in, 287
    dynamic interplay in, 287
    overview, 279–284, 286–287

Narcissism (Nar) subscale, 220
National Audit Office (NAO), 308
National Autistic Society, 208, 209
National Drug Treatment Monitoring System, 179
National Institute for Health and Care Excellence (NICE) guidelines
    ADHD, 77
    antipsychotic medication, 170
    antisocial personality disorder, 90
    Autistic Spectrum Disorder, 209–210
    conduct disorder, 259
    depression, 135
    early intervention, 242–243
    intervention recommendations, 152, 266–267

PTSD, 155
    schizophrenia treatment in adults, 171
    on self harm, 138, 143
    substance misuse, 177
National Institute for Health and Care Excellence (NICE) guidelines
    cognitive behavioral therapy, 254
National Specification for Substance Misuse for Juveniles in Custody, 308
National Suicide Prevention Strategy, 137
NATO Guidance on Psychosocial Care for People Affected by Disasters and Major Incidents, 24
needs assessment approaches, 45–46
negative, intrusive parenting, 13
negative emotionality of parents, 19
negative reinforcement processes, 16
neurobiological factors, 20, 86
neurocircuitry of individual violence, 86–88
neurocognitive deficits, 11
neurodevelopmental impairment and youth crime
    antisocial behavior and, 70
    assessments for, 77, 78
    case example, 78
    cognitive empathy, 71–72
    comorbidity, 191
    discrimination and criminalisation, 74–75
    educational and family intervention, 75–76
    educational disengagement, 72–73
    emotional regulation, 72
    executive function deficits, 70–71
    introduction, 68, 69t
    learning disability, 74–75
    management of, 78
    parenting practices, 74
    peer group influence, 73–74
    policy and practice implications, 75
    prevalence in custodial youth, 312
    prevalence of, 68–70, 70t
    social and environmental risk factors, 72
    youth gangs, 110–111
    youth justice interventions, 76–77
neuropsychological deficits, 13, 14, 15, 85
New Zealand Department of Corrections, 183
New Zealand Ministry of Health, 181
NHS Health Advisory Service (NHS HAS), 32
nomological net in youth psychopathy, 220–222
non-fatal shootings, 94

non-shared environmental influences, 12
Non Suicidal Self Injurious Behaviour (NSIB), 138
Non Suicidal Self Injury (NSSI), 138
nonverbal communicative deficits, 202
North West Juvenile Project (NWJP), 42
'nuisance' behaviours, 126

Offending, Crime and Justice Survey (OCJS), 108, 112
Office for National Statistics, 166
Office of the Children's Commissioner, 41
Operation New Hope Intervention, 113
Oppositional Defiant Disorder (ODD)
  comorbidity, 203, 247
  early interventions, 239, 241
orbitofrontal cortex, 71, 86–87
organ donation, 296
organised crime groups, 83
origins of offending, 11–12
'out-of-sight, out-of-mind' response, 315
over-controlled/reserved sex offenders, 122
over-restrictive parenting, 5
overt behavior, 85

parent child interaction therapy (PCIT), 243
Parent Management Training – Oregon (PMT-O), 243
parental consent for treatment, 293
parental responsibility, 291, 294
parenting practices
  antisocial parents, 15
  attachment security, 17
  behavioral parenting training, 90, 244, 267
  good-enough parenting, 5, 8
  good practices, 243
  influences on antisocial behavior, 16–17
  intervention, 75–76
  lack of boundaries, 8
  maternal depression, 19
  negative, intrusive parenting, 13, 19
  negative emotionality of parents, 19
  neurodevelopmental impairment and youth crime, 74, 75–76
  over-restrictive parenting, 5
  parent-over-child authority, 243
  reduced supervision and substance misuse, 180
  under-reactive parenting, 5
Pathways to Desistance study, 184
peer group influences
  deviance, 18, 20

homicide offending, 98
impact of, 267
introduction, 12, 15
neurodevelopmental impairment and youth crime, 73–74
rejection and ADHD, 191
social support, 33, 114
victimization and rejection, 15
perinatal influences in antisocial behavior, 15–16
peripheral nervous system, 68
Perry Preschool intellectual enrichment program, 104
personal psychosocial resilience, 27
personality disorder and schizophrenia, 168
pervasive developmental disorder – unspecified/not otherwise specified (PDD-NOS), 201. See also autism spectrum disorders
pharmacotherapy, 156, 209–210
'phase-orientated' approach to interventions, 130
physical aggression, 12
physical needs and assessment, 46–48
physical restraint of custodial youth, 318–319
Pittsburgh Youth Study (PYS), 94, 95–96, 97, 101
play during adolescence, 3
police community support officers (PCSOs), 302
polydrug use, 178, 308
The Positive Parenting Program (Triple P), 243
post-assessment intervention services, 131
Post-Traumatic Stress Disorder (PTSD)
  with Adjustment Disorder, 154
  cognitive behavioral therapy, 255
  conclusion, 162–163
  diagnosis and prevalence, 152–153
  female-specific components, 115, 125
  introduction, 152
  overview, 152–154
  pharmacotherapy, 156
  psychological interventions, 155–156
  rates of, 42, 44
  sexually abusive behaviors, 126
  trauma systems therapy, 158–159
  trauma theory, 153–154
poverty and deprivation, 8
Practice Parameter for the Assessment and Treatment of Children and Adolescents with Substance Use Disorders, 181

Practice Parameters from the American Academy of Child and Adolescent Psychiatry, 183
Practice Standards for Young People with Substance Misuse Problems, 181, 184
pragmatic formulation, 227
precipitating factors in psychopathy, 228
predisposing factors in psychopathy, 228
prefrontal cortex, 3, 72, 86–88
pregnancy/prenatal influences, 15–16
Primary Care Trusts, 307
Prison and Probation Ombudsman (PPO), 139
Prison Reform Trust, 139
Problem Solving Skills Training (PSST-P), 240, 244
programme integrity principle, 261
Project Safe Neighbourhoods Prevention, 113
promiscuity behaviors, 125
prostitution, 125
protective factors in psychopathy, 228
psycho-education around trauma, 155
psychoactive substances, 180
psychological first aid (PFA), 35
psychological interventions for PTSD, 155–156
Psychologically Informed Planned Environments (PIPEs), 314
psychopathy. See youth psychopathy
Psychopathy Checklist Revised' (PCL-R), 217–218
Psychopathy Checklist Youth Version (PCL:YV), 219–220, 221–222
psychosexual development, 2
psychosocial resilience
  adaptive capacities, 30f, 30–31
  adaptive coping/responses, 28, 35
  collective psychosocial resilience, 29
  conclusions, 36–37
  defined, 26–27
  distress and disorders and, 31
  epidemiology of, 29–31
  factors of, 28t–29
  forensic mental healthcare, 33–34, 34f
  interventions for, 35–36, 194
  introduction, 24–26, 31–33
  model of care, 34
  overview, 26, 31
  personal psychosocial resilience, 27
  resilience, defined, 26
  self-regulation, 35
  social support/identity, 35–36
  summary, 31
  systemic notions of, 33
  three generations of, 26

puberty, 1, 20
pupil referral unit (PRU), 269

QbTest, 193

racial concerns with homicide
    offenders and victims, 101
Randomised Controlled Trial's
    (RCT's), 255, 268, 272–273
reactive attachment disorder, 126
reading/reading comprehension
    difficulties, 48
Reasoning and Rehabilitation
    programme (R&R), 259, 260
receptive plasticity state of brain, 3
recidivism, 192, 271
recording information in risk
    assessment, 59
recovery in psychosocial resilience, 28
referral orders, 302, 303
rehabilitation challenges with
    schizophrenia, 172–173
relationship deficits, 202
relationship-focused services, 114
reparative experience in therapy, 9–10
repeat scenario in risk assessment, 63
Report of the committee of enquiry into
    children and young people who
    sexually abuse other children
    (NCH), 121
resettlement and aftercare provision
    (RAP), 0= 305, 308
responsivity principle, 261
restorative conferencing, 302
restorative justice (RJ), 302–303
restraint
    minimising and managing physical
        restraint, 304
    physical restraint of custodial youth,
        318–319
    Restraint Advisory Board, 318, 319
Restraint Advisory Board (RAB), 318,
    319
reverse causation, 16
risk assessment/formulation. *See also*
    antisocial behavior risk factors;
    assessment of young offenders
    additional processes, 64–65
    background example, 58, 60t, 61t
    case example, 57–59, 60t, 61t
    collateral information, 57–59
    common mistakes, 65–66
    conclusion, 66
    interviews, 57
    introduction, 55
    management plan, 63–64
    monitoring in, 63
    overview, 59–62
    principles of practice, 57
    protective factors, 59

recording information, 59
resilience approach, 46, 47f
risk formulation, 59–62
stepping-stone pattern of risk, 110
suicide, 139–141, 140–141t, 142–143
tools for, 55
twist scenario in risk assessment, 63
risk classification principle, 260
risk management strategies
    Assessment, Care in Custody and
        Teamwork, 144
    cognitive beahvioral therapy, 145
    dialectical behavioural therapy,
        144–145
    good practice in management of
        self-harm, 144
    listeners and support, 144
    multisystemic therapy, 145
    place of care, 144
    promising interventions, 145t,
        144–145
    suicide, 144–145
    supervision and restriction to access,
        63, 144
Risperidone Disruptive Behaviour
    Study Group, 248
Royal College of Paediatrics and Child
    Health, 51, 184
Royal College of Psychiatrists, 181

safer school partnerships (SSPs), 302
Salford Needs Assessment Schedule for
    Adolescents (SNASA), 44, 45, 46
schizophrenia
    assessment of young offenders,
        169–170, 172
    case example, 168, 172
    conclusions, 173–174
    diagnosis, 166–167
    early onset schizophrenia, 167
    epidemiology, 167–168
    introduction, 166
    links with aggression, 168
    medication, 170–171
    mortality and, 167
    personality disorder and, 168
    presentation to services, 168–169
    psychological interventions, 171
    rehabilitation challenges, 172–173
    therapeutic approaches, 171–172
    treatment in young offenders, 169,
        170–172
school-based early interventions,
    246–247
Scottish Law Commission, 290
screening and assessment. *See also*
    assessment of young offenders
    assessment *vs.*, 41–42
    speech language difficulties with
        TBI, 50

substance misuse, 181–182, 182f
suicide concerns, 142–144
toxicology screening, 183
Screening Questionnaire Interview for
    Adolescents (SQIFA), 45
Secure Accommodation Orders, 291
secure attachment style, 223
secure environments for youth offenders
    accreditation and effective
        governance, 319
    coherent framework of, 316
    conclusions, 319–320
    daily regime, 315
    integrated approach, 317–318
    introduction, 312
    managing transitions, 314–315
    mental health provisions for
        custodial youth, 312–314
    overview, 312, 315–317
    safety and security in, 316
    sentencing, 314
    status of child, 318
    transitions into/out of, 315
    use of physical restraint, 318–319
Secure Training Centres (STCs), 304,
    314, 318
segregation by gender, 127
selective serotonin reuptake inhibitors
    (SSRIs), 156
self-concept and trauma, 224
self-control skills, 240
self-esteem, 8, 136, 192
self-harm
    alcohol misuse, 182
    assessment and protective factors,
        141–142
    case example, 143
    conclusions, 145–146
    coping typologies, 142
    defined, 138
    depression and, 135
    early detection, 146
    good practice in management of
        self-harm, 144
    introduction, 135, 137–138
    overview, 44, 142
    potential risk of, 315
    prevalence of, 138–139
    risk factors, 139–141, 140t–141t
    scale of problem, 139
    self-strangulation /hanging, 139
    in youth gangs, 110
self-management skills, 314
self-medication phenomenon, 180
self-mutilating technique, 128
self-regulation in psychosocial
    resilience, 35
self-strangulation /hanging, 139
Sendai Framework for Disaster Risk
    Reduction (2015–30), 34

sense of coherence (SOC), 28, 31
serious situations during adolescence, 5–7
serotonergic functioning, 13, 89
service provision effectiveness, 131
sex hormones, 3
sex offenders, 122
    antisocial/impulsive sex offenders, 122
    confident/aggressive sex offenders, 122
    juvenile sexual offender, 121, 122
    over-controlled/reserved sex offenders, 122
    personality variables of, 122
    unusual/isolated sex offenders, 122
sexual abuse, 115, 180, 279
sexual attraction to younger children, 206
sexual behaviors, age-appropriate, 4, 124
Sexual Offences Act (2003), 124
sexual prowess in adolescents, 4
sexually harmful behavior
    appropriate vs. inappropriate, 123f, 123
    autism spectrum disorder, 126–128
    case example, 129
    classification of, 122
    concerning sexual behaviors, 124
    definitions, 121–122
    effectiveness of service provision, 131
    gender-related issues, 125
    Good Lives Model, 130–131
    incidences of, 122
    intervention approaches, 128–130
    introduction, 121
    learning disabilities, 125–126
    mental health needs, 126
    over-controlled/reserved sex offenders, 122
    socio-sexual knowledge and understanding, 127
    very concerning sexual behaviors, 124–125
shaming concerns, 65
shop-lifting charges during adolescence, 6
Short Form Physical Health Survey Subscale, 47
Short Term Assessment of Risk and Treatability: Adolescent Version (START), 57
short-term distress, 31
single-nucleotide polymorphisms, 89
sleep patterns in adolescence, 3, 166
SNAP-IV Scale, 193
social cognition, 14
Social Communication Questionnaire, 45

social-emotional reciprocity deficits, 202
social identity theory, 29, 35–36
social isolation and alcohol misuse, 182
Social Learning Theory, 243
social stimuli sensitivity, 20
social support from peers, 33
socialised delinquent groups, 124
socio-cultural issues with trauma, 159
socio-economic status (SES), 89, 111–112
socio-sexual knowledge and understanding, 127
somatic marker hypothesis, 87
stability in personality functioning, 222
Standard Minimum Rules for the Administration of Juvenile Justice, 295
Stanford-Binet 5th edition, 48
status of child in secure environments, 318
stepping-stone pattern of risk, 110
Stop Now And Plan program, 245–246
story-telling therapy, 286
street gangs, 107
street therapy, 114, 115
street triage, 305–306
stress-regulating mechanisms, 13
Structured Assessment of Protective Factors for violence risk – Adolescent Version (SAPROF-AV), 240
Structured Assessment of Protective Factors for violence risk – Youth Version (SAPROF-YV), 56, 240
Structured Assessment of Violence Risk in Youth (SAVRY), 56, 57, 60t, 61t, 64–66, 193
structured professional judgement (SPJ), 55, 57, 66
substance misuse
    ADHD and, 191–192
    assessment and screening, 181–182, 182f, 185
    case example, 185
    comorbidity, 42, 180–181
    conclusion, 185–186
    in custodial youth justice, 307–308
    defined, 178
    developmental pathways, 178–179
    formulation and diagnosis, 185
    health and, 305–306
    impact on youth gangs, 111
    individual violence and, 89
    introduction, 177–178
    life expectancy with drug misuse, 178
    polydrug use, 178, 308
    prevalence, 179–180
    psychoactive substances, 180

resettlement and aftercare provision, 308
    schizophrenia and, 166
    services in YOTs, 306
    toxicology screening, 183
    treatment/management approaches, 183–185
    use vs. induced disorders, 178
    youth gangs, 110
    Youth Offending Teams, 305–306
substance use disorder (SUD), 178, 191–192
suicide concerns
    case example, 143
    conclusions, 145–146
    contagion, 141
    death statistics, 139
    depression, 135, 136
    early detection, 146
    formulation of attempt, 143
    intervention approach, 257–258
    introduction, 135, 137–138
    motivational factors, 142
    non-suicidal outpatients, 258
    overview, 142
    prevalence of, 138–139
    related behavior, 138
    risk factors, 139–141, 140–141t, 142–143
    risk management strategies, 144–145
    screening and assessment, 142–144
    treatment, 143
    in youth gangs, 110
suicide related behaviour (SRB), 141
supervision in risk assessment management, 63, 144
Systemic Family Practice (SFP), 137
systemic notions of psychosocial resilience, 33
systemic treatment for risky behaviours
    advantages of, 274
    conclusions, 275
    functional family therapy, 269–271
    introduction, 266
    limitations of, 274–275
    milieu therapy, 273–274
    Multidimensional treatment foster care, 271–272
    multisystemic therapy, 268–269, 273
    review of, 267–268
    risk factors, 266
    traditional interventions, summary, 266–267

targeted intervention, 103
TEACCH Report, 128
technology impact on youth gangs, 112–113
teenagers. See adolescence

Tele-health, defined, 263
temperament concerns, 11, 12–13
temporal sequencing, 227
Test of Adolescent and Adult Language, 3rd Edition (TOAL-3), 49
tetrahydrocannabinol in cannabis, 179
therapeutic relationship, 9–10, 159
'3Ds' model of youth psycopathy, 61
three generations of psychosocial resilience, 26
toddler tantrums, 5
topographical analysis, 227
toxicology screening, 183
traditional intervention. See interventions
transference, 278
trauma. See also complex trauma
  affective experiences, 31
  arts psychotherapies, 285
  callous-unemotional (CU) traits, 225–226
  developmental trauma disorder, 157, 224
  early interpersonal trauma, 157–158
  group behavior, 29
  impact on child self-concept, 224
  impact on youth gangs, 111
  individual trauma focused work, 162
  interpersonal traumas, 156
  introduction, 26
  negative impact of, 152
  psycho-education around trauma, 155
  self-concept and, 224
  sexually harmful behavior, 130
  socio-cultural issues with, 159
trauma systems therapy, 153–154, 158–159
traumatic brain injury (TBI)
  cognitive empathy and, 71
  educational disengagement, 73
  emotional regulation, 72
  executive function deficits, 71
  intelligence (IQ) assessments, 255
  loss of consciousness, 46
  neurodevelopmental impairment, 68
  parenting practices, 74
  rehabilitation difficulties, 76
  screening for speech language difficulties, 50
  support guidelines, 77
traumatic reinactment, 158
treatment. See also systemic treatment for risky behaviours
  ADHD, 193–196
  assessment based, 241
  child therapies, 244
  depression, 137
  early interventions, 241

individual violence, 89–90
interventions for treatment staff, 36
mentalisation based treatments, 258–259
in natural environment, 243
parental consent for, 293
schizophrenia, 169, 170–172
substance misuse, 183–185
suicide concerns, 143
treatment as usual (TAU), 255
truancy concerns, 84
Tuberous Sclerosis Complex (TSC), 201
turmoil in adolescence, normal vs. pathological, 4
Twins Early Development Study, 88
twist scenario in risk assessment, 63

UK Offending, Crime and Justice Survey, 108, 109
under-reactive parenting, 5
United Nations Convention on the Rights of the Child, 289, 295
United Nations Declaration on the Rights of the Child, 295
Universal Declaration of Human Rights, 295
universal prevention, 103
unusual/isolated sex offenders, 122
US Department of Justice, 177
US National Gang Centre, 113
User Voice Study (2011), 181

very concerning sexual behaviors, 124–125
victim safety planning, 63
victims-offender mediation, 302
violence
  amygdala and, 88
  attachment security, 17
  behavioural re-enactments, 111, 154
  case example, 84
  in children, 217
  conclusion, 91
  cortex and, 86–88
  developmental pathways to, 83–85
  genetic factors, 88–89, 90
  integrated model of aggression and violence, 86
  introduction, 83
  left cerebral hemisphere, 86
  neurobiological factors, 86
  neurocircuitry, 86–88
  neurocircuitry of individual violence, 86–88
  physically abused groups, 124
  risk factors for, 191
  schizophrenia and, 168
  treatment for, 89–90
  weapons and youth gangs, 112

weapons and youth gangs, 112
Wechsler Abbreviated Scale for Intelligence (WASI), 49
Wechsler Intelligence Scale for Children (WISC), 48
Werther effect, 141
WHO/EURO Multicentre Study on Suicidal Behaviour, 138
wider systemic change approach, 115
Woodcock Johnson-III, 49
World Health Organisation, 177, 179, 184
Wrap around services, 118

Youth Crime Action Plan, 169
Youth Forensic Services Development, 181
Youth Inclusion Programmes (YIPs), 302
Youth Inclusion Support Panels (YISPs), 302
Youth Justice Board (YJB)
  establishment, 300
  report, 108, 112
  responsibilities, 300
youth justice interventions, 76–77
Youth Justice System (YJS) services
  asset of, 301
  community sentences, 303
  components of, 301
  Comprehensive Health Assessment Tool, 307
  conclusions, 309
  custodial sentences, 304
  health and substance misuse, 305–306
  intensive resettlement, 305
  international perspectives, 301
  introduction, 300
  Key Elements of Effective Practice, 308–309
  minimising and managing physical restraint, 304
  overview, 300–301
  psychoactive drugs, 177
  referral orders, 302, 303
  resettlement and aftercare provision, 308
  resettlement consortia, 305
  restorative justice, 302–303
  safeguarding approach, 301
  safer school partnerships, 302
  substance misuse in custodial youth justice, 307–308
  success in, 308
Youth Offending Teams, 301
Youth Restorative Disposal, 303

Youth Level of Service/Case Management Inventory (YLS/CMI), 56
Youth Offender Institutions (YOIs), 304, 313, 314
Youth Offender Panel (YOP), 303
Youth Offending Service (YOS), 160
Youth Offending Teams (YOTs)
  attendance surveys, 32
  custodial healthcare, 307
  health services within, 305
  overview, 301
  practitioners, 108
  schizophrenia, 169
  in secure environments, 312
  substance misuse and, 305–306

youth psychopathy
  assessment protocols, 219–220
  attachment and trauma, 222–226, 225f
  avoidant-ambivalent attachment style, 223
  case example, 218, 229–233t
  conclusions, 226, 233–234
  developmental dilemmas, 222
  disorganized attachment style, 223
  equifinality and trauma, 222–223
  '5Ps' model in, 61
  formulation of traits, 227–229
  insecure-ambivalent attachment style, 223
  introduction, 217–219
  nomological net, 220–222
  perpetuating factors in, 228
  perspectives on, 219
  precipitating factors in, 228
  predisposing factors in psychopathy, 228
  protective factors in, 228
  psychopathology, origins, 278–279
  secure attachment style, 223
  '3Ds' model, 61
  understanding of, 218–219
Youth Psychopathy Inventory (YPI), 219
Youth Rehabilitation Order (YRO), 304
Youth Restorative Disposal (YRD), 303